JERUSALEM

JERUSALEM

One City

Three Faiths

Karen Armstrong

Alfred A. Knopf   New York   1996

THIS IS A BORZOI BOOK
PUBLISHED BY ALFRED A. KNOPF, INC.

Copyright © 1996 by Karen Armstrong
All rights reserved under International and Pan-American
Copyright Conventions. Published in the United States
by Alfred A. Knopf, Inc., New York,
and simultaneously in Canada by Random House of Canada Limited, Toronto.
Distributed by Random House, Inc., New York.

ISBN: 0-679-43596-4
LC: 96-75888

Manufactured in the United States of America
First Edition

For my mother, Eileen Armstrong

Contents

Maps and Diagrams

Acknowledgments

Writing is a solitary and sometimes lonely occupation, but I should like to thank my agents, Felicity Bryan, Peter Ginsberg, and Andrew Nurnberg, as well as my editors, Jane Garrett and Stuart Proffitt, for their support and encouragement. I am also grateful to Roger Boase, Claire Bradley, Juliet Brightmore, Katherine Hourigan, Ted Johnson, Anthea Lingeman, Jonathan Magonet, Toby Mundy, and Melvin Rosenthal for their expertise, their patience, advice, and help. Finally, my thanks to Joelle Delbourgo, my erstwhile editor at Ballantine, who first suggested that I should write this book and always gave me the benefit of her immense enthusiasm and encouragement.

Introduction

In Jerusalem, more than in any other place I have visited, history is a dimension of the present. Perhaps this is so in any disputed territory, but it struck me forcibly the first time I went to work in Jerusalem in 1983. First, I was surprised by the strength of my own reaction to the city. It was strange to be walking around a place that had been an imaginative reality in my life ever since I was a small child and had been told tales of King David or Jesus. As a young nun, I was taught to begin my morning meditation by picturing the biblical scene I was about to contemplate, and so conjured up my own image of the Garden of Gethsemane, the Mount of Olives, or the Via Dolorosa. Now that I was going about my daily business among these very sites, I discovered that the real city was a far more tumultuous and confusing place. I had, for example, to take in the fact that Jerusalem was clearly very important to Jews and Muslims too. When I saw caftaned Jews or tough Israeli soldiers kissing the stones of the Western Wall or watched the crowds of Muslim families surging through the streets in their best clothes for Friday prayers at the Ḥaram al-Sharif, I became aware for the first time of the challenge of religious pluralism. People could see the same symbol in entirely different ways. There was no doubting the attachment of any of these people to their holy city, yet they had been quite absent from *my* Jerusalem. Still, the city remained mine as well: my old images of biblical scenes were a constant counterpoint to my firsthand experience of twentieth-century Jerusalem. Associated with some of the most momentous events of my life, Jerusalem was somehow built into my own identity.

Yet as a British citizen, I had no political claim to the city, unlike my new colleagues and friends in Jerusalem. Here again, as Israelis and Palestinians presented their arguments to me, I was struck by the vivid immediacy of past events. All could cite, in sometimes minute detail, the events leading up to the creation of the State of Israel in 1948 or the Six-Day War in 1967. Frequently I noted how these depictions of the past centered on the question of who had done what *first*. Who had been the first to resort to violence, the Zionists or the Arabs? Who had first noticed the potential of Palestine and developed the country? Who had lived in Jerusalem first, the Jews or the Palestinians? When they discussed the troubled present, both Israelis and Palestinians turned instinctively to the past, their polemic coursing easily from the Bronze Age through the Middle Ages to the twentieth century. Again, when Israelis and Palestinians proudly showed me around *their* city, the very monuments were drawn into the conflict.

On my first morning in Jerusalem, I was instructed by my Israeli colleagues how to spot the stones used by King Herod, with their distinctively beveled edges. They seemed ubiquitous and a perpetual reminder of a Jewish commitment to Jerusalem that could be dated back (in this case) to the first century BCE—long before Islam appeared on the scene. Constantly, as we passed construction crews in the Old City, I was told how Jerusalem had been utterly neglected by the Ottomans when they

Separated by decades of hostility, Israelis and Palestinians both claim that Jerusalem belongs to them. The question could deepen the rift and make peace and coexistence impossible.

had ruled the city. It had come to life again only in the nineteenth century, thanks, largely, to Jewish investment—look at the windmill built by Sir Moses Montefiore and the hospitals funded by the Rothschild family. It was due to Israel that the city was thriving as never before.

My Palestinian friends showed me a very different Jerusalem. They pointed out the splendors of the Ḥaram al-Sharif and the exquisite *madāris,* Muslim schools, built around its borders by the Mamluks as evidence of the Muslim commitment to Jerusalem. They took me to the shrine of Nebī Mūsā near Jericho, built to defend Jerusalem against the Christians, and the extraordinary Umayyad palaces nearby. When we drove through Bethlehem once, my Palestinian host stopped the car beside Rachel's roadside tomb to point out passionately that the Palestinians had cared for this Jewish shrine for centuries—a pious devotion for which they had been ill rewarded.

One word kept recurring throughout. Even the most secular Israelis and Palestinians pointed out that Jerusalem was "holy" to their people. The Palestinians even called the city al-Quds, "the Holy," though the Israelis scornfully waved this aside, pointing out that Jerusalem had been a holy city for Jews *first,* and that it had never been as important to the Muslims as Mecca and Medina. But what did the word "holy" mean in this context? How could a mere city, full of fallible human beings and teeming with the most unholy activities, be sacred? Why did those Jews who professed a militant atheism care about the holy city and feel so possessive about the Western Wall? Why should an unbelieving Arab be moved to tears the first time he stood in the Mosque of al-Aqsā? I could see why the city was holy to Christians, since Jerusalem had been the scene of Jesus's death and resurrection: it had witnessed the birth of the faith. But the formative events of both Judaism and Islam had happened far away from Jerusalem, in the Sinai Peninsula or the Arabian Hijaz. Why, for example, was Mount Zion in Jerusalem a holy place for Jews instead of Mount Sinai, where God had given the Law to Moses and made his covenant with Israel? Clearly, I had been wrong to assume that the holiness of a city depended upon its associations with the events of salvation history, the mythical account of God's intervention in the affairs of humanity. It was to find out what a holy city was that I decided to write this book.

What I have discovered is that even though the word "holy" is bandied around freely in connection with Jerusalem, as though its meaning were self-evident, it is in fact quite complex. Each one of the three monotheistic religions has developed traditions about the city that are remarkably similar. Furthermore, the devotion to a holy place or a holy city is a near-universal phenomenon. Historians of religion believe that it is one of the earliest manifestations of faith in all cultures. People have developed what has been called a sacred geography that has nothing to do with a scientific map of the world but which charts their interior life. Earthly cities, groves, and mountains have become symbols of this spirituality, which is so omnipresent that it seems to answer a profound human need, whatever our beliefs about "God" or the supernatural. Jerusalem has—for different reasons—become central to the sacred geography of Jews, Christians, and Muslims. This makes it very difficult for them to see the city objectively, because it has become bound up with their conception of themselves and the ultimate reality—sometimes called "God" or the sacred—that gives our mundane life meaning and value.

There are three interconnected concepts that will recur in the following pages. First is the whole notion of God or the sacred. In the Western world, we have tended to view God in a rather anthropomorphic and personalized manner, and as a result, the whole notion of the divine frequently appears incoherent and incredible. Since the word "God" has become discredited to many people because of the naïve and often unacceptable things that have been asserted and done in "his" name, it may be easier to use the term "sacred" instead. When they have contemplated the world, human beings have always experienced a transcendence and mystery at the heart of existence. They have felt that it is deeply connected with themselves and with the natural world, but that it also goes beyond. However we choose to define it—it has been called God, Brahman, or Nirvana—this transcendence has been a fact of human life. We have all experienced something similar, whatever our theological opinions, when we listen to a great piece of music or hear a beautiful poem and feel touched within and lifted, momentarily, beyond ourselves. We tend to seek out this experience, and if we do not find it in one setting—in a church or synagogue, for example—we will look elsewhere. The sacred has been experienced in many ways: it has inspired fear, awe, exuberance, peace, dread, and compelling moral activity. It represents a fuller, enhanced existence that will complete us. It is not merely felt as a force "out there" but can also be sensed in the depths of our own being. But like any aesthetic experience, the sense of the sacred needs to be cultivated. In our modern secular society, this has not always been a priority, and so, like any unused capacity, it has tended to wither away. In more traditional societies, the ability to apprehend the sacred has been regarded as of crucial importance. Indeed, without this sense of the divine, people often felt that life was not worth living.

This is partly because human beings have always experienced the world as such a painful place. We are the victims of natural disasters, of mortality, extinction, and human injustice and cruelty. The religious quest has usually begun with the perception that something has gone wrong, that, as the Buddha put it, "Existence is awry." Besides the common shocks that flesh is heir to, we all suffer personal distress that makes apparently unimportant setbacks overwhelmingly upsetting. There is a sense of abandonment that makes such experiences as bereavement, divorce, broken friendship, or even losing a beloved object seem, sometimes, part of an underlying and universal ill. Often this interior dis-ease is characterized by a sense of separation. There appears to be something missing from our lives; our existence seems fragmented and incomplete. We have an inchoate feeling that life was not meant to be thus and that we have lost something essential to our well-being—even though we would be hard put to explain this rationally. This sense of loss has surfaced in many ways. It is apparent in the Platonic image of the twin soul from which we have been separated at birth and in the universal myth of the lost paradise. In previous centuries, men and women turned to religion to assuage this pain, finding healing in the experience of the sacred. Today in the West, people sometimes have recourse to psychoanalysis, which has articulated this sense of a primal separation in a more scientific idiom. Thus it is associated with memories of the womb and the traumatic shock of birth. However we choose to see it, this notion of separation and a yearning for some kind of reconciliation lies at the heart of the devotion to a holy place.

The second concept we must discuss is the question of myth. When people have tried to speak about the sacred or about the pain of human existence, they have not been able to express their experience in logical, discursive terms but have had recourse to mythology. Even Freud and Jung, who were the first to chart the so-called scientific quest for the soul, turned to the myths of the classical world or of religion when they tried to describe these interior events, and they made up some new myths of their own. Today the word "myth" has been rather debased in our culture; it is generally used to mean something that is not true. Events are dismissed because they are "only" myths. This is certainly true in the debate about Jerusalem. Palestinians claim that there is absolutely no archaeological evidence for the Jewish kingdom founded by King David and that no trace of Solomon's Temple has been found. The Kingdom of Israel is not mentioned in any contemporary text but only in the Bible. It is quite likely, therefore, that it is merely a "myth." Israelis have also discounted the story of the Prophet Muḥammad's ascent to heaven from the Ḥaram al-Sharif in Jerusalem—a myth that lies at the heart of the Muslim devotion to al-Quds—as demonstrably absurd. But this, I have come to believe, is to miss the point. Mythology was never designed to describe historically verifiable events that actually happened. It was an attempt to express their inner significance or to draw attention to realities that were too elusive to be discussed in a logically coherent way. Mythology has been well defined as an ancient form of psychology, because it describes the inner reaches of the self which are so mysterious and yet so fascinating to us. Thus the myths of "sacred geography" express truths about the interior life. They touch on the obscure sources of human pain and desire and can thus unleash very powerful emotions. Stories about Jerusalem should not be dismissed because they are "only" myths: they are important precisely *because* they are myths.

The Jerusalem question is explosive because the city has acquired mythical status. Not surprisingly, people on both sides of the present conflict and in the international community frequently call for a rationalized debate about rights and sovereignty, divorced from all this emotive fiction. It would be nice if this were possible. But it is never safe to say that we have risen above our need for mythology. People have often tried to eradicate myth from religion in the past. Prophets and reformers in ancient Israel, for

The Shrine of the Book in West Jerusalem houses the Dead Sea Scrolls. The sexual imagery embodied in the shrine shows how deeply the secular State of Israel has assimilated the ancient myths of sacred geography.

example, were extremely concerned to separate their faith from the mythology of the indigenous Canaanites. They did not succeed, however. The old stories and legends surfaced again powerfully in the mysticism of Kabbalah, a process that has been described as the triumph of myth over the more rational forms of religion. In the history of Jerusalem we shall see that people turned instinctively toward myth when their lives became particularly troubled and they could find no consolation in a more cerebral ideology. Sometimes outer events seemed so perfectly to express a people's inner reality that they immediately assumed mythical status and inspired a burst of mythologized enthusiasm. Two such events have been the discovery of the Tomb of Christ in the fourth century and the Israeli conquest of Jerusalem in 1967. In both cases, the people concerned thought they had left this primitive way of thinking far behind, but the course of events proved too strong for them. The catastrophes which have befallen the Jewish and the Palestinian people in our own century have been of such magnitude that it has not been surprising that myth has once again come to the fore. For good or ill, therefore, a consideration of the mythology of Jerusalem is essential, if only to illuminate the desires and behavior of people who are affected by this type of spirituality.

The last term that we must consider before embarking on the history of Jerusalem is symbolism. In our scientifically oriented society, we no longer think naturally in terms of images and symbols. We have developed a more logical and discursive mode of thought. Instead of looking at physical phenomena imaginatively, we strip an object of all its emotive associations and concentrate on the thing itself. This has changed the religious experience for many people in the West, a process that, as we shall see, began in the sixteenth century. We tend to say that something is *only* a symbol, essentially separate from the more mysterious reality that it represents. This was not so in the premodern world, however. A symbol was seen as partaking in the reality to which it pointed; a religious symbol thus had the power of introducing worshippers to the sacred realm. Throughout history, the sacred has never been experienced directly—except, perhaps, by a very few extraordinary human beings. It has always been felt in something other than itself. Thus the divine has been experienced in a human being—male or female—who becomes an avatar or incarnation of the sacred; it has also been found in a holy text, a law code, or a doctrine. One of the earliest and most ubiquitous symbols of the divine has been a place. People have sensed the sacred in mountains, groves, cities, and temples. When they have walked into these places, they have felt that they have entered a different dimension, separate from but compatible with the physical world they normally inhabit.

For Jews, Christians, and Muslims, Jerusalem has been such a symbol of the divine.

This is not something that happens automatically. Once a place has been experienced as sacred in some way and has proved capable of giving people access to the divine, worshippers have devoted a great deal of creative energy to helping others to cultivate this sense of transcendence. We shall see that the architecture of temples, churches, and mosques has been symbolically important, often mapping out the inner journey that a pilgrim must take to reach God. Liturgy and ritual have also heightened this sense of sacred space. In the Protestant West, people have often inherited a mistrust of religious ceremonial, seeing it as so much mumbo-jumbo. But it is probably more accurate to see liturgy as a form of theater, which can provide a powerful experience of the transcendent even in a wholly secular context. In the West, drama had its origins in religion: in the sacred festivals of ancient Greece and the Easter celebrations in the churches and cathedrals of medieval Europe. Myths have also been devised to express the inner meaning of Jerusalem and its various shrines.

One of these myths is what the late Romanian-American scholar Mircea Eliade has called the myth of eternal return, which he found in almost all cultures. According to this mode of thought, all objects that we encounter here on earth have their counterpart in the divine sphere. One can see this myth as an attempt to express the sense that our life here below is somehow incomplete and separated from a fuller and more satisfactory existence elsewhere. All human activities and skills also have a divine prototype: by copying the actions of the gods, people can share in their divine life. This *imitatio dei* is still observed today. People continue to rest on the Sabbath or eat bread and drink wine in church— actions which are meaningless in themselves—because they believe that in some sense God once did the same. The rituals at a holy place are another symbolic way of imitating the gods and entering their fuller and more potent mode of existence. The same myth is also crucial to the cult of the holy city, which can be seen as the replica of the home of the gods in heaven; a temple is regarded as the reproduction of a particular deity's celestial palace. By copying its heavenly archetype as minutely as possible, a temple could also house the god here on earth.

In the cold light of rational modernity, such myths appear ridiculous. But these ideas were not worked out first and then applied to a particular "holy" location. They were an attempt to explain an experience. In religion, experience always comes before the theological explanation. People first felt that they had apprehended the sacred in a grove or on a mountain peak. They were sometimes helped to do so by the aesthetic devices of architecture, music, and liturgy, which lifted them beyond themselves. They then sought to explain this experience in the poetic language of mythology or in the symbols of sacred geography. Jerusalem turned out to be one of those locations that "worked" for Jews, Christians, and Muslims because it did seem to introduce them to the divine.

One further remark is necessary. The practices of religion are closely akin to those of art. Both art and religion try to make some ultimate sense of a flawed and tragic world. But religion is different from art because it must have an ethical dimension. Religion can perhaps be described as a moral aesthetic. It is not enough to experience the divine or the transcendent; the experience must then be incarnated in our behavior towards others. All the great religions insist that the test of true spirituality is practical compassion. The Buddha once said that after experiencing enlightenment, a man must leave the mountaintop and return to the marketplace and there practice compassion for all living beings. This also applies to the spirituality of a holy place. Crucial to the cult of Jerusalem from the very first was the importance of practical charity and social justice. The city cannot be holy unless it is also just and compassionate to the weak and vulnerable. But sadly, this moral imperative has often been overlooked. Some of the worst atrocities have occurred when people have put the purity of Jerusalem and the desire to gain access to its great sanctity before the quest for justice and charity.

All these underlying currents have played their part in Jerusalem's long and turbulent history. This book will not attempt to lay down the law about the future of Jerusalem. That would be a presumption. It is merely an attempt to find out what Jews, Christians, and Muslims have meant when they have said that the city is "holy" to them and to point out some of the implications of Jerusalem's sanctity in each tradition. This seems just as important as deciding who was in the city *first* and who, therefore, should own it, especially since the origins of Jerusalem are shrouded in such obscurity.

JERUSALEM

R. Danube

Black Sea

CAUCASUS MTS.

MACEDONIA

Troy

HATTI

PHRYGIA

Mycenae

LYDIA

MITANNI

Caspian
Sea

GREECE

CILICIA

ASSYRIA

Haran

Nineveh

CRETE

Antioch

Ugarit

Ashur

MEDIA

CYPRUS

R. Tigris

Mediterranean
Sea

Sidon

Damascus

R. Euphrates

AKKAD

LIBYA

Jerusalem

Babylon

Nippur

ELAM

Gaza

SUMER

Susa

Memphis

Ur

SINAI

Eridu

EGYPT

River Nile

NAJD

El-Amarna

HIJAZ

Yathrib

N

Thebes

W   E

Mecca

S

Red
Sea

Persian
Gulf

0   miles   300

0   kilometers   500

Syene

THE ANCIENT NEAR EAST

1

ZION

W<small>E KNOW NOTHING</small> about the people who first settled in the hills and valleys that would eventually become the city of Jerusalem. In tombs on the Ophel hill, to the south of the present walls of the Old City, pottery vessels have been found which have been dated to 3200 BCE. This was the time when towns had begun to appear in other parts of Canaan, the modern Israel; in Megiddo, Jericho, Ai, Lachish, and Beth Shan, for example, archaeologists have unearthed temples, houses, workshops, streets, and water conduits. But there is as yet no conclusive evidence that urban life had begun in Jerusalem at that period. Ironically, the city which would be revered as the center of the world by millions of Jews, Christians, and Muslims was off the beaten track of ancient Canaan. Situated in the highlands, which were difficult to settle, it was outside the hub of the country. Development in the Early Bronze Age was mainly confined to the coastal plain, the fertile Jezreel Valley, and the Negev, where the Egyptians had established trade depots. Canaan was a potentially rich country: its inhabitants exported wine, oil, honey, bitumen, and grain. It also had strategic importance, linking Asia and Africa and providing a bridge between the civilizations of Egypt, Syria, Phoenicia, and Mesopotamia. But even though the springs around the Ophel hill had always attracted hunters, farmers, and temporary settlers—flints and shards have been found there dating from the Paleolithic Age—Jerusalem, as far as we know, played no part in this early florescence.

In the ancient world, civilization was always a precarious achievement. By about 2300 BCE there were virtually no cities left in Canaan. Because of either climatic change, foreign invasion, or internecine warfare, urban life disappeared. It was also a time of upheaval and instability throughout the Near East. Egypt saw the destruction of what is known as the Old Kingdom (c. 2613–2160 BCE). The Akkadian dynasty of Mesopotamia was overthrown by the Amorites, a Western Semitic people who established a capital at Babylon. Urban sites were abandoned throughout Asia Minor, and Ugarit and Byblos, on the Phoenician coast, were destroyed. For reasons that we do not understand, Syria remained unscathed and nearby towns in northern Canaan, such as Megiddo and Beth Shan, managed to survive longer than their southern neighbors. Yet in all these regions the struggle to create an ordered environment where people could lead a more secure and fulfilled life continued. New cities and new dynasties appeared and old settlements were restored. By the beginning of the second millennium the old towns of Canaan were inhabited once more.

We know very little about life in Canaan at this period. No central government developed in the country. Each town was autonomous, having its own ruler and dominating the surrounding countryside, rather as in Mesopotamia, where civilization had begun. Canaan remained an intensely regional country. There was no large-scale trade or industry, and there were such sharp differences of terrain and climate that the various districts tended to remain distinct and cut off from one another. Few people lived in the highlands, the Judaean steppes, or the Jordan Valley, where the river was not navigable and led nowhere. Communications were difficult, and people did not travel much from one part of the country to another. The main road linking Egypt and Damascus went up the coast from Gaza to Jaffa and then cut inland to avoid the swamps around Mount Carmel toward Megiddo, the Jezreel Valley, and the Sea of Galilee. Naturally these regions remained the most densely populated, and it was this area which interested the pharaohs of the Twelfth Dynasty when they began to extend their influence northward toward Syria during the twentieth and nineteenth centuries BCE. Canaan, which the Egyptians called "Retinu," did not actually become a province of Egypt, but the pharaohs dominated the country politically and economically. Sesostris III, for example, did not hesitate to march up the coastal road to subdue local rulers who were becoming too powerful and independent. Even so, the pharaohs showed relatively little interest in other parts of Canaan, and despite the general Egyptian overlordship, towns such as Megiddo, Hazor, and Acco developed into fortified city-states. By the end of the nineteenth century, settlers had also begun to penetrate the hill country and built cities there. Shechem became the most powerful of these fortified highland towns: in area it may have been as large as thirty-seven acres, and it controlled a considerable part of the

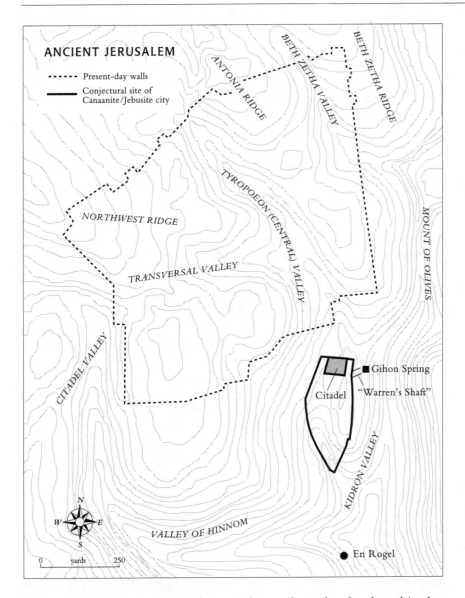

ANCIENT JERUSALEM

- - - - - Present-day walls
──────── Conjectural site of
Canaanite/Jebusite city

ANTONIA RIDGE

BETH ZETHA VALLEY

BETH ZETHA RIDGE

TYROPOEON (CENTRAL) VALLEY

NORTHWEST RIDGE

MOUNT OF OLIVES

TRANSVERSAL VALLEY

CITADEL VALLEY

■ Gihon Spring

Citadel   "Warren's Shaft"

KIDRON VALLEY

N
W E
S

VALLEY OF HINNOM

0   yards   250

● En Rogel

countryside. Cities, such as Hebron and Jerusalem, also developed in the southern hills.

This is the point when Jerusalem can be said to have entered history. In 1961 the British archaeologist Kathleen Kenyon discovered a wall, nearly six and a half feet thick, running along the eastern slope of the Ophel hill with a large gate near the Gihon Spring. She concluded that this town wall continued around the southern end of the hill and along the western slope. In the north it disappeared under a later city wall. Kenyon also found pottery between the wall and the rock scarp which dated to about 1800 BCE. The city was most vulnerable in the north, and later the citadel of Zion was built there; it is possible that there was also a fortress in the north of the city during the eighteenth century BCE. The walls were built quite low down the eastern slope of the Ophel, possibly to include access to an underground tunnel to the Gihon Spring.[1] The British engineer Charles Warren had discovered this tunnel in 1867: it started at an opening in the rock within the city, descended obliquely, and then plunged vertically to meet the water which had been conveyed from the Gihon by means of another horizontal tunnel. Jugs and pitchers could be lowered down the shaft during a siege. Similar devices have been discovered at Megiddo, Gezer, and Gibeon. Kenyon believed that the shaft was in use during the Bronze Age, but her theory has been disputed: some doubt that the inhabitants would have had the technological skill to build such a system at this stage. But recent geological findings indicate that "Warren's Shaft," as it is known, is not entirely man-made; it is a natural sinkhole along a joint in the limestone, which the ancient Jerusalemites could well have modified and enlarged.[2]

Settlers were probably attracted to the Ophel because of its proximity to the Gihon. The site also had strategic advantages, lying at the point where the foothills of the highlands give way to the Judaean desert. The Ophel could not support a large population—the city covered an area of little more than nine acres—but three steep valleys gave the settlers formidable protection: the Kidron Valley to the east, the Valley of Hinnom (or Gehenna) to the south, and the Central Valley, now largely silted up, which the Jewish historian Flavius Josephus called the Tyropoeon Valley, to the west.[3] Even though the town was not one of the most important cities of Canaan, it seems to have come to the attention of the Egyptians. In 1925, sherds were bought in Luxor which, when reassembled, made up about eighty dishes and vases inscribed with an ancient hieratic script. When this was deciphered, the texts were found to contain the names of countries, towns, and rulers alleged to be the enemies of Egypt. These vases would then be smashed in a rite of sympathetic magic designed to bring about the downfall of the recalcitrant vassals. The vases have been dated to the reign of Pharaoh Sesostris III (1878–1842 BCE); they include the names of nineteen Canaanite cities, one of which is "Rushalimum." This is the first mention of the city in any historical record. The text also names two of its princes, Yq'rm and Shashan. In another of these so-called Execration Texts, thought to have been inscribed a century later, "Rushalimum" is cursed again, but this time the city appears to have only one ruler. From this slender shred of evidence, some scholars have inferred that during the eighteenth century, Jerusalem, like the rest of

Canaan, had evolved from a tribal society with a number of chieftains to an urban settlement governed by a single king.[4]

Here we should pause to consider the name of the city. It seems to have incorporated the name of the Syrian god Shalem, who was identified with the setting sun or the evening star. Canaan may have been dominated politically by Egypt, but in cultural and religious affairs the chief influence was Syria. In Hazor, Megiddo, and Shechem, temples of this period have been unearthed that have clearly been built on a Syrian model. They are constructed according to the same basic plan as the king's palace, underlining the fact that all rule was seen to derive from the gods. The laity were forbidden to enter the Hekhal, or cult hall, just as they were denied access to the king's presence. They could glimpse the god's effigy, which was placed in a niche at the end of the hall, from the courtyard, through the open doors of the Hekhal. No Bronze Age temple has been unearthed in Jerusalem, but the city's name shows that the inhabitants were also open to Syrian religion. The names of the Jerusalem princes in the Execration Texts indicate that, like the people of Syria, the Jerusalemites were of Western Semitic origin and shared the same worldview.

The name "Rushalimum" can probably be translated as "Shalem has founded."[5] In the ancient world of the Near East and the Mediterranean, settlement and town-planning were regarded as divine enterprises. The Ophel hill would have appealed to the first colonists because of its water supply and its strategic advantages, but the name of the city shows that the initiative came from the god. At this date, all cities were regarded as holy places, an alien concept for us in the modern West, where the city is often experienced as a godforsaken realm in which religion has an increasingly marginal role. But long before people began to map their world scientifically, they had evolved a sacred geography to define their place in the universe emotionally and spiritually. Mircea Eliade, who pioneered the study of sacred space, pointed out that reverence for a holy place preceded all other speculation about the nature of the world.[6] It is to be found in all cultures and was a primordial religious conviction. The belief that some places were sacred, and hence fit for human habitation, was not based on an intellectual investigation or on any metaphysical speculation into the nature of the cosmos. Instead, when men and women contemplated the world about them, they were drawn irresistibly to some localities which they experienced as radically different from all others. This was an experience that was basic to their view of the world, and it went far deeper than the cerebral level of the mind. Even today our scientific rationalism has not been able to replace the old sacred geography entirely. As we shall see, ancient conceptions of holy topography still affect the history of Jerusalem and have been espoused by people who would not normally consider themselves religious. Men and women have formulated this perception of sacred space in different ways over the centuries, but in their discussion of the special status of a city such as Jerusalem certain themes tend to recur, indicating that they speak to some fundamental human need.[7] Even those who have no interest in any of the traditionally holy cities and have no belief in the supernatural often have special places to which they like to repair. Such sites are "sacred" to us because they are inextricably bound up with our conception of ourselves; they may be associated with a profound experience that transformed our lives, with memories of early childhood, or with a person who was important to us. When we visit such places, we can perhaps recall the experience of enhanced life that we once had there, an experience which momentarily convinced us that despite the distressing and arbitrary nature of much of our mundane existence, it had some ultimate meaning and value, even if we would find it hard to explain this insight in rational terms.

In the ancient world, just as in traditional societies in our own day, people tried to explain their sacred geography by saying that the world had been created by the gods. It was not, therefore, neutral territory: the landscape had something to say to humanity. When they regarded the cosmos, men and women discerned a level of existence which transcended the frailties and limitations that impeded their own lives. This represented a fuller and more powerful dimension, a reality that was at one and the same time other than they and yet deeply familiar. To express their sense of affinity with the sacred realm, they often personified it, imaging it forth in gods and goddesses with personalities similar to their own. Because they sensed this divine element in the natural world, these deities were also associated with the sun, the wind, or the life-giving rain. People told stories about these deities which were not intended to describe events that had actually happened but were a tentative attempt to express the mystery that they experienced in the world. Above all, men and women wanted to live as closely as possible to this transcendent reality. To say that they sought the meaning of life could be misleading, since the phrase suggests a clear formula that sums up the human condition. In fact, the goal of the religious quest has always been an experience, not a message. We want to feel truly alive and to fulfill the potential of our humanity, living in such a way that we are in tune with the deeper currents of existence. This search for superabundant life— symbolized by the potent, immortal gods—has informed all great religions: people wanted to get beyond the mortality and triviality of mundane experience to find a reality that would complement their human nature. In the ancient world, men and women felt that without the possibility of living in contact with this divine element, life was insupportable.[8]

Hence, as Eliade has shown, they would settle only in places where the sacred had once manifested itself, breaking down the barrier that divided the gods from humanity. Perhaps the god Shalem had revealed himself on the Ophel hill and thus made the place peculiarly his own. People could journey there, knowing that it was possible to make contact with the god in the city that he had marked out for himself. But the sacred did not only erupt into the mundane world in apparitions and epiphanies. Anything that stood out from its surroundings and ran counter to the natural order could be a hierophany, a revelation of the divine. A rock or a valley that was particularly beautiful or majestic might indicate the presence of the sacred because it could not easily be fitted into its surroundings. Its very appearance spoke of *something else*.[9] The unknown, the alien, or even the perfect seemed to the men and women of archaic societies to point to something other than themselves. Mountains which towered above the earth were particularly potent symbols of transcendence; by climbing to the summit, worshippers could feel that they had ascended to a different plane, midway between heaven and earth. In Mesopotamia, the great temple-towers known as ziggurats were designed to resemble hills; the seven levels of these huge stone ladders represented the seven heavens. Pilgrims thus imagined themselves climbing through the cosmos and at the top they could meet their gods.[10] In Syria, a more mountainous region, there was no need to create artificial hills: real mountains were experienced as sacred places. One which would be very important in the history of Jerusalem would be Mount Zaphon, the present Jebel al-Aqra, twenty miles north of Ugarit at the mouth of the Orontes.[11] In Canaan too, Mounts Hermon, Carmel, and Tabor were all revered as holy places. As we know from the Hebrew psalms, Mount Zion to the north of the Ophel hill in Jerusalem was also a sacred site. It is impossible for us to see the mountain's natural contour, since it has been concealed by the vast platform built by King Herod in the first century BCE to house the Jewish Temple. But in its natural state, Mount Zion may have stood out dramatically from the surrounding hills in such a way that it seemed to embody the sacred "other" and marked the place out as "holy."

Once a spot had been experienced as sacred, it was radically separate from its profane environs. Because the divine had been revealed there, the place became the center of the earth. This was not understood in any literal, geometric manner. It would not matter to the inhabitants of Jerusalem that nearby Hebron was also regarded as a sacred "center."

Nor when psalmists or rabbis later claimed that Mount Zion was the highest place in the world were they at all disturbed by the fact that the Western Hill, on the other side of the Tyropoeon Valley, was obviously higher than Zion. They were not describing the physical geography of the city but its place on their spiritual map. Like any other sacred hill where the divine had revealed itself, Zion was felt to be exalted because people felt closer to heaven there. It was "the center" of their world for the same reason: it was one of the places where it was possible to make contact with the divine that alone gave reality and point to their lives.

In archaic societies, people would settle only in places where such contact was possible. Eliade noted that the Australian Achilpa tribe became entirely disoriented when the sacred pole which they carried around with them on their travels was broken. It represented their link with the sacred: once it had been broken, the Achilpa simply lay down to die.[12] We are meaning-seeking creatures, and once we have lost our orientation, we do not know how to live or to place ourselves in the world. That was why cities in the ancient world were built around shrines and temples which housed the divine Presence. The sacred was the most solid reality and gave substance to our more fragmented existence. The sacred could be experienced as frightening and "other." The German historian Rudolph Otto explained in his classic book *The Idea of the Holy* that it could sometimes inspire dread and horror. Yet it was also *fascinans,* exerting an irresistible attraction because it was recognized as profoundly familiar and something that was essential to humanity. Only by associating themselves with this more potent reality could human beings ensure that their societies would survive. Civilization was fragile: cities could disappear almost overnight, as they did in Palestine during the Early Bronze Age. They could not hope to endure if they did not share to some degree the more potent and effective life of the gods.

Sometimes this search for the sacred and the cult of a holy place was associated with the nostalgia for paradise. Almost every culture has a myth of a golden age at the dawn of time, when communication with the gods was easy and intimate. The divine was felt not as a distant, eruptive force but as a fact of daily life. Humanity enjoyed enhanced powers: there was no death, no sickness, no disharmony. People longed to return to this state of primal bliss and harmony, feeling that this is what life should have been like had it not been for some original lapse.[13] Today we may no longer believe in an earthly paradise or a Garden of Eden, but the yearning for something different from the flawed present persists. There is an innate conviction that life was not *meant* to be like this: we hanker for what might have been, mourn the transitory nature of earthly existence, and feel outraged by death. We are haunted by a sense of more perfect relationships and imagine a world of harmony and wholeness, where we would feel completely in tune with our surroundings, instead of having to battle against them. This longing for an inaccessible paradise that remains irretrievably lost surfaces today in popular songs, in fiction, and in the utopian fantasies of philosophers, politicians, and advertisers. Psychoanalysts associate this nostalgia with the pain of separation we experienced at birth, when we were ejected violently and forever from our mother's body. Today many people seek this paradisal harmony in art, drugs, or sex; in the ancient world, men and women sought it by living in a place where, they believed, the lost wholeness could be recovered.

We have no direct information about the religious life in Jerusalem during the eighteenth century BCE, however. In fact, after the Execration Texts there is no further mention of Jerusalem for some time. It was a time of prosperity in Canaan. During the seventeenth century, the pharaohs were too preoccupied with domestic affairs to bother about "Retinu," and the country prospered. There were no more aggressive Egyptian campaigns; local culture could flourish. Some towns of Canaan became full city-states: architecture, furniture, pottery, and jewelry have been unearthed at such sites as Megiddo, Hazor, and Shechem. But no pottery from the seventeenth to the fifteenth century has been found in Jerusalem. For all we know, the city may even have ceased to exist during these years.

It is not until the fourteenth century BCE that we can be certain that the site was inhabited again. By that time, Egypt had managed to reassert its presence in Canaan. The pharaohs were now in conflict with the new Hittite empire in Anatolia and the Hurrian Kingdom of Mittani in Upper Mesopotamia. They needed to ensure that Canaan, an important transit country, was firmly under their control. In 1486, Pharaoh Thutmose III had put down a rebellion of Canaanite and Syrian princes at Megiddo and reduced "Retinu" to a mere dominion of Egypt. The country was divided into four administrative districts, and the princes of the city-states of Canaan became vassals of the pharaoh. They were bound to him by a personal oath and forced to pay heavy tribute. In return they seem to have expected more help and support than the pharaoh was actually prepared to give. Yet the princes still enjoyed a fair measure of independence: Egypt did not have the means to control the country completely. The princes could raise armies, fight against one another, and annex new territory for themselves. But other great powers were beginning to be interested in Canaan. Hurrians from the Kingdom of Mitanni had started to establish themselves in the country by the beginning of the fifteenth century. They are the people who are called

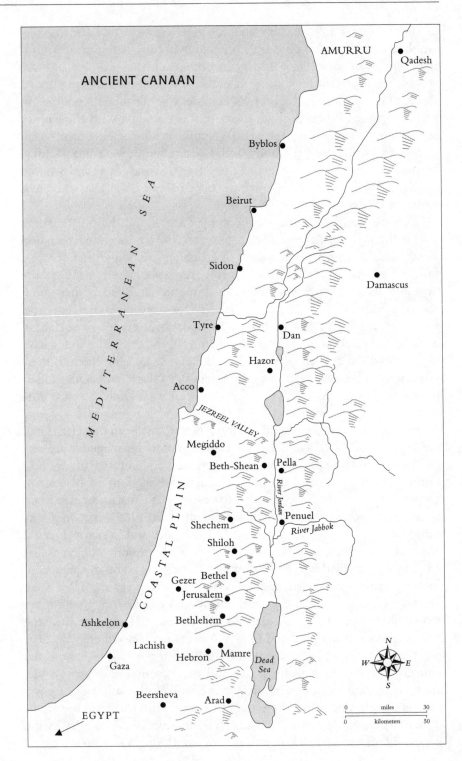

ANCIENT CANAAN

AMURRU

Qadesh

MEDITERRANEAN SEA

Byblos

Beirut

Sidon

Damascus

Tyre

Dan

Hazor

Acco

JEZREEL VALLEY

Megiddo

Beth-Shean

Pella

River Jordan

Penuel

River Jabbok

Shechem

Shiloh

COASTAL PLAIN

Gezer

Bethel

Jerusalem

Bethlehem

Ashkelon

Lachish

Mamre

Hebron

Dead Sea

Gaza

Beersheva

Arad

N
W   E
S

0   miles   30
0   kilometers   50

EGYPT

"Hivites" or "Horites" in the Bible. Unlike the local people, they were of Aryan stock, and though they did not come as conquerors, they exerted such strong influence that the Egyptians started to call Canaan "Huru" or "Hurrian Land." The Hurrians often gained positions of power in the city-states; they lived alongside the native population and taught them their Akkadian language, which became the official diplomatic tongue, and cuneiform writing.

Hurrian influence was strong in Jerusalem,[14] which emerges in the fourteenth century as one of the city-states of Canaan—albeit one of lesser importance than Hazor or Megiddo. Its territory now extended as far as the lands of Shechem and Gezer. Its ruler was Abdi-Hepa, whose name is Hurrian. Our knowledge of Jerusalem at this point is derived from the cuneiform tablets discovered at Tel el-Amarna in Egypt in 1887 CE, which seem to have been part of the royal archives of Pharaoh Amenhotep III (1386–49 BCE) and his son Akhenaten (1350–34 BCE). They consist of about 350 letters from the princes of Canaan to the pharaoh, their overlord, and show that the country was in turmoil. The city-states were at war with one another: Prince Lab'ayu of Shechem, for example, was pursuing a ruthlessly expansionist policy and had extended his territory as far north as the Sea of Galilee and westward as far as Gaza. The princes also complained of internal enemies and begged the pharaoh for help. It also appears that Egypt, then at war with the Hittites, gave them little support. The unrest in Canaan probably did not displease the pharaoh, since it meant that the city-states were unable to take a united stand against Egyptian hegemony.

Six of the Amarna letters are from Abdi-Hepa of Jerusalem, who does not appear to have been one of the more successful rulers of Canaan. He protests his loyalty to the pharaoh in extravagant terms, plangently appealing for help against his enemies—help that was not forthcoming. Abdi-Hepa could make no headway against Shechem and in the end lost all his allies. There were also uprisings in the city of Jerusalem itself. Yet Abdi-Hepa did not want Egyptian troops to be sent to Jerusalem. He had already suffered enough at the hands of the poorly trained and inadequately supplied Egyptian soldiers, who, he complained, had actually broken into his palace and tried to kill him. Instead he asked the pharaoh to send reinforcements to Gezer, Lachish, or Ashkelon. Unless help came from Egypt, the land of Jerusalem would surely fall to his enemies.[15]

Abdi-Hepa almost certainly never received his troops: indeed, at this time the hill country was fast becoming a demilitarized zone.[16] The fortified town of Shiloh, for example, was abandoned and 80 percent of the smaller highland settlements had disappeared by the early thirteenth century. Some scholars believe that it was during this period of unrest that the people whom the Bible calls the Jebusites established themselves in Jerusalem. Others claim, on the basis of the literary evidence, that the Jebusites, who were closely related to the Hittites, did not arrive in the country until after the fall of the Hittite empire, which was situated in what is now northern Turkey, in about 1200 BCE.[17] It is impossible to be certain about this one way or the other. Certainly, the archaeological investigations do not, as yet, indicate a change in the population of Jerusalem at the end of the Late Bronze Age (1550–1200 BCE). It has also been suggested that the Jebusites were simply an aristocratic family who lived in the citadel, separately from the people in the town itself.[18] It could, therefore, have been the Jebusites who repaired the old fortifications on the Ophel and built a new district on the eastern slope between the wall and the summit of the hill. Kathleen Kenyon unearthed a series of stone-filled terraces which, she believed, made this steep terrain habitable and replaced the old straggling houses and plunging streets. The work took a long time; Kenyon claimed that the project was begun in the mid-fourteenth century but was not completed until the early thirteenth century. Some of the walls were thirty-three feet high, and construction was often interrupted by such natural disasters as earthquakes and soil erosion.[19] As well as providing accommodation, this new structure was probably also part of the city's defenses. Kenyon thought that it could have been the "Millo" mentioned by the biblical writers:[20] since some of the later kings of Judah made a point of repairing the Millo, it probably had a military function. It may well have been part of the city's fortress on the crest of the Ophel. It has been suggested that the name "Zion" did not refer to the whole city of Jerusalem but originally denoted the fortress which protected the town on its northern and more vulnerable side.

During the Amarna period, Jerusalem seems to have remained loyal to Shalem, its founder-god. Abdi-Hepa speaks in his letters to the pharaoh of "the capital of the land of Jerusalem, of which the name is Beit-Shulmani [House of Shalem]."[21] But scholars believe that the Hurrians brought a new god to the city: the storm god Baal, who was worshipped by the people of Ugarit on the Syrian coast.[22] We know about Baal's cult there from the cuneiform tablets which were discovered at Ras Shamra (the modern city on the site of ancient Ugarit) in 1928. We should pause briefly to consider it, because it would have a great impact on the spirituality of Jerusalem.

Baal was not the chief god of the Syrian pantheon. His father was El, who would also make an appearance in the Hebrew Bible. El lived in a tent-shrine on a mountain, near the confluence of two great rivers which were the source of the world's fertility. Each year the gods used to assemble there to take part in the Divine Council to establish the laws of the universe. El, therefore, was the fount of law, order, and fecundity, without which no human civilization could survive. But over the years, like other high gods, El became a rather remote figure, and many people were attracted by his more dynamic son Baal, who rode upon the clouds of heaven and hurled lightning from the skies to bring the life-giving rain to the parched earth.

But Baal had to fight to the death to secure the earth's fruitfulness. In the Near East, life was often experienced as a desperate struggle against the forces of chaos, darkness, and mortality. Civilization, order, and creativity could be achieved only against great odds. People told stories about the mighty battles fought by the gods at the dawn of time which brought light out of darkness and order out of chaos and kept the lawless elements of the cosmos within due and manageable bounds. Thus in Babylon, the liturgy commemorated the battle of the young warrior god Marduk, who slew the sea-monster Tiamat, split her carcass in two, and created the world. There were similar stories about Baal. In one myth, he fought the seven-headed sea-monster Lotan, who is called "Leviathan" in the Hebrew Bible. In almost all cultures, the dragon or the monster has symbolized the unformed and the undifferentiated. By slaying Lotan, Baal had halted the slide back to the formless waste of chaos from which all life—human and divine—had sprung. The myth depicts a fear of extinction and annihilation that, especially in these early days of civilization, was a perpetual possibility.

The same terror can be felt in the stories of Baal's other battles, against the sea and the desert—two natural forces that threatened these early cities of the Near East. The sea represented everything that the civilized world was not and everything it feared. It had no boundaries, no shape. It was vast, open, and unformed. At the same time, the barren steppes constantly threatened to encroach on the fertile land, which alone was suitable for human habitation. The myths of Ugarit told the story of Baal's desperate fight with Yam-Nahar, the god of the seas and rivers, and Mot, the god of death, sterility, and drought. Mot in particular was death imagined as a voracious force, insatiably craving human flesh and blood. Baal overcame both these foes only with great difficulty: the battle with Mot was especially frightening, since, it seems, Baal was taken prisoner in the underworld—Mot's domain—the "abyss" of fearful nothingness. During Baal's imprisonment the earth was scorched by drought and reduced to desert. Finally Baal prevailed. Yet his victory was never complete. Yam and Mot both survived: the frightening power of Chaos was a perennial possibility and Death the most ineluctable of certainties. Gods and men had to join forces and fight an endless battle against them.

To celebrate his victory, Baal asked El's permission to build a palace for himself. This was quite common in ancient myth. After Marduk had created the world, gods and humans worked together to build the city of Babylon at the center of the earth. At Bab-ilani ("The Gate of the Gods") the deities could assemble each year to take part in the Divine Council: it was their home in the mundane world of men and women, who knew that they could gain access to them there. At the center of the city, they also built Marduk's great temple of Esagila, his palace in the city. There he lived and imposed the divine order, through his vicegerent the king. Architecture was thus seen as a divinely inspired exercise. The great stone cities, temples, and ziggurats seemed such colossal achievements that the human beings who had created them appeared to have transcended themselves. They were a permanent reminder of the human–divine victory against formlessness and disorder.

In the Near East, culture has always involved a struggle against the sterility and drought of the desert, which constantly threatens to obliterate all human achievement.

Similarly, Baal could not rule over the gods without a palace. Once he was properly housed in his celestial mansion of gold and lapis lazuli above Mount Zaphon, Baal had truly become "Lord," as

his name suggests. Henceforth, Baal alone would rule gods and men alike. As he proclaimed:

> [For] I alone am he that shall be king over the gods,
> [that] indeed fattens gods and men,
> that satisfies the multitudes of the earth.[23]

In his temple, Baal and his consort, Anat, celebrated their great victories which had restored order to the world:

> Did I not destroy Yam the darling of El . . .
> Was not the dragon captured and vanquished?
> I did destroy the wiggling serpent,
> the tyrant with seven heads.[24]

The people of Ugarit, who lived just twenty miles from Baal's dwelling on Zaphon, felt that because they lived in Baal's territory they shared in his victory. In the hymns of Ugarit, Baal calls Zaphon "the holy place, the mountain of my heritage . . . the chosen spot . . . the hill of victory." Zaphon was the center of their world. It was a "holy mountain," a "beautiful height," and the "joy of the whole earth."[25] Because Baal lived there, he had made Zaphon an earthly paradise of peace, fertility, and harmony. There he would "remove war from the earth. Pour out peace in the depths of the earth." "Love would increase in the depths of the fields."[26] To make sure that they would also enjoy this divine fertility and peace, the people of Ugarit built a temple which was a replica of Baal's palace on Mount Zaphon. They copied it down to the last detail that had been revealed to them, so that, according to the principle of *imitatio dei,* Baal would dwell with them too. Thus heaven would come to earth in their city and they would create an enclave of life as it was meant to be in the midst of a dangerous world.

Baal's presence among them in his temple made human life possible in Ugarit. When the people entered the temple, they felt that they had entered another dimension of existence and were once again in communion with the natural and divine rhythms of life that were normally hidden from them. They could hear

> The speech of wood and the whisper of stones,
> the converse of heaven with the earth
> Of the deeps with the stars.
> . . . lightning which the heavens do not know,
> Speech which men do not know
> And the multitude of the earth do not understand.[27]

In the ancient world, the temple was often experienced as a place of vision, where people learned to see further and in a different way. They were stretching themselves imaginatively to see into the life of things. The liturgy and the architecture of the temple were part of that creative effort to imagine a fuller and more intense mode of existence. But it was also a program for action. In their ritual, the people of Ugarit reenacted the battles of Baal and his enthronement on Mount Zaphon in a sacred drama. This autumnal festival marked the start of the New Year: Baal's victories were repeated and imitated so that the lifegiving rain would fall once again and the city be preserved in safety against the lawless forces of destruction. This enthronement ceremony also made Ugarit part of Baal's "eternal heritage,"[28] a haven—or so they hoped—of peace and plenty.

A central figure in the liturgy was the person of the king, who sat enthroned, his head glistening with the oil of victory as Baal's representative. Like other kings in the Near East, he was regarded as the viceroy of the god and had clearly defined duties. At this point, the people of the Near East did not have extravagant hopes of religion. "Salvation" for them did not mean immortality: that was a prerogative of the gods alone. Their aim was more modest: to help the gods to sustain a decent, ordered life on earth, holding hostile forces at bay. War was an essential part of the king's duties: the enemies of a city were often identified with the forces of chaos, because they could be just as destructive. Yet war was waged for the sake of peace. At his coronation, a Near Eastern king would often swear to build temples for the gods of his city and keep them in good repair. Thus the city's lifeline to the divine world would be preserved intact. But he also had a duty to build canals for the city and to ensure that it was properly fortified at all times. No city was worthy of the name if it could not provide its citizens with security from their enemies. At the beginning and end of the Babylonian *Epic of Gilgamesh,* the people of Uruk were exhorted to admire the strength and craftsmanship of the city walls:

> *Inspect the foundation terrace and examine the brickwork*
> *If its brickwork be not of burnt bricks*
> *and if the seven [wise men] did not lay its foundations.*[29]

King Gilgamesh had tried to transcend the human condition; he had left his city and gone to seek eternal life. His quest failed, but, the poet tells us, at least he had been able to ensure that his city was safe from attack, and had anchored himself in Uruk, the one place on earth that he was meant to be.

But a Near Eastern king also had another task. He had to impose the law, which was widely regarded as a divine creation which had been revealed to the king by the gods. In a famous stele, the great eighteenth-century Babylonian king Hammurabi is shown standing in front of the enthroned god Shemesh and receiving the laws from him. In his law code, he asserts that he was appointed by the gods

> to cause justice to prevail in the land,
> to destroy the wicked and the evil,
> that the strong might not oppress the weak.[30]

Besides maintaining the physical fabric of the city, the king was bound to preserve its social order. It was no good building fortifications against external foes if exploitation, poverty, and discontent were likely to cause instability within the city. The king therefore presented himself as the shepherd of his people, as Hammurabi explained in the epilogue of his code:

> I made the people rest in friendly habitations;
> I did not let them have anyone to terrorize them. . . .
> So I became the beneficent shepherd whose scepter
>   is righteous;
> My benign shadow is spread over the city.
> In my bosom I carried the people of Sumer and Akkad;
> They prospered under my protection;
> I have governed them in peace;
> I have sheltered them in my strength.[31]

In Ugarit too the king was supposed to take good care of widows and orphans:[32] by making sure that justice and fair dealing prevailed in the city, he would also ensure that famine and drought would be held at bay and the land would remain fertile. Both were essential to the divine order. A city could not be a peaceful, fecund enclave unless the welfare of the people was a top priority.[33] Throughout the Near East, this ideal of social justice was crucial to the notion of sacred kingship and the holy city. People were very much aware that only a privileged elite was able to enjoy the benefits of civilization. The fragile order could easily be overturned by an angry peasantry. Hence the battle for social justice was crucial to the ideal of the city of peace.

Just how crucial can be seen in the history of Ugarit, where some 7,000 city dwellers, who were mostly dependents of the palace, were supported by a mere 25,000 peasants in the surrounding countryside. This elaborate civilization was built on the backs of the poor—a perception that might be reflected in the stories of Baal's battles, which show creativity and order as dependent upon the subjugation of another. Eventually the system proved unworkable, and in the thirteenth century the economy collapsed, the villages were deserted, and the city-states of the region could not defend themselves against the invasions of the "sea peoples" from the Aegean islands and Anatolia. The quest for greater social equity was not just a pious fantasy. It was essential to the healthy running of the holy city and would remain so. We shall see in the history of Jerusalem that oppressive regimes would sometimes sow the seeds of their own downfall.

We have no direct evidence about the religious life of Jerusalem during the Bronze Age. Archaeologists have found no trace of a Jebusite temple, and no texts similar to those at Ugarit have been unearthed to give us detailed information about the cult of Mount Zion. Yet there are uncanny similarities between the Ugaritic texts and some of the Hebrew psalms that were used in the Israelite cult on Mount Zion. Phrases from the hymns of Ugarit appear in the psalms that celebrate the enthronement of the God of Israel on Mount Zion. They praise his victory over "Leviathan" and the dragon on the day of creation. Mount Zion is also called the city of peace, the holy mountain, and the eternal heritage of its god. Occasionally "Zion" is even called "Zaphon" in the Hebrew Bible. We know that the Hurrians also told stories about Baal and his temple on Zaphon, and scholars have therefore concluded that they brought the cult of Baal with them to Jerusalem and this would one day introduce the Ugaritic notion of a holy city of peace to the Israelite cult on Mount Zion.[34]

Because urban civilization depended upon the labor of peasants, social justice became central to the ideal of a holy city of peace in the ancient Near East.

The people of Near Eastern antiquity yearned for security, and it seems that Jerusalem was able to

provide its people with the safety for which they longed. The city was able to survive the unrest of the thirteenth century, when so many settlements of the Canaanite hill country were abandoned. The Bible indicates that the Jebusite citadel of Zion was considered impregnable. In the twelfth century, there were new threats and new enemies. Once again, Egypt began to lose control of Canaan; the Hittite empire was destroyed and Mesopotamia ravaged by plague and famine. Yet again the achievements of civilization were shown to be frail and flawed. There were large-scale migrations, as people sought a new haven. As the great powers declined, new states emerged to take their place. One of these was Philistia on the southern coast of Canaan. The Philistines may have been among the "sea peoples" who invaded Egypt, were repelled, and were made the vassals of the pharaoh. Ramses III may have settled the Philistines in Canaan to rule the country in his stead. In their new territory, they adapted to the local religion and organized themselves into five city-states at Ashkelon, Ashdod, Ekron, Gath, and Gaza. As Egypt grew weaker, Philistia became virtually independent and may even have become the de facto ruler of Canaan. But during the eleventh century, the inhabitants of Canaan had to encounter a new power in the land. A kingdom was forming in the hill country which was bigger and entirely different in kind from any previous Canaanite entity. Eventually Jebusite Zion found itself entirely surrounded by an aggressive new power: the Kingdom of Israel, which would change its destiny forever.

ISRAEL

WHO WERE the Israelites? The Bible tells us that they came originally from Mesopotamia. For a time they settled in Canaan, but
in about 1750 BCE the twelve tribes of Israel migrated to Egypt during a
famine. At first they prospered in Egypt, but their situation declined and
they were reduced to slavery. Eventually—in about 1250 BCE—they
escaped from Egypt under the leadership of Moses and lived a nomadic
life in the Sinai Peninsula. Yet they did not regard this as a permanent
solution, because they were convinced that their god, Yahweh, had
promised them the fertile land of Canaan. Moses died before the Israelites reached the Promised Land, but under his successor, Joshua, the
tribes stormed into Canaan and took the country by the sword in the
name of their God, an event that is usually dated to about 1200 BCE.
The Bible speaks of terrible massacres. Joshua is said to have subdued
"the highlands, the Negev, the lowlands, the hillsides, and all the kings
in them. He left not a man alive."[1] Each of the twelve tribes was allot-
ted a portion of Canaan, but between the territory of the tribes of
Judah and Benjamin one city held out: "The sons of Judah could not
drive out the Jebusites who lived in Jerusalem," the biblical writer
admits. "The Jebusites lived in Jerusalem side by side with the sons of
Judah, as they still do today."[2] Eventually, Jerusalem would become central to the religion of Israel, but the first time the city is mentioned
unequivocally in the Bible it appears as enemy territory.

Yet in recent years, scholars have become skeptical about the biblical
account. Archaeologists have found signs of destruction in some
Canaanite sites, but nothing that can be linked definitively with Israel.
There is no sign of any foreign invasion in the highlands, which would

become the Israelite heartland.[3] Even the biblical writers concede that Joshua's conquest was not total. We are told that he could not defeat the Canaanite city-states nor make any headway against the Philistines.[4] A careful examination of the first twelve chapters of the Book of Joshua shows that most of the action was confined to a very small area of the territory of Benjamin.[5] Indeed, the Bible leaves us with the distinct impression that the conquest of Joshua was something of a nonevent. There are still scholars—particularly in Israel and the United States— who adhere to the view that the Israelites did conquer the country in this way, but others are coming to the conclusion that instead of erupting violently into Canaan from the outside, Israel emerged peacefully and gradually from *within* Canaanite society.

There is no doubt that Israel had arrived in Canaan by the end of the thirteenth century. In a stele commemorating the successful campaign of Pharaoh Merneptah in 1207 BCE, we find this entry among the other conquests: "Israel is laid waste, his seed is not." But this is the only non-biblical reference to Israel at this time. It used to be thought that the *hapiru* or *apiru* mentioned in various inscriptions and documents of the fourteenth century were forerunners of Joshua's "Hebrew" tribes. But it appears that the *hapiru* were not an ethnic group but, rather, a class within Canaanite society. They were people who had become social outcasts, banished from the city-states for economic or political reasons. Sometimes they became brigands, sometimes they hired themselves out as mercenaries.[6] Certainly they were perceived as a disruptive force in Canaan: Abdi Hepa himself was very worried indeed about the *hapiru*. The Israelites were first called "Hebrews" while they were themselves an outgroup in Egypt, but they were not the only *hapiru* in the region.

Instead, scholars today tend to associate the birth of Israel with a new wave of settlement in the central highlands of Canaan. Archaeologists have uncovered the remains of about one hundred unfortified new villages in the hill country north of Jerusalem, which have been dated to about 1200 BCE. Hitherto this barren terrain had been unsuitable for farming, but there had recently been technological advances that made settlement feasible. The new settlers eked out a precarious existence by breeding sheep, goats, and oxen. There is no evidence that the settlers were foreigners: the material culture of these villages is substantially the same as that of the coastal plain. Archaeologists have therefore concluded that the settlers were almost certainly native Canaanites.[7] It was a time of great unrest, especially in the city-states. Some people may well have preferred to take to the hills. Their lives were hard there, but at least they were free of the wars and economic exploitation that now characterized life in the decaying cities on the coast. Some of the settlers may have been *hapiru,* others nomads, compelled during these turbulent times to change their lifestyle. Could this migration from the disintegrating Canaanite towns have been the nucleus of Israel? Certainly this is the area where the Kingdom of Israel would appear during the eleventh century BCE. If this theory is correct, the "Israelites" would have been natives of Canaan who settled in the hills and gradually formed a distinct identity. Inevitably they clashed from time to time with the other cities, and tales of these skirmishes form the basis of the narratives of Joshua and Judges.

Yet if the Israelites really were Canaanites, why does the Bible insist so forcefully that they were outsiders? Belief in their foreign origin was absolutely central to the Israelite identity. Indeed, the story of the Pentateuch, the first five books of the Bible, is dominated by the story of Israel's search for a homeland. It is inconceivable that the entire story of the Exodus is a fabrication. Perhaps some *hapiru* did flee the pharaoh's corvée (forced labor) and later join the Canaanite settlers in the hill country. Even the Bible hints that not all of the people of Israel had taken part in the Exodus.[8] Ultimately the religion and mythology of these newcomers from Egypt became the dominant ideology of Israel. The stories of a divine liberation from slavery and the special protection of the god Yahweh may have appealed to Canaanites who had themselves escaped from oppressive and corrupt regimes and had become aware that they were taking part in an exciting new experiment in their highland settlements.

Israelites did not begin to write their own history until after they had become the major power in the country. Scholars have traditionally found four sources embedded in the text of the Pentateuch. The earliest two writers are known as "J" and "E" because of their preferred use of "Yahweh" and "Elohim" respectively as titles for the God of Israel. They may have written in the tenth century, though some would put them as late as the eighth century BCE. The Deuteronomist ("D") and Priestly ("P") writers were both active during the sixth century, during and after the exile of the Israelites to Babylon. In recent years this source criticism has failed to satisfy some scholars and more radical theories have been suggested, as, for example, that the whole of the Pentateuch was composed in the late sixth century by a single author. At present, however, the four-source theory is still the customary way of approaching these early biblical texts. The historical books that deal with the later history of Israel and Judah—Joshua, Judges, and the books of Samuel and Kings—were written during the Exile by historians of the Deuteronomist school ("D"), whose ideals we shall discuss in Chapter 4. They were often working with earlier sources and chronicles but used them to further their own theological interpretation. The Chronicler, who was probably writing in the mid-fourth century BCE, is even more cavalier with his sources. None of our authors, therefore, was writing objective history that would satisfy our standards today. What they show is how the people of their own period saw the past.

This is especially true of the stories of Abraham, Isaac, and Jacob, the three patriarchs of Israel. These could have been written nearly a thousand years after the events they purport to describe. They are legends, and not historical in our sense. The biblical writers knew nothing about life in nineteenth- and eighteenth-century Canaan—there is no mention of the strong Egyptian presence in the country, for example—but the tales of the patriarchs are important because they show how the Israelites were beginning to shape a distinct identity for themselves at the time when J and E were writing. By this time, Israelites believed that they had all descended from a common ancestor, Jacob, who had been given the new name of Israel ("May God show his strength!," or, alternatively, "One who struggles for God") as a sign of his special relationship with the Deity. Jacob/Israel had twelve sons, each of whom was the ancestor of one of the tribes. Next the Israelites looked back to Jacob's grandfather Abraham, who had been chosen by God to be the founder of the new nation. So strong was their conviction that they were not of Canaanite stock originally that they wanted to trace their ancestry back to Mesopotamia. In about 1850 BCE, they believed that God had appeared to Abraham in Haran and told him: "Leave your country, your family and your father's house for the land I will show you."[9] That country was Canaan. Abraham did as he was told and left Mesopotamia, but he lived in Canaan as a migrant. He owned no land there until he bought a burial plot for his wife in the Cave of Machpelah at Hebron.

Crucial to the patriarchal narratives is the search for a homeland. Abraham, Isaac, and Jacob remained highly conscious of their alien status in Canaan.[10] As soon as he describes Abraham's arrival, J makes a point of reminding the reader: "At that time the Canaanites were in the land."[11] This is an important point. In the history of Jerusalem and the Holy Land, Jews, Christians, and Muslims have all found other people in possession. They have all had to cope with the fact that the city and the land have been sacred to other people before them and the integrity of their tenure will depend in large part upon the way they treat their predecessors.

The perception that other people were established in Canaan before the Chosen People can, perhaps, be seen in God's persistent choice of the second son instead of the first. Thus Abraham had two sons. The first was Ishmael, who was born to his concubine Hagar. Yet when Isaac was miraculously born to Abraham's aged and barren wife, Sarah, God commanded Abraham to sacrifice his oldest son. Ishmael would also be the father of a great nation, but Abraham's name must be carried on through Isaac. Consequently the patriarch dispatched Hagar and Ishmael to the desert east of Canaan, where they would certainly have perished had God not protected them. They were of little further interest to the biblical writers, but, as we shall see in Chapter 11, a people who claimed to be the descendants of Ishmael would arrive in Jerusalem centuries later. In the next generation too, God preferred the second son. Isaac's wife, Rebecca, felt her twin babies fighting in the womb, and God told her that two nations were at war in her body. When the twins were born, the second arrived grasping the heel of his brother, Esau. Consequently he was called Ya'aquob: the Heel-Holder or Supplanter.[12] When the twins grew up, Jacob managed to trick the aged Isaac into giving him the blessing that should by rights have gone to the older son. Henceforth Esau was also dismissed to the eastern lands. Yet neither J nor E discounts the claims of the rejected older siblings. There is real pathos in the story of Hagar and Ishmael, and the reader is made to sympathize with Esau's distress. When J and E were writing, the Israelites did not perceive their ownership of the Promised Land as a cause for crude chauvinism: the process of establishing themselves as a nation in their own land was painful to others and morally perplexing.

There is none of the militant zeal of Joshua, who was commanded by God to wipe out all the altars and religious symbols of the indigenous people of Canaan. This was a later Israelite ideal. Both J and E show the patriarchs behaving for the most part with respect toward the Canaanites and honoring their religious traditions. According to them, the patriarchs did not seek to impose their own God on the country, nor did they trample on the altars of the native people. Abraham seems to have worshipped El, the high god of the country. It was only later that El was fused imaginatively with Yahweh, the God of Moses. As God himself told Moses from the burning bush: "To Abraham and Isaac and Jacob I appeared as El Shaddai; I did not make myself known to them by my name Yahweh."[13] In the meantime, the land of Canaan had to reveal its own sanctity to the patriarchs, who waited for El to show himself to them in the usual sites.

Thus Jacob stumbled unawares upon the sanctity of Beth-El. He lay down to sleep at what seemed to be an unremarkable spot, using a stone as a pillow. But the site was in fact a *maqom* (a "place"), a word with cultic connotations. That night Jacob dreamed of a ladder standing in the ground beside him reaching up to heaven. It was a classic vision, reminding us of the ziggurats of Mesopotamia. At the top of the ladder was the

God of Abraham, who now assured Jacob of his protection and favor. When he woke, Jacob was overcome with the dread that often characterizes an encounter with the sacred: "Truly God is in this place and I never knew it!" he said in awe. What had seemed to be an ordinary location had proved to be a spiritual center that provided human beings with access to the divine world. "How awe-inspiring this place is! This is nothing less than a house of God [*beth-el*]; this is the gate of heaven!"[14] Before leaving, Jacob upended the stone on which he had been lying and consecrated it with a libation of oil to mark the place out as radically separate from its surroundings.

Later generations of Israelites would strongly condemn the Canaanite *matzevot,* or standing-stones, which were used as symbols of the divine. But J and E found nothing odd about Jacob's pious action here. When they were writing, Israelites were not monotheists in our sense. Yahweh, the God of Moses, was their God, and some believed that Israelites should worship him alone. But they believed that other gods existed, and, as we know from the writings of the prophets and historians, many Israelites continued to worship other deities. It seemed absurd to neglect gods who had long ensured the fertility of Canaan, and could be encountered in its sacred "places" (*bamoth*). We know that other deities were worshipped by the Israelites in Jerusalem right up until the city was destroyed by Nebuchadnezzar in 586 BCE. We shall see that Israelites honored the fertility goddess Asherah, the consort of El, in their Temple in Jerusalem as well as a host of Syrian astral deities; they also took part in the fertility rites of Baal. It was not until the exile to Babylon (597–39) that the people of Israel finally decided that Yahweh was the *only* God and that no other deities existed. They would then become very hostile indeed to all "pagan" worship. But when J and E, the earliest biblical writers, imagined the religion of their forefathers, they found nothing offensive in the notion that Jacob had seen his God in a pagan cult place and had marked this theophany with a *matzevah*.

Sometimes, therefore, the religious experiences of the patriarchs—especially those described by J—would seem rather dubious to later generations of Israelites. Thus Jews came to believe that it was blasphemous to represent their God in human form, but J shows him appearing to Abraham as a man. Abraham is sitting outside his tent at Mamre, near Hebron, when three strangers approach. With typical Near Eastern courtesy, the patriarch insists that they all sit down while he prepares a meal for them. Then the four men eat together, and in the course of the conversation it transpires quite naturally that these three visitors are really the God of Abraham and two of his angels.[15] Jews cherished this story, however, which also became very important to Christians, who regarded it as an early manifestation of God as Trinity. One of the reasons why this Mamre epiphany is so important is that it expresses a truth which is central to monotheism. The sacred does not manifest itself only in holy places. We can also encounter the divine in other human beings. It is essential, therefore, that we treat the men and women with whom we come in contact—even complete strangers—with absolute honor and respect, because they too enshrine the divine mystery. This is what Abraham discovered when he ran out joyfully to meet these three travelers and insisted on giving them all the refreshment and comfort he could. This act of compassion and courtesy led to a divine encounter.

Social justice and concern for the poor and vulnerable were crucial to the concept of sanctity in the Near East, as we have seen. It was essential to the ideal of a holy city of peace. Very early in the Israelite tradition we find an even deeper understanding of the essential sacredness of humanity. Perhaps we can see this in the stark and terrible tale of God's temptation of Abraham. He commanded the patriarch to take Isaac—"your son, your only son, whom you love"—and offer him as a human sacrifice in "the land of Moriah."[16] Since Abraham had just lost his older son, Ishmael, this would seem to mean the end of God's promise to make Abraham the father of a great nation. It made a mockery of his life of faith and commitment. Nevertheless, Abraham prepared to obey and took Isaac to the mountaintop which God had prescribed. But just as he was about to plunge the knife into Isaac's breast, an angel of the Lord commanded him to desist. Instead, Abraham must sacrifice a ram caught by its horns in a nearby thicket. There is no mention of Jerusalem in the text, but later, at least by the fourth century BCE, "the land of Moriah" would come to be associated with Mount Zion.[17] The Jewish Temple was thought to have been built on the place where Abraham had bound Isaac for sacrifice; the Muslim Dome of the Rock also commemorates Abraham's sacrifice of his son. There was a symbolic reason for this identification, because on this occasion Yahweh had let it be known that his cult must not include human sacrifice—a prohibition that was by no means universal in the ancient world—but only the sacrifice of animals. Today we find even the notion of animal sacrifice repellent, but we should realize that this practice, which was absolutely central to the religion of antiquity, did not indicate any disrespect for the animals. Sacrifice tried to engage with the painful fact that human life depended on the killing of other creatures— an insight that also lay at the heart of the combat myths about Marduk and Baal. Carnivorous humanity preyed upon plants and animals in order to survive: there were guilt, gratitude, and reverence for the beasts who were sacrificed in this way—a complex of emotions that may have inspired the prehistoric paintings in the caves of Lascaux. Today we carefully shield ourselves from the realization that the neatly packaged joints of meat we buy in the butcher shop come from other beings who have laid down their lives for our sake, but this was not the case in the ancient world. Yet it is also significant that in later years, the Jerusalem cult was thought to have been established at the moment when it was revealed that the sacredness of humanity is such that it is never permissible to sacrifice another human life—no matter how exalted the motivation.

After his ordeal, Abraham called the place where he had bound Isaac "Yahweh sees," and E glossed this by quoting a local maxim: "On Yahweh's mountain [it] is seen."[18] On the sacred mountain, midway between earth and heaven, human beings could both see and be seen by their gods. It was a place of vision, where people learned to look in a different way. They could open the eyes of their imagination to see beyond their mundane surroundings to the eternal mystery that lay at the heart of existence. We shall see that Mount Zion in Jerusalem became a place of vision for the people of Israel, though it was not their only holy place in the earlier phase of their history.

Jerusalem played no part in the formative events in which the new nation of Israel found its soul. We have seen that even at the time when the books of Joshua and Judges were written, some Israelites saw

The coffin of Prime Minister Yitzhak Rabin, who was killed on 4 November 1995 by a fellow-Jew who claimed to be acting in God's name. It was a chilling example of the danger in any spirituality which fails to recognize that the sacred is enshrined in each human person.

the city as an essentially foreign place, a predominantly Jebusite city. The Patriarchs were associated with Bethel, Hebron, Shechem, and Beersheva but do not seem to have noticed Jerusalem during their travels. But on one occasion Abraham did meet Melchizedek, King and Priest of "Salem," after his return from a military expedition. The king presented him with bread and wine and blessed him in the name of El Elyon, the god of Salem.[19] Jewish tradition has identified "Salem" with Jerusalem, though this is by no means certain,[20] and the meeting was thought to have taken place at the spring of En Rogel (known today as Bir Ayyub: Job's Well) at the conjunction of the Kidron and Hinnom valleys.[21] En Rogel was certainly a cultic site in ancient Jerusalem and seems to have been associated with the coronation of the kings of the city. Local legend made Melchizedek the founder of Jerusalem, and its kings were seen as his descendants.[22] Later, as we see in the Hebrew psalms, the Davidic kings of Judah were told at their coronation: "You are a priest of the order of Melchizedek, and for ever,"[23] so they had inherited this ancient title, along with many other of the Jebusite traditions about Mount Zion. The story of Melchizedek's meeting with Abraham may have been told first at the time of King David's conquest of the city to give legitimacy to his title: it shows his ancestor honoring and being honored by the founder of Jerusalem.[24] But the story also shows Abraham respond-ing with courtesy to the present incumbents of the city, offering Melchizedek a tithe of his booty as a mark of homage, and accepting the blessing of a foreign god. Again, the story shows respect for the previous inhabitants of Jerusalem and a reverence for their traditions.

Melchizedek's god was called El Elyon, "God Most High," a title later given to Yahweh once he had become the high god of Jerusalem. El Elyon was also one of the titles of Baal of Mount Zaphon.[25] In the ancient world, deities were often fused with one another. This was not regarded as a betrayal or an unworthy compromise. The gods were not seen as solid individuals with discrete and inalienable personalities but as symbols of the sacred. When people arrived in a new place, they would often merge their own god with the local deity. The incoming god would take on some of the characteristics and functions of his or her predecessor. We have seen that in the imagination of Israel, Yahweh, the god of Moses, became one with El Shaddai, the god of Abraham. Once the Israelites arrived in Jerusalem, Yahweh was also linked to Baal El Elyon, who was almost certainly worshipped on Mount Zion.

Jerusalem does not figure at all in the stories of the Exodus of the Israelites from Egypt, which became absolutely central to their faith. The biblical account of these events has mythologized them, bringing out their spiritual, timeless meaning. It does not attempt to reproduce them in a way that would satisfy the modern historian. It is essentially a story of liberation and homecoming that has nourished Jews in many of the darkest moments of their long and tragic history; the message of the Exodus also inspires Christians who are struggling with injustice and oppression. Even though Jerusalem plays no part in the story, the Exodus traditions would become significant in the spirituality of the Israelites on Mount Zion. The incidents can also be seen as versions of the Near Eastern creation and combat myths, except that instead of taking place in primordial time they are seen to happen in the mundane world and what comes into being is not a cosmos but a people.[26] The combat myths of Baal and Marduk ended with the construction of a city and a temple: the Exodus myth concludes with the building of a homeland. During these years, Israel passed from a state of chaos and nonbeing to a divinely established reality. Instead of splitting the carcass of a sea-monster to create the world, as Marduk did, Yahweh divided the Sea of Reeds to let his people escape from Pharaoh and his pursuing army. Instead of slaying the demonic hordes, like Marduk, Yahweh drowned the Egyptians. As always the new creation depended upon the destruction of others—a motif that would frequently recur in the future history of Jerusalem. Finally the people of Israel had passed through the divided waters to safety and freedom. In all cultures, immersion signified a return to the primal waters, the original element, an abrogation of the past and a new birth.[27] Water thus had the power to restore—if only temporarily—the pristine purity of the beginning. Their passage through the Sea of Reeds made Israel Yahweh's new creation.

Next the Israelites traveled to the holy mountain of Sinai. There, in the time-honored way, Moses climbed to meet his god on the summit, and Yahweh descended in the midst of a violent storm and volcanic eruption. The people kept their distance, as instructed: the sacred could be dangerous for the uninitiated and, at least in the Israelite tradition, could be approached only by a carefully instructed elite. On Mount Sinai, Yahweh made Israel his own people, and as a seal of this covenant, he gave Moses the Torah, or Law, which included the Ten Commandments, though, as we shall see, the Torah would not become central to the religious life of Israel until after the exile to Babylon.

Finally, before they were permitted to enter the Promised Land, the Israelites had to undergo the ordeal of a forty-year sojourn in the desert. This was no romantic interlude. The Bible makes it clear that the people constantly complained and rebelled against Yahweh during these years: they longed for what seemed, in retrospect, the easier life they had enjoyed in Egypt. In the Near East the desert was associated with death and primeval chaos. We have seen that Mot, the Syrian god of the desert, was also the voracious god of the Abyss, the dark void of death and mortality. Desert was thus a sacred area that had, as it were, gone awry and become demonic.[28] It remained a place of utter desolation in the Israelite imagination: there was no nostalgia for the wilderness years of the Exodus, as some biblical critics have imagined. Instead, the prophets and biblical writers recalled that God had made Israel his people "in the howling wilderness of the desert";[29] the desert was "a land unsown" where "no one lives"; it was "void of human dwelling," the land of "no-kingdom-there,"[30] It constantly threatened to encroach on the settled land and reduce it to the primal no-thingness. When they imagined the destruction of a city, Israelites saw it reverting to desert and becoming once again "the plumb-line of emptiness," the haunt of pelicans, hedgehogs, and satyrs, where there was "no man at all."[31] For forty years—a phrase that is used simply to denote a very long time indeed—the Israelites had to struggle through this demonic realm, entering a state of symbolic extinction before their God brought them home.

God had not entirely deserted his people in the wilderness, however. Like other nomadic peoples,

In Moses's time, the Law gave the Israelites access to the divine in the desolate wilderness. Today Jewish settlers engage in prayer and in study of the Torah in the West Bank, occupied by Israel since 1967, believing that they will thus reestablish the sacred link between the Chosen People and its God.

the Israelites possessed a portable symbol of their link with the divine realm which kept them in being. Where the Australian Aborigines carried a sacred pole, the Israelites carried the Ark of the Covenant, a shrine that would be of great importance to them in Jerusalem. Most of the descriptions of the Ark in the Bible come from the later sources, so it is difficult to guess what it was originally like. It seems to have been a chest which contained the tablets of the Law and was surmounted by two golden cherubim: their outstretched wings formed the back of a throne for Yahweh.[32] We know that an empty throne was often used as a symbol for the divine: it invited the god to sit among his worshippers. Henceforth the Throne would come to stand as a symbol of the divine Presence in the Jewish tradition. The Ark was thus an outward sign of Yahweh's presence. It was carried by members of the tribe of Levi, who were the appointed priestly caste of Israel: Aaron, Moses's brother, was the chief priest. Originally the Ark seems to have been a military palladium, since its sacred power—which could be lethal—provided protection against Israel's enemies. J tells us that when the Israelites began their day's march, the cloud representing Yahweh's presence would descend over the Ark and Moses would cry: "Arise, Yahweh, may your enemies be scattered!" At night, when they pitched tent, he would cry: "Come back, Yahweh, to the thronging hosts of Israel!"[33] The Ark enclosed the Israelites in a capsule of safety, as it were; it rendered the Abyss of the desert habitable because it kept them in touch with the sacred reality.

We know very little about the early life of Israel in Canaan. P believes that once they had settled in the hill country, the Israelites set up a tent for the Ark in Shiloh: P imagined Yahweh giving very precise instructions about this tabernacle to Moses on Mount Sinai. If the Ark was indeed originally enshrined in a tent, Yahweh was very like El, who also lived in a tent-shrine, was the source of law, and, when he appeared as El Sabaoth ("El of Armies"), was enthroned on cherubim. In the Book of Samuel, however, the Ark seems to have been housed in the Hekhal (or cult hall) of a more conventional temple in Shiloh.[34] But Israelites seem to have worshipped at a number of other temples, in Dan, Bethel, Mizpah, Oprah, and Gibeon, as well as at outdoor *bamoth*. Some Israelites would have worshipped other gods, alongside Yahweh, who was felt to be a foreign deity who had not yet properly settled in Canaan. He was still associated with the southern regions of Sinai, Paran, and Seir. They imagined him leaving this territory, when his people were in trouble, and riding on the clouds to come to the help of his people: this is how he appears in some of the earliest passages of the Bible.[35] The Israelites may even have developed a liturgy which reenacted the theophany of Mount Sinai, with braying trumpets reproducing the thunder and incense recreating the thick cloud that had descended on the mountain-top. These elements would also later appear in the Jerusalem cult. The ceremony thus imitated the decisive appearance of Yahweh on Sinai, and this symbolic reenactment would have created a sense of Yahweh's presence among his people yet again.[36] Unlike most of the Near Eastern gods, therefore, Yahweh was at first regarded as a mobile deity who was not associated with one fixed shrine. Yet the Israelites also commemo-rated their liberation from Egypt. Over the years the old spring festival was used to recall the Israelites' last meal in Egypt, when the Angel of Death passed them by but slew all the firstborn sons of the Egyptians. Eventually, this family feast would be called Passover (Pesaḥ).

By about 1030 BCE, the people of the northern hill country had a strong sense of kinship and solidarity. They thought of themselves as a dis-tinct people with a common ancestry. They had been ruled till then by a series of "judges" or chieftains, but eventually they aspired to establish a monarchy like the other peoples of the region. The biblical authors have mixed feelings about this move. They show Samuel, the last of the judges, as bitterly opposed to the idea: he warns the people of the oppression and cruelty that a king would inflict upon them.[37] But in fact the creation of the Kingdom of Israel was a natural and, perhaps, an inevitable develop-ment.[38] The great powers in Assyria, Mesopotamia, and Egypt were in eclipse at this time, and other, smaller states had appeared to fill the power vacuum: Ammon, Moab, Edom. The Israelites found themselves sur-rounded by aggressive competitors who were eager to conquer the Canaanite highlands. Ammonites and Moabites infiltrated their territory from the east and the Philistines harried them from the west. On one occasion the Philistines sacked and destroyed the city of Shiloh, carrying off the Ark of the Covenant as a war trophy. They quickly returned it, however, once they experienced the deadly power of this palladium. Now that it was no longer protected by a shrine or a temple, the Israelites also found the sanctity of the Ark frightening, so they lodged it in a pri-vate house in Kireath-Jearim, on the border of their land.[39] All this polit-ical turbulence probably convinced the Israelites that they needed the strong leadership of a king, and, reluctantly, Samuel anointed Saul of the tribe of Benjamin as the first King of Israel.

Saul ruled over a larger territory than any previous king in Canaan. It included the whole of the central highlands, on both sides of the Jordan, north of the city-state of Jerusalem, which was still ruled by the Jebusites. (See map.) In the Bible, Saul is a tragic figure: deserted by his God for daring to take initiative in a cultic matter, prey to paralyzing bouts of depression, and slowly watching his power ebb away. Yet even in this critical narrative, we can see that Saul's achievements were con-

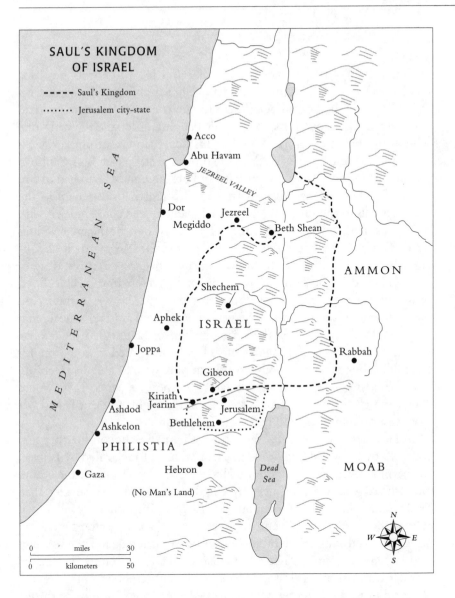

SAUL'S KINGDOM
OF ISRAEL

- - - - - Saul's Kingdom
·········· Jerusalem city-state

MEDITERRANEAN SEA

Acco
Abu Havam
JEZREEL VALLEY
Dor
Megiddo
Jezreel
Beth Shean
AMMON
Shechem
Aphek
ISRAEL
Joppa
Rabbah
Gibeon
Kiriath Jearim
Ashdod
Jerusalem
Ashkelon
Bethlehem
PHILISTIA
Gaza
Hebron
Dead Sea
MOAB
(No Man's Land)

N
W E
S

0   miles   30
0   kilometers   50

siderable. Ruling from Gibeon, which contained the most important Yahwist temple in Israel, Saul steadily increased his territory, and the people of the hills joined him voluntarily. For nearly twenty years he was able to hold his kingdom against his enemies, until he and his son Jonathan were killed by the Philistines at the battle of Mount Gilboa in about 1010 BCE. After his death, he was eulogized in some of the most moving poetry in the Bible:

> *Saul and Jonathan, loved and lovely,*
> *neither in life, nor in death, were divided.*

Swifter than eagles were they,
stronger were they than lions.[40]

This lament was sung not by one of Saul's loyal followers but by a rebel who had fled his court. David had been a highly privileged warrior in Saul's kingdom: he had been the intimate friend of Jonathan and had been given the hand of Michal, Saul's daughter. He was the only one who could bring comfort to Saul in his depression, soothing away his despair with song and poetry. Yet, the biblical historians tell us, Saul had become jealous of David's popularity and prestige, and David had to run for his life. First he had lived with a band of partisans as *hapiru* in the deserted hills to the south of Jerusalem. Finally he had allied himself with the Philistines, the deadly enemies of Israel. When he heard of Saul's death, David of the tribe of Judah was living in the Negev town of Ziklag, which had been given to him by his new overlord, Achish, King of Gath.[41] David is one of the most complex characters in the Bible. Poet, musician, warrior, rebel, traitor, adulterer, terrorist, he was certainly no paragon, even though—later—he would be revered as Israel's ideal king. After Saul's death, Ishbaal, the surviving son of Saul, ruled his father's northern Kingdom of Israel, while David established a kingdom for himself in the sparsely inhabited southern hills, with a capital at Hebron. The Philistines may have encouraged this venture, since they would thus, through their vassal, have a toehold in the highlands. But David was playing a double game and had larger ambitions.

In Jerusalem, the Jebusites thus found themselves uncomfortably surrounded by two rival kingdoms: the Kingdom of Israel, ruled by Ishbaal, in the north, and the Kingdom of Judah, ruled by David, in the south. But Ishbaal was a weak ruler: his kingdom was probably smaller than Saul's had been, and he antagonized his most important commander, who defected to David. Eventually, seven and a half years after David had been crowned king in Hebron, Ishbaal was murdered, and the assassins fled to David's court. David's hour had come. He carefully dissociated himself from Ishbaal's death by having his murderers executed. As the husband of Saul's daughter Michal, he had a tenuous claim to the throne of the Kingdom of Israel. Soon representatives of the tribes of the northern kingdom came to David, made a treaty with him in the Temple of Yahweh in Hebron, and anointed him King of Israel. David was now ruler of the United Kingdom of Israel and Judah. But in the middle of his territory was the Jebusite city-state of Jerusalem, which he intended to make his capital.

3

CITY OF DAVID

THE JEBUSITES were convinced that David would never be able to conquer their city. Jerusalem may not have been the most venerable or powerful of the Canaanite city-states, but, compared with David's upstart kingdom, it was of considerable antiquity, was powerfully fortified, and, over the years, had earned the reputation of being impregnable. When David's troops arrived at the foot of the Ophel, the Jebusites jeered contemptuously: "You will not get in here. The blind and the lame will hold you off."[1] Perhaps they even paraded the blind and the lame of the city on the walls, as was the custom of the Hittite army, to warn any soldier who dared to penetrate the stronghold of his fate.[2] But David refused to be intimidated. The first man to strike down a Jebusite, he vowed, would become the commander of his army. His old comrade Joab, son of Zeruiah, took up the challenge, possibly by climbing up "Warren's Shaft," the water conduit that led from the Gihon Spring into the city.[3] We do not know exactly how David conquered Jerusalem: the biblical text is both incomplete and obscure. But his conquest of the city proved to be a watershed, and its effects still reverberate today. A city which had hitherto been of only secondary importance in Canaan had been drawn into the ambit of the tradition that would eventually become historical monotheism. This would make it one of the most sacred—and hence one of the most disputed—places in the world.

David could not have foreseen this. When he conquered the city in about the year 1000 BCE, he would simply have been relieved to have overcome this alien Jebusite enclave in the heart of his United Kingdom and to have found a more suitable capital for himself. The union of Israel and Judah was fragile. The northern kingdom still regarded itself as a distinct entity, and the people would have had mixed feelings about submitting to David, the erstwhile traitor. To have continued to rule from Hebron would have been unwise, since it would have allied David too clearly with his own southern Kingdom of Judah. The old city-state of Jerusalem, however, was neutral territory, as it had belonged to neither Israel nor Judah and had no connection with any of the old tribal traditions. Because David had conquered the city with his own troops, it became, according to the custom of the region, his personal property, and he renamed it ʾIr David: City of David.[4] It would thus remain neutral, unaffiliated with either Judah or Israel, and David could treat the city and its environs as his own royal domain. There were also strategic advantages. Jerusalem was well fortified and more central than Hebron. High up in the hill country, it would be secure from sudden attack by the Philistines, by the tribes of Sinai and the Negev, or by the new kingdoms of Ammon and Moab on the east bank of the River Jordan. In his new capital, David was now undisputed king of a continuous stretch of land in the hill country, the largest unified state ever achieved in Canaan.

What was David's capital like? By the standards of today, the city was tiny, comprising some fifteen acres and consisting, like other towns in the area, of little more than a citadel, a palace, and houses for the military and civil personnel. It could not have accommodated many more than two thousand people. The Bible does not tell us that David conquered the *city,* however: our authors emphasize that he captured "the fortress of Zion" and that he went to live in "the citadel."[5] There is a passage in the Book of Joshua which calls Jerusalem "the flank of the Jebusites," suggesting that the city of "Jerusalem" may have been seen as separate from "the fortress of Zion."[6] David may thus have simply seized control of the Jebusite citadel in what amounted to a military coup d'état. The Bible makes no mention of a massacre of the population of Jerusalem like those described in the Book of Joshua. Nor is there any hint that the Jebusite inhabitants of Jerusalem were driven out of the city and replaced by Yahwists. It is not impossible, then, that David's conquest was merely a "palace coup" by means of which he and a few of his closest associates replaced the Jebusite king and his immediate entourage, leaving the Jebusite city and its population intact. We can only speculate but, as we have seen, the first time Jerusalem is mentioned in the Bible, the author tells us that Jebusites and Judahites were *still* living in the city side by side.

Thus, David, who was famous for his wholesale slaughter of Philistines and Edomites, may well have been a just and merciful conqueror of Jerusalem. He not only treated the existing inhabitants of the city with respect but even worked closely with them, incorporating them into his own administration. Joshua would have torn down the altars of the Jebusites and trampled on their sacred symbols. But there is no record of David interfering in any way with the local cult. Indeed, we shall see that Jebusite religious ideas and enthusiasms were actually brought into the worship of Yahweh in Jerusalem. J sees David as another Abraham: he believes that David's kingdom fulfilled the ancient promises, since the descendants of Abraham had indeed become a mighty nation and had inherited the Land of Canaan.[7] But David was also like Abraham in honoring the faith of the people of the country.

In the ʾIr David, there was, therefore, a creative interaction of Jebusite and Israelite traditions. Araunah, who may have been the last Jebusite king, was allowed to keep his estate outside the city walls on the crest of Mount Zion. David also took over the old Jebusite administration. The Canaanite city-states had developed a political and fiscal bureaucracy over the centuries, whereas the Israelites and Judahites of the hill country would have had neither the experience nor the expertise to administer a city-state. Most of them were probably illiterate. It made sense, therefore, to keep the old administration and to make use of the Jebusite officials, who would be able to help him to keep the city running smoothly and to ensure that David enjoyed good relations with his new Jebusite subjects. David's behavior in Jerusalem indicates that the Israelites did not yet consider it a sacred duty to hold aloof from the people of the country: that would not become the norm in Israel until after the Babylonian exile. When the Egyptians controlled Canaan, they had probably taught the people their methods of administration: in the Bible we see that the Davidic and Solomonic court was identical to that of Egypt. It had a grand vizier, a secretary for foreign affairs, a recorder in charge of internal matters, and a "king's friend." So the system that was in place during the Amarna period was still operating during the reign of David's son Solomon. Some of Solomon's officials had non-Semitic names,[8] and David almost certainly took over the Jebusite standing army. These were the *kereti* and *peleti* ("Cretans" and "Philistines") of the Bible: they were mercenaries who formed David's personal bodyguard. There was, therefore, very little disruption after King David's conquest of the city, which retained its Jebusite character. Its new name—ʾIr David—never became popular. Most people continued to use the old pre-Davidic names, Jerusalem and Zion.

Indeed, the royal family may have had Jebusite blood, since it is possible that David actually married a Jebusite woman. Later there would be strict laws forbidding Israelites to marry foreigners, but neither David nor Solomon had any scruples about this. David had seduced Bathsheba, the wife of "Uriah the Hittite," one of the Jebusite officers of his army.

(The Jebusites, it will be recalled, were related to the Hittites.) So that he could marry Bathsheba, David had arranged Uriah's death by having him placed in a particularly dangerous position in a battle against the Ammonites. Bathsheba's name may originally have been "Daughter of the Seven Gods" (which was written as *sibbiti* in cuneiform but became *sheva,* "seven," in Hebrew).[9] The son born to David and Bathsheba was thus half Jebusite. He was given the good Israelite name Jedidiah ("Beloved of Yahweh"), as a sign that he had been chosen as David's heir, but the name his parents gave him was Solomon, which may have been connected with Shalem, the ancient deity of Jerusalem. The Chronicler, however, connects it with the Hebrew *shalom:* unlike his father, Solomon would be a man of "peace."[10]

Other famous Jerusalemites who would become very important in the Jewish tradition may also have been Jebusites. One of these was the prophet Nathan.[11] We are told of the origins of nearly every other prophet in the Bible, but Nathan is introduced without even a patronymic. Perhaps he was the adviser of the Jebusite king; if so, he would have been a very helpful mediator between David and his new Jebusite subjects. Thus Nathan rebuked David sternly after the death of Uriah, not because he was imbued with Mosaic morality but because such a flagrant abuse of power would have been reprehensible in any Near Eastern monarch who had vowed to establish justice in his kingdom. The murder of Uriah could also have gravely damaged David's relations with the Jebusite population. Zadok, the chief priest of Jerusalem, may also have been a Jebusite, though this has been hotly disputed in the past.[12] Later, as we shall see, all the priests of Israel had to prove that they were Zadok's descendants, since by that time Zadok had become a symbol of Jewish authenticity. But Zadok is a Jebusite name. Later the Chronicler gave him an impeccable genealogy which traced his ancestry back to Aaron, but it is five generations longer than the number of generations which were supposed to have elapsed between David and Aaron.[13] Perhaps the Chronicler also incorporated Zadok's own Jebusite lineage. To have dismissed the chief priest of El Elyon could have alienated the local people. To satisfy the Israelites, David appointed Abiathar, a descendant of the old priesthood of Shiloh, to serve alongside Zadok. But Abiathar would not long survive David's death, and it was Zadok who became the chief priest of Jerusalem. Nevertheless, the sight of an Israelite and a Jebusite priest serving side by side was emblematic of the coexistence that David wanted to establish in Jerusalem. He needed symbols that could unite his increasingly disparate kingdom and hold its various elements together. David called one of his sons Baalida, showing that he was open to the local Zion traditions, and many of the Jebusites' old cultic practices on Mount Zion would blend fruitfully with the Israelite traditions of Yahweh in Jerusalem.

One of David's first acts was to move the Ark of the Covenant, which was still lodged in Kireath-Jearim on the western border of his kingdom, into Jerusalem. This was an inspired, if perilous, decision. The people of the northern kingdom who still felt uneasy about David would have been impressed by the presence of the Ark, which enshrined their most sacred traditions, in his city. It would legitimize his rule and also transform Jerusalem, which had no religious significance for Yahwists, into a holy place. But David's first attempt to transfer the Ark ended in tragedy. It was not up to human beings to establish a holy place on their own initiative: the sanctity of a site had to be revealed. Yahweh had often been envisaged as a mobile god in the past, but he could not be moved about at the mere whim of a king. A sacred object is potentially dangerous and can be approached only by those who have taken the proper precautions. This became fatally apparent during the Ark's first journey when Uzzah, one of the attendants, put out his hand to steady it when it seemed in danger of falling from the cart, and was killed instantly. The Ark symbolized Yahweh's presence, and the incident showed that David was attempting to bring a mighty and unpredictable power into the city, not a pious souvenir. If Yahweh came to live in Zion it would be because he—and he alone—had chosen to do so.

Three months later, David tried again. This time Yahweh did allow the Ark to enter the territory of Jerusalem without mishap. David danced and whirled before the Ark, clad only in a brief linen garment, like a priest. Periodically he stopped the procession and sacrificed a sheep and a goat. Finally the Ark was carried into the tent-shrine that had been prepared for it beside the Gihon Spring, with great ceremony and rejoicing.[14] By deigning to dwell in the City of David, Yahweh gave an unequivocal sign that he had indeed chosen David to be King of Israel. Henceforth, Yahweh's choice of Zion as a permanent home was inextricably linked to his election of the House of David. This became clear when David decided that it was time to build a temple for Yahweh in Jerusalem. When he first mooted the idea to Nathan, the prophet was enthusiastic. It was the duty of a Near Eastern monarch to build a house for the god on whom his rule depended. But Yahweh had other plans: he told Nathan that he had always led the life of a wanderer in a tent. He did not want a house for himself; instead, he would build a house for David, a dynasty that would last forever.[15]

Perhaps Nathan feared that it was too soon for David to dethrone El Elyon by building a temple to a foreign god within Jebusite Jerusalem.

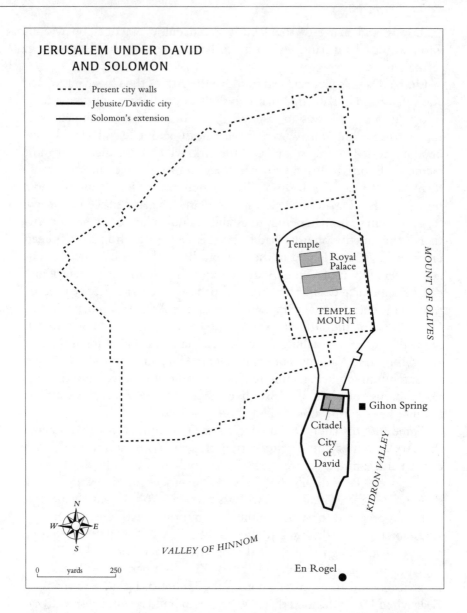

David may have chosen the site of the Gihon Spring, outside the walls, out of respect for Jebusite sensibilities. Or perhaps the tribes of Israel and Judah were averse to the idea: they may have become attached to Yahweh's nomadic image and been reluctant to see him becoming like all the other gods of Canaan, confined to a particular sanctuary. Perhaps people feared the power that such a temple would bring to David. The biblical writers may have included the story of Yahweh's refusal of a temple because they were disturbed that David, their ideal king, had

Religion is still used as grounds for appropriating territory in the Near East today. On the festival of Passover, Jewish settlers on the Israeli-occupied West Bank march through Arab territory, a "pilgrimage" that establishes an aggressive Jewish presence in what they believe is their holy land.

failed to build a temple for his God. The Chronicler thought that David had been denied this high honor because he had shed too much blood and that Solomon had been given the privilege because he was a man of peace.[16] We have seen that building had a religious significance in the cities of the ancient world. David had achieved other construction work in Jerusalem, as befitted a king. He had built himself a palace of cedar wood brought from the Lebanon; he had repaired the "Millo," a word that seems to puzzle the biblical writers but probably referred to the old terraces on the Ophel. He had also built the Tower of David, a new citadel. To accommodate the growing number of civil servants, craftsmen, and soldiers that his expanding empire required, he had enlarged the city, breaking down the walls at one point to do so. But just as Moses, who had led the people out of Egypt, had died on the threshold of the Promised Land, David had led the people of Yahweh into Jerusalem but had not been permitted to build the temple that would one day make this Jebusite city the holiest place in the Jewish world.

He had at least been able to prepare the ground by purchasing the site of the future Temple of Solomon from Araunah, who may have been the last Jebusite king. David had sinned, our authors tell us, by ordering a census. This was always an unpopular measure, because it was usually a prelude to taxation and forced labor. As a result, God sent a plague upon the kingdom which killed seventy thousand people in three days. Finally David saw Yahweh's "angel" standing beside the threshing floor of Araunah on Mount Zion, with his arm outstretched toward the city below. David could only avert the plague, he was informed by a court prophet, by building an altar to Yahweh on the site of this theophany. The biblical writers show David and Araunah working harmoniously together during this crisis. The incident is reminiscent of Abraham's purchase of the Cave of Machpelah from Ephron the Hittite. Like Ephron, Araunah wanted to give the place away without charging David a single shekel, but David, who could simply have annexed the area, behaved with admirable courtesy and respect toward his predecessor and insisted on paying the full price.[17] Today many scholars believe that the site may have been one of the holy places of Jebusite Jerusalem: threshing floors were often used in Canaan for public meetings or prophetic divination or in the fertility cult of Baal, and a floor such as that owned by Araunah, in a high exposed position at the entrance of the city, could well have been used in the cult.[18] The biblical writers do not mention this, perhaps because they were disturbed by the possibility of their Temple having been built on a pagan *bamah* (cult place), but such continuity was common in antiquity. Araunah shows no anger but seems quite willing to share this sacred space with David, even offering to pay for the first sacrifice on the new altar. Holiness was not something that human beings could own or feel possessive about. The theophany had shown that the place belonged to the gods, and in the next generation, the children of David and of Araunah would pray together on Mount Zion.

David is also said to have collected the materials for a new temple, sending to his ally Hiram, King of Tyre, for cedarwood and juniper. The Chronicler in particular cannot bear the idea that David took no part in the building of the Temple. He tells us that Yahweh had revealed the plan of the future sanctuary in minute detail and that David then passed on these divine instructions to his son Solomon.[19] The Temple could thus be built "in accordance with what Yahweh with his hand had written in order to make the whole work clear for which he was providing the plans."[20] A king could not choose the site of a temple: it had to be built at a site which had been revealed as one of the "centers" of the world. That is why kings so often chose sites of former temples which were known to yield access to the divine. In the same way, an architect was not expected to be original when he designed a new temple. It was to be a *symbol*. The Greek from which this word derives means that two things have been put together, and in the premodern world this idea was taken very seriously. It was the basis of ancient religion. A temple had to be a copy of the god's heavenly home, and it was this likeness which linked the celestial archetype with its earthly replica here below, making the two in some sense one. This close similarity was what made it possible for the deity to reside in his mundane sanctuary as he did in his heavenly palace. Consequently the plans of a temple had to be revealed, as they were to David, so that the dimensions and furnishings of the god's home in the world above could be accurately reproduced on earth.

Yet there was also a strong political element in all this. By conveying the Ark to Jerusalem, David was gradually appropriating the city. First he had brought the most sacred object of his people to the foot of the Ophel and then, by purchasing the threshing floor of Araunah, was preparing the way for Yahweh's eventual enthronement in his own temple on Mount Zion. Under Solomon, Yahweh would become the El Elyon of Jerusalem, its Most High God. In the same way, David was building a small empire for himself step by step. First he subjugated the Philistines; indeed, he may have defeated them in the Valley of Rephaim, southwest of Jerusalem, before he conquered the city. At some stage, he must also have incorporated the other city-states of Canaan into his empire, though the Bible does not mention this. They may have accepted vassal status. Finally he subdued the neighboring kingdoms of Moab and Edom, together with a substantial area in Syria. (See map.) The Israelites did not forget the Kingdom of David: never again would they be so politically powerful. There is no mention of the kingdom in any of the other Near Eastern texts of the period, however, and for this reason it has been thought by some to be a fantasy which, like the stories of the Patriarchs, has no real historical basis. But the general scholarly consensus is that the United Kingdom of Israel and Judah did indeed exist. Too many political, economic, and commercial details in the biblical account mesh with what we know of Near Eastern society at this time for the empire of David to be an entire fabrication. Mesopotamia and Egypt were both in decline, preoccupied with their own affairs, and may have had no contact with the Davidic state. Moreover, the Bible does not idealize the kingdom. Alongside the glowing descriptions, we also read of a nation bitterly divided against itself, exceeding its resources, and clearly heading for a crisis.

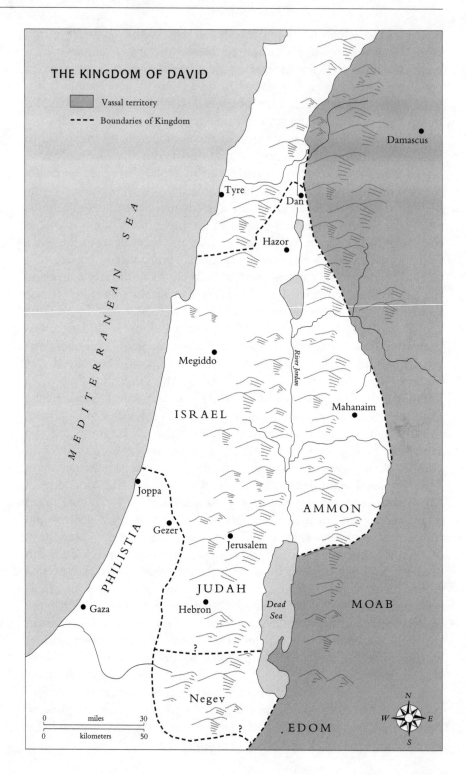

THE KINGDOM OF DAVID

Vassal territory

- - - Boundaries of Kingdom

MEDITERRANEAN SEA

Tyre

Dan

Hazor

Damascus

Megiddo

ISRAEL

River Jordan

Mahanaim

Joppa

Gezer

Jerusalem

AMMON

PHILISTIA

Gaza

JUDAH

Hebron

Dead Sea

MOAB

Negev

EDOM

0 — miles — 30

0 — kilometers — 50

N W E S

David may have been a hero posthumously, but he was not universally loved in his own lifetime. His son Absalom led a revolt against him, erecting a monument to himself at the spring of En Rogel, a cult-place associated with the Jebusite monarchy, and was acclaimed King of Israel and Judah at Hebron. The situation was so grave that David had to flee Jerusalem and crushed the revolt, which had popular support, only with his superior military capability. The union between Israel and Judah was also fragile, since David seems to have favored his own Kingdom of Judah. After Absalom's revolt, the whole of Israel seceded from his United Kingdom, and again David could reassert his power only by using force. At the very end of his life, there was a split between the Jebusites and the Israelites in Jerusalem. As David lay dying, his eldest surviving son, Adonijah, had himself crowned at En Rogel with the backing of the old *garde* of Hebron, including Joab, the commander, and Abiathar, the priest. What can perhaps be called the Jebusite faction obtained David's support for a countercoup. Nathan, Zadok, and Bathsheba, accompanied by the old Jebusite army of *kereti* and *peleti*, took Solomon to Yahweh's shrine beside the Gihon Spring and crowned him there with great fanfare. Adonijah immediately surrendered, and together with Joab he was eventually executed, while Abiathar the priest was banished. When David died, the Jebusite party could be said to have triumphed over the newcomers to Jerusalem.

Under David, Jerusalem ceased to be a minor Canaanite city-state and became the capital of an empire. Under Solomon, who began his reign in about 970 BCE, Jerusalem acquired a regional status and doubled in size. Solomon had a huge harem of princesses, the daughters of allied or subject kings. He also achieved the rare distinction of marrying one of the pharaoh's daughters. The kingdom now had a powerful army of chariots—the latest in military technology—and a fleet at Ezion Geber on the Gulf of Aqaba. Solomon became an arms dealer, trading chariots and horses with Egypt and Cilicia. The Bible tells us that the Queen of Sheba (in modern Yemen) came to visit Solomon, attracted by his reputation for wisdom. The story may reflect the growing importance of Solomon's kingdom, since if he had started to trade in the Red Sea this might have upset the Sabean economy. Solomon achieved legendary status; his wealth and wisdom were said to be prodigious, and, as befitted a successful king, he embarked on a massive building project, restoring the old fortress cities of Hazor, Megiddo, and Arad.

Jerusalem became a cosmopolitan city and was the scene of Solomon's most ambitious construction program. Extending the city to the north, Solomon built a royal acropolis on the site of Araunah's old estate on the crest of Mount Zion: its plan, as far as we can tell from the biblical sources, was similar to other tenth-century acropolises which have been unearthed at several sites in Syria and northwestern Mesopotamia. It consisted of an elaborate Temple to Yahweh and a royal palace for the king, which, significantly, took nearly twice as long to build as the Temple.[21] There were also other buildings: the cedar-pillared House of the Forest of Lebanon, whose function is not entirely clear to us; a treasury; the Judgment Hall, containing Solomon's magnificent ivory throne; and a special palace for the daughter of the pharaoh, Solomon's most illustrious wife.

None of this has survived. Our knowledge of the Temple, which proved to be the most important of these buildings, is derived entirely from the biblical writers, who dwelt lovingly on every remembered detail, sometimes long after the building itself had been destroyed. It was dedicated to Yahweh and designed to house the Ark of the Covenant. Unlike most Near Eastern temples, it contained no effigy of the presiding deity to symbolize his presence, since from the time he had revealed himself to Moses in the burning bush Yahweh had refused to be defined or represented in human iconography. But in every other respect, the Temple conformed to the usual Canaanite and Syrian model. It was built and probably designed by Tyrian craftsmen and seems to have been a typical example of Syrian imperial architecture.[22] Ordinary worshippers did not enter the temple buildings, and the sacrifices were performed in the courtyard outside. The sanctuary itself was quite small and consisted of three parts: the Vestibule (Ulam), at the eastern end; the cult hall (Hekhal); and, up a short flight of steps, the Holy of Holies (Devir), which housed the Ark and was hidden by a curtain of blue, crimson, and purple linen.[23] (See diagram.) The furniture shows how thoroughly the Jerusalem cult of Yahweh had accommodated itself to the spiritual landscape of the Near East. Apart from the Ark, there were no obvious symbols of the Exodus. Instead, the Bible tells us, there were two large golden candlesticks in the Hekhal, together with a golden table for shewbread, and an incense altar of gold-plated cedarwood. There was also a bronze serpent, later said to have been the one used by Moses to cure the people of plague, but which was probably connected with the old Jebusite cult.[24] At the entrance of the Ulam were two freestanding pillars, known enigmatically as "Yakhin" and "Boaz," and outside,[25] in the open courtyard, stood the imposing altar of sacrifice and a massive bronze basin, supported by twelve brazen oxen, representing Yam, the primal sea. The walls of the Temple, within and without, were covered with carved figures of cherubs, palm trees, and open flowers.[26] Syrian influence is clear. The bronze sea recalled Baal's battle with Yam-Nahar, the oxen were common symbols of divinity and fertility, while the pillars Yakhin and

CONJECTURAL PLAN
OF SOLOMON'S TEMPLE

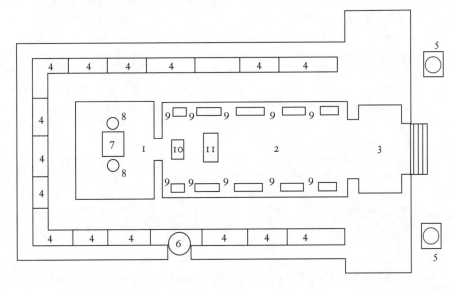

1. Devir (Holy of Holies)
2. Hekhal (the cult hall)
3. Ulam (Vestibule)
4. Chambers
5. Jachin and Boaz pillars
6. Winding staircase
7. The Ark
8. The Cherubim
9. Tables for candlesticks
10. Incense altar
11. Table of shewbread

Boaz may have been Canaanite standing-stones (*matzevot*). The biblical authors refer to the Canaanite rather than the Hebrew calendar when they describe the building of the Temple, and its dedication in the month of "Ethanim" (September/October) could have coincided with the autumn festival of Baal, which celebrated his victory over Mot and his enthronement on Mount Zaphon. In the Israelite tradition, this festival would be known as Sukkoth (Tabernacles), and eventually, as we shall see, this agricultural celebration would be reinterpreted and linked to the Exodus.

Yet the Temple, teeming with apparently "pagan" imagery, became the most cherished institution in Israel. Some prophets and reformers would feel unhappy about it and urge the people to return to the purer religion of the Exodus, but when Solomon's Temple was destroyed by Nebuchadnezzar, most Israelites felt their world had come to an end. Perhaps we should not be surprised that most of the people found these symbols of Canaanite and Syrian myth compatible with the religion of the Ark and the Exodus. We have seen that the legends of the Exodus had transposed, in another key, the old myths of Baal and Marduk. If we see the Exodus story as merely a historical event which is "true," then Baal's battle with Yam is simply a fantasy that is "false." But if instead we look for the inner meaning of the Exodus events and experience its power as a timeless truth, we can see that the brazen sea in the courtyard of Solomon's Temple was not entirely out of place. Both speak of that endless battle with the powers of darkness and of a rite of passage. Just as Jews remind themselves that every generation must regard itself as having escaped from slavery in Egypt, the presence of Yam was a reminder that the forces of chaos were never entirely overcome. Placed at the threshold of the Temple, which housed the divine Presence, it was a reminder of the challenge and effort that the creativity inspired by the sacred seems to inspire and require.

We know from the psalms which are connected with the Jerusalem cult of Yahweh that the Temple was imaginatively associated with Mount Zion. Once the Ark was installed there, the site became for the Israelites a "center" that linked heaven and earth and also had its roots in the underworld, represented by the primal sea. Like the Sacred Mountain, the Temple was a symbol of the reality that sustains the life of the cosmos. Like Jacob's lad-

A rabbi prays near the site of the Temple Mount in Jerusalem today. Still drawn by the great holiness of Solomon's Temple, he seeks to get as close as he can to its foundations, which now lie beneath the Muslim Ḥaram al-Sharif.

der, it represented a bridge to the source of being, without which the fragile mundane world could not subsist. Because it was built in a place where the sacred had revealed itself in the past, worshippers could hope to make contact with that divine power. When they entered the holy precincts, they had stepped into another dimension which, they believed, existed contemporaneously with the mundane world and kept it in being. Mount Zion had become radically different from the surrounding territory, therefore: in Hebrew the word for "holy" (*kaddosh*) means "other," "set apart." The very plan of the building, with its three-tiered gradations of sanctity culminating in the Devir (the Holy of Holies), symbolized the transcendence of the sacred. Entry to the Devir was prohibited to all except the priests; it remained silent, void, and inaccessible. Yet since it enshrined the Ark and the Presence, it tacitly bore witness to the fact that the sacred could enter the world of men and women: it was at once immanent and transcendent.

Built on the summit of the sacred mountain of Zion, the Temple also represented the Garden of Yahweh, as described by J in the second and third chapters of Genesis.[27] The great candlesticks resembled branched trees, covered with almonds and flowers; the palm trees and flowers on the doors and walls of the Hekhal also recalled the garden where the cherubim had walked at the beginning of time; there was even a serpent. J may have been writing during the reign of King Solomon, but even if he lived at a later date, he had clearly been influenced by the spirituality of the Temple. When Marduk created the world, he built a temple, but, J tells us, after Yahweh completed the creation, he planted a garden, where he walked in the cool of the evening and conversed familiarly with the first human beings at the dawn of history.

In the Eden story, we can see what the divine meant for the Israelite worshippers in Solomon's Temple. As in all the myths of the lost paradise, Eden was a place where there had been easy access to the heavenly world. Indeed, Eden was itself an experience of the sacred. It was, J says, the source of the world's fertility; in its midst was a river that divided into four streams once it had left the garden and fructified the rest of the earth: one of these streams was called the Gihon. In the Temple there were two large candlesticks; in Eden there were two trees, which, with their power to regenerate themselves each year, were common symbols of the divine. Eden was an experience of that primal wholeness which human beings all over the world sought in their holy places. God and humanity were not divided but could live in the same place; the man and woman did not know that they were different from each other; there was no distinction between good and evil. Adam and Eve, therefore, existed on a plane that transcends all opposites and all divisions: it is a unity that is beyond our experience and is quite inconceivable to us in our fragmented existence, except in rare moments of ecstasy or insight. It was a mythical description of that harmony which people in all cultures have felt to have been meant for humanity. Adam and Eve lost it when they "fell" and were ejected from the divine presence and barred from Eden. Yet when the worshippers entered Solomon's Temple, its imagery and furnishings helped them to make an imaginary return to the Garden of Yahweh and to recover—if only momentarily—a sense of the paradise they had lost. It healed in them that sense of separation which, we have seen, lies at the root of the religious quest. The liturgy and architecture all aided this spiritual journey to that unity which is inseparable from the reality that we call "God" or the "sacred."

These ideas are also implicit in J's story of the Tower of Babel, which describes the creation of a perverse holy place. Instead of waiting for the sacred site to be revealed to them, human beings themselves take the initiative. "Come . . . let us build ourselves a town and a tower with its top reaching heaven." This attempt to scale the heavens is an act of pride and self-aggrandizement: the men concerned want to "build a name for themselves." The result is not unity but discord and fragmentation. To punish these people for their presumption, God "scattered them thence over the whole face of the earth" and muddled their language so that they could no longer understand one another. Henceforth the place was called Babel, "because God had confused (bll) the language of the whole earth there."[28] J's story reveals a profound hostility towards Babylon and its imposing ziggurats. Instead of being a "gate of the gods" (bab-ilani), it was the source of the alienation, disharmony, and disunity that characterizes mundane existence at its worst. Quite different was the worshippers' experience in Zion, the city of peace (shalom) and reconciliation. There the people of Israel could congregate on the holy mountain that God himself had established as his heritage, not on an artificially constructed sacred mountain rooted in human ambition and the lust for power.

The Temple built by Solomon on Mount Zion gave pilgrims and worshippers an experience of God. In the following chapter, we will see that many of them hoped to have a vision of Yahweh there. Instead of being cast adrift in the world, like the builders of Babel, many of them felt that they had come home when they entered Yahweh's Temple. As a symbol of the sacred, the Temple was also the source of the world's fertility and order.[29] But, as in the other countries of the Near East, its great sanctity was inseparable from the pursuit of what we would today call "social justice." This is an important point. Now that they had a monarchy of their own, the people of Israel and Judah naturally adopted the local ideal of sacral kingship. The king was Yahweh's mashiach, his "anointed one." On the day of his coronation on Zion, God's "holy mountain," God adopted him as his son.[30] His palace was next to the Temple, and his throne of judgment was beside Yahweh's throne in the Devir. His task was to impose the rule of God and to ensure that God's own justice prevailed in the land. The psalms tell us that the king had to "defend the poorest, save the children of those in need, and crush their oppressors."[31] If this justice prevailed, there would be peace, harmony, and fertility in the kingdom.[32] Yahweh would provide them with the security which was so earnestly and continually sought for in the ancient world: because Zion was now Yahweh's heritage, it was, therefore, "God-protected for ever."[33] But there could be no security and no *shalom* if there was no justice in Zion.

The ideal is expressed in three words which recur constantly in the Jerusalem psalms: *mishpat, tzedek,* and *shalom.*[34] The word *mishpat* is a legal term meaning "judgment" or "verdict," but it also denotes the harmonious rule of Yahweh on Mount Zion. When the Ark of the Covenant was carried into the Devir, Yahweh was enthroned on his holy mountain and he was henceforth the real King of Jerusalem, the earthly king being merely his human representative. The human king's task was to impose *tzedek.* In Canaan, *tzedek* (justice, righteousness) was an attribute of the sun god, who brought hidden crimes to light, righted the wrongs done to the innocent, and watched over the world as a judge. Once Yahweh had been enthroned on Zion, *tzedek* became his attribute too: he would see that justice was done in his kingdom, that the poor and vulnerable were protected, and that the strong did not oppress the weak. Only then would Zion become a city of *shalom,* a word that is usually translated as "peace," but has as its root meaning "wholeness," "completeness"—that sense of wholeness and completeness which people sought in their holy places. Hence *shalom* includes all manner of well-being: fertility, harmony, and success in war. The experience of *shalom* negated the anomie and alienation that is the cause of so much human distress on earth. It was, as we have seen, also a sense of the peace which is God. But Jerusalem could not be a holy city of *shalom* if there was no *tzedek* or "righteousness" in the land. All too often, the people of Israel would forget this. They would concentrate on the holiness and integrity of Jerusalem; they would fight for its purity. But, as the prophets reminded them, if they neglected the pursuit of justice, this would inevitably entail the loss of *shalom.*

By building his Temple and enthroning Yahweh on Zion, Solomon was in Canaanite terms formally taking possession of the land in the name of the Davidic dynasty. Yahweh was now the ruler of Jerusalem, and because Israel was his people, the land became theirs. Baal's palace on Mount Zaphon had made the surrounding territory his inalienable heritage; now Zion belonged to Yahweh, as *his* eternal inheritance. The Temple and Yahweh's enthronement, therefore, were the basis for Solomon's claim to Jerusalem as the eternal heritage of the House of David. The construction of the Temple was an act of conquest, a means of occupying the Promised Land with divine backing. The edifice proclaimed that Israel's days of wandering had come to an end; the people of the United Kingdom had finally come home and established themselves in a place where they could live in close intimacy with the divine.

Yet Solomon was ultimately a disappointment. The Deuteronomist historian, writing in the sixth century BCE, regarded him as an idolater. Solomon built shrines to the gods of all his foreign wives in Jerusalem; he also worshipped the gods of his neighbors: Astarte, goddess of Sidon; Milcom, the god of Ammon; and Chemosh, the god of Moab. There were altars to Milcom and Chemosh in the hills to the east of Jerusalem.[35] It was because of this infidelity, D believed, that the United Kingdom of Israel and Judah disintegrated after Solomon's death. But D was writing from an entirely different perspective. By the sixth century, the Israelites were becoming true monotheists; they were beginning to believe that Yahweh was the *only* god and that all other deities were false. But Solomon and his subjects did not yet share that belief. Just as nobody found it strange that the Temple was full of pagan imagery, so too the other shrines and temples that Solomon built in Jerusalem would probably have been regarded as a courtesy to his wives. They did not affect Yahweh's position. He was still the King of Zion and presided over the lesser gods in their smaller establishments, rather as the psalmists depicted him presiding over the other gods in the Divine Council.

If Solomon failed, it was probably because he did not pursue *tzedek*. The political economy of his kingdom was weak. Empires fall when they have outrun their resources, and despite Solomon's alleged riches, the nation was stretched beyond its limits. Solomon had bought costly building materials from Hiram, King of Tyre, and could not repay his debt. He was therefore obliged to cede twenty towns to Tyre, probably in western Galilee. Despite his powerful army, Solomon could not hold on to the territory he had inherited from David. First Edom and then Damascus fell away and regained their independence. But even more serious was the dissatisfaction and malaise within the kingdom itself. David had favored his own Kingdom of Judah and had nearly lost the allegiance of the Kingdom of Israel in consequence. Solomon did not learn from this. It seems that he exploited Israel, treating it as conquered territory instead of as an equal partner. He divided the northern part of the country into twelve administrative units, each of which was obliged to provision the court for one month a year and provide men for the corvée. There is no mention of any similar arrangement for the southern Kingdom of Judah.[36] Furthermore, people were bitterly resentful of the corvée itself. Forced labor was a fact of life in the ancient world: David had also resorted to conscription, and nobody had objected. Solomon, however, needed a vast amount of manpower for his huge building program. This damaged the economy, since the buildings themselves were not productive and the corvée took the men away from the land and the cities where the wealth of the country *was* produced. Worse, the conscription represented a glaring injustice. We are told that thirty thousand of the men of Israel were forced into the corvée, but we read of no such conscription in Judah.[37] The people of Israel were angry, and some dreamed of breaking away from Jerusalem.

We have seen that the cult of justice in the ancient world was not a pious dream, but rooted in sound political sense. Kingdoms had fallen because of social unrest. We have seen that Ugarit was destroyed in the thirteenth century because its system placed too great a burden on the peasantry. Solomon's kingdom would also disintegrate because the king had not dealt equitably with his subjects—it was a salutary lesson for his successors. Solomon was aware that his kingdom was in danger. In the last years of his life, we read that Jeroboam, one of the Israelite officers of the corvée, fell afoul of the king. It was said that one of the northern prophets had foretold that Solomon's kingdom would be split in two and that Jeroboam would rule the ten northern tribes of Israel.[38] It seems likely, therefore, that Jeroboam was planning an insurrection. Solomon tried to have him assassinated, but Jeroboam fled to Egypt, taking refuge in the court of Pharaoh Shishak. He did not have to remain long in exile. Shortly afterward, Solomon died, after a long reign of forty years, in about 930 BCE. He was buried with his father in the ʾIr David and was succeeded by his son Rehoboam. Immediately the disaster that Solomon had feared struck the United Kingdom of Israel and Judah.

CITY OF JUDAH

REHOBOAM INHERITED an impoverished and alienated king-dom. His rule was accepted in Judah, but the northern Kingdom of Israel had been drained dry by Solomon's ambitious building pro-gram, which had yielded little income and had required a conscription that deprived large areas of the country of productive labor. When Rehoboam went to meet the elders of Israel at Shechem to have his rule ratified there, they told him that they would accept him as king only if he reduced the burden of taxation and conscription. It was a difficult decision: if Rehoboam granted this request, he would have to renounce the imperial dream of his grandfather David forever and accept a lower standard of living for his court. Few rulers would have made this choice, and it is not surprising that Rehoboam rejected the advice of his older and more experienced counselors in favor of the hard-line policy of his younger henchmen, who could see that reduced taxation in Israel would mean a drastic decline in their own lifestyle. Rehoboam returned to the elders of Israel with a contemptuous answer: "My father beat you with whips; I am going to beat you with loaded scourges."[1] Immediately the elders seceded from the United Kingdom, the master of the corvée was stoned to death, and Rehoboam was forced to hurry back to safety in Jerusalem.

Henceforth the kingdoms of Israel and Judah went their separate ways. Jeroboam became King of Israel, establishing a capital at Tirza and making the old shrines of Bethel and Dan royal temples. Later King Omri of Israel (885–74) built a new capital at Samaria, which became the most elegant and luxurious city in the region. The Kingdom of Israel was far larger and wealthier than Judah: it was close to the major

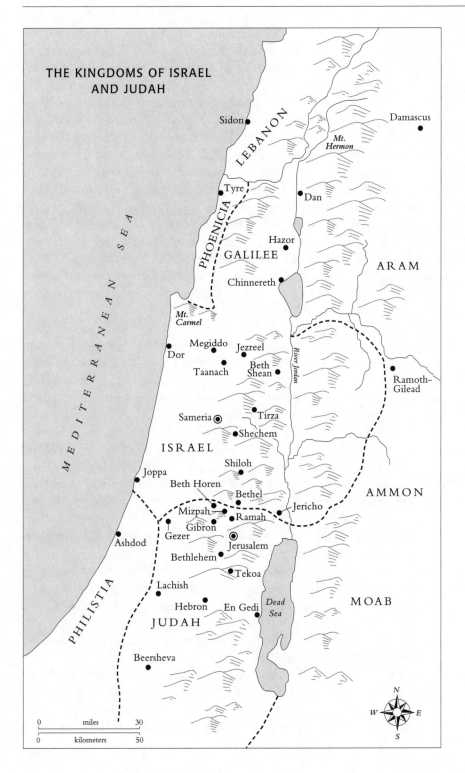

THE KINGDOMS OF ISRAEL
AND JUDAH

Sidon

Damascus

LEBANON

*Mt.
Hermon*

Tyre

Dan

PHOENICIA

Hazor

GALILEE

ARAM

Chinnereth

*Mt.
Carmel*

MEDITERRANEAN SEA

Megiddo

Jezreel

Dor

Beth
Shean

Taanach

River Jordan

Ramoth-
Gilead

Sameria

Tirza

Shechem

ISRAEL

Shiloh

Joppa

Beth Horen

Bethel

AMMON

Mizpah

Ramah

Jericho

Gibron

Gezer

Jerusalem

Ashdod

Bethlehem

Tekoa

Lachish

Dead
Sea

MOAB

Hebron

En Gedi

PHILISTIA

JUDAH

Beersheva

N
W E
S

| 0 | miles | 30 |
| 0 | kilometers | 50 |

roads and included most of the territory owned by the most prosperous of the old city-states. By contrast, the Kingdom of Judah was isolated and lacking in resources, consisting almost entirely of steppe and mountainous land that was difficult to farm. Naturally the kings of Judah bitterly regretted the loss of Israel and accused the northern kingdom of apostasy, though all that had happened was the restoration of the status quo ante, before the union under David. For some fifty years after the collapse of the United Kingdom, Israel and Judah were at war, and as the weaker state, Judah was particularly vulnerable. Rehoboam was able to secure Jerusalem from an attack by Pharaoh Shishak, who had tried to establish a presence in Canaan, only by making him a substantial payment from the Temple treasury. During the reign of King Asa of Judah (911–870), the armies of Israel actually reached Ramah, five miles north of Jerusalem. This time the king saved the city by appealing to the Aramaean Kingdom of Damascus, which attacked Israel from the rear. Henceforth Israel was embroiled in a series of bloody territorial wars with Damascus and left Judah alone.

Beset on all sides by powerful enemies who sought to overthrow their kingdom, the people of Judah increasingly turned for help to Yahweh of Zion. We know that, in common with other people in the ancient Near East, they tended to identify their enemies—Israel, Egypt, or, later, Damascus—with the primal forces of chaos. Like the sea or the desert, these earthly enemies could easily overturn the fragile security of their state and reduce the little world that had been created in Judah to the kind of desolate waste that was thought to have prevailed before the gods had established the habitable earth. This may seem a fanciful idea, but we still talk in similar terms today when we speak of our enemies as occupying an "evil empire" which could reduce "our world" to chaos. We still tend to perceive life as a struggle between the forces of light and darkness, fearing a return to the "barbarism" that could overthrow everything that "we" have created. We have our own rituals—memorial services, wreath-laying, processions—which are designed to evoke an emotional response and make past battles present to us. We vividly recall the time when "we" seemed to stand alone against a hostile world. We feel hope, pride, and renewed commitment to continue the struggle. The people of ancient Jerusalem had similar stratagems, based on the old Canaanite mythology which they had made their own.

Instead of looking back to their own battles, they commemorated Yahweh's struggle against the forces of chaos at the beginning of time. In their temples throughout the Near East, the battles of such gods as Marduk and Baal were commemorated annually in elaborate cere-

monies, which were at one and the same time an exultant celebration
of the divine victory and an attempt to make this power available in the
present, since only a heavenly warrior, it was thought, could establish
the peace and security on which their city depended. The rituals of the
ancient world were not simply acts of remembrance: they reproduced
the mythical stories in such a way that they were felt to occur again, so
that people experienced the eternal, unseen struggle at the heart of existence and participated in the primordial divine conquest of the chaos-
monsters. Again, as in the building of a temple, likeness was experienced
as identity. Imitating these divine battles in symbolic dramas brought this
action into the present or, more properly, projected the worshippers into
the timeless world of myth. The rituals revealed the harsh reality of existence, which seemed always to depend upon pain and death, but also
made it clear that this struggle would always have a creative outcome.
After emerging victoriously from his mortal encounters with Yam and
Mot, Baal had been enthroned on Mount Zaphon, which had become
his home forever. From Zaphon, Baal had established the peace, fertility,
and order which his enemies had sought to overcome. When this victory was commemorated in Ugarit, the king took Baal's place, anointed
like his heavenly prototype for the task of establishing peace, fruitfulness,
and justice in his realm. Each autumn, Baal's enthronement was celebrated in the month of Ethanim, and this festival made the divine energies which had been unleashed in those primal struggles at the dawn of
time available in Ugarit for another year.

Before Solomon's Temple was built in Jerusalem, there was, as far as
we know, little or no interest in Yahweh as a creator-god. The myths of
the Exodus showed him creating a people, not the cosmos. But once he
had been ritually enthroned in the Devir on Mount Zion, his cult took
on many of the aspects of the worship of Baal El Elyon which had preceded it. Possibly under the influence of Zadok, Jebusite ideas fused with
the old Israelite mythology. Like Baal, Yahweh was now said to have bat-
tled with the sea monster Lotan, who became "Leviathan" in Hebrew.[2]
He had tamed the primal waters of chaos, which would otherwise have
flooded the earth, and had "marked the bounds it was not to cross and
made it fast with a bolted gate."[3] Like Marduk, he had split another sea
monster—this one called Rahab—in two when he laid the foundations
of the world.[4] Later these myths of a violent creation were replaced by
P's calm and peaceful account of the establishment of primal order in
the first chapter of Genesis. But the Bible shows that the people of Judah
also had stories that conformed more closely to the spirituality of their
neighbors and that in times of crisis they turned readily to this "pagan"

mythology. The combat myth was consoling because it proclaimed that however powerful the forces of destruction, order would always prevail. It would not do so automatically, however. Priests and kings had a responsibility to renew this primal victory annually in their Temple in order to bring the embattled city of Jerusalem an infusion of divine power. Their task was to put their people in touch with the great mystery that sustained the world, face up to the unavoidable terror of existence, and learn to see that what appeared to be frightening and deadly had a positive aspect. Life and order would triumph over violence and death; fertility would follow a period of drought and sterility, and the threat of extinction would be averted because of the divine power in their midst.

The early psalms show how thoroughly the people of Judah had absorbed this spirituality. Sometimes they are simply a restatement of the old myths of Ugarit:

> *Yahweh is great and supremely to be praised:*
> *in the city of our God*
> *is his holy mountain, its peak as it rises*
> *is the joy of the whole world.*

> *Mount Zion is the heart of Zaphon,*
> *the city of the Great King,*
> *here among her palaces*
> *God proved to be her fortress.*[5]

Yahweh would fight for Jerusalem, just as Baal had fought for his heritage at Ugarit: his presence made the city an inviolable enclave against the enemies that lurked without. Jerusalemites were told to admire the fortifications of Zion—"counting her towers, admiring her walls, reviewing her palaces"—as the people of Uruk had admired the bastions built by Gilgamesh. After their tour of inspection, they would conclude that "God is here!"[6] At the beginning of time, Yahweh had set up boundaries to keep everything in its proper place: walls and security arrangements had a similar religious value in keeping the threat of extinction and chaos at bay. The city could never fall: Yahweh was the citadel of his people and would break the bow and snap the spear of their foes.[7] They would not even have to fear if the whole cosmic order crashed around them: God was their shelter and strength. The people of Judah need not worry if the mountains tumbled into the sea and the waters roared and heaved.[8] Within their city, Yahweh had established a haven of *shalom*: wholeness, harmony and security. In the Jerusalem liturgy, the people saw the old Exodus myths in the context of Yahweh's creation of the world. He had made himself the king of the whole earth when he had defeated Leviathan and Rahab, and he sustained it in being. Liberating the people from Egypt revealed his plans for the whole of humanity.[9]

Critics have attempted to reconstruct the liturgy from the psalms, but their more detailed claims are probably extravagant. We know very little about the Jerusalem cult in this early period. Yet there does seem to have been a focus on Yahweh's kingship on Mount Zion. It is likely that the feast of Sukkoth was a celebration of his enthronement on the sacred mountain during the dedication of the Temple by King Solomon. Just as Baal's return to his palace on Mount Zaphon after the defeat of Mot had restored fertility to the land, Yahweh ensured the fertility of Zion and its environs, and this too was celebrated in this ancient agricultural festival. With music, applause, and acclamation, Yahweh was felt to rise up to his throne in the Devir, accompanied by the blast of trumpets.[10] Perhaps the braying instruments, the cultic shout, and the clouds of incense filling the Temple reproduced the theophany on Mount Sinai, when Yahweh appeared to his people in the midst of a volcanic eruption.[11] Perhaps there was a procession from the Gihon to the Temple, which retraced Yahweh's first journey up Mount Zion. He was experienced in this liturgy as so great a

Jews select palm branches for the rituals of Sukkoth in Jerusalem today. Even though it is now primarily a historical festival commemorating the Israelites' forty years in the desert, Sukkoth still retains its links with the original harvest festival.

force that he was not only King of Zion but "the Great King of the whole world."[12] He was acquiring preeminence over other deities:

> For you are Yahweh
> Elyon over the world
> far transcending all the other gods.[13]

Long before the Israelites developed the formal doctrine of monotheism, the rituals and ceremonies on Mount Zion had begun to teach the people of Judah at an emotional if not a notional level that Yahweh was the only god who counted.

But the Zion cult was not just a noisy celebration. The early pilgrimage psalms show that it was capable of creating an intensely personal spirituality. A visit to the Temple was experienced as an ascent (aliyah). As they climbed from the Valley of Hinnom, making their way up the steep hills of Jerusalem toward the peak of Zion, they prepared themselves for a vision of Yahweh.[14] It was not just a physical ascent but an "ascent inward" to the place where the inner world met the outer world. There was a sense of homecoming:

> The sparrow has found its home at last,
> the swallow a nest for its young—
> your altars, Yahweh Sabaoth.[15]

The imagery of rest and of the establishment of a permanent abode had been present in the discourse about the Temple ever since David had first suggested the idea of a house for Yahweh in Jerusalem.[16] The cult of the Temple had helped the people of Judah to attach themselves to the world. The creation myths insisted that everything in the universe had its appointed place. The seas had been bounded by Yahweh to prevent them from overwhelming the dry land. Now Yahweh was in his special place on Zion, and that had made it a secure home for the Judahites. They too, as a holy people, were in their specially appointed place. Outside the walls of the city were destructive enemies who could reduce their world to formless chaos, but within this enclave the people could create their own world. The sense of joy and belonging that the Zion temple evoked expressed their satisfaction at being, emotionally and physically, in the right place. Attendance at the Temple was not a dreary duty. The psalmist "yearns and pines" for Yahweh's courts; his whole being sings for joy there.[17] Pilgrims felt empowered by having found an orientation; they felt liberated from the endless flux of relativity and meaninglessness. Their mythology spoke of the long years of wandering in the wilderness, where human beings could not hope to live. Now in the Temple, the still point of the turning world, pilgrims could feel fully alive, experiencing existence at its most intense: a single day in the courts of the Temple was worth a thousand elsewhere.[18]

Still, this did not mean that Yahweh was the only god who was worshipped in Jerusalem. The Deuteronomist historian judges the kings of Israel and Judah according to a single criterion: good kings are those who promote the worship of Yahweh alone and suppress the shrines, cult places (*bamoth*), and *matzevot* (standing stones) of rival deities; bad kings are those who encourage these foreign cults. The result is that, despite D's long narrative, we know very little about events in Jerusalem during this period, since we hear almost nothing about the kings' other activities. And even in telling us of the kings who *were* true to Yahweh alone, D cannot conceal the fact that under these rulers as well other cults continued to flourish in the city. Thus King Jehoshaphat (870–848) is praised for his fidelity to Yahweh alone, yet D is forced to admit that the *bamoth* of other gods still functioned. Furthermore, Jehoshaphat had no problem about marrying his son Jehoram to Princess Athaliah, daughter of King Ahab and Queen Jezebel of Israel, who was a devout worshipper of Baal. She brought his Phoenician cult with her to Jerusalem and built a temple for him in the city, which was served by the Sidonian priest Mattan.

The marriage of Jehoram and Athaliah may have sealed a treaty whereby the Kingdom of Judah became the vassal of Israel: henceforth both Jehoshaphat and Jehoram fought on Israel's side in its campaigns against Damascus. The ninth and eighth centuries saw a new prosperity in the Near East. Even Judah's fortunes improved, since Jehoshaphat won striking victories against Moab, Ammon, and Seir. But a fresh danger was arising. From their capital in Nineveh, the kings of Assyria, in what is now Iraq, were building an empire of unprecedented power and strength. Their chief ambition was to expand westward towards the Mediterranean coast and, in an attempt to prevent this Assyrian advance, Israel and Damascus stopped fighting each other and united in a coalition with other small states of Anatolia and the steppes. But this coalition was defeated in 863 at the battle of Qarqar on the River Orontes. Both Israel and Damascus were forced to become vassals of Assyria. The Kingdom of Judah, however, was too insignificant to interest the Assyrians and maintained its independence.

Yet these were not peaceful years in Jerusalem. When Queen Athaliah became regent after the death of her son in 841, she tried to wipe out the Davidic dynasty by killing, so she thought, all the legitimate heirs to the throne. Some six years later, the Temple priests and the rural aristocracy organized a coup and crowned Jehoash—Athaliah's infant grandson, who had managed to escape the carnage—in the Temple. They then executed Athaliah and pulled down her temple to Baal. The city was also threatened by external foes: Jehoash had to make a substantial payment from the Temple treasury to prevent the King of Damascus from attacking Jerusalem, and during the reign of a later king of Judah, Amaziah (796–81), the army of Israel sacked the royal palace and the Temple in Jerusalem, demolishing part of the city wall before returning to Samaria. Yet this did not diminish the people's faith in Zion's impregnability. Indeed, under King Uzziah (781–40),[19] the city went from strength to strength despite the fact that the king was smitten with leprosy. The walls damaged in the Israelite attack were repaired, and the old citadel on the Millo was replaced with a new fortress between the city and the Temple, called the Ophel. Jerusalem became an industrial center, and the population increased: it seems that the city had begun to spread beyond the walls down into the Tyropoeon Valley and onto the Western Hill opposite Mount Zion. At this point, Assyria was in a state of temporary eclipse and had been forced to retreat from the region, so the Kingdom of Israel also enjoyed a period of affluence and de facto independence.

Yet this prosperity led to social disorders: the more sensitive people became acutely aware of an unacceptable gulf between rich and poor, and prophets arose in both the northern and the southern kingdoms to fulminate against injustice and oppression. At their coronation, the kings of the Near East vowed to protect the poor and the vulnerable, but people seemed to have lost sight of this ideal. Ever since Abraham had entertained his god at Mamre, Yahwism had indicated that the sacred could be encountered in one's fellow human beings as well as in temples and holy places. Now the new religions that were beginning to develop all over the civilized world during this period (which historians call the Axial Age) all insisted that true faith had to be characterized by practical compassion. The religion of Yahweh was also beginning to change to meet the new circumstances of the people. The Hebrew prophets began to insist on the prime importance of social justice: it was all too easy for a religious symbol such as the Temple to become a fetish, an end in itself and an object of false security and complacency.

None of the prophets of the Axial Age was as devoted to the Jerusalem Temple as Isaiah, who received his prophetic call in the sanctuary in 740, the year of King Uzziah's death. Isaiah was a member of the royal family and must also have been a priest, since he was standing in the Hekhal, watching the clouds of incense fill the hall and listening to the great cultic shout, when he suddenly saw through the imagery of the Temple to the fearful reality behind it. He perceived Yahweh seated on his heavenly throne symbolized by the Ark, surrounded by the seraphim. The Temple was a place of vision, and now Isaiah became aware as never before of the sanctity that radiated from the Devir to the rest of the world: "Holy, holy, holy is Yahweh Sabaoth," cried the seraphim, "his glory fills the whole world."[20]

The Temple was therefore crucial to Isaiah's vision. The holy mountain of Zion was the center of the earth, because it was the place where the sacred reality had erupted into the mundane world of men and women to bring them salvation. The Zion cult had celebrated Yahweh's universal kingship, and now Isaiah looked forward to the day when "all the nations" would stream to "the mountain of the Temple of Yahweh," urging one another to make the *aliyah* to Jerusalem: "Come, let us go up to the Temple of the God of Jacob."[21] It would be a universal return to the Garden of Eden, where all creatures would live in harmony, the wolf with the lamb, the panther with the kid, the calf and the lion cub.[22] The holy mountain of Jerusalem would see the creation of a new world order and the recovery of that lost wholeness for which humanity yearns. Isaiah's vision of the New Jerusalem has never been forgotten. His hope for an anointed king, a Messiah, to inaugurate this era of peace laid the foundations of the messianic hope that would inspire monotheists in all three of the religions of Abraham. Jews, Christians, and Muslims would all see Jerusalem as the setting for God's final intervention in human history. There would be a great judgment, a final battle at the end of time, and a procession of repentant unbelievers making their way to Jerusalem to submit to God's will. These visions continue to affect the politics of Jerusalem to the present day.

Yet Isaiah's templocentric prophecy begins with an oracle that seems to condemn the whole Zion cult.

> *What are your endless sacrifices to me?*
> *says Yahweh.*
> *I am sick of holocausts of rams*
> *and the fat of calves . . .*
> *who asked you to trample over my courts?*[23]

Elaborate liturgy was pointless unless it was accompanied by a compassion that seeks justice above all and brings help to the oppressed, the orphan, and the widow.[24] Scholars believe that this prophecy may not have been the work of Isaiah himself but was included with his oracles by the editors. It reflects a perception shared by other prophets, however. In the northern kingdom, the prophet Amos had also argued that the Temple rituals had formed no part of the original religion of the Exodus. Like Isaiah, Amos had had a vision of Yahweh in the Temple of Bethel, but he had no time for a cult that became an end in itself. He represented God as asking: "Did you bring me sacrifice and oblation in the wilderness for all these forty years?" Yahweh wanted no more chanting or strumming on harps; instead, he wished justice to flow like water and integrity to pour forth in an unending stream.[25] Amos imagined God roaring aloud from his sanctuary in Jerusalem because of the injustice that he saw in all the surrounding countries: it made a mockery of his cult.[26] As the religion of Yahweh changed during the Axial Age, justice and compassion became essential virtues, and without them, it was said, devotion to sacred space was worthless. The Jerusalem cult also enshrined this value, proclaiming that Yahweh was concerned above all with the poor and the vulnerable. Zion was to be a refuge for the poor, and, as we shall see, Jews who regarded themselves as the true sons of Jerusalem would call themselves the Evionim, the Poor. Yet it seems that in Jerusalem "poverty" did not simply mean material deprivation. The opposite of "poor" was not "rich" but "proud." In Jerusalem, people were not to rely on human strength, foreign alliances, or military superiority but on Yahweh alone: he alone was the fortress and citadel of Zion, and it was idolatry to depend arrogantly upon mere human armies and fortifications.[27]

Then, as now, there would always be people who preferred the option of devoting their religious energies to sacred space over the more difficult duty of compassion. Isaiah's long prophetic career shows some of the dangers that could arise from the Jerusalem ideology. During the reign of King Ahaz of Judah (736–16), Assyria reappeared in the Near East and the kings of Damascus and Israel formed a new coalition to prevent the Assyrians, under King Tiglathpileser III, from controlling the region. When King Ahaz refused to join this confederation, Israel and Damascus marched south to besiege Jerusalem. Isaiah tried to persuade Ahaz to stand firm: The son that his queen was about to bear would restore the Kingdom of David; he would be called Emanu-El ("God with us"), because he would usher in the reign of peace when men and women would live in harmony with the divine once more. Before this child reached the age of reason, the kingdoms of Damascus and Israel would be destroyed; there was no reason for panic or for foreign alliances with other princes.[28] Ahaz should rely on Yahweh alone.

To Isaiah's disgust, Ahaz was unwilling to take the risk of following his counsel; the king chose instead to submit to Tiglathpileser and become a vassal of Assyria, which promptly invaded the territories of Damascus and Israel and deported large numbers of their inhabitants. By 733, Israel had been reduced to a small city-state based on Samaria, with a puppet king on the throne. It was not the policy of Assyria to impose its religion upon its vassals, but Ahaz seems to have wanted to make some kind of cultic gesture to his new overlord. An Assyrian-style altar replaced the old altar of sacrifice in the Temple courtyard, and henceforth there would be a new enthusiasm in Judah for cults involving the sun, moon, and constellations, which were appearing at this time in other parts of the Near East.

Isaiah had little time for Ahaz, but the king had at least saved his country. The same cannot be said for the child whom Isaiah had hailed as Emanu-El: Hezekiah succeeded his father in about 716, and, D tells us approvingly, he devoted himself to Yahweh alone. He closed down all the *bamoth* dedicated to other gods, tore down the *matzevot*,

The military might of Assyria: In this stele (c. 745 BCE) soldiers besiege a city with battering rams and are merciless toward their captives.

and smashed the bronze serpent in the Hekhal of the Jerusalem Temple. The Chronicler tells us that the priests took a leading role in this reform movement and threw out the paraphernalia of the foreign cults that had crept into the Temple. He also says that Hezekiah ordered all the people of Israel and Judah to assemble in Solomon's Temple in Jerusalem to celebrate the Passover, a feast that had hitherto been held in the home.[29] This is unlikely, since the Passover was not celebrated in the Temple until the late sixth century; the Chronicler was probably projecting the religious practices of his own day back onto Hezekiah, about whom he is most enthusiastic. In fact, we do not know exactly what Hezekiah intended by this reform: it seems to have had no lasting effect. He may have been trying to dissociate himself from the syncretizing policies of his father and to take the first steps toward throwing off Assyrian hegemony. The story of his summoning the people of Israel to Jerusalem could indicate that he had dreams of reviving the United Kingdom, as Isaiah had foretold. Israel was no longer a threat, and there must have been a certain schadenfreude in Judah about the demise of this former enemy. For the first time since the split, Judah was in the stronger position, and by summoning the remaining Israelites to the city of David, Hezekiah may have been nurturing Isaiah's messianic vision.

If there were such hopes, however, they were definitively crushed in 722 when, after a futile revolt against Assyria, Samaria was defeated and destroyed by Shalmaneser V. The Kingdom of Israel was reduced to an Assyrian province called Samerina. Over 27,000 Israelites were deported to Assyria and were never heard of again. They were replaced by people from Babylon, Cuthnah, Arad, Hamah, and Sephoraim, who worshipped Yahweh, the god of their new country, alongside their own gods. Henceforth the name "Israel" could no longer be used to describe a geographical region, and it survived as a purely cultic term in Judah. But not all the Israelites had been deported. Some stayed behind in their old towns and villages and tried, with the help of the new colonists, to rebuild their devastated country. Others probably came to Judah as refugees and settled in and around Jerusalem. They brought with them ideas that may have been current in the north for some time and that would have a significant effect on the ideology of Jerusalem.

Perhaps because of such an influx from the former Israel, Jerusalem seems to have expanded to three or four times its former size by the end of the eighth century. Two new suburbs were built: one on the Western Hill opposite the Temple, which became known as the Mishneh—the Second City. The other developed in the Tyropoeon Valley and was called the Makhtesh—the Hollow. The new Assyrian king Sargon II adopted more liberal policies toward his vassals, which gave Jerusalem

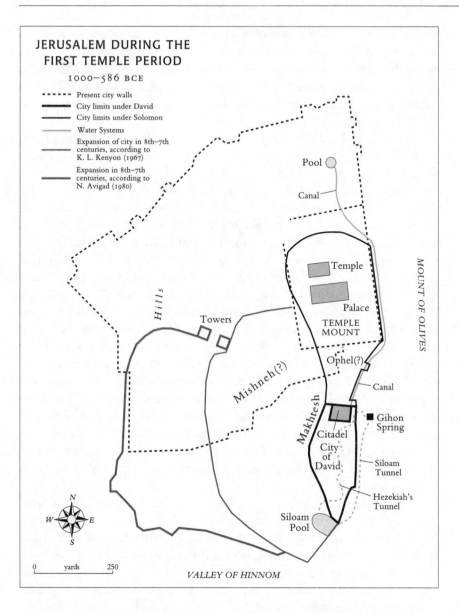

JERUSALEM DURING THE FIRST TEMPLE PERIOD

1000–586 BCE

- - - - - Present city walls
───── City limits under David
───── City limits under Solomon
───── Water Systems
───── Expansion of city in 8th–7th centuries, according to K. L. Kenyon (1967)
───── Expansion in 8th–7th centuries, according to N. Avigad (1980)

Pool

Canal

Hills

Towers

Temple

Palace

TEMPLE MOUNT

MOUNT OF OLIVES

Mishneh(?)

Ophel(?)

Canal

Makhtesh

Citadel

City of David

Gihon Spring

Siloam Tunnel

Hezekiah's Tunnel

N
W — E
S

Siloam Pool

0   yards   250

VALLEY OF HINNOM

special privileges and economic advantages. But instead of learning from the fate of the northern kingdom, Hezekiah seems to have let his prosperity go to his head. When Sargon died in 705, Jerusalem was at the center of a new coalition of discontented vassals who hoped to throw off the Assyrian yoke: he was joined by the kings of Tyre and Ashkelon, and Egypt's pharaoh gave promises of help. Another rebellious coalition had sprung up in Mesopotamia, led by Merodach-baladan, King of Babylon, who sent envoys to Jerusalem to inspect its storehouses and fortifications. Hezekiah made elaborate preparations for war. He improved the water supply by digging a new tunnel, seventeen hundred feet long, through the bedrock from the Gihon to the Pool of Siloam and had built a new city wall to protect this pool and, perhaps, the Mishneh. He was clearly proud of his military capability in a way that was far removed from the spirit of the Jerusalem "Poor."

He soon realized the folly of his arrogance: it was impossible for Jerusalem to withstand the power of Assyria. Once Sennacherib, the new king, had quelled the revolts in Babylon and other parts of Mesopotamia, he began to move westward toward Jerusalem. Egypt sent no troops, Transjordan and Phoenicia went down like dominoes before the Assyrian army, and finally, Sennacherib's soldiers arrived outside the city. Hezekiah sent gifts and tribute in an attempt to stave off the disaster, but to no avail. The prophet Micah, a disciple of Isaiah, foretold that Jerusalem would soon be reduced to a heap of rubble and Zion would become a plowed field.[30] But Isaiah still insisted that all was not lost: Yahweh, the fortress of Zion, would protect his city. Reliance upon diplomacy and military preparations had indeed proved futile, but Yahweh's presence would repel the enemy.[31] And, against all odds, Isaiah's predictions were dramatically fulfilled. We are not sure what happened. The Chronicler simply says that Yahweh sent his "angel" to destroy the Assyrian army and Sennacherib was forced to return home.[32] The most reasonable explanation was that the Assyrians were decimated by plague, but nobody in Jerusalem wanted to hear prosaic facts. They naturally saw this deliverance as a miracle. Yahweh had indeed proved to be a mighty warrior who had brought salvation to his people, as the cult had always proclaimed.

This extraordinary event had a fatal effect upon the politics of Jerusalem. In former years, such kings as Rehoboam and Asa had saved their city by natural diplomacy. They did not believe that the cult of Yahweh on Zion permitted them to throw caution to the winds; on the contrary, they had a duty to fight with every weapon in their power against their enemy, joining their effort to the titanic struggle of Yahweh. But later generations of Jerusalemites felt that the impregnability of their city was such that they would be saved by miraculous intervention—a form of religiosity that reduces spirituality to magic. Hezekiah was hailed as a hero after Sennacherib's retreat, but his reckless policy had brought his country to the brink of ruin. In the Assyrian annals, Sennacherib claimed that he had plundered forty-six of Hezekiah's walled cities and innumerable villages; a large percentage of the population had been deported and Hezekiah had lost almost all his territory. Jerusalem was once again a small city-state. It was a hard legacy for his small son Manasseh, who came to the throne in 698 and ruled in Jerusalem for fifty-five years. The biblical writers regard Manasseh as the worst king Jerusalem ever had. To distance himself from Hezekiah, he entirely reversed his father's religious policies, seeking Judah's greater integration within the region and abandoning a dangerous particularity. He set up altars to Baal and reestablished the *bamoth* in the countryside. The practice of human sacrifice was instituted in the Valley of Hinnom, which henceforth retained an aura of horror. An effigy of Asherah was installed in the Temple, possibly in the Devir itself, and in the courtyard Manasseh built houses for the sacred prostitutes. Zion was now dedicated to the fertility cult of Asherah; there were also altars to other astral deities.[33] The most fervent Yahwists were naturally appalled by these measures, but they were probably acceptable to some of the people. We know from the prophet Hosea that the fertility cult of Baal had been widespread in the northern kingdom before 722. But for over 270 years, Yahweh had been the Elyon in Jerusalem, and to the prophets who predicted dire punishments this dethronement was rank apostasy and gross ingratitude for the deliverance of 701. Yet Manasseh probably believed that it was essential to appease Assyria and to abjure the Yahwistic chauvinism of his father. His long reign gave Judah time to recuperate and Manasseh was able to recover some of the territory that Hezekiah had lost.

Manasseh's most severe critics were probably the Deuteronomist reformers, who were developing a new form of Yahwism during his reign and who looked askance at the cult of Zion. They may well have come to Jerusalem from the northern kingdom after the catastrophe of 722. They would then have seen the old temples of Israel cast down by the Assyrians, and could no longer believe that a man-made shrine could be a link between heaven and earth and save the people from their enemies. To many people in the Axial Age, the sacred was experienced as an increasingly distant reality: a new gulf had opened between heaven and earth. The Deuteronomists found it inconceivable that God could live in a human building. When D described the dedication of the Jerusalem Temple by King Solomon, he put on the king's lips words which struck at the base of the Zion cult. "Yet will God really live with men on the earth?" Solomon muses incredulously. "Why, the heavens and their own heavens cannot contain you. How much less this house that I have built!"[34] God dwelt in heaven, and it was only his "name"—a shadow of himself—that was present in our world. For the Deuteronomists, the Zion cult depended too heavily on the old Canaanite mythology. They wanted a religion that was based on history, not on symbolic stories that had no basis in fact. In many ways, they are closer to us today in the modern West. They did not believe, for example, that Israel's claim to

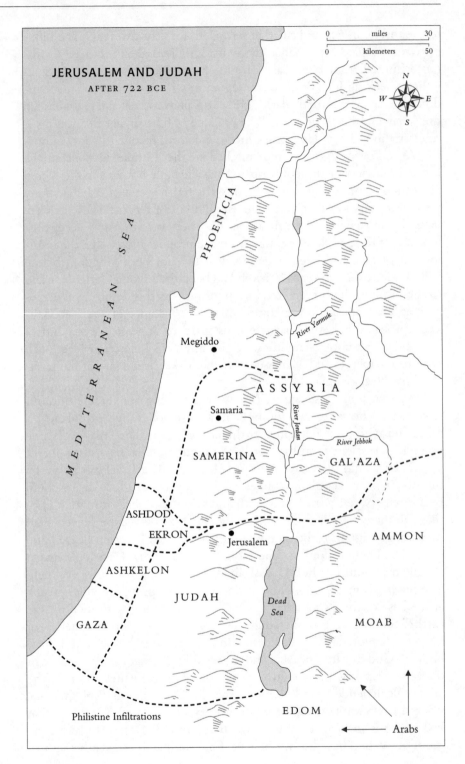

0 — miles — 30

0 — kilometers — 50

JERUSALEM AND JUDAH
AFTER 722 BCE

N
W · E
S

M E D I T E R R A N E A N   S E A

PHOENICIA

River Yarmuk

Megiddo ●

A S S Y R I A

Samaria ●

River Jordan

River Jebbok

SAMERINA

GAL'AZA

ASHDOD

EKRON

Jerusalem ●

AMMON

ASHKELON

JUDAH

Dead Sea

GAZA

MOAB

EDOM

Philistine Infiltrations

Arabs

the land of Canaan rested on Yahweh's enthronement on Mount Zion. Instead, they developed the story of Joshua's divinely inspired conquest of Canaan to show that Israel had won the land, with the help of God, by force of arms. The feast of Sukkoth, they insisted, was just a harvest festival; it did not celebrate Yahweh's enthronement on Mount Zion.[35]

Above all, the Deuteronomists wanted the Israelites to worship Yahweh alone and to turn their backs on all other gods. Northern prophets, such as Elijah and Hosea, had long preached this message, but ever since the days of King Solomon there had been a tradition of syncretism in Jerusalem. As far as the Deuteronomists were concerned, the policies of Manasseh were the last straw. They believed that at the time of the Exodus the Israelites had undertaken to worship Yahweh alone and in Chapter Twenty-four of the Book of Joshua they showed the Israelites formally ratifying this choice in a covenant treaty. Under the tutelage of Joshua, they had cast away all alien gods and given their hearts to Yahweh instead. The Deuteronomists were not yet monotheists: they believed that other gods existed, but thought that Israel had been called to worship Yahweh alone.[36]

We have seen that the experience of the liturgy in the Jerusalem Temple had already brought some of the people of Judah to this point. The Zion ritual proclaimed that Yahweh alone was king and superior to other gods. But in the eyes of the Deuteronomists, the Zion cult was flawed and inauthentic. They did not want to abolish temples altogether: they were too central to religion in the ancient world, and at this date it was probably impossible to imagine life without them. But instead they proposed that Israel should have only *one* sanctuary, which could be closely supervised to prevent foreign accretions from creeping into the cult. Originally, they may have had Shechem or Bethel in mind, but after 722 the Jerusalem Temple was the only major Yahwistic shrine in a position to become the central sanctuary, so, reluctantly, the reformers had to settle for this. Even so, when they described Moses looking forward to this central shrine in the Promised Land, they were careful to avoid the mention of "Zion" or "Jerusalem": instead, they make Moses refer vaguely to "the place where Yahweh your god has chosen to set his name."[37]

There was no possibility of the Deuteronomists' ideal coming into effect under Manasseh, but unexpectedly their chance came during the reign of his grandson Josiah (640–609). The time was right. Throughout the Near East, people were obscurely aware that the old order was passing away. The experience of living in the new giant empires of Assyria and of its rising competitor Babylon had given the population a wider global perspective than ever before. Technological advance had also given them a greater control of their environment. People could not see the world in the same way as their ancestors, and inevitably their religious ideas changed too. In other parts of the world, it had also been found necessary to reform the old paganism. During the Axial Age, Taoism, Confucianism, Hinduism, Buddhism, and, finally, Greek rationalism took the place of the old faith, and there was a similar movement toward change in Judah. But as antiquity died, people from Egypt to Mesopotamia were possessed by a *fin de siècle* nostalgia for an idealized past. This was congenial to the Deuteronomists' vision of the "golden age" of Israel during the Exodus and the period of the judges; it was a past that was largely fictitious but more attractive than the confusions of the present.

As part of this nostalgic return to the past, Josiah had decided to restore the Temple of Solomon, which, after three hundred years, must have been in serious need of repair. While the work was in progress, the chief priest Hilkiah discovered a scroll which may have been part of the text that we know as the Book of Deuteronomy. When the scroll was read to Josiah, the young king was shocked to discover that God's favor did not rest on Israel unconditionally as a result of his eternal election of the House of David; it was wholly dependent, rather, upon the observance of the Mosaic Law.[38] It was no longer sufficient to rely on Yahweh's presence in his Temple on Mount Zion. Josiah's extreme reaction to this new theology shows that the Law had not been central to the religious life of Judah. The cult and the rule of the king, Yahweh's Messiah, had been the foundation of Judah's polity hitherto: now the Torah, the Law of Moses, should become the law of the land.

Accordingly, Josiah began his reform, and, like all such reformations, it was an attempt to re-create the past. First, all the elders of Judah were summoned to renew the ancient covenant in the Temple. The people vowed to cast away alien gods and commit themselves to Yahweh alone. Next the cults had to be purged, and D's account shows the ubiquity of these "pagan" cults in Jerusalem. All the cult objects in the worship of Baal, Asherah, and the astral deities were carried out of the city and burned in the Kidron Valley. The Temple was also cleared of the *matzevot* and the houses of sacred prostitutes dedicated to Asherah in the courtyard:

> He desecrated the furnace in the Valley of Hinnom so that no one could make his son or daughter pass through the fire in honor of Moloch. He did away with the houses that the kings of Judah had dedicated to the sun at the entrance to the Temple of Yahweh. . . . The altars on the roof that the Kings of Judah had built, with those that Manasseh had built in the two courts of the Temple of Yahweh, the King pulled down and broke them to pieces on the spot. . . . The King desecrated the *bamoth* facing Jerusalem to the south

of the Mount of Olives, which Solomon, King of Israel, had built for Astarte, the Sidonian abomination, for Chemosh, the Moabite abomination, and for Milcom, the Ammonite abomination. He also smashed the sacred pillars, cut down the sacred poles, and covered the places where they had stood with human bones.[39]

There is a worrying violence in this catalogue of destruction. It marked the start of Israel's abhorrence of "idolatry," which seems to fill prophets, sages, and psalmists with a furious and violent disgust. Perhaps this is because Israelites felt the attraction of these old religious symbols so strongly that they could not simply set them peaceably to one side, as the Buddha would be able to do when he reformed the old paganism of India. Yet "idolatry" is part of the religious quest, because the sacred never manifests itself to humanity directly but always through something other: in myths, objects, buildings, people, or human ideas and doctrines. All such symbols of the divine are bound to be inadequate, because they are pointing to a reality that is ineffable and greater than human beings can conceive. But the history of religion shows that when a people's circumstances change, the old hierophanies cease to work for them. They no longer reveal the divine. Indeed, they can become obstacles to religious experience. It is also possible that people can mistake the symbol— the stone, the tree, or the doctrine—for the sacred reality itself.

There was clearly such a religious transition in Judah at the time of Josiah. For three hundred years, the people of Jerusalem had found spiritual sustenance in the other religious symbols of Canaan, but now they seemed so flawed that they appeared evil. Instead of looking *through* the *matzevot* to the mysterious reality they symbolized, Josiah and Hilkiah could see only an obscenity. There was a strain that would also become apparent in the later monotheistic traditions. This denial expressed itself with particular ferocity in the northern territories, the lands that had once been the Kingdom of Israel. Assyria was now in decline and no longer in control of its province of Samerina. Josiah's campaign there was probably part of a *reconquista,* another attempt to restore the United Kingdom of David. But here his reformation became savage and brutal. Josiah demolished the ancient altar at Bethel, which the "apostate" Jeroboam had made the royal shrine of Israel. In revenge, Josiah broke up its stones and beat them to powder. Then he desecrated the *bamah* by digging up corpses in a nearby cemetery and burning the bones on the site of the altar. He repeated this act in all the old cultic places of Israel and murdered their priests, burning their bones too upon their own altars. This cruelty and fanatical intolerance is a far cry from the courtesy shown by Abraham to other religious traditions. There is also no sign here of that absolute respect for the sacred rights of others, which the prophets had insisted was the litmus test of true religiosity. This is the spirit that the Deuteronomist historians would praise in Joshua, when he had—so they claimed—ruthlessly slaughtered the Israelites' predecessors in Canaan in the name of his god. Sadly, this spirit would henceforth become a part of the spiritual climate of Jerusalem.

For Josiah's reform was also a campaign for Zion. He was attempting to implement the Deuteronomic ideal by making Jerusalem the one and only shrine of Yahweh in the whole of Israel and Judah. All other holy places were to be destroyed and desecrated to preserve this central sanctity. Josiah's particular vehemence at Bethel was inspired partly by the fact that this royal temple had dared to challenge Jerusalem. Northern priests were killed, but the priests of the country shrines of Judah were simply taken from their destroyed *bamoth* and moved to Jerusalem, where they took their places in the lower echelons of the Zion priesthood. The exaltation of Jerusalem had inspired destruction, death, desecration, and dispossession. Where the prophets had preached mercy and compassion as an essential concomitant to the cult, Josiah's reform saw the honor and integrity of the holy city as paramount.

The reform did not last, even though the spirit that it had unleashed would remain. In 609, Josiah made a bid for total political independence, when he attacked Pharaoh Necho II, who was trying to establish an Egyptian presence in the country. The Judaean and Egyptian armies fought at Megiddo, and Josiah was killed at the first encounter. Necho immediately tightened his grip on Judah by deposing Josiah's son Jehoahaz, the choice of the Judaean aristocracy, in favor of his brother Jehoiakim. But the Egyptians did not retain control of Jerusalem. In 605, Nebuchadnezzar, King of Babylon, defeated Assyria and Egypt, and Babylon became the greatest power in the Near East. Like the other states in the area, Judah became a vassal of Babylon, and at first it seemed that it could prosper under this new empire. Jehoiakim was confident enough to build himself a splendid palace in the Mishneh suburb. Yet it was not long before a fatal chauvinism returned to Jerusalem. The king switched allegiance to Egypt, which was attempting a comeback, and thus defied the might of Babylon. Prophets assured the people in the old way that Yahweh's presence on Zion would protect Jerusalem against Nebuchadnezzar, as it had done against Sennacherib. The opposition to this suicidal tendency was led by Jeremiah, the son of Josiah's colleague Hilkiah. He warned the people that, on the contrary, Yahweh would destroy Jerusalem as he had once destroyed Shiloh, and for this blasphemy he faced the death penalty. Jeremiah was acquitted but still continued to wander through the streets of Jerusalem warning of the impending catastrophe. They were treating Zion as a fetish, he proclaimed, when they repetitively chanted the slogan "This is the Temple of Yahweh!" like a magic spell.[40] But Yahweh would protect them only if they turned away from alien gods and observed the laws of compassion, treating one another fairly and refusing to exploit the stranger, the orphan, and the widow.

Before Nebuchadnezzar arrived to punish his contumacious vassal, Jehoiakim died and was replaced by his son Jehoiachin. Jerusalem was besieged almost immediately by the Babylonian army and three months later capitulated in 597 BCE. Since the city had surrendered, there were no mass executions and the city was not destroyed. Nebuchadnezzar contented himself with plundering the Temple and deporting the Judaean leadership to Babylon. The Deuteronomist tells us that only the poorest people were left behind. The king and his bureaucracy were taken, together with ten thousand members of the aristocracy and the military and all blacksmiths and metalworkers.[41] These were standard procedures in ancient empires to prevent further rebellion and the manufacture of weapons. Yet, incredibly, the people who remained behind had still not learned their lesson. Nebuchadnezzar placed Zedekiah, another of Josiah's sons and the uncle of Jehoiachin, on the throne, and in about the eighth year of his reign he also rebelled against Babylon. This time there was no mercy. Jerusalem was besieged by the Babylonian army for eighteen months until the wall was breached in August 586 BCE. The king and his army tried to escape but were captured near Jericho, and Zedekiah had to watch his sons being executed before he was blinded and carried off to Babylon in chains. Then the Babylonian commander began systematically to destroy the city, burning down the Temple of Solomon, the royal palace, and all the houses of Jerusalem. All the precious Temple furnishings were taken off to Babylon, though, curiously, there is no mention of the Ark of the Covenant, which disappeared forever: subsequently there would be much speculation about its fate.[42] In the ancient world, the destruction of a royal temple was tantamount to the destruction of the state, which could not survive without a "center" linking it to heaven. Yahweh had been defeated by Marduk, god of Babylon, and the Kingdom of Judah was no more. A further 823 people were deported in three stages, leaving behind only the laborers, villagers, and plowmen.

Jeremiah was not among the deportees, possibly because of his pro-Babylonian stance. Once disaster had struck, Jeremiah, prophet of doom, became the comforter of his people. It was perfectly possible to serve Yahweh in an alien land, he wrote to the exiles: they should settle down, plant gardens, build houses, and make a contribution to the life of their new country.[43] No one would miss the Ark: its day was over. There would be "no thought for it, no regret for it, no making of another."[44] One day, the exiles would return to buy land "in the district around Jerusalem, in the towns of Judah, the highlands, the lowlands, and the Negev."[45]

The destruction of the Temple should have meant the end of Yahweh. He had failed to protect his city; he had shown that he was not the secure fortress of Zion. Jerusalem had indeed been reduced to a desert waste-land. The forces of chaos had triumphed and the promise of the Zion cult had been an illusion. Yet even in ruins, the city of Jerusalem would prove to be a religious symbol that could generate hope for the future.

5

EXILE AND RETURN

THE DESTRUCTION of Jerusalem and its Temple was in some profound sense the end of the world. Yahweh had deserted his city and Jerusalem had become a desert wasteland, like the formless chaos that had preceded creation. The destruction was an act of de-creation, like the Flood that had overwhelmed the world at the time of Noah. As Jeremiah had predicted, the desolate landscape, from which even the birds had fled, seemed to presage the overturning of cosmic order: the sun and the moon gave no light, the mountains quaked, and no people could be seen on earth at all.[1] Poets recalled with horror the memory of the Babylonian troops rushing through the Temple courts and the sickening sound of their axes hacking away at the cedar panels.[2] They longed for vengeance and dreamed of smashing the heads of Babylonian babies against a rock.[3] The people of Judah had become a laughingstock: no wonder the gentile nations asked derisively, "Where is their god?"[4] Without a temple, there was no possibility of making contact with the sacred in the ancient world. Yahweh had disappeared, Jerusalem was a heap of rubble, and the people of God were scattered in alien territory.

When a city had been destroyed in the Near East, it was customary for the survivors to sit among the ruins to sing dirges, similar to those sung at the funeral of a beloved relative. The Judahites and Israelites who had been left behind seem to have mourned their city twice a year: on the ninth day of the month of Av, the anniversary of the destruction, and at Sukkoth, the anniversary of the Temple's dedication. On one occasion, we know of eighty pilgrims coming from the northern towns of Shechem, Shiloh, and Samaria to the ruined city, with shaven heads and torn garments.[5] The Book of Lamentations may have preserved some of these dirges, chanted by the elders who sat upon the ground in the usual posture of mourning, clad in sackcloth and with ashes sprinkled on their foreheads. The poems give us a poignant picture of the desolation of the site. Instead of a populous city, its streets thronged with worshippers, there remained only empty squares, crumbling walls, and ruined gates haunted by jackals. But the lamentations also painfully evoke the psychological effects of catastrophe, which can make the survivors abhorrent to themselves. Those who had died in 586 were the lucky ones: now people reared in luxury clawed at rubbish heaps for food, tender-hearted women had killed and boiled their own babies, and beautiful young men wandered through the ruined streets with blackened faces and skeletal bodies.[6] Above all, there was a crippling sense of shame. Jerusalem, the holy city, had become unclean. People who used to admire her now eyed her with contempt, "while she herself groans and turns her face away," her garments covered in menstrual blood.[7] Even in their evocation of despair, however, the lamentations had gone beyond the point of blaming the Babylonians. The authors knew that Yahweh had destroyed the city because of the sins of the people of Israel.

Jerusalem was no longer habitable, and the country south of the city had been too badly damaged for settlement. In the extreme south of the former Kingdom of Judah, the land was overrun by Edomites, who laid the foundations of the future Kingdom of Idumea. Most of the Judahites who had stayed behind in 586 either migrated to Samerina or settled to the north of Jerusalem at Mizpah, Gibeon, or Bethel. The Babylonians had installed Gedaliah, a grandson of King Josiah's secretary, as governor of the region, and from his residence at Mizpah he tried to establish some measure of normality. The Babylonians also attempted to build up the country by giving the lands of the deportees to those who had stayed, people who had previously been among the poorest and most exploited sector of Judah. Yet this bid for the loyalty of the former Kingdom of Judah failed. In 582, officers of the old Judaean army who had fled to the Transjordan returned, and their leader, Ishmael, a member of the House of David, murdered Gedaliah and many of his entourage. The coup failed, because Ishmael failed to win the grassroots support of the people, and he escaped to Ammon. Many of the more politically active people also emigrated to Egypt to escape the wrath of Babylon. We hear nothing more about the fortunes of Jerusalem and Judah for another fifty years.

Despite the pain of their uprooting, the deportees had an easier time. They were not persecuted in Babylon, and King Jehoiachin lived at the court and retained his royal title.[8] The exiles were settled in some of the most attractive and important districts in and around Babylon, near the "great canal" of the Chebar, which brought the waters of the Euphrates to the city. They probably translated the Babylonian place-names into Hebrew: some, for example, lived in a neighborhood called Tel Aviv, Springtime Hill. The exiles followed Jeremiah's advice and became well integrated into Babylonian society. They were allowed to meet freely, buy land, and establish businesses. Many quickly became prosperous and respected merchants; some gained office at court. They may have been joined by descendants of the Israelites who had been deported to Babylonia in 722, since a number of the deportees mentioned in the Bible were members of the ten northern tribes.[9]

Babylon was both a shock and a challenge: the magnificent city was more sophisticated and cosmopolitan than any of the towns they had seen back home. With its fifty-five temples, Babylon had a religious world far more complex than the old paganism of Canaan. Yet some of its myths would seem strangely familiar. Yahweh had been defeated by Marduk, and now that they were living in his territory it would have seemed natural to many of the deportees to adopt the local faith. Others probably worshipped Babylonian deities as well as Yahweh and gave their children such names as Shameshledin ("May [the god] Shamesh judge!") or Beliadach ("Bel protects!").[10]

The Deuteronomists urged the Israelites to teach the divine commandments to their children (Deuteronomy 6:7). The Temple was destroyed, but in Babylon the exiles learned to find God in the Law of Moses, making of the sacred text a new shrine.

But others clung to their old traditions.

The Deuteronomists must have felt vindicated by the tragedy of 586: they had been right all along. The old Canaanite mythology that had encouraged Judahites to believe that Zion was impregnable had indeed been a delusion. Instead, they urged their fellow countrymen to concentrate on the Law of Moses and the covenant that Yahweh had made with the people of Israel before they had ever heard of Jerusalem. The Law would prevent the exiles from losing their identity in the melting pot of Babylon. During these years, the exiles codified regulations and practices that marked them out from their pagan neighbors. They circumcised their male children, refrained from work on the Sabbath, and adopted special food laws that distinguished them as the people of the covenant. They were to be a "holy" people, as distinct and separate as their God.

Others found comfort in the old mythology, however, and felt that the ancient symbols and stories of Zion spoke more eloquently to their condition. The history of religion shows that in times of crisis and upheaval, people turn more readily to myth than to the more rational forms of faith. As a form of psychology, myth can penetrate deeper than cerebral discourse and touch the obscure cause of distress in the farthest reaches of our being. In our own day, we have seen that exile involves far more than a change of address. It is also a spiritual dislocation. Having lost their unique place in the world, exiles can feel cast adrift and lost in a universe that has suddenly become alien. Once the fixed point of "home" has gone, there is a fundamental lack of orientation that makes everything seem relative and aimless. Cut off from the roots of their culture and identity, people can feel that they are in some sense withering and becoming insubstantial. Thus the French anthropologist R. P. Trilles records that after they had to leave their ancestral land, the Gabon Pygmies felt that the whole cosmos had been disturbed. Their creator was angry with them, the world had become a dark place—"night and again night"—and their exile had also uprooted the spirits of their ancestors, who now wandered lost in distant, inaccessible realms, eternally displaced.

> *Are they below, the spirits? Are they there?*
> *Do they see the offerings set out?*
> *Tomorrow is naked and empty.*
> *For the Maker is no longer with us there,*
> *He is no longer the host seated with us at our fire.*[11]

The loss of homeland meant that the link with heaven, which alone made life supportable, had been broken. In the sixth century, the Judahite exiles expressed this by saying that their world had come to an end.

Those who wished to remain loyal to Yahwism and the traditions of their ancestors had a serious problem. When the exiles asked: "How can we sing one of Yahweh's songs in an alien land?"[12] they were not simply giving voice to their homesickness but facing a theological dilemma. Today religious people believe that they can make contact with their God wherever they are in the world: in a field, supermarket, or church. But in the ancient world, prayer in our sense was far from common. In exile the Judaeans developed the practice of lifting up their hands, turning in the direction of Jerusalem, and speaking words of praise or entreaty to Yahweh precisely as a substitute for sacrifice, which was the normal way to approach the deity.[13] But this type of prayer was a novel idea and would not have occurred to the first deportees as a matter of course. The exile would teach the Judaeans the more interior spirituality of the Axial Age. When they first arrived in Babylonia in 597 the exiles would probably have felt that they had been taken away from Yahweh's presence. His home was in Zion, and they could not build a temple to him in Babylon, as we would build a church, synagogue, or mosque, because according to the Deuteronomist ideal there was only one legitimate shrine for Israel and that was in Jerusalem. Like the Gabon Pygmies, the exiles must have wondered whether their Maker was actually with them in this strange city. Hitherto Israelites had gathered for communal worship only in places associated with a revelation of Yahweh or some other type of hierophany. But there was no known instance of a Yahwistic theophany in Babylonia.

Then, out of the blue, Yahweh made an appearance in Tel Aviv. Among the first batch of deportees to arrive in Babylon in 597 was the priest Ezekiel. For the first five years, he stayed alone in his house and did not speak to a soul. Then he was—literally—knocked out by a shattering vision of Yahweh which left him stunned for an entire week. A cloud of light had seemed to approach him from the north in the midst of which he saw a huge chariot drawn by four of the cherubim, strange beasts not unlike the *karibu* carved on the palace gates of Babylon. When he tried to describe this apparition, Ezekiel was at pains to show that it lay beyond normal words and concepts. What he had seen was "something . . . shaped *like* a throne and high upon this throne was a being that looked *like* a man." In the dense confusion of storm, fire, and tumultuous noise, Ezekiel knew that he had glimpsed "something that looked like the glory [*kavod*] of Yahweh."[14] Like Isaiah, Ezekiel had glimpsed the extra-ordinary Reality that lay behind the symbols of the Temple. The Ark of the Covenant—Yahweh's earthly throne—was still in the Temple in Jerusalem, but his "glory" had arrived in Babylon. It was indeed a "revelation," an unveiling: the great curtain separating the

Hekhal from the Devir in Solomon's Temple had represented the farthest limit of human perception. Now that veil had been pulled to one side, though Ezekiel was careful to distinguish between Yahweh himself and his "glory," a manifestation of his Presence which made the ineffable reality of the sacred apprehensible to human beings. The vision was a startling reformulation of an older theology. In the very earliest days, Israel had experienced God as mobile. He had come to his people from the Sinai to Canaan on the wings of the cherubim. Now the cherubim had conveyed him to his people in exile. He was not confined to either the Temple or the Promised Land, like so many of the pagan gods who were associated indissolubly with a particular territory.

Furthermore, Yahweh chose to be with the exiles, not with the Judaeans who were still living in Jerusalem. Ezekiel had his vision in about 592, some six years before the destruction of the city by Nebuchadnezzar, but in a later vision he realized that Jerusalem was doomed because even though they were on the brink of disaster the Judaeans back home were still worshipping other gods and ignoring the terms of their covenant with Yahweh. One day Ezekiel was sitting in his house in Tel Aviv with the exiled elders of Judah when "the hand of the Lord Yahweh" fell upon him and he was taken in spirit to Jerusalem. There he was led on a conducted tour of the Temple and was horrified to see people bowing before alien gods within the sacred precincts. These "filthy practices," he was told, had driven Yahweh from his house, and Ezekiel watched the cherubim spread their wings, the wheels of the great chariot-throne begin to move, carrying the "glory of Yahweh" out of the city of Jerusalem and disappearing over the Mount of Olives to the east of the city. He had decided to come to the community of exiles instead, and now that Yahweh was no longer living in Zion, the destruction of Jerusalem was only a matter of time.[15]

But Yahweh also promised the prophet that one day he would return to his city, taking the same route over the Mount of Olives, and reestablish his residence on Mount Zion. There would be a new exodus, as the scattered exiles were brought home, and a new creation in which the land would be transformed from a desolate wasteland to become "like the garden of Eden." It would be a time of healing and integration: Judah and Israel would be reunited under a Davidic king and, as in Eden, Yahweh would live among his people.[16] It would be the end of separation, alienation, and anomie and a return to that original wholeness for which people longed. Jerusalem was central to this vision. Some fourteen years after the destruction of the city by Nebuchadnezzar, either Ezekiel or one of his disciples had a vision of a city "on a very high mountain" whose name was Yahweh Sham: "Yahweh is there."[17] The city was an earthly paradise, a place of peace and fertility in the old sense. Just as the stream had welled up in the midst of the Garden of Eden and flowed down the sacred mountain to fructify the rest of the world, Ezekiel saw a river bursting up from beneath the city's Temple, leaving the sacred precincts and bringing life and healing to the surrounding territory. Along the banks of this river there grew trees "with leaves that never wither and fruit that never fails . . . good to eat and the leaves medicinal."[18] As they experienced the pain of severance and dislocation, the exiles turned to the ancient myths to imagine a return to the place where they were supposed to be.

Yet Ezekiel was not simply clinging to the past but shaping a new vision for the future. As he contemplated the city of Yahweh Sham, he created a new sacred geography. The Temple in the middle of the city was a replica of Solomon's Temple, which was now in ruins. Its vestibule (Ulam), cult hall (Hekhal), and inner sanctum (Devir) represented the gradations of holiness: each zone was more sacred than the last.[19] As of old, the sacred could only be approached in stages and not everybody was to be permitted to approach the inner circles of sanctity. This concept would be central to Ezekiel's vision and would form the basis of his new map of the ideal world. The Temple differed from Solomon's in two important respects, however. The palace of the king was no longer next door to the Temple, and the Temple buildings were now surrounded by two walled courts.[20] The holiness of Yahweh was to be segregated more carefully than before from the profane world. God was becoming a more transcendent reality, more radically separate (kaddosh) from the rest of mundane existence. J, the first biblical writer, had imagined Yahweh sitting and talking with Abraham as a friend, but for Ezekiel, a man of the Axial Age, the sacred was a towering mystery that was overwhelming to humanity. But despite the essential "otherness" of the divine reality, it was still the center of the world of men and women and the source of their life and potency, a reality that was symbolized in Ezekiel's vision by the paradisal river. Ezekiel now described the Promised Land in a way that bore no relation to its physical geography. Unlike the city of Jerusalem, for example, Yahweh Sham was in the very center of the Land, which was far bigger than the joint kingdoms of Israel and Judah had ever been, stretching as far as Palmyra in the north and to the Brook of Egypt in the west.[21] Ezekiel was not attempting a literal description of his homeland but was creating an image of a spiritual reality. The divine power radiates from the city of Yahweh Sham to the land and people of Israel in a series of concentric circles, each zone diluting this holiness as it gets farther from the source. The Temple is the nucleus of the world's reality; the next zone is the city which enfolds it.

Surrounding the city and Temple is a special area, occupied by the sacred personnel: the king, priests, and Levites. This district is holier than that occupied by the rest of the twelve tribes of Israel, who inhabit the rest of this sacred territory. Finally, beyond the reach of this holiness, is the rest of the world, occupied by the other nations (Goyim).[22] Just as God is radically separate from all other beings, so too Israel, the holy people grouped around him, must share his holy segregation and live apart from the pagan world. It was an image of the kind of life that some of the exiles were trying to establish for themselves in Babylon.

We do not know whether Ezekiel intended this vision as a blueprint for the earthly Jerusalem. It was clearly utopian: at this point, the city, Temple, and much of the land were in ruins and there seemed no hope that they would ever be rebuilt. Ezekiel's model could have been designed as a mandala, an object of contemplation. When his mysterious visionary guide shows him this new temple, he does not tell him that this is the way the next Temple must be built. The vision has quite another function:

> Son of man, describe this Temple to the House of Israel, to shame them out of their filthy practices. Let them draw up the plan, and if they are ashamed of their behavior, show them the design and plan of the Temple, its exits and entrances, its shape, how all of it is arranged, the entire design and all its principles.[23]

If they wanted to live in exile as they had in Jerusalem, with Yahweh in their midst, the Judaean exiles had to make themselves into a sacred zone, so to speak. There must be no dangerous fraternizing with the Goyim and no flirting with Marduk and other false gods. The House of Israel must make itself into a house for the God who had chosen to dwell among them. By meditating on this idealized cultic map, the Israelites would learn the nature and meaning of holiness, where every person and object had its place. They must find a center for their lives and a new orientation. It must have been consoling for the exiles, who must frequently have felt marginal in Babylon, to realize that they were closer to the center of reality than their pagan neighbors, who were not even on the map. A displaced people would have found this new description of where they really stood profoundly healing.

We can see a little more clearly what this holy lifestyle involved when we examine the Priestly writings ("P") that were also begun in exile. P's work appears throughout the Pentateuch but is especially apparent in the books of Leviticus and Numbers. P rewrote the history of Israel from the priestly perspective, and he has much in common with Ezekiel, who, it will be remembered, was also a priest. When P described the wanderings of the Israelites in the desert and codified the laws that God was supposed to have given them on Mount Sinai, he imagined a similar series of graded zones of holiness. In the heart of the Israelite camp in the wilderness was the Tabernacle, the tent-shrine that housed the Ark of the Covenant and the "glory" of Yahweh. This was the holiest area, and only Aaron, the high priest, was permitted to enter the Holy of Holies. The camp was also holy, however, and had to be kept clear of all pollution because of the Presence in its midst. Outside the camp was the godless realm of the desert. Like Ezekiel, P also saw Yahweh as a mobile god. In his portable shrine, he was continually on the move with his people. P never mentioned Jerusalem. This is partly because his narrative ends before the Israelites enter the Promised Land and long before the city was captured by King David. But, unlike the Deuteronomists, P did not seem to have envisaged a special "place" where Yahweh could set his name. In P's vision, Yahweh has no fixed abode: his "glory" comes and goes and his "place" is with the community. For P, Israel became a people when Yahweh decided to live among them. He believed that this accompanying Presence was as important as the Law: he made Yahweh reveal the plan of his portable Tabernacle to Moses on Mount Sinai at the same time as he revealed the Torah. Again, P's was a consoling vision: it assured the exiles that Yahweh could be with his people wherever they were, even in the chaos of exile. Had he not already moved about with them in the desolate wasteland of Sinai?

The priests of Jerusalem had probably always had their own esoteric law: P's chronicle was an attempt to popularize this and make it available to the laity. Because their old world had been destroyed by Nebuchadnezzar, the exiles had to build a new one. The creation was central to P's vision, but he jettisoned the old combat myths, which were so closely associated with temples and fixed holy places. Instead he concentrated on the essence of those stories: the ordering of chaos to create a cosmos. In P's creation account in the first chapter of Genesis, Yahweh brings the world into being without fighting a mortal battle with Leviathan, the sea monster. Instead, he peacefully separates one element of the primal *tohu vohu* from all others. Thus he separates night from day, light from darkness, sea from dry land. Boundaries are set up and each component of the cosmos is given its special place. The same separation and creative ordering can be discerned in the Torah, as described by P. When the Israelites were commanded to separate milk from meat in their diet or the Sabbath from the rest of the week, they were imitating Yahweh's creative actions at the beginning of time. It was a new type of ritual and *imitatio dei* which did not require a temple or an elaborate liturgy but could be performed by men and women in the apparently humdrum ordering of their daily lives. By this ritual repetition of the divine creativity, they were building a new world and bringing order to their disrupted and dislocated lives in exile.

Many of the commandments (*mitzvoth*) are concerned with putting things in their correct place. The anthropologist Mary Douglas has shown that the beings and objects labeled "unclean" in the priestly code have stepped outside their proper category and invaded a realm that is not their own. "Filth" is something in the wrong place, whether an alien god in Yahweh's temple or mildew on clothes, something which has left the world of nature and penetrated the realm of human culture. Death is the greatest impurity of all, since it is the most dramatic reminder of the fragility of culture and our inability to control and order the world.[24] By living in an ordered cosmos, Israelites would build the kind of world imagined by Ezekiel, centered on the God in their midst. While the Temple had stood in Jerusalem, it had given them access to the sacred. Now the *mitzvoth* would restore the intimacy that Adam and Eve had enjoyed with Yahweh when he had walked with them in the Garden. By means of the *mitzvoth,* the exiled Judaeans would create a new holy place which kept the confusion and anomaly of chaos at bay. But P was not simply concerned with ritual purity: crucial to his Holiness Code were the *mitzvoth* relating to the treatment of other human beings. Alongside the laws about worship and agriculture in the Holy Land are such stern commandments as these:

> You must not steal nor deal deceitfully or fraudulently with your neighbor. . . .
> You must not be guilty of unjust verdicts. You must neither be partial to the little man nor overawed by the great. . . .
> You must not slander your own people, and you must not jeopardize your neighbor's life.
> You must not bear hatred for your brother in your heart. . . .
> You must not exact vengeance, nor must you bear a grudge against the children of your people. You must love your neighbor as yourself.[25]
>
> If a stranger lives with you in your land, do not molest him. . . . You must count him as one of your countrymen and love him as yourself—for you yourselves were once strangers in Egypt.[26]

Social justice had always been the concomitant to the devotion to a holy place and to temple ritual: in the Canaanite myths, the Zion cult and the oracles of the prophets. P goes further: there must be not only justice but love, and this compassion must also extend to people who do not belong to the House of Israel. The Goyim might be off Ezekiel's map of holiness, but they must be included in the ambit of Israel's love and social concern.

As the memory of the Temple became idealized in exile, the priests acquired a new prestige. Both P and Ezekiel stressed the role of the priesthood in the community. Originally there had been no priestly caste in Israel; David and Solomon had both performed priestly functions. But gradually the Temple service and the interpretation of the Law had been assigned to the tribe of Levi, who were supposed to have carried the Ark in the wilderness. Ezekiel narrowed this down still further. Because the Levites had condoned the idolatry in the Temple, they were demoted to a subsidiary role. Henceforth they would perform only menial tasks in the new Temple, such as preparing the animals for sacrifice, singing in choir, and keeping watch at the Temple gates. Only those priests who were direct descendants of Zadok would be allowed to enter the Temple buildings and perform the liturgy.[27] This injunction would be the cause of much future strife in Jerusalem, and it is ironic that the authentic traditions of Israel were to be enshrined in the House of Zadok the Jebusite. The more exclusive nature of the priesthood reflected the growing transcendence of God, whose sanctity was more dangerous than ever to the uninitiated and unwary. Both P and Ezekiel gave detailed instructions regarding the behavior of the priests in the sanctuary of Yahweh. When they entered the Hekhal, for example, they must change their clothes, since they were passing to a realm of sanctity that demanded a higher standard of purity. The high priest alone was permitted to enter the Devir, and that only once a year.[28] The new regulations enhanced the Israelites' sense of the holiness of Yahweh, who was a reality that was entirely separate from all other beings and could not be approached in the same way.

It is a striking fact that these elaborate descriptions of the sanctuary, its liturgy, and the priesthood were evolved at a time when there was no hope of their being implemented. The Temple was in ruins, but the most creative exiles imagined it as a fully functioning institution and drew up an intricate body of legislation to regulate it. In Chapter 8 we shall see that the rabbis did the same. Thus the most detailed Jewish texts regarding sacred space and the sanctity of Jerusalem describe a situation that no longer existed at the time of writing. "Jerusalem" had become an internalized value for the exiled Judaeans: it was an image of a salvation that could be achieved far from the physical city in the desolate territory of Judah. At about the same time in India, Siddhartha Gautama, also known as the Buddha, discovered that it was possible to enter into the ultimate reality by the practice of meditation and compassion: it was no longer essential to walk into a temple or other sacred area to attain this transcendent dimension. In the spirituality of the Axial Age it was sometimes possible to bypass the symbols and experience the sacred in the depths of the self. We have no idea how their contemporaries understood the writings of Ezekiel and P. Doubtless they hoped that one day the Temple would be rebuilt and Jerusalem restored to them. Yet it remains true that when they finally had the chance to return to Jerusalem, most of the exiles elected to stay in Babylon. They did not feel that their physical presence in Jerusalem was necessary, since they had learned to apprehend the values of Zion in a new way. The religion that we know as Judaism originated not in Judaea but in the diaspora and would be conveyed to the Holy Land in the future by such emissaries from Babylon as Nehemiah, Ezra, and Hillel.

Ezekiel and P had both been able to look beyond the earthly symbols of their faith to the eternal reality to which they pointed. Neither mentioned Jerusalem directly in their vision of the future, and P concluded his narrative on the threshold of the Promised Land. Their vision was essentially utopian, and perhaps they did not expect it to be fulfilled in their own lifetime. Their attitude to Jerusalem may have been similar to its use in the Passover seder today, where the words "Next year in Jerusalem!" always refer to the future messianic age and not to the earthly city. When Ezekiel imagined the return to Zion, he looked forward to a spiritual transformation: Yahweh would give his people "a new heart" and "a new spirit." In the same way, Jeremiah had foretold that one day the Law would no longer be inscribed on stone tablets but deep in the hearts of the people.[29] If they did look forward to a redemption, the architects of the new Judaism did not believe that it would be accomplished by a political program alone. They understood that salvation meant more than a new Temple and a new city: these could only be symbols of a more profound liberation.

Yet suddenly it seemed that political redemption was at hand. It might indeed be possible for the Judaean exiles to return to the land of their fathers and rebuild Jerusalem. People in Babylon who were becoming increasingly disenchanted with the rule of King Nabonidus, the successor of Nebuchadnezzar, were watching the career of Cyrus II, the young King of Persia, with much interest. Since 550, when he had conquered the Kingdom of Medea, he had been steadily building a vast empire for himself, and by 541 Babylon was entirely surrounded by Cyrus's territory. The priests of Marduk were especially heartened by Cyrus's propaganda, since they felt that Nabonidus had neglected their cult. Cyrus, on the other hand, promised that he would restore the temples of the empire and honor the gods. He would rebuild the ruined cities and restore a universal peace in his domains. This message also appealed to the anonymous Judaean prophet who is usually known as Second Isaiah. He hailed Cyrus as the Messiah: he had been anointed by Yahweh for the special task of rebuilding Jerusalem and its Temple. Second Isaiah turned instinctively to the old myths and liturgy of Zion. Through his instrument Cyrus, Yahweh would initiate a new creation and a new exodus. He would overcome the current enemies of Israel as he had once overcome Leviathan and Rahab, and the Judaean exiles would return to Zion through the desert, which had lost its demonic power.[30]

This return would have implications for the whole of humanity: the returning exiles would be the pioneers of a new world order. Once they had returned to Jerusalem, they would at once rebuild the Temple and the "glory" of Yahweh would return to its holy mountain. Once again, he would be enthroned in his own city "in the sight of all the nations."[31] The Jerusalem liturgy had long proclaimed that Yahweh was not only the king of Israel but the king of the whole world. Now, thanks to Cyrus, this was about to become a demonstrable reality. The other gods were cowering in terror: Bel and Nebo—important Babylonian deities—were cringing; their effigies were being carted off ignominiously on the backs of common beasts of burden.[32] Those foreign gods who had seemed to lord it over Yahweh had been made redundant. Henceforth all the nations of the world—Egypt, Cush, Sheba—would be forced to submit to Israel, dragged to Jerusalem in chains and forced to admit:

> With you alone is God, and he has no rival:
> there is no other god.[33]

The Zion liturgy had always asserted that Yahweh was the only god who counted; with Second Isaiah that insight had developed into an unequivocal monotheism. As the setting for this world triumph, Jerusalem would be more glorious than ever before. It would glitter with precious stones: rubies on the battlements, crystal on the gates, and the city walls would be encrusted with jewels—a splendor that amply demonstrated the integrity and sanctity of the city within.[34]

These hopes were brought one step nearer to fulfillment in the autumn of 539, when Cyrus's army defeated the Babylonians at Opis on the River Tigris. A month later, Cyrus entered Babylon and was enthroned as the representative of Marduk in the Temple of Esagila. At once he carried out what he had promised. Between September and August 538, all the effigies of the Assyrian gods which had been captured by the Babylonians were returned to their native cities and their temples were rebuilt. At the same time, Cyrus issued a decree stating that the Temple of Jerusalem should be rebuilt and its vessels and cultic furniture restored. Cyrus's Persian empire was run along entirely different lines from the empires of Assyria and Babylon. He gave his subjects a certain autonomy because it was cheaper and more efficient: there would be less resentment and rebellion. Rebuilding the temples of the gods was one of the chief duties of any king, and Cyrus probably believed that he would not only earn the gratitude of his subjects but also win divine favor.

Accordingly, some months after his coronation in Babylon, Cyrus handed over the gold and silver vessels which Nebuchadnezzar had confiscated from the Jerusalem Temple to one Sheshbazzar, a "prince" (*nasi*) of Judah. He set out with 42,360 Judaeans, together with their servants and two hundred singers, for the Temple.[35] If the returning exiles had left Babylon with the prophecies of the Second Isaiah ringing in their ears, they must have come down to earth very quickly when they arrived in Judah. Most of them had been born in exile and had grown up amid the magnificence and sophistication of Babylonia. Judah must have seemed a bleak, alien place. There could be no question of building a new Temple immediately. First the returning exiles had to establish a viable community in the desolation. Few of them actually stayed in Jerusalem, which was still in ruins, and the majority settled in more comfortable parts of Judah and Samerina. Some of those who stayed may have settled in the old city, while others established themselves in the countryside south of Jerusalem, which had remained uninhabited since 586.

We hear nothing more about the Golah, the community of exiles, until 520, the second year of the reign of Darius, King of Persia. By this time Sheshbazzar was no longer in charge of the Golah in Judah: we have no idea what happened to him. The building work had come to a standstill, but enthusiasm revived when, shortly after Darius's accession, Zerubbabel, the grandson of King Jehoiachin, arrived in Jerusalem from Babylon with Joshua, the grandson of the last chief priest to officiate in the old Temple. Zerubbabel had been appointed high commissioner (*peha*) of the province of Judah. He was the representative of the Persian government, but he was also a scion of the House of David, and this put new heart into the Golah. All the immigrants gathered together in Jerusalem to build a new altar on the site of the old, and when it was finished, they began to offer sacrifice and observe the traditional festivals there. But then the building stalled again. Life was still a struggle in Jerusalem: the harvests had been bad, the economy deplorable, and it was difficult to be enthusiastic about a Temple when there was not enough to eat. But in August 520 the prophet Haggai told the immigrants that their priorities were all wrong. The harvests could not improve until the Temple had been built: the House of Yahweh had always been the source of the fertility of the Promised Land. What did they mean by building houses for themselves and leaving Yahweh's dwelling place in ruins?[36] Duly chastened, the Golah went back to work.

The foundations of the Second Temple were finally laid by the autumn of 520. On the feast of Sukkoth, they were rededicated in a special

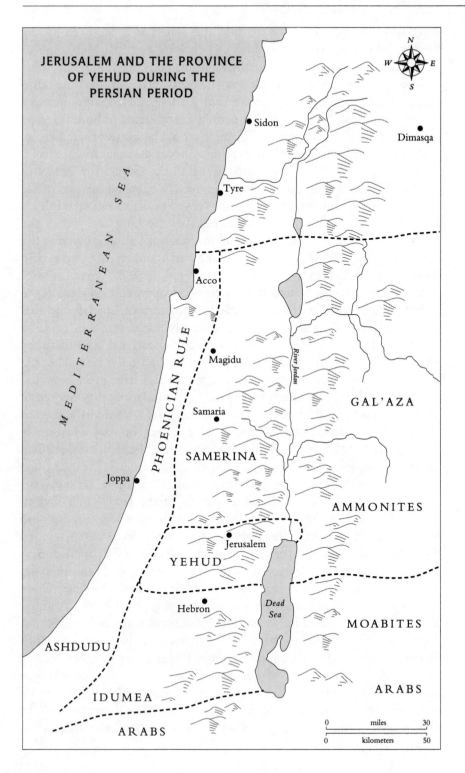

JERUSALEM AND THE PROVINCE
OF YEHUD DURING THE
PERSIAN PERIOD

Sidon

Dimasqa

M E D I T E R R A N E A N   S E A

Tyre

Acco

PHOENICIAN RULE

Magidu

River Jordan

GAL'AZA

Samaria

SAMERINA

Joppa

AMMONITES

Jerusalem

YEHUD

Hebron

Dead
Sea

MOABITES

ASHDUDU

IDUMEA

ARABS

ARABS

0   miles   30
0   kilometers   50

ceremony. The priests processed into the sacred area, followed by the Levites, who were singing psalms and clashing cymbals. But some of them were old enough to remember the magnificent Temple of Solomon, and when they saw the modest site of its successor they burst into tears.[37] From the very start, the Second Temple was a disappointment and an anticlimax for many of the people. Haggai tried to boost morale: he assured them that the Second Temple would be greater than the old. Soon Yahweh would rule the world, as Second Isaiah had foretold. Zerubbabel would be the Messiah, ruling all the Goyim on Yahweh's behalf.[38] Haggai's colleague Zechariah agreed. He looked forward to the day when Yahweh would come back to dwell on Zion and establish his reign through the two messiahs: Zerubbabel the king and Joshua the priest. It was important not to rebuild the walls of Jerusalem, so that the city would be able to accommodate the vast numbers of people who would shortly flock to live there.[39]

But not everybody shared this vision of an open city. As soon as the people of Samerina, in the old northern Kingdom of Israel, found that work on Yahweh's new Temple was seriously under way, they came to Zerubbabel and offered their services. The Chronicler tells us that they were the descendants of the foreigners who had been settled in the country by the Assyrians in 722. Some would also have been Israelites, members of the ten northern tribes, and others Judaeans, the children of those who had stayed behind in 586. Naturally these Yahwists wished to help with the rebuilding of Zion. Zerubbabel, however, brusquely refused.[40] The Golah alone constituted the "true" Israel; they alone had been commissioned by Cyrus to rebuild the Temple. Thereafter these other Yahwists were seen not as brothers but as "enemies," known collectively as the Am Ha-Aretz, the "people of the land." In Babylon, Ezekiel and P had seen all the twelve tribes as members of Israel and worthy of holiness. Only the Goyim, the gentile nations, were excluded from the sacred area. But the returning exiles had an even narrower perspective. The Am Ha-Aretz were regarded as "strangers," but the exiles were not prepared to welcome them into their city as the Holiness Code had enjoined. Consequently, instead of bringing peace to the country, the new Jerusalem became a new bone of contention in the Holy Land. The biblical authors tell us that henceforth the Am Ha-Aretz "set out to dishearten and frighten the Judaeans from building any further."[41] They tried to enlist the support of Persian officials, and on one occasion in about 486 the governor of Samerina wrote to warn King Xerxes that the Judaeans were building the walls of Jerusalem without permission. In the ancient world, this was usually regarded as an act of rebellion against the imperial power, and the work was forcibly stopped until Cyrus's original decree was discovered in the royal archive at Ecbatana.

Meanwhile the building of the Second Temple continued slowly. We hear no more of Zerubbabel after his rejection of the Am Ha-Aretz. Perhaps the messianic hopes of Haggai and Zechariah had alarmed the Persian government. He could have been removed from office when King Darius passed through the country in 519. No member of the House of David was appointed *peha* of the subprovince of Judah again. But despite the failure of this messianic dream, the immigrants did succeed in completing their Temple on 23 Adar (March) 515. It was built on the site of Solomon's Temple, of course, to ensure continuity with its sacred traditions. It also reproduced the old tripartite plan of Ulam, Hekhal, and Devir. It was separated from the city by a stone wall: a double gateway led into an outer court surrounded by various offices, storehouses, and apartments for the priests, which were built into the walls. Another wall separated this courtyard from an inner court where the altar of sacrifice stood, made of white, unhewn stone. This time, however, there was no royal palace on the Zion acropolis, since Judah no longer had a king. Another crucial difference was that the Devir was now empty, as the Ark of the Covenant had vanished without trace. The vacancy symbolized the transcendence of Yahweh, who could not be represented by any human imagery, but others may have felt that it reflected his seeming absence from this new Temple. The extravagant hopes of the Second Isaiah were not fulfilled. If Yahweh's "glory" did come and take up residence in the Devir, nobody would have known it. There was no dramatic revelation to the Goyim, and the gentile nations did not troop to Jerusalem in chains. There was a new sense of God's immense distance from the world, and in these first years of the Second Temple the very idea that the transcendent Deity could dwell in a house seemed increasingly ridiculous:

> *Thus says Yahweh:*
> *With heaven my throne*
> *and earth my footstool*
> *what house could you build me?*
> *what place could you make for my rest?*[42]

All people could do was to hope against hope that Yahweh would condescend to come down to meet them.

Instead of being drawn to splendid temples as in the past, Yahweh was more attracted these days by a "humbled and contrite spirit."[43] The cult of the First Temple had been noisy, joyful, and tumultuous. Worship in the Second Temple tended to be quiet and sober. In exile, the Golah had become aware that its own sins had been responsible for the destruction of Jerusalem, and the cult reflected the "broken and crushed heart" of the Golah. This was especially apparent in the new festival of Yom Kippur, the Day of Atonement, when the chief priest symbolically laid the sins of the people onto a goat, which was then driven out into the desert. But this enabled Israel to approach the sacred once more. Yom Kippur was the one day in the year when the chief priest entered the Devir as the people's representative. The element of expiation was also evident in the sacrifices that were offered daily in the Temple court. The people would bring bulls, sheep, goats, or pigeons as "guilt" or "sin" offerings, according to their means. They would lay their hands on the animal's head as a symbol of its surrender to Yahweh. After the beast had been killed, parts of it were given to the person who offered it, and he or she would share it with family and friends. The communion feast on earth mirrored the restored harmony with the divine.

Even though Yahweh never returned to Zion in the way that Second Isaiah had predicted, people continued to dream of the day when he would create "a new heaven and a new earth" in Jerusalem. The old hopes did not die, and Jerusalem became a symbol of that final salvation: integration, harmony, intimacy with God, and a return to paradise. The New Jerusalem would be like no other city: everybody would live a long and happy life there; everybody would be settled in his own place. There would be no weeping in the city, and the pain of the past would be forgotten. The gentiles would be astonished by the city of peace, which would establish life as it had been meant to be.[44] But other people were more disillusioned. There were social problems in the city, some prophets pointed out, and the inhabitants still flirted with the old paganism.[45] There were worries about the new exclusive attitude of the Golah: should not the City of God be open to everybody, as Zechariah had suggested? Perhaps Jerusalem should open its doors to foreigners, outcasts, and eunuchs—people regarded as "unclean" by the priests. Yahweh had proclaimed, "My house will be a house of prayer for all the peoples": one day he would bring these outsiders into the city and let them sacrifice to him on Mount Zion.[46]

Yet in the fifth century, there seemed little chance of Jerusalem's becoming a cult center for either Judaeans or gentiles. The city was still largely in ruinous condition and underpopulated. Jerusalem might even have suffered fresh damage in 458 during the disturbances that broke out all over the Persian empire when King Xerxes ascended the throne. In about 445 the news of the city's plight reached Susa, the Persian capital, and shocked the community of Judaeans there. One of the leading members of this community was Nehemiah, who held the post of cupbearer to King Artaxerxes I. He was so distressed to hear of the humiliation of the Golah in Jerusalem, whose walls were still in ruins, that he wept for several days in penitence for the sins that his people and family had committed, which had caused this calamitous state of affairs. Then he begged the king to allow him to go to Judah and rebuild the city of his ancestors. The king granted his request and appointed Nehemiah the *peha* of Judah, giving him letters of recommendation to the other governors in the region and promising him access to timber and other building materials from the royal park.[47] Artaxerxes probably hoped that Nehemiah would be able to bring stability to Judah: a reliable Persian bastion so near to Egypt would enhance the security of his empire.

The books of Ezra and Nehemiah consist of a number of unrelated documents, which an editor has attempted to string together. He thought that Ezra and Nehemiah were contemporaries and makes Ezra arrive in Jerusalem before Nehemiah. But there are good reasons for dating Ezra's mission much later, in 398, during the reign of King Artaxerxes II.[48] So Nehemiah probably set out from Susa in about 445. He would have regarded his post as a religious challenge, since the building of fortifications had long been a sacred duty in the Near East. When he arrived in Jerusalem, he stayed in the city incognito for three days and then went out secretly one night to ride around the walls. He paints a grim picture of the old fortifications "with their gaps and burned-out gates." At one point he could not even find a path for his horse.[49] The next day he made himself known to the elders, urging them to put an end to this shame and indignity. The whole city responded in a massive cooperative effort, priests and laity working side by side, and managed to erect new walls for the city in a record fifty-two days. It was a dangerous task. By this time relations with the Am Ha-Aretz had seriously deteriorated, and Nehemiah constantly had to contend with the machinations of some of the local dynasts: Sanballat, governor of Samerina; Tobiah, one of his officials; and Gershen, governor of Edom. The situation was so tense that the builders constantly feared attack: "each did his work with one hand while gripping his weapon with the other. And as each builder worked, he wore his sword at his side."[50] There was no attempt to fortify the old Mishneh suburb on the Western Hill. Nehemiah's city simply comprised the old 'Ir David on the Ophel. From the biblical text we can see the way it was organized. The markets were ranged along the western wall of the city; the priests and temple servants lived next to the Temple on the site of the old Ophel fortress. Artisans and craftsmen inhabited the southeastern quarters, while the military were concentrated in the northern district, where the city was most vulnerable. Nehemiah also built a citadel, probably northeast of the Temple on the site later occupied by the Hasmonean and Herodian

ten thousand by organizing a lottery whereby every tenth man had to move into the city.[51] The settlers who "volunteered" in this way were regarded as performing a pious action. During Nehemiah's twelve years in Jerusalem, the city gradually superseded Mizpah as the capital of the province: he built a residence for the *peha* in Jerusalem. Gradually the city became the center of the life of the Golah in Judah. But there was a power struggle going on within Jerusalem itself: some of the priests had close links with the Am Ha-Aretz, including Sanballat, who seems to have been the most dangerous of Nehemiah's opponents. He also had to curb the greed of some of the wealthier citizens, who were seizing the sons and daughters, vineyards and fields of the poor, when they proved unable to pay off their loans with interest. With considerable popular support, Nehemiah forced the nobles and officials to take a solemn oath to stop charging interest.[52] It was an attempt to make Jerusalem a refuge for the poor once again, but it naturally antagonized the upper classes, who tended to turn more and more to their allies in the neighboring territory. There seems to have been considerable tension in the country. Sanballat, Tobiah, and Gershen could see perfectly well that fortifying the city was a bid for political control and preeminence.

In his second term of office, which began in about 432, Nehemiah also made new legislation to prevent members of the Golah from marrying the local people. He expelled the chief priest Eliashib, who was married to Sanballat's daughter; Eliashib took up residence in Samaria, where he was probably joined by other malcontents from the priestly caste. The question of mixed marriage became an increasingly contentious issue in Jerusalem. Nehemiah's legislation was not designed to ensure the purity of the race in the twentieth-century sense but was an attempt to express the new sacred geography developed in exile by such prophets as Ezekiel in social terms: the Golah must live apart from the Goyim, as befitted God's holy people. In Babylon, the exiles had been concerned to preserve a distinct Judaean identity, centered on the presence of Yahweh in Israel. The same centripetal pull was also evident in social life. The Torah obliged the people of Israel to marry beyond the basic family unit, but it was considered better to marry people who were as closely related as was legally possible. People inside the family were regarded as acceptable marriage partners, while those outside were undesirable. These series of concentric circles stopped at the border of Israel: the Goyim, who were off the holiness map, were literally beyond the pale.[53] A marriage "outside" was equivalent to leaving the sacred enclave and going out into the godless wilderness, where the scapegoat was dispatched on Yom Kippur. It was an attempt to make Israel a "holy" and separate people and defined the Judaean identity by marking out the people who were "outside" and "not–like–us." But in Judah, the Golah were being asked to reject people who had once been members of the Israelite family but had now been pushed into the role of strangers and enemies.

During the fifth century, the exiles in Babylon had been engaged in a remarkable religious reform, which resulted in the religion of Judaism. The question of identity was still crucial: the exiles had stopped giving their children Babylonian names, preferring such names as Shabbetai, which reflected their new religious symbols. The Torah now played a central role in their religious lives and had taken the place of the Temple. By observing the *mitzvoth,* the Judaeans of Babylon could make themselves a sacred community which enshrined the divine Presence and established God's order on earth. But that meant that the ordinary Jews had to be instructed in the intricacies of the Torah by experts. One of these was Ezra, who "had devoted himself to the study of the Law of Yahweh, to practicing it and to teaching Israel its laws and customs."[54] He may also have been the minister for Jewish affairs at the Persian court. In 398 he was sent by Artaxerxes II to Judah with a fourfold task. He was to accompany a party of Jews who wished to return to their homeland; he would take gifts from the Jewish community in Babylon to the Temple; once he had arrived in Judah, he was "to conduct an inquiry into the situation in Judah and Jerusalem on the basis of the law of [their] god"; and finally, he had to instruct the Jews in the Levant in this law.[55] The laws of other subject peoples were under review at this time. Artaxerxes was supporting the cult of the Jewish Temple, which was central to the life of the province of Judah. He had to be sure that it was compatible with the interests and security of the empire. As a legal expert in Babylon, Ezra may have worked out a satisfactory *modus vivendi* between the Torah and the Persian legal system, and Artaxerxes needed to be certain that this law was also operating in Judah. Ezra would promulgate the Torah in Jerusalem and make it the official law of the land.[56]

The biblical writer sees Ezra's mission as a turning point in the history of his people. Ezra's journey to Judah is described as a new exodus and Ezra himself, the lawgiver, as a new Moses. He arrived in Jerusalem in triumph, but was appalled by what he found: priests and Levites were still colluding with the Am Ha-Aretz and continued to take foreign wives. The people of Jerusalem were chastened to see the emissary of the king tear his hair and sit down in the street in the posture of mourning for a whole day. Then he summoned all the members of the Golah to a meeting in Jerusalem: anybody who did not attend would be cast out of the community and have his property confiscated. On New Year's Day (September/October), Ezra brought the Torah to the square in front of the Water Gate and, standing on a wooden dais and surrounded by the leading citizens, he read the Law to the assembled crowd, explaining it as he went along.[57] We have no idea what he actually read to them: was it the whole of the Pentateuch, the Book of Deuteronomy, or the Holiness Code? Whatever its content, Ezra's Law was clearly a shock to the people, who had obviously never heard it before. They were so tearful that Ezra had to remind them that this was a festival day, and he read aloud the passage from the Torah which commanded the Israelites to live in special booths during the month of Sukkoth, in memory of their ancestors' forty years in the wilderness. He sent the people into the hills to pick branches of myrtle, olive, pine, and palm, and soon Jerusalem was transformed by the leafy shelters that appeared all over the city. The new festival had replaced the old Jebusite rites of Sukkoth; now a new interpretation linked it firmly to the Exodus traditions. There was a carnival atmosphere in the city during the next seven days, and every evening the people assembled to listen to Ezra's exposition of the Law.

The next assembly was a more somber occasion.[58] It was held in the square in front of the Temple, and the people stood trembling as the torrential winter rains deluged the city. Ezra commanded them to send away their foreign wives, and special committees were set up to examine individual cases. Women and children

"Israel does not acknowledge us." Excluded from Jerusalem, the Am Ha-Aretz built their own temple on Mount Gerizim in Samerina. Today the Samaritans, their descendants, still worship there and practice their own form of Judaism.

were sent away from the Golah to join the Am Ha-Aretz. Membership of Israel was now confined to the descendants of those who had been exiled to Babylon and to those who were prepared to submit to the Torah, which had now become the official law code of Jerusalem. The lament of the people who had now become outcasts may have been preserved for us in the book of Isaiah:

> For Abraham does not own us
> and Israel does not acknowledge us;
> yet you, Yahweh, yourself are our father. . . .
> We have long been like people who do not rule,
> people who do not bear your name.[59]

A ruthless tendency to exclude other people would henceforth become a characteristic of the history of Jerusalem, even though this ran strongly counter to some of Israel's most important traditions. As one might expect, there were many people who opposed this new tendency. They did not want to sever all relations with the people of Samerina and the surrounding countries. They feared that Jerusalem would become parochial and introverted and that the city would suffer economically. But others responded to the new legislation with enthusiasm. We know very little about Jerusalem in the generations succeeding Ezra, but within the next eight generations the Law had become as central as the Temple to the spirituality of the people of Judah. When these two sacred values were imperiled, there was a crisis in Jerusalem which nearly resulted in the city's losing its new Jewish identity.

6

ANTIOCH IN JUDAEA

WHEN ALEXANDER OF MACEDON defeated Darius III, King of Persia, beside the River Issus in October 333 BCE, the Jews of Jerusalem were shocked, because they had been loyal vassals of Persia for over two hundred years. Josephus Flavius, the first-century Jewish historian, tells us that the high priest refused at first to submit to Alexander because he had taken a vow to remain loyal to the last Persian king but, as a result of a dream, capitulated when Alexander promised that throughout his empire the Jews would continue to be governed according to their own Law.[1] In fact, it is most unlikely that Alexander ever visited Jerusalem. At first the Macedonian conquest made very little difference to the lives of the people of Judah. The Torah continued to be the official law of the province, and the administration which had operated under the Persians probably remained in place. Yet the legend of Alexander's dealings with the high priest was significant, because it illustrated the complexity of the Jewish response to Hellenism. Some Jews instinctively recoiled from the culture of the Greeks and wanted to cling to the old dispensation; others found Hellenism congenial and saw it as profoundly sympathetic to their own traditions. The struggle between these opposing factions would dominate the history of Jerusalem for nearly three hundred years.

Hellenism had been gradually penetrating the Near East for decades before the triumph of Alexander. The old cultures of the region were beginning to crumble and would all be indelibly affected by the Greek spirit. But the Jews of Jerusalem had probably had little direct contact with the Greeks: such elements of Hellenistic culture as did come their way had usually been mediated through the coastal cities of Phoenicia, which could translate it into a more familiar idiom. Jerusalem was once more off the beaten track and had become rather a backwater. It was not on any of the main trade routes. The caravans that stopped at the nearby cities of Petra and Gaza had no reason to go to Jerusalem, which was a poor city, lacking the raw materials to develop an industry. Introverted, its life revolving around the Temple and its supposedly ancient Torah, Jerusalem paid little heed to international politics and seemed more in tune with the past than with the modernity infiltrating the region from the west.

All that changed when Alexander the Great died in Babylon on 13 June 323. The only possible heir was a minor, and almost immediately fighting broke out among the leading generals for control of the empire. For the next two decades the lands conquered by Alexander were convulsed by the battles of these six *diadochoi* ("successors"). As a crucial transit region, Judaea was continuously invaded by armies on the march from Asia Minor or Syria to Egypt, with their baggage, equipment, families, and slaves. Jerusalem was conquered no fewer than six times during these years, and its inhabitants became painfully aware that the long period of peaceful isolation was over. The Jews of Jerusalem first experienced Hellenism as destructive, violent, and militaristic. The Macedonian *diadochoi* had erupted into the country as arrogant conquerors who took little notice of the native population except insofar as it could serve their interests. Greek art, philosophy, democracy, and literature, which have played such an important role in the development of Western culture, would not have impressed the inhabitants of Jerusalem in these terrible years. They would probably have agreed with the Sanskrit writer who described the Greeks as "powerful and wicked."

In 301, Judaea, Samerina, Phoenicia, and the whole of the coastal plain were captured by the forces of Ptolemy I Soter, the "successor" who had recently established a power base for himself in Egypt. For the next hundred years, Jerusalem remained under the control of the Ptolemies, who needed the province of Syria as a military buffer against attack from the north.

Like most ancient rulers, the Ptolemies did not interfere overmuch in local affairs, though they introduced a more streamlined and efficient type of administration that was flexible enough to treat the different regions of their Kingdom differently. Some parts of the province were crown lands that were ruled directly by royal officials; so were the new ports founded by the Ptolemies at Joppa and Strato's Tower and the new military colonies at Beth Shan, Philotera and Pella. The rest of the country had more freedom to manage its own affairs. The Phoenician cities of Tyre, Sidon, Tripoli, and Byblos were allowed significant freedoms and privileges. Greek colonists arrived in Syria and established *poleis,* modeled on the democratic Greek republics, in such towns as Gaza, Shechem, Marissa, and Amman, which were virtually self-governing. Greek soldiers, merchants, and entrepreneurs swarmed into these settlements to take advantage of the new opportunities in the east, and the local people who learned to speak and write in Greek became "Hellenes" themselves and were allowed to enter the lower ranks of the army and administration.

The *polis* was alien to many of the most deeply rooted traditions of the region. Hellenistic culture was secular. It depended upon an intelligentsia that was independent of both palace and temple. Instead of being ruled by a divinely appointed ruler or by a priestly elite, the *polis* kept government separate from religion. *Gymnasia* also appeared in these new Greek cities, where the young men were trained according to the Hellenistic ideal. They studied Greek literature and underwent a rigorous physical and military training, developing mind and body simultaneously. The *gymnasion* was the institution that bound the Greeks together in their far-flung empire. It had its own religious ethos. Like the Olympic Games, the athletic competitions of the young men were religious celebrations in honor of Hermes and Heracles, the patrons of the *gymnasia.* Usually the native people were not allowed to enter the *gymnasion;* it was a privilege reserved for the Greeks. But the Ptolemies did permit foreigners to be admitted. That was how the Jews of Alexandria came to be trained in the *gymnasion* there and were able to achieve a unique fusion of Greek and Jewish culture. The Greeks were materialistic and sometimes shocking, but many of the local people found this new culture seductive. For some it was as irresistible as Western culture is to many people today in the developing world. It attracted and repelled; it broke taboos, but for that very reason many found it profoundly liberating.

At first, Jerusalem was not affected by these new ideas. It was not a *polis* and therefore had no *gymnasion.* Most of the inhabitants would have been horrified by the idea of Hermes being honored in Yahweh's city and appalled to see youths exercising in the nude. Judaea was of no great interest to the Ptolemies. The Jews there constituted a distinct *ethnos* ("nation"), which was ruled by the *gerousia,* a council of elders which was based in Jerusalem. The Torah continued as the official law of the *ethnos,* which thus remained what it had been under the Persians: a temple state governed by its priests. The Ptolemies may have appointed a local agent (*oikonomos*) to keep an eye on Judaean affairs, and, at least in time of war, they would have installed a garrison in the city. But for the most part, the Jews were left to their own devices. Their chief link with the Egyptian government was the tribute of twenty talents that they were obliged to pay each year.

But it was inevitable that Jerusalem would eventually be dragged into the Greek world, which was transforming the rest of the country. During the reign of Ptolemy II (282–46), a Jerusalemite called Joseph managed to secure the job of collecting the taxes of the whole province of Syria. For over twenty years he was one of the most powerful men in the country. Joseph belonged to the Tobiad clan and may have been a descendant of the Tobiah who had caused Nehemiah such trouble. If so, the Tobiads refused to allow their lives to be circumscribed by the Torah; they still liked to make contact with foreigners and would not submit to the more exclusive ethos of the Jerusalem establishment. The Tobiad estate at Ammantis in Transjordan had become one of the Ptolemaic military colonies. Joseph was obviously at home in the Greek world, and he was able to introduce the high finance of the Hellenes into Jerusalem, becoming the first Jewish banker. Many of his fellow Jews were proud of Joseph's success: a novella quoted by Josephus, which tells the story of his career, clearly delights in his cleverness, chicanery, and skills as an entrepreneur.[2] The author praises Joseph for rescuing his people from poverty and enabling them to share in the economic boom that the Ptolemies had brought to the region.

The Tobiads became the pioneers of Hellenism in Jerusalem. They wanted their city to discard the old traditions, which they found inhibiting and parochial. They were not alone in this. Many people in the Greek empire experienced a similar desire to shake off ancestral customs that suddenly seemed oppressive. Instead of seeing their world as an enclave, in which it was essential that limits, borderlines, and frontiers be clearly drawn and defined, many people were looking for larger horizons. The *polis* was a closed world, but many Greeks now considered themselves cosmopolitans: citizens of the whole cosmos. Instead of regarding their homeland as the most sacred value, since it gave them their unique place in the world, Greeks became colonialists and world travelers. The conquests of Alexander had opened up the globe and made the *polis* seem petty and inadequate. The very boundlessness that had seemed chaotic and threatening to their ancestors now seemed exciting and liberating. Jews in the Greek world also shared this rootlessness and wanted to become citizens of humanity rather than members of a chosen people, hampered by a law that had become constricting. By the end of the third century, some Jews had begun to acquire the rudiments of a Greek education and were giving their children Greek names.

Others found all this extremely threatening. They clung to the old traditions centered on the Temple. In particular, the lower classes, who were not able to share in the new prosperity, tended to turn more fervently than ever to the Law, which ensured that each thing had its place and that order could prevail in society only if people and objects were confined to the category to which they belonged. The conservative Jews naturally gravitated toward the priests, the guardians of Torah and Temple. Their leaders were the Oniads, a priestly family of Zadokite descent whose members had for some time been the chief priests of Jerusalem. The Oniads themselves were attracted to the Greek ideal, and some of them had Greek names. But they were determined to maintain the old laws and traditions on which their power and privileges depended.

Toward the end of the century, it became clear that the Ptolemies might lose Syria to the Seleucid dynasty, which ruled the Greek kingdom of Mesopotamia. In 219 the young, ambitious Seleucid king Antiochus III invaded Samaria and the Phoenician coastline, and he was able to hold his own in these territories for four years. Even though he was eventually driven back by Ptolemy IV Philopater, it seemed likely that he would be back. Because the Tobiads had been closely associated with the Ptolemies since Joseph had become their chief tax collector, the more conservative Jews of Jerusalem supported the Seleucids and hoped that they would gain control of the country. Since the Tobiads became embroiled in an internal family dispute, the energetic high priest Simon II of the Oniad family achieved considerable influence in the city and supported the Seleucid cause. After Antiochus had invaded the country again in 203, his Jewish supporters helped him to conquer the citadel of Jerusalem in 201, though his troops were thrown out of the city the following year by the Ptolemies. In 200, Jerusalem was subjected to a long siege and suffered severe damage before Antiochus was able to take it back again.

By this time the Seleucids had conquered the whole country, which they called the province of Coele-Syria and Phoenicia. Different administrative arrangements were once again made for the various political units: the Greek and Phoenician cities, the military colonies, and the crown lands. With the help of Jewish scribes, Antiochus drew up a special charter for the *ethnos* of Judaea and rewarded his supporters in Jerusalem. Simon II was made head of the *ethnos,* which meant that the priestly conservative party had gained ascendancy over the Hellenizing Tobiads. The Torah continued to be the law of the land, and the Jewish senate (*gerousia*) remained the governing body. The charter made special arrangements for the Temple which reflected the sacred geography of the Jews but introduced even more exclusive measures than had Nehemiah and Ezra. To preserve the purity of the shrine, the city of Jerusalem had to be free of all impurity. A proclamation on the city gates now forbade the breeding or slaughter of "unclean" animals in Jerusalem. Male Jews were not permitted to enter the inner court of the Temple, where the sacrifices were performed, unless they went through the same ritual ablutions as the priests. Gentiles were also forbidden to enter the inner court. This was an innovation that had no basis in the Torah but reflected the hostility of the more conservative Jews of Jerusalem toward the gentile world. It would have made a strong impression on Greek visitors to the city. They would have found it natural that the laity were excluded from the Temple buildings: in almost any temple of antiquity, priests were the only people to enter the inner sanctum. But in Greece, anybody was allowed to go into the temple courts, provided that he performed the usual rites of purification. Now Greek visitors to Jerusalem found that they were relegated to the outer court, with the women and the Jews who were in a state of ritual impurity. Because they did not observe the Torah, foreigners were declared "unclean." They must keep to their place, beyond the pale of holiness.

But for Jews who were within the ambit of the sacred, the Temple cult yielded an experience of the divine that brought a new clarity and sense of life's richness. Ben Sirah, a scribe who was writing in Jerusalem during the early Seleucid period, gives us some idea of the impact of the Temple liturgy on the faithful when he describes Simon performing the ceremonies of Yom Kippur. This was the one day in the year that the high priest was permitted to enter the Devir on behalf of the faithful. When he emerged, he brought its great sanctity with him out to the people. The sacred aura that seemed to surround Simon is compared to the sun shining on the golden roof of the Temple, to a rainbow amid brilliant clouds, to an olive tree laden with fruit and a cypress soaring toward the heavens.[3] Reality became heightened and was experienced more intensely: the sacred brought out its full potential. In Simon's day, the office of high priest had achieved an entirely new status. It became a symbol of the integrity of Judaism and played an increasingly important role in the politics of Jerusalem. Ben Sirah believed that the high priest alone had the authority to give a definitive interpretation of the Torah.[4] He was a symbol of continuity: the kingship of the House of David had lasted only a few generations, but the priesthood of Aaron would last forever.[5] By this date, Yahweh had become so exalted and transcendent in the minds of his people that it was dangerous to utter his name. When they came across the Hebrew consonants YHWH in the text of the Torah, Jews would now substitute such a synonym as "Adonai" ("Lord") or "El Elyon" ("Most High"). Only the high priest could pronounce the divine name, and then only once a year on Yom Kippur. Ben Sirah also praised Simon for his building work in Jerusalem.

He repaired the city walls and Temple porches which had been damaged in the siege of 200. He also excavated a large reservoir—"as huge as the sea"—north of the Temple Mount, which became known as the Pool of Beth-Hesda (Aramaic: "House of Mercy"). Traditionally, building had always been considered a task for a king, but Antiochus had not agreed to pay for these repairs: he had simply exempted the cost of the building from the city's tax. So Simon had stepped into the breach, acting, as it were, as king and priest of Jerusalem.[6]

Ben Sirah was a conservative. He deplored the materialism that had crept into the city now that so many people had been infected by the mercenary ways of the Greeks. The Greeks liked to blame the Levantines for their venality, but in fact this was a vice that they themselves had brought into the region from the West. In the old days, the Zion cult had insisted that Jerusalem be a refuge for the poor; but now, Ben Sirah complained, Jerusalemites considered poverty a disgrace and the poor were pushed callously to one side in the stampede for wealth.[7] And yet, however much Ben Sirah distrusted those Jews who flirted with Greek culture, he was not himself immune to the lure of Hellenism. Why should the young Jews of Jerusalem not study the works of Moses as the young Greeks studied the works of Homer in the *gymnasia*? This was a revolutionary suggestion. Hitherto laymen might learn extracts from the Torah by heart, but they were not expected to read it themselves: the Law was expounded to them by the priests. But Ben Sirah was no priest; he was a Jewish intellectual who believed that the Torah could become the basis of a liberal education for all male Jews. Fifty years later, Ben Sirah's grandson, who translated his book into Greek, took this type of study for granted.[8] Throughout the Near East, the old religions which opposed the Hellenistic challenge were themselves being subtly changed by their contact with the Greek world. Judaism was no exception. Jews like Ben Sirah had already begun to adapt the Greek educational ideal to their own traditions and thus laid the foundation of rabbinic Judaism. Even the discipline of question and answer, later developed by the rabbis, would show the influence of the Socratic method.

But other Jews wanted to go further: they were hoping to receive a wholly Greek education and did not believe that this would be incompatible with Judaism. Soon they would clash with the conservatives in Jerusalem. The first sign of the rift occurred in about 180, when the high priest Onias III, the son of Simon II, was accused of hoarding a large sum of money in the Temple treasury. King Seleucus IV immediately dispatched his vizier Heliodorus from Antioch to Jerusalem to recover the money, which, he believed, was owed to the Seleucid state. By this date, enthusiasm for the Seleucids had waned in the city. In 192,

Antiochus III had suffered a humiliating defeat at the hands of the advancing Roman army, which had annexed Greece and much of Anatolia. He was allowed to keep his throne only on condition that he paid an extremely heavy indemnity and annual tribute. His successors were, therefore, always chronically short of money. Seleucus IV probably assumed that since the charter obliged him to pay all the expenses of the Jerusalem cult out of his own revenues, he had the right to control the Temple finances. But he had reckoned without Jewish sensitivity about the Temple, which now surfaced for the first time. When Heliodorus arrived in Jerusalem and insisted on confiscating the money in the Temple coffers, the people were overcome with horror. Onias became deathly pale and trembled convulsively; women ran through the streets, clad in sackcloth, and young girls leaned out of their windows calling on heaven for aid. The integrity of the Temple was saved by a miracle. As he approached the treasury, Heliodorus was struck to the ground in a paralytic fit. Afterward he testified that he had seen the Jewish god with his own eyes.

The incident was a milestone: henceforth any attack on the Temple was likely to provoke a riot in Jerusalem. Over the years, the Temple had come to express the essence of Judaism; it had been placed in the center of the emotional map of the Jews, constituting the heart of their beleaguered identity. It was regarded as the core of the nation, the source of its life, creativity, and survival. The Temple still exerted a centripetal pull on the hearts and minds of those Jews who carried out the directives of the Torah. Even in the diaspora, Jews now turned toward Jerusalem when they prayed and had begun to make the long pilgrimage to the holy city to celebrate the great festivals in the Temple. The psalms, prayers, and sacred writings all encouraged them to see the Temple as paradise on earth, an objective correlative for God himself. As Jews struggled to preserve a distinct identity in the midst of a world that urged them to assimilate, the Temple and its city had become an embattled enclave. Gentiles were not allowed anywhere near the Temple buildings, and any attempt to violate that holy separateness was experienced collectively by the people as a rape. This was not a rational position: it was a gut reaction, instinctive and immediate.

But the crisis of 180 did not end with Heliodorus's stroke. There were insinuations that Onias had somehow been responsible for his illness and he felt bound to go to the Seleucid court to clear his name. But he had played into the hands of his enemies. While he was at Antioch, his ambitious brother Joshua—or Jason, as he preferred to be called—curried favor with King Seleucus and offered him a hefty bribe in return for the high priesthood. Seleucus was only too happy to agree, and Onias was forced to flee the court and was later murdered. But high priest Jason was not a conservative like his brother. The Torah had become meaningless to him, and he wanted his people to enjoy the freedoms of a wider world by adopting the Greek lifestyle. Soon after he had taken office, King Seleucus was also murdered, by his brother Antiochus Epiphanes, and Jason offered the new king a further sum of money, asking in return that the old charter of 200 be revoked. He did not want Judah to continue to be an old-fashioned temple state based on the Torah. Instead, he hoped that Jerusalem would become a *polis* known as Antioch after its royal patron. Ever in need of cash, Antiochus accepted the money and agreed to Jason's program, which, he hoped, would consolidate his authority in Judah.

But Jerusalem could not become a *polis* overnight. A significant number of the citizens had to be sufficiently versed in Greek culture to become Hellenes before the democratic ideal could be imposed on the city. As an interim measure, Jason probably had leave to establish a society of "Antiochenes," who were committed to the Hellenizing project. A *gymnasion* was established in Jerusalem, provocatively close to the Temple, where the young Jews had the opportunity to study Homer, Greek philosophy, and music; they competed naked in the sporting events. But until Jerusalem was a full-fledged *polis,* the Torah was still the law of the land, and it is therefore unlikely that Hermes and Herakles were honored in the Jerusalem *gymnasion.* Jason's plans received a good deal of popular support during this first phase. We hear of no opposition to the *gymnasion* in the biblical sources. As soon as the gong sounded for the athletic exercises, the priests used to hurry down from the Temple Mount to take part. Priests, landowners, merchants, and craftsmen were all attracted to the challenge of Hellenism and probably hoped that a more open society would improve Jerusalem's economy. There had always been opposition to the segregationalist policies of Nehemiah and Ezra, and many of the Jews of Jerusalem were attracted by the Greek ideal of world citizenship. They did not feel that Judaism was necessarily incompatible with the Hellenic world. Perhaps Moses could be compared to a lawgiver such as Lycurgus? The Torah was not necessarily a sacrosanct value: Abraham had not obeyed the *mitzvoth,* for example. Had he not eaten milk and meat together when he entertained Yahweh at Mamre? There was no need for Jews to separate themselves so fanatically from the *goyim.* By making friends with their neighbors and enjoying cultural and economic exchange with them, Jews could return to the primal unity that had prevailed before the human race had been split up into different tribes and religions after the building of the Tower of Babel. When King Antiochus Epiphanes visited Jerusalem in 173, he was given an enthusiastic welcome. Jason led the people through the streets in a torchlight procession in honor of their new patron. It may have been on this occasion that Jerusalem formally became a *polis*—a development which most of the population applauded.

But then the Hellenizers went too far. In 172, Jason sent a priest called Menelaus to Antioch with the money he had promised to Antiochus. Menelaus treacherously abused this trust by offering the king yet another bribe in order to secure the high priesthood for himself. Yet again, Antiochus needed the money and Menelaus returned to Jerusalem as high priest. Jason was deposed and fled for his life. He found a refuge on the Tobiad estate near Amman, on the other side of the Jordan. But the people could not accept Menelaus as high priest: although a member of a priestly family, he was not a descendant of Zadok and was, therefore, ineligible for this office. Menelaus compounded his mistake by plundering the Temple treasury in order to find the money he had undertaken to pay to Antiochus. Disillusioned, most of the people of Jerusalem abandoned the society of "Antiochenes," who now became a small minority group, wholly dependent upon the Seleucid king.

At the Western Wall in Jerusalem, Jews dedicate a new Torah scroll for their synagogue. After the persecution by Antiochus Epiphanes, there was a new passion for the Law in Judaea.

The Hellenizers resorted to some very dubious tactics, but it would be a mistake to see them as

cynics who simply wanted the good life and the fleshpots of Greece. Most of them were probably quite sincere in their desire for a less exclusive Judaism. In our own day, Jews have tried to reform their traditions in order to embrace modernity and have attracted a wide following. One of the chief failings of these Hellenizing reformers was that they did not keep Antiochus fully informed about the change of heart in Jerusalem, and so he may not have realized how unpopular their project had become. Menelaus pressed on with the conversion of the city to a *polis*. He renamed Jerusalem "Antioch in Judaea" and continued to encourage the *gymnasion,* the ephebate (an organization which trained young men in military, athletic, and cultural pursuits), and the Hellenistic games. But the reform suffered a severe setback in 170 when, following a report that Antiochus had been killed in an encounter with the Romans in Egypt, Jason attempted a coup. He marched into the city and forced Menelaus and the other Antiochenes into the citadel. Antiochus was still very much alive, however, and he descended upon the city in fury, putting Jason once again to flight. Construing the coup as a rebellion against his authority, he plundered the Temple treasury and stormed into the Temple buildings, removing the golden incense altar, the lampstand, the Veil of the Devir, and all the vessels and censers he could lay hands on. His violation of these most sacred precincts was never forgotten, and in future Antiochus would be seen as the archetypal enemy of the Jewish people. Jerusalem was now reduced from a *polis* in the making to a mere military colony, ruled by Menelaus with the support of a Syrian garrison. But this was not sufficient to secure law and order in the city. The following year Antiochus had to send another regiment, which invaded Jerusalem on the Sabbath and tore down part of the city walls. The Syrians then built a new fortress overlooking the Temple enclosure called the Akra, which became the Seleucid headquarters in Jerusalem. In effect the Akra became a separate district, inhabited by pagan troops and Hellenist Jews, where the Greek gods were worshipped.

But this was not all. Possibly at the behest of Menelaus and his Antiochenes, Antiochus issued an edict which left an indelible impression on the Jewish spirit and made it emotionally impossible for many Jews to accommodate the gentile world. This decree revoked the charter of 200 and outlawed the practice of the Jewish faith in Judah. This was the first religious persecution in history. The Temple liturgy was forbidden, as was the Sabbath rest, circumcision, and the observance of the purity laws. Anybody who disobeyed the edict was put to death. Women who circumcised their sons were paraded around the city and flung with their babies from the walls to the valleys below. A mother watched all seven of her sons die; in her zeal for the Law, she cheered each of her sons to their deaths, before being executed herself. A ninety-year-old man called Eliezar went to his death rather than swallow a morsel of pork. Once people had started to die for the Torah, it became sacred to Jews in an entirely new way.

As a result of this edict, the Temple Mount was transformed. Antiochus broke down the gates and walls that had separated the sacred space from the rest of the city and, deliberately defying the proscriptions of the Torah, planted trees that transformed the sanctuary into a sacred grove, Greek-style. The Temple buildings, which had been plundered by Antiochus two years earlier, remained empty and desolate. On 25 Kislev (December) 167, conservative Jews were horrified to hear that an "abomination"—probably a *matzevah,* a standing stone—had been set up next to the altar of sacrifice. With its trees and open altar, the sanctuary now resembled an old *bamah*; indeed, there were still shrines like this at Mamre and on Mount Carmel. The Temple was now dedicated to Zeus Olympios, but this did not necessarily mean that the Jews were being forced to worship the Greek deity. *Olympios* was simply a synonym for "heaven" at this date: the area had thus been dedicated to the God of Heaven, a title that could apply to Yahweh as to any other high god.[9]

The Hellenizers probably believed that they were returning to the simpler religion of Abraham, who had worshipped their god at similar shrines before Moses had introduced the complexities of the Torah.[10] We shall see in future chapters that other monotheists had similar plans to restore this primordial religion in Jerusalem. In their worship of the God of Heaven they seem to have been attempting to create a rationalized cult that would appeal to all men of goodwill—to the Greeks in the Akra as well as to the Antiochene Jews. Their program was not dissimilar to the deism of the French *philosophes* of the eighteenth-century European Enlightenment. But these ideas were utterly abhorrent to the majority of Jews. For the first time an apocalyptic piety entered Judaism which looked forward to a final victory of the righteous at the End of History. Subsequently this type of faith would appear in all three of the monotheistic traditions when a cherished way of life came under attack, as in Jerusalem under Antiochus Epiphanes. Instead of adopting the rationalized, secular ethos of the Greeks, the apocalyptic writers defiantly reasserted the values of the old mythology. When the present looked hopeless, many Jews found comfort in the visions of a triumphant future. To give these "revelations" authority, they were often attributed to such august figures of the past as the prophet Daniel or to Enoch, the patriarch who was said to have been taken up to heaven at the end of his life.

The scenario of the Last Days as conceived by these seers always followed a similar pattern. God would gather the twelve tribes of Israel together from all the lands of their dispersion and bring them to Jerusalem. Then he would lead them to victory in terrible battles, reminiscent of the divine struggles at the beginning of time: now the people of Israel would eliminate all their enemies, who incarnated the evils of chaos and destruction, and create a better world. Some, however, looked forward to the conversion of the Goyim to the religion of Yahweh. The setting for this final act of redemption was always Jerusalem. Now that Mount Zion had been desecrated by pagans and Jewish renegades, the apocalyptic authors of the books of Daniel, Jubilees, and Enoch looked forward to a future era when the city would be purified and God would build a new Temple. At a time when there were no native kings in the Greek empire, people imagined a Jewish Messiah who would lead them to their final triumph. These visions were a defiant assertion of Jewish identity at a moment when it seemed particularly imperiled. It was an attempt to keep faith in hopeless circumstances and was not confined to a small minority. Apocalyptic piety would permeate most religious movements during the second and first centuries and could inspire sober intellectuals—such as Ben Sirah—as well as revolutionaries. Nor were the Jews alone in their new visionary fervor. The Greeks had been much impressed by the mystical feats of the priests of Egypt, the magi of Persia, and the Brahmans of India, who seemed far more spiritual than their own sages. This gave the subject peoples of the East a much-needed infusion of self-esteem. The Greeks might be very clever, but their elaborate discourse was merely "arrogant" and "impotent." They could devise "empty concepts" and had a facility for marshaling effective arguments, claimed a hermetic text of the time, "but in reality the philosophy of the Greeks is just the sound of words." This assertion of their own native traditions was an attempt to put the sophisticated conquerors in their place.[11]

Some of these visionaries imagined themselves flying through the air to the highest heaven. The idea of God living in a temple was beginning to lose its compelling power in many parts of the Near East. In Egypt and Persia, visionaries of the second and first centuries had begun to bypass the earthly symbol and travel directly to the celestial world of the gods. These mystical journeys reflected the new rootlessness of the age: spirituality was no longer earthed in a particular place. Some people—though by no means all—were seeking a freedom that was not of this world and a different kind of spiritual expression. Jewish mystics also began to make these imaginary flights. The word "apocalypse" means "unveiling": like the prophets, these visionaries claimed to have seen what lay behind the Veil of the Devir. Like that of Amos, Isaiah, and Ezekiel, their vision of God was deeply conditioned by the Jerusalem cult. The Devir had once held the Ark, God's Throne on earth. Now, in the second century, visionaries imagined ascending directly to God's heavenly palace and approaching his celestial Throne. One of these early visions is recounted in the First Book of Enoch (c. 150 BCE). Instead of going into the Jerusalem Temple to have his vision, he imagined himself flying through the air, propelled by the winds, to God's great marble house in heaven, which was surrounded by "tongues of fire" and "fiery cherubim." These were not whimsical flights of fancy. Later we read of Jewish mystics preparing themselves for this mystical ascent by special disciplines, similar to those evolved by yogis and contemplatives all over the world. The Jewish visionary would fast, place his head between his knees, and murmur certain praises of God to himself as a mantra. As a result of these spiritual exercises, the mystic "will gaze into the inner-most recesses of his heart and it will seem as if he saw the seven halls [of the divine Palace] with his own eyes, moving from hall to hall."[12] Like all true meditation, this was an "ascent inward."

Even though the visionary felt that he could bypass the earthly replica of God's palace, the Temple still dominated the way he approached his God, and this shows that its architecture had been experienced as a spir-itual reality by the people. It had embodied their inner world and would continue to do so long after the Jerusalem Temple had ceased to exist. Just as the worshipper could approach God by walking through the zones of holiness in Jerusalem, so Enoch must approach God in carefully graded stages in the heavenly world. First he had to leave the profane world and enter the divine sphere, just as the pilgrim to Jerusalem would enter the Temple courts. Most would have to stop there, but Enoch imagined himself as a spiritual high priest. First he was taken into a house which, like the Hekhal, was filled with cherubim. Finally he was ushered into a second, greater palace, the heavenly equivalent of the Devir, where he saw the Throne and the "Great Glory sitting on it," amid streams of living fire.[13] There Enoch was entrusted with a message for his people, and, like the high priest on Yom Kippur, he left the Throne Room and returned to bring its holiness to his fellow Jews. This type of mysticism would continue to inspire Jewish contemplatives until it was absorbed into the disciplines of Kabbalah during the Middle Ages.

Some Jews opposed the Greeks with visions, others resorted to arms. After the Seleucid troops had taken up residence in the Akra and desecrated the Temple Mount, many of the more devout Jews felt that they could no longer live in Jerusalem. Among these émigrés was the Hasmonean family, the aged priest Mattathias and his five sons. They took up residence in the village of Modein, but when the royal officials arrived to establish the new rationalized cult of the God of Heaven,

Mattathias and his sons fled to the hills. They were followed by other pious Jews, who left all their possessions behind and "lived like wild animals in the hills, eating nothing but wild plants to avoid contracting defilement."[14] They also conducted a campaign against those Jews who had submitted to Antiochus's edict, overturning the new Greek altars and forcibly circumcising the baby boys. When Mattathias died in 166, his son Judas, nicknamed Maccabeus ("Hammer-Headed"), took control of the movement and began to lead attacks against the Greek and Syrian troops. Since the Seleucids were busily occupied in Mesopotamia, where the Parthians were trying to drive them from their holding, Judas's campaign achieved an unexpected success.[15] By 164, Antiochus was forced to rescind his infamous edict and Judas gained control of Jerusalem, though he could not dislodge the Greeks and Antiochene Jews from the Akra.

When Judas and his companions saw the burned temple gates and the sacred grove on Mount Zion, they rent their garments and prostrated themselves in grief. They then set about purifying the site, refurbishing the Temple buildings and, finally, lighting the lamps on the seven-branched candlestick in the Hekhal. On 25 Kislev, the day on which the Seleucids had desecrated the sanctuary three years earlier, the Temple was rededicated.[16] The partisans processed through the Temple courts carrying palms and leafy branches as they did on Sukkoth. Finally they decreed that this festival of Chanukah ("Dedication") should be celebrated annually by the whole Jewish people.

The rebellion of the Maccabees was able to succeed because of the internal power struggles in the Seleucid camp. By playing one pretender to the throne off against another, Judas and his successors managed to consolidate their position. In 161, Judas made an alliance with Rome, which doubtless strengthened his hand.[17] Finally in about 152 BCE, the Hasmonean movement received official recognition when one of the Seleucid pretenders made Jonathan, Judas's brother and successor, governor of the *ethnos*. Not to be outdone, his rival appointed Jonathan high priest. On the festival of Sukkoth 152, Jonathan donned the sacred vestments for the first time, and the people were awestruck by this astonishing reversal.[18] Jonathan held his own until 143, when he was kidnapped and killed by yet another pretender to the Seleucid throne. His brother Simon was able to reassert Hasmonean ascendancy and got himself appointed ruler of the *ethnos* and high priest by the new Seleucid king, Demetrius II. Judah became independent of the Greek empire, and for the first time in centuries, Judaeans were free of pagan control. The following year, the Greeks and the Antiochene Jews who were still occupying the Akra surrendered to Simon and the citadel was razed to the ground—a task which, according to Josephus, took three years. The anniversary of its conquest was celebrated as a national festival.[19]

The Hasmonean revolution began as a popular rebellion, passionately opposed to the Greek culture of the imperial power. But the state that came into being under Simon and his successors soon had many of the features that had offended the rebels in the first place. When Menelaus had secured the high priesthood, devout Jews had been shocked because he was not a Zadokite. Now the Hasmonean rulers had become high priests, but though they were a priestly family, they were not descended from Zadok either. There also seemed little to choose between this Jewish regime and the pagan dynasties. The Hasmoneans were good soldiers and clever diplomats but no paragons. Simon was actually murdered by his own sons. Yet after centuries of obscurity and humiliation, most Judaeans felt extremely proud of the Hasmoneans' achievements. When Simon's son John Hyrcanus (134–104) began to conquer some of the neighboring territory, it must have seemed as though the glorious days of King David had returned. By about 125, the Seleucids had been so weakened by their internal power struggles and wars against the Parthians that it was not difficult for Hyrcanus to take control of Samaria. His first act was to destroy the temple which the Samaritans had built to YHWH on Mount Gerizim, near Shechem. John also extended his borders to the south into Idumea, forcing the inhabitants to convert to Judaism and accept circumcision. As in so many revolutions, the rebel regime had become almost indistinguishable from the power it had replaced. Like the Seleucids, the Hasmoneans had become imperialists who were insensitive to the religious traditions of their subjects.

Further, the *ethnos* was, ironically, becoming a thoroughly Hellenized state. Under John Hyrcanus, Jerusalem had once again expanded onto the Western Hill overlooking the Temple Mount. This became the home of the wealthier aristocratic and priestly families, who could enjoy cooler breezes and healthier air than the poorer inhabitants of the old 'Ir David below. This western district became more and more like a Greek city. Very few remains of the Hasmonean period have been found, but it almost certainly had a marketplace (*agora*) surrounded by colonnades on the highest point of the Western Hill. The Hasmoneans had closed Jason's *gymnasion,* of course, but there was a *xystos* in the western part of the city, a square which in a normal *polis* was used for athletic competitions but which in Jerusalem probably functioned simply as a public meeting place. One of the Hasmonean monuments that has survived is the tomb of the priestly family of Bene Hezir in the Kidron Valley, which shows an interesting fusion of Greek and Oriental style. Finally, on the eastern slope of the Western Hill, the Hasmoneans built a palace

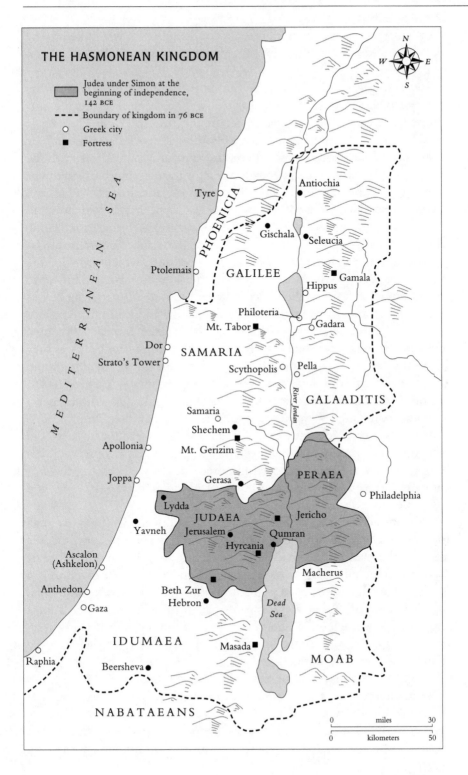

THE HASMONEAN KINGDOM

Judea under Simon at the beginning of independence, 142 BCE

Boundary of kingdom in 76 BCE

○ Greek city

■ Fortress

MEDITERRANEAN SEA

PHOENICIA

Tyre

Antiochia

Gischala

Seleucia

Ptolemais

GALILEE

Gamala

Hippus

Philoteria

Mt. Tabor

Gadara

Dor

SAMARIA

Strato's Tower

Scythopolis

Pella

River Jordan

GALAADITIS

Samaria

Shechem

Mt. Gerizim

Apollonia

Gerasa

PERAEA

Joppa

Philadelphia

Lydda

Jericho

JUDAEA

Yavneh

Jerusalem

Qumran

Hyrcania

Ascalon
(Ashkelon)

Macherus

Anthedon

Beth Zur

Hebron

*Dead
Sea*

Gaza

IDUMAEA

Masada

MOAB

Raphia

Beersheva

NABATAEANS

0   miles   30

0   kilometers   50

for themselves with a splendid view of the Temple;[20] it was linked to the old city and the Temple Mount by a bridge that spanned the Tyropoeon Valley.

Yet despite these Hellenistic features, the Temple still dominated the city, physically, politically, and spiritually. The Temple especially impressed the author of a romance set in the time of King Ptolemy II which was written during the early Hasmonean period. Aristeas, as he calls himself, described the shrine on the crest of Mount Zion, with the houses and streets huddled beneath like seats in an amphitheater. He was fascinated by the sight of the huge curtain at the entrance of the Hekhal, "which resembled a door in every respect" except that "it was always in motion and undulated from the bottom to the top as the air passed along the pavement beneath."[21] He also admired the elaborate system of cisterns under the pavement of the Temple enclosure, which provided the water to wash away the blood of the sacrificial victims. He laid his ear to the ground and claimed that he could hear the water murmuring below. Above all, Aristeas was struck by the demeanor and skill of the priests, who worked ceaselessly, sacrificing one beast after another with total concentration. They needed their "surpassing bodily strength"[22] as they lifted the carcasses and tossed the limbs high into the air, catching them in one hand. Most of their work was very unpleasant, but nobody had to be ordered back to work after the prescribed break. The whole operation was conducted without a sound. The stillness in the Temple courts was almost eerie. "So great is the silence everywhere that one would suppose that there was no one in the place," Aristeas observed, "although the priests number seven hundred and they who bring the victims to the Temple are many; but everything is done with awe and reverence for its great sanctity."[23]

But not all the Jews of Judaea shared this admiration. They were all passionately attached to the Temple, but a significant number of people felt that the Hasmoneans had damaged its integrity. These difficult years had led to the emergence of three sects in Judaea; they involved only a small percentage of the total population but were extremely influential. Their widely divergent views meant that in future it would be almost impossible for the Jews of Judaea to take a united stand against an external enemy, though, as we shall see in the following chapter, the one issue that could instantly bond them was any threat to the holiness of the Temple. The Saducees were the chief supporters of the Hasmoneans. The members of this sect came from the priestly and wealthier classes who lived in the Upper City on the Western Hill. They had become Hellenized and wanted good relations with their pagan neighbors, but were also committed to such ancient symbols of their nation as the king and the Temple and its liturgy. Like other nationalistic movements in the Near East at this time, their Judaism tended toward the archaic: fidelity to an idealized past was a way of rooting their new Greek enthusiasms with their own traditions. The Saducees would not accept any adaptation of the written Torah. They believed that the Hasmoneans were like King David, who had also combined priesthood with monarchy. But other Jews were so horrified by the Hasmoneans that they withdrew completely from Jewish society to make a new exodus into the wilderness. Their leader, known as the Teacher of Righteousness, may have been the High Priest who had been forcibly retired when Jonathan was appointed to the post. Only a Zadokite could hold this high office, and Jonathan had therefore polluted the sanctity of the Temple. Some of his followers, who are known as the Essenes, lived in a monastic-style community at Qumran by the Dead Sea. Others were less extreme: they lived in the towns and cities of Judah and continued to worship in the Temple, even though they were convinced that it had been hopelessly contaminated. The Essenes nurtured fierce apocalyptic dreams of a final reckoning when God would redeem the Holy City and rebuild their Temple. During the reign of John Hyrcanus, their numbers swelled to about four thousand and an Essene community was founded in Jerusalem.

The most popular and influential of these three parties, however, was that of the Pharisees, who were committed to an exact and punctilious observance of the Torah. They were also convinced that the Hasmonean rulers should not hold the High Priesthood and came to believe that the people would be better off under foreign rule than under these bad Jews. The Pharisees may have been behind the revolt that broke out in Jerusalem at the beginning of John Hyrcanus's reign, which the king put down mercilessly.[24] They also opposed the rule of his son Alexander Jannaeus (105–76) and could have been among the rebels who attacked the king in the Temple as he officiated at the ceremonies of Sukkoth, pelting him with the citrus fruits they were carrying in procession. Immediately afterward, Alexander executed six thousand people.[25] On another occasion, after another revolt, Alexander had eight hundred rebels crucified in Jerusalem and butchered their wives and children before their eyes as they hung upon their crosses, while he himself looked on, feasting and carousing with his concubines.[26] This horrific occasion seemed proof to many of the people that the monarchy, which had inspired such high hopes, had become just one more Hellenistic despotism.

Alexander had continued the conquest of new territory and ruled over a much-extended kingdom on both sides of the Jordan. When he seized new territory, the non-Jewish inhabitants were given the option

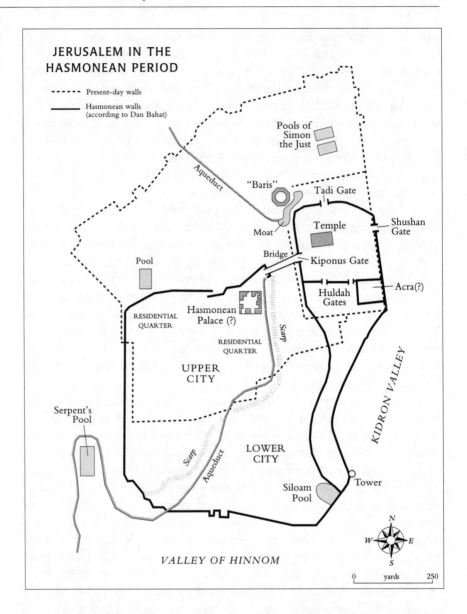

of conversion to Judaism; those who refused were expelled from the country. He was aware that his rule was not universally popular, and on his deathbed he advised his wife, Salome, who was to succeed him, to give power to the Pharisees. He knew the extent of their influence and hoped that "they could dispose the nation favorably toward her."[27] This she did, but it did not save the dynasty. After her death in 67 BCE, her two sons—Hyrcanus II and Aristobulus II—became involved in a murderous struggle for the kingship and high priesthood, with the help of various outside powers. The most important of these allies was Antipater, the Idumean who had served as governor of the region under Alexander and who now supported Hyrcanus. Both Hyrcanus and Aristobulus appealed to Pompey, the Roman general who arrived in Antioch in 64 BCE and deposed the last of the Seleucid kings. The Pharisees also sent a delegation to Pompey, asking him to abolish the monarchy in their country too, since it was alien to their religious traditions.

Jerusalem became the battleground of these warring factions. Aristobulus II and his supporters barricaded themselves in the Temple and burned the bridge over the Tyropoen Valley. Hyrcanus II and Antipater had possession of the Upper City, and they invited the Roman army in as their allies: a Roman garrison was installed in the Hasmonean palace, and Pompey pitched his camp north of the Temple Mount at the city's most vulnerable spot. Aristobulus held out for three months. Josephus tells us that the Roman general was astonished by the devotion of the Temple priests, who carried on with their sacrifices without appearing to notice the missiles raining down upon the Temple courts. The priests did not even stop their work when the Roman troops finally breached the defenses and swarmed into the Temple courts in

The blowing of the shofar, or ram's horn, which this rabbi is performing at the Western Wall to usher in the Jewish New Year, is intended to instill feelings of awe. A call to repentance and a reminder of the Last Days, this ancient practice expresses the sobriety and solemnity of Second Temple ritual.

September 63 BCE, followed by Hyrcanus's troops.[28] Twelve thousand Jews were killed in the ensuing slaughter, and to the horror of the entire Jewish nation, Pompey entered the Temple buildings, walked through the Hekhal, and looked into the dark holiness of the Devir. Anxious to appease the people, he instantly withdrew and gave orders that the sanctuary be purified. But the Roman occupation of the country that they called Palestina[29] had begun with a violation of the Temple, and the Jews watched their new masters warily lest this sacrilege be repeated.

DESTRUCTION

AFTER HIS VICTORY, Pompey imposed harsh terms upon the defeated Hasmonean kingdom. The Jews would be allowed to rule Judaea, Idumea, Peraea, and Galilee, but in future the Yahwists of Samaria and the gentile inhabitants of the coastal plain, the Greek cities, the Phoenician coast, and the Decapolis would manage their own affairs. The people who had refused to convert to Judaism and been expelled from the country were now permitted to return. Aristobulus II was taken to Rome in chains, but Pompey rewarded his allies. Antipater had control of the army and was in charge of Judaea but had to report to the Roman legate in Damascus. Hyrcanus II was made high priest, which pleased those who still felt sympathy for the Hasmoneans. But Jerusalem had lost much of its political status: Pompey had razed its walls to the ground, and it was now merely the capital of a landlocked subprovince which was divided from Galilee by territory controlled by Samaritans and gentiles who had no reason to feel friendly toward their Jewish neighbors.

The Hasmoneans attempted to reassert their power. At one point Aristobulus actually escaped from his captors and managed to reestablish himself in Jerusalem, where he began to rebuild the walls. In 57 BCE, Gabinus, the Syrian legate, put down this insurrection and Aristobulus and his son Alexander were sent back to Rome. But Palestine was of strategic importance to the Romans, and they did not wish to antagonize their Jewish subjects unduly. Aristobulus's other children were permitted to stay in Palestine, Hyrcanus remained high priest, and the Hasmoneans remained a potent presence in the country. Yet Antipater still held more power than anybody else. He was a shrewd ruler and respected by the Jews, even though his family were only recent converts to Judaism and, as Idumeans, were regarded as ethnically distinct. Antipater and his sons never forgot that they owed their position to Rome, however, and kept a careful eye on the turbulent politics of the empire, adroitly switching sides when a patron fell from power. Thus in 49 BCE, when Pompey was defeated by Julius Caesar, Antipater had been prescient enough to back the winning side. Caesar rewarded him for his support by making him the full prefect of Judaea and allowing him to rebuild the walls of Jerusalem. The port of Joppa and the Jezreel Valley were returned to the Jews and Antipater's two sons were appointed *tetrarchs* (district commissioners) under him: Herod was made tetrarch of Galilee and Phasael tetrarch of Judaea. They had inherited their father's political astuteness, which they sorely needed during these troubled years. On 15 March 44 BCE, Julius Caesar was assassinated in Rome by a conspiracy of senators headed by Marcus Brutus and Gaius Cassius. In the same year, Antipater was murdered by an old family foe. Herod and Phasael became clients of Cassius but continued to watch the developments in Rome very carefully. When Octavian, Julius Caesar's grandnephew and adopted son, and Mark Antony declared war on Brutus and Cassius, Herod and Phasael were ready to change sides again, if necessary. After the battle of Philippi, in 42 BCE, when Brutus and Cassius were defeated, Phasael and Herod were befriended by Mark Antony, who now controlled the eastern provinces of the Roman empire. Rome was about to embark on a new era of peace and prosperity and Herod and Phasael enjoyed its patronage.

Yet in 40 BCE the Romans temporarily lost control of Palestine, when the Parthians of Mesopotamia broke through their lines of defense, invaded the country, and installed the Hasmonean prince Antigonus in Jerusalem as their client. Phasael was taken prisoner and forced to commit suicide in captivity, but Herod was able to escape to Rome, where he impressed the Senate as a Jew who was capable of holding the country on Rome's behalf. The senators named Herod King of the Jews, and in 39 BCE he returned to Palestine. He conquered Galilee with the help of Mark Antony, and laid siege to Jerusalem in 37, taking the city four months later after a horrible massacre. Thousands of Jews were killed in the narrow streets and the Temple courts where they had sought sanctuary, and Antigonus the Hasmonean was executed by Mark Antony at Herod's request, even though this was the first time that the Romans had inflicted capital punishment on a subjugated king.

Once installed in Jerusalem as King of the Jews in Palestine, Herod was left in total control. The Romans withdrew, rightly judging that the province would be secure under his leadership. Despite his brutal conquest of Jerusalem, Herod had supporters among the Jews. The Pharisees were still opposed to the Hasmoneans and backed his claim. Herod also took the precaution of marrying Mariamne, a Hasmonean princess, which gave him a legitimacy of sorts in the eyes of Hasmonean supporters. In 36 BCE he appointed Mariamne's younger brother Jonathan to the high priesthood, but this proved to be a mistake. The people burst into tears of emotion when the young Hasmonean donned the sacred vestments at Sukkoth and called out rapturously to him in the streets. Herod immediately had Jonathan murdered and replaced by a safe candidate of his own. Throughout his life, Herod was ruthless about eliminating any challenge to his rule. Nonetheless, he was a gifted king and was able to impose peace on his potentially unstable kingdom. There were no uprisings in Judaea until the very end of his reign.

It is a mark of his power that Herod was able to appoint and depose high priests at will without inspiring a revolution. We have seen that the office aroused strong passions, and hitherto high priests had held the post for life; under Herod, the high priest became a political appointee. Even so, the priesthood lost none of its luster. High priests were never regarded as mere political pawns. Herod found it necessary to keep the ceremonial robes of the high priest locked up in the citadel, releasing them only for the major festivals. As soon as the priest put on these sacred garments, he was enveloped in a celestial aura and was empowered to approach YHWH on the people's behalf. The control of these vestments continued to be a matter of priority in Jerusalem, and only the emperor could authorize their permanent release to the priestly caste. The man who wore them assumed the mantle of divine power and could be a threat to the throne.

While Herod was a devout enough Jew after his own fashion, he was also happy to accommodate other religions in and around Palestine. Unlike the Hasmoneans, he did not interfere with the religious lives of his subjects, and he regarded the Hasmonean policy of forcing people to convert to Judaism as politically inept. Herod built temples to the Greek and Roman gods in gentile cities within and without his own kingdom, and when Emperor Octavian declared himself to be divine, Herod was one of the first people to build a temple in his honor in Samaria, which he renamed Sebaste, the Greek equivalent of the emperor's new title, Augustus. By this time, Herod had switched allegiance yet again, after his patron Mark Antony had been defeated by Octavian at the battle of Actium. In 22 BCE, Herod began to build the city of Caesarea in honor of Augustus on the site of the old port of Strato's Tower. The city contained temples in honor of Roman deities, an amphitheater, and a harbor that rivaled Piraeus. It was a gift to his pagan subjects. As a result,

Herod, the Jewish king, was a respected figure in the pagan world: one of the last Greco-Roman honors to be accorded him was the presidency of the Olympic Games.

Yet Herod was equally careful to avoid offending the Jews, and he would not have dreamed of building a pagan temple in Jerusalem. As part of his ambitious building program—the largest ever accomplished by a minor ruler—he transformed the Holy City and made it one of the most important *metropoleis* of the east. Ever mindful of security, Herod's first act was to build a massive fortress, begun in 35 BCE on the site of the citadel built by Nehemiah at the city's most vulnerable point, north of the Temple Mount. Since he was still friends with Mark Antony, he called the new fortress Antonia after his patron. It was built on a precipitous rock, seventy-five feet high, whose steep slope was faced with polished slabs of stone to make it almost impossible to climb. The rectangular citadel rose sixty feet above this, with four towers rising from each corner, and was capable of housing a large garrison. But despite its formidable military appearance, the Antonia was as luxurious as a palace. It was surrounded by a deep moat called the Struthion, which separated the fortress from the new suburb of Bezetha that was developing in the north. Here he probably built the double reservoir that can still be seen today, near the Pool of Beth-Hesda excavated by Simon the Just.

Herod did not begin the real transformation of Jerusalem until about 23 BCE, when he had just won a good deal of respect in Palestine by his efficiency in providing food and grain for the people during the famine of 25–24. Many Jerusalemites had been ruined and were able to find employment as builders once work had begun in the city. Herod began by building a palace for himself in the Upper City on the Western Hill; it was fortified by three towers, which he named after his brother Phasael, his beloved wife Mariamne the Hasmonean, and his friend Hippicus. They all had solid bases, some fifteen meters high; the base of what is probably Hippicus can still be seen in the Jerusalem Citadel and is known as the Tower of David. The palace itself consisted of two large buildings, one of which was called Caesareum in honor of Octavian, which were joined by enchanting water gardens, where the deep canals and cisterns were lined with bronze statues and fountains. Herod seems to have also redesigned the streets of the Upper City into a gridded system, which made traffic and town planning easier. In addition, the Upper City had a theater and a hippodrome, though we do not know the exact location of these buildings. Every five years, games were held in honor of Augustus, which drew crowds of distinguished athletes to Jerusalem.

Under Herod, Jerusalem became an imposing and distinguished city, the home of about 120,000 permanent inhabitants. He rebuilt the city

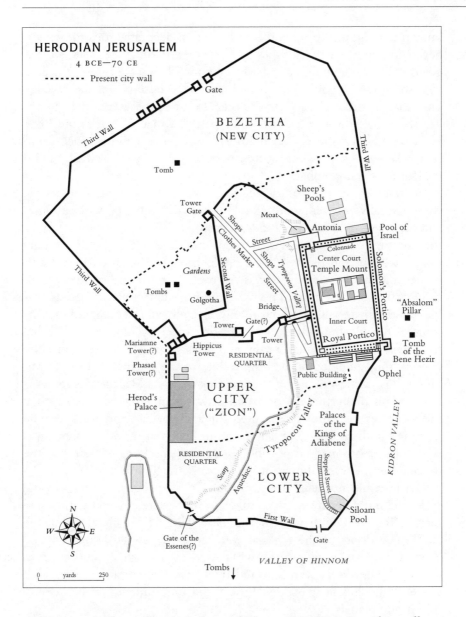

HERODIAN JERUSALEM
4 BCE—70 CE
- - - - - - Present city wall

Gate

BEZETHA
(NEW CITY)

Third Wall

Third Wall

Tomb

Third Wall

Sheep's
Pools

Tower
Gate

Moat

Antonia

Pool of
Israel

Shops

Clothes Market

Street

Colonnade

Second Wall

Shops

Tyropoeon Valley

Center Court

Temple Mount

Solomon's Portico

Gardens

Tombs

Street

Golgotha

Bridge

Inner Court

"Absalom"
Pillar

Tower

Gate(?)

Tower

Royal Portico

Tomb
of the
Bene Hezir

Mariamne
Tower(?)

Hippicus
Tower

RESIDENTIAL
QUARTER

Phasael
Tower(?)

Public Building

Ophel

Herod's
Palace

UPPER
CITY
("ZION")

Palaces
of the
Kings of
Adiabene

KIDRON VALLEY

RESIDENTIAL
QUARTER

Tyropoeon Valley

Stepped Street

N

W E

S

Scarp

Aqueduct

LOWER
CITY

Siloam
Pool

First Wall

Gate of the
Essenes(?)

Gate

VALLEY OF HINNOM

Tombs

0   yards   250

walls, but scholars still argue about their exact course. Josephus tells us
that the First Wall surrounded the Upper City and the Lower City on
the site of the ancient 'Ir David. The Second Wall provided an added
line of defense and encircled the new commercial quarter extending
from the Antonia to the old north wall built by the Hasmoneans.[1] There
were other, humbler palaces in the Lower City, notably that of the royal
family of Adiabene of Mesopotamia, who had converted to Judaism.
They also built the large mausoleum outside the city walls which is

known today as the Tomb of the Kings. Other decorated rock tombs also began to appear in the hills and valleys surrounding the walls, so that corpses did not contaminate the Holy City. They were often protected by a stone which could be rolled to cover the entrance of the cavelike sepulcher in the rock face. The most famous of these Herodian tombs can still be seen in the Kidron Valley, near the mausoleum of the Bene Hezir family. It consists of a memorial pillar and a nearby rock tomb which later pilgrims would call respectively the Pillar of Absalom and the Tomb of Jehoshaphat.

In about 19 BCE, Herod decided to rebuild the Temple. The people were naturally worried: would the king tear down the present buildings and find that he lacked the funds to continue? Would he be faithful to the prescriptions in the Torah? Herod's buildings were often startlingly innovative, but the plan of the Temple had been revealed by God to Moses and David, and there was no room for originality. Herod was careful to allay these fears. The work did not begin until he had assembled all the materials, and he carefully reproduced the plan and dimensions of the old buildings. To ensure that the laity did not violate the forbidden areas, Herod had a thousand priests trained as masons and carpenters; they alone could be responsible for the Hekhal and the Devir. Herod himself never entered the building that would always be remembered as his masterpiece. Construction was planned in such a way that the sacrifices were not interrupted for a single day, and work on the Temple buildings was completed within eighteen months. This continuity of worship made it possible for Herod's building to be called the Second Temple even though it was actually the Third.

Herod could not alter the size or shape of the shrine, but he could make the buildings more beautiful. The walls were covered with white marble, threaded with reddish and blue veins "like the waves of the sea."[2] The doors of the Hekhal were covered in gold and decorated above with "golden vines from which depended grape clusters as tall as a man."[3] The doors were covered by a priceless curtain, woven with scarlet, blue, and purple linen thread and embroidered with the sun, moon, and planets.

Even though the Temple buildings had to remain quite small, Herod could satisfy his love of immensity by extending the Temple platform. This was a huge project that took some eighty years—Herod did not live to see the task finished—and employed eighteen thousand workmen. When completed, the platform covered an area of about thirty-five acres, many times its original size. Since the plaza now extended far beyond the crest of Mount Zion, it had to be supported by a massive substructure of vaults and piers. The new supporting walls, Josephus tells

The Western Wall—the western supporting wall of the Temple platform built by King Herod. When the Muslims restored the wall in the eighth century CE, their smaller stones at the top could not match the massive slabs used by Herod.

us, were "the greatest ever heard of":[4] some of the stones weighed between two and five tons. Since Herod did not want to extend the Temple platform to the east, the old eastern wall, which coincided with the city wall, remained in place. Henceforth that side of the Temple Mount was associated with Solomon, the first builder on Zion. The western supporting wall was the longest of these new constructions, measuring some 530 yards from the Antonia to its southern extremity. At the foot of this western wall was the Lower Market, which belonged to the priests and was very popular with tourists and pilgrims. Shops were built right against the wall, covering the first three courses of stones. The city council buildings and the national archive were also located at the foot of the western wall. On the Temple platform itself, the supporting walls were surmounted on three sides by colonnaded porches in the Greek fashion, rather like the porticos on the Ḥaram al-Sharif today. The whole southern end of the platform consisted of a large pillared covered area, similar to the basilica in a Roman forum, which gave people shelter from the rain and shade in the summer. This Royal Portico was about the size of Salisbury Cathedral, six hundred feet long and soaring to one hundred feet at its highest point. Towering above the southern supporting wall, covered in gleaming white marble, it was an awe-inspiring sight. From a distance, the Temple Mount was a brilliant spectacle. The gold on the sanctuary "reflected so fierce a blaze of fire that those who tried to look at it were forced to turn away," recalled Josephus. "It seemed in the distance like a mountain covered in snow, for any part not covered in gold was dazzling white."[5] It is not surprising that long after it had been destroyed, the rabbis would claim: "Whoever has not seen the Temple of Herod has never seen a beautiful building in his life."[6]

Pilgrims could enter the Temple courts in one of two ways. They could either climb the imposing staircase leading up to the Royal Portico, or cross two bridges which spanned the street at the foot of the western supporting wall. Once on the platform, visitors found that an intricate arrangement of courts, each one more holy than the last, led to the central sanctity of the Devir. (See diagram.) First pilgrims entered the Court of the Gentiles, which was open to everybody. It was separated from the Court of the Israelites (for male Jews in a state of ritual purity) by an elegant balustrade. Notices warned foreigners not to proceed further, on pain of death. Beyond the barrier was the Court of the Women, a screened-off area with a raised gallery which enabled the women to watch the sacrifices in the altar court. Next came the Court of the Levites and finally the Court of the Priests, which contained the great altar of sacrifice.

This gradual approach to the inner sanctum reminded pilgrims and worshippers that they were making an *aliyah* (ascent) to a wholly different order of being. They had to prepare themselves by undergoing various rites of purification which heightened this sense by putting them at some distance from their normal lives. They were about to enter the separate sphere of their holy God, and for the duration of their visit they had to be in the same state of ritual purity as the priests. In particular, they had to be cleansed of any contact with death, the greatest impurity of all, which it was impossible to avoid in daily life: one could inadvertently step on the site of an ancient grave without realizing it. But any of the great changes of life, such as childbirth, were also impure, not because they were considered dirty or sinful but because the God they were about to approach was beyond such alteration and pilgrims had symbolically to share this immutability if they were to be in the place where he was. If pilgrims could not be purified by the local priest before leaving home, they would have to wait in Jerusalem for seven days before going up to the Temple Mount. They had to refrain from sex during this period, and on the third and seventh day, they would be ritually sprinkled with water and ashes and take a ritual bath. This enforced wait was a time of spiritual preparation and self-scrutiny. It reminded pilgrims of the interior journey they must make as they "ascended" to the ultimate reality and entered a wholly different dimension.

When they finally climbed up to the Temple platform with the animal that they were taking for sacrifice in the Altar Court, pilgrims felt that they had stepped into a more intense mode of existence. The whole of reality was somehow condensed into this segregated space. By this time, the symbolism of the Temple appears to have changed: it was now experienced as a microcosm of the entire universe. Josephus, who once served in the Temple as a priest, explained its cosmic imagery. The Court of the Gentiles was still associated with Yam, the primal sea, which stood over and against the ordered world of the sacred, a perpetual challenge to be borne in mind and overcome. The Hekhal, on the contrary, represented the whole of the created world; its curtain symbolized the four elements and the "whole vista of the heavens"; the lamps on the great candlestick stood for the seven planets, and the twelve loaves of shewbread recalled the signs of the Zodiac and the twelve months of the year. The incense altar with its thirteen spices "from sea and land (inhabited and uninhabited) signified that all things came from God and for God."[7] Philo of Alexandria (c. 30 BCE to c. 41 CE), who came once to Jerusalem as a pilgrim, was also familiar with this symbolism.[8] A Platonist, he also pointed out that the furniture of the Hekhal represented the heavenly archetypes and made those Ideals, which lay beyond our experience, intelligible and visible.[9] The layout and design of the Temple Mount thus traced the path to God. You passed from the ordinary mundane world into the marginal realm of chaos, the primal sea, and the Goyim to the ordered world that God had created, but you saw it in a different way. The world was now revealed as leading inexorably to God; one journeyed through life on earth to the divine, just as the high priest walked through the Hekhal to the ultimate reality, which lay beyond and gave meaning to the whole. This, of course, was symbolized by the Devir, separated from the Hekhal and the visible world by yet another veil. The Devir was empty because it stood for something that transcended our senses and concepts: "Nothing at all was kept in it," Josephus tells us; "it was unapproachable, inviolable, and invisible to all."[10]

The utter separateness of the holy God was emphasized by the fact that only the priests could draw near to the heart of the Temple's sanc-

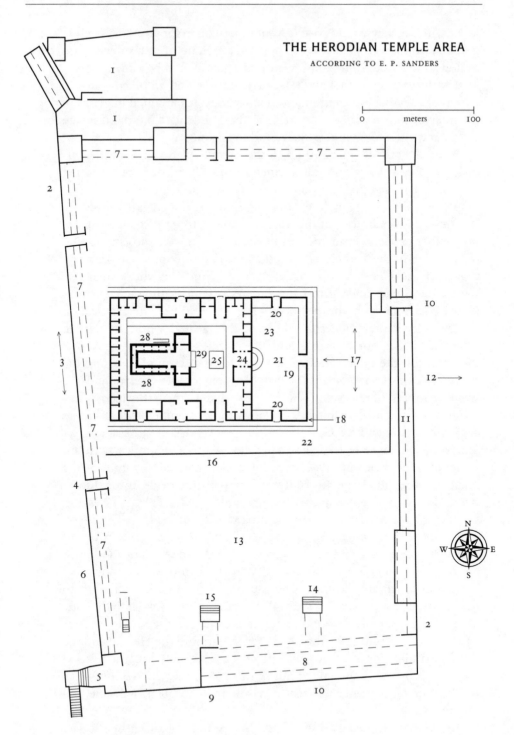

THE HERODIAN TEMPLE AREA
ACCORDING TO E. P. SANDERS

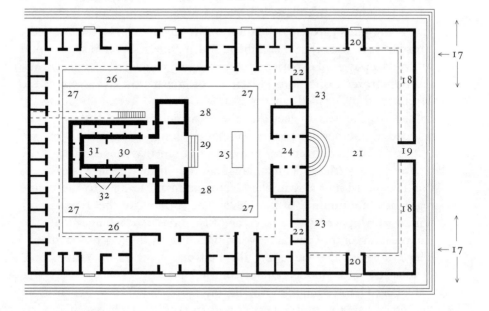

THE INNER COURTS AND THE SANCTUARY

ACCORDING TO E. P. SANDERS

0   meters   50

1. The Antonia Fortress
2. Supporting wall
3. Street beside the western supporting wall
4. "Wilson's Arch" spanning the Tyropoeon Valley
5. "Robinson's Arch" leading to the street below
6. Shops
7. Porticoes
8. Royal Portico
9. Exit gate
10. Entrance gate
11. "Solomon's Portico"
12. Mount of Olives

13. Court of the Gentiles
14. Entrance to the Plaza, connected by a tunnel to (10)
15. Exit to the Plaza, connected by a tunnel to (9)
16. Balustrade and steps prohibited to gentiles
17. Inner platform and steps
18. Inner wall
19. Eastern gate for male Israelites
20. Southern and northern gates for women Israelites

21. Court of the Women
22. Inner porticoes
23. Wall separating men from women
24. Second eastern gate for male Israelites
25. The altar for burnt sacrifices
26. Court of the Israelites
27. Parapet separating priests from laymen
28. Court of the Priests
29. Entrance to sanctuary
30. Hekhal
31. Devir
32. Upper floors

tity. Josephus explains that the vestments of the high priest also had cosmic significance: his tunic symbolized heaven and earth and the upper garments the four elements. This was fitting, since the high priest officiated in the Hekhal as the representative not only of the "whole human race but also for the parts of nature, earth, water, air, and fire."[11] But when he entered the Devir on Yom Kippur, the high priest changed into white linen garments, the dress of the angels, who were also mediators between the celestial and the mundane spheres. Sacred space could still yield a powerful experience of a presence which transcended all anthropomorphic expression. The rituals of preparation, the ascent of the Mount, and the graded sanctity of the courts and Temple buildings all helped worshippers to feel that they had entered into and been enveloped by another dimension that existed alongside normal life and yet was utterly distinct from it. The degrees of sanctity were similar to the platforms on a Mesopotamian ziggurat; they made the level surface of the Temple Mount a symbolic sacred mountain leading to the divine realm at the "summit" of the Devir. The imagery of the Temple presented worshippers with a landscape that threw into stronger relief the real meaning of the mundane world which lay at the heart of existence. The whole of life—including the destructive forces of Yam—could yield access to the hidden sanctity of the Devir.

During Herod's reign, more pilgrims were drawn to Jerusalem from the rest of Palestine and the diaspora than ever before: between 300,000 and 500,000 would be likely to assemble for the great feasts of Passover, the harvest festival of Weeks or Pentecost, and Sukkoth.[12] Despite the emphasis on purification, these festivals were not gloomy, somber affairs. Pilgrimages gave families the chance to take a vacation together. During the long journey to Jerusalem, pilgrims would eat and drink wine together at night, joke, laugh, and sing popular songs. When they arrived in Jerusalem, festivities really got under way. Pilgrims would put up in private homes or in the synagogues of the city. Some preferred to camp in the hills and valleys outside. They had to bring a special pilgrimage tithe to spend in Jerusalem, which did not have to be put to pious use. You could buy red meat, wine, or some other treat. In this relaxed atmosphere, new friendships were formed and pilgrims came away with an enhanced sense of Jewish solidarity: the bonds of charity were thus strengthened alongside the cultic bond to God.[13]

The festivals themselves were also a time of rejoicing. There was still a holiday atmosphere during the eight days of Sukkoth, as the people camped in their leafy booths all over the city. Passover was an especially popular festival. Each family group would sacrifice a paschal lamb in the Temple and eat it together that evening in a festive supper that recalled the liberation of their people from Egypt. A particularly vibrant festival was the Feast of the Water Drawing, which symbolically united the upper and lower worlds. Israelite cosmology now conceived of the earth as a capsule surrounded by water: the upper waters were male, while the dangerous, subterranean waters were female, like Tiamat: they cried out to be united. As Jerusalem was at the "center" of the world, it was a place where all the levels of existence could meet. Once a year, the "stoppers" to the underworld were symbolically opened and the upper and lower waters mingled, while the people rejoiced. Later the rabbis would say that whoever had not experienced this festival had never known joy in his life.[14] It recognized the power of primal chaos, which needed to invade the world to ensure the vitality, creativity, and fruitfulness of the coming year.

The Temple remained the pivot of Jewish spirituality during Herod's reign, but some of the Jews were beginning to explore other paths to God. We have seen that some had started to bypass the Temple in mystical flight to the Reality it symbolized, especially in the diaspora. Jews also congregated in synagogues and meeting places, where they could study the Torah and enter the spiritual realm without traveling to Jerusalem.[15] Even in Palestine, some Jews had begun to experience God in the community of the faithful. Thus the Pharisees were still devoted to the Temple. In Herod's day, the school of Shammai urged Pharisees to segregate themselves more strictly than ever from the pagan world: they should not eat with gentiles, speak Greek, or accept gifts from gentiles. This was partly designed to enhance the purity of the Temple, which had long depended on the support of pagan rulers. But the exclusive community envisaged by Shammai also mirrored the ancient sacred geography, which had placed the gentiles beyond the reach of holiness.

Shammai's rival Hillel was also concerned with purity and segregation, but he also stressed the importance of charity. During the Hasmonean period, the ideal of compassion seems to have got lost. After the trauma of Antiochus Epiphanes, the emphasis had been on the purity of Jerusalem and its Temple and not on the social concern which had always been regarded as an essential concomitant of the Zion cult. Now Hillel's Pharisees saw deeds of charity and loving-kindness as the most important *mitzvoth* of the Torah: they could be as effective an atonement as sacrifice in the Temple.[16] Some of the Pharisees would form special fraternities, whose associates (*chaverim*) pledged themselves to live perpetually in the state of ritual purity that was necessary for Temple worship. It was a symbolic way, perhaps, of living continually in God's presence in their own homes and making their tables as sacred as the great altar in the Court of the Priests. When the *chaverim* ate together, their meals of fellowship became sacred occasions, like the meals of the priests who ate the sacrificial victims.[17] This type of piety made each home a temple and brought the sacred reality of Jerusalem into the humblest house.

Similarly, by the end of Herod's reign the Qumran sect also regarded their community of true Israelites as a new, spiritual temple. They would have no truck with the contaminated Temple in Jerusalem, but in their self-imposed exile, the sectarians would go into the dining room as into a sacred shrine. They also lived like the priests who were the constant denizens of the Temple: before eating, they would bathe in cold water and dress in linen loincloths just as the priests did when they ate the sacrificial meat. The prayers of the group were regarded as a substitute for sacrifice. But this was only a provisional arrangement. The sectarians looked forward to the day when, led by two messiahs—one priest and one layman—they would fight the forces of darkness in a final war to liberate Jerusalem. Then the Holy City would be reclaimed and God would rebuild the Temple. The Qumran sectarians called themselves the Evionim: the Poor. They alone were the true inhabitants of Zion, which had always been seen as a haven for the poor and humble. When they looked forward to this New Jerusalem, they used terms and phrases that were customarily applied to God:

> I will remember you, O Zion, for a blessing;
> with all my might, I love you;
> your memory is blessed forever.[18]

In the Torah, Jews had been commanded to love YHWH alone with all their might; he was the only source of blessing, and his memory alone was blessed forever. The use of these phrases in the Qumran hymn was not accidental: the sectarians were precise and jealous monotheists. But the divine never revealed itself to humanity directly, and for centuries Jerusalem had been one of the primary symbols that had enabled Jews to experience the inaccessible God. For the Qumran sectarians, Zion was inseparable from the peace, blessing, and salvation that were integral to an experience of God, and despite the sad state of the earthly city under Herod, it was still a most sacred and religious value.

But Qumran was an expression of the more militant forms of Judaism that were beginning to surface in Palestine. Throughout the Greco-Roman world, people were beginning to nurture dreams of nationalistic nostalgia. Temples were restored and old myths revived, especially those with a "resistance" motif. Hence the apocalyptic visions of Qumran revived the ancient myths of combat which had led to the foundation of a Temple, the building of a city, and the creation of right order.

Similarly, the ordinary Jewish worshipper saw the great festivals as celebrating the sacredness of the nation and the homeland. Passover was a festival of national liberation; the harvest festival of Weeks (Shavuoth) reminded Jews that the land belonged to YHWH alone—not to Rome. Sukkoth, which recalled the nation's years in the desert, was also the anniversary of the dedication of the Temple. When they congregated in such vast numbers before their God in the national shrine, feelings ran high, though Herod was such a powerful ruler that they did not dare to express them until 4 BCE, when they heard he was on his deathbed.

The occasion was significant. Herod had recently erected a golden eagle, the symbol of Jupiter and imperial Rome, over the Temple Gate. He had gone too far. When the news came that Herod was actually dying, Judas and Matthias, two respected teachers, hinted to their disciples that this was a splendid opportunity to bring the eagle down. Any such action was very dangerous, but what a glorious thing it would be to die for the Torah of their fathers! Accordingly, the young men climbed up onto the roof of the Royal Portico, lowered themselves down on stout ropes, and hacked the eagle down with axes. But they had been premature. Galvanized into action by sheer rage, Herod rose from his bed, postponed his death, and sentenced the young men and their teachers to death. When he died a few days later, his mortal agony was said to have been a punishment for the execution of these holy "martyrs."[19] It should be noted that this was a limited protest. There was as yet no attempt—nor even, possibly, the will—to assassinate Herod or dispense with Roman hegemony. The cause of this demonstration was the pollution of the Temple, and its sole objective was to get rid of this defilement. This would continue to be the case. As long as a ruler left the Temple alone, the Jews were prepared to tolerate him, but any threat to the Temple from any source could lead to violence, bloodshed, and fearful reprisals.

Herod had killed his beloved wife Mariamne in 29 BCE, and three of his sons shortly before his death, because he believed—in both cases, with reason—that they were plotting against him. Herod had kept his three surviving sons, Archelaus, Philip, and Antipas, on such a tight rein, delegating no power, that he had no idea which of them was capable of taking his place. When he died, he left two wills, so the fate of his kingdom was left to Augustus, who summoned the three sons to Rome. But on the eve of their departure, as the pilgrims poured into Jerusalem to celebrate Passover, passions were still running high about the recent deaths of the holy martyrs. Local Jews staged a demonstration of mourning, which filled the city with the sound of weeping and lamentation. The pilgrims quickly caught the mood of rage, fear, and grief. Finally, finding he could not control the mob, Archelaus sent his troops into the Temple courts just after the first paschal lambs had been sacrificed. Three thousand people were killed. Yet again the shrine had been desecrated, but this time not by a pagan symbol but by Jewish troops shedding Jewish blood. Five weeks later, while Archelaus was in Rome, there was another riot in Jerusalem during the pilgrim festival of Pentecost, and Sabinus, prefect of Syria, had to send a legion into Judaea. When it arrived in Jerusalem, tens of thousands of local Jews and pilgrims barricaded the streets and attacked the Roman soldiers. Sabinus could contain the mob violence only by setting fire to the porticoes on the Temple Mount. Afterward the Romans crucified two thousand of the rebels around the city walls.[20]

There were also other disturbances in other parts of Palestine, and this must have convinced the Senate that Herod was irreplaceable as King of the Jews. Archelaus returned to Judaea as the mere ethnarch of Judaea; Antipas and Philip were made tetrarchs of Galilee, Peraea, and the other northern regions. They were successful district commissioners and managed to hold on to their positions for many years. But Archelaus pursued such ruthless policies toward both Jews and Samaritans that he was deposed and banished in 6 CE. Henceforth Judaea was ruled by Roman prefects, who made the new city of Caesarea their capital—a safe and respectful distance from the turbulent sanctity of Jerusalem. There was unrest in Galilee during the first days of this Roman occupation, but it would be a mistake to imagine that the whole of Jewish Palestine was passionately opposed to Rome. This would never be the case. Some Jews had sent a deputation to Augustus after Herod's death specifically asking him to send a Roman governor to Palestine: the Pharisees in particular were still opposed to any form of Jewish monarchy. The Roman occupation of Palestine was not ideal, but Rome was no worse and a good deal better than some of the other empires which had ruled the Jews in the past. With a few sad exceptions, most of the Roman officials did their best to avoid offending the Jews' religious sensibilities and tried to cooperate with the high priest. For their part, the high priests were also anxious to keep the peace. They kept a careful lookout for troublemakers, not because they were sycophantic quislings but because they did not want Jews to die as pointlessly as they had in the riots that followed Herod's death. It was now essential that the high priests be men of caliber; in 18 CE, Caiaphas took office and became the ablest high priest of the Roman period.

But not even Caiaphas could control the angry mob when the Temple was violated again in 26 CE by the new prefect, Pontius Pilate, who had provocatively sent his troops into Jerusalem under cover of darkness

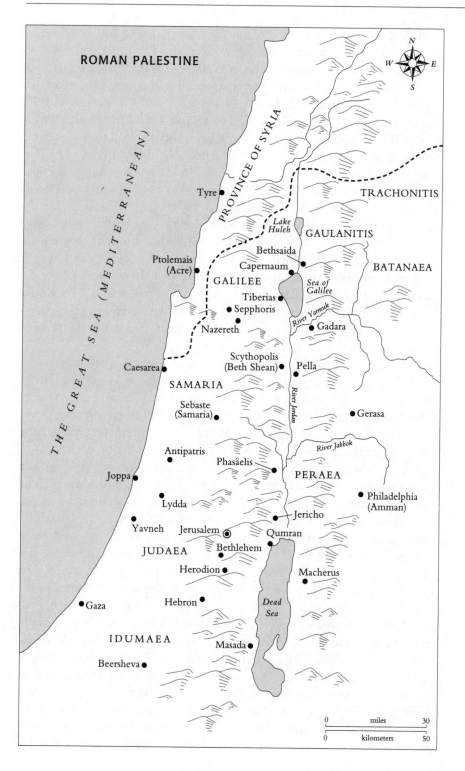

with standards sporting the portrait of Caesar. These had been raised aloft in the Antonia, a stone's throw from the Devir. When the Jews woke up to this abomination the next day, old fears that dated back to Antiochus Epiphanes surfaced once again, and an angry mob marched all the way to Caesarea and camped around Pilate's residence. Usually the Jews of Judaea were too divided to mount a solid front, but a threat to the Temple produced instant unity. Yet it did not lead to violence on this occasion. Perhaps the Jews had learned a hard lesson in 4 BCE. This time they resorted to passive resistance. For five days they simply lay outside Pilate's house until he summoned them to the amphitheater of Caesarea, telling them that he was now ready to give them an answer. As soon as the crowd had assembled, Pilate gave a sign to his troops, who appeared on all sides with swords drawn. If he had thought to scare the Jews into acquiescence, Pilate was badly mistaken. As one, the Jews fell to the ground and bared their necks, crying that they would rather die than break their laws. Pilate was astonished and realized that he would have to give in.[21] The offending standards were removed from the Antonia, and peace was restored, though the incident had made the Jews of Judaea even more fearful for the Temple's safety.

Four years later the Temple was threatened again. A small procession, headed by a man riding on a donkey, came down the Mount of Olives, through the Kidron Valley, and into Jerusalem. There were cries of "Hoshannah!" and "Save us, Son of David!" Some people cut down branches and waved palm shoots. Word went around that the young man was Jesus, a prophet from Nazareth in Galilee. As he drew near to the city, it was said that Jesus wept: Jerusalem would not accept him, and in the not-too-distant future it would suffer a fearful punishment. The Holy City would be surrounded by its enemies and razed to the ground, and its inhabitants slaughtered. Not one stone would be left standing. Then, as if to give point to his words, Jesus entered the city and made straight for the Temple. He made a whip of short cords and drove out the money-changers and vendors of sacrificial pigeons from the Court of the Gentiles. "Does not scripture say: My house will be called a house of prayer?" he demanded. "You have turned it into a robber's den."[22] It was the week before Passover, and Jesus spent a lot of time preaching in the Temple courts. He foretold that Herod's magnificent Temple would shortly be laid waste. "You see those great buildings?" he asked his disciples. "Not a single stone will be left on another: everything will be destroyed."[23] Mark, author of the earliest of the four gospels that describe Jesus's life, tells us that as soon as the chief priests heard about Jesus's demonstration in the Court of the Gentiles, they were resolved to get rid of him. Any threat to the Temple, especially during the crowded and emotional festival of Passover, was likely to lead to violence, which, in turn, could result in dreadful reprisals. Jesus was a risk that the Jewish people could not afford.

What did Jesus mean by his provocative outburst in the Temple? We can only speculate, since the gospels do not give us much information. Jesus had already acquired a following in the small towns and villages of Galilee, where he had worked as a healer and an exorcist. The people called him a prophet. We do not know whether Jesus claimed to be the Messiah—our sources are ambiguous; he certainly made no attempt to raise an army to drive the Romans out of Palestine, as other would-be messiahs had attempted to do in the country regions after Herod's death. Zechariah had foretold that the Messiah would be a humble ruler and would come to them riding on an ass. Perhaps Jesus's procession into the city had been a demonstration, showing the people that in God's Kingdom, Jerusalem would be ruled by the Poor, not by a militaristic king like Herod. Jesus evidently believed that the Day of YHWH was at hand. Like other apocalyptic seers, he foresaw the return of the Twelve Tribes to Israel and claimed that they would be ruled by twelve of his disciples.[24] It was also generally thought that after his final victory, YHWH would build a new Temple in Jerusalem, where he would be worshipped by all the nations. When he drove out the money changers and pigeon-sellers, Jesus was not protesting against the commercial abuse of sacred space. Such vendors were essential to the running of any temple in late antiquity and would have occasioned no outrage. Instead, Jesus was probably making another prophetic gesture to demonstrate the imminent End when Herod's beautiful Temple would be replaced by a shrine not made with human hands. There was nothing startlingly original about Jesus's pronouncements, but during the feast of national liberation the authorities might well have feared that they could inspire a demonstration against Rome.

Caiaphas would have been as familiar with the apocalyptic implications of Jesus's gestures as anybody else in Judaea. But he could not allow provocative talk about the Temple so soon after Pilate's attempted violation had brought the nation to the brink of catastrophe. On the first day of the festival he had Jesus arrested but let his disciples go free—a sign that he did not regard him as a major political threat. At his trial, Jesus was accused of vowing to destroy the Temple, but the witnesses could not agree and the charge was dropped. Caiaphas managed to get a conviction on a charge of blasphemy, however, and, since the Jews did not have the authority to inflict capital punishment, Jesus was sent to Pilate for sentencing. Pilate had Jesus scourged, condemned him to death by crucifixion, and forced him to carry his cross from the Praetorium through the streets of Jerusalem to a hill outside the city walls called Golgotha: the Place of the Skull (Latin: Calvarius). There Jesus was executed together with two bandits. Victims of crucifixion could linger for hours, but Jesus died quite quickly. As the Sabbath was approaching, his friends were anxious to bury him before sundown, so Joseph of Arimathea, a member of the Sanhedrin (the Jewish governing council), got permission from Pilate to inter the body in his own tomb. This was one of the new cavelike sepulchers cut into the hillside conveniently near Golgotha. Jesus was buried hastily, the stone was pushed into place, and his friends resolved to come back to anoint the body properly after the Sabbath.

That should have been the end of the matter. But soon there were rumors that Jesus had risen from the dead. It was said that the women had found the tomb empty when they arrived there early on Sunday morning. Some of his disciples and relatives had visions of Jesus, walking, talking, and eating as though he were alive. Many people believed that the righteous would be raised from the dead on the Day of the Lord. Had Jesus been raised in advance of this imminent event? Perhaps he had been the Messiah, the forerunner of the coming redemption? Finally, during the festival of Weeks,

The Garden of Gethsemane on the lower slopes of the Mount of Olives, where Jesus prayed in agony before his arrest, was one of the earliest places venerated by the Christians of Jerusalem: most of the first Christian sacred sites were located outside the city walls.

while the disciples were praying together in a room in Jerusalem, they felt that they had been possessed by the spirit of YHWH and were convinced that this was the start of the new age foretold by the prophets when God's presence would be felt more immediately than ever before. The members of the Jesus sect seemed to demonstrate this Presence: they performed miracles of healing, spoke in strange tongues, prophesied, and had visions. The idea that a man who had suffered the shameful death of crucifixion had been the Messiah was astonishing, but the sect soon attracted new converts and was eventually accepted as an authentic Jewish movement by the Sanhedrin at the behest of the distinguished Pharisee Gamaliel.[25] Certainly Jesus's disciples did not think that they had founded a new religion: they continued to live as fully observant Jews and went every day in a body to worship in the Temple. Like the sectarians at Qumran, they called themselves the Evionim, the Poor: they gave their possessions away and lived a communal life, trusting in God for subsistence like the birds of the air and the lilies of the field.[26] Theirs was an attractive piety which was admired by many of their fellow Jews. Soon, they believed, Jesus would return in glory and it would be clear to everyone that the Kingdom of God had finally arrived.

The movement spread to nearby cities and towns. There was a large assembly or church in Jerusalem and others in Lydda, Joppa, Caesarea, Galilee, and Damascus. The Jerusalem church was led in these early days by three of Jesus's leading disciples—Peter, James, and John—who were known as the "Pillars."[27] A particularly important member was Jesus's brother James, who was known as the Tzaddik, the Righteous Man. He had not been a follower of Jesus during his lifetime, but after the crucifixion he had been one of the first to see his risen brother in a vision; he would become a dominant member of the church, and by 50 CE would be its leader. James was held in high regard in Jerusalem. He lived a peculiarly austere life and was so scrupulous about ritual purity that, it was said, he was allowed to wear the priestly robes and to pray in the Court of the Priests. He also had good relations with the Pharisees and was respected by the Qumran community. James the Tzaddik shows how well integrated the Jesus sect was with Jewish religious life in Jerusalem. Far from abandoning the Torah, James and the Jerusalem church were committed to observance of every single *mitzvah*. Not one syllable of the law could pass away. The followers of Jesus were expected to go beyond the Torah's prescriptions and become perfect Jews: if the Torah said "Thou shalt not kill," they must not even get angry; if the Torah forbade adultery, they must not even look lustfully upon a woman.[28] Their duty was to live as exemplary Jews, worshipping in the Temple daily, until Jesus returned.

But in about 36 CE, it seems that some members of the Jesus movement clashed with mainstream Jews about the Temple. The Jerusalem
community included some Greek-speaking Jews from the diaspora, who
appear to have felt at a disadvantage among the Judaeans.[29] Their leader
was Stephen, a charismatic speaker whose preaching gave great offense
in the city. Like Jesus, he was hauled before the Sanhedrin and accused
of speaking against the Torah and the Temple. The speech that Luke,
who is traditionally held to be the author of the Acts of the Apostles,
puts on Stephen's lips is almost certainly not historical, but it may reflect
a tendency that later became common in the diaspora churches and had
its roots in this early conflict. Luke makes Stephen dwell on the number
of times God had revealed himself to his people *outside* Jerusalem: in
Mesopotamia, Haran, Egypt, Midian, and Sinai. Even Solomon had realized that God could not dwell in a man-made building.[30] Stephen so
enraged the Sanhedrin that they rushed him outside the city and stoned
him to death. Then, Luke says, they turned their wrath on the rest of the
church. But not, apparently, on the "Pillars" and the original Palestinian
followers of Jesus.[31] It was probably only the Hellenes, the Greek-
speaking Jews, who had to flee the city, taking refuge first in the countryside and then founding churches in Phoenicia, Cyprus, and Antioch.

It was at Antioch that the followers of Jesus were first called "Christians" because of their assertion that Jesus had been the Christos, the
Anointed One, the Messiah.[32] The Antiochan Christians were joined in
about 40 by another diaspora Jew who had originally been fanatically
opposed to the Christian movement but had been converted by an overpowering vision of Jesus while traveling to Damascus to persecute the
church there. Paul of Tarsus quickly became one of the Christian leaders of Antioch. He had an entirely different conception of Christianity
from the Pillars of Jerusalem. In the last chapter we saw that during this
period many people in the Greek world were beginning to find their
ancestral traditions constricting. We know very little about Paul's early
life, but it seems as though he was one of the people who were looking
for something new. He had studied Torah under Gamaliel and joined the
Pharisee sect, but had come to experience the Torah as a burden that was
destructive of his personal liberty. It could not bring him salvation,
peace, and union with God.[33] After his vision on the road to Damascus,
Paul came to believe that Jesus had replaced the Torah as God's primary
revelation to the world. The death and resurrection of Jesus had opened
a new phase in salvation history. Jew and gentile alike could now enter
the New Israel by means of the initiatory rite of baptism, which incorporated them mystically into Christ. There was, therefore, no need for
Christians to observe the dietary laws, to keep themselves separate from

the Goyim, or to practice circumcision, because these were the marks of the old covenant, which had now been superseded. All who lived "in Christ" were now sons of God and children of Abraham, whatever their ethnic origin.

Paul's arresting revisionist interpretation of the gospel gained adherents in the diaspora not because it could be proved rationally nor because it was consistent with the historical facts of Jesus's life and death. Paul's view of Jesus appealed because it was so profoundly in tune with other religious developments in the Greco-Roman world at this time. As the American scholar Jonathan Z. Smith explains, there was a spiritual shift in late antiquity which was beginning to transform the old Temple cultus by giving the cosmos a human shape instead:

> Rather than a city wall, the new enclave protecting men against external, hostile powers will be a human group, a religious association or a secret society. Rather than a return to chaos or the threat of decreation, the enemy will be described as other men or demons, the threat of evil or death. Rather than a sacred place, the new centre and chief means of access to divinity will be a divine man. . . .[34]

Smith traces these changes in Egypt in the story of Thessalos the Magician; he looks forward to the cult of the holy man in Syria during the fourth and fifth centuries CE. But we have also seen that this tendency had already appeared in Palestinian Judaism: the Pharisees and the Qumran sect had regarded their religious association as a new temple. Now the Christians were beginning to make the transition from Temple to divine man. Instead of the old rituals of pilgrimage and purification, the new Christian rites of passage would be conversion, initiation, and identification with the man Jesus, who had achieved divine status when he was raised by God from the dead.[35] Paul would teach Christians that Jesus was the locus of salvation; he would rescue them not from primal chaos but from the demonic powers of sin and death.

This assertion would seem blasphemous to many Jews as well as to the Pillars and their followers in Jerusalem. They found it shocking to think that the divine could be experienced in a mere man. But, as we have seen, the sacred always manifests itself in something other than itself. Considered objectively, a city or a temple was just as unsuitable a vehicle of the divine as a human being. Any symbol of the sacred, be it a building, a city, a literary text, a law code, or a man, is bound to be inadequate. The essential paradox at the heart of the religious quest is that the sacred manifests itself in the profane, the absolute in the relative, the eternal in the temporal. Indeed, like forms of Indian mysticism, Christianity would find the shock of this contradiction redemptive: the divine shows its love and also its sovereign freedom in adapting itself to an inferior mode of being.[36] The real mystery is that the sacred can be manifest at all. Paul's dramatic conversion on the road to Damascus illustrated what conversion would mean to many of the early Christians. It represented a reversal, a turning of old sacred values on their head, which many people were beginning to find liberating.

Henceforth Christianity would not be rooted in a particular place. The new Christian hero was not James the Tzaddik in the Jerusalem Temple but Paul the traveler, who had no abiding city in this world and is shown perpetually on the move. Still, the severance from Jerusalem was painful. There was a bitter clash between Paul and the mother church after James discovered that the Christians of Antioch were not eating kosher meat and were consorting freely with the Goyim. A compromise was reached whereby Paul was put in charge of the gentile mission. The prophets had always looked forward to the gentile nations coming to pay homage to YHWH in Jerusalem in the messianic age. Paul was now able to point out to the Pillars that the Goyim were indeed beginning to arrive in his churches. They manifestly possessed the Spirit as fully as the Jewish Christians, so was it appropriate for James to turn them away by making unrealistic demands about circumcision and observance of the whole of the Torah? In return for autonomy in the gentile mission, Paul promised that his converts would help the Evionim, the Poor of Jerusalem. Throughout his mission, Paul gave this collection for the Jerusalem church top priority. It was an important symbol of continuity, a way for his converts to express their spiritual debt to Judaism and a fulfillment of the ancient prophecy.[37] The gentiles really were bringing gifts to Jerusalem, so the final redemption must truly be at hand.

But when Paul actually arrived in Jerusalem with the money during the festival of Weeks, 58 CE, his presence in the Temple caused a riot and he was arrested by the Romans for causing a disturbance. He was accused of bringing one of his gentile converts past the balustrade and into the Court of the Israelites.[38] It is most unlikely that Paul had contravened the Law in this way, because one of his guiding principles was to be "all things to all men" and to cater to people's religious sensitivities. Yet he did believe that the old barriers had come down and that the gentiles were no longer strangers in the Kingdom of God. Not only had the Torah been abrogated by the resurrection of Christ, the old sacred geography which had relegated the goyim to the margins of holiness had also been revoked. As Paul explained to his Ephesian converts, Jesus had "broken down the barrier which used to keep [Jews and Gentiles] apart" and therefore "you are no longer aliens or foreign visitors; you are citizens like all the saints, and part of God's household." Indeed, the Christians now formed a spiritual temple and were "being built into a house where God lives."[39] Similarly to the Qumran sectarians, Paul's Christians believed that God now dwelt on earth in the community of the faithful. Like other people in late antiquity, the Christians were beginning to bypass the earthly Temple and felt that they had already entered into the spiritual reality—the "heavenly Jerusalem"—which it symbolized.[40] But for those Jews who still believed that the Temple on Mount Zion provided the most certain means of access to God, this was blasphemous. Paul's very presence in the Temple in 58 was felt as a threat, and, like Jesus and Stephen before him, Paul lost his freedom and ultimately his life because he had jeopardized the sanctity of Zion. Eventually, Luke tells us in the Acts of the Apostles, Paul was sent to Rome as a prisoner, since he had claimed his right as a Roman citizen to be tried by Caesar himself. Like the Jewish reformers at the time of Antiochus Epiphanes, Paul, the rootless man of late antiquity, wanted to be a citizen of the world, not a son of Jerusalem. We do not know Paul's ultimate fate. Legend has it that he died during the persecution of the Emperor Nero in 64, yet long after his death, the churches that he had founded in the Diaspora remained true to his Christian vision, and one day, ironically, these gentile Christians would make their own claim to Jerusalem.

The Jews had become even more defensive about their Temple since Pilate's time, because its holiness had been seriously imperiled yet again. In 41, Emperor Gaius Caligula had given orders that his statue be erected in the Jerusalem sanctuary. When Petronius, the legate of Syria, arrived at the port of Ptolemaïs to carry out this difficult task, he had been confronted by "tens of thousands of Jews" with their wives and children massed on the plain in front of the city. They refused to give an inch in the ensuing negotiations, even though Caligula threatened that the entire population would be taken into captivity if they continued to resist. Yet again the Jews resorted to nonviolent methods, neglecting to harvest their crops, which meant that it was impossible for the Romans to collect the annual tribute. Some believed that God would step in to save them, and, indeed, he appeared to do so when the emperor was assassinated in Rome before he could carry out his threats.[41]

To appease the Jews, Caligula's successor, Claudius, appointed Herod's grandson Agrippa King of Jewish Palestine, and Jerusalem flourished under his brief rule. Agrippa expanded the Upper and Lower Markets in the Tyropoeon Valley and planned a third city wall around the northern district of Bezetha. His death in 44 was a severe blow. His son Agrippa II was too young to rule, so Claudius sent a new Roman governor to Judaea, but this time with the lower rank of procurator. The young King Agrippa II retained a high position in the government. There were signs of unrest in Palestine. A prophet called Theudas persuaded about four hundred people to follow him into the desert, where God would bring deliverance and liberate the Jews from Rome. Another prophet rose up under the procurator Felix (52–59), promising that he would drive the Romans from Jerusalem. Neither prophet attracted much of a following, and the Romans were able to crush them without much difficulty. Feelings could still explode during the national festivals. Thousands of Jews were trampled to death in the Temple courts at Passover during the procuratorship of Cumanus (48–52), when one of the soldiers on guard on the portico roof exposed himself and made obscene gestures to the crowds of pilgrims below. But despite these disturbances, Jerusalem continued to flourish. There were extremists who resorted to terrorism in the Holy City in a desperate attempt to end Roman hegemony, but during these years a *modus vivendi* with Rome seemed to have been established. In 59, King Agrippa II was allowed to take up residence in the old Hasmonean palace: Herod's palace was now used as the residence of the procurator when he visited Jerusalem. The Temple was finally completed, and eighteen thousand workers were employed paving the city streets. Jerusalem had been granted a certain autonomy: Agrippa and the high priest governed the city jointly and cooperated amicably with the procurator in Caesarea.

But in 60, Rome began to appoint men of lesser caliber as governors of Judaea. Alibinus (60–62) was said to have taken bribes from the Jewish bandits who terrorized all who cooperated with Rome, and Gessius Florus (64–66) continued this practice. When riots broke out between the Jewish and Syrian residents of Caesarea, Florus found that he needed more cash and took the fatal step of commandeering money from the Temple treasury. Instantly the city exploded into violence, and the Jews fought the Roman cohorts in the streets. When he failed to restore order, Florus withdrew, asking for help from Cestius Gallus, the governor of Syria. Gallus arrived in Palestine in mid-November prepared for war. He encamped on Mount Scopus and advanced on the northern suburb of Bezetha, but then, for some unexplained reason, he withdrew to Emmaus, hotly pursued by Jewish partisans. There his legion was defeated and the Jews killed more than five thousand Roman soldiers.

During this crisis, the Jews were engaged in their own internal struggles. The rebels did not command universal support. Many of the rural aristocracy as well as Jews in such towns as Sepphoris and Tiberias were opposed to the war against Rome. The Saducees, too realistic to imagine that the Jews could defeat the might of Rome, had abandoned their dream of Jewish independence. Many of the Pharisees were more concerned with religion than politics and realized that the Jews of the Diaspora would be seriously jeopardized by a Jewish revolt against Rome. King Agrippa tried to persuade the rebels to make peace: did they imagine that they were stronger than the Gauls, the Germans, or the Greeks, who had all been forced to submit to the power of the Roman empire? Josephus himself defected to the Roman side, convinced that the rebels had embarked on a suicidal cause. But a new, radical party of Zealots arose to oppose the moderates. They believed that Rome was in decline and that the Jews had a good chance of success. Had not the Maccabees shaken off foreign control and established an independent Jewish kingdom? They regarded those Jews who wanted to make peace as traitors to Zion and would not allow them to take part in the Temple liturgy. Only a small percentage of the Jewish population of Palestine supported the Zealots, and there was dissension even within their own ranks. Some of the more extreme withdrew to the fortress of Masada by the Dead Sea and took no further part in the war for the city. The Zealots were still fighting one another in Jerusalem after the defeat of Cestius Gallus, when it was clear that war with Rome was inevitable.

It was probably at this point that the Jewish Christians decided to leave Jerusalem. There had been occasional signs of strain between their church and the Jewish establishment. James the Pillar had been executed, and in 62, James the Tzaddik himself had been condemned to death by the high priest for "breaking the law," even though eighty Pharisees protested to Rome on James's behalf and died with him. The leadership of the Jerusalem church now passed to Simeon, Jesus's cousin. He led his community to Pella in Transjordan: Jesus had foretold the destruction of Jerusalem, and the Christians knew that the city was doomed. Other Jews were resolved to fight to win. While they waited for Rome to avenge the defeat they had inflicted on Gallus, the Jewish residents of Jerusalem hastily built the Third Wall, which had been planned by Agrippa I, around Bezetha.

The Jews were unlucky that Rome dispatched its ablest general to quell the Jewish revolt. In 67, Vespasian arrived in Palestine and began systematically to defeat the pockets of resistance in Galilee. In 70, however, Vespasian was made emperor and returned to Rome, leaving his son Titus in charge of the Jewish war. Titus promptly began the siege of Jerusalem in February of that year. By May he had broken through the new northern wall, and a week later he demolished the Second Wall around the markets. The fighting now centered around the Temple itself. In late July the Romans captured the Antonia and began to bombard the Temple courts. The last sacrifice was offered on 6 August. But still the Jews did not give up. Many of the Zealots continued to believe that because God dwelt in the city, it could not fall. One prophet insisted that at the eleventh hour God would intervene miraculously to save his people and his Temple.[42]

And so, when the Roman troops finally broke into the inner courts of the Temple on 28 August, they found six thousand Jewish Zealots waiting to fight to the death. The Greek historian Dio Cassius (d. 230) says that the Jews defended themselves with extraordinary courage, deeming it an honor to die in the defense of their Temple. Right up to the end, they observed the purity laws, each fighting in his appropriate place and, despite the danger, refusing to enter forbidden areas: "The ordinary people fought in the forecourt and the nobility in the inner courts, while the priests defended the Temple building itself."[43] Finally they saw the Temple catch fire, and a terrible cry of horror arose.[44] Some flung themselves onto the swords of the Romans, others hurled themselves into the flames. But once the Temple had gone, the Jews gave up. They showed no interest in defending the Upper City or continuing the struggle from other fortresses nearby. Some asked leave to go out into the desert in the forlorn hope that this new exodus would lead to a new national liberation. The rest watched helplessly as Titus's officers efficiently demolished what was left of the Temple buildings, though, it was said, the western wall of the Devir was left standing. Since this was where the divine Presence had been thought to rest, Jews drew some consolation from this.[45] But it was poor comfort. For centuries the Temple had stood at the heart of the Jewish world, and it was central to the Jewish religion. Once again it had been destroyed, but this time it would not be rebuilt.

8

AELIA CAPITOLINA

THE TEMPLE MOUNT was now a heap of rubble. Apart from the western wall of the Devir, only the huge walls supporting the Temple platform had survived the onslaught. Once they had dealt with the Temple, Titus's soldiers began to smash the elegant mansions in the Upper City and pulled down Herod's beautiful palace. Archaeologists have revealed how thoroughly and ruthlessly the Roman troops went about their task. Houses collapsed and lay buried under piles of debris that were never cleared away. The Tyropoeon Valley was completely blocked with fallen masonry and silted up by the torrents that poured down the hillsides during the winter rains. The city walls were wholly demolished except for a section to the west of the Upper City: this served to protect the Camp of the Tenth Legion Fretensis, which now occupied the site of Herod's palace. Visitors found it difficult to believe that Jerusalem had ever been an inhabited city. The emperors were at pains to warn the Jews against attempting any further rebellion. For years after 70 they struck coins depicting a Jewish woman with bound hands sitting desolately under a palm tree, with the legend JUDAEA DEVICTA or JUDAEA CAPTA. The emperors Vespasian (70–79), Titus (79–81), Domitian (81–96), and Trajan (98–117) all ordered the Tenth Legion to hunt out and execute any Jew who claimed to be a descendant of King David. But the Romans tried to be fair. Palestine was now a full province of the empire, yet King Agrippa II, who had tried to keep the peace, was allowed to retain his title and rule Galilee, on the understanding that it would revert to Rome after his death. All Jewish land was confiscated and in theory became the property of the emperor, but in practice the Romans left most of the former owners in actual possession, recognizing that nearly all the surviving landlords of Palestine had been opposed to the revolt.

But despite these measured policies, the Roman victory continued to be a source of pain and humiliation for the Jews. They were reminded of it in so many distressing ways. The half-shekel Temple tax paid by all adult male Jews was now donated to the Temple of Jupiter on the Capitoline Hill in Rome. In 81 a magnificent triumphal arch was erected in Rome to celebrate Titus's victory, depicting the sacred vessels that had been carried away. A century later these objects were still proudly displayed in the imperial capital. Rabbi Eleazar said that he had seen the Temple Veil, which was still stained with the blood of the sacrificial victims, and the high priest's headband inscribed with the words "Sacred to YHWH."[1] In Jerusalem, the soldiers of the Tenth Legion could display the imperial eagles freely now and make sacrifices to their gods in the ruined streets. They may also have built a shrine to Serapis-Asclepius, god of healing, near the Pool of Beth-Hesda.[2]

Jerusalem, the center of the Jewish world, was now little more than a base for the Roman army. The Tenth Legion has left little trace of its long sojourn, since the soldiers probably lived in wooden huts and tents beside Herod's three great towers—Hippicus, Phasael, and Mariamne—which Titus had allowed to remain. Roman soldiers and Syrian and Greek civilians were also brought to live in the desolate city. But some Jews remained. A few houses had been left standing on the hill to the south of the Roman camp, which Josephus had mistakenly called Mount Zion. By the time of his writing, people had forgotten that the original 'Ir David had been on the Ophel hill; they assumed that David had lived in the Upper City in the better part of town, where their own kings and aristocrats had their residences. Today this western hill is still called Mount Zion, and, to distinguish it from the original, I propose to adopt the commonly used alternative spelling "Mount Sion." Once a measure of calm had returned to the area, a small number of Jews settled on Mount Sion; they could not worship on the Temple Mount, since it had been totally polluted, but they built seven synagogues on this southern hill. Our sources are the Christian historians Eusebius of Caesarea (264–340) and Epiphanius of Cyprus (c. 315–403), who had access to local traditions and tell us that after the destruction of Jerusalem, the Jewish Christians returned from Pella and settled alongside the Jews on Mount Sion under the leadership of Simeon. They used to meet in one of the houses that had survived destruction, which was later identified with the "Upper Room" where the disciples had seen the risen Christ and received the Holy Spirit. Epiphanius tells us that on their return from Pella, the Jewish Christians settled around the Upper Room "in the part of the city called Sion, which part was exempted from destruction, as also were some of the dwellings around Sion and seven synagogues . . . like monks' cells."[3] Eusebius makes it clear that the Jerusalem church continued to be entirely Jewish, ruled by Jewish "bishops."[4] They shared many of the ideals of their Jewish neighbors on Sion. Unlike Paul's converts, they did not believe that Jesus had been divine: after all, some of them had known him since he was a child and could not see him as a god. They viewed him simply as a human being who had been found worthy to be the Messiah. They probably honored the places in Jerusalem that were associated with Jesus, especially the Mount of Golgotha and the nearby rock tomb whence Jesus had risen from the dead. Many Jews liked to visit the tombs of their revered masters, and it would have been natural for them to commemorate Jesus's sepulcher. Some of them began to engage in mystical speculation about Golgotha, the Place of the Skull. There was a Jewish legend that Adam had been buried on Mount Moriah, the site of Solomon's Temple; by the second century, Jewish Christians said that he had been buried at Golgotha, the place of Adam's skull.[5] They were beginning to evolve their own mythology about Jerusalem, and this notion expressed their belief that Jesus was the new Adam, who had given humanity a fresh start. During this tragic period, many Jews entered their church: perhaps the idea of a crucified Messiah who had risen again helped them to hope for the revival of their old cult.

Others turned to asceticism. In the rabbinical writings we hear of Jews who wanted to ban meat and wine, since these could no longer be offered to God in the Temple. Life could not continue as before: Jews must express their changed status in rituals of mourning and abstinence. The loss of the Temple was a profound shock. Thirty years after the destruction, the author of the Book of Baruch suggests that the whole of nature should mourn: now that the Temple had gone, there was no need for the earth to bring forth a harvest nor the vine to yield grapes; the heavens should withhold their dew and the sun dim its rays:

> For why should light rise again
> Where the light of Zion is darkened?[6]

The Temple had represented the heart of the world's meaning, the core of the faith. Now life had neither value nor significance, and it seems that in these dark days many Jews lost their faith. It is not true, as has often been asserted, that the Jews had wholly outgrown their Temple. Even those Jews who had begun to evolve other ways of experiencing the divine believed that Jerusalem and its sanctuary were central to their religion. Jews would need all their creativity to survive this devastating loss.

During the siege of Jerusalem, the distinguished Pharisee Rabbi Yohanan ben Zakkai was smuggled out of the city in a coffin. Like many of the Pharisees, he had been totally opposed to the revolutionary extremism of the Zealots. The mass suicide in 73 of the Zealots of Masada, who preferred to die rather than submit to Rome, was repugnant to him. As a result of his determined moderation, he and his companions were the only Jewish leaders to retain credibility after the destruction of the Temple. Rabbi Yohanan approached Emperor Vespasian to ask his permission to found a school where Jews could study and pray: this, he insisted, would be a spiritual center, not a hotbed of revolutionary fervor. He was given leave to establish the academy of Yavneh on the coast, and there he and his fellow rabbis, many of whom had served as priests in the Temple, began to build a new Judaism. When the Jews lost their Temple in 586, they had found consolation in the study of Torah. Now at Yavneh and the other similar academies that developed in Palestine and Babylonia, the rabbis who are known as the Tannaim began to codify the body of oral law which had been developing over the centuries. Finally, this new law code would be called the Mishnah. It would become a symbolic new Jerusalem where Jews could experience the divine Presence wherever they happened to be. The rabbis taught that whenever a group of Jews studied the Torah together, the Shekhinah, God's Presence on earth, would sit among them.[7] Many of the laws were concerned with the Temple ritual, and to this day when Jews study this legislation they are engaged in an imaginary reconstruction of the lost Temple in which they recover a sense of the divine at its heart. Once the Tannaim had completed their work, later generations of rabbis known as the Amoraim would begin to comment on *their* exegesis. Finally the Talmud would enshrine these rabbinical discussions, wherein Jews argued—and continue to engage in passionate debate about their Torah—over the centuries, overcoming the barriers of place and time. The accumulated layers of commentary and interpretation would become, as it were, the walls of a symbolic Temple surrounding the Presence that Jews could glimpse during their studies.

The rabbis also stressed that charity and compassion could now replace the old animal sacrifices.

> Once, as Rabbi Yohanan ben Zakkai was coming forth from Jerusalem, Rabbi Joshua followed after him and beheld the Temple in ruins.
>
> "Woe to us," Rabbi Joshua said, "that this, the place where the iniquities of Israel were atoned for, is laid waste!"
>
> "My son," Rabbi Yohanan said, "be not grieved. We have another atonement as effective as this. And what is it? It is acts of loving-kindness, as it is said: 'For I desire mercy and not sacrifice.'"[8]

Practical compassion had long been seen as an essential accompaniment to the Zion cult: now acts of charity alone would have to atone for the sins of Israel—a revolutionary idea in the ancient world, where religion was still almost unimaginable without some form of sacrifice. Now that the Temple was gone, the rabbis would teach their fellow Jews to experience God in their neighbor. Some taught that the *mitzvah* "Thou shalt love thy neighbor as thyself" was "the great principle of Torah."[9] Offenses against a fellow human being were now said to be equivalent to a denial of God himself, who had made men and women in his image. Murder was, therefore, not merely a crime in Jewish law but a sacrilege.[10] God had created a single man at the beginning of time to teach us that whoever destroyed a single human life would be punished as though he had destroyed the whole world; similarly, to save a life was to redeem the whole world.[11] To humiliate anybody, even a *goy* or a slave, was tantamount to destroying God's image.[12] Jews must realize that their dealings with others were sacred encounters. Now that the divine could no longer be experienced in sacred space, Jews must find it in their fellow human beings. The Pharisees had always stressed the importance of charity. But now the loss of the Temple had helped them to make that transition toward a more humane conception of the sacred, which we noted in the previous chapter.

The rabbis had not given up hope that one day their Temple would be rebuilt: the last time the Temple had been destroyed, there had been a restoration against all the odds. But they believed that it was wiser and safer to leave this rebuilding to God. Yet Jews must not forget Jerusalem. The rabbis drew up legislation to discourage emigration from Palestine and demanded that the Eighteen Benedictions be recited three times a day, in place of the Morning and Evening Sacrifice. Jews must recite these prayers wherever they were: if they were traveling, they should dismount and turn their faces in the direction of Jerusalem, or at least direct their hearts toward the ruined Devir.[13] These benedictions show that in spite of everything, Jerusalem was still regarded as God's habitation:

> Be mindful, O Lord our God, in thy great mercy towards Israel, thy people, and towards Jerusalem, thy city, and towards Zion, the abiding place of thy Glory, and towards thy Temple and towards thy habitation, and towards the Kingdom of the House of David, thy righteous anointed one. Blessed be Thou, O Lord our God, the builder of Jerusalem.[14]

Some rabbis imagined the Shekhinah (the personified divine presence) lingering still beside the western wall of the Devir, which had, providentially, survived the destruction.[15] Others saw the Shekhinah leaving Jerusalem reluctantly, by slow degrees: for three years it had "stayed continuously on the Mount of Olives, and was crying out three times a day."[16] Jews remembered that Ezekiel had seen a vision of the Glory of YHWH returning to Jerusalem over the brow of the Mount of Olives, so they liked to gather there as a declaration of faith in God's eventual return to their Holy City.

Other Jews turned more readily to mysticism for consolation. This was a form of spirituality that the rabbis sometimes mistrusted, but the mystics themselves found no incompatibility between their mystical flights to God's heavenly Throne and rabbinic Judaism. Indeed, they frequently ascribed their visions to some of the more distinguished rabbis in the academies. After the loss of the Temple, Throne Mysticism acquired a wholly new relevance. The earthly replica had, alas, been destroyed, but its celestial archetype was indestructible, and Jews could still reach it in their imaginary *aliyah* to the divine realm. Thus the author of 2 Baruch, who was writing some thirty years after the destruction of the Temple, insisted that the heavenly Jerusalem was eternal. It had been "with God" from before the beginning of time and "was already prepared from the moment that I decided to make Paradise." It was graven forever on the palms of God's hands, and one day this heavenly reality would descend to earth once more.[17] It would take physical form again in an earthly city on the old sacred site, and God would dwell among his people in the mundane world. At about the same time, the author of 4 Enoch had a similar vision of the incarnation of the celestial Jerusalem. The earthly Zion had suffered and died but its heavenly counterpart was still with God. One day "the city that is now invisible [shall] appear."[18] This new Jerusalem would be the earthly paradise: those who dwelt within it would enjoy a perfect intimacy with God; sin would be vanquished and death swallowed up in victory.[19] The anguish of severance, loss, and dislocation which had descended upon the Jewish world in 70 CE would be overcome and the primal harmony of Eden restored.

Jewish Christians also had Throne Visions. During the reign of Domitian, when the Christians were being persecuted by the Roman authorities, an itinerant preacher called John had a vision of the heavenly Temple, in which the martyrs were the new priests, clad in their white garments and serving before the throne. He imagined the celestial liturgy of Sukkoth but found a crucial difference from the old cult. There had always been a void at the heart of the Second Temple: once the Ark was lost, the Devir was empty. But John saw Christ, mysteriously identified with God himself, seated on the heavenly throne. He was, therefore, the fulfillment of the old Zion cult. Yet these Christians still shared the hopes of their fellow Jews and looked forward to a final restoration. One day the heavenly Jerusalem would descend to earth. In a final vision, John saw "the holy city, coming down from God out of heaven. It had all the radiant glory of God."[20] There would be no Temple in this New Jerusalem because Christ had taken its place. The divine man was now the principal locus of the "glory." But Jerusalem was still such a potent symbol to a Jewish Christian like John that he could not imagine God's final apocalypse without it. The celestial city would have to take physical form on earth for the Kingdom to be complete. At last the earthly paradise would be restored and the river of life well up from beneath God's throne to bring healing to the whole world.[21]

Jews and Christians were experiencing their God in remarkably similar ways. They respectively saw Jerusalem and Jesus as symbols of the sacred. Christians were beginning to think about Jesus in the same way as some of the Throne Mystics were envisaging Jerusalem: as the incarnation of a divine reality that had been with God from the beginning and that would bring salvation from sin, death, and the despair to which humanity is prone. But despite this similarity, Jews and Christians were starting to feel extremely hostile and defensive toward one another. As far as we know, there were no gentile Christians living on Mount Sion or in the ruined city of Jerusalem. They were interested in the heavenly Jerusalem, as described by John the Preacher, but had no interest in the earthly city. In the gospels of Matthew, Luke, and John, written during the eighties and nineties, we can see the way that Christians who subscribed to Paul's version of Christianity were beginning to regard Jerusalem and the Jewish people.

Interestingly, it was Luke, the gentile Christian, who had the most positive view of the parent faith. His gospel begins and ends in Jerusalem: it starts with the vision of Zacharias, the father of John the Baptist, in the Hekhal and finishes with the disciples returning to Jerusalem after watching Jesus ascend to heaven from the Mount of Olives. They "went back to Jerusalem full of joy; and they were continually in the Temple praising God."[22] Continuity is very important to Luke, as it was for most people in late antiquity. Innovation and novelty were suspect, and it was crucial for religious people to know that their faith was deeply rooted in the sanctities of the past. Hence Luke, like Paul himself, did not want to sever all links with Jerusalem and Judaism. Jesus commands the disciples to begin their preaching in the Holy City, which is still the center of the world and the place where every prophet must meet his destiny. In the Acts of the Apostles, Luke makes his hero Paul very respectful of the Jerusalem church and deferential to James the Tzaddik. He paints a highly idealized picture of this early cooperation and tries to hide the bitterness that seems in fact to have characterized the relations of Paul and James. Luke shows Paul, like Jesus before him, feeling obliged and impelled to make the journey to Jerusalem, even though he is putting his life in danger. But Luke is equally clear that Christians cannot stay in Jerusalem: they must take the gospel from the Holy City to "all Judaea and Samaria and then to the ends of the earth."[23] Luke's favorite name for Christianity is "the Way": the followers of Jesus are continual travelers, with no abiding city in this world.

Matthew and John, however, were far less positive about either Jerusalem or the Jewish people. Both were Jewish converts to Paul's church, and their work may reflect some of the debates that were currently raging between Jews and Christians on such topics as the nature of Christ and the status of Jerusalem. Matthew has no doubts about the earthly Zion. It had once been a sacred place—he is the only evangelist to call it the Holy City—but it had rejected Jesus and put him to death, and, foreseeing this, Jesus had prophesied its destruction. Jerusalem had become the Guilty City. When Matthew makes Jesus describe the catastrophe that will befall the city in 70, he links it with the cataclysms that will occur at the End of History. He saw the destruction of Jerusalem as an eschatological event that heralded Jesus's glorious return.[24] When Jesus died on the hill of Golgotha outside the city, the Veil separating the Hekhal from the Devir had split in two: the old Temple cult had been abrogated, and now everybody—not merely the old priestly caste of the Jews—could gain access to the divine in the person of Christ. John emphasizes this even more strongly. Like others at this time, he insisted that God was no longer to be found in a Temple but in a divine man. In the Prologue to his gospel, he asserts that Jesus is the Logos, the "Word" that had existed "with God" from before the beginning of time and that God had uttered to create the world. This heavenly reality had now descended to earth, taken flesh, and revealed God's "glory" to the human race.[25] John was writing in Greek. There was no Greek equivalent of the Hebrew term "Shekhinah," which Jews were careful to distinguish from the utterly transcendent reality of God itself. Besides seeing Jesus as the incarnate "Word" and the "glory" of God, John may also have seen him as the Shekhinah in human form.[26]

But like Matthew, John was extremely hostile to the Jews and shows them repeatedly rejecting Christ. Both evangelists thus laid the ground for the antagonism to the Jewish people that would lead to some of the most shameful incidents of Christian history. Increasingly, as we shall see, Christians found it impossible to tolerate their spiritual predecessors and from a very early date saw the integrity of their own faith as dependent upon the defeat of Judaism. Thus John indicates that Jesus set out by rejecting the Temple cult: he makes Jesus go to Jerusalem and drive the money changers out of the Court of the Gentiles at the very beginning of his mission, not at the end. He tells the Jews: "Destroy this Temple, and in three days I will raise it up." John explains that he was "speaking of the Temple of his body."[27] Henceforth the risen body of the Logos would be the place where people would encounter the divine Presence. There was a confrontation between Jesus and the most sacred institution in Judaism from the start, therefore, and the days of the Temple were numbered. Jesus made it clear that holy places such as Jerusalem, Mount Gerizim, and Bethel had been superseded.[28] The Shekhinah had withdrawn from the Temple precincts,[29] and by rejecting this revelation the Jews had allied themselves with the forces of darkness.

The Christians must have seen the hand of God in the next development in Jerusalem. In 118, the Roman general Publius Aelius Hadrianus became emperor, one of the ablest men who ever held this office. His ambition was not to extend the empire but to consolidate it. Hadrian wanted to build a strong and united polity, a brotherhood in which all citizens, regardless of their race and nationality, could feel at home. One of the chief ways in which he tried to publicize and implement this ideal was by the royal progress through his imperial domains. Hadrian spent almost half his reign on the road with a huge and magnificent entourage, which was meant to give bystanders the impression of a whole capital city on the march. In each city he would hear petitions and present gifts to the local people, hoping to leave behind the image of a benign and powerful government. He particularly liked to leave a permanent memento of his visit, in the form of a building or monument: a temple for Zeus in Athens or aqueducts in Athens, Antioch, Corinth, and Caesarea. This would provide a physical link with Rome and permanently embody the emperor's benevolence toward his people. When Hadrian arrived in Jerusalem in 130, he decided that his gift to the people of Judaea would be a new city. The generous emperor would replace the unsightly ruin and desolate army base of Jerusalem with a modern metropolis called Aelia Capitolina: it would thus bear his own name and honor the gods of the Capitol in Rome, who would be its patrons.

Hadrian's plan filled the Jewish people with horror. There was actually going to be a temple to Jupiter on Mount Zion, the site of YHWH's holy Temple. Shrines to other deities would also appear all over the city. Over the centuries, the names "Jerusalem" and "Zion" had become central to the identity of Jews all over the world: they were inseparable from the name of its God. Now these names were to be replaced with the names of a pagan emperor and his idols. Jewish Jerusalem had been in ruins for sixty years: now it would be buried by order of the imperial power. It could never rise again. Zion and all that it stood for would vanish from the face of the earth. Hitherto the people of Jerusalem had experienced war and destruction; they had twice watched a victorious army raze the city to the ground, several times seen their Temple polluted and the walls demolished. But this was the first time that a building project had been experienced as an inimical act. Building had always been a religious activity in Jerusalem: it had held the threat of chaos and annihilation at bay. But now construction and building had become a weapon in the hands of the victorious empire. Aelia Capitolina would annihilate Jewish Jerusalem, whose shrine had symbolized the whole of reality and the innermost soul of its people. All this would disappear under the Roman city. This imperial building program would be an act of de-creation: chaos would come again. It would not be the last time in the history of Jerusalem that a defeated people would have to watch their holy city and its beloved landmarks disappear under the streets, monuments, and symbols of a hostile power and feel that its very self had been obliterated.

To be fair to Hadrian, he almost certainly had not foreseen this reaction. Who would not prefer a pleasant, modern city to this miserable ruin? The construction would bring employment, and the new metropolis wealth to the area. As they stood, the ruins of Jerusalem were an unhealthy reminder of past enmity, which must be transcended in the interests of brotherhood and amity. Jews and Romans must put the past behind them and work together for the peace and prosperity of the region. Hadrian had no love for Judaism, which appeared to him a primitive religion. The stubborn particularity of the Jews militated against the ideal of a culturally united empire: they must be dragged—by force, if necessary—into the modern world. Hadrian would not be the first ruler to destroy, in the name of progress and modernity, traditions that were inextricably bound up with a nation's sense of identity. In 131 he issued a set of edicts designed to make the Jews abandon their

A letter written in Aramaic by Bar Kochba, requesting palm branches, myrtles, citrons, and willows for the rituals of Sukkoth. It is possible that Bar Kochba tried to revive the cult on the ruined Temple Mount.

peculiar customs and fit in with everybody else in the Greco-Roman world. Circumcision—a barbaric practice, in his view—the ordination of rabbis, the teaching of Torah, and public Jewish meetings were all outlawed. This was another blow to Jewish survival. Once these edicts had been passed, even the most moderate rabbis realized that another war with Rome was unavoidable.

This time the Jews were not going to be caught unawares. Their new campaign was meticulously planned and organized down to the smallest detail. No fighting occurred until all preparations were in place. The revolt was led by Simon Bar Koseba, a hardheaded, practical soldier, who led his troops in guerrilla warfare, carefully avoiding pitched battle. Once the Tenth Legion had been forced to leave Jerusalem to fight the Jews in the countryside, Bar Koseba's soldiers occupied the city. With the help of his uncle Eleazar, a priest, Bar Koseba forced all the remaining gentiles to leave the city and probably tried to resume as much of the sacrificial cult as possible on the Temple Mount. The great Rabbi Akiva, one of the greatest scholars and mystics of his day, hailed Bar Koseba as the Messiah and liked to call him Bar Kokhba, "Son of the Star." We have no idea whether Bar Koseba regarded himself in this light: he was probably too busy planning his highly successful campaign to have much time for eschatology. But coins were struck in Jerusalem bearing the legend SIMON THE PRINCE and ELEAZAR THE PRIEST, which could mean that they saw themselves as the kingly and priestly messiahs who had been regarded as the joint redeemers of Jerusalem since the time of Zerubbabel. Other coins bore the words FOR THE LIBERATION OF JERUSALEM. But it was hopeless. Bar Koseba and his men were able to keep their rebellion going for three years. Eventually Hadrian had to send one of his very best generals, Sextus Julius, to Judaea. The Jewish army was too small to hold out indefinitely against the might of Rome, and Jerusalem—still lacking either walls or fortifications—was impossible to defend. The Romans systematically wiped out one Jewish stronghold after another in Judaea and Galilee. Dio Cassius tells us that the Romans took fifty fortresses, devastated 985 villages, and killed 580,000 Jewish soldiers: "as to those who perished by hunger, pestilence, or fire, no man could number them. Thus almost the whole of Judaea was laid waste."[30] Finally in 135, Bar Koseba was driven out of Jerusalem and killed in his last citadel at Bethar. But the Jews had also been able to inflict such heavy casualties on the Romans that when Hadrian reported the victory to the Senate he could not use the customary formula "I am well and the army is well."[31] The Jews were no longer regarded as a miserable, defeated race. Their conduct in this second war had won the grudging respect of Rome.

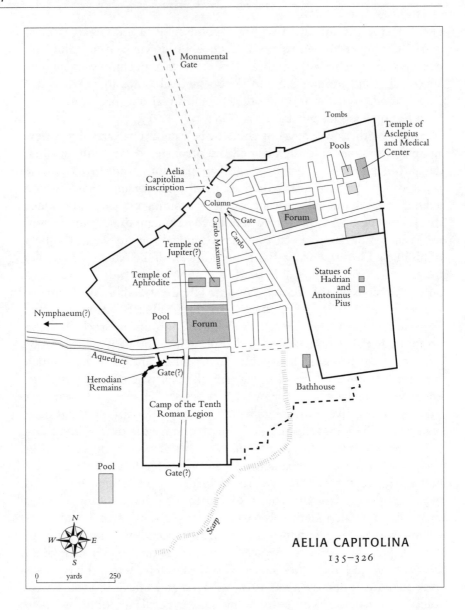

This, however, gave the Jews little comfort. After the war, Jews were banned from Jerusalem and the whole of Judaea. The little community on Mount Sion was disbanded, and there were no Jewish communities left in the city's environs. The Jews of Palestine now concentrated in Galilee: Tiberias and Sepphoris became their chief cities. They had to hear the painful news of the final obliteration of the Holy City and the creation of Aelia Capitolina. The work was entrusted to the legate

Rufus Timeius. First the city and the ruins had to be plowed over, following an ancient Roman rite for the founding of a new settlement.[32] To the Jews, this seemed a fulfillment of the prophecy of Micah: "Zion shall be plowed as a field."[33] Next Hadrian transformed the desolate site into an up-to-date Hellenic city, with temples, a theater, public baths, a pool dedicated to the nymphs (which may have been thought to have healing properties), and two marketplaces. One forum was in the east of the city, near what is now Stephen's Gate, the other on the second-highest point of the Western Hill on what is now Muristan Square. The Camp of the Tenth Legion remained on the former site of Herod's palace, on the highest point in town. Hadrian built no new city walls but instead erected a series of monumental arches. One was about 440 yards north of the city to commemorate his victory over Bar Koseba; another marked the main entrance to Aelia on the site of the present Damascus Gate; two others appeared in each of the forums. The arch in the eastern forum is known today as the Ecce Homo Arch, because Christians thought that it was the place where Pilate had displayed Jesus to the people, crying: "Behold the man!"[34] The chief entrance gate in the north of Aelia led into a square with a column, which supported a statue of the emperor. The two main streets of Aelia (known as *cardines,* the "hinges," of the city) issued from the square inside the main northern entrance gate: one *cardo* ran along the route of today's Valley Street (Tariq al-Wad), while the Cardo Maximus followed the ridge of the Western Hill. Hadrian also laid down a grid of streets that is still, roughly, the basis of the city's thoroughfares today.

Far more distressing to the Jews, however, were the religious symbols that appeared triumphantly in the Holy City of YHWH. Aelia was indeed dedicated to the three Capitoline gods, Jupiter, Juno, and Minerva, but after the Jewish War, Hadrian seems to have thought better of locating the Temple of Jupiter on the old Temple Mount. No visitor ever reports seeing a pagan temple on Herod's platform, but they did see two statues there: one of Hadrian and the other of his successor, Antoninus Pius. The Temple of Jupiter could have been built beside the chief commercial forum of Aelia on the Western Hill. A temple to Aphrodite was also built beside the western forum on the site of the Golgotha hill. Christians would later accuse Hadrian of deliberately desecrating this holy place, but it is most unlikely that the emperor had even registered the existence of the obscure church of Jewish Christians in Jerusalem. St. Jerome (c. 342–420) believed that this temple was dedicated to Jupiter but that the peak of the Golgotha hill protruded above the platform of the sanctuary surmounted by a statue of Aphrodite, although he does not explain how a temple to Jupiter came to have such a prominent statue of the goddess. Because the ground was so uneven in this part of the city, the architects had to fill in depressions by building supporting walls for a plaza, rather as Herod had done on the Temple Mount, though on a smaller scale. Aelia was now an entirely pagan, gentile city, indistinguishable from any other Roman colonial settlement. By the third century the town had spread eastward and there was extensive building at the southern end of the Temple Mount. When the Tenth Legion left Aelia in 289, the Romans built a new city wall. Jewish occupation of the city seemed a thing of the past.

Yet, surprisingly, the Jews' relations with Rome improved during these years. Emperor Antoninus Pius (138–61) relaxed Hadrian's anti-Jewish legislation, and the practice of Judaism became legal once more. The Bar Kokhba war had shown Rome that it was important to send able men to Judaea who had firsthand knowledge of the region, and the rabbis obviously appreciated this. They often praised the conduct of the Roman legates.[35] In Galilee they were allowed to develop a new type of leadership: in 140, Rabbi Simon, a descendant of Hillel, was proclaimed patriarch. Gradually he assumed monarchical powers and came to be recognized as head of all the Jews of the Roman empire. Since Simon was also said to be a descendant of King David, he united the ancient with the modern, rabbinic authority. The patriarchate gave Jews a new political focus that compensated in some small degree for their loss of Jerusalem; it reached its apogee under Simon's son Judah I (200–20), who was known as "the Prince" and lived in regal splendor. He was said to be a personal friend of Emperor Marcus Aurelius Antoninus (206–17), who was not of Roman descent, and therefore did not despise foreigners, and was particularly interested in Judaism.

Like most of the rabbis, the patriarchs believed that it was essential to accept the political situation. There were a few radicals, such as Rabbi Simeon ben Yohai, who lived as a fugitive in hiding from the Roman authorities until his death in 165. But the majority were convinced it was dangerous for Jews to nurture dreams of reconquering Jerusalem and rebuilding the Temple. Jews should wait for God to take the initiative. "If children tell you, Go build the Temple—do not listen to them," warned Rabbi Simeon ben Eliezar.[36] This task was reserved for the Messiah. Instead, the rabbis made other places the focus of Jewish spiritual life. Developing an insight of the Pharisees, they taught that the home had in some sense replaced the Temple, calling the family house a *mikdash m'at* ("small sanctuary"): the family table replaced the altar, and the family meal replicated the sacrificial cult. In the same way, the synagogue was also a reminder of the Temple. The building itself had an element of holiness and, like the vanished Jerusalem sanctuary, had a hierarchy of sacred places in which only certain people were allowed. The women had their own section, as in the Temple; the room where the sacrifice was conducted was holier; then came the *bimah* (reading desk) and, finally, the Ark containing the scrolls of the Torah, the new Holy of Holies. Thus people could still approach the inner sanctum step by step. The *bimah* was usually placed on a higher level so that it became a symbolic sacred mountain: when a member of the congregation was called upon to read the Torah, he still had to make an ascent (*aliyah*) as he mounted the podium. Under the rabbis, the Sabbath also acquired a new importance. Observing the Sabbath rest was now held to be a fore-taste of the world to come: once a week, therefore, Jews could enter another dimension of existence. Shabbat had become a temporal temple, where Jews could meet their God in consecrated time, instead of in sacred space.

Now that Jerusalem had become inaccessible to Jews and the Temple had gone, the rabbis had had to develop their understanding of the divine Presence. What had it meant to say that God dwelt in a man-made building? Had he been present nowhere else? The rabbis would often compare the

After the destruction of Jerusalem in 70 CE, the Jewish home came to replace the lost Temple. At Passover, Jews could no longer sacrifice lambs in the traditional manner; instead, they commemorate their liberation from Egypt with a family meal at which the father, clad in white, officiates as a priest, the table becomes a new altar, and the candlesticks recall the Temple Menorah.

Presence in the Devir to the sea, which could entirely fill a cave without reducing the amount of water in the sea as a whole. Again, they frequently asserted that God was the Place of the world but the world was not his place.[37] His immensity could not be contained by the physical world; on the contrary, God contained the earth. Some of the rabbis even suggested that the loss of the Temple had liberated the Shekhinah from Jerusalem. The exiles in Babylon had believed that YHWH had left the Temple to join them in exile.[38] Now the rabbis insisted that throughout Jewish history the Shekhinah had never deserted Israel but had followed them wherever they went: to Egypt, to Babylon, and back to Jerusalem in 539.[39] Now the Shekhinah had gone into exile with the Jews yet again. It was present whenever Jews studied Torah together; it skipped from one synagogue to another and stood at the door of the synagogue whenever Jews recited the *Shema.*[40] Indeed, God's presence with Israel had made the Jewish people a temple for the rest of the world. In the old days, YHWH's Temple on Zion had been the source of the world's fertility and order. Now this function was performed by the Jews: "Were it not for [God's presence in Israel]", the rabbis argued, "the rain would not come down, nor would the sun shine."[41] But always the emphasis was on community. God's presence was conditional upon the unity and charity of the people. It was felt when two or three Israelites studied Torah *together;* prayer was not valid unless ten men assembled to form a *minyan;* if Jews prayed "with devotion, with one voice, one mind, and one tone" the Shekhinah would be in their midst; if not, it ascended to heaven to listen to the harmonious worship of the angels.[42]

Yet just as the Babylonian exiles had evolved a sacred geography when there was no possibility of returning to their holy land, the rabbis still praised the holiness of Jerusalem long after the city had been polluted and the Temple destroyed. They still put Zion and the Devir at the center of the Jewish map of the world:

> There are ten degrees of holiness: the land of Israel is holier than other lands. . . . The walled cities of the land of Israel are still more holy . . . within the walls of Jerusalem is still more holy. . . . The Temple Mount is still more holy . . . the rampart is still more holy . . . the Court of the Women is still more holy . . . the Court of the Israelites is still more holy . . . the Court of the Priests is still more holy . . . the space around the Altar is still more holy . . . the Hekhal is still more holy . . . the Devir is still more holy, for none may enter therein save only the high priest on Yom Kippur.[43]

The rabbis continued to speak of Jerusalem in the present, even though the building no longer existed: the reality that it symbolized—God's presence on earth—was eternal, however, and still worthy of contemplation. Each level of holiness was more sacred than the last, and as the worshipper gradually ascended to the Holy of Holies, the groups of people who were permitted to enter were progressively reduced. As in the former exile, this spiritual geography had no practical relevance but was a mandala, an object of contemplation. The rabbis now insisted that all the key events of salvation had taken place on Mount Zion: the primal waters had been bound there on the day of creation; Adam had been created from its dust; Cain and Abel had offered their sacrifices there, as had Noah after the Flood. The Temple Mount had been the site of Abraham's circumcision, his binding of Isaac, and his meeting with Melchizedek; finally the Messiah would proclaim the New Age from Zion and redeem the world.[44] The rabbis were not interested in historical fact. They would not have been perturbed to hear that Noah's Ark had first touched down on Mount Ararat, not on Mount Zion, or that another ancient tradition located Abraham's meeting with Melchizedek at En Rogel. Jerusalem was a symbol of God's redemptive Presence in the world, and in that sense all saving events must have taken place there. Now that it was a forbidden city, Jerusalem was a more effective symbol of transcendence than ever. Whatever the physical state of Aelia, the spiritual reality that the Temple and city had replicated was eternal. We shall see that Jews continued to meditate on the ten levels of holiness for centuries when Jerusalem was still closed to them or the Temple Mount in alien hands. It became a model which helped them to imagine how God could make contact with humanity and also a map of their internal world.

Yet by the beginning of the third century, some Jews were beginning to renew contact with the earthly Jerusalem. The ban was still on the statute books, but under the sympathetic emperor Marcus Aurelius Antoninus, the Romans did not enforce it as strictly as before. First, some Jews of humbler rank had begun to slip through the Roman lines. Simon of Kamtra, a donkey driver, told the rabbis that in the course of his work he often had to pass the Temple Mount: did he really have to tear his clothes *every* time he saw the ruins?[45] Then Rabbi Meir was given permission to live in Aelia with five or six of his pupils, though this small community survived only a few years.[46] There were certainly no Jews living permanently in Jerusalem after the death of Patriarch Judah I in 220. Yet by the middle of the third century, Jews were allowed to go to the Mount of Olives and mourn the Temple from afar. At some point after this—we do not know exactly when—they were also given permission to go up to the ruined Temple Mount on the ninth day of the Jewish month of Av, the anniversary of the Temple's destruction. According to a document found in the Cairo Geniza, the pilgrims would begin by standing barefoot on the Mount of Olives, gazing at the ruins, and tearing their garments, crying: "This sanctuary is destroyed!" Then they would go into Aelia, climb up to the Temple platform, and weep "for the Temple and the people and the House of Israel." These sad rites were very different from the old joyful pilgrimages, because the Jews now encountered desolation and emptiness instead of a Presence. Yet the annual ceremony on the Temple Mount helped them to face up to their grief, confront it, and come through on the other side. The ceremony would end with prayers of thanksgiving, and then the pilgrims would "circle all the gates of the city and go around all its corners, make a circuit and count its towers," just as their forefathers had done when the Temple was still standing.[47] They were not deterred by the fact that these gates had been built by the Romans; this was a symbolic rite of passage from despair to hope. In circling the city as though it still belonged to them, the pilgrims were looking forward to the final messianic deliverance: "Next year in Jerusalem!"

After the Bar Kokhba war, the Jewish Christian community had also been expelled from Aelia, because, whatever their religious persuasion, the ban had applied to them too as circumcised Jews. But some of the Greek and Syrian colonists imported by Hadrian were probably Christians, because we hear of a wholly gentile church in Aelia thereafter.[48] These non-Jewish Christians took over the "Upper Room" on Mount Sion, which was outside Aelia proper and had therefore been spared by Hadrian's contractors. This was just an ordinary private house: Christianity was not yet one of the permitted religions of the Roman empire and, indeed, was often persecuted by the authorities. Christians were not permitted to build their own places of worship. But they liked to call the house of the Upper Room the "Mother of the churches," since this was where Christianity came into being. The gentile Christians also possessed a throne which, they believed, had belonged to James the Tzaddik, the first "bishop" of Jerusalem. There were not many other Christian "holy places" in Aelia, however. The city that Jesus had known had now been obliterated by Hadrian's new town. Golgotha, for example, was now buried under the Temple of Aphrodite, and Christians would not want to worship there. But, Eusebius tells us, the site was "pointed out" to visitors.[49] Melito, bishop of Sardis, had seen it when he visited Palestine in 160, and he told his flock back home that Golgotha was now in the middle of the city.[50] In Jesus's day, of course, Golgotha had been outside the walls, but now the buried hillock was next to Aelia's main forum.

Not many Christians came to Palestine as pilgrims. Eusebius says that "crowds" came "from all over the world" to visit Jerusalem,[51] but even he could only name four pilgrims, one of whom was Melito, who had absolutely no interest in the city of Aelia. It was "worthless now because of the Jerusalem above."[52] Melito had come to Palestine for scholarly, not devotional, reasons: he hoped to further his biblical studies by researching the country's topology. Gentile Christians were primarily interested in the heavenly Jerusalem, as described by John in the Book of Revelation—a text that was quoted more frequently in the second century than any other Christian scripture. They looked forward to the New Jerusalem that would descend to earth at the end of time and transform its earthly counterpart.[53] But nobody was particularly interested in visiting Aelia. Eusebius was writing apologetics: he wanted to get Christianity legalized, and he probably exaggerated the number of pilgrims to demonstrate the universal appeal of his faith. There is no evidence that Jerusalem was a major pilgrim center for Christians during the second and third centuries. In fact, gentile Christians tended to agree with the gospels of Matthew and John. Jerusalem was now the Guilty City because it had rejected Christ. Jesus had said that in future people would not gather in such holy places as Jerusalem but would worship him in spirit and truth. Devotion to shrines and holy mountains was characteristic of paganism and Judaism, both of which Christians were anxious to transcend.

Thus Jerusalem had no special status on the Christian map. The bishop of Caesarea was the chief prelate of Palestine, not the bishop of Aelia. When Origen, the illustrious Christian scholar, settled in Palestine in 234, he chose to establish his academy and library in Caesarea. When he traveled around the country he was, like Melito, chiefly interested in biblical topology. He certainly did not expect to get a spiritual experience by visiting a mere geographical location, however august its associations. It was, he believed, only pagans who sought God in a shrine and thought that the gods dwelt "in a particular place."[54] It was interesting to visit a place such as Bethlehem, where Jesus had been born, and see the manger (which had—apparently—been preserved), because it proved that the gospel story was accurate. But Origen was a Platonist. In his view, Christians should liberate themselves from the physical world and seek the wholly spiritual God. They should not cling to earthly places but "seek the heavenly city in place of the earthly."[55]

Yet even though there was no widespread cult of Jerusalem, it seems that the local Christians of Aelia liked to visit sites outside the city connected with Jesus. Eusebius tells us that they frequented the summit of the Mount of Olives, whence Jesus had ascended to heaven; the Garden of Gethsemane in the Kidron Valley, where he had prayed in agony before his arrest; and the River Jordan, where he had been baptized by John the Baptist.[56] Grottoes were regarded as particularly numinous places in the Greco-Roman world, and Aelia's Christians also visited two caves. The first was in Bethlehem, the birthplace of Jesus; the second was on the Mount of Olives, where the risen Christ was said to have appeared to the apostle John.[57] Christians did not go to these caves to remember Jesus the man; there was, as yet, little interest in Jesus's earthly life. The caves were important because they had witnessed a theophany: in both, the incarnate Logos had been revealed to the world.

But the cave on the Mount of Olives had an added significance. It was said to be the place where Jesus had instructed his disciples about the forthcoming destruction of Jerusalem and the Last Days.[58] The Christians seem to have been much stirred by the sight of the Jews mourning their lost Temple on the Mount of Olives. Origen found these ceremonies pathetic and misguided, but he also noted that the plight of the Jews was another proof of the veracity of the gospels. Prophecy and inspired oracles were very important in late antiquity, so the fact that Jesus had accurately predicted the destruction of the Jewish Temple would have impressed Origen's pagan adversaries. Ever since they had rejected Jesus, he pointed out, "all the institutions in which the Jews took such pride, I mean those connected with the Temple and the Altar of Sacrifice and the rites which were celebrated and the vestments of the high priests, have been destroyed."[59] This was profoundly satisfying. The Christians of Aelia seem to have developed their own counter-ceremony on the Mount of Olives. Eusebius says that they liked to go up to the cave there "to learn about the city being taken and devastated."[60] Looking down on the desolate Temple platform, with the statues of the victorious emperors, they could contemplate the defeat of Judaism and the survival of their own faith, which may not have been winning many converts in Palestine at this time but was making great strides in the rest of the empire. As they meditated on Roman Aelia, reflecting on the fact that it had been built on the ruins of the Guilty City, they had visual proof of the truth of their own religion. Yet there was a disquieting note. Like the rabbis, Jesus and Paul had both stressed the supreme importance of charity and loving-kindness. In fact, Jesus had gone so far as to say that Christians should love their enemies. But these third-century Christians seem to have indulged in some rather unholy gloating when they contemplated the fate of the Jews who had dwelt in this city before them. Monotheists have always had to come to terms with the fact that previous occupants of Jerusalem venerated it as a holy city, and the integrity of their own tenure often depends upon their response to this fact. The Christians of Aelia did not seem to have got off to a good start here: it did not seem as though the experience of living in the city where Christ had died and risen again had inspired them to live up to their noblest ideals.

Eusebius became bishop of Caesarea in 313, a date of great significance for the Christians of the Roman empire. Like Origen, Eusebius was a Platonist and had no interest in shrines or sacred space. Christianity, in his view, had left these primitive enthusiasms behind. There was nothing special about Palestine, he asserted: "it in no way excels the rest [of the earth]."[61] Aelia was simply the Guilty City: it was quite unworthy of veneration and helpful to Christians only insofar as it symbolized the death of Judaism. By this time few people even remembered the original name of the city: Eusebius himself always called it Aelia. For him—as for most gentile Christians—"Jerusalem" meant the heavenly Zion, a reality that was entirely out of this world. But in 312, Constantine had defeated his imperial rival Maxentius at the battle of Milvian Bridge and attributed his victory to the God of the Christians. In 313, the year of Eusebius's accession, Constantine declared that Christianity was one of the official religions of the Roman empire. From being persecuted, marginalized, with no stake in this world, no political power and no holy cities, Christianity would now begin to acquire a mundane dimension. Ultimately this would radically change the way that Christians saw "Aelia."

9

THE NEW JERUSALEM

CONSTANTINE had become emperor in the West after his victory at the Milvian Bridge. In 323 he went on to defeat Licinius, emperor of the eastern provinces, and become sole ruler of the Roman world. Constantine always attributed his astonishing rise from obscurity to the God of the Christians, and though he had very little understanding of its theology and delayed his baptism until he was on his deathbed, he would continue to be loyal to the church. He also hoped that once it was legalized, Christianity could become a cohesive force in his far-flung empire. In Palestine only a tiny minority of the total population was then Christian, but during the third century Christianity had emerged as one of the most important religions of the empire and one of the largest in numbers of adherents. By 235, Christians could boast of a "Great Church" with a single rule of faith. It had begun to attract highly intelligent men who could interpret this originally Semitic religion in a way that the broad Greco-Roman world could understand. During the years of persecution the church had evolved an efficient administration, which was a microcosm of the empire itself: it was multicultural, catholic, international, and ecumenical and was run by capable bureaucrats. Now that Constantine had made the church *religio licta,* Christians could come out of hiding and make a distinctive contribution to public life, and Constantine hoped to channel its power and skill into the *imperium.*

Yet he would not promote Christianity at the expense of other faiths. Constantine was a realist and knew that he could not afford to antagonize his pagan subjects. He retained the title *pontifex maximus,* and the old sacrificial cult of the empire continued unabated. Constantine did find one way to begin to express his vision of the new Christian Rome—by a huge building program. In Rome he built shrines at the tombs of the Christian martyrs and a *martyrium,* or mausoleum, similar to those commemorating Roman emperors, to St. Peter the Apostle. These new church buildings were nothing like the ancient temples: they were not designed as cosmic symbols, and the newly emancipated church had yet to evolve a public ceremonial liturgy. But these basilicas had started to appear alongside the pagan symbols of Rome, and showed that Christianity had begun to take its place in the world. In Rome, however, the central sites were already occupied by pagan buildings, and Constantine's *martyria* had to be confined to marginal areas. But no such restrictions applied in the new imperial capital he built for himself on the Bosphorus, on the site of the ancient Greek city of Byzantium. Constantinople could be a wholly Christian city, where the cross could be displayed proudly and centrally and statues of biblical heroes could adorn its squares. Yet Constantinople had no history: the emperor, who had a near-magical belief in the power of symbols, knew that his Christian empire must be shown to have roots in a venerable past if it was to express that continuity which was such a crucial value in late antiquity.

One of Constantine's most ardent supporters in the early years of his reign was Eusebius, bishop of Caesarea. After Milvian Bridge, Eusebius hailed the emperor as a new Moses who had cut down Maxentius as Moses had smitten the Egyptians.[1] He also called Constantine a second Abraham, one who would restore the pure monotheism of the patriarchs.[2] Abraham, Isaac, and Jacob, he argued, had had no Temple and no elaborate Torah: Eusebius pointed out that they had worshipped God wherever they found themselves, simply, in spirit and truth.[3] Eusebius had stood on the Mount of Olives like the other Christians of the region contemplating the ruined Temple Mount. He found it a grim irony that the citizens of Aelia had pillaged the stones of the Temple to build their pagan shrines and theaters.[4] The fate of the Temple was clear proof that God no longer wanted that showy type of sacrificial ritual. He wanted them to follow the spiritual religion preached by Jesus, which did not depend on temples or holy places. Like Origen, Eusebius had no time for sacred geography. God would not come to those who sought him in "lifeless matter and dusky caves" but only to "souls purified and prepared with clear and rational minds."[5] The Law of Moses required believers to hurry to one single holy place but Eusebius imagined Christ saying:

> I, giving freedom to all, teach men not to look for God in a corner of the earth, nor in mountains, nor in temples made with hands, but that each should worship and adore him at home.[6]

He had come to teach men the primordial religion of Abraham, free from irrational mythology and carnal imagery.

With considerable satisfaction, Eusebius gazed at the suburb of Mount Sion, imagining, like all his contemporaries, that this had been the site of the biblical Zion. Now instead of being a center of study and learning, Mount Sion was merely "a Roman farm, like the rest of the country. Indeed, with my own eyes, I have seen bulls plowing there and the holy place sown with seed."[7] Devastated and deserted, the present state of "Zion" proved that God had indeed abandoned the city. It is interesting, however, that Eusebius never mentioned that Mount Sion was also the Christian center of Aelia. By the beginning of the fourth century, the local Christians had started to argue that, as the "Mother of the churches," Aelia should have higher ecclesiastical status than Caesarea, which had no sacred associations. Besides displaying the throne of James the Tzaddik, they had also begun to identify some of the ruins on Mount Sion as important biblical landmarks: one old house was thought to be the residence of Caiaphas, another the palace of King David. There was a pillar that was supposed to be the place where Jesus had been scourged by Pilate. Yet Eusebius ignored these developments. In the *Onomasticon,* his guide to the place-names of the Bible, he had pointed out that the geography of Palestine "proved" the accuracy of the gospels: the towns and villages were exactly where the evangelists said. But Eusebius never cited the sites on Mount Sion as proofs or witnesses of the life of Christ. He may as a historian have been rightly skeptical of their authenticity, but he could also have been aware that Makarios, the bishop of Aelia, was using these places to support his campaign to make Aelia the metropolitan see of Palestine instead of Eusebius's own see of Caesarea.

The conflict between Caesarea and Aelia came out into the open in 318, when Eusebius and Makarios found themselves on opposite sides of a doctrinal controversy that threatened to split the whole church down the middle. Arius, a charismatic presbyter of Alexandria, had put forward the argument, which he was able to back up with an impressive array of biblical texts, that Jesus, the incarnate Logos, was not divine in the same way as God the Father: he had been created by God before the beginning of time.[8] Arius did not deny the divinity of Christ—he called Jesus "strong God" and "true God"—but he did not think that he was divine by nature. God the Father had conferred divinity upon him as a reward for Jesus's perfect obedience.[9] Jesus himself had said that his Father was greater than he. Arius's ideas were not new, nor were they, at this date, obviously heretical. The great Origen had had a rather similar view of Jesus. Christians had long believed that Jesus was God, but they had as yet no agreement about what this actually meant. If Jesus was divine,

were there not in fact two gods? Was it not idolatry to worship a mere
man? Arius may have expressed his theology more clearly and forcefully
than his predecessors, but many of the bishops had similar notions, and
at the beginning of the dispute it was by no means clear why—or even
whether—Arius was wrong.

Arius was opposed by his bishop, Alexander, and the bishop's brilliant
young assistant Athanasius, who argued that the Logos was God in
exactly the same way as God the Father. He shared the same nature as
God the Father and had been neither begotten nor created. Had the
Logos been a mere creature, called by the Father from a primal, abysmal
nothingness, he would not have been able to save humanity from death
and extinction. Only the One who had created the world had the
strength to save it, so Jesus, the Logos made flesh, must share the Father's
essential divinity. His death and resurrection had redeemed human
beings from sin and mortality, and now, by incorporation into Christ, the
god-man, men and women could also become divine.

The conflict grew heated, and bishops were forced to take sides. In
Palestine, Makarios sided with Athanasius and Eusebius with Arius,
whose theology bore some resemblance to his own. Again, it must be
emphasized that when he took this position, Eusebius was not flying in
the face of the official doctrine of the church. There was, as yet, no
orthodox teaching on the person and nature of Christ. Eusebius was one
of the leading Christian intellectuals of his generation, and his views
were similar to those espoused by several previous theologians. Athanasius saw Christ's coming as dramatic and unique, but Eusebius's interpretation of Christianity stressed its quiet continuity with the past.
Athanasius saw the incarnation of the Logos as an absolutely unparal-
leled event in world history: the divine had erupted into the mundane
sphere in an entirely unprecedented way. Jesus was, therefore, the one
and only revelation of God. Eusebius did not believe this. In his view,
God had revealed himself to humanity before. The Logos had appeared
to Abraham in human form at Mamre;[10] Moses and Joshua had experienced similar epiphanies. So the Logos had simply returned to earth in
Jesus of Nazareth.[11] The incarnation was not a unique event but clarified
theophanies of the past. God's revelation of himself to humanity was an
ongoing process.

Athanasius saw the *salvation* of the world as Jesus's most important
achievement. Eusebius did not see it quite in this light; certainly Jesus
had saved us, but his principal task was to be a *revelation* of God to the
world. Jesus had been a theophany: by looking at him, human beings
could form some idea of what the invisible, indescribable God was like.
One of Jesus's chief objectives had been to remind Christians of the

essentially spiritual nature of religion. Over the centuries, men and women had forgotten Abraham's pure spirituality and had muddied their faith with such physical emblems as the Torah and the Temple. Jesus had come to remind us of this ancient purity. Thus we should not focus on Christ's humanity: Eusebius once wrote a sharp letter to Constantia, the emperor's sister, who had foolishly asked him for a picture of Jesus. Christians should look through the flesh to the divine essence of the heavenly Logos. After his sojourn on earth, the Logos had returned to the spiritual realm, and Christians should follow him there. The attachment of permanent value to Jesus's humanity was as perverse and irrational as the Jews' attachment to an earthly city. Christians were engaged in a constant *katharsis,* or purification. They must learn to read Scripture in a more spiritual way, looking for the timeless truth within the historical event. Thus Jesus's resurrection was not the dramatic, eruptive act that Athanasius envisaged; it simply revealed the immortality that was natural to the human condition.

These were clearly imponderable issues, impossible to prove one way or the other, yet the dispute was threatening to tear the church apart. This was infuriating to Constantine, who could not understand the theology but had no intention of allowing these intellectual quibbles to divide the institution that was supposed to be cohesive and unitive. By the beginning of 325, Athanasius's party had won his support, excommunications were issued against the "Arian" leaders, and Constantine summoned all the prelates of the church to a council to sort the matter out once and for all. Thus it happened that Eusebius—then sixty-five years old and one of the most eminent bishops in the church—found that when he arrived at Nicaea in May to take part in the council, he had been excommunicated. His rival Makarios, however, who had managed to pick the winning side, was in a very strong position: surely his colleagues would see that it was intolerable that the bishop of Aelia, the Mother of the churches, should be subject to the heretical bishop of Caesarea.

The Council of Nicaea issued an official creed that expressed Athanasius's ideas but was unable to bring peace to the church. Most of the bishops would have espoused views midway between those of Athanasius and Arius and probably regarded both as extreme and eccentric. Under pressure from the emperor, however, all the bishops save two brave Arian supporters signed the creed for the sake of peace; but afterward they continued teaching as before. Again, they were not contumaciously embracing heresy. The Council of Nicaea was the first ecumenical council of the church, and there was as yet no tradition to insist that its decrees were "infallible." The bishops understandably felt that their own views should also be heard, and the result was that the Arian controversy dragged on for another sixty years. One of the prelates who signed the creed was Eusebius, but after the council he immediately began to campaign against Athanasian "orthodoxy." He wrote a treatise called *Theophany*, which put forward his view of Jesus, and, as he had always supported Constantine, was able to gain the emperor's ear. In 327, two years after Nicaea, Eusebius's moderate party gained the ascendancy and the ban on Arius was lifted.

Yet if the Council of Nicaea had little effect on theological realpolitik, it would have immense repercussions on the history of Jerusalem. First, Makarios had been able to exploit his position: the seventh canon of the council insisted that "custom and ancient tradition" decreed that the bishop of Aelia should hold an honored position in the church, though he was still subordinate to the metropolitan bishop of Caesarea. Makarios did not get everything he wanted, but it seems likely that it was at Nicaea that he proposed a scheme that would have far more impact on the status of Aelia than a cautiously worded conciliar directive and would do far more to ensure the eventual victory of Athanasius's theology than the creed signed by the reluctant bishops. Makarios asked Constantine's permission to demolish the Temple of Aphrodite and unearth the Tomb of Christ, which was said to be buried beneath it.

This proposal immediately appealed to Constantine, who, a pagan at heart, did not share Eusebius's lofty disdain for holy places. He wanted to visit Palestine himself, and his mother-in-law, Eutropia, had already begun her trip to the Land of the Bible. Constantine also knew that his Christian empire needed symbols and monuments to give it a historical resonance. Makarios's extraordinary plan was also very risky. The vast majority of the inhabitants of Aelia were pagan, and they would not take kindly to having one of their principal temples destroyed. They would have to agree if the excavations had imperial backing, but it was nearly two hundred years since Hadrian's contractors had built the Temple of Aphrodite. How certain could the Christians be that Golgotha and the tomb really were under that shrine? The pagans of Aelia would be understandably enraged if they lost their temple for nothing. Emperor and church alike would suffer an unacceptable embarrassment, not to mention the fact that if the excavations drew a blank, this might reveal a worrying lacuna at the heart of imperial Christianity.

Nevertheless, Constantine gave his permission, and work began immediately after the council under the supervision of Makarios. There were two sites, which were worked on simultaneously. First, Constantine had ordered a house of prayer to be built beside the Cardo Maximus, the main street of Aelia, some yards east of the supposed site of Golgotha.

This was a relatively straightforward project, and the construction proceeded swiftly, without a hitch. The second task was much more onerous. The Temple of Aphrodite had to be demolished, the supporting platform dismantled, and the ground beneath leveled. This massive undertaking had a twofold religious dimension. First, the Christians were delving beneath the pagan city to make contact with the historical roots of their faith. During the persecutions, the murderous hatred of the pagan establishment led Christians to believe that the world was against them. They had developed an otherworldly theology, certain that they had no abiding city here below. But since Constantine's succession, they had experienced a spectacular reversal and were beginning to feel that they had a stake in this world after all. This act of holy archaeology would lay bare the physical roots of their faith and enable them to build literally on these ancient foundations. A new Christian identity was also in the process of being constructed. The second aspect of this building project was less positive. The creation of the new Christianity involved the dismantling of paganism, eloquently symbolized by the destruction of Aphrodite's temple. The demolition took on the character of a ritual purification. Paganism was "filth": every last trace of the temple was to be obliterated, the materials cast out of the city, and even the soil beneath transported to a "far distant spot" because "it had been polluted by the defilements of pagan worship."[12] The new birth of Christianity involved the rooting out and undermining of paganism, which had the very ground cut from beneath it.

As the excavations proceeded, Makarios and his colleagues must have had some bad moments: they knew that they had to find something. Yet it was two years before the grand discovery was made. A rock tomb was unearthed beneath the old Temple platform and was immediately declared to be the sepulcher of Christ. Even Eusebius, who had every reason to be skeptical, did not question the authenticity of this relic. Although the discovery had been eagerly anticipated, the find stunned the Christian world. Eusebius described the event as "contrary to all expectation," and even Constantine felt that it "surpassed all astonishment."[13] One of the reasons for this amazed acceptance was probably that the event fitted so closely with the internal dimension of what seemed to be happening that it appeared to have a mythical quality. Three hundred years earlier, Jesus had risen from that tomb. Now the tomb itself had risen, as it were, from its own untimely grave, just as Christians were witnessing an unlooked-for resurgence of their faith.

The rock tomb had been found in an ancient quarry which had been obliterated by Hadrian's builders. Now it had to be disengaged from the surrounding hillside in such a way that the mass of rock surrounding the

cave was retained. Then a circular space about 38 yards in diameter had
to be cut around it to clear the site for the circular martyrium commissioned by the emperor. That meant that about 16,500 cubic feet of rock
had to be hacked by pickaxes into building blocks that could be used for
the monument. It was a huge undertaking and this round shrine—
which would be called the Anastasis, or Resurrection—was not finished
until long after Constantine's death. For many years, the tomb in its
huge block of cliff remained outside in the open air, while the ground
was prepared. At the same time as they unearthed the tomb, the workers
also discovered what they identified as the rocky hillock of Golgotha.
Since what remains of this rock is today almost entirely encased in the
Golgotha chapel of the Holy Sepulcher Church, it is difficult to imagine
how it appeared originally. Excavations undertaken in 1961 suggest that
"Golgotha" was a vertical block of stone, about ten meters high, which
had probably stood by itself in the corner of the quarry. At its base was a
cave, which may long before Jesus's time have been a tomb. Could this
stone column have been a memorial stone, similar to those found in the
Kidron Valley? By the time Jesus was crucified, earth had accumulated
around the block to form a hillock, from which the rock protruded like
a skullcap, giving the hill its name of Golgotha: the Place of the Skull.

Thus the excavations had brought to light not one holy site but two:
the hill on which Jesus had been crucified and the tomb in which he had
been buried. Meanwhile, Constantine's basilica was nearing completion.
Constantine wanted the church to be the finest in the world. No expense was to be spared, and the building was financed by contributions
from all the governors of the eastern provinces. Space was limited, however, so the basilica was quite small: it cannot have exceeded 44 by 30
yards. It had five naves, one of which included the Rock of Golgotha,
and ended in a semicircular apse at the western end, nearest the tomb.
For Eusebius, the only contemporary writer to record his impressions,
the basilica was a place of wondrous beauty. It was lined inside and out
by slabs of variegated marble and polished stone; the interior "was finished with carvings of panel work, and, like a great sea, covered the
whole basilica with its endless swell, while the brilliant gold with which
it was covered made the whole temple sparkle with rays of light."[14] The
basilica of St. Constantine was usually known as the Martyrium, because
it was a "witness" to the resurrection and a memorial to Christ.

It was thus a complex site, which introduced the worshipper to the
tomb, the new Holy of Holies, step by step, rather like the old Jewish
Temple. (See diagram.) Visitors entered the Martyrium from the Cardo
Maximus in the heart of pagan Aelia. Its three doors were left ajar, so that
strangers could glimpse the splendors of the church and feel moved to

Today an elaborate shrine covers the remains of the rock of Golgotha within the Holy Sepulcher Church. The discovery of this relic led Christians to concentrate on Christ's crucifixion in an entirely new way.

enter. First, they had to walk through a courtyard before entering the basilica, which was itself simply another step along the way. All the western doors of the basilica opened into the large courtyard in front of the tomb, designed to accommodate crowds of pilgrims. A garden was planted there in memory of the garden where the women had first seen the risen Christ. Constantine had taken possession of the center point of Roman Aelia and transformed it into a Christian holy place. He had built a New Jerusalem beside the forum of Aelia. Hitherto Aelia had been off the spiritual map of most gentile Christians, and in the city itself the church had been marginalized, located outside the walls in the largely uninhabited suburb of Mount Sion. Now Constantine had demonstrated the centrality of the new faith to his empire. It was a gesture that immediately captivated the Christian imagination. As soon as the tomb had been discovered and the lovely basilica completed, Christians

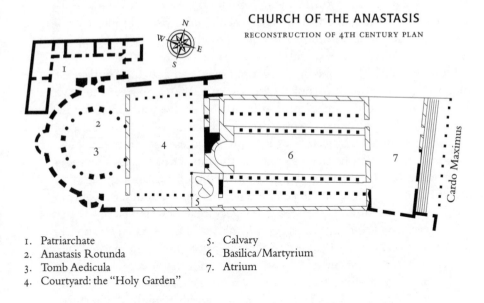

CHURCH OF THE ANASTASIS

RECONSTRUCTION OF 4TH CENTURY PLAN

1. Patriarchate
2. Anastasis Rotunda
3. Tomb Aedicula
4. Courtyard: the "Holy Garden"
5. Calvary
6. Basilica/Martyrium
7. Atrium

started to evolve their own mythology about the place, which located it at the heart of their spirituality. They recalled the old Jewish-Christian tradition that Adam had been buried at Golgotha. Soon they had also come to believe that Abraham had bound Isaac for sacrifice there. This new Christian holy place had started to inspire the same kind of belief and legend as the old Jewish Temple. It had become a symbolic "center," where the divine power had touched the frail world of humanity in a unique way. It represented a new start for humanity, a fulfillment of the religion of Abraham and a new era in Christian history.

Yet Christians had thought that they were above this type of piety. They had proudly proclaimed that theirs was a purely spiritual faith that was not dependent upon shrines and holy places. Their startling response to the discovery of the tomb shows that the myths of sacred geography are deeply rooted in the human psyche. A sudden shock or an unexpected reunion with one of the physical symbols of our faith and culture can reawaken this enthusiasm for sacred space, particularly after a period of persecution when people have experienced the threat of annihilation in an especially acute manner. It is never safe to assume that we have outgrown these primal myths: even in the secular, scientific world of the twentieth century, we are not immune to their appeal, as we can see in Jerusalem today. When they looked at the resurrected tomb, the Christians felt a shock of recognition and, for the first time, were impelled to root themselves in a physical place, make a home for themselves in the mundane world and appropriate this sacred area. This healing link with the past enabled them to place themselves right in the center of Roman Aelia, abandon their marginal position, and take up an entirely new place in the world.

Nobody could have been more opposed to the whole notion of sacred space than Eusebius, but the discovery of the tomb seems to have touched him to the core of his being, so that he was forced to revise some of his former beliefs. Now that he was back in favor with Constantine, Eusebius had the task of interpreting these astonishing events. He found that when he tried to explain the impact of this archaeological find, he had to resort to the kind of mythological language he had hitherto despised. Its significance could not be explained in terms of reason but only according to the old imagery that described the deeper workings of the mind and heart. The tomb was a theophany: an apparition, in physical form, of something previously hidden and inaccessible. It reproduced the miracle of Christ's resurrection from the dead, which now seemed to Eusebius to have been a victory over the powers of darkness, not unlike those described in the old combat myths. "The most holy cave received what was an exact emblem of its coming to life," he wrote in his official *Life of Constantine*, "for after its descent into darkness it again came forth into light, and afforded to those who came to see a clear insight into the history of the wonders which had there been wrought."[15] The destruction of the Temple of Aphrodite had been a triumph over the powers of evil, for it had been "the haunt of an impure demon called Aphrodite, a dark shrine of lifeless idols." Abominations had been practiced there, "foul oblations on profane and accursed altars." But the God of light who illumines men's hearts had inspired Constantine to order a *katharsis* of this filth. "As soon as his orders were given, the contrivances of deceit were cast down from on high to the ground, and the dwelling places of error, images, and demons and all were overthrown and utterly destroyed."[16] The tomb had reproduced the whole Christian experience, for its discovery had been simultaneously a revelation, a resurrection, and a victory for the forces of light. Hitherto Eusebius had seen the resurrection in much calmer terms: now he had started to invest this event with some of the drama it had in Athanasius's theology.

Eusebius does not seem to have been very interested in the Rock of Golgotha: he never mentions it. But the sight of the cave, so recently hewn out of the rocky hillside, moved him profoundly. He was struck by its solitude—"standing out erect and alone in a level land"—and by the fact that no other body had ever been placed there.[17] It was an emblem of the uniqueness of Christ's victory. When he looked at the tomb, the events of Christ's life became vivid for Eusebius in an entirely new way. If we are not able to envisage the place in which something happened to us, it is very difficult to recall it in any detail. Seeing this place bridged the gap between past and present in a way that mere hearsay could not do. Eusebius acknowledged that the sight of the tomb "spoke louder than all words."[18] Other Christians would find that it made sense of Athanasius's theology of incarnation. Instead of looking through the human figure of Jesus to the divinity, as Eusebius had advised, they would want to see and touch the places associated with his humanity and find that Jesus the man was a powerful symbol of God's link with the world.

Eusebius had not entirely reversed his opinions, however. He continued to call the city Aelia: there was nothing holy about this pagan metropolis, and it was "not only base but impious" to imagine that there was, "the mark of an exceedingly base and petty thinking."[19] The name "Jerusalem" applied only to the tomb and to Constantine's new buildings on the Western Hill. The rest of the city was as profane and guilty as ever. Eusebius called the Constantinian complex the *New* Jerusalem precisely because it was "built over against the old."[20] It was utterly distinct from the old Jewish city which had been cursed by Christ. Indeed, the New Jerusalem gave Christians yet another vantage point from which to contemplate the defeat of Judaism. Situated on one of the highest points of the Western Hill, the Martyrium towered above the desecrated Temple Mount. It was a graphic illustration of the resurgence of the new faith, which now enjoyed imperial backing while Judaism was entirely off the map of Aelia. To that extent the establishment of the New Jerusalem reinforced Eusebius's former beliefs. Christianity had now been able to come out of hiding and put down roots in the mundane world. It was now able to take its place alongside the other institutions of the empire and was acquiring a wholly new identity. The New Jerusalem was an important part of this process. But this new Christian self was based on a destructive rejection of the older religious traditions, and this had become obvious in Aelia. The New Jerusalem was "built over *against*" its predecessors: its establishment had entailed a violent uprooting of pagan religion, a demonization of older traditions, and a contemptuous assertion of superiority over Judaism. Christians would make sure that Jews were never permitted to live in Jerusalem while they were in power there. The old ban remained on the imperial statute books. Christianity may have been liberated from oppression but it was still embattled and defensive, poised in an attitude of resolute and destructive opposition to its rivals. Persecution does not always make its victims compassionate. From the start the New Jerusalem involved the exclusion and denigration of others in a way that was far removed from the compassionate ethic of Jesus.

Eusebius therefore continued to see Aelia as hopelessly contaminated by both Judaism and paganism. He also continued to ignore the new "holy places" on Mount Sion and may have used his influence with Constantine to ensure that they got no imperial funding. They were too important to his rival Makarios: the bishop of Aelia had certainly achieved a coup by masterminding the discovery of the tomb, but in the coming years Eusebius was able to ensure that *his* theology was also reflected in the Christianization of Palestine. Thus when Eutropia, Constantine's mother-in-law, visited the country, Eusebius, as metropolitan, almost certainly had the honor of conducting her around the sites. At Mamre, near Hebron, he drew her attention to the dubious worship going on at the very place where Abraham had received his theophany. Abraham, it will be recalled, was very important to Eusebius, and he would have been horrified by the festival in which Jews, Christians, and pagans celebrated the patriarch on the site of his sacred oak tree. Each year, people came from the various districts of Palestine, Phoenicia, and Arabia to hold an annual fair and a magnificent feast, to which everybody contributed: Jews, Christians, and pagans would pray to God or to Zeus Olympios, the God of all; they would call upon the angels, make libations of wine and burn incense; pagans would sacrifice an ox or a sheep. It was a decorous occasion; people used to wear their best clothes for the festival and there was no licentiousness or debauchery. But Eusebius had no time for this ecumenical gathering, which seemed to him an unholy consorting with false religion. He made sure that Eutropia informed Constantine about the festival in a way that would get Makarios into trouble. Since Mamre was in Makarios's diocese, Constantine wrote him a stern letter, rebuking him for permitting these "unhallowed pollutions." The letter shows that Constantine had already begun to be influenced by Eusebius's theology. It was at Mamre that the religion of the Logos had been founded; "there first did the observance of the holy law receive its beginning; there first did the Savior himself with the two angels vouchsafe the manifestation of his presence to Abraham."[21] A new basilica was built beside Abraham's altar, well and oak tree by the emperor whom Eusebius had hailed as the second Abraham.

Constantine had intended to visit Palestine himself, but was prevented by the continued rumblings of the Arian conflict which kept him occupied in Constantinople. Instead he sent his mother, the dowager empress Helena Augusta. Helena's "pilgrimage" to the Holy Land has been enshrined in Christian legend as an act of personal piety, but in fact her tour of the eastern provinces in 326 was an imperial progress that finished with a grand flourish in Jerusalem. Like Hadrian, Constantine used the progress to advertise his particular conception of the Roman empire: the sight of the aged dowager and her huge entourage praying at the Christian holy places was a powerful symbol of Constantine's Christian Rome. Hadrian had built temples, stadia, and aqueducts during his progress: Aelia Capitolina had been his gift to the people of Palestine. Now Helena donated new churches. She had arrived during the planning of the Martyrium and the excavations for the tomb. She may even have been present when the tomb was discovered in 327. Again, Eusebius probably had the job of escorting Helena around Palestine, and he may have suggested the location of the two new churches commissioned by the empress. He had always been enthusiastic about the two caves—one in Bethlehem at Christ's birthplace and the other on the Mount of Olives—which had been sites of theophanies of the incarnate Logos. The caves thus expressed his view of the revelatory nature of Jesus's mission. Helena herself had Arian sympathies, and she may have been responsive to Eusebius's doctrines. At all events, the dowager commissioned two new basilicas to consecrate these caves. Eusebius might well have been pleased to have a holy place established in Bethlehem: the new basilica of the Nativity would deflect Christians' attention from Aelia and the New Jerusalem. The basilica on the Mount of Olives, known as the Eleona, seventy meters from the summit, commanded a magnificent view of the city. As in Constantine's complex of buildings, the basilica at both the Eleona and Bethlehem was separate from the actual "holy place." On the Mount of Olives, staircases led down from the basilica into the sacred cave so that the pilgrims could visit the holy place without disturbing the liturgy. Again, the architecture ensured that worshippers approached the inner sanctum step by step, so that they had time to prepare their minds and hearts.

Helena's visit was soon shrouded in legend. By the middle of the fifth century, Christians tended to believe that she rather than Constantine and Makarios had supervised the excavations at Golgotha. It was also said that she had discovered the relic of the cross on which Jesus had died. In his account of Helena's visit to Palestine, Eusebius never mentioned the finding of the True Cross. We have no contemporary description of this archaeological discovery, but by 390 the cross was part of the Jerusalem scene and portions of the relic had been distributed all over the Christian world. It must have been produced at some time during the excavations of 325–27, and it is not impossible that Helena was involved in this discovery. In the early fourth century, Christians did not dwell overmuch on the Crucifixion as a distinct event in itself. It was seen as inextricably bound up with the Resurrection. Christ's death and his rising from the tomb were seen as two aspects of a single mystery. But the experience of worshipping in Jerusalem would teach Christians to focus on the Crucifixion by itself, as we shall see in the following chapter, and Christ's agonizing death came more to the forefront of the Christian imagination. Ultimately people would not remember the discovery of the tomb; the more famous event would be the legend of Helena's finding of the True Cross.

Before the Golgotha excavations, there had been no pilgrimages to Jerusalem, but once the tomb had been discovered pilgrims started to come from all corners of the Roman empire, even from the distant West. The first to leave an account of his travels came from Bordeaux in 333, his immense journey made slightly easier by the military roads that now linked Europe with the imperial capital at Constantinople. The pilgrimage must have been an astonishing experience, but the Pilgrim's laconic *itinerarium* gives little clue to his feelings: it is merely a catalogue of the biblical sites and the events associated with them. The Pilgrim was utterly single-minded. He did not pause to look at the great monuments of classical antiquity but concentrated solely on places mentioned in the Bible. His guides may have been Jews, since many of the sites he visited were connected with what Christians now called the "Old Testament" and some of the lore he cites was known only in the Jewish tradition. Pilgrimage was still a novel Christian devotion, and the early pilgrims probably had to rely on the Jewish residents of Palestine before they had established their own tours. Nor was the Pilgrim much interested in Jesus's earthly life: he must have passed through Galilee, but he did not bother to visit Nazareth or Capernaum. Instead, he made straight for Jerusalem and headed first for the Temple Mount, pausing only to note the pagan healing cult that still flourished at the Pool of Beth-Hesda.

The Pilgrim's is the first description of the Temple Mount since 70. Over the years, it had become a rather ghostly, sinister place. There was a crypt, the Pilgrim tells us, where King Solomon was said to have tortured devils, and on the site of the Temple itself were stains of the blood of the prophet Zechariah, who had been killed during the persecution of King Jehoash.[22] The marks of the nails made by the Jewish soldiers could still be seen. The desolate platform was associated in the Christian mind with the violence and apostasy of the Jewish people. The Pilgrim described the Jewish mourning rites that were still held there on the Ninth of Av. Not far from the two statues of Hadrian, he says, "there is a perforated stone [*lapis perfusus*], to which the Jews come every year and anoint it, bewail themselves, rend their garments and so depart."[23] The Pilgrim is the only person to mention this stone. Was he referring to the outcrop of rock protruding above Herod's platform, which is today enshrined in the Muslim Dome of the Rock? Was this rock, which is not mentioned in the Bible, beginning to be associated with the Stone of Foundation (Even Shetiyah) in the Devir, mentioned by the rabbis? Or was this stone merely a dramatic piece of fallen masonry? It is not impossible that the Pilgrim, who does not seem to have seen these reported Jewish ceremonies himself, was simply misinformed.

But Christians were beginning to colonize the site imaginatively themselves: the Pilgrim noted a turret still standing at the southeast corner of the platform, which he identified with the "pinnacle of the Temple" where Jesus was tempted by Satan.[24] There was a room in this tower where Solomon was said to have written the Book of Wisdom, and in time this site would be associated with the martyrdom of James the Tzaddik. From the Temple Mount the Pilgrim passed through the Pool of Siloam to the Christian areas of Aelia. On Mount Sion, he was shown the house of Caiaphas, the column where Jesus had been beaten, and "David's palace." He also saw a "synagogue," which may have been a ruin from the days when the Jews had lived in this suburb, or the Pilgrim could have been referring to the house of the Upper Room.[25] Once he had entered the city proper, he saw a ruin in the Tyropoeon Valley, which he believed to be the Praetorium where Jesus had been tried by Pilate. Then he proceeded to Golgotha, where Constantine's basilica was still being built: the "little hill of Golgotha where the Lord was crucified" and the tomb (*crypta*) were still standing in the open.[26] The Pilgrim betrayed no emotion when he saw the New Jerusalem. What is impressive is the huge effort that he had made to get to the Holy Land, which was beginning to be a magnet capable of drawing Christians from the other side of the known world.

In September 335, Constantine's basilica at Golgotha was finally completed and the bishops of all the dioceses in the eastern provinces were summoned to Aelia for the dedication at state expense, together with important imperial officials. It was a momentous occasion. On 17 September, Constantine was to mark the thirtieth anniversary of his accession to the position of Caesar by consecrating the New Jerusalem. For the first time the Martyrium and its courtyards were crowded with distinguished pilgrims. Christians may still have constituted only a small minority in Aelia; the New Jerusalem was merely a little enclave in a pagan city, and all the other new holy places were actually outside the city walls; but the dedication was billed as an imperial event, and it was clear that Christianity was the coming religion of Rome.

Eusebius was one of the many bishops who preached that day, and he used the occasion to promote his own theology. Very cleverly he reassured the absent emperor, who had been unable to attend the ceremony, that his Christian experience was not incomplete simply because he had not come to Aelia. The Logos could visit him in Constantinople just as easily as in the New Jerusalem. Throughout his sermon, he insisted that the Logos had descended to earth to wean humanity away from the physical world. Athanasius had just been deposed and exiled, and Eusebius believed that his moderate party had carried the day. The tomb was undoubtedly a holy place and had immense emotional power, but Christians must not make a fetish of this relic or treat it as an idol. They must always look through the earthly symbols to the spiritual reality beyond.

But Eusebius was now an old man. His view of Christianity and Jerusalem had been standard when he had become bishop of Caesarea in 313, but since then the lives of Christians had been utterly transformed. A whole generation had grown up in a world where Christians were no longer persecuted and no longer hourly expected Christ's Second Coming. They felt at home in the Roman empire, and this inevitably altered their religious perceptions. They wanted to find God here on earth instead of straining endlessly for the things above, and they found Athanasius's incarnational theology more congenial than Eusebius's wholly spiritual doctrine. Some still preferred the Christianity of Arius and Eusebius, but there was a definite shift toward the doctrines of Nicaea. When Eusebius died in 340, he was succeeded as bishop of Caesarea by an ardent Arian, but Makarios was replaced as bishop of Aelia by Maximus, a devout Athanasian. One of his first acts was to build a church around the Upper Room on Mount Sion. He received no imperial grant and had to fund the building himself, so the new basilica was very modest compared with the splendid Constantinian creations. But the Sion basilica became increasingly important. There, it was believed, Jesus had eaten the Last Supper with his disciples, had instituted the Eucharist, and had appeared after the Resurrection. Above all, the Holy Spirit had descended on the apostles there, so that the Upper Room was the birthplace of the church and the Mother of all other churches.

This was certainly the view of Cyril, who became bishop of Aelia in 349. He described his devotion to Jerusalem eloquently in his sermons. The descent of the Spirit on the festival of Pentecost "here in this city of Jerusalem," he claimed, gave the church there "preeminence in all things."[27] The bishops of Aelia would continue to campaign for the primacy of the church in Palestine. Cyril was one of the new generation of Christians. He was five years old when the tomb had been unearthed, and found nothing odd in calling Jerusalem a "holy city." Christ had descended to earth and taken flesh in nearby Bethlehem, he had redeemed the world on Golgotha, ascended to heaven from the Mount of

Olives, and sent down the Spirit to the disciples in the Upper Room. How could the city not be holy when it had witnessed the salvation of the world? The city was not guilty because of the Crucifixion: the Cross was not a shame and a disgrace but the "glory" and the "crown" of Jerusalem.[28] Eusebius had tended to ignore the cross, but Cyril saw the physical death of Jesus as a crucial event in its own right. The cross was the ground of salvation, the basis of our faith, the end of sin. God had rejected the Temple, not the city; he had not condemned Jerusalem but only the Jews. This new positive theology still contained the old rejection and denial and gave it a disturbing new twist. For Cyril, Jerusalem was not the Guilty City: he simply removed the burden of guilt from the city and placed it squarely on the shoulders of the Jews.

Unlike Eusebius, Cyril believed that the humanity of Christ had religious value in itself. There was no need to discount it and seek the spiritual essence of the Logos. By taking a body, God had voluntarily and permanently allied himself with the human race. The image of Jesus the man revealed God's eternal disposition toward us. There was no need to reject the physical world; you could actually use it to seek God. Thus Cyril believed that the holy places of Jerusalem—he never called it Aelia—could bring Christians into contact with the divine. They were the places where God had touched our world, so they now had spiritual potency. They gave Christians an experience of God by breaking down the barrier of space—if not the barrier of time—between them and the life of Jesus. Cyril liked to emphasize that the saving events had happened "in the very city in which we are now."[29] The descent of the Spirit at Pentecost had happened over three hundred years ago, but in another sense it had happened "among us" in Jerusalem.[30] When Christians came into contact with objects that Jesus had touched—the cross, the tomb, the very ground they stood on—they could reach across the years to the absent Christ. "Others merely hear," Cyril liked to say, "but we see and touch."[31] By following literally in Jesus's footsteps, treading where he had trod, the distant events of Jesus's life became a present reality for the pilgrims. Of course, Christ was not confined to a single locality; Christians could experience his presence anywhere in the world. But a visit to the holy places enabled them to stand in space that was still pregnant with the divine Presence.

The New Jerusalem was obviously distressing to the Jews. A small group of zealots may have tried to prevent this Christian building in the Holy Land.[32] It seemed incredible that Christianity, a bastard and apostate form of Judaism, should now have imperial backing. They had been prepared to fight to the death to prevent the building of Aelia Capitolina, but they had since made friends with some of the emperors, and

until Constantine it had not been beyond the bounds of possibility that
the Romans would one day allow the Jews to rebuild their Temple. But
these new Christian buildings in and around Jerusalem were creating
facts that would make it very difficult—if not impossible—for a future
emperor to restore Jerusalem to the Jewish people. Constantine had even
initiated a building project in Galilee, where Jews were in a majority, and
a missionary offensive had been launched in Sepphoris, Tiberias, Capernaum, and Nazareth. Some Jews felt acute despair; others looked for the
Messiah.[33] Most of the rabbis, however, continued to preach moderation. They reminded their people of the catastrophes that had befallen
the Jewish nation when it had attempted to rebel against Rome in the
past. This peculiar imperial preference for Christianity could only be a
temporary enthusiasm.

Yet the position of the Jews continued to deteriorate under the Christian emperors. Constantine himself took no new measures to oppress
the Jewish people, but after his death in 337 his
successors introduced new legislation forbidding
intermarriage between Jews and Christians and
prohibiting Jews from owning slaves—measures
which were designed to isolate the Jews and to
cripple Jewish industry. In 351, Jews revolted in

*The theology of such Christians
as Cyril established the Greek
Orthodox devotion to Jerusalem
which persists to the present day.
Jerusalem was no longer the
Guilty City: the cross is now
regarded as the "glory" and
"crown" of the Christian holy
city.*

Sepphoris, Tiberias, and Lydda, but the Romans suppressed the revolt humanely. In 353, however, Constantius II enacted new legislation, forbidding Christians to convert to Judaism and entering on the empire's official statute books a description of the Jews as "savage," "abominable," and "blasphemous."[34] Jesus had preached a religion of love and forgiveness, but now that Christians had come into power they were beginning to stigmatize Jews as the enemies of society, pushing them to the margins and making them outcasts as the Christians had once been.

The position of the Jews seemed hopeless. The Christians had appropriated their Scriptures, called themselves the new Israel, and had now set about annexing the Jews' Holy City through an imperially funded building program. "Why do you take what is ours," asked a Jew during a debate with Christians, "and make it your own?"[35] Then, suddenly, redemption seemed at hand. In 361, Constantius II died and was succeeded by his nephew Julian.

Julian had been brought up as a Christian. But eventually he came to detest the new faith, which he saw as inimical to Rome's most sacred traditions. Vigorously at odds with Constantine's vision of Christianity as a force promoting empire-wide cohesion, he was now passionately committed to the old pagan religion. He was not alone. Paganism was in fact still alive and well and would continue to flourish all over the empire until the fifth century. To the many people who still loved the old gods and the ancient rites, Christianity represented, as it did to Julian, a flagrantly impious casting off of hallowed traditions. There was widespread anxiety that some fearful catastrophe might ensue if the old gods did not receive their due; the old sacrifices and sanctities must be observed. Pagans, moreover, were deeply offended by the Christian belief in Jesus—a man who had died a disgraceful death—as divine, a notion decidedly counter to their own conceptions of the sacred. When, therefore, the new emperor declared his intention to restore the ancient faith of their fathers to its rightful place in the Roman world, he could rely on the ardent support of great numbers of his subjects.

The Jews, for their part, must have felt at first that they had little to gain from this pagan ruler. But it soon became clear that Julian had a revolutionary plan for Jerusalem.

CHRISTIAN HOLY CITY

O N 19 JULY 362, Jewish delegates from Syria and Asia Minor—
but not, apparently, from the patriarchate in Tiberias—arrived at
Antioch for a meeting with Emperor Julian. They had been summoned
as part of Julian's great plan for the empire. To replace the newfangled
religion of Christ, he wished to see sacrifice offered in all the imperial
domains to the One God, the Supreme Being, who was worshipped
under many names: Zeus, Helios, or God Most High, as he was sometimes called in the Jewish Scriptures. Already in each region, Julian, as
pontifex maximus of Rome, had appointed pagan priests to oppose the
Christian bishops; towns which had never adopted Christianity were
given special privileges, and Christians were being gradually removed
from public office. Although the emperor also disapproved of some
aspects of Judaism, he admired the Jews' fidelity to their ancient faith.
His teacher Iambilicus had taught him that no prayer could reach God
unless it was accompanied by sacrifice; the Jews, however, were no
longer able to celebrate their ancestral rituals. This could only be damaging to the interests of the empire, whose well-being depended upon
the support of God.

When, therefore, the Jewish elders were assembled before him, Julian
asked them why they no longer offered sacrifice to God according to the
Law of Moses. He knew the reason perfectly well, but he was deliberately
setting the stage for the Jews to request the resumption of their cult. The
elders duly explained: "We are not allowed by our Law to sacrifice outside the Holy City. How can we do it now? Restore to us the city, rebuild
the Temple and the altar, and we shall offer sacrifices as in days of old."
This was exactly what Julian wanted to do, not least because it would deal

such a bitter blow to the Christian argument that the defeat of Judaism proved the truth of their, the Christians', scriptures. Now the emperor told the elders: "I shall endeavor with the utmost zeal to set up the Temple of the Most High God."[1] Immediately after the meeting, Julian wrote to Patriarch Hillel II and to all the Jews of the empire, promising to make Jerusalem a Jewish city once more: "I will rebuild the holy city in Jerusalem at my expense and will populate it, as you have wished to see it for these many years."[2]

There was wild enthusiasm in the Jewish communities. The *shofar* was blown in the streets, and it seemed as though the Messiah would shortly arrive. Many Jews turned viciously on the Christians, who had lorded it over them for so long.[3] Crowds of Jews began to arrive in Jerusalem, thronging its streets for the first time in over two hundred years. Others sent contributions for the new Temple. The Jews built a temporary synagogue in one of the ruined porches on the Temple Mount, and Julian may even have asked the Christian inhabitants to restore the property that belonged by rights to the Jewish people. He appointed his scholarly friend Alypius to supervise the building of the Temple and began to amass the materials. Special silver tools were prepared, since the use of iron was forbidden in the construction of the altar. On 5 March 363, Julian and his army left for Persia, where, the emperor believed, the success of his campaign would prove the truth of his pagan vision. When he returned, he promised that he would personally dedicate the Temple as part of the victory celebrations. After the emperor's departure, Jewish workers began to uncover the foundations of the old Temple, clearing away the mounds of rubble and debris. Work continued throughout April and May. But the patriarch and the rabbis of Galilee regarded the venture with deep misgiving:[4] they were now convinced that the Messiah alone could rebuild the Temple. How could a Temple built by an idolater be blessed by God, and what would happen if Julian did not return from Persia?

Now it was the Christians' turn to contemplate an imperial building program that wholly ignored their claim to the Holy City. For fifty years the church had seemed to be going from strength to strength, but Julian's apostasy had shown Christians how vulnerable they really were. The old paganism still flourished, and over the years a great deal of pent-up hostility had accumulated against the church. In Paneas and Sebaste the pagans had actually rioted against Christianity when Julian's edicts were published. His plan to restore the old religion was not an impractical dream, and the Christians knew that. On the day that the work began on the Temple Mount, the Christians of Jerusalem assembled in the Martyrium to implore God to avert this disaster. Then they processed to the Mount of Olives, singing the Jewish psalms that they had made their own. From the spot where generations of Christians had meditated on the defeat of Judaism, they gazed aghast at the purposeful activity on the Temple platform. They had become so accustomed to seeing the decline of Judaism as the essential concomitant to the rise of their own church that the Jewish workmen below seemed to be undermining the fabric of the Christian faith. Bishop Cyril, however, begged them not to lose hope: he confidently foretold that the new Temple would never be completed.

On 27 May, Cyril's prophecy seemed to come true. An earthquake shook the entire city in what seemed to the Christians to be a display of divine wrath. Fire broke out in the vaults underneath the platform, as gases, which had been gathering in the underground chambers, exploded, setting fire to the building materials stored there. According to Alypius's official report, huge "balls of fire" (*globi flammarum*) erupted from the ground, injuring several workmen.[5] By this time, Julian had already crossed the Tigris and burned his bridge of boats. He was now beyond the reach of communications, so Alypius probably decided to wait for further news from the front after this setback. A few weeks later, Julian was killed in battle and Jovian, a Christian, was proclaimed emperor in his stead.

The Christians made no effort to conceal their jubilation after this "miracle": there was talk of a giant cross appearing in the sky, stretching from the Mount of Olives to Golgotha. Other people claimed that crosses mysteriously appeared on the clothes of many pagans and Jews in Jerusalem. These extreme reversals could only intensify the hostility between Christians and Jews. Jovian banned the Jews from Jerusalem and its environs yet again, and when they came to mourn the Temple on the Ninth of Av, the rituals had acquired a new sadness. "They come silently and they go silently," wrote Rabbi Berakiah, "they come weeping and they go weeping."[6] The ceremonies no longer ended in thanksgiving and a bracing procession around the city. Christians regarded these rites with a new harshness. When the biblical scholar Jerome saw this "rabble of the wretched" process to the Temple Mount, he decided that their feeble bodies and tattered clothes were outward signs of their rejection by God. The Jews "are not worthy of compassion," he concluded,[7] with a callousness that showed scant regard for the teaching of Jesus and Paul, who had both declared charity to be the highest religious duty. To Jerome's fury, by the end of the fourth century the Jews seemed to have recovered their nerve. They still proclaimed that the ancient prophecies would be fulfilled. They pointed to Jerusalem, confidently predicting: "There the sanctuary of the Lord will be rebuilt."[8] At the end of time, the Messiah would come and rebuild the city with gold and jewels.

Christians did not forget that they had nearly lost their holy city. They could no longer take their tenure for granted and were determined to establish such a strong Christian presence in Palestine in general and Jerusalem in particular that they could never be dislodged again. The character of the city changed as the Christians gradually began to achieve a majority. By 390 the city was full of monks and nuns and foreign visitors came to Jerusalem in large numbers,[9] returning home with tales of the Holy City and enthusiastic descriptions of its impressive liturgy; others stayed on permanently. Jerome was just one of the new settlers who came from the the West toward the end of the fourth century: some had come as pilgrims, others as refugees from the Germans and Huns who had started to bring down the Roman empire in Europe. This influx from the West increased when Theodosius I, a fervent Spanish Christian, became emperor in 379. He arrived in Constantinople on 24 November 380, with an entourage of pious Spaniards who were committed to implementing his aggressive orthodoxy. In 381, Theodosius put an end to the long Arian controversy by declaring Nicene Christianity to be the official creed of the Roman empire. Ten years later, he banned all pagan sacrifice and closed down the old shrines and temples. Some of the women in the court, such as Empress Aelia Flacilla, had already distinguished themselves in Rome by attacking pagan shrines and building splendid churches in honor of the martyrs. Now they brought this militant Christianity to the East.

The chief focus of Theodosian Christianity in Jerusalem was the hostel on the Mount of Olives which had been founded in 379, the year of Theodosius's accession, by two Western Christians: Rufinus, an old friend of Jerome's, and Melania, an aristocratic lady of Spanish descent. She had embraced the ascetical life after her husband's death and become a formidable Christian scholar. As soon as her children were old enough to take care of themselves, she had left Europe and toured the new monasteries in Egypt and the Levant before coming to Jerusalem to found her own monastery. On the Mount of Olives, men and women could live a life of prayer and penance, teach, study, and provide shelter and hospitality to pilgrims. Melania and Rufinus involved themselves closely in the life of the city, and their monks and nuns took a full part in the developing liturgy, acting as interpreters to pilgrims from the West who could not understand the Greek used in the services, nor the Aramaic of the local translators. Melania and Rufinus were both passionate Nicene Christians and maintained close links with the court at Constantinople and with the monastic movement abroad.

Jerome and his friend Paula stayed at Melania's hostel during their pilgrimage to Jerusalem in 385, and it became their model for their own community in Bethlehem. At first, Jerome had praised Melania to the skies, but he was an irascible man, not given, as we have seen, to the practice of Christian charity, and soon he had permanently fallen out with her as a result of a theological quarrel. After that Jerome had never a good word to say about the Mount of Olives establishment. He sneered at its comfortable lifestyle, which reminded him of the wealth of Croesus;[10] he stigmatized the worldliness of Melania's community, with its cosmopolitan atmosphere and links with the court. The "solitude" of Bethlehem was far more suitable as a setting for the monastic life, he argued, than the pagan bustle of Jerusalem, "a crowded city with its command, its garrison, its prostitutes, actors, jesters, and everything which is usually found in cities."[11] The Bethlehem community was more close-knit and introverted, consisting in the main of admirers of Jerome. For years he fought a bitter campaign against Melania, but her reputation spread in the West and pilgrims continued to be inspired by her example.

One of these was Poemenia, a member of the royal family, who also toured the monasteries of Upper Egypt before coming to Jerusalem in 390. There she built a church on the summit of the Mount of Olives to mark the spot of Christ's ascension into heaven. Poemenia's church, which has not survived, was surmounted by a large, glittering cross that dominated the skyline. It was a round church, enclosing a rock on which pilgrims believed that they could see Christ's footprint. Other buildings were also appearing in the vicinity. At one end of the Kidron Valley, a church was erected on the site of the tomb of the Virgin Mary; at the other end of the valley, some monks had decided that the tomb of the Bene Hezir was the grave of James the Tzaddik, and they converted it into a church. In about 390 an elegant church was erected on the site of the Garden of Gethsemane. Theodosian Christianity laid great stress on shrines, and these churches created new facts in front of Jerusalem. The pagans of the city now had to confront an increasingly assertive Christian presence, as new churches appeared and new sites were annexed inside and outside the walls.

Christians also took over the city on their principal feast days, when huge crowds spilled out of the churches onto the streets, marching all around Jerusalem and the surrounding countryside. Christianity was no longer a clandestine faith: people no longer had to meet unobtrusively in one another's homes to celebrate their Eucharist. They could develop their own public liturgy. In Rome they used to gather around the tombs of the martyrs, weeping and shouting aloud as they listened to an account of their passion and death. They paraded with their bishop through the streets from one church to another, gradually imposing their own sacred

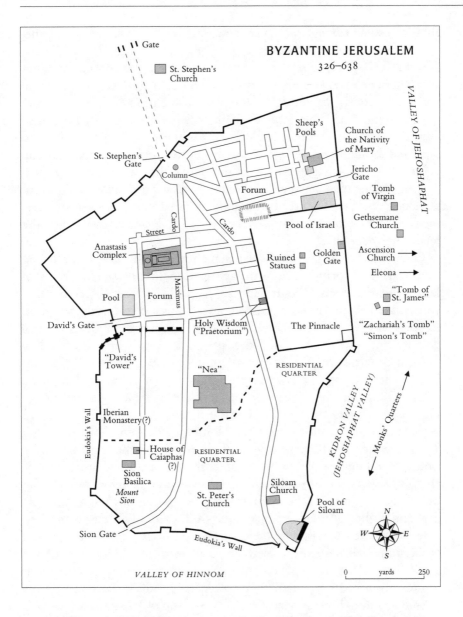

Gate

St. Stephen's
Church

BYZANTINE JERUSALEM
326–638

St. Stephen's
Gate

Column

Sheep's
Pools

Church of
the Nativity
of Mary

Jericho
Gate

Forum

Tomb
of Virgin

Cardo

Cardo

Street

Anastasis
Complex

Pool of Israel

Gethsemane
Church

Ruined
Statues

Golden
Gate

Ascension
Church

Eleona

Pool

Forum

Maximus

"Tomb of
St. James"

David's Gate

Holy Wisdom
("Praetorium")

The Pinnacle

"Zachariah's Tomb"
"Simon's Tomb"

"David's
Tower"

"Nea"

RESIDENTIAL
QUARTER

Eudokia's Wall

Iberian
Monastery(?)

House of
Caiaphas
(?)

RESIDENTIAL
QUARTER

KIDRON VALLEY
(JEHOSHAPHAT VALLEY)

Monks' Quarters

Sion
Basilica

Mount
Sion

St. Peter's
Church

Siloam
Church

Sion Gate

Eudokia's Wall

Pool of
Siloam

N
W   E
S

VALLEY OF JEHOSHAPHAT

VALLEY OF HINNOM

0   yards   250

topography upon the old pagan capital. There was a similar development in Jerusalem, which was starting to transform pagan Aelia into a Christian holy city. We see this in the writings of Egeria, a devout Spanish pilgrim who arrived in Constantinople in 381, just as the bishops were assembling for the council which would make Athanasius's doctrine of the incarnation the official teaching of the church.[12] Egeria shared to the full the Theodosian enthusiasm for shrines. She embarked on a lengthy tour of the Near East, venturing as far afield as Mesopotamia, treating the

Bible as a sort of *Blue Guide*. Whenever she and her companions identified a sacred site, they would read the appropriate passage from Scripture
"on the very spot" (*in ipso loco*), a phrase which recurs constantly in her
account. Egeria was far more effusive than the taciturn Bordeaux pilgrim:
she was obviously thrilled to see the places which most Christians could
only imagine. The Bible came to life before her eyes. As Cyril had suggested, proximity to the place where a miracle or a theophany had
occurred brought these distant events closer and the Bible reading
became a sacramental reenactment that made the past a present reality.
The only difference between this new Christian ritual and the old Temple cults was that the latter had commemorated mythical events of primordial time, while the New Testament episodes had occurred in the
relatively recent past.

Once Egeria had arrived in Jerusalem, however, this holy sight-seeing
gave way to a formal liturgical participation in the sacred events of
Jesus's life, death, and Resurrection. The whole Christian community
would take part in carefully planned processions to the appropriate spot.
Egeria speaks of immense crowds filling the courtyards of Golgotha and
flowing out into the streets. On September 14 the city was filled to
bursting point with monks and nuns from Mesopotamia, Syria, and
Egypt who had come to celebrate the eight days of Enkainia, the festival
which celebrated the dedication of Constantine's New Jerusalem and
Helena's discovery of the True Cross. Enkainia also roughly coincided
with Sukkoth, the anniversary of Solomon's dedication of the Jewish
Temple, which Christians saw as a foreshadowing of the later, more glorious event. Pilgrims had to be in good physical condition: liturgical celebration in Jerusalem involved more than decorous hymn singing and
listening to sermons. The participants were required to spend whole
days and nights on their feet, marching from one holy place to another.
They celebrated Christmas week, starting on 6 January, with a solemn
procession each night from Bethlehem to Jerusalem. They would not
arrive at the tomb, now enclosed in the recently completed Anastasis
Rotunda, until dawn, when they would take only a short rest before
attending a four-hour service. On the afternoon of Palm Sunday, crowds
gathered at the Eleona Basilica on the Mount of Olives for a service, followed by a march down the mountainside, through the Kidron Valley,
and back into the city. Bishop Cyril rode behind the procession on a
donkey, just as Jesus had done when he arrived in Jerusalem, the children
waved palm and olive branches and the congregation sang hymns, chanting periodically: "Blessed is he who comes in the name of the Lord."
Egeria tells us that the procession moved slowly, so as not to weary the
people, and it was late at night before they arrived at the Anastasis. Pen-

tecost was especially exhausting. After the usual Sunday Eucharist, Cyril led a procession to the Sion Basilica to celebrate the descent of the Spirit *in ipso loco,* but, not content with that, the crowds spent the afternoon walking to the top of the Mount of Olives in memory of the Ascension. After that they processed slowly and gently back to the city, stopping at the Eleona Basilica for vespers, an evening service in Constantine's Martyrium, and, finally, midnight prayers back at the Basilica of Holy Sion.

These celebrations inevitably changed the Christian experience. Hitherto there had been little interest in the individual events of Jesus's earthly life. Jesus's death and resurrection had been seen as a single revelation, a *mysterium* which had disclosed the way that human beings, through the Logos, would themselves return to God. But now the monks, nuns, clerics, laity, and pilgrims of Jerusalem were being encouraged to focus on specific incidents for some considerable time. In the week leading up to Easter, for example, they followed in Jesus's footsteps, reading at the appropriate places the gospel account of Jesus's betrayal by Judas, his last supper, and his arrest. It was an extraordinarily emotional experience. Egeria tells us that when the crowds listened to the story of Jesus's arrest in the Gethsemane Church, "there is such a moaning and groaning of all the people,

Processional crosses stacked against the wall of the Ethiopian monastery on the roof of the Holy Sepulcher Church. Since the fourth century, Christians have marched through the streets of Jerusalem following in Jesus's footsteps, and thus acquired an enhanced appreciation of the meaning of the incarnation.

with weeping, that the groans can be heard almost at the city."[13] There was a new sympathy for Jesus the man; the crowds were learning to live through the experience of his suffering with him, day by day, and were acquiring an enhanced appreciation of what this pain had meant to him. Eusebius had told Christians not to dwell upon the physical form which the Logos had temporarily assumed during his brief sojourn on earth, but the Jerusalem liturgy was changing all that. Christians were now concentrating on Christ's human nature. Ever since Constantine had established the New Jerusalem, the rock of Golgotha had stood near the tomb: every day there were separate prayers around the rock as well as at the Anastasis, so people were getting used to meditating on the Crucifixion as a distinct event. On Good Friday the faithful would process one by one to the small chapel behind the rock to kiss the relic of the True Cross. Eusebius had never shown much interest in the Crucifixion, but now these emotive celebrations were forcing Christians to consider the human implications of Christ's death and to meditate upon what it meant for the incarnate Logos to die.

Matter was no longer something to be cast aside; Christians were beginning to find that it could introduce them to the sacred. Pilgrims were developing a very tactile spirituality. They wanted to touch, kiss, and lick the stones that had once made contact with Jesus. When Jerome's disciple Paula arrived at the tomb, she first kissed the stone which had been rolled away from the cave on Easter Sunday morning. Then, "like a thirsty man who had waited long and at last comes to water, she faithfully licked the very place where he had lain."[14] Paula's contemporary Paulinus of Nola explained: "The principal motive which draws people to Jerusalem is the desire to see and touch the places where Christ is present in the body."[15] In other parts of the world, Christians experienced the divine power when they touched the bones of the martyrs, which embodied their holiness. The great Cappadocian theologian Gregory of Nyssa (338–95) pointed out that "they bring eye, mouth, ear, and all senses into play."[16] Because God had been incarnated in human form, Christians had now begun to experience the physical as sacred and able to transmit eulogia ("blessing"). Gregory had visited Palestine himself, and though he had misgivings about the new vogue for pilgrimage, he admitted that the holy places of Jerusalem were different. They had "received the footprints of Life itself."[17] God had left a trace of himself in Palestine, just as perfume lingered in a room after the wearer had left. Pilgrims now took rocks, soil, or oil from the lamps in the holy places back home with them; one particularly fervent pilgrim had actually bitten off a chunk of the True Cross when he had kissed it on Good Fri-

This medieval map charts the sacred geography experienced by
Christians. Jerusalem is placed at the center of the world and, with
a blithe disregard for the physical facts, Rome, France (Gallia), and
England (Anglia) are much nearer to the Holy City than Egypt.
The unknown, foreign and alien world is depicted as monstrous
and pushed to a marginal position.

The Dome of the Chain is seen here beside the golden Dome of the Rock. A symbol of spiritual ascent and integration, the dome has been used in mosques and shrines throughout the Islamic world.

The Aqsa Mosque exemplifies the inclusive nature of the Muslim concept of holiness: filled with light, the mosque welcomes the world into the sacred area. It is an expression of tawḥid, *the sacralization of the whole of existence.*

This sixteenth-century Persian depiction of the Night Journey shows Muḥammad, seated on Burāq, flying from Mecca to Jerusalem with the angel Gabriel, a mythical event which bound the two holy cities inextricably together in the Muslim imagination. From the Ḥaram in Jerusalem, Muḥammad is said to have ascended to heaven, a perfect act of surrender to God, which became the paradigm of the Islamic spiritual journey.

The Ḥaram al-Sharif and the Western Wall, one of the holiest and most disputed areas in Jerusalem. The Dome of the Rock and the Aqsa Mosque (with the silver dome at right) now occupy the immense platform built on top of Mount Zion by King Herod for the Jewish Temple. Below, Jews pray at the Western Wall, their last link with the ancient Temple. On the left, beneath the Dome of the Rock, is the Tanzikiyya Madrasah. In front of the Western Wall is the huge plaza which replaced the Maghribi Quarter, demolished by the Israelis in 1967. On the right, beneath the Aqsa Mosque, is the area appropriated by Israeli secularists for archaeological excavations after the Six-Day War. In the background can be seen the Mount of Olives, where, in the apocalyptic mythology of Jews, Christians, and Muslims, the faithful will gather for judgment on the Last Day.

Holy places often cause dissension, but they can also unite. Here, in a rare moment of amity and cooperation, Armenian, Coptic, and Franciscan priests stand beside the shrine containing the tomb of Christ in the Holy Sepulcher Church.

Ultra-Orthodox Jews, who may be—as some ultra-Orthodox are—opposed to the secular State of Israel, pray at the Western Wall beside Israeli soldiers who are committed to defending their country.

Sacred space can reveal surprisingly common ground among the three religions of Abraham, which now coexist so uneasily in Jerusalem. These elaborate palm crosses recall the palms carried by Jews during Sukkoth. Since the fourth century, Christians have carried palm branches in procession from the Mount of Olives to the Holy Sepulcher Church on Palm Sunday and, like Jews on Sukkoth, they cry "Hosanna!," the Hebrew shout of acclaim.

The rock in the Mosque of the Ascension on the Mount of Olives, which is believed to bear the imprint of Jesus's left foot. This holy place, whence Jesus ascended to heaven, is revered by both Muslims and Christians.

This Renaissance map of Palestine shows that the Christians of Europe were beginning to move away from the old sacred geography. The Holy Land is still golden and special, but the world is now seen scientifically and literally, a development which would eventually make the notion of sacred space incomprehensible to many Westerners.

day. People wanted to make the holiness of Jerusalem effective and available in their hometowns.

Christian archaeology had begun with the spectacular dig at Golgotha. Now new excavations unearthed the bodies of saints and biblical heroes in other parts of Palestine. What was thought to be the body of Joseph the Patriarch was exhumed at Shechem, now known as Neapolis, and transferred to Constantinople. Jerome described the crowds who lined the roads when the bones of the prophet Samuel were carried from Palestine to the imperial capital; they felt as though the prophet himself were present.[18] These expropriations of holy bones were an attempt to give the new Christian city of Constantinople a link with the sacred past that it would otherwise have lacked. Yet it was also an attempt to appropriate Jewish history: if the church was, as it claimed, the new Israel, it followed that these saints of the Old Covenant would be more truly at home in Christian territory than in cities frequented by the perfidious Jews. In 415 the Eastern emperor Theodosius II publicly reprimanded the Jewish patriarch Gamaliel II and stripped him of the rank of *praefectus praetorio*. The emperor thus set in motion a process that would bring the patriarchate to an end in 429, a step which, the ecclesiastical leaders believed, would hasten the inevitable demise of Judaism.[19]

In December 415, a parish priest made another archaeological discovery that seemed connected to the humiliation of the Jewish patriarch. Lucian, a presbyter of the village of Kfar Gamala on the coastal plain, had a dream in which Rabbi Gamaliel I, the teacher of St. Paul, appeared to him. The great Pharisee told Lucian that he had been secretly converted to Christianity but had kept this hidden out of fear of the Jews. When Stephen, the first Christian martyr, was killed outside the walls of Jerusalem for attacking the Torah and the Temple, Gamaliel had taken the body and buried it on his estate here at Gamala; later he himself was buried beside the martyr, together with Nicodemus, the young Jew who had once had a clandestine meeting with Jesus by night. The next day Lucian made some investigations and unearthed three tombs with Hebrew inscriptions, just as the rabbi had told him in his dream. Immediately he informed his bishop of this wonderful discovery.

Now it happened that Bishop John of Jerusalem was presiding at a church council at nearby Lydda, now called Diospolis. He had been deciding the fate of the British monk Pelagius, who had scandalized the Western Christians in Jerusalem by denying the doctrine of original sin, though John himself could see little harm in Pelagius's theology. As soon as he heard Lucian's news, however, he set off posthaste to Kfar Gamala, accompanied by the bishops of Sebaste and Jericho. When Stephen's tomb was opened, the air was filled with such sweet scent, Lucian recalled, that "we thought we were in Paradise."[20] This was a common experience at the tombs of the martyrs. The body of the saint who was now in heaven had created a link between this world and the next. The place had thus become a new "center" of holiness that enabled the worshippers to enter the realm of the sacred and gave them an experience of the power and healing presence of God. At the martyrs' tombs in Europe the faithful were healed by the tangible aura of holiness which filled the shrine when the story of the martyr's passion was read aloud; a sweet fragrance filled the air, and people cried aloud as they experienced the divine impact.[21] Now Christians started to arrive at Kfar Gamala from all over Palestine, and seventy-three sick people were cured.

John, however, had no intention of allowing Kfar Gamala to become a center of pilgrimage but was determined to use this miraculous find to enhance his own position. Like his predecessors, he wanted to improve the status of the see of Jerusalem and had recently rebuilt the basilica on Mount Sion, the Mother of all the churches. Now he decided that it was only right that Stephen should be buried in this new basilica, on the site of the church where he had served as a deacon, and on 26 December the bones were transferred to Mount Sion. Yet this discovery, which brought healing and holiness to Christians, was inherently inimical to Judaism. Stephen had died because he had attacked the Torah and the Temple; he had been a victim of the Jews. The revelation that the great Rabbi Gamaliel, the ancestor and namesake of the present patriarch, had been a closet Christian undermined the Jewish integrity of the patriarchate. Still, Christian growth was seen as inextricably involved with a rejection of the parent faith.

The court of Theodosius II was consumed by a passion for asceticism. Indeed, it resembled a monastery, and Pulcheria, the emperor's sister, lived in its midst as a consecrated virgin. Inevitably this reign saw the resurgence of monasticism in and around Jerusalem. Jerome's hostility had so poisoned the Holy City for Melania and Rufinus that they had returned to Europe in 399, though family considerations had also played a part in Melania's decision to leave. But in 417 her granddaughter, usually known as Melania the Younger, arrived in Jerusalem with her husband, Pionius. Together they founded a new double monastery on the Mount of Olives for about 180 monks and nuns. Melania also built a *martyrium,* a shrine for relics, next to Poemenia's church. Twenty years later, Peter, a prince of the Kingdom of Iberia,[22] who had been living in the imperial court of Constantinople, arrived in Jerusalem to found a monastery at the so-called Tower of David, which was in fact part of the

Herodian tower Hippicus. He also brought Melania a gift of relics for her *martyrium* on the Mount of Olives.

Monks had also started to come from all parts of the Christian world to colonize the Judaean desert, drawn to this beautiful but desolate region by the sanctity of Jerusalem. One of the earliest of these monastic pioneers was the Armenian monk Euthymius (d. 478), who founded about fifteen monasteries in spectacular locations between Masada and Bethlehem. He was regarded by his contemporaries as a second Adam: his career was thought to have launched a new era for humanity.[23] In their monasteries, the monks planted gardens and fruit trees, making the desert bloom and reclaiming this demonic realm for God. Each settlement was thus a new Eden, a new beginning. There monks could live a paradisal life of intimacy with God, like the first Adam. The monasteries were thus a new kind of holy place, part of a Christian offensive against the powers of darkness, where people called to the monastic life could return to the primal harmony and wholeness for which human beings continue to yearn. Soon Latins, Persians, Indians, Ethiopians, and Armenians were flocking to the Judaean monasteries. One of Euthymius's most influential disciples was Sabas (439–531), a Cappadocian who had deliberately chosen to settle in Judaea because of its proximity to the holy places. As with all true sacred space, the site of his monastery was revealed to him by God in a vision, and for five years Sabas lived alone, high up in a cliff, nine miles south of Jerusalem overlooking the Brook Kidron. Then disciples began to join him, each living in a separate cave until gradually the area became a new monastic city in the desert. Living alone, denying their natural need for sex, sleep, food, and social intercourse, the monks believed that they would discover for themselves human powers that God had given the first Adam; they would thus reverse the effects of the Fall and share in God's own holiness. Yet Sabas also had another aim. "It was necessary for him to colonize [the desert]," explained his biographer, "to fulfill the prophecies about it of the sublime Isaiah."[24] Second Isaiah had promised that the desert would burst into flower and become a new Eden: now Sabas and his monks believed that these holy settlements would bring the final redemption foretold by the prophets one step nearer, except now the recipients would not be the Jewish people but Christians.

Like most of the institutions of Christian Jerusalem, therefore, the new monastic venture had an inbuilt hostility toward the Jews. This had become tragically apparent during the pilgrimage of Empress Eudokia, the wife of Theodosius II, in 438. Eudokia was a convert to Christianity: she was the daughter of a distinguished Athenian philosopher and was herself a learned woman. As an intelligent convert, she does not seem to have shared the apparently ingrained Christian aversion to Judaism and had given the Jews permission to pray on the Temple Mount on holy days other than the Ninth of Av. Naturally this must have appalled many of the Christians, though Eudokia's high rank made it impossible to protest. Her astonishing edict gave some Jews hope of an impending redemption: it was said that a letter circulated to the Diaspora communities urging Jews to come to celebrate the festival of Sukkoth in Jerusalem so that the Kingdom could be established there.[25] Sukkoth happened to coincide with the empress's visit to Palestine. On the first day of the festival, while Eudokia was in Bethlehem, Jews began to congregate on the Temple Mount in large numbers.

They were not alone. The Syrian monk Bar Sauma, who was famous for his violence against Jewish communities, had also arrived in Jerusalem for Sukkoth. He was careful to stay innocently in a monastery, but other monks were also lurking on the Temple platform while the Jews were processing around its ruined courts waving their palm branches for the first time in centuries. Suddenly, Bar Sauma's biographer tells us, they were attacked by a miraculous shower of stones which rained down upon them from heaven. Many Jews were killed on the mount; others died as they tried to escape, and their bodies filled the streets and courtyards of the city. But the survivors acted quickly, seized eighteen of Bar Sauma's disciples, and marched them off to Bethlehem, still clutching their palm branches, to confront Eudokia with the evidence. The empress found herself in great danger. Monks rushed into the city from their desert monasteries, and soon the streets of Jerusalem and Bethlehem were packed with an angry monastic mob who made it clear that if Eudokia passed sentence on the prisoners they would burn her alive. When the imperial legate arrived from Caesarea, six days later, he was afraid to enter Jerusalem and was only permitted to examine the prisoners in Bar Sauma's presence. A compromise was reached when the governor's investigators arrived with the news that the Jews who had been killed on that fatal night had died of natural causes. Bar Sauma sent a herald through the streets proclaiming: "The cross has triumphed!" The mob took up the cry, and Bar Sauma was carried in a jubilant procession to Mount Sion, where he celebrated a victory mass in the basilica.

Eudokia's visit ended on a more positive note. On 15 May 439, she dedicated a small shrine in honor of St. Stephen outside the northern gate of the city on the very spot where it was believed he had been executed. The next day she carried a relic of the saint to Melania's *martyrium* on the Mount of Olives before returning to Constantinople. Despite her rather checkered experiences there, she had been happy in

Palestine, and when she had a disagreement with the imperial family in 444, especially with the emperor's pious sister Pulcheria, she was banished to Jerusalem. Because of her high rank she became the ruler of Palestine and built many new churches and hospices in and around Jerusalem: one at the Pool of Siloam, where Jesus had healed a blind man, one in honor of St. Peter on the site of Caiaphas's supposed residence on Mount Sion, and one in honor of Holy Wisdom on what was mistakenly thought to have been the site of Pilate's Praetorium in the Tyropoeon Valley, west of the Temple Mount. Eudokia also built a palace for herself at the southeast corner of the Temple Mount, beneath the "Pinnacle of the Temple"; later this residence would become a convent for six hundred nuns. She is also said to have built a new city wall for Jerusalem, which extended the city limits southward to include the old 'Ir David on the Ophel and Mount Sion.[26]

While she was ruling in Jerusalem, Eudokia became involved in the continuing doctrinal dispute about the person and nature of Christ. In 431 the Council of Ephesus had condemned the teachings of Nestorius, patriarch of Constantinople, who had declared that Jesus had two natures, human and divine: Mary had not been Theotokos, the God-Bearer, but only the mother of Jesus the man. After the council, Nestorius's supporters in northern Syria founded their own breakaway church. Other Christians were unhappy with the official Nicene Orthodoxy for other reasons. Eutyches, an aged abbot of a monastery near Constantinople, went the other way, insisting that Jesus had only one nature (*mone physis*). It had been the divine Logos who had been born of the Virgin Mary and died on the cross. This offended the Orthodox, because the "Monophysites," as they were called, seemed to have lost sight of Jesus's humanity, which for them was apparently swallowed up by Christ's overwhelming divinity. Many bishops and monks in Syria, Palestine, and Egypt espoused Monophysitism as a declaration of independence from Constantinople: they too formed separatist churches, represented in Jerusalem today by the Copts, Ethiopians, Armenians, and Syrian Jacobites. They were not simply supporting national independence, however, but were addressing the central religious question: how could the transcendent divinity establish a link with the world of human beings? In the old days, people had thought that temples established this connection with the sacred. Christians, however, had come to the astonishing conclusion that God had permanently allied himself to humanity in the person of Jesus, the god-man. The various Christological formulations were all stumbling attempts to see how this could have come to pass.

Eudokia, partly because of her quarrel with Pulcheria and the imperial family, supported the Monophysites in Jerusalem, as did Juvenal, the bishop of the city. He was rebuked by the bishop of Rome, Pope Leo the Great, who complained that it was outrageous that Juvenal, the custodian of the holy places, should teach a doctrine that virtually denied the humanity of Christ. As the successor of St. Peter, the chief disciple of Jesus, the bishop of Rome was widely regarded as the chief prelate in the church. Leo now put the weight of his authority behind the doctrine of the incarnation, writing an official "tome" which argued that the gospels constantly stressed the coexistence of humanity and divinity in Jesus. The holy places in Jerusalem, he claimed, were "unassailable proofs" that God had joined himself to the material world. For over a hundred years, Christians' experience at these sacred sites had provided incontrovertible evidence that the physical objects with which the incarnate Logos had made contact had the power to introduce people to the sacred. They were an eloquent reminder of the physical reality of Jesus's humanity. Leo's *Tome* provided the text used at the new ecumenical council of the church which Pulcheria summoned to Chalcedon in Asia Minor in 451. At this council, Bishop Juvenal crossed the floor to join the Orthodox and was rewarded with the prize that had been sought by bishops of Jerusalem since the time of Makarios. The see of Jerusalem became a patriarchate that now took precedence over the sees of Caesarea, Beth Shan, and Petra.

When Eudokia and the Christians of Jerusalem heard of Juvenal's defection, they not unnaturally felt betrayed, and they appointed Theodosius, a Monophysite, as their new bishop. Hordes of angry monks poured into Jerusalem from the Judaean monasteries, so that when Patriarch Juvenal arrived home with a guard of soldiers he was mobbed. He fled to the desert, where he lived in hiding in Rubra, to the west of Qumran. But the confusion of the church troubled Eudokia, and when Bishop Theodosius died in 457 she asked advice of the famous Syrian ascetic Simeon Stylites. He told her to consult Euthymius, the Armenian monastic leader, and Eudokia was so impressed by his teaching that she submitted to Orthodox doctrine. Anastasius, the Orthodox patriarch who had been appointed to replace Juvenal, took up residence in the new palace which Eudokia had built for him near the Anastasis. Her last project was to build a church and monastery for St. Stephen on the site of the modest shrine she had dedicated in 439. The bones of the martyr were carried there on 15 June 460, and four months later Eudokia herself died and was buried in the church.

Jerusalem was now a center of Nicene Orthodoxy, but the doctrinal conflict still raged in other churches, since many Eastern Christians regarded Chalcedon as an unworthy compromise. They also resented the doctrinal control exerted by the court. Future emperors, such as Zeno

(474–91) and Anastasius (491–518), tried to appease these dissidents, fearing a split in the empire. Other groups also resented Byzantium. In 485 the Samaritans declared independence of Constantinople and crowned their own king: their revolt was cruelly put down by Emperor Zeno, who desecrated their place of sacrifice on Mount Gerizim, where he built a victory church in honor of Mary Theotokos.

The oppressive measures taken by the Christian emperors was beginning to alienate increasing numbers of their subjects, and this ultimately damaged the empire. The emperor Justinian (527–65), for example, was committed to Chalcedonian Orthodoxy. His efforts to suppress Monophysitism in some of the eastern provinces meant that whole sectors of the population were seriously disaffected. He also made it impossible for Jews to support the empire. Justinian's Orthodoxy saw the destruction of Judaism as mandatory, and he published edicts that virtually deprived the Jewish faith of its status as *religio licta* in the imperial domains. Jews were forbidden to hold civil or military posts, even in such cities as Tiberias and Sepphoris where they were in a majority. The use of Hebrew was forbidden in the synagogues, and if Passover fell before Easter, Jews were not allowed to observe the festival on the correct date. Jews remained defiant. The Beth Alpha synagogue in Galilee, which may have been built at this time, could reflect a continued hope for the restoration of Jerusalem. The mosaic floor depicts the binding of Isaac, a tradition associated with the Temple Mount, and the cultic instruments used in the Temple, including the menorah and the palm branches and citrus fruits of Sukkoth, a festival which some Jews had come to associate with the Messiah.

Part of Justinian's offensive against dissident groups was his building program in and around Jerusalem. He restored Zeno's victory church on Mount Gerizim and rebuilt Helena's Nativity Basilica in Bethlehem, which had been badly damaged during the Samaritan revolt. His most impressive building in Jerusalem was the new Church of Mary Theotokos on the southern slope of the Western Hill. The church had been planned as a monument to Orthodoxy by the monk Sabas and Patriarch Elias during the reign of the Monophysite emperor Anastasius. The Nea, as the complex was known locally, was an impressive feat of engineering. Justinian had given very clear directions about its size and proportions, and since there was simply not enough room on the hill, the architects had to build huge vaults to support the church, monastery, and hospice with three thousand beds for the sick. The Nea was unique in Jerusalem, since it commemorated a doctrine and not an event in the life of Christ and the early church. It never quite won the hearts of the city's Christians, and they made no move to restore it after its destruction in an earthquake of 746. It is, however, clearly visible on a mosaic map of Jerusalem during the reign of Justinian, which was discovered in a church at Madaba in present-day Jordan in 1884.

The Madaba mosaic map shows the two columned *cardines* and the western supporting wall of the city, as well as the Basilica of Holy Sion and Eudokia's Church of Holy Wisdom[28] in the supposed site of Pilate's Praetorum. The map reflects the sacred geography of the Christian world which had developed since the time of Constantine. Palestine is depicted as the Holy Land: the map not only marks the biblical sites but also the new buildings, monuments, and monasteries by which the Christians had transformed the country into sacred space. Jerusalem, bearing the legend "The Holy City of Jerusalem," is at the center of the map and had now been enshrined at the heart of the Christian world. Before the discovery of the tomb, Christians had been taught to discount the earthly city and concentrate on the heavenly Jerusalem. By the end of the fourth century, they had been fused in the Christian imagination, as we can see in the mosaic in the Church of St. Pudenziana in Rome, which shows Christ teaching his disciples in heaven: behind him Constantine's new buildings at Golgotha are clearly visible. Jerusalem had thus become a holy Christian city, though not always a city of charity. All too often, the revelation of the city's sacred character had been accompanied by internecine Christian struggles, power games, and the suppression of rival faiths.

When Justinian and Zeno wanted to make an emphatic statement about the power of Christian Orthodoxy, they had both built churches in honor of Mary Theotokos. The image of the Mother of God holding the infant Christ had become the rallying cry of Orthodoxy because it expressed the central paradox of the incarnation: it showed that the Logos had accepted the extreme vulnerability of infancy out of love for the world. The tenderness of the relationship between Mary and her son expressed God's almost sensuous love for the human race:

> Thou didst stretch out thy right arm, O Theotokos, thou didst take him and make him lie on thy left arm. Thou didst bend thy neck and let thy hair fall over him. . . . He stretched out his hand, he took thy breast, as he drew into his mouth the milk that is sweeter than manna.[29]

In a similar way, Christian pilgrims fondled and kissed the stones and wood that had once touched the incarnate Logos. This type of tactile spirituality shows how the incarnation and the Jerusalem cult could have enabled Christians to see sexual love as a means of transcendence, a development which, sadly, never came about in the Christian tradition. It is also tragic that this poignant vision of divine tenderness could not

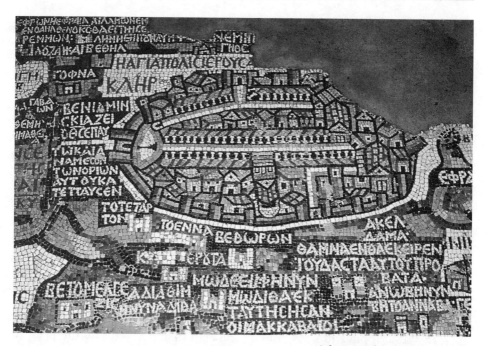

A fragment of the Madaba Mosaic Map, which precisely charts the main features of Christian Jerusalem at the time of Justinian. The two Cardines, built originally by Hadrian and clearly visible here, are still the main thoroughfares of the Old City.

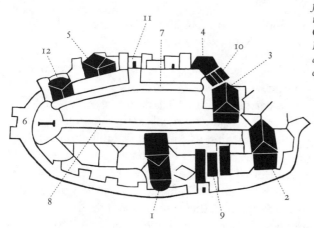

1. The Golgotha buildings
2. Basilica of Holy Sion
3. The "Nea" Church
4. Church of Holy Wisdom
5. Beth-Hesda Church of Mary's Nativity
6. Bab al-Amud (Gate of the Column), This is the current Arab name for the Damascus Gate, which preserves the memory of the column erected there by Hadrian's builders.

7. Cardo (today's Tariq al-Wad)
8. Cardo Maximus (today's Tariq Khan al Zeit).
9. Herodian Towers at today's Jaffa Gate
10. Western Wall: Western supporting wall of the Temple platform built by King Herod
11. Today's Lion Gate
12. Empress Eudokia's Palace

inspire Christians to a greater love and compassion for their fellow men. Unfortunately, the pathos of the Logos's vulnerability does not seem to have helped some Christian inhabitants of Jerusalem to lay aside their own egotistic lust for power and control.

Yet the physical approach to the spiritual gave many pilgrims a profound religious experience. It also made Jerusalem a natural center of Nicene Orthodoxy despite its earlier dalliance with Monophysitism. In 511 when Emperor Anastasius had been trying to impose a Monophysite patriarch upon the Jerusalem church, the monk Sabas had tried to explain that the experience of living in the holy city made it impossible for pilgrims and people to discount the humanity of Christ: "We, the inhabitants of Jerusalem, as it were, touch with our hands each day the truth through these holy places in which the mystery of our great God and Savior took place."[30] At some of the holy places Jesus was thought to have left a physical trace: he had literally impressed the stones indelibly with his presence. His footprint could be seen on the rock in the Ascension Church and on a stone in Eudokia's Church of Holy Wisdom, where, it was said, Jesus had stood before Pilate.[31] Theodosius, a Western pilgrim who visited Jerusalem in about 530, saw the print of Jesus's body on the pillar on Mount Sion. He had

> clung to it while he was being scourged, his hands, arms, and fingers sank into it, as if it were wax, and the marks appear to this day. Likewise his whole countenance, his chin, nose, and eyes, are impressed on it.[32]

Clinging to the stone, Jesus had in his extremity left a permanent impression of God's perpetual embrace of humanity and the material world in his person. The earthly city of Jerusalem was now felt to be imbued with divine power, as a result of Jesus's actions there. The very dew had healing properties, according to Antoninus, a pilgrim from Piacenza who visited Jerusalem in about 570. Christians bathed in the Pool of Siloam and the Pool of Beth-Hesda, the old site of the Asclepius cult, which had been replaced by a church in honor of the Virgin Mary's nativity. Many cures were effected in these healing waters.[33]

The holy places were like the icons which were beginning to be seen as providing another link with the celestial world. The icon was not intended as a literal portrait of Jesus or the saints. Like any religious symbol, it was mysteriously one with the heavenly being it represented on earth. As the eighth-century monk Theodore of Studios remarked: "Every artificial image . . . exhibits in itself, by way of imitation, the form of its model. . . . the model [is] the image, the one in the other."[34] In rather the same way, the pilgrims who "imitated" Christ by following in his footsteps during the great processions around the city had become "living icons," momentarily one with the Logos himself. So too, the holy places were not mere mementos but were experienced as earthly replicas of the divine. A pilgrim's ampulla of this period shows the Rock of Golgotha, surmounted by a jeweled cross donated by Theodosius II, but the four rivers of Paradise are also depicted flowing from the rock. When they visited Golgotha, pilgrims were now shown the place where Adam had been created by God at the beginning of time. Golgotha was thought to be on the site of the Garden of Eden. It had become a symbol which gave pilgrims that experience of returning to Paradise which, as we have seen, has been such an important motif in the religious quest. Pilgrims did not visit Golgotha and the tomb as modern travelers visit a historical site: these earthly relics of Christ's life on earth introduced them to a transcendence. This for a time assuaged that sense of separation and loss that lies at the root of so much human pain and gave them intimations of an integrity and wholeness which they felt to be their "real" state.

The creation of Christian Jerusalem had wholly shifted the sacred center of the city, which had formerly been Mount Zion and the Temple Mount. When the Bordeaux Pilgrim visited Jerusalem, he had started his tour there and then proceeded to the newer, Christian shrines. By the sixth century, Christians scarcely bothered to glance at the Temple platform. All the events that had once been thought to have occurred on Mount Zion were now located at Golgotha, the New Jerusalem. The Bordeaux Pilgrim had sited the murder of Zechariah at the Temple Mount and had seen the bloodstains on the pavement. Now pilgrims were shown the altar where Zechariah had been slain in Constantine's Martyrium. The altar on which Abraham had bound Isaac and where Melchizedek had offered sacrifice—incidents formerly associated with Zion—were also displayed near Golgotha. There too was the horn which had contained the oil that had anointed David and Solomon, together with Solomon's signet ring.[35] This transition represented another Christian appropriation of Jewish tradition, but it also showed that the holiness of the New Jerusalem was so powerful that it pulled the tradition of the old Jerusalem into its orbit.

Yet the power of the holy city could not hold its earthly enemies at bay. The Byzantine empire was weak and internally divided, and its subjects were alienated from Constantinople. In 610, King Khosrow II of Persia judged the time right to invade Byzantine territory and began to dismember the empire. Antioch fell in 611, Damascus two years later, and in the spring of 614 the Persian general Shahrbaraz invaded Palestine, pillaging the countryside and burning its churches. The Jews of Palestine, who had happier memories of Persian than of Roman rule, came to their aid. On 15 April 614, the Persian army arrived outside the walls of Jerusalem. Patriarch Zacharias was ready to surrender the city but a group of young Christians refused to allow this, convinced that God would save them by a miracle. The siege lasted for nearly three weeks, while the Persians systematically destroyed all the churches and shrines outside the city, including St. Stephen's church, the Eleona basilica, and the Ascension Church. At the end of May, Jerusalem fell amid scenes of horrific slaughter. In his eyewitness account, the monk Antiochus Strategos says that the Persians rushed into the city like wild boars, roaring, hissing, and killing everyone in sight: not even women and babies were spared. He estimated that 66,555 Christians died, and the city was vandalized, its churches, including the Martyrium, set aflame. Survivors were rounded up, and those who were skilled or of high rank were taken into exile, including Patriarch Zacharias.

When the deportees reached the summit of the Mount of Olives and looked back on the burning city, they began to weep, beat their breasts, and pour dust over their heads, like the Jews whose mourning rituals they had so thoroughly despised. When Zacharias sought to calm them, he uttered a lament for the Christian Holy City which had now become inseparable from the idea and experience of God:

> O Zion, do not forget me, your servant, and may your Creator not forget you. For if I forget you, O Jerusalem, let my right hand wither. Let my tongue cleave to the roof of my mouth if I do not remember you. . . . I adore you, O Zion, and I adore him who dwelled in you.[36]

The Christians had sharply differentiated their experience in Jerusalem from that of the Jews. Now as they went into exile in their turn, they turned naturally to the gestures and psalms of their predecessors in the Holy City, and like the Jews they spoke of God and Zion in the same breath. With the exiles went the relic of the True Cross together with other implements of the Passion of Christ that had been kept in the Martyrium: the spear that had pierced his side, the sponge and the onyx cup that he was supposed to have used at the Last Supper. They passed into the possession of Queen Meryam of Persia, who was a Nestorian Christian.

When they left Jerusalem to continue their campaign, the Persians left the city in the charge of the Jews, their allies in Palestine. Messianic hopes soared: visionaries looked forward to the imminent purification of the land by the Messiah and to the rebuilding of the Temple. Some contemporaries even hint that sacrifice was resumed on the Mount during this period, that booths were built once again during Sukkoth and that prayers were recited at the ruined city gates.[37] But in 616, when the Persians returned to Palestine, they took over control of the city. They had now realized that if they were to pacify the country, they had to make some concessions to the Christian majority. Withdrawal of Persian support spelled the end of any realistic hope for the restoration of Jerusalem to the Jewish nation.

In 622, Heraklius, Emperor of Byzantium, resumed the offensive against Persia, campaigning for six years in Persian territory until he arrived outside Ctesiphon, where Khosrow II was assassinated in a palace coup. Persia and Byzantium made peace and both powers evacuated each other's territory, but they were both exhausted by the long years of destructive warfare and would never truly recover. Nevertheless, the Christians of Jerusalem were jubilant. On 21 March 629, Heraklius entered Jerusalem in a splendid procession, carrying the relic of the True Cross. The "Golden Gate" in the eastern supporting wall of the Temple Mount may have been built in honor of his triumphal entrance. The emperor marched through the city streets to the Anastasis and returned the cross to its rightful home. Both the Martyrium and the Rotunda shrine around the tomb had been damaged in 614, but the buildings were still standing. Modestos, a monk of the Judaean desert, had taken charge of the repairs, and since Zacharias had died in exile, Heraklius appointed Modestos patriarch of Jerusalem in recognition of his services. Heraklius had issued an official pardon to the Jews for their collaboration with Persia but found that he had to make some gestures to appease the Christians. A new edict banned the Jews from Jerusalem yet again; some Jews accused of killing Christians or burning churches during Persian rule were executed, while others fled to Persia, Egypt, or the desert. Those who remained in Galilee were forbidden to recite the Sh'ma in public or to hold services in the synagogue more than once a week. In 634, Heraklius commanded all the Jews of his empire to be baptized. Yet again a Christian emperor had totally alienated his Jewish subjects, and Heraklius would find it impossible to gain their support three years later, when the empire was again in deadly peril.

The Christians were exultant. Yet again, as after the reign of the apostate Julian, their Holy City had been restored to them. This time they would never let it go. The fervent Orthodox monk Sophronius, who became patriarch of Jerusalem in 633, wrote two poems describing his love of the city. He imagined himself running from one place to another, kissing the stones and weeping over the sites of the Passion. For Sophronius the tomb represented the earthly paradise:

> O light-giving Tomb, thou art the ocean stream of eternal life and the true river of Lethe. I would lie at full length and kiss that stone, the sacred center of the world, wherein the tree was fixed which did away with the curse of

[Adam's] tree. . . . Hail to thee, Zion, splendid sun of the world, for whom I long and groan by day and by night.[38]

The experience of living in Jerusalem had impelled the Christians to develop a full-blown sacred geography, based on the kind of mythology they had once despised. They now saw Jerusalem as the center of the world, the source of life, fertility, salvation, and enlightenment. Now that they had died in such great numbers for their city, it was dearer to them than ever. The restoration of Jerusalem to the Christian emperor seemed an act of God. But in 632, the year before Sophronius became patriarch, a prophet who had followed the recent developments in Jerusalem with interest died in the Arabian settlement of Yathrib. Five years later, an army of his friends and followers arrived outside the walls of Jerusalem.

BAYT AL-MAQDIS

MUHAMMAD IBN ABDALLAH, the new prophet of Mecca in the Hijaz, did not believe that he was about to found a new world religion when he received his first revelation in 610, the same year that King Khosrow II invaded Byzantine territory. Muḥammad, a merchant famous in Mecca for his integrity, had long been concerned about the spiritual malaise he could discern in the city. Mecca was enjoying a greater material prosperity than ever before, but as a direct result, some of the old tribal values were being undermined. Instead of taking care of the weaker members of society, in the old way, people had become preoccupied with building up their private fortunes. Some people felt obscurely dissatisfied with the old paganism, which no longer seemed adequate now that they were beginning to enter the modern world. It was widely believed that Allah, the high god of the Arabian pantheon whose name simply means "God," was in fact the deity who was worshipped by the Jews and the Christians. Yet those Jews and Christians with whom they came in contact often taunted the Arabs because God had sent them no revelation or prophet of their own.

All this changed forever in the month of Ramadan in 610 CE, when Muḥammad felt overwhelmed by a terrifying divine presence and found the words of a divinely inspired scripture pouring from his lips. For the next twenty-two years, Muḥammad continued to receive new revelations from Allah, which were later collected by his followers in the Arabic scripture known as the Qur'ān, the Recitation. At last God had spoken to the Arabs in their own language and had brought them into the community of true believers. Thus Muḥammad did not see his revelation as new; what was revealed through him was simply the old religion of the one God worshipped by the Jews and the Christians. It called upon the people of Mecca to make an existential surrender (*islām*) of their whole lives to God. If they lived in the way that Allah desired and built a just and decent society, they would prosper and be in harmony with the divine laws that were fundamental to existence.

Islām, therefore, did not mean submission to something alien. From the perspective of the Qur'ān, it was a profoundly natural act. God had sent prophets and messengers to all the people on the face of the earth to tell them the way they ought to live. Only by surrendering to this divine imperative could people fulfill the potential of their humanity. It was rebellion (*kufr*) against God that was unnatural, ungrateful, and perverse, because it was a denial of reality. It could bring only disorder and disruption into the lives of individuals and societies. A *muslim,* one who made this surrender to God, on the other hand, would find that life had harmony, purpose, and direction, because he or she would at last be in tune with the way things were supposed to be; Muslims were thus returning to the original perfection that God had envisaged for men and women when he had first created the world.

The whole of *islām,* therefore, can be seen as a quest for wholeness, a return to the paradise that human beings had lost. Yet there was nothing whimsical or escapist about the Qur'ān or its prophet. Not only was Muhammad a spiritual genius, he had political gifts of a very high order. In the Qur'ān, God gives very clear and concrete commands. It is wrong to build a private fortune and good to share your wealth equally; the first religious duty is to create a society where the poor and vulnerable are treated with respect. Like the Hebrew prophets, Muhammad stressed the prime duty of practical compassion: care for the poor, the orphan, the widow, and the oppressed was a Muslim's first responsibility. The Qur'ān does not demand intellectual submission to a complex set of religious doctrines—indeed, it has no time for theological speculation about matters that nobody can prove one way or the other. As in Judaism, God was experienced in a moral imperative rather than in orthodoxy.

The message of the Qur'ān had immediate relevance in Mecca, then (as noted) in the throes of a capitalistic revolution in which the more vulnerable members of Muhammad's tribe of Qureish had been pushed aside in the stampede for wealth. Many of the first people to respond to the Qur'ān were slaves, women, and other disadvantaged people, particularly from among the poorer and less successful clans. The Meccan establishment, however, had no desire to change the status quo. Its members were appalled when Muhammad also commanded them to neglect the worship of the traditional gods and worship Allah alone; this seemed an act of impiety to the traditions of their ancestors and an apostasy from the ancient sanctities of Arabia. The Meccan aristocracy persecuted the small Muslim community and in 622 Muḥammad was forced to leave Mecca with some seventy Muslim families for the settlement of Yathrib, some 250 miles to the north. This *hijrah* ("migration") marks the start of the Muslim era, because it was at this point that Muḥammad was able to put his ideals fully into practice and form the first community (*ummah*) whose social system and spirituality embodied the teachings of the Qurʾān.

The next ten years were dangerous and frightening for the Muslims, and the growing *ummah* constantly faced the prospect of extermination. The *hijrah* had been a shocking, even a blasphemous, action. By abandoning their tribe, the Muslims had violated one of the most sacred values of Arabia: the tie of blood. They had torn away from their true place in the world and cast themselves adrift in an extremely hostile world where the individual could not usually survive without the support of the tribal group. The *ummah* was subject to an ongoing threat of war with the powerful city of Mecca. It also had to contend with the antagonism of some of the Jews and pagans of Yathrib, who did not want to join this revolutionary society based on ideology rather than kinship. Some Jews and pagans plotted to kill Muḥammad; others

Islam as the religion of peace and unity. At Zeita, in the Israeli-occupied West Bank, Muslims kiss each other's hand, a greeting customary in the ummah *at the time of the Prophet Muḥammad.*

were prepared to betray the *ummah* to Mecca. If they had been successful, the Muslims would certainly have all been killed in a vicious Meccan vendetta. Death and massive slaughter did occur. Muslims lost their
lives in desperate battles against Mecca, and, in their struggle for survival,
three of the most important Jewish tribes of Yathrib were either
expelled from the settlement or massacred. But eventually the Prophet
brought peace to Arabia, which had hitherto been torn apart in an
unstoppable cycle of tribal violence and vendetta. One tribe after
another joined Muḥammad's *ummah,* and eventually, in 630, even the
proud city of Mecca voluntarily opened its gates to the Muslim army
and Muḥammad occupied his hometown without bloodshed.

Islam's birth had been violent, but the Qurʾānic ideal was harmony
and unity. The very word *islām* derives from the same root as *salām*
("peace"). The great ideal of the Qurʾān was *tawḥīd,* "making one."
Individual Muslims should order their lives so as to make God their chief
priority: when they had achieved this personal integration, they would
experience within that unity which was God. The whole of human
society also had to achieve this unity and balance and bring all its activities under the aegis of the sacred. Muslims were thus engaged in a ceaseless struggle (*jihād*) to restore all things, in the human and in the natural
world, to the primal perfection envisaged by God. Consequently there
must be no divisive sectarianism in religion. Originally Muḥammad
believed that the Jews and Christians belonged to the same faith. He was
shocked to discover that they had quarreled about doctrinal matters that
nobody could prove one way or the other. It was also extremely painful
to him when most of the Jews of Yathrib refused to accept him as an
authentic prophet and closed their doors to the Muslims. The Qurʾān
therefore instructed Muslims to return to the original, pure religion of
Abraham, who had lived before either the Torah or the gospel and had,
therefore, been neither a Jew nor a Christian. He had simply been a
muslīm, one who had made this total surrender of his life to God.[1] From
the more friendly Jews of Yathrib, Muḥammad learned that the Arabs
were thought to be the descendants of Abraham's son Ishmael: they
too could call themselves children of Abraham, like the Jews and the
Christians.

But Muḥammad was also convinced that not all Jews and Christians
subscribed to this exclusive sectarianism, and, despite his own desperate
struggle with the Jews, he insisted that all his followers must respect the
ahl al-kitāb, those who followed an earlier revelation:

> Do not argue with the followers of an earlier revelation otherwise than in
> the most kindly manner. . . . Say: "We believe in that which has been
> bestowed from on high upon us, as well as that which has been bestowed

upon you: for our God and your God is one and the same, and it is to him that we all surrender ourselves."[2]

Over and over again the Qur'ān insists that the revelation to Muhammad did not cancel out the teaching of previous prophets: Adam, Noah, Abraham, Isaac, Ishmael, Job, Moses, David, Solomon, and Jesus.[3] The Qur'ān was simply a restatement and a reminder of the single message that God had sent down to all peoples. It was idolatry to prefer a creed or an institution to God himself, who transcends all human systems. By returning to the original faith of Abraham, Muslims would make God, not a religious establishment, the goal of their lives.

This vision of the essential unity of the religious quest of humanity would profoundly affect Muslim policy in Jerusalem. Muslims had a rather different sacred geography from their predecessors. Because everything came from God, all things were good, so there was no essential dichotomy between the "sacred" and the "profane" as in Judaism. The aim of the *ummah* was to achieve such integration and balance between divine and human, interior and exterior worlds, that such a distinction would become irrelevant. There was no intrinsic "evil"; no "demonic" realm, standing over against the "good." Even Satan would be forgiven on the Last Day. Everything was holy and had to be made to realize its sacred potential. All space, therefore, was sacred and no one location was holier than another. Yet Islam is a realistic faith, and Muhammad knew that human beings need symbols on which to focus. Consequently, from the earliest years, the Muslims were taught to regard three places as sacred centers of the world.

The first of these was Mecca. At the heart of the city was a cube-shaped granite shrine of considerable antiquity known as the Ka'bah. It was widely regarded as the holiest place in Arabia. Each year the tribes would assemble from all over the peninsula to take part in the arduous and intricate rites of the *hajj* pilgrimage, Christian Arabs alongside the pagans. By Muhammad's time, the Ka'bah was dedicated to the Nabatean deity Hubal and surrounded by effigies of the Arabian pantheon, but it may well originally have been the shrine of Allah, the high god. Like most sacred space, the Ka'bah was thought to stand at the center of the world: the gate of heaven was positioned directly above it, so it was a place where the divine world had made itself accessible to the mundane. Embedded in the wall of the Ka'bah was the Black Stone, a meteorite which had once dropped from the sky, linking heaven and earth. Like the Herodian Temple in Jerusalem, the Meccan sanctuary (*haram*) represented the whole of reality, and the Ka'bah represented being itself. The box-shaped shrine also symbolized the earth, its four corners radiating from a central point. Worshippers circled around the shrine at a steady trot, not unlike the *pas gymnastique,* in the ritual of *ṭawāf,* seven circumambulations that followed the direction of the sun. They were thus putting themselves symbolically in tune with the rhythms and motions of the cosmos—taking the right direction and the right path. In nearly all cultures, the circle is a symbol of perfection and eternity. By means of these circumambulations, Arabs passed from mundane reality to a sense of transcendent wholeness. *Ṭawāf* was a meditative exercise: circling around the still, small point of the turning universe, pilgrims learned to orient themselves, finding their own center and priorities. To this day, pilgrims who perform the *ṭawāf* with other worshippers describe the bonds of their ego dissolving as they become one with the people. The holiness of the Kaʿbah was protected by a sacred area with a twenty-mile radius. It became a sanctuary where all violence was forbidden and thus a refuge from the ceaseless tribal warfare. This had been responsible for Mecca's commercial success. Arabs could meet there in relaxed circumstances, trading with one another without fear of enemy attack.

Muḥammad felt deeply attracted to the Kaʿbah. He liked to pray in the Ḥaram, recite the Qurʾān there, and perform the *ṭawāf.* He was drawn by the legend that was probably current in pre-Islamic Arabia that Adam, the first man, had built the earliest shrine on this sacred spot. It was, therefore, the first temple built in God's honor in the whole world. The Meccan Ḥaram had been the site of the Garden of Eden, where Adam had been created, had named the animals, and had been honored by all the angels.[4] Mecca thus represented that lost paradise, which could be momentarily recovered by performing the traditional rites of this holy place. The shrine was later rebuilt by Seth, Adam's son; by Noah after the Flood; and by Abraham and Ishmael.[5] Finally it had been rebuilt by Qusayy ibn Qilāb, the ancestor of the Meccan tribe of Qureish. The Kaʿbah linked the past with the present, the human with the divine, the internal world with the external.

Yet when Muḥammad taught his first converts to prostrate themselves in prayer before Allah as an outward sign of their interior *islām,* he told them to turn away from the Kaʿbah to face Jerusalem. The Kaʿbah was now contaminated by idols, so Muslims must focus on the spiritual center of the Jews and Christians who worshipped Allah alone. This *qiblah* ("direction of prayer") marked their new orientation away from their tribe toward the primordial faith of the whole of humanity. It also expressed Muḥammad's sense of solidarity and continuity with the *ahl al-kitāb.* Then in January 624, when it became clear that most of the Jews of Yathrib would never accept Muḥammad, the *ummah* declared its independence of the older traditions. Muḥammad made the congregation turn around and pray facing Mecca instead. This change of *qiblah* has been described as one of Muḥammad's most creative gestures. It marked a return of the Muslims to the primordial faith of Abraham before it was split into warring sects by the Jews and Christians; it was an attempt to find a lost unity, represented by the primal shrine rebuilt by Abraham, the true *muslīm*. Since the Ka'bah had no associations for either Jews or Christians, the Muslims were tacitly declaring that they would bow to none of the established religions but only to God himself:

> Verily, as for those who have broken the unity of their faith and become sects—thou hast nothing to do with them. . . .
> Say: "Behold, my Sustainer has guided me to a straight way through an ever-true faith—in the way of Abraham, who turned away from all that is false, and was not of those who ascribe to aught beside Him."
> Say: "Behold, my prayer, and [all] my acts of worship, and my living and my dying are for God alone."[6]

The change of *qiblah* was also consoling for the Meccan Muslims who made the *hijrah* to Yathrib and were now living in exile. It healed their sense of dislocation and symbolically directed them toward the sacred associations of home.

When Muhammad entered Mecca in triumph in 630, his first act was to purify the Ka'bah by smashing the idols and removing the effigy of Hubal. Two years later, shortly before his death, he performed the old pagan rites of the *hajj,* giving them a new, monotheistic interpretation. They now became a symbolic reenactment of the experience of Hagar and Ishmael after Abraham had abandoned them in the wilderness. Mecca would remain the holiest place in the Muslim world and the Ḥaram became a symbolic expression of the Islamic religious experience. The Qur'ān constantly reminds Muslims that we can only speak of God in terms of "signs" and "symbols" (*ayāt*). Each one of its verses is called an *āyah,* a "similitude," and such images as paradise or the Last Judgment are also symbols, since God and his doings can be expressed by human beings only in figurative form. Muslims are therefore used to thinking symbolically and could see the holiness of Mecca, the primordial sacred space, reflecting the whole dynamic of the Islamic vision. Just as there is only one God and one religion made manifest in many forms, so too there is one sacred space—Mecca—that is revealed plurally. All subsequent holy places in the Islamic world would derive their holiness from Mecca and can be seen as extensions of this central sanctity. So too the cosmos is an *āyah* of God and reveals his presence in phenomena. All other shrines in the Islamic world would thus be modeled on Mecca, the archetypal symbol of the sacred: this would be an expression of *tawḥīd,* the sacralization and unification of the universe.

One of the most holy of these other places was Jerusalem. Muslims never forgot that the holy city of the *ahl al-kitāb* had been their first *qiblah*. This city had been a symbol that had helped them to form a distinct Islamic identity, to turn their backs on the pagan traditions of their ancestors and seek a new religious family. Jerusalem had been crucial in this painful process of severance and would always occupy a special place in the Muslims' spiritual landscape. It remained a vital symbol of Islam's sense of continuity and kinship with the *ahl al-kitāb,* whether or not Jews and Christians were willing to acknowledge this. Muslims called the city *madinat bayt al-maqdis,* the City of the Temple. It had long been a spiritual center of their monotheistic predecessors. The great prophets David and Solomon had prayed and ruled there: Solomon had built a sacred mosque. The city was associated with some of the holiest prophets, including Jesus, whom the Muslims held in high esteem, even though they did not believe that he was God.

Later Muslims could claim that the Prophet Muḥammad had also visited Jerusalem, conveyed there miraculously from Mecca one night by God:

> Limitless in His glory is He who transported His servant by night from the Inviolable House of Worship [*al-masjid al-ḥaram*] to the Remote House of Worship [*al-masjid al-aqsa*]—the environs of which We had blessed—so that We might show him some of Our symbols [*ayāt*].[7]

The "Inviolable House of Worship" was certainly the Kaʿbah but there is nothing in the Qurʾān to link the Remote Mosque with Jerusalem. But later, probably some generations after Muḥammad, Muslims had made this identification. They said that one night in about 620, before the *hijrah,* when Muḥammad was praying beside the Kaʿbah, he was carried by the angel Gabriel to Jerusalem. They flew through the night on a winged horse named Burāq and alighted on the Temple Mount. There they were greeted by a large crowd of prophets, Muḥammad's predecessors, after which Gabriel and Muḥammad climbed through the seven heavens up a ladder (*al-miʿrāj*) which extended from the Temple Mount to the divine Throne. Prophets presided over each one of the celestial spheres—Adam, Jesus, John the Baptist, Joseph, Enoch, Aaron, Moses, and, finally, Abraham at the threshold of the divine realm. There Muḥammad received the final revelation, which took him beyond the limits of human perception. His ascent to the highest heaven had been the ultimate act of *islām,* a return to the unity whence all being derives. The story of Muḥammad's Night Journey (*al-isrāʾ*) and Ascension (*al-miʿrāj*) is clearly reminiscent of the Throne Visions of Jewish mystics. More important, it symbolized the Muslims' conviction of continuity and solidarity with the older faiths. The flight of their Prophet from the Ka'bah to the Temple Mount also revealed the transference of Mecca's holiness to Jerusalem, *al-masjid al-aqsā*. There was a divinely established connection between the two cities.

But Jerusalem was only the third-holiest site in the Islamic world. The second was Yathrib, the home of the first *ummah,* which Muslims called *al-madinah,* "*the* City." When Muḥammad took his small group of converts to Medina, he had also conveyed the holiness of Mecca, the primal sacred space, to this new city. After his death, Muḥammad was revered as the Perfect Man by Muslims: he was not divine—Muḥammad had tirelessly warned Muslims not to deify him as the Christians had deified Jesus—but his faith, virtue, and surrender to God had been so wholehearted that he had forged in his own person a living link (*qutb*) between heaven and earth. Muslims, therefore, combined the ancient symbolism of sacred space with the more recent cult of the holy human being. People as well as places could link the celestial and the mundane. Because it had been the Prophet's home, Medina had also become a place where heaven touched earth, especially at Muḥammad's tomb, where his presence was most concentrated. Medina was also holy because the *ummah* had come into existence there. On the same principle of *tawḥīd,* all future Islamic cities and states participated in the primal sanctity of Medina, which had become a symbol of the attempt to bring the whole of human life under God's rule.

In the same way, all future mosques built in the Islamic world were modeled on the first humble mosque that Muḥammad built in Medina. It was a rough building that expressed the austerity and simplicity of the early Islamic ideal. Tree trunks supported the roof, a stone marked the *qiblah,* the direction of prayer, and Muḥammad stood on a stool to address the congregation. These would all be represented in later mosques by columns supporting the roof, the *miḥrāb,* a niche indicating the orientation to Mecca, and the pulpit (*minbar*) for the preacher. They would also have a courtyard, like the one in Medina which played a crucial role in the life of the first *ummah.* Muḥammad and his wives lived in little apartments or huts around the periphery of this courtyard. The poor of the city could congregate there to receive alms, food, and care. Public meetings to discuss social, political, and military as well as religious matters were also held in the courtyard. Similarly today the mosque remains a center of all kinds of activity in the Muslim community and is not used exclusively for religious functions.

This is often surprising—even shocking—to Jews and Christians, who regard holiness as essentially separate from the profane world. They imagine that Muslims cannot really regard their mosques and sanctuaries as sacred if they chat with their friends there or "exploit" its sanctity by holding political rallies. But this is to misunderstand the Islamic concept of the sacred, which is not seen as separate (*kaddosh* in Judaism) but something that informs the whole of life. When Muḥammad set up house with his wives in the courtyard of the mosque, he showed that the sexual, the sacred, and the domestic could—and, indeed, must—be integrated. Similarly, politics, welfare, and the ordering of social life must be brought into the ambit of holiness and under the rule of God. Holiness in Islam was thus seen as inclusive rather than exclusive: the Christians of Medina were allowed to worship in the mosque, an expression of the continuity of the Islamic tradition with the gospel. The multifaceted function of the mosque was thus an expression of *tawḥīd,* the sacralization of the entire spectrum of human life.[8] Further, since all space is inherently sacred, the mosque should not be cordoned off from its surroundings. The Prophet is reported to have said: "Revile not the world for the world is God," and the Qurʾān constantly urges Muslims to regard the beauty and order of the earth as *ayāt.* Thus trees, which were prohibited on the Temple Mount, are encouraged in a Muslim sanctuary; there will be fountains in the courtyard, and the mosques will be full of light; birds can fly around during the Friday prayers. The world is to be invited into the mosque, not left outside. The principles of Medina would also become apparent in Jerusalem, the third-holiest place in the Islamic world.

When Muḥammad died on 6 June 632, he had united almost the whole of Arabia under his leadership. But so endemic was tribal warfare to the peninsula that there was a real danger the *ummah* would fall apart after his death. Many of the tribes who had allied themselves to Medina were more attached to the Prophet than to his religion, and when he died they no longer felt bound to obey his successor (*khalīfah*) Abu Bakr or to pay the religious tax (*zakat*) to the Islamic treasury. Local "prophets" set out to rival Muḥammad and broke away from the *ummah;* Abu Bakr had to fight a pitiless campaign against the rebel tribes of Asad, Tamim, Ghatafan, and Hanīfah. Once he had crushed the rebellion, Abu Bakr may well have decided to alleviate internal tensions by employing the unruly energies within the *ummah* against external foes. Whatever the case, in 633 Muslim armies began a new series of campaigns in Persia, Syria, and the Iraq. By the time Abu Bakr died in 634, one Arab army had driven the Persians from Bahrein and another had penetrated Palestine and conquered Gaza.

These wars were almost certainly not inspired by religious motives: nothing in the Qurʾān encouraged Muslims to believe that they had a duty to conquer the world for Islam. There are indications, however, that at the end of his life Muḥammad had plans to bring more Arabs into the *ummah:* in 630 he had led military expeditions to the northern regions of the Arabian Peninsula. At this stage, however, Islam was still not a missionary religion like Christianity. Muḥammad had not expected Jews or Christians to convert to Islam unless they especially wished to do so, because he believed that they had received valid revelations of their own. In these early days, the Muslims regarded Islam as the religion given to the Arabs, the sons of Ishmael, just as Judaism was a faith for the sons of Jacob. The old idea that the Bedouin converts to Islam immediately rushed out of Arabia to impose their new religion on a reluctant world by force of arms has been completely quashed by modern historians. Most of the Muslim generals probably had more mundane motives. For centuries the nomads of the harsh Arabian steppes had sought to break out of the peninsula to find more fertile land and better pasturage. Hitherto they had been held in check by the armies of two great powers, Byzantium and Persia. But the Muslims began their external campaigns in 633 in the face of a power vacuum. Persia and Byzantium were both exhausted after long years of warfare against each other. Some of the troops employed by the two empires to turn back the Muslim armies were Arabs, who felt an ethnic bond with the invaders. The tribe of Ghassān on the Arabian border, for example, had long been clients of Constantinople, with the assigned mission of holding the Arabian nomads at bay. But they were resentful that Byzantium had recently withheld their subsidies, and were ready to defect to the armies of the *ummah,* not for religious reasons, but out of a vague sense of Arab solidarity. Other, Aramaic and Semitic elements in both Syria and the Iraq were either indifferent to the Arab invasion or enthusiastic about it. We have seen that in the Byzantine empire, the oppressive policies of the Christian emperors had thoroughly alienated the Monophysite "heretics" and the large Jewish population. They were not inclined to support the Byzantines, and the Jews in particular welcomed Muslim armies into Palestine. For these complex reasons, the Muslim armies were able to conquer with relative ease a considerable amount of territory in the old empires.

After Abu Bakr's death, the Caliph ʿUmar, one of the most austere and passionate Companions of the Prophet, continued the military campaigns in both Persia and Byzantium. Although the Muslims were beginning to become quite rich, ʿUmar continued to live as simply as Muḥammad had done. He always wore an old, patched woolen tunic; he carried his own baggage, like any other soldier, and insisted that his officers do the same. Islam thus arrived in Palestine as an energetic faith, in the flush of its first enthusiasm. The Byzantine emperor Heraklius, by contrast, had alienated many of his subjects and, sick with depression and in the grip of a spiritual crisis, feared that the Muslim invasion was a sign of God's displeasure. The Arab armies continued their advance into Palestine. On 20 August 636, the Muslims defeated the Byzantine troops at the battle of Yarmuk. In the midst of the fighting, the Ghassānids defected from Byzantium and went over to their fellow Arabs. With the help of the Jews, the Muslims began to subjugate the rest of the country. Heraklius paused only to make a quick dash to Jerusalem to retrieve the True Cross and then left Syria forever. By July 637 the Muslim army was encamped outside the walls of Jerusalem.

The patriarch Sophronius valiantly organized the defense of the city with the help of its Byzantine garrison, but by February 638[9] the Christians were forced to surrender. Tradition has it that the patriarch refused to deliver the Holy City to anybody but Caliph ʿUmar. One of the earliest Muslim sources claims that ʿUmar was not present in person but only visited Jerusalem at a later date. But most scholars still believe that ʿUmar came to receive the city's surrender. He was in Syria at the time, and, given the status of Jerusalem in early Islam, it is very likely that he would have wanted to preside over this momentous occasion. The traditional account says that Sophronius rode out of the city to meet ʿUmar and then escorted the caliph back into Jerusalem. ʿUmar must have looked incongruous amid the splendidly dressed Byzantines, as he rode into the city on a white camel wearing his usual shabby clothes, which he had refused to change for the ceremony. Some of the Christian observers felt that the caliph was being hypocritical: they were probably uncomfortably aware that the Muslim caliph embodied the Christian ideal of holy poverty more faithfully than their own officials.

ʿUmar also expressed the monotheistic ideal of compassion more than any previous conqueror of Jerusalem, with the possible exception of King David. He presided over the most peaceful and bloodless conquest that the city had yet seen in its long and often tragic history. Once the Christians had surrendered, there was no killing, no destruction of property, no burning of rival religious symbols, no expulsions or expropriations, and no attempt to force the inhabitants to embrace Islam. If a respect for the previous occupants of the city is a sign of the integrity of a monotheistic power, Islam began its long tenure in Jerusalem very well indeed.

ʿUmar had asked to see the holy places, and Sophronius took him straight to the Anastasis. The fact that this magnificent complex of buildings commemorated the death and resurrection of Jesus would not have pleased the caliph. The Qurʾān reveres Jesus as one of the greatest of the prophets but does not believe that he died on the cross. Unlike Jesus,

Muḥammad had been a dazzling success in his own lifetime, and Muslims found it hard to believe that God would allow a prophet to die in such disgrace. The Arabs seem to have picked up the Docetist and Manichean idea, current in many areas of the Near East, that Jesus had only *seemed* to die: the figure on the cross was only a phantom, a simulacrum. Instead, like Enoch and Elijah, Jesus had ascended triumphantly to heaven at the end of his life. Later Muslims would express their contempt for the Christian belief by calling the Anastasis *al-qumāmah* ("the Dungheap") instead of *al-qiyāmah* ("the Resurrection"). ʿUmar, however, showed no such chauvinism, even in the excitement of an important military victory. While he was standing beside the tomb, the time for Muslim prayer came around, and Sophronius invited the caliph to pray where he was. ʿUmar courteously refused; neither would he pray in Constantine's Martyrium. Instead he went outside and prayed on the steps beside the busy thoroughfare of the Cardo Maximus. He explained to the patriarch that had he prayed inside the Christian shrines, the Muslims would have confiscated them and converted them into an Islamic place of worship to commemorate their caliph's prayer in the *bayt al-maqdis*. ʿUmar immediately wrote a charter forbidding Muslims to pray on the steps of the Martyrium or to build a mosque there.[10] Later he prayed in the Nea and, again, was careful to ensure that it would remain in Christian hands.

But the Muslims needed a place where they could build a mosque without annexing Christian property. They were also anxious to see the famous Temple of Solomon. According to the traditionist al-Walīd ibn Muslīm, Sophronius tried to pass off the Martyrium and the Basilica of Holy Sion as the "mosque of David," but eventually he led ʿUmar and his entourage to the Temple Mount. Ever since the Persian occupation, when the Jews had resumed worship on the platform, the Christians had used the place as the city rubbish dump. When ʿUmar reached the old ruined gates of the Temple, says the Muslim historian Mujīr al-Dīn, he was horrified to see the filth, "which was then all about the holy sanctuary, had settled on the steps of the gates so that it even came out into the streets in which the gate opened, and it had accumulated so greatly as almost to reach up to the ceiling of the gateway."[11] The only way to get up to the platform was to crawl on hands and knees. Sophronius went first and the Muslims struggled up behind. When they arrived at the top, the Muslims must have gazed appalled at the vast and desolate expanse of Herod's platform, still covered with piles of fallen masonry and garbage. The shock of this sad encounter with the holy place whose fame had reached them in far-off Arabia was never forgotten: Muslims claimed that they called the Anastasis *al-qumāmah,* "the Dungheap," in retaliation for the impious behavior of the Christians on the Temple Mount.

ʿUmar does not seem to have spent any time on this occasion examining the rock, which would later play such an important part in Islamic piety. Once he had taken stock of the situation, he threw handfuls of dung and rubble into his cloak and then hurled it over the city wall into the Valley of Hinnom. Immediately his followers did the same.[12] This act of purification was not dissimilar to the excavations at Golgotha under Constantine. Yet again, a newly triumphant religion was seeking to establish itself in Jerusalem by delving beneath the impiety of the previous occupants to make physical contact with the foundations of the faith.

The Muslims' arrival in Jerusalem was an event of immense importance. At the *hijrah,* the first Meccan converts had painfully torn themselves away from their home and most sacred traditions. Now the Arab armies had started to penetrate a world that was alien in its sophistication and culture to anything known in Arabia, which had hitherto been beyond the pale of civilization. They had to confront mythologies and religious and political traditions that were deeply challenging to their new faith. The Islamic armies were on the move perpetually, cut adrift from their roots. But now they had possession of the *bayt al-maqdis,* the home of some of the greatest of the prophets and their first *qiblah.* It was a homecoming of sorts, a physical "return" to the city of their fathers in religion. Islam could now graft itself physically onto these ancient traditions in a way that symbolized the continuity and wholeness of the Qurʾānic vision. As part of their mandate to sacralize the world, Muslims also had a duty to reconsecrate a place that had been so horribly desecrated.

As soon as the platform had been cleared, ʿUmar summoned Kaʿb ibn Aḥbar, a Jewish convert to Islam and an expert in the *isrāʾīliyāt* or, as we would say, "Jewish studies." It came naturally to the Muslims to consult the Jews about the disposition of the site that had been sacred to their ancestors. Both the Jewish and the Muslim sources make it clear that Jews took part in this reclamation of the Mount. ʿUmar is also said to have traveled to Jerusalem with a group of rabbis from Tiberias. The distinguished tenth-century historian Abu Jafar at-Ṭabarī says that ʿUmar began his meeting with Kaʿb by reciting Surahs 17 and 18 of the Qurʾān, which tell the stories of David, Solomon, and the Temple. Then he asked Kaʿb to point out the best place on the Mount for prayer. Kaʿb chose a spot north of the rock, assuming—almost certainly incorrectly— that it was the site of the Devir. If they prayed there, Muslims could orient themselves toward both Mecca and the Jewish Holy of Holies.[13] This is almost certainly legendary, since it was fifty years before the Muslims showed any interest in the rock. But the story does show Muslims holding on to the principle of Islamic independence of the older faiths. ʿUmar refused Kaʿb's suggestion and decided to build his mosque at the southern end of the platform, on the site of Herod's Royal Portico, where the present Mosque of al-Aqsā stands. There the Muslims would face only Mecca when they prayed. ʿUmar's was a humble wooden building, in keeping with the austere ideal of early Islam. The first person to describe it was the Christian pilgrim Arculf, who visited Jerusalem in about 670 and was struck by its contrast with the magnificent Temple that had preceded it: "The Saracens now frequent a four-sided house of prayer, which they have built rudely, constructing it by raising boards and great beams upon some remains of ruins."[14] It was large, however, able to accommodate three thousand worshippers. By this time, the Arab tribes of the region had converted to Islam and would have come to ʿUmar's mosque for the Friday prayers.

None of the Christians of the city were obliged to convert to Islam, however. Indeed, conversion was not encouraged until the eighth century. Ṭabarī quotes a document that is supposed to be the covenant agreement between ʿUmar and the Christians of Jerusalem. It is almost certainly not authentic, but it does accurately express Muslim policy regarding a conquered people.

> [ʿUmar] grants them security, to each person and their property: to their churches, their crosses, to the sick and the healthy, to all the people of their creed. We shall not station Muslim soldiers in their churches. We shall not destroy their churches nor impair any of their contents or their property or their crosses or anything that belongs to them. We shall not compel the people of Jerusalem to renounce their beliefs and we shall not do them any harm.[15]

Like the other subject people of the Islamic empire, the Jews and Christians of Palestine became "protected minorities" (*dhimmis*): they had to give up all means of self-defense and could not bear arms. Instead, the Muslims provided military protection for which the *dhimmis* paid a poll tax (*jizyah*). In Jerusalem it seems that each family had to pay one dinar per year. Christian pilgrims had to pay a dinar as an entrance fee if they came from outside the Islamic empire, so that they became *dhimmis* during their stay.[16] The *dhimmi* system was not perfect. Later Islamic law evolved some rather humiliating legislation: *dhimmis* were not allowed to build without permission; their places of worship must not tower above the mosque; they had to bow when they presented the *jizyah* tax, were forbidden to ride on horseback, and had to wear distinctive clothing, although these rules were not often rigidly enforced. The system granted the *dhimmis* religious freedom but not equality: they were subject to the Muslims and had to accept Muslim supremacy. But the system did enable people of different faiths to coexist in relative harmony and ensured that, in the main, subject peoples were treated with decency and legality. It was certainly a vast improvement on Byzantine law, which, increasingly, had persecuted such minorities as Monophysites, Samaritans, and Jews.

Not surprisingly, therefore, Nestorian and Monophysite Christians welcomed the Muslims and found Islam preferable to Byzantium. "They did not inquire about the profession of faith," wrote the twelfth-century historian Michael the Syrian, "nor did they persecute anybody because of his profession, as did the Greeks, a heretical and wicked nation."[17] Orthodox Christians obviously had to make a more difficult adjustment. Sophronius had wept when he saw ʿUmar standing on the Temple Mount and remembered the "abomination of desolation" foretold by the prophet Daniel. He is said to have died broken-hearted a few weeks later. Some Christians had apocalyptic fantasies of a Greek emperor liberating Jerusalem and preparing the way for the Second Coming of Christ.[18] The Christians of Jerusalem now found themselves cut off from Constantinople, which seemed to forget all about them. No patriarch was appointed to replace Sophronius until 691. They had to watch the transformation of the Temple Mount, whose desecration had been so important to them. Many probably resorted to the psychological expedient of denial: Christian pilgrims such as Arculf scarcely register the presence of Muslims in their Holy City. Perhaps Christians believed subconsciously that if they ignored the "Saracens" they would cease to exist.[19] It was not difficult for them to do so. Christians retained their majority in the city, and even Muslims would acknowledge that Jerusalem was largely a city of *dhimmis*. Christian holy places had nearly all centered on the Western Hill, and this remained an entirely Christian area. The Muslim conquerors did not settle in that part of town, even though it was cooler and healthier than their own quarters at the foot of their Ḥaram. Muslims were also forbidden to go into those churches that still remained on the Mount of Olives and in the Kidron Valley, especially the Ascension Church and the Tomb of the Virgin—both of which commemorated sites and events that Muslims revered. Christians were allowed to build and restore their churches freely: indeed, during the seventh and eighth centuries there was quite a spate of church-building in Syria and Palestine. Christians were still allowed to hold their processions and services. The only place where Muslims congregated in large numbers was on their Ḥaram,[20] the old Temple Mount, and this place had never played any part in the Christian liturgy.

Immediately after the conquest, ʿUmar agreed with Sophronius that Jews would not be permitted to reside in Jerusalem. When conquering a new city, ʿUmar generally reinforced the status quo, and Jews had long been banned from Jerusalem and its environs. Later, however, this arrangement was revoked. There seemed no good reason to deny the Jews the right to live in the City of David. ʿUmar invited seventy Jewish families from Tiberias to settle in Jerusalem: they were assigned the district around the Pool of Siloam at the southwest corner of the Ḥaram. This neighborhood had been devastated at the time of the Persian conquest in 614 and was still littered with debris and rubble. The Jews cleared this away, using the old stones for their new houses. They were also allowed to build a synagogue—known as "the Cave"—near Herod's western supporting wall, possibly in the vaults underneath the platform.[21] Some sources say that the Jews were allowed to pray on the platform itself, just as the Christians had been allowed to pray in the Medina mosque. Some of the *dhimmis*—Jews and Christians—were employed as guards and servants on the Ḥaram, a privilege which exempted them from paying the *jizyah*.[22] Jews were probably willing to do this because the Muslim conquest had given them new hope. The Byzantine emperors had outlawed Judaism, and Heraklius had been on the point of forcing Jews to be baptized. They had been as willing to support the Muslims as they had the Persians, especially since this new form of monotheism was much closer to Judaism than Christianity. Perhaps some believed that Islam was merely a stage in the Ishmaelites' conversion to the true faith. The Muslims had not only liberated them from the oppression of Byzantium but had also given Jews rights of permanent residence in their Holy City. It is not surprising that this reversal inspired some apocalyptic dreams, especially since the Muslims had attempted to purify the Temple Mount. Were they clearing the way for the building of the new and definitive Temple by the Messiah? Toward the end of the seventh century, a Hebrew poem hailed the Arabs as the precursors of the Messiah and looked forward to the ingathering of the Jewish exiles and the restoration of the Temple.[23] Even when the Messiah failed to arrive, Jews continued to look favorably on Islamic rule in Jerusalem. In a letter written in the eleventh century, the Jerusalem rabbis recalled the "mercy" God had shown his people when he allowed the "Kingdom of Ishmael" to conquer Palestine. They were glad to remember that when the Muslims arrived in Jerusalem, "there were people from the children of Israel with them; they showed them the spot of the Temple and they settled with them until this very day."[24]

The Muslim conquest of Palestine did not mean that the country was suddenly overrun with Arabs from the Hijaz. Ethnically, the population

of Palestine remained as mixed as it had ever been. The Muslim conquerors were not permitted to settle down in their new territories. They
remained a small military caste who lived apart from the local people in
special military compounds. Some of the generals were allowed to build
estates, but only in unoccupied territory. In Jerusalem, as we have seen,
the Muslims did not attempt to settle in the more salubrious part of
town but in a district at the base of their Ḥaram next to the Jewish
Quarter. Jerusalem remained a largely Christian city with one Muslim
sacred area. Muḥammad once said that anybody who spoke Arabic was
an Arab, rather as Greek speakers had been called Hellenes. Over the
years, the inhabitants adopted Arabic as their main language, and today
we call their descendants—Muslim and Christian—Arabs.

When setting up their own administration in Palestine—"Filasṭīn" in
Arabic—the Muslims took over the old Byzantine system, which had
divided the country into three sections. Now Jerusalem was included in
the Jund Filasṭīn, which included the coastal plain and the highlands of
Judaea and Samaria. The Jund Urdunn comprised Galilee and the western part of Peraea, while the Jund Dimashq covered the old Moab and
Edom. The Arabs continued to call Jerusalem either *bayt al-maqdis* or
"Ilya" (Aelia). Their esteem for the city can be seen in the caliber of the
people who were appointed to govern it. Muʿāwiyah ibn Abī Sufyān, a
future caliph, became the governor of the whole of Syria and Palestine
(which the Arabs called al-Sham). Uwaymir ibn Saʿd, one of the most
important Muslim officers, was put in charge of the Jund Filasṭīn and
was known for his decent treatment of the *dhimmis*. ʿUbādah ibn al-
Samīt, one of the five leading experts in the Qurʾān, became the first
qāḍī (Islamic judge) of Jerusalem. Other eminent Companions of the
Prophet, such as Fairuz at-Dailami and Shaddad ibn Aws, also settled in
Jerusalem, drawn by the holiness of the city.

After its auspicious beginning, the Islamic empire seemed in danger of
falling apart when ʿUmar was killed in 644 by a Persian prisoner of war.
It is one of the tragedies of religion that it frequently fails to live up to
its most treasured ideals. Thus Christianity, the religion of love, had often
expressed itself in Jerusalem in hatred and contempt. Now Islam, the
faith of unity and integration, seemed to fall prey to disintegration and
sectarianism. There had been tension between the caliphs and the
Prophet's family regarding the leadership of the *ummah* ever since
Muḥammad's death. Ultimately this conflict would lead to the
Sunni/Shiite split. ʿUmar was succeeded by ʿUthmān ibn ʿAffān, one of
the first Companions of the Prophet and a member of the aristocratic
Umayyad clan. His main contribution to Jerusalem was to create and

endow a large public garden at the Pool of Siloam for the city's poor. ʿUthman was a pious but ineffective leader, and when he was murdered in 656 by a group of officers, they proclaimed ʿAlī ibn Abī Ṭālib, the Prophet's closest living male relative, as the fourth caliph. At once civil war broke out between ʿAlī and Muʿāwiyah, ruler of al-Sham and now the leader of the Umayyad clan. He insisted that ʿUthman's murderers be delivered to him for punishment. The war dragged on until ʿAlī was stabbed to death in 661 by a member of a new fanatical sect. Six months later, Muʿāwiyah was proclaimed caliph in Jerusalem. He was the first caliph of the Umayyad dynasty, which would rule the Islamic empire for nearly a century.

Muʿāwiyah immediately moved the capital of the empire from Medina to Damascus. This did not mean that he was abandoning the old religious ideal, as has sometimes been suggested. Muslims now ruled an empire that extended from Khurasan in the east to what is now Libya in North Africa. By the end of the Umayyad period, the Islamic empire would stretch from Gibraltar to the Himalayas. It was essential that the capital be more central and that the Muslims integrate fully with the territories they had conquered. It was also part of the Muslim mission to sacralize the world: Muslims must move outward and bring the holiness of God to the outer reaches of the empire, not cling to their holy places at home. The move to Damascus was good for Palestine, which was now close to the seat of power and prospered culturally and economically. Muʿāwiyah had been governor of al-Sham for nearly twenty years, and he had learned to love Jerusalem. He would make a point of visiting the city whenever he was in Palestine, even though an attempt was once made on his life there. Muslims collected his words of praise for *bayt al-maqdis,* which show that the Muslims had acquired much Jerusalem lore from the *dhimmis.* The city was "the place where the people will gather and arise on the Day of Judgment"; it was a place that sanctified the people who lived there; the whole of al-Sham was "the chosen land of Allah to which he will lead the best of his servants." Once when he was preaching in the Ḥaram the caliph said: "God loves the area between the two walls of this mosque more than any other place in the world."[25] The Muslims who worshipped there might be far from Mecca, but they could experience its holiness in the Jerusalem Ḥaram.

There was more dissension in the empire after the death of Muʿāwiyah, since some of his Muslim subjects refused to accept the caliphate of his son Yazid. In 680 al-Ḥusayn, the son of ʿAlī and grandson of the Prophet, led an insurrection against the Umayyads and was cruelly slaughtered with his pitifully small band of followers at Kerbala in the Iraq. Henceforth Kerbala would become a holy city to the Shiah, who believed that the *ummah* should be ruled by a direct descendant of Muḥammad. Yet despite the holiness of Kerbala, the Shiis still revered their imams (leaders), who descended from Muḥammad and ʿAlī. Each imam was regarded as the *quṭb* of his generation: he provided Muslims with direct access to heaven by sharing in the holiness of Muḥammad, the Perfect Man.

There was another rebellion against the Umayyads in 683 when Caliph Yazīd fell mortally ill. Abdallah ibn al-Zubayr proclaimed himself caliph and seized the holy city of Mecca. He remained in power there until 692 but could not win the support of the whole *ummah*. After the death of Yazīd, Marwān I (684–85) and his son ʿAbd al-Malik (685–705) were able to reestablish Umayyad power in Syria, Palestine, and Egypt and then in the rest of the empire. ʿAbd al-Malik, a particularly able ruler, began the process of replacing the old Byzantine and Persian systems with a new Arab administration: a centralized monarchy built on the theocratic ideal.

The Dome of the Rock, built by Caliph Abd al-Malik and completed in 691. By restoring the Temple Mount and erecting the first major Islamic building there, Muslims expressed their conviction that their new faith was rooted in the sanctity of the older traditions.

Once he had established a measure of peace and security, Caliph ʿAbd al-Malik could turn his attention to Jerusalem, to which, like all the Umayyads, he was devoted. He repaired the city walls and gates, which had been damaged in the

recent disturbances, and built the Dar Imama, a residence for the governor of Ilya, near the Ḥaram. But ʿAbd al-Malik's greatest contribution to the city was undoubtedly the Dome of the Rock, which he commissioned in 688. Islam had its own holy places; it had an Arabic scripture of extraordinary power and beauty. But Islam had no great monuments, and in Jerusalem, a city filled with magnificent churches, the Muslims felt at a disadvantage. They must have wanted to show the Christians, who, if Arculf's reaction was typical, sneered at their humble wooden mosque on the Ḥaram, that they also had a formidable vision to express. In the tenth century, the Jerusalem historian Muqaddasī noted that all the churches of al-Sham were so "enchantingly fair" and the "Dome of Qumāmah so great and splendid that ʿAbd al-Malik feared that "it would dazzle the minds of the Muslims." They wanted monuments that were "unique and a wonder to the world."[26] So ʿAbd al-Malik decreed that there would be a new dome to challenge the Dome of the Anastasis on the Western Hill and the extraordinary Church of the Ascension on the Mount of Olives, which, when illuminated at night, shone so brightly that it was one of the great sights of Jerusalem.[27] To make sure that the new Muslim building was equally brilliant, ʿAbd al-Malik employed craftsmen and architects from Byzantium, and two of the three people in charge of the construction may have been Christians.[28] Despite this input from the *dhimmis,* however, the first great Muslim shrine carried an unmistakably Islamic message.

The caliph chose to build his dome around the rock that protruded from the Herodian pavement toward the northern end of the platform. Why did he choose to honor this rock, which is not mentioned in either the Bible or the Qurʾān? Later Muslims would believe that Muḥammad had ascended to heaven from the Rock after his Night Journey and that he had prayed in the small cave beneath. But in 688 this event had not yet been definitively linked with Jerusalem: had ʿAbd al-Malik intended to commemorate the *miʿrāj* of the Prophet, he would certainly have inscribed the appropriate Qurʾānic verses somewhere in the shrine. But he did not do so. We do not know whence the devotion to the Rock originates. The Bordeaux Pilgrim had seen Jews anointing a "pierced stone" on the Temple mount, but we cannot know for certain that this was the Rock. In the second century, the Mishnah speaks of a "stone of foundation" (*even shetiyah*) which had been placed beside the Ark in the days of David and Solomon, but the rabbis do not tell us whether this stone was still in place in Herod's Temple, nor do they identify it with the Rock on the devastated Temple Mount. It is likely that both Jews and Muslims assumed that the Rock marked the site of the Holy of Holies in the Temple, though the present scholarly consensus is that it

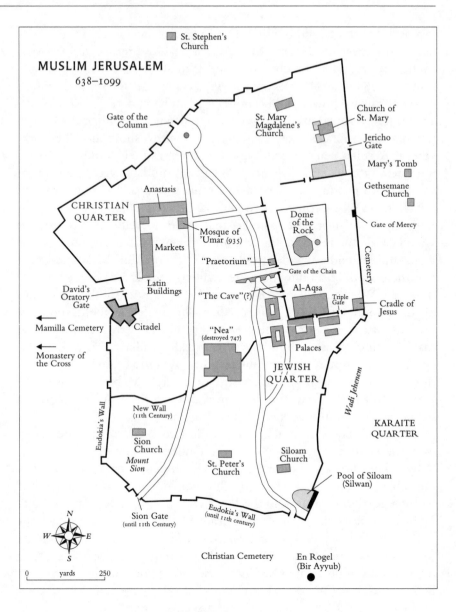

did not.[29] If so, they would naturally see the Rock as the "center of the earth," a place which had always yielded access to heaven. After the building of the Dome of the Rock, Jews and Muslims would both develop legends about the Rock, so the Muslim shrine might have stimulated the Jewish imagination. Both Jews and Muslims came to regard the Rock as the foundation of the Temple, the center of the world, the entrance to the Garden of Eden and the source of fertility—all the usual imagery associated with a monotheistic holy place. From a very early date, the Muslims felt that a visit to their new shrine took them back to the primal harmony of paradise.

Some scholars have recently suggested that ʿAbd al-Malik did not choose the site himself. Their theory is that during the Persian occupation, the Jews had begun to rebuild their Temple on the Mount and that when Heraklius reconquered the city, he commissioned an octagonal victory church to celebrate the Christian triumph over Persia and Judaism. The foundations had been laid, but the Greeks had to abandon their plan when the Arabs invaded Palestine. ʿAbd al-Malik would have been able to build on these Byzantine foundations when work began on the Dome of the Rock in 688.[30] It is a controversial theory to explain a building which, in one sense, is unique in the Islamic world. The Dome of the Rock is not a mosque. There is no *qiblah* wall to orient the faithful toward Mecca and no large space for prayer. Instead, the Rock takes up the central position and two circular walkways have been created around it, marked by forty pillars. The Dome of the Rock is a shrine, a reliquary. It would not have been an unusual building in Jerusalem, however. It was surrounded by famous churches which all enshrined rocks and caves: the Rotunda of the Anastasis around the cave-tomb; the Martyrium containing the Rock of Golgotha; the Nativity Church over the cave of Christ's birth; and the Ascension Church encircling the rock imprinted with Jesus's footstep. These sites all commemorated the Incarnation. Now ʿAbd al-Malik's magnificent new building rose up to defy them.

Inside the Dome, the major inscription over the arches of the inner arcade is devoted almost exclusively to the Qurʾānic verses denying the shocking notion that God had sired a son. It is addressed to the "Followers of the Gospel" and warns them against inaccurate and dangerous statements about God:

> The Christ Jesus, son of Mary, was but God's apostle—[the fulfillment of] His promise which he had conveyed unto Mary—and a soul created by Him. Believe then in God and his apostle and do not say "[God] is a trinity." Desist [from this assertion] for your own good. God is but One God: utterly remote is He in his glory from having a son.[31]

The Muslims were in a minority in Jerusalem; the Christian majority probably regarded their conquerors with disdain, seeing them as primitive barbarians. But the Dome of the Rock, rising majestically from the most ancient holy place in Jerusalem, was a dramatic assertion that Islam had arrived and was here to stay. It issued an imperious call to the Christians to revise their beliefs and return to the pure monotheism of Abraham.[32]

The Jews must have approved of this inscription. Not all of them gazed aghast at this Muslim building project on their Temple Mount. In about 750 the Jewish author of "The Mysteries of Rabbi Simeon ben Yohai" saw the building as a prelude to the messianic age. He praises the Muslim caliph as "a lover of Israel" who had "restored the breaches of Zion and the breaches of the Temple." He "hews Mount Moriah and makes it all straight and builds a mosque there on the Temple Rock [*even shetiyah*]."[33] But the Dome of the Rock also had a message for the Jews. It occupied the site of their Temple, which had itself been built on the place where Abraham had sacrificed his son. Now the sons of Ishmael had established themselves on this sacred site. The Jews were not the only children of Abraham and should remember that he had been neither a Jew nor a Christian but a *muslīm*.

It is more likely that the Dome of the Rock was an assertion of Muslim identity than that it was designed to deflect the *hajj* from Mecca, which was still in the hands of Ibn al-Zubayr. This theory was first proposed by the ninth-century Iraqi historian Yaʿqūbī, who tells us that the circular walkways were designed for the *tawāf*: "the people began to walk round [the Rock] as they walk round the Kaʿbah."[34] This is most unlikely. The ambulatories of the Dome of the Rock are far too small for the complex ritual of *tawāf,* and if replacing Mecca had been the caliph's aim, it would have been far simpler merely to reproduce the Kaʿbah than to go to all the trouble

Inside the Dome of the Rock. The rock and the circular dome symbolize the spiritual ascent to wholeness and perfection.

of designing the elaborate Dome. No other contemporary historian mentions this blasphemous project of the caliph, which would have shocked the whole Muslim world, and ʿAbd al-Malik showed nothing but the deepest piety toward Mecca and the Kaʿbah. Yaʿqūbī was strongly opposed to the Umayyads, and this theory can almost certainly be dismissed as propaganda.

Had the Dome of the Rock simply been a political ploy or designed to score points against the *dhimmis,* however, it would never have won the hearts of the Muslim people. Instead, it became the archetype of all future Muslim shrines. When pilgrims and worshippers entered this building, they found that it perfectly symbolized the path that all must follow to find God.[35] As such, the design may have been inspired by the new metaphysics of the Sufis, the mystics of Islam, who started to come to live in Jerusalem from a very early date. We have seen the importance of symbolism in Islam. Because God was incomparable, the Muslims would eventually forbid all figurative art in their places of worship, but the patterns and shapes of geometry were permitted, because they reflected the ideal world of the imagination. They pointed to the underlying structure of existence to which Muslims must attune themselves if they were to find the harmony, peace, and unity of God. In the Meccan Ḥaram, the square of the Kaʿbah had led to the circle of the *tawāf,* reflecting the journey from earth to eternity. There was a similar pattern in the Jerusalem shrine. The Rock and its cave symbolize the earth, the origin and starting point of the quest. It is surrounded by an octagon, which, in Muslim thought, is the first step away from the fixity of the square. It thus marks the beginning of the ascent toward wholeness, perfection, and eternity, replicated by the perfect circle of the Dome.

The Dome itself, which would become such a feature of Muslim architecture, is a powerful symbol of the soaring ascent to heaven. But it also reflects the perfect balance of *tawḥīd:* its exterior, which reaches toward the infinity of the sky, is a perfect replica of its internal dimension. It illustrates the way the divine and the human, the inner and the outer worlds fit and complement one another as two halves of a single whole. The very colors of the shrine also convey a message. In Islamic art, blue, the color of the sky, suggests infinity, while gold is the color of knowledge, which in the Qurʾān is the faculty which brings Muslims an apprehension of God.

The Dome of the Rock had been built on the site of the first *qiblah* of the Muslims. The place was known to have been a spiritual "center"; in the cave underneath the Rock, Muslims pointed out the spots where Abraham, David, Solomon, and Elijah had prayed. Some could see Enoch's footprint on the Rock, believing that he had ascended thence to heaven. This was one of the places where heaven and earth met; it had helped Muslims to start on their journey to God, and the symbolism of ʿAbd al-Malik's shrine delineated the process of that return to the ultimate reality, an ascent that was also, as the Sufis were discovering, a descent within. We have seen that the architecture of the Temple continued to shape the Jewish spirit long after the building itself was destroyed. Now the Dome of the Rock, the first major piece of Muslim architecture, had become a spiritual map for Muslims.

As such this basic design would often be used for the mausoleum of a man or woman who had been revered as a *qutb,* a link between heaven and earth. In its turn too, the Dome of the Rock had replicated the basic symbolism of Mecca. Yaʾqūbi's story of the Dome's being designed as a substitute for Mecca is almost certainly false, but it does at least reveal the kinship that Muslims felt between the two. At the very beginning of Muslim history, the first *qiblah* had, briefly, been a substitute for the Kaʿbah. Both sites were seen as the Garden of Eden, the center of the earth, and were associated with Adam and with Abraham and the sacrifice of his son. This replication of the central holiness of Mecca in myth and in the architecture of other shrines was not slavish imitation. It was itself a symbol of that struggle for unity, the desire to restore all things to their original perfection by relating everything to the Source.

This became clear in the new traditions about the holiness of Jerusalem that had begun to circulate in the Islamic world by the end of the seventh century—some obviously influenced by the *isrāʾīliyāt.* Jews had always imagined the Temple as the source of the world's fertility, and now Muslims proclaimed, "All sweet water originates from beneath the Rock." The Last Judgment would take place in Jerusalem; God would defeat Gog and Magog there; the dead would arise and congregate in the Holy City on the Last Day. To die in Jerusalem was a special blessing: "He who chose to die in Jerusalem, has died as if in heaven." All prophets longed to be buried there. Before his death, even "Adam commanded that he be brought to Jerusalem for burial." It was said that Muḥammad's friends had wanted to bring his body to be buried in Jerusalem, the resting-place of the prophets and the place of Resurrection. Jerusalem was the natural end of all holy men and holy objects: on the Last Day the Kaʿbah itself would be brought to Jerusalem—a frequently recurring myth which shows how deeply fused the two were in the Muslim imagination.[36]

Caliph al-Walīd I, who succeeded ʿAbd al-Malik in 705, continued to build up the holiness and majesty of the Ḥaram. In 709 he ordered the construction of a new mosque to replace ʿUmar's rough building, on the site of the present Mosque of al-Aqsā. Unlike the Dome of the

Rock, this mosque has been frequently destroyed, rebuilt, and altered. Al-Walīd's mosque was destroyed shortly afterward in an earthquake, and very little survived. We know that it had a marble pavement and columns; later it would be criticized as too long and narrow. The caliph also repaired Herod's supporting walls and extended them upward, though he could not match the massive size of the Herodian stones. Around the walls of the platform, the caliph built colonnades, rather like the ones there today. Finally the old residential quarters in the immediate vicinity of the Ḥaram were cleared to make room for some magnificent imperial buildings. The gates at the southern end of the platform were rebuilt and a complex of public buildings erected, the most spectacular of which was a large palace, two stories high, with its rooms arranged around a central courtyard. The upper story was linked to the Ḥaram by a bridge leading directly into the new mosque. A series of other colonnaded buildings extended to the west and north, along the western supporting wall. There was a hostel for pilgrims, a bathhouse, a barracks, and other public structures. Finally the old Herodian bridge to the Ḥaram from the street known today as the Street of the Chain (Tariq al-Silsila) was reconstructed. This is the largest building complex the Umayyads ever built: did al-Walīd intend to make Jerusalem the capital of the Islamic empire?[37]

Certainly al-Walīd's son Sulayman (715–17) was deeply drawn to Jerusalem and, Mūjīr al-Dīn says, "conceived the plan of living in Jerusalem and making it his capital and bringing together there great wealth and a considerable population."[38] Sulayman had been proclaimed caliph in the city, and delegations had come to the *bayt al-maqdis* to pledge loyalty. Like his namesake Solomon, Sulayman liked to receive the people on the Temple Mount sitting under a domed building near the Dome of the Rock, which was furnished with a carpet, cushions, and divans. Yet his plan of making Jerusalem his capital came to nothing. Jerusalem was too inconveniently situated to be the center of a huge empire. Sulayman recognized this when he built the new city of Ramleh, near Lydda, which became the administrative capital of the Jund Filastīn. It also drew much of the power and prosperity of Jerusalem away to the coast. It was probably impossible for the Umayyads to make a capital of a city which had such an overwhelming Christian majority. But this did not mean that they did not value Jerusalem, as has sometimes been argued. From the earliest times, Muslims had tended to keep their capital away from the holiest places of the region. Muḥammad did not move his capital from Medina to Mecca once he had conquered the city, though he left his followers in no doubt that Mecca was the more sacred place. The first caliphs had kept their capital at Medina, and a similar pattern can be seen in the choice of Ramleh over Jerusalem. Even the Jews, who had no doubts at all about the sanctity of Jerusalem, preferred to live in Ramleh: the Jewish community in the new city was always much larger than the one in Jerusalem.

By the middle of the eighth century, the empire was in turmoil. In 744, Caliph al-Walīd II was murdered and the tribes of both the Jund Filasṭīn and the Jund Urdunn rebelled against his son Yazid, and they continued to oppose his tolerant attitude to the *dhimmis* long after the revolt was suppressed. The rebellion continued in al-Sham against Marwān II, Yazīd's successor, in the course of which the caliph destroyed the walls of Jerusalem, Hims, Damascus, and other cities as a precautionary measure. Jerusalem suffered more damage on 11 September 747 when an earthquake wrecked the city. The eastern and western sides of the Dome of the Rock came down, as did al-Walīd's mosque, the Umayyad palace, and Justinian's Nea Church. Many of the Muslims who lived near the Ḥaram were killed, and, fearing aftershocks, the inhabitants lived in the hills for nearly six weeks. The earthquake heralded the political collapse of the Umayyad dynasty. The descendants of ʿAbbas, the uncle of Muḥammad, had long challenged the Umayyads from their base at Humayma in Transjordan. In 749 they joined forces with Abu Muslīm of Khurasan, who had managed to unite all the opponents of the caliphate into a single party. In January, Caliph Marwān II suffered his final defeat on the great Zaʿb river, east of the Tigris, and shortly afterward the remaining Umayyads were slaughtered at Antipatris in Palestine. Abu al-ʿAbbas al-Saffah became the first ʿAbbasid caliph. But the ʿAbbasids moved their capital to the new city of Baghdad, and this would have serious consequences in Jerusalem.

12

AL-QUDS

THE MUSLIMS had established a system that enabled Jews, Christians, and Muslims to live in Jerusalem together for the first time. Ever since the Jews had returned from exile in Babylon, monotheists had developed a vision of the city that had seen its sanctity as dependent upon the exclusion of outsiders. Muslims had a more inclusive notion of the sacred, however: the coexistence of the three religions of Abraham, each occupying its own district and worshipping at its own special shrines, reflected their vision of the continuity and harmony of all rightly guided religion, which could only derive from the one God. The experience of living together in a city that was sacred to all three faiths could have led monotheists to a better understanding of one another. Unfortunately, this was not to be. There was an inherent strain in the situation. For over six hundred years there had been tension between Jews and Christians, particularly regarding the status of Jerusalem. Each believed the other was in error, and living side by side in the Holy City did not improve matters. Some Muslims were also beginning to abandon the universal vision of the Qurʾān and to proclaim Islam the one true faith. Sufis and philosophers all tried to reassert the old ideal in their different ways, but an increasing number of Muslims began to take it for granted that Islam had superseded the older traditions. Once monotheism makes such exclusive assertions, coexistence becomes very difficult. Since each faith assumes that it—and it alone—is right, the proximity of others making the same claim becomes an implicit challenge that is hard to bear. As each of the three religions tried to assert a distinct identity and an inherent superiority, tension increased in the *bayt al-maqdis* during ʿAbbasid rule.

One reason for the increased anxiety in the city was the caliphate's decision to move to Baghdad, which became the new capital of the Islamic empire in 762. Jerusalem still had a symbolic importance for the ʿAbbasid caliphs, but they were not ready to lavish as much money and attention on al-Sham and the *bayt al-maqdis* as their predecessors. Jerusalem had too many associations with Umayyad rule. Where the Umayyad caliphs had regularly visited the Holy City and were familiar figures about town, the ʿAbbasids were remote celebrities, and a visit from any one of them was a major event, but at first the caliphs still found it necessary to visit Jerusalem as a symbol of their legitimacy. As soon as Caliph al-Mansur finally succeeded in establishing his rule in 757, he visited Jerusalem on his way home from the *hajj*. The city was in a sorry state. The Haram and the Umayyad palace were still in ruins after the earthquake of 747. When the Muslims asked the caliph to restore al-Walīd's mosque at the southern end of the Haram, he simply replied that he had no money, but he suggested that the gold and silver plating of the Dome of the Rock be melted down to pay for the repairs. The ʿAbbasids would not neglect the Haram, but they would not adorn it as munificently as the Umayyads. No sooner had the mosque been restored than it was brought down again by yet another earthquake in 771. When Caliph al-Mahdi came to the throne (775–85), he gave orders that it be rebuilt and enlarged. This time all the provincial governors and the commanders of the local garrisons were told to foot the bill. The new mosque was far more substantial than the old and was still standing when Muqaddasī wrote his description of Jerusalem in 785. It had a beautiful dome and was now much wider than before: what remained of the Umayyad building stood "like a beauty spot in the midst of the new."[1]

The mosque was now called *al-masjid al-aqsā,* "the Remote Mosque": it was now definitely identified with the Night Journey of Muhammad, which had been briefly mentioned in the Qurʾān.[2] The first full account of the Prophet's visionary experience in Jerusalem appears in the biography written by Muhammad ibn Ishaq (d. 767), which tells how Muhammad was conveyed miraculously from Mecca to the Temple Mount by Gabriel, the angel of Revelation; he then ascended through the seven heavens to the divine throne. Some Muslims interpret the story literally, and believe that Muhammad journeyed physically to Jerusalem and ascended to heaven in the body. Others, including ʿĀʾishah, the Prophet's favorite wife, have always insisted that it was a purely spiritual experience. It was natural for Muslims to associate this flight to God with Jerusalem. Ever since the Dome of the Rock was completed in 691, the Haram had been a powerful image of the archetypal spiritual ascent. Sufis were drawn

irresistibly to the *bayt al-maqdis.* At about the time the Aqsā Mosque was
being restored, the celebrated woman mystic Rabi ʿa al-Adawiyya died in
the city and was buried within sight of the Dome on the Mount of
Olives. Abu Ishaq Ibrāhīm ibn Adham, one of the founders of Sufism,
also came all the way from Khurusan to live in Jerusalem. The Sufis were
teaching Muslims to explore the interior dimension of Islamic spirituality: the motif of return to the primal Unity is crucial in their understanding of the mystical quest, and Muḥammad's Night Journey and
miʿrāj became the paradigm of their own spiritual experience. They saw
Muḥammad as losing himself in ecstasy before the divine throne. But this
annihilation (*fanāʾ*) was merely the prelude to his total recovery (*baqāʾ*)
of an enhanced and fulfilled humanity.

Sufis began to cluster around the Ḥaram: some even took up residence in the colonnaded porches around the borders of the platform, so
that they could contemplate the symbolism of the Dome and the Rock
from which Muḥammad had begun his ascent. Their presence could
have been a beneficial influence in Jerusalem, since the Sufis developed
an outstanding appreciation of the value of other faiths. While the jurists
and clergy (*ʿulamāʾ*) who were developing Islamic law tended to stress
the exclusive claims of Islam, Sufis remained true to the universalism of
the Qurʾān. It was quite common for a Sufi mystic to cry in ecstasy that
he or she was neither a Jew, a Christian, nor a Muslim and was at home
equally in a mosque, synagogue, church, or temple, because having experienced the loss of ego in *fanāʾ,* he or she had transcended these man-
made distinctions. Not all Muslims could reach these mystical heights,
but they were deeply influenced by Sufi ideas; in some parts of the
empire, Sufism would become the dominant Islamic piety, though in
these early days it was regarded as rather marginal and dubious.

Now that Muḥammad was thought to have visited Jerusalem, the city
was regarded as doubly holy. It had always been revered as the City of the
Temple, a spiritual center of the earth, but it was now also associated
with the Prophet, the Perfect Man, whose mystical flight (*al-isrāʾ*) from
Mecca to Jerusalem had reinforced the link between the two holy
places. Muḥammad had, as it were, conveyed in his own person the primal sanctity of Mecca to the Distant Mosque in Jerusalem. Like that of
Mecca and Medina, the sanctity of Jerusalem had been enhanced by the
presence of the archetypal Man, who had provided a new link between
heaven and earth. The story of Muḥammad's *miʿrāj* made this quite
clear. By this time, Muslims were beginning to see the life of the Prophet
as a theophany. He had not been divine, of course, but his career had
been an *āyah,* a symbol of God's activity in the world and of the perfect human surrender to Allah. During the eighth and ninth centuries,

A Muslim studying the Qurʾān, the word of God, in the Aqsā Mosque. Through such study Muslims make contact with the divine and learn how to surrender to God in the smallest details of their daily lives.

scholars had begun to compile the collections of Muḥammad's maxims (*aḥādīth*) and customary practice (*sunnah*). These formed the basis of Islamic Law (*sharīʿah*) and of each Muslim's daily life. The *sunnah* taught Muslims to imitate the way Muḥammad spoke, ate, washed, loved, and worshipped so that in the smallest details of their lives they were participating in his perfect *islām*. The symbolic act of repetition linked Muslims with the eternal prototype: Muḥammad, who represented humanity as God had intended it to be.

Few of the stories about Muḥammad's life displayed his perfect surrender to God as eloquently as the *miʿrāj* from the Ḥaram in Jerusalem to the highest heaven. For Muslims it was an archetypal image of the return that all human beings had to make to the source of existence. Muslims who came to pray in Jerusalem thus evolved a symbolic way of imitating the external events of the *isrāʾ* and the *miʿrāj* as a way of participating in the mystical flight of the Prophet. They hoped in this way to approximate to some degree his internal disposition of total surrender. Their new *sunnah* on the Ḥaram was not unlike the ritual processions of the Christians, which followed in the footsteps of Jesus around Jerusalem. During the eighth and ninth centuries—we are not sure exactly when—a number of small shrines and oratories began to appear on the Ḥaram. (See map.) Just north of the Dome of the Rock was the smaller Dome of the Prophet and the Station of Gabriel.[3] These little shrines marked the places where Muḥammad and the angel had prayed with the other prophets before the golden ladder (*al-miʿrāj*) rose before them. Nearby was the Dome of the Miʿrāj, where the Prophet began his ascent to the divine throne. Muslims also liked to pray at the southern gate of the Ḥaram, which was now known as the Gate of the Prophet, because, it was said, Muḥammad had entered the city there with Gabriel walking ahead of him, illuminating the darkness with a light as strong as the sun. Then they would go to a place in the southwest corner of the Ḥaram where Burāq, Muḥammad's heavenly steed, had been tethered after the journey from Mecca.

But other shrines on the Ḥaram recalled the presence of other prophets, and here again we can see Sufi influence. Muslim pilgrims to Jerusalem were being taught to honor the holy men and women who had lived, prayed, and suffered in the city before them. The Dome of the Chain, east of the Dome of the Rock, was said to be the place where King David had judged the Children of Israel. He had made use of a special chain of light, which possessed the faculty of unmasking liars. At the northern end of the Ḥaram was the Chair of Solomon, where the king had prayed after he finished building the Temple. Some of the gates of the Ḥaram were also associated with Jewish history: the Israelites had carried the Ark through the Gate of the Divine Presence (Bab al-Ṣakina) and prayed for forgiveness at the Gate of Repentance (Bab Hitta) on Yom Kippur. But Jerusalem was also the city of Jesus, and the Qurʾān tells a number of stories about his birth and childhood. It says that when Mary was pregnant, Zachariah, the father of John the Baptist, took care of her and that food was provided miraculously. When he was a baby, Jesus spoke prodigiously from his cradle; it was an early *āyah* of his prophethood.[4] Now Muslim visitors to the Ḥaram would pray at the Oracle of Zakariyya in the northeastern corner of the platform and at two shrines in the vaults under the pavement: the Oratory of Mary (Mihrab Mariam) and the Cradle of Jesus (Mahd Isa). Finally, Muslims looked from the parapet to the Valley of Hinnom (Wadi Jahannum) and the Mount of Olives, which would be the scene of the Last Judgment and the Resurrection. They called the "Golden

THE NOBLE SANCTUARY

AL-ḤARAM AL-SHARIF

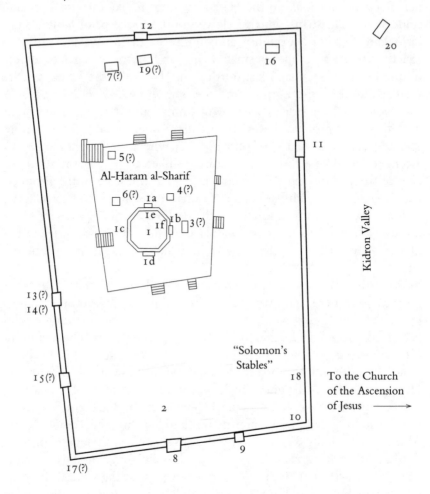

1. Dome of the Rock
1a. Gate of Paradise
1b. Gate of the Angel Israfil
1c. Gate of the Angel Gabriel
1d. Gate of the Aqsa Mosque
1e. Black Paving Stone
1f. The Cave
2. Al-Aqsa Mosque
3. Dome of the Chain
4. The Treasury
5. Dome of the Prophet

6. Dome of the Ascension of the Prophet
7. "Chair" or "Stool" of Solomon
8. Gate of the Prophet
9. Gate of Repentance
10. Oratory of Mary and Cradle of Jesus
11. Gate of Mercy ("Golden Gate")
12. Gate of the Tribes
13. Gate of the Divine Presence
14. Gate of David

15. Gate of Remission
16. Oratory of Zachariah (mentioned in 9th century)
17. Place where Gabriel fettered al-Buraq
18. Oratory of Zachariah (first mentioned in 11th century)
19. Oratory of David (first mentioned in 11th century)
20. Kanisat Mariam (Church of Mary)

Gate" in the eastern wall of the Ḥaram the Gate of Mercy (Bab al-Rahma). This would be the dividing line between the blessed and the damned mentioned in the Qurʾān:[5] after the Judgment, the Ḥaram would be paradise and the Valley of Hinnom hell. In the rooms over the gate, the Sufis had established a convent with a mosque, where they could meditate on the approaching end.

Caliph al-Hārūn al-Rashid (786–809) was the first ʿAbbasid ruler who felt no compulsion to visit Jerusalem, even though he came several times to Syria on his return from the *ḥajj*. The ʿAbbasids were beginning to free themselves from the holy city which had been so important to the hated Umayyads. Hārūn's court at Baghdad was of legendary splendor and the scene of a great cultural florescence. But in fact the caliphate had begun its decline: Hārūn was not able to impose his rule effectively outside of the Iraq, and already local commanders were beginning to establish dynasties in other parts of the empire. They would usually rule in the name of the caliph but enjoyed a de facto independence. At this date, Palestine experienced the decay of the central government economically: under the Umayyads, the country had flourished, but now the ʿAbbasids were beginning to exploit the region, to drain it of its wealth and resources. A plague also wiped out large numbers of the population, and the Bedouin began to invade the countryside, pillaging the towns and villages and fighting their own tribal wars on Palestinian territory. In Umayyad times, the Bedouin had fought for the caliphate; now, increasingly, they became the scourge of the country. The unrest led to the first signs of overt tension between the local Muslims and the Christians in Jerusalem. Bedouin attacked the Judaean monasteries, and the Christians on the Western Hill became aware that the economically deprived Muslims were beginning to resent their affluence. Their churches seemed to represent vast wealth, and in times of hardship Muslims would become enraged by stories of Christian treasure.

To the people of Jerusalem, Hārūn al-Rashid was a remote and unpopular figure, but to the Christians of Western Europe he was a benign personage who had recognized the worth of their own emperor. On Christmas Day 800, Pope Leo III crowned Charles, King of the Franks, the Holy Roman Emperor of the West. The coronation was attended by monks from Jerusalem. The Byzantines refused to recognize Charles's elevation: they were appalled at the idea of an illiterate barbarian assuming the imperial purple. Charles would have to look farther afield for allies, and, like his father, he made approaches to Baghdad. The people of the West were thrilled to have an emperor once again: it seemed that the obscurity and darkness that had fallen upon Europe after the collapse of Rome was finally beginning to lift. They called

Charles "Charlemagne," "Charles the Great," and saw him as the king of a new Chosen People. His capital at Aachen was to be a New Jerusalem, and his throne there had been modeled upon the throne of King Solomon. Instinctively as they sought a new Western identity, the people of Europe reached out for the Holy City of Jerusalem, which had inspired them to make the long and arduous pilgrimage ever since the discovery of the Tomb of Christ. Charlemagne had already exchanged gifts with Caliph Hārūn, and the patriarch of Jerusalem had sent him a gift of relics and the keys of the Anastasis. The caliph was probably glad of a new foreign ally and allowed Charles to build a hospice in Jerusalem opposite the Anastasis, together with a church and a splendid library. Charles also commissioned a building in the Kidron Valley containing twelve rooms for pilgrims and with an estate of fields, vineyards, and a market garden. The new emperor had a base in Jerusalem: his new empire could be said to be rooted in the center of the earth.

In fact, Charles's empire did not survive his death, but the people of Europe never forgot his brief renaissance nor his links with Jerusalem. Later historians and chroniclers claimed that the caliph had been so impressed by Charles that he had wanted to give him the whole of the Holy Land;[6] others said that he had put Charles in charge of the Christians of Jerusalem. It became firmly established in the Western consciousness that even though Hārūn had not been able to give Palestine to Charles, he had made him the owner of the Anastasis. This holy place, therefore, belonged by rights to them.[7] It was a belief that would surface perniciously three hundred years later at the time of the Crusades, when the West achieved another more permanent revival. But some of these imperial dreams could have been expressed by the European monks, priests, and nuns who came out to run Charles's new establishments in Jerusalem. In 807 there were riots in the Nativity Church between Greeks and Latins. Eastern and Western Christians, who were developing very different interpretations of their religion, felt an instinctive doctrinal aversion to one another that led to violence in one of the holiest places in the Christian world. It was also the start of a long and disgraceful antagonism in Jerusalem.

For the Muslims, the new Latin buildings on the Western hill merely underlined the increasing power and wealth of the Christians of Jerusalem. Their own caliph seemed to be neglecting the holy city, whereas the Christian kings spared no expense in securing a foothold there. The Jacobites, a Syrian Monophysite sect, had also built a new monastery dedicated to Mary Magdalene just north of the Ḥaram. These were grim years in Palestine. From 809 to 813 there was civil war in the empire as Hārūn's two sons fought over the succession. When that was settled by the accession of Caliph al-Mamūn, Jerusalem was shaken by yet another earthquake, which gravely damaged the dome of the Anastasis, and by a plague of locusts, which devastated the countryside and led to severe famine. The Muslims, whose quarters beside the Ḥaram were in the more unhealthy part of the town, were forced to leave Jerusalem for a few weeks. When they returned, they were furious to discover that Patriarch Thomas had seized the opportunity to repair the dome of the Anastasis, which was now nearly as big as the Dome of the Rock. The Muslim residents of the city complained bitterly to the imperial commander that the Christians had contravened Islamic law, which clearly stated that none of the *dhimmis'* places of worship should be higher than or as large as a mosque or other sacred building of the *ummah*.

This was a worrying new development, the sort of problem which would continually recur in Jerusalem. Construction had long been an ideological weapon in the city; since the time of Hadrian it had been a means of obliterating the tenancy of previous owners. Now buildings were becoming a way for the communities of Jerusalem to express their hostility toward one another. The Muslims had always felt edgy about the Christians' magnificent churches in the *bayt al-maqdis,* but such display had been easier to bear in the Umayyad period, when the caliphs were willing to pour money into Islamic Jerusalem and into the country as a whole. But now that they were economically deprived and felt abandoned by the caliphate, Muslims found the size of the Anastasis dome intolerable. Islam had burst into Palestine as a confident religion, but a new insecurity had made the religious buildings, formerly symbols of transcendence, come to stand for their own imperiled identity. The Christians too had almost certainly intended the enlargement of their own dome as an aggressive statement of their own power and position in the city. They may have been conquered by Islam, but they would not long remain inferior dependents.

In the end a compromise was reached. The patriarch managed to escape a beating by pointing out that the burden lay with his accusers to prove that the old dome had been smaller than the new—a ruse actually suggested to him by a Muslim, whose family received a regular allowance from the grateful patriarchate for the next fifty years. Caliph al-Mamūn soothed Muslim feelings by ordering new building work on the Ḥaram: eastern and northern gates to the platform were constructed, and the Dome of the Rock was thoroughly refurbished. Al-Mamūn also took the opportunity to expunge the name of the Umayyad ʿAbd al-Malik from the principal inscription, replacing it with his own, though he had the sense not to change the date. In 832 the caliph issued new coins bearing the words "al-Quds": "the Holy," the new Muslim name for Jerusalem.

But the Christians continued to use their religious symbols to undermine Muslim confidence. In the early ninth century, we read for the first time of the annual ceremony of the Holy Fire in the Anastasis on the evening before Easter Sunday. Crowds gathered expectantly in the Rotunda and the Martyrium, which were both in total darkness. The patriarch then intoned the usual evening prayers from behind the tomb, and then suddenly, as if from heaven, a clear white flame appeared within the shrine. Immediately the congregation, who had been waiting in a tense, strained silence, burst into noisy, exultant jubilation. They yelled sacred texts at the tops of their voices, waved their crucifixes in the air, and shrieked with joy. The patriarch passed the flame to the Muslim governor, who always attended the ceremony, and then to the crowds, who had brought their own candles with them. Then they dispersed, carrying the holy fire to their own homes and shouting "Hasten to the religion of the Cross!" as they stormed through the streets. The event seemed to disturb the Muslims, who are our major source of information about the ceremony at this early stage. Each year the governor had to write a report to the caliph, and on one occasion in 947, Baghdad officials actually tried to stop it, reprimanding the patriarch for the "magic ritual" and claiming that "you have filled all Syria with your Christian religion and you have destroyed our customs."[8] The Muslims tried to discount the apparent "miracle" as a sordid trick, and everybody had his own theory as to how it was done. But they could not quite convince themselves that there was nothing in it. They were appalled by the unrestrained joy of the crowds, whose "abominations," according to Mūjīr ad-Dīn, "make one shudder with horror."[9] The sober worship of Islam had nothing comparable, and for these few tumultuous hours the ceremony seemed to blot out the Muslim presence in Jerusalem in a way that fed Muslim anxiety during this difficult time. Each year the Christians seemed to prove the superiority of their faith, and the Muslims could not entirely dismiss this demonstration.

The decline of ʿAbbasid power meant that the imperial authorities found it increasingly difficult to keep order in Palestine. In 841 all the inhabitants of Jerusalem—Jews, Christians, and Muslims—fled in panic from the city during a peasants' revolt, whose leader, Tamim Abu Harb, claimed to be restoring Umayyad rule. He and his followers plundered the city, attacking mosques and churches. The Anastasis escaped total destruction only because of a large bribe offered by the patriarch. It was thus a relief when in 868 the local Turkish commander, Aḥmad ibn Tulun, seized power in Egypt and established an independent state there, which also controlled Syria and Palestine. He was able to restore law and order, the economy improved, and trade picked up. Ibn Tulun was particularly gracious to the *dhimmis.* He appointed a Christian governor in Jerusalem and restored the churches which had been damaged and fallen into disrepair. He also allowed a new Jewish sect to establish itself in Jerusalem.

Daniel al-Qumusi emigrated from Khurasan to Jerusalem with a small band of companions in about 880. They were members of the obscure sect of the Karaites, Jews who rejected the Talmud and based their lives entirely on the Bible. Once they arrived in Jerusalem, however, Daniel gave Karaism an entirely new messianic dimension. In Palestine he came across documents belonging to the Qumran sect, which had recently been unearthed by a dog belonging to the Bedouin. These ninth-century Dead Sea Scrolls convinced Daniel that the exile of the Jews would shortly end. If Jews left their comfortable homes in the Diaspora and settled in sufficient numbers in Jerusalem, they would hasten the coming of the Messiah. Christians and Muslims from all parts of the world came to Jerusalem; why could Jews not do the same? Each Diaspora community should send at least five settlers to swell the Jewish presence in the Holy City. Sahl ibn Masliah, Daniel's disciple, painted a poignant picture of Jerusalem as a city yearning for its true sons. Neglecting the city was almost equivalent to abandoning God himself: "Gather ye to the Holy City and gather in your brethren," he pleaded in his texts and letters, "for at present you are a nation which does not long for its Father in Heaven."[10]

The propaganda of Daniel and Sahl bore fruit, and Karaites began to arrive in Jerusalem. Ibn Tulun allowed them to establish a separate quarter for themselves outside the city walls, on the eastern slope of the Ophel. Since Karaites did not observe the laws of the Talmud regarding food and purity, they could not live with the "Rabbanates," as they called the majority of Jews who accepted the authority of the rabbis. They also practiced an asceticism that was unusual in Judaism, dressing in sackcloth and, in Jerusalem, refraining from meat. They built a cheese factory for themselves on the Mount of Olives. Jews had wept over their ruined Temple on the Ninth of Av for centuries, but the Karaites made this lamentation a way of life. They organized continuous prayer shifts at the city gates, when they would bewail the "desolation" of their holy city in Hebrew, Persian, and Arabic. They believed that the prayers of the Mourners of Zion, as they were called, would force God to send the Messiah and rebuild Jerusalem as a wholly Jewish city. The Rabbanates looked askance at these rituals. They had become very wary of all forms of messianism, which had time and again been the cause of tragedy and unacceptable loss of Jewish life. They believed that God would send the Redemption in his own good time and that it was blasphemous to try to hasten it. Indeed, some rabbis went so far as to forbid Jews to make the *aliyah* to Jerusalem in the hope of bringing the Messiah.

Tulunid rule came to an end in 904, when the ʿAbbasids regained control of Palestine. But they could not hold on to it for long. In 935, Muḥammad ibn Tugh, a Turk from central Asia, seized control of Egypt, Syria, and Palestine, ruling nominally in the name of the Caliph of Baghdad but enjoying a complete de facto autonomy. He and his successors assumed the Asian royal title *ikhshid*. Other dynasties were also rising to power in other parts of the empire, with the result that Palestine was often a battleground for these competing dynasts in their endless struggle for power. To make matters worse, the Greek emperors of Byzantium had seized the opportunity offered by the manifest disorder in the Muslim empire to declare a holy war against Islam. During the tenth century, the Byzantines recovered territory in Cilicia, Tarsus, and Cyprus with the avowed aim of recovering Jerusalem for the true faith.

Inevitably these Greek victories led to a further deterioration of Muslim–Christian relations in Jerusalem. Usually Muslims were able to accept the Christian majority in al-Quds. There was occasional trouble and a residual unease, centering on such matters as the Holy Fire, but they recognized the Christian claim to the city and assumed that there would always be a Christian presence in al-Quds. At the height of his war with Byzantium, the *ikhshid* was able to write to the Christian emperor reminding him that Jerusalem was holy to both faiths. It was

> the sacred land, in which there are the Aqṣā Mosque and the Christian Patriarch. Jews and Christians make pilgrimages there; it is where the Messiah and his mother were born; and it is the place where the Sepulchres of the two are found.[11]

Muslims took part in Christian festivals in a secular way. At Enkainia they celebrated the beginning of the grape harvest; the feast of St. George was the day to sow new seed. The festival of St. Barbara marked the onset of the rainy season. Muslims accepted the fact that Christians were there to stay. But when the Greeks began their holy war and there was bellicose talk about the liberation of Jerusalem, the tension became unbearable. In 938, Christians were attacked during their Palm Sunday procession and the Muslims set fire to the gates of the Martyrium. Both the Anastasis and the Golgotha Chapel were badly damaged. In 966, after a fresh spate of Byzantine victories, Patriarch John IV urged the emperor to proceed immediately to the reconquest of Jerusalem. At once Muslims and Jews attacked the Anastasis, set fire to the roof of the Martyrium, and looted the Basilica of Holy Sion. The patriarch was dragged from the oil vat where he had been cowering during the riot and was burned at the stake.

The *ikhshid* had tried to prevent these hostilities. As soon as John issued his unwise plea to the emperor, troops had been dispatched from Cairo to protect the patriarch. Afterward the *ikhshid* apologized to the emperor for the damage to the churches and offered to rebuild them himself at his own expense. The emperor curtly refused: he would rebuild the holy city himself—with the sword. It was a vicious circle: Greek victories led to reprisals against the Christians, and this "persecution" only fueled the Byzantine holy war effort.[12] It was natural that the Muslims would become defensive about al-Quds: they did not imagine that, in the event of a Greek victory, the Christians would deal as magnanimously with its inhabitants as ʿUmar. For the first time they began to look farther afield than the Haram and built a new mosque on the Western Hill near the Anastasis, which they dedicated to the Caliph ʿUmar. It was the first Muslim building in Christian Jerusalem. Situated provocatively close to their holiest place, the mosque reminded Christians who were the real rulers of Jerusalem and, perhaps, also reminded Muslims of ʿUmar's courteous behavior in the Anastasis—a far cry from their own in recent years.

The *ikhshids* were ejected from Palestine, first by the Shii sect of the Qarmatis and then by the Shii Fatimids of Tunisia, who conquered Ramleh in May 970. For the next thirteen years, the countryside of Palestine was laid waste in a series of campaigns in which Fatimids, Qarmatis, Bedouin, and ʿAbbasid troops all fought one another for the control of the region. Eventually the Fatimids were able to establish their own rival Shii caliphate in 983, moving their capital from Kairouan to Cairo. An uneasy peace settled on the country. The Arab tribes frequently rebelled, but the Jews gave the Fatimids unqualified support. The caliph signed a truce with Byzantium, and arrangements were made to restore the Anastasis and the Martyrium, which had been without a roof since 966. This truce put the Christians in a stronger position, and the tension in the city abated.

Yet an undercurrent of unease remained. When the local geographer Muqaddasī wrote his description of Jerusalem in 985, he saw it as a city of *dhimmis:* "everywhere the Jews and the Christians have the upper hand."[13] The Christians were the most privileged people in Jerusalem: they were much richer than the Jews and more literate than the Muslims. Muqaddasī was intensely proud of his city. There was no building to rival the Dome of the Rock anywhere else in the Muslim world; the climate was perfect, the markets clean and beautifully appointed, the grapes enormous, and the inhabitants paragons of virtue. Not a single brothel could be found in Jerusalem, and there was no drunkenness. But Muqaddasī did not paint an entirely glowing picture. The public baths were filthy, food expensive, taxes heavy, and the Christians rude. He was particularly worried about the decline of intellectual stimulus in Jerusalem. Hitherto, great Muslim scholars, such as al-Shafiʿi, founder of one of the four schools of Islamic jurisprudence, had often come to visit Jerusalem, drawn by the holiness of the city. Now that the Shii Fatimids were in power, the number of visitors from the Sunni world had understandably declined. The Fatimids had established a study center (*dār al-ʿilm*) to propagate Shiite ideals: they had dreams of conquering the whole Islamic world and probably clamped down on the public teaching of the Sunnah. Muqaddasī complained of the Fatimid controls: there were guards at every gate and tight curbs on trade. Above all, there was a lack of scholarly debate. There were very few reputable *ʿulamāʾ* in the city: "Jurists [*fuqahāʾ*] remain unvisited, and erudite men have no renown; also the schools are unattended for there are no lectures."[14] True, there was not an entire dearth of scholarship: the Qurʾān readers had their circles in the city, the Hanifah law school had a study group in the Aqsā Mosque, and Sufis met in their hostels [*khawāniq*]. But such learning as there was tended to be conservative and defensive, adopting the most literal interpretation of the Qurʾān, possibly as a reaction against what Muqaddasī called the "peculiar customs" of the Shiah.[15] Muqaddasī had traveled widely and missed in his own city the easy exchange of views that was the norm in other parts of the Islamic world.

In October 996, the Fatimid caliph al-ʿAziz died in Cairo and was succeeded by his son al-Hākim, a pious, austere man who was passionately committed to the Shii ideal of social justice. Yet he was of a troubled disposition, given to outbursts of fanatical rage and cruelty. His mother had been a Christian, and it is likely that many of the caliph's problems sprang from a conflicted identity. At first the caliph's evident sympathy with the Christians boded well for the Christians of Jerusalem. Al-Hākim appointed his uncle Orestes patriarch and appeared to desire close personal links with the community there. In 1001 he concluded a further truce with Emperor Basil II of Byzantium, which made a great impression on his contemporaries. It seemed as though Islam and Christianity were about to enter a new era of friendship and peace.

Then, out of the blue in 1003, the caliph ordered the destruction of St. Mark's Church in Fustat, which, he claimed, had been built without permission in flagrant contravention of Islamic law. In its place, al-Hākim built the Mosque of al-Rashida, enlarging it during the construction so that it covered the nearby Jewish and Christian cemeteries. There followed ordinances ordering further confiscation of Christian property in Egypt, the burning of crosses, and the building of small mosques on the roofs of churches. The caliph was also disturbed by rumors of trouble in

Palestine: it was said that the Christians and Byzantines had been behind recent Bedouin raids there, which threatened to escalate into full-blown revolution. Everything came to a head one Easter when the caliph noticed a large group of Coptic Christians setting off to Jerusalem "with a great and offensive display." They looked like *hajjis* en route to Mecca. He asked Qutekin al-Adudi, the Shii propagandist, what was happening and heard about the immense riches of the Anastasis Church. At Easter vast numbers of Christians of the highest rank went to pray there. Even the Byzantine emperors were said to have visited Jerusalem incognito: "they carry there immense sums of silver, vestments, dyed cloths and tapestries . . . and over the course of a long period a considerable number of objects of immense value have been amassed."[16] All the pent-up envy of the Christians, fear of their powerful contacts abroad, and worry about the Christian challenge to the Muslim faith can be discerned here. Worst of all, al-Adudi told the caliph, was the ceremony of the Holy Fire, a trick "that made a great impression on [Muslim] spirits and introduces confusion in their hearts."[17]

This account certainly introduced panic into the already confused heart of al-Hākim. In September 1009, the caliph gave orders that both the Anastasis and the Martyrium of Constantine be razed to the ground. Even the foundations of the churches and chapels must be uprooted. Yarukh, the Fatimid governor of Ramleh, carried out the work with deadly thoroughness. All the buildings on the site of Golgotha were torn down, except for a few portions of the Rotunda which, explained the Christian historian Yahya ibn Sa'īd, "proved too difficult to demolish."[18] These fragments have survived and been incorporated into the present building. The tomb, its shrine, and the rock of Golgotha were hacked to pieces with pickaxes and hammers and the ground leveled off, though, Yahya hinted, a small fragment of the tomb remained behind. All the rest of the stone was carried out of the city. It was an entirely uncharacteristic act by an Islamic ruler and filled even the caliph's Muslim subjects with unease. Next new legislation introduced measures designed to separate the *dhimmis* from the *ummah* and force them to convert to Islam. Christians had to wear heavy crosses around their necks and Jews a large block of wood. In 1011 the Jews of Fustat were stoned as they followed a funeral cortège. The synagogue in Jerusalem was desecrated and its scrolls burned. Many *dhimmis* were terrorized into accepting Islam; others held firm, though some Christians took the option of escaping over the border into Byzantium.

The next people to suffer from the caliph's dementia were the Muslims. In 1016, al-Hākim declared that he was an incarnation of the divinity and had been sent to bring a new revelation to the human race. He substituted his own name for that of God in the Friday prayers. This naturally appalled Muslims throughout the Islamic world. There were riots in Cairo, and since Muslims were inevitably more incensed about this blasphemy than Christians, al-Hākim turned his wrath upon them. In 1017 the decrees against Christians and Jews were revoked and the Christians had their property restored to them. Muslims, on the other hand, were forbidden to fast during Ramadan or to make the *hajj*. Those who disobeyed were horribly tortured. The caliph seemed to glide through these violent events in a dream of his own: he wandered through the streets of Cairo unnoticed during the riots, unmolested by the angry mob. One night in 1021 he simply rode out of Cairo alone into the desert and was never seen again.

The mad caliph had left Christian Jerusalem in ruins: somehow a new shrine would have to be built over what was left of the tomb and the Golgotha rock. In 1023, Sitt al-Mulk, al-Hākim's sister, sent Patriarch Nicephorus of Jerusalem to Constantinople to report on the situation. But the following year, the Bedouin tribe of Jarrah rose against the Fatimids yet again, seized control of the roads in Palestine, and systematically laid waste to the countryside. Conditions were so bad in Jerusalem that there could be no thought of building. The position of the Jews was particularly desperate. During the tenth century, the Jewish community of Jerusalem had slightly increased when refugees fleeing disturbances that had broken out in Baghdad and North Africa during the 940s settled in Palestine. Most of the new immigrants preferred to live in Ramleh or Tiberias, however. Jerusalem, one of them wrote, is a town that had been "cursed. . . . its provisions are brought from afar and its sources of livelihood are limited. Many come there rich and there become poverty-stricken and depressed."[19] The Christians held the most affluent and prestigious positions: Jews worked as bankers, dyers, and tanners,[20] though there was little work to be had. Nevertheless, despite these problems, the Jews had moved their governing body from Tiberias to Jerusalem during the tenth century, so that Jerusalem was once again the administrative capital of Palestinian Jewry. Despite their sufferings under al-Hākim, the Jews remained staunchly supportive of the Fatimid government. For their loyalty during the Bedouin rebellion of 1024 they were rewarded by merciless taxation. Many Jews went to prison because they could not pay their debts. There was starvation and destitution, and many Jews died. Others were "empty, naked, sad, poor," wrote Solomon Ha-Kohn, the gaon, or head, of the governing council. "Nothing remained to a man in his house, even a garment for himself or houseware."[21] The suffering continued. Other Bedouin invaded Palestine from the north and the Fatimid caliph al-Zahīr did not regain control of the country until 1029. To strengthen his position, he made a new treaty with Byzantium, promising that the Christians would be allowed to rebuild the

Anastasis. The year 1030 was the first peaceful year that Palestine had enjoyed for almost a century. The Turkish governor al-Dizbiri immediately began the task of bringing order to the shattered country.

Muslims had their own rebuilding to do in Jerusalem. In 1017 the Dome of the Rock had collapsed, and, possibly as part of a fund-raising campaign, the Muslim scholar al-Wasiti published the first anthology of Traditions in Praise of Jerusalem (*fadā'il al-quds*). Now the various maxims (*ahādīth*) about Jerusalem attributed to the Prophet, caliphs, and sages, which had been circulating in the Islamic world since the Umayyad period, could be read in one volume. There had been much tension in the holy city, and, most recently, the disaster of al-Hākim's persecution had made all three faiths defensive, but al-Wasiti's collection was faithful to the old Muslim ideal of integration. Many of the maxims quoted come from the *isrā'īliyāt* and others recalled the presence of the prophet Jesus in Jerusalem. Al-Quds was still acknowledged to be sacred to all the children of Abraham. We can also see how indissolubly Jerusalem had been fused imaginatively with Mecca and Medina. Al-Wasiti, for example, attributes this *hadīth* to the Prophet:

> Mecca is the city that Allah exalted and sanctified and created and surrounded by angels one thousand years before creating anything else on earth. Then he joined it with Medina and united Medina to Jerusalem and only a thousand years later he created [the rest of the world] in a single act.[22]

On the Last Day, paradise would be established in Jerusalem like a bride, and the Ka'bah and the Black Stone would also come from Mecca to al-Quds, which was the ultimate destination of the whole of humanity.[23] Indeed, the two cities of Mecca and Jerusalem were already physically connected in local lore. During the month of the *hajj* to Mecca, on the night when the pilgrims stood in vigil on the plain of 'Arafat, it was said that the water from the holy well of Zamzam, near the Ka'bah, came underground to the Pool of Siloam. On that night the Muslims of Jerusalem held a special festival there. The legend was a picturesque way of expressing the belief that the holiness of Jerusalem was derived from the primal sanctity of Mecca, a process that would be illustrated at the End of Time when the holiness of Mecca would be transferred to al-Quds for all eternity. When that final integration took place, there would be paradise on earth.

The local people certainly felt that Mecca and Jerusalem shared the same sanctity. It was probably during the early eleventh century that Muslims who could not make the *hajj* to Mecca would gather in Jerusalem during the days of the pilgrimage. On the night when the *hajjis* stood in vigil on the plain of 'Arafat, just outside Mecca, crowds of country people and Jerusalemites would gather on the Haram platform and in the Aqsā Mosque facing Mecca, standing all night and praying in loud voices as though they were in ʿArafat. On the Eid al-Adha, the last day of the *hajj*, they would perform the customary sacrifice on the Ḥaram—again, as if they were in Mecca. Some *hajjis* liked to combine their pilgrimage with a pious visit (*ziyārah*) to Jerusalem, putting on there the special white robes traditionally worn for the *hajj* and entering the required state of ritual purity. Some Muslims objected to this innovation. There were traditions which had the Prophet actually advising his followers against going to Jerusalem. But though some of the more exuberant expressions of the devotion to al-Quds were frowned upon in certain circles, it was generally accepted that it was one of the three holy cities of Islam. Muhammad says in this most famous *hadīth*: "You shall only set out to three mosques, the Ḥaram mosque [in Mecca], my mosque [in Medina], and the Aqsā mosque."

Governor al-Dizbiri began the restoration of the Dome of the Rock immediately, spurred on by Caliph al-Zahīr, who was especially interested in the Ḥaram. The wooden beams that were inserted to support the Dome at this time are still in place today. But then, alas, yet again disaster struck. Palestine was hit by an especially violent earthquake on 5 December 1033. Fortunately it happened before sundown, so not many people

Today huge crowds of Muslims assemble on the Ḥaram every Friday afternoon—not simply during the month of the hajj—for communal prayers.

were in their homes. It was days before anybody dared to go indoors, and the population camped in the hills surrounding the city. A whole new building program was needed. The supporting walls of the Ḥaram had to be repaired, and al-Zahīr ordered work to begin on a new city wall, a project which continued for over a generation. The Aqsā Mosque had been badly damaged in the quake: all fifteen of the aisles north of its dome had been destroyed. Work began at once, and the new mosque was complete when the Persian traveler Nasir-i-Khusraw visited Jerusalem in 1047. The mosque was now much narrower: the damaged aisles had been replaced by a nave, spanned by seven arches. Nasir described with admiration the beautiful carpets, the marble flags, the 280 marble columns, and the exquisite enamelwork on the Dome.

By the mid-eleventh century, Jerusalem seemed to have made a valiant recovery. Nasir suggests that there were about 20,000 families living in the city, which would put the overall population at about 100,000. He was impressed by Jerusalem's excellent markets and high buildings. Each craft had its own *sūq,* the town had many excellent craftsmen, and goods were plentiful and cheap. Nasir also mentioned a large hospital, generously endowed, where medicine was taught, and two Sufi hostels (*khawāniq*) beside the mosque where they lived and prayed. One congregation of Sufis had made an oratory in the cloister beside the northern wall of the Ḥaram. Nasir walked meditatively around the shrines and oratories on the Ḥaram platform, going from one "station" to another and recalling the prayers and strivings of the prophets. He imagined the Prophet Muḥammad praying beside the Rock before his *miʿrāj,* laying his hand upon it so that the Rock rose up to meet him, creating the cave beneath. He also communed with the other prophets, thinking especially of King David at the Gate of Repentance and asking for forgiveness for himself. He prostrated himself in prayer at the Cradle of Jesus. As in the Christian holy places, the prophets had left a physical impression behind them. Nasir contemplated the marks that Mary had made when she gripped the marble columns during her labor and—somewhat cautiously—reported that the footsteps of Abraham and Isaac could be seen on the Rock itself.

Nasir was also able to visit the new Anastasis Church, which was completed in 1048 with funds donated by Emperor Constantine IX Monomarchus. Nasir found it extremely beautiful and was quite fascinated by the paintings and mosaics depicting Jesus, the prophets, and the Last Judgment, since he was unaccustomed to figural art in places of worship. The new church was very different from the Constantinian buildings. No attempt had been made to rebuild the Martyrium, and there was now just a field full of stones, broken columns, and masonry in the place where the basilica had been. The new church around the tomb was built on the remains of the Rotunda which had escaped al-Hākim's demolition team. Monomarchus's new building transformed the former Roman mausoleum. The builders added an upper story and an apse, linked to the Rotunda by a great arch. (See diagram.) There had always been a courtyard in front of the Anastasis, and now this was enlarged to include the remains of Golgotha in the southeast corner and the Chapel of Adam behind it. New chapels dedicated to St. John, the Trinity, and St. James were added to the old baptistery wing, and on the Golgotha side of the courtyard were chapels connected with various incidents of the Passion.

Nasir had felt no tension when he visited the new church. He was able to walk in freely and obviously felt quite at home with the pictures of familiar prophets, such as Abraham, Isaac, Jacob, and Jesus. But the Christians had not been able to forget the distress and destruction they had experienced during the past century and still felt vulnerable. In 1055, while the new city walls were under construction, the governor told the Christians that they would have to finance the wall in their own part of town. Since they had no means of paying, they turned to Constantine IX, who eagerly seized the chance of intervening in the life of the Holy City. After negotiations with the caliph, it was agreed that Constantine would provide the money for the new wall on condition that only the Christians would reside in that part of the city. Thus by 1063 the Christians of Jerusalem had their own exclusive quarter. It was bounded by the outside wall from the Citadel at the western gate of the city to the northern gate. Internally, the boundary ran along the old Cardo Maximus until the intersection leading back to the Citadel. Thanks to Constantine IX, they now had "no other judge or lord than the Patriarch."[24] The Byzantines had managed to achieve a protectorate of sorts, a Christian enclave that was separate from the Muslim city and backed by a foreign power. One of the buildings in what was now known as the "Patriarch's Quarter" was the Hospital of St. John the Almoner, which was built at about this time on the site of Charlemagne's old hospice by the people of Amalfi in Italy. The people of Western Europe were making another attempt to recover from the chaos of the Dark Ages. Merchants from the Italian cities had started to trade with the East, and since the Amalfitans had come to play a key role in Fatimid commerce, they easily got permission from the caliph to build a monastery for Italian Benedictine monks which offered accommodation to pilgrims from their city.

Other newcomers to Jerusalem were the Armenians. Like the Europeans, they had been coming to visit the Holy City ever since the fourth

THE ANASTASIS RESTORED
REBUILT BY EMPEROR CONSTANTINE IX, 1048

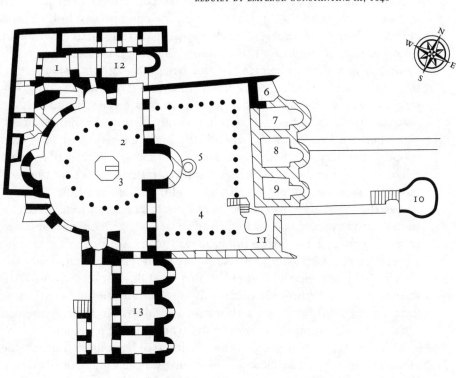

1. Patriarchate
2. Anastasis Rotunda
3. Tomb Aedicula
4. Courtyard: the "Holy Garden"
5. Omphalos
6. Holy Prison
7. Chapel of the Flagellation
8. Chapel of the Crown of Thorns
9. Chapel of the Division
   of the Garments
10. Crypt of St. Helena
11. Calvary
12. Chapel of St. Mary
13. Baptistery wing

century. Many had stayed on as monks and ascetics. Now they brought the new church on Mount Sion, which had been built in the 1030s by the Georgian monk Prochore at the same time as he built the Monastery of the Cross outside the city walls. The Armenians acquired the Sion church from the Georgians some forty years later and made it their cathedral. It was dedicated to St. James (or "Surp Hagop," as he was called in Armenian). In its main shrine, the Kilkhateer, was the head of James the "Pillar," the apostle of Jesus who had been beheaded in Jerusalem in about 42 CE. Under the high altar was the tomb of James

the Tzaddik, the first "bishop" of Jerusalem, who had long been venerated by Christians on Mount Sion. Once they were installed, the
Armenian monks gradually began to build a convent for their patriarch
and the Brotherhood of St. James, which included priests, bishops, and
deacons. Over the centuries, the Armenian patriarchs patiently bought
land and houses adjoining the convent buildings until they eventually
owned an almost unbroken ring of properties in the southwest corner of
the city. When Armenian pilgrims decided to stay in Jerusalem, they
were assigned a house in the developing Armenian quarter and became
part of a permanent secular community supporting the brotherhood.
They became known as the *kaghakatsi,* inhabitants of Jerusalem, and
adopted the city as their own. For their parish church, they were
assigned the Chapel of the Holy Archangels (Hristagabed) near the center of the convent, which was thought to be on the site of the house of
Annas, the priest who had helped Caiaphas to condemn Jesus to death.
In its courtyard, there was an ancient olive tree where Jesus was supposed
to have been tied. Gradually the *kaghakatsi* came to form a sizable and
separate community. The Armenians were Monophysites, but, unlike the
Greek Orthodox and the Latin Catholics, they did not receive converts,
so they remained ethnically distinct. By the end of the nineteenth century, there would be about a thousand *kaghakatsi,* and the Armenian
Quarter would comprise a tenth of the whole city of Jerusalem.

More and more pilgrims were flocking to Jerusalem during the
eleventh century. The influx was particularly noticeable from Western
Europe, where pilgrimage was promoted by the reforming monks of the
Abbey of Cluny in Burgundy as a way of instructing the laity in true
Christian values. In the millennial year 1000, according to the Burgun-
dian annalist Raoul Glaber, an "immeasurable multitude" of nobles and
common folk took to the road, determined to reach Jerusalem: they
came from Italy, Gaul, Hungary, and Germany and were largely inspired
by apocalyptic ideas.[25] People recalled the old prophecies, dating from
the late Roman period, which had foretold that before the End of Days
an emperor from the West would be crowned in Jerusalem and would
fight the Antichrist there. The Book of Revelation indicated that this
final battle would take place a thousand years after Christ's victory over
Satan,[26] so in the year 1000, pilgrims congregated in Jerusalem to witness
the Second Coming. Like the Karaites, they probably believed that their
presence in the Holy City would force God to send down the New
Jerusalem and a better world order. When the End of Days failed to
occur, people began to wonder whether 1033, the thousandth anniversary of the crucifixion, was a more appropriate date; there was severe
famine in Europe that year, and, Glaber tells us, many people imagined

that this catastrophe heralded the Last Days. First the peasants, then the established classes of society, and finally the rich nobles began "to stream towards the Saviour's Tomb in Jerusalem." Glaber was convinced that never before had the Holy City witnessed such a press of people, and the pilgrims were convinced that this "presaged nothing else than the coming of the miserable Antichrist, which must indicate the coming end of the world."[27] There was a desperation in the Christianity of Western Europe, as people struggled out of the long period of barbarism and disorder toward Jerusalem, an emblem of salvation.

The great Western pilgrimage of 1064 was very different. Led by Arnold, bishop of Bamberg, these crowds of pilgrims were not traveling in holy poverty. Life in Europe had improved, and the German grandees flaunted their wealth and magnificence proudly—and rashly. The Bedouin tribes were always on the lookout for pilgrim bands, knowing that even the humblest might have gold pieces sewn into their rough cloaks. The spendor of the German pilgrimage was an open invitation: tribes attacked the pilgrims, who died in droves almost within sight of the Holy City. Every thirty years or so, there had been a huge mass pilgrimage from Europe. As the century drew to a close, it was time for another of these Western expeditions, but the pilgrims who arrived in the Holy City in 1099 would come with a sword, prepared not only to defend themselves but to fight and kill.

Jewish pilgrims and settlers were also inspired to make the *aliyah* to Jerusalem, and, like the Christians, were often impelled by catastrophe at home. When the nomadic Berbers invaded Kairouan during the 1050s, Jews and Muslims both migrated to Palestine to escape the devastation; other immigrants arrived from Spain in flight from penury and starvation. Some of these Jewish "Maghribis," as these Westerners were called, settled in the Holy City, but the hard conditions there made them homesick for their homes at the other end of the Islamic world. Joseph ha-Kohn described the lot of Jerusalem's Jews, "eaten by the swallowers . . . devoured by the insolent . . . the poor, the destitute, squeezed and mortgaged." The presence of Christians and Muslims was intolerable. As if life were not bad enough, Jews had to listen to "the noise of the Edom [Christian] masses" during their pilgrimages and "the five-fold mendacious voice [of the Muslim muezzin] which never stops."[28] Since the Jerusalem community was entirely dependent on alms from Fustat and Ramleh, any plague or drought there meant that they went hungry.

Yet despite these hardships, Jewish pilgrims continued to make the journey to Jerusalem, especially during the month of Tishri, when they would gather there to celebrate Sukkoth, coming from as far away as Khurasan. They had developed their own rituals for this messianic festival.

First pilgrims and residents would circle the city walls, praying at the Ḥaram gates as of old. Then they would climb the Mount of Olives, singing psalms as they made the ascent. There, wrote the gaon Solomon ben Judah, they would stand "facing the Temple of God on the holidays, the place of the Divine Presence, his strength and his footstool."[29] Despite the melancholy sight of the Temple Mount covered with Muslim shrines, these enormous Jewish rallies on the Mount of Olives were convivial and joyous. Jews would greet one another warmly and embrace with emotion. They liked to gather around a large stone on the mountain which was thought to mark the spot where the Shekhinah had rested when leaving Jerusalem. Here the Jerusalem Gaon would preach his annual sermon. Unfortunately a sectarian hostility clouded the friendliness of this gathering: the gaon would take out a Torah scroll and solemnly excommunicate the Karaites, who had their own camp on the mountain opposite the Rabbanates. This excommunication nearly always led to serious quarreling and even to unseemly brawling, and Gaon Solomon, a peaceable man, wanted to abolish the custom. The Muslim authorities also insisted that the excommunications cease, maintaining that Rabbanates and Karaites both had the right to practice their faith as they saw fit.

The Fatimid occupation of Jerusalem had been a mixed blessing for the city. Soon the inhabitants had to face a new enemy from the north. In about 1055, Turkish tribes, recent converts to Sunni Islam, took control of northern Syria in the name of the ʿAbbasid caliph and the Sunnah. They were gifted administrators and excellent soldiers. Because the Seljuk family played a key role in these campaigns, these Turkomans ("Noble Turks") are often called Seljuks, though not all their leaders were members of this family. In 1071, the Turkish leader Alp Aslan smashed through the defense lines of the Byzantines at Manzikurt in Armenia, and soon the Turks had overrun most of Asia Minor. Meanwhile, Atsiz ibn Abaq led the holy war against the Shiites, invading Palestine, conquering Ramleh, and laying siege to Jerusalem. The city surrendered in June 1073, and the inhabitants were amazed at the restraint of the conquerors. Atsiz had issued an amnesty for all the people of Jerusalem, and he ordered his men not to touch anything and not to plunder the great wealth in the city. He even appointed guards to protect the churches and mosques. The Fatimid garrison—composed of Turks, Sudanese, and Berbers—remained in the city; the Turks went over to the Seljuks, and the others stayed on as private citizens.

The Turkish occupation meant that Jerusalem was now back in the Sunni sphere. Scholars began to return to Jerusalem, and the city enjoyed a renaissance after the Fatimid repression of intellectual life. Turkoman rule brought prosperity to the city. In 1089 a new mosque was built, and two of the four schools of Islamic jurisprudence, the Shafi'i and the Hanafi, founded establishments in the city. The Turks rebuilt the old church commemorating the birthplace of the Virgin Mary beside the Pool of Beth-Hesda and transformed it into a Shafi'i *madrasah,* under the leadership of Sheikh Nasr al-Maqdisi. *Ḥadīth* and *fiqh* (jurisprudence) studies flourished in Jerusalem once again: Mūjīr ad-Dīn listed the eminent scholars who came to teach and write in al-Quds, including Abu al-Fath Nasr and al-Tartushi, the great jurist from al-Andalus. In 1095 the eminent Sunni scholar Abu Hamid al-Ghazzālī came to Jerusalem to pray and meditate; he took up residence in the little convent above the Gate of Mercy, where he practiced Sufi exercises. In Jerusalem he wrote his famous treatise *The Revival of the Religious Sciences,* which, as we shall see in Chapter 14, became the blueprint of the reformed Sunnah. At about the same time, the Spanish traveler Abu Bakr ibn al-ʿArabi visited Jerusalem and found it so stimulating that he decided to stay for three years. He was impressed by the two law schools, where prominent scholars gave regular lectures and seminars, using methods of debate and discussion that were unknown in al-Andalus. He was also impressed by the dialogues between Muslim intellectuals and the *dhimmis,* where Jews, Christians, and Muslims explored many topics of religion and spirituality together.

There was strife in the city. In 1077 the pro-Fatimid groups in Jerusalem rebelled against the Turks while Atsiz was campaigning in Egypt. The *qāḍī* imprisoned all the Turkish women and children and barricaded them into the Citadel; he also confiscated Turkish property. This time when Atsiz appeared outside the city walls there was no mercy. When the city surrendered, his soldiers massacred about three thousand of the inhabitants, sparing only those who had sought sanctuary in the Ḥaram. The Christians in the Patriarch's Quarter were safe, however. Not so the Jews, who had always been loyal supporters of the Fatimids and may not have enjoyed the same Tulunid patronage as the Christians. They describe Turkoman rule as a time of catastrophe, speaking of widespread destruction and ruin, the burning of harvests, the razing of plantations, plunder, and terrorism. The Jewish Yeshiva moved from Jerusalem to Tyre during this period, and leading Muslims who supported Fatimid rule were also forced to leave the country. Yet most of the population seemed able to block out these violent disturbances. Ibn al-ʿArabi was astonished by the way the inhabitants went about their daily business during a small uprising. A rebel had entrenched himself in the citadel, the governor's archers were bombarding him, and the soldiers, divided into two factions, began to fight one another. If such a thing had happened in al-Andalus, fighting would have broken out all over the city, shops would have been closed, and normal life would have been entirely disrupted. Instead, Ibn al-ʿArabi watched with amazement the way life went on as usual in this relatively small town:

> No market was closed because of these disturbances, no one of the commoners participated in it by making violence, no ascetic left his place in the Aqsā Mosque and no discussion was suspended.[30]

The inhabitants of Jerusalem had been through so many violent reversals during the previous two hundred years that they had acquired a lordly indifference to such relatively minor vicissitudes.

Despite such occasional outbursts, therefore, Jerusalem prospered under Turkoman rule and became the most important city of Palestine. Ramleh had never fully recovered from the 1033 earthquake, but Jerusalem now had new walls, impressively restored buildings, and a thriving cultural life and had become an international city, visited each year by thousands of pilgrims from all over the world. Yet even as Ibn al-ʿArabi was enjoying its amenities, a catastrophe was approaching the city which not even the Jerusalemites could regard with their usual phlegm. The Fatimids had not abandoned Palestine: in August 1098, the Shii caliph al-Afdal conquered the city after a siege of six months, to the joy of Fatimid supporters. But less than a year later, in June 1099, the Christian Crusaders from Europe arrived in the hills outside Jerusalem. When they first caught sight of the Holy City, the whole army was convulsed with a fearful ecstasy. Soldiers wept and screamed aloud, their delight mingling with rage as they saw the golden Dome of the Rock majestically dominating the spectacle of *their* Holy City. Then the Crusader army settled outside the walls of Jerusalem, where, says the anonymous author of the *Gesta Francorum,* rejoicing and exulting, they laid siege to the city.

13

CRUSADE

AFTER THE BATTLE of Manzikurt in 1071, the Byzantines had lost almost the whole of Asia Minor to the Seljuks and found that Islam was virtually on their doorstep. Yet the power of the Turkomans was waning, and it seemed to Emperor Alexius Comnenus I that a few brisk campaigns might settle them once and for all. Early in 1095 he asked Pope Urban II for military help, expecting to be sent a few detachments of the Norman mercenaries who had fought for him before. The pope, however, had more ambitious plans. Later in the year he addressed the clergy, knights, and poor people of Europe at the Council of Clermont and preached a holy war of liberation. He begged the knights to stop fighting one another in the pointless feudal wars that were tearing Europe apart and to go to the aid of their fellow Christians in Anatolia, who had been subject to the Muslim Turks for over twenty years. Once they had freed their brethren from the yoke of the infidel, they should march to Jerusalem to liberate the tomb of Christ from Islam. There would be the Peace of God in Europe and the War of God in the Near East. We have no contemporary record of the actual words of Urban's speech, but it seems certain that he saw this expedition, which would become known as the First Crusade, as an armed pilgrimage, similar to the huge massed pilgrimages which had already made their way to the Holy City three times during the eleventh century. Hitherto pilgrims had been forbidden to bear arms; now the pope had given them a sword. At the end of his speech, Urban received an immense ovation. The vast crowd shouted with one voice, "*Deus hoc vult!*": "God wills this!"

The response was extraordinary, widespread, and immediate. Popular preachers spread the word, and in the spring of 1096 five armies of about sixty thousand soldiers accompanied by hordes of noncombatant peasants and pilgrims with their wives and families set off on the road to Jerusalem. Most of them died on the perilous journey through Eastern Europe. They were followed in the autumn by five more armies of some 100,000 men and a crowd of priests. As the first detachments struggled toward Constantinople, it seemed to Princess Anna Comnena as though "the whole West, and as much of the land as lies beyond the Adriatic Sea to the Pillars of Hercules—all this, changing its seat, was bursting forth into Asia in a solid mass with all its possessions."[1] The emperor had asked for conventional military help and found that he had inspired what seemed like a barbarian invasion. The Crusade was the first cooperative venture of the new West as it emerged from the Dark Ages. All classes were represented: priests and prelates, nobles and peasants. They were all seized by a passion for Jerusalem. It is not the case that the Crusaders were merely seeking land and wealth: crusading was grim, frightening, dangerous, and expensive. Most Crusaders returned home having lost their possessions, and they would need all their idealism merely to survive. It is not easy to define the Crusader ideal, since these pilgrims all had very different conceptions of their expedition. The higher clergy probably shared Urban's ideal of a holy war of liberation to enhance the power and prestige of the Western church. Many of the knights saw it as their duty to fight for Jerusalem, the patrimony of Jesus, as they would fight for the rights of their feudal lord. The poorer Crusaders seemed inspired by the apocalyptic dream of a New Jerusalem. But Jerusalem was the key. It is unlikely that Urban would have got the same response if he had made no mention of the tomb of Christ.

But this idealism had a dark underside; it soon became apparent that the victory of Christ would mean the death and destruction of others. In the spring of 1096 a band of German Crusaders massacred the Jewish communities of Speyer, Worms, and Mainz along the Rhine. This had certainly not been the pope's intention, but it seemed ridiculous to these Crusaders to march thousands of miles to fight Muslims—about whom they knew next to nothing—when the people who had actually killed Christ (or so the Crusaders believed) were alive and well on their very doorsteps. These were the first full-scale pogroms in Europe; they would be repeated every time a new Crusade was preached. The lure of Christian Jerusalem thus helped to make anti-Semitism an incurable disease in Europe.

The Crusading armies which left in the autumn of 1096 were more orderly than their predecessors, and they did not turn aside to kill Jews. Most reached Constantinople in good order. There they swore that they would faithfully return territory that had previously belonged to Byzantium, though as events proved, some had no intention of keeping their vow. It was a good time to attack the Seljuks: their early solidarity had given way to factional strife, and the emirs were fighting one another. The Crusaders made a good start, and they inflicted defeats on the Turks at Nicaea and Dorylaeum. But it was a long journey, food was scarce, and the Turks pursued a scorched-earth policy. It took the Crusaders three years of unimaginable hardship to reach Jerusalem. When they arrived at Antioch, they laid siege to this powerfully fortified city during the terrible winter of 1097–98; over the course of the siege, one man in seven starved to death and half the army deserted. Yet, against the odds, the Crusaders were ultimately victorious, and when they stood at last before the walls of Jerusalem in 1099, they had changed the map of the Near East. They had destroyed the Seljuk base in Asia Minor and created two new principalities governed by Western rulers: one in Antioch, under the Norman Bohemund of Tarentino, and the other in Armenian Edessa, ruled by Baldwin of Boulogne. Yet their victories had been hard-won. A fearful reputation had preceded these ironclad warriors. There were dark rumors of cannibalism at Antioch, and the barbaric Christians from Europe were known to be utterly ruthless and fanatical in their religious zeal. Many of the Greek Orthodox and Monophysite Christians of Jerusalem, alerted by these alarming tales, fled to Egypt. Those who remained behind were expelled from the city by the Muslim governors, together with the Latin Christians, who were rightly suspected of sympathy with the Crusaders. Their knowledge of the city and the terrain proved extremely valuable to the Crusaders during the siege.

The Crusader leaders deployed their troops around the walls. Robert the Norman was posted near the ruined Church of St. Stephen in the north; Robert of Flanders and Hugh of St. Poll were placed on the southwest of the city; Godfrey of Bouillon, Tancred, and Raymund of St. Gilles encamped opposite the citadel, while another army was posted on the Mount of Olives to ward off an attack from the east. Then Raymund moved his Provençal troops to defend the holy places outside the walls on Mount Sion. At first the Crusaders made little progress. They were still not accustomed to besieging the stone cities of the East, which were far larger and more imposing than most towns in Europe, and they lacked the skill or the materials to build siege engines. Then a Genoese fleet arrived in Jaffa and dismantled its ships of masts, cords, and hooks, which enabled the Crusaders to build two towers or "belfreys," which could be wheeled up to the walls—a device that was unfamiliar to the Muslims. Finally on 15 July 1099, a soldier in Godfrey's army managed to break into the city from one of these towers, and the rest of the Crusaders followed, falling on the Muslim and Jewish defenders of the city like the avenging angels of the Apocalypse.

For three days the Crusaders systematically slaughtered about thirty thousand of the inhabitants of Jerusalem. "They killed all the Saracens and the Turks they found," said the author of the *Gesta Francorum* approvingly, "they killed everyone, whether male or female."[2] Ten thousand Muslims who had sought sanctuary on the roof of the Aqsā were brutally massacred, and Jews were rounded up into their synagogue and put to the sword. There were scarcely any survivors. At the same time, says Fulcher of Chartres, a chaplain in the army, they were cold-bloodedly appropriating property for themselves. "Whoever first entered a house, whether he was rich or poor, was not challenged by any other Franks. He was to occupy and own the house or the palace and whatever he found in it as if it was entirely his own."[3] The streets literally ran with blood. "Piles of heads, hands and feet were to be seen," says the Provençal eyewitness Raymond of Aguiles. He felt no shame: the massacre was a sign of the triumph of Christianity, especially on the Ḥaram:

> If I tell the truth it will exceed your powers of belief. So let it suffice to say this much, at least, that in the Temple and the Porch of Solomon, men rode in blood up to their knees and bridle reins. Indeed, it was a just and splendid judgment of God that this place should be filled with the blood of unbelievers since it had suffered so long from their blasphemies.[4]

Muslims and Jews were cleared out of the Holy City like vermin.

Eventually there was no one left to kill. The Crusaders washed and processed to the Anastasis, singing hymns with tears of joy rolling down their faces. Standing around the tomb of Christ, they sang the Office of the Resurrection, its liturgy seeming to herald the dawn of a new era. As Raymund saw it:

> This day, I say, will be famous in all future ages, for it turned our labors and sorrows into joy and exultation; this day, I say, marks the justification of all Christianity, the humiliation of paganism, the renewal of faith. "This is the day that the Lord hath made, let us rejoice and be glad therein," for on this day the Lord revealed himself to his people and blessed them.[5]

This was a view quickly adopted by the establishment of Europe, who had probably been horrified at the first news of the massacre. But the Crusade had been such a resounding success—against all odds—that they came to believe it had enjoyed God's special blessing. Within ten years, three learned monks—Guibert of Nogent, Robert the Monk, and Baldrick of Bourgeuil—had written accounts of the First Crusade which entirely endorsed the belligerent piety of the Crusaders. Henceforth the Muslims, hitherto regarded with relative indifference, would be viewed in the West as a "vile and abominable race," "absolutely alien to God" and fit only for "extermination."[6] The Crusade had been an act of God on a par with the Exodus of the Israelites from Egypt; the Franks were now the new chosen people of God: they had taken up the vocation that the Jews had lost.[7] Robert the Monk made the astonishing claim that the Crusaders' conquest of Jerusalem was the greatest event in world history since the Crucifixion.[8] Soon the Antichrist would arrive in Jerusalem and the battles of the Last Days would begin.[9]

But the Crusaders themselves were nothing if not practical, and before any of these apocalyptic triumphs occurred, the city had to be cleared up. William of Tyre says that the bodies were burned with great efficiency so that the Crusaders could make their way to the holy places "with greater confidence"[10]—without, presumably, suffering the inconvenience of tripping over severed limbs. But in fact the task was too great, and bodies were still lying around the city five months later. When Fulcher of Chartres arrived in Jerusalem to celebrate Christmas that year, he was horrified:

> Oh, what a stench there was around the walls of the city, both within and without, from the rotting bodies of the Saracens slain by ourselves at the time of the capture of the city, lying wherever they had been hunted down.[11]

Overnight, the Crusaders had turned the thriving and populous city of Jerusalem into a stinking charnel house. There were still piles of putrefying corpses in the streets when the Crusaders held a market three days after the massacre. With great festivities and celebration, they sold their loot, blithely unconcerned about the carnage they had inflicted and the hideous evidence lying at their feet. If a respect for the sacred rights of their predecessors is a test of the integrity of any monotheistic conqueror of Jerusalem, the Crusaders must come at the bottom of anybody's list.

They had not looked further than the conquest and had no clear idea about how the city should be governed. The clerics believed that the Holy City should be run by a patriarch on theocratic lines, the knights wanted one of their own to be its lay ruler, while the poor, who exerted considerable influence on the Crusaders, were hourly expecting the New Jerusalem and wanted no conventional government at all. At length a compromise was achieved. Since the Greek Orthodox patriarch had been expelled by the Muslims during the siege, the Crusaders appointed Arnulf of Rohes, the chaplain of Robert of Normandy, to fill the office, replacing a Greek by a Latin. They then chose Godfrey of Bouillon, an unintelligent but pious young man of enormous physical courage, as their leader. Godfrey declared that he could not wear a crown of gold in the city where his Savior had worn a crown of thorns and took the title "Advocate of the Holy Sepulcher." The city would be ruled by the patriarch, but Godfrey would give him military protection (*advocatia*). A few months later, Daimbert, archbishop of Pisa, arrived in Jerusalem as the official papal legate. He summarily deposed Arnulf, assumed the patriarchate himself, and banished all the local Christians— Greeks, Jacobites, Nestorians, Georgians, and Armenians—from the Anastasis and the other churches of Jerusalem. Pope Urban had given the Crusaders the mandate of helping the Oriental Christians, but now they were extending the intolerance of their predecessors in the Holy City to the people of their own faith. On Easter Sunday 1100, Godfrey gave Patriarch Daimbert "the city of Jerusalem with the Tower of David and all that pertained to Jerusalem,"[12] on condition that the advocate could make use of the city while he conquered more land for the kingdom.

This was the most pressing task for the Crusaders. Their conquest of Jerusalem had not liberated the whole of Palestine for the church. The Fatimids were still in control of many parts of the country, including the vital coastal cities. Godfrey began to conduct raids against the Fatimid bases backed up by the Pisan fleet. By March 1100, the emirs of Ascalon, Caesarea, Acre, and Arsuf had surrendered and accepted Godfrey as their overlord. The sheikhs of Transjordan followed suit, while Tancred established a principality in Galilee. Yet the situation was precarious. The kingdom now had defensible borders, but for the next twenty-five years it would have to struggle to survive, surrounded as it was by bitterly hostile enemies.

The Crusaders' chief problem was manpower. Once Jerusalem had been won, most of their soldiers went home, leaving only a skeleton army behind. Jerusalem was particularly desolate. It had recently housed about 100,000 people, but now only a few hundred lived in the empty, ghostly city. As William of Tyre said, "the people of our country were so few in number and so needy that they scarcely filled one street."[13] They huddled together for security in the Patriarch's Quarter around the Holy Sepulcher.[14] The rest of the city remained uninhabited, its streets dangerously haunted by prowlers and Bedouin who broke into the empty houses. Jerusalem could not be adequately defended: when Godfrey led his soldiers on a raid, there were only a few noncombatants and pilgrims left to ward off an attack. Once the hostilities died down, Muslims and Jews began to filter back to such cities as Beirut, Sidon, Tyre, and Acre, and Muslim peasants remained in the countryside. But after the conquest of Jerusalem, the Crusaders promulgated a law banning Jews and Muslims from the Holy City; the local Christians were also expelled, because the Crusaders suspected them of complicity with Islam. To the unsophisticated Westerners, these Palestinian, Coptic, and Syrian Christians seemed indistinguishable from Arabs. However holy the city, few of the Franks wanted to live in Jerusalem, now only a shadow of its former self. Most preferred the coastal towns, where life was easier and there were more opportunities for trade and commerce.

Immediately after the conquest, Godfrey moved into the Aqsā Mosque, which became the royal residence, and he converted the Dome of the Rock into a church called the "Temple of the Lord." The Ḥaram meant a great deal to the Crusaders. The Byzantines had shown no interest in this part of Jerusalem, but the Crusaders had come to believe that they were the new Chosen People and that it was therefore fitting that they should inherit this Jewish holy place. From the first, it played an important part in the spiritual life of Crusader Jerusalem, and Daimbert made the "Temple of the Lord" his official residence. The importance of the Ḥaram to the Crusaders can be seen by the fact that the patriarch and his advocate chose to live in this lonely outpost, which was far away from the main Crusader quarters on the Western Hill. Their nearest neighbors were the Benedictine monks whom Godfrey had installed in the Tomb of the Virgin Mary in the Kidron Valley.

Godfrey's reign was short. In July 1100 he died of typhoid fever and was buried in the Anastasis, which the Crusaders preferred to call the Church of the Holy Sepulcher. Patriarch Daimbert made ready to assume secular as well as spiritual leadership, but was outmaneuvered by Godfrey's brother Baldwin, count of the Crusader state of Edessa in Armenia, who was summoned to Jerusalem by his fellow countrymen of Lorraine. Baldwin was far more intelligent and worldly than his brother. Having trained for the priesthood in his youth, he was better educated than most laymen, and he had tremendous physical presence. He would make the Crusader Kingdom of Jerusalem a viable possibility, When Baldwin arrived in the holy city on 9 November 1100, he was greeted with tumultuous joy not only by the Franks but by the local Christians who waited for him outside the city. Baldwin realized that if the Franks were to survive in the Near East, they needed friends, and since the Jews and Muslims were out of the question, that meant that the Greek, Syrian, Armenian, and Palestinian Christians were their natural allies. Baldwin himself had an Armenian wife and had won the confidence of the Christians of the East, whom Daimbert had treated with such contempt.

On 11 November, Baldwin was crowned "King of the Latins" in the Nativity Church in Bethlehem, the city of King David. He had no scruples about wearing a golden crown in Jerusalem or being called a king. Under his leadership, the Crusaders went from one triumph to another. By 1110, Baldwin had conquered Caesarea, Haifa, Jaffa, Tripoli, Sidon, and Beirut. The Crusaders now established a fourth state: the County of Tripoli. In these conquered towns, the population was slaughtered and the mosques were destroyed, and Palestinian refugees fled to the safety of Islamic territory. The memory of these massacres and dispossessions made it very hard for the Crusaders to establish normal relations with the local people in later years. The Crusaders seemed unstoppable, yet the Seljuk emirs and the local dynasts put up no serious opposition. Still locked into their personal quarrels, they found it impossible to form a united front. There was no hope of a riposte from Baghdad. The caliphate was now incurably weak and could not take these wars in far-away Palestine seriously. As a consequence, the Crusaders were able to found the first Western colonies in the Near East.

Baldwin also had to solve the problem of Jerusalem, which was still a deserted shell with scarcely any inhabitants. The Franks were still leaking away to the more affluent cities on the coast. They were mostly peasants and soldiers, not craftsmen and artisans, so it was difficult for them to make a living in a city which had relied on local light industry. By the Law of Conquest of 1099, the people who had taken part in the Crusade were empowered to become landowners and householders. They were now free of the feudal hierarchy of Europe and, as freedmen, could own property. Some of these "burgesses," as they were called, were now the owners of houses in Jerusalem or of estates and villages in the surrounding countryside. To keep them from leaving the city, Baldwin introduced a law which gave the possession of a house to anybody who had lived in it for a year and a day: this prevented people from deserting their estates during a crisis in the hope of returning when times were easier. The burgesses would become the backbone of Frankish Jerusalem; they would work in the city as cooks, butchers, shopkeepers, and smiths. But there were not enough of them.

Baldwin hoped to bring the local Christians back to the churches and monasteries of Jerusalem, and in 1101 he was given a heaven-sent opportunity. On the night before Easter, the crowds waited as usual for the miracle of the Holy Fire. Nothing happened: the divine light failed to appear. Presumably the Greeks had taken the secret with them and were not inclined to divulge it to the Latins. The failure looked bad: had the Franks displeased God in some way? At length, Daimbert suggested that the Latins follow him to the Temple of the Lord, where God had answered the prayers of Solomon. The local Christians were asked to pray too. The next morning, it was announced that the fire had appeared in two of the lamps beside the tomb. The message from heaven seemed clear. The Armenian historian Matthew of Edessa claimed that God had been angry that "the Franks expelled from the monasteries the Armenians, the Greeks, the Syrians, and the Georgians" and had only deigned to send the fire because the Eastern Christians had asked for it.[15] The keys of the tomb were restored to the Greeks, and the other denominations were permitted to return to their shrines, monasteries, and churches in the Holy City.

Henceforth the King of Jerusalem became the protector of the local Christians. The higher clergy remained Latin, but there were Greek canons in the Holy Sepulcher Church. When the Jacobites returned from Egypt, where they had fled in 1099, the Monastery of Mary Magdalene was restored to them. The Armenians were especially favored, since there were now Armenian members of the royal family. Baldwin had created a special link with Armenia, and the community and Convent of St. James prospered. Important Armenian dignitaries and notables came to Jerusalem as pilgrims, bearing rich gifts: embroidered vestments, golden crosses, chalices, and crucifixes encrusted with precious stones, which are still used on major feast days, and illuminated manuscripts for the convent library. The Armenians were also given the custody of the Chapel of St. Mary in the Holy Sepulcher Church.

Finally in 1115, Baldwin was able to solve the population problem in Jerusalem by importing Syrian Christians from the Transjordan, who had become *personae non gratae* in the Muslim world since the Crusader atrocities. Baldwin lured them to the city by promising them special privileges and settled them in the empty houses in the northwest corner of the city. They were allowed to build and restore churches for their own use: St. Abraham's near Stephen's Gate and St. George's, St. Elias's, and St. Jacob's in the Patriarch's Quarter.

Baldwin's policy must have worked, because from this point Jerusalem developed and the population reached some thirty thousand. It was a capital city once again, and also the chief metropolis of all the Frankish states because of its religious significance. This brought new life and zest to Jerusalem. In some ways, it was organized like a Western city. The Muslim *sharī͑ah* court was replaced by three courts for civil and criminal offenses: the High Court for the nobility, the Court of the Burgesses, and the Court of the Syrians, a lesser body, run by and for the local Christians. The Crusaders kept the markets which had developed in the old Roman forum beside the Holy Sepulcher and along the Cardo. They probably learned about the organization of the *sūq* from the local Christians, because they kept the Oriental system of having separate markets for poultry, textiles, spices, and takeaway food. Franks and Syrians traded together, but on opposite sides of the street. Jerusalem could never become a trading center, since it was too far from the main routes. Merchants from the Italian cities, who established communes in the coastal towns and played an important role in urban life there, did not bother to establish themselves in Jerusalem. The city remained—as always—depen-

This seal of the Templars, which shows two of the knights sharing the same horse, reflects the early idealism of the Poor Soldiers of Jesus Christ before they became rich and powerful.

dent upon the tourist trade. Baldwin had scotched the clerical idea of running Jerusalem as a theocracy. Once he had got rid of Daimbert,[16] he chose patriarchs who were content with a subservient role. From 1112 the patriarch had complete jurisdiction in the old Christian Quarter, but Baldwin ruled the rest of the city, and the kingdom was freer of ecclesiastical control than any contemporary European state.

It was ironic that after the fanatical religiosity of its inception, Crusader Jerusalem became a rather secular place. As soon as they were settled, the Franks also began to transform it into a Western city. They began in 1115 with the Dome of the Rock, another sign of the importance of this site in Frankish Jerusalem. The Crusaders had no clear idea of the history of this building. They realized that it was not the Temple built by King Solomon, but seem to have thought that either Constantine or Heraklius had graced the site of the holy Temple with a building which the Muslims had impiously converted for their own use. In 1115 they began, as they thought, to restore it to its pristine purity. A cross was put atop the Dome, the Rock was covered with a marble facing to make an altar and choir, and the Qur'ānic inscriptions were covered with Latin texts. It was a typical Crusader venture, aiming to blot out Muslim presence as though it had never been. Yet the craftsmanship was of the highest order: the grille built by the Crusaders around the Rock is one of the finest surviving pieces of medieval metalwork. It also took years: the "Temple of the Lord" was not officially consecrated until

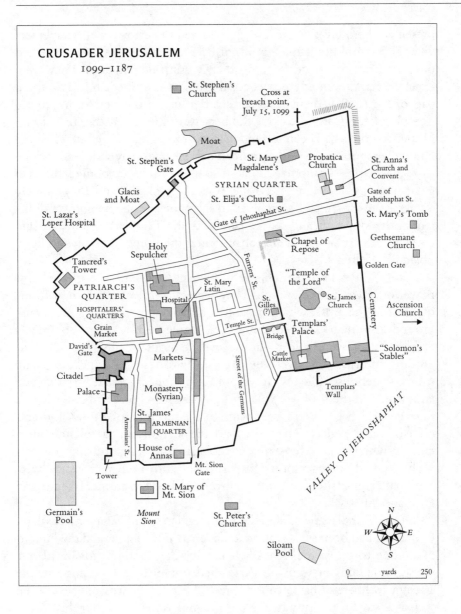

CRUSADER JERUSALEM
1099–1187

St. Stephen's Church

Cross at breach point, July 15, 1099

Moat

St. Stephen's Gate

St. Mary Magdalene's

Probatica Church

St. Anna's Church and Convent

SYRIAN QUARTER

Glacis and Moat

St. Elija's Church

Gate of Jehoshaphat St.

St. Lazar's Leper Hospital

Gate of Jehoshaphat St.

St. Mary's Tomb

Chapel of Repose

Gethsemane Church

Holy Sepulcher

Tancred's Tower

Furriers' St.

"Temple of the Lord"

Golden Gate

PATRIARCH'S QUARTER

St. Mary Latin

St. Gilles (?)

St. James Church

Ascension Church

HOSPITALERS' QUARTERS

Hospital

Temple St.

Templars' Palace

Cemetery

Grain Market

David's Gate

Bridge

"Solomon's Stables"

Citadel

Markets

Cattle Market

Street of the Germans

Palace

Monastery (Syrian)

Templars' Wall

St. James' ARMENIAN QUARTER

VALLEY OF JEHOSHAPHAT

Armenians' St.

House of Annas

Tower

Mt. Sion Gate

St. Mary of Mt. Sion

Germain's Pool

Mount Sion

St. Peter's Church

Siloam Pool

N
W E
S

0   yards   250

1142. North of the new church, the Crusaders built cloisters for the Augustinians and converted the Dome of the Chain into a chapel dedicated to James the Tzaddik, who was believed to have been martyred on the Temple Mount.

At first there was no money to renovate the Aqsā Mosque, which had been badly damaged and plundered during the conquest. Baldwin had even been forced to sell the lead off the roof. Then, in 1118, a small band of knights who called themselves the Poor Fellow Soldiers of Jesus Christ presented themselves to the king and offered to perform a charitable service. They would police the roads of Palestine and protect the unarmed pilgrims from the Bedouin and other Muslim desperadoes. They were exactly what the kingdom needed, and Baldwin immediately gave them part of the Aqsā as their headquarters. Because of their proximity to the Temple of the Lord, the Poor Soldiers were known as the Templars.[17] Hitherto monks had been forbidden to bear arms and fight, but when the church recognized the Templars as an official *ordo,* sacred violence was—to some degree—canonized. These soldier monks embodied the two great passions of the new Europe, war and worship, and they quickly attracted new recruits. They helped to solve the chronic manpower problem of the kingdom, and during the 1120s the Templars became an élite corps in the crusading armies, abandoning the purely defensive military objective of their origins.

Ironically, the Poor Knights soon became rich and one of the most powerful orders in the church. They were able to refurbish their headquarters in the Aqsā, which became a military compound. The underground Herodian vaults became their stables. Known as "Solomon's Stables," they were able to house over a thousand horses with their grooms. Internal walls were built inside the mosque to make separate rooms: storehouses filled with weapons and supplies, granaries, baths, and lavatories. On the roof were pleasure gardens, pavilions, and cisterns, and the Templars had added a west wing to the mosque for a new cloister, a refectory, and cellars. They also laid foundations for a splendid new church, which was never completed. Again, the craftsmanship was of a high standard. The sculpture in particular, with a characteristic "wet-leaf" patterning, shows an imaginative blend of Byzantine, Islamic, and Romanesque style.

Yet the Templars illustrated the main tendency of Crusader Jerusalem. Crusading had been seen as an act of love: the pope had urged the knights of Europe to go to the help of their Christian brethren in the Islamic world; thousands of Crusaders had died out of love for Christ in the attempt to liberate his patrimony from the infidel. Crusading was even seen as a way for the laity to live out the monastic ideal.[18] But this "love" had been expressed in violence and atrocity. In the career of the Templars too, charity and concern for the poor and oppressed had quickly modulated into military aggression. All violence had been forbidden on the Ḥaram; now the Aqsā had been transformed into a barracks and a military arsenal. Soon the round Templar churches, modeled on the Anastasis, began to spring up in towns and villages all over Europe, reminding Christians there that the whole of Christendom was mobilized for a holy war in the defense of Jerusalem.

We can see the same trend in the Templars' rivals, the Knights Hospitaler, who were based in the old Latin Hospice of St. John the Almoner in the Patriarch's Quarter. Gerard, the abbot, had assisted the Crusaders during the siege of Jerusalem, and after the conquest he was joined by a group of knights and pilgrims who felt called to care for the poor and needy. Hitherto, knights would never have dreamed of degrading themselves in the menial tasks of nursing, but under Gerard they voluntarily shared the humble lives of the poor and dedicated themselves to charitable work. Like the Templars, the Hospitalers embodied the ideal of holy poverty, which had been so important during the First Crusade, and, again, the Hospitalers soon attracted many vocations in both Palestine and Europe. In 1118, Gerard died and was replaced by Raymund of Le Puy, who did much to promote the order in Europe, but, like the Templars, the Hospitalers were entirely Jerusalem-centered. In their rule, the word *outremer* ("overseas") refers to Europe. By the mid-twelfth century, the Hospitalers had also become soldiers and fought in the Crusading armies, their charity leading inevitably to militarism. Yet they never abandoned their charitable work. In the huge and magnificent compound they built for themselves south of the Holy Sepulcher, the brothers cared for

Like these Christian pilgrims to Jerusalem, the Crusaders believed that they were following in Jesus's footsteps. They had taken up their cross (sewing red crosses on their clothes at the beginning of their expedition) and were ready to lay down their lives for his sake and for the defense of his holy city. But the sword was also central to their vision.

about a thousand sick people all the year round and distributed quantities of alms, clothing, and food to the poor. A stone's throw from the Holy Sepulcher, the Hospital represented the more attractive face of Crusading.

Pilgrims were always most impressed by the Hospital. They were beginning to discover a very different Jerusalem. The Byzantines had not directed pilgrims to the Temple Mount, for example. They had seen the place as a mere symbol of the defeat of Judaism, and the Temple Mount played no part in their liturgy. But as early as 1102, when the British pilgrim Saewulf visited Jerusalem, he was proudly escorted around the shrines of the Ḥaram, which had quickly been given a Christian significance. The Gate of Mercy was now seen as the place where Joachim and Anna, the parents of the Virgin Mary, had first met. Another of the Ḥaram gates was the "Beautiful Gate," where St. Peter and St. John had cured a cripple. The Dome of the Rock was now revered as the Temple where Jesus had prayed all his life: his footprint could be seen on the Rock. The Ḥaram also played a crucial role in the liturgy of the Crusaders.[19] All their major ceremonies now included a procession to the "Temple of the Lord": it was now central to the Palm Sunday celebrations, for example. Another major change in the devotional life of the city was that many of the sites of the Passion, which had originally been located on Mount Sion, seemed to be shifting to the north of town. Saewulf, for example, found that the pillar where Christ had been scourged was now in the Holy Sepulcher Church instead of Mount Sion. Pilgrims were also beginning to be taught that the Praetorium, where Pilate had sentenced Jesus to death, was not in the Tyropoeon Valley as before but north of the Temple Mount, on the site of the Antonia fortress. This change could have been inspired by the Templars, who might have wanted this holy place in their district of Jerusalem.

Baldwin I died in 1118 and was succeeded by his cousin Baldwin of Le Bourg, count of Edessa, a pious but genial man, who was devoted to his Armenian wife and four daughters. Baldwin was the first king to be crowned in the Holy Sepulcher Church instead of the Bethlehem basilica. He processed through the streets, where the balconies and roofs were festooned with Oriental rugs, and, in the presence of the patriarch, bishops, and Latin and local clergy, he vowed before the tomb of Christ to protect the church, the clerics, and the widows and the orphans of the Kingdom of Jerusalem. He also took a special oath of loyalty to the patriarch. After the ceremony, the king processed to the Temple of the Lord, where he laid his crown on the altar, before proceeding to a banquet in the Aqsā, served by the city's burgesses. In 1120, Baldwin vacated his quarters in the Aqsā, leaving the mosque entirely to the Templars, and took up residence in a new palace near the citadel, where he was closer to the heart of Crusader Jerusalem.

In 1120, Baldwin attended the Council of Nablus, which tried to curb the tendency of some of the younger generation to assimilate with the local culture. In the early years of the kingdom, Fulcher of Chartres had enthusiastically told the people of Europe: "Westerners, we have become orientals! The Italians and the Frenchmen of yesterday have been transplanted and become men of Galilee and Palestine."[20] This was certainly an exaggeration, but over the years the Franks had changed. A whole generation had grown up in the East with no memories of Europe. They took baths—a practice that was almost unheard of in the West; they lived in houses instead of wooden shacks and wore soft clothes and the *keffiyeh*. Their wives wore veils, like the Muslim women. This shocked the pilgrims from home: the Franks of Palestine seemed to be going native, and since the Islamic world had achieved a far higher standard of living than Europe at this point, they had adopted what seemed to these more rugged Christians a decadent and effete lifestyle. Many of the Palestinian Franks had realized that some degree of accommodation was essential if they were to survive. They had to trade with Muslims and establish normal relations. Baldwin II even slightly relaxed the ban that excluded Jews and Muslims from Jerusalem. Muslims were now permitted to bring food and merchandise to the city and stay there for limited periods. By 1170 there was also a family of Jewish dyers living near the royal palace.

But this assimilation was superficial. During the 1120s the Franks were adapting old fortresses and building a ring of new castles around their kingdom, as a bulwark against the hostile Muslim world. A line of fortified churches and monasteries also encircled Jerusalem at Ma'ale Adumin, on the Jericho road, Hebron, Bethany, Nabi Samwil, al-Birah, and Ramallah. The Crusaders were not breaking down the barrier of hatred that now existed between Western Christianity and Islam but erecting massive stone walls against their neighbors. Their states became artificial Western enclaves that remained alien and inimical to the region. They were military states, poised aggressively and constantly ready to strike. The twelfth century was a time of immense creativity in Europe, but not in the Crusader kingdoms. There the chief innovations were the military orders and military architecture. Their chief intellectual passion was Western law. The Franks made no real attempt to plumb the intellectual and cultural riches of the Near East and therefore put down no real roots. Their energies were concentrated on survival, and the societies they created were essentially artificially preserved against their surroundings.

Yet the Crusaders tried to be creative and to leave their mark on the alien country they had conquered. In 1125 the Franks began an intensive building program in Jerusalem. Not even Herod built as much as they did in Palestine. They were trying to make themselves feel at home by building Europe in the Holy Land. Consequently their buildings and churches show few signs of Byzantine or Muslim influence; nor did the Crusaders keep abreast of the new architectural developments in Europe. They remained in a Romanesque time warp, untouched by the Gothic, building churches that looked like the ones they had known at home before the Crusade. First they began a massive reconstruction of the Holy Sepulcher Church, which was to be completed in time for the fiftieth anniversary of their conquest of the city in 1149. Then they built an exquisite Romanesque church dedicated to St. Anna, the mother of the Virgin Mary, beside the Pool of Beth-Hesda. The site had been venerated by Christians as the birthplace of the Virgin since the sixth century. Now it became a Benedictine convent and church. Despite their cruelty and fear, the Franks still retained some understanding of spirituality. In the Church of St. Anna the eye is drawn directly to the high altar by the line of columns in the nave; the bare simplicity means that there are no distractions, while the light falling into the church from different directions creates subtle patterns of shadow and a sense of distance.

The Franks also restored the churches in the Kidron Valley and the Mount of Olives: the Church of Gethsemane and the Tomb of the Virgin, where the Crusaders also built a monastery and decorated the crypt with frescoes and mosaics. The round Church of the Ascension was also rebuilt and decorated with Parian marble. This church also became part of the Crusaders' war machine and reflects their embattled piety. It was, the pilgrim Theodorich tells us, "strongly fortified against the infidels with towers, both great and small, with walls and battlements and night patrols."[21] The Eleona Basilica had been destroyed by the Persians in 614 and had never been rebuilt; on this site the Crusaders built two churches to commemorate Jesus's teaching of the Lord's Prayer and the Apostle's Creed to his disciples. The Basilica of Holy Sion had been ruined by al-Hākim and had never been restored. Now the Crusaders repaired the "Mother of all the churches," enclosing many of the ancient shrines: the Chapel of St. Stephen, where the martyr's body had been laid before being transferred to Eudokia's church; the Upper Room of the Last Supper; and, next door, the Chapel of Pentecost, decorated by a picture of the descent of the Spirit. On the floor below was the "Galilee Chapel," where Jesus had appeared to his apostles after the Resurrection.[22] While they were restoring this chapel, the Crusaders made a discovery that they did not quite know how to deal with. One of the old

walls fell in to reveal a cave, containing a golden crown and scepter.
Today some scholars think that it may have been an ancient synagogue.
The workmen rushed in panic to the patriarch, who consulted with a
Karaite ascetic. They decided that they had stumbled upon the Tomb of
David and the Kings of Judah. For centuries, people had confused
Mount Sion with the original 'Ir David on the Ophel hill. It had long
been assumed that the citadel beside the west gate of the city had been
David's fortress, and Herod's Hippicus tower was generally known as the
Tower of David. It was probably inevitable that one day somebody
would "discover" his tomb on Mount Sion. The patriarch wanted to
investigate the cave, but the workmen were too frightened. The patriarch then "ordered the place to be closed up and hidden," said the Jewish traveler Benjamin of Tudela, who visited Jerusalem in about 1170,
"so that to this day the Tombs of David and the Kings of Judah cannot
be identified."[23] Later, however, the Tomb of
David would be uncovered by the Crusaders and
made part of the Basilica of Holy Sion—the cause
of much trouble in the future.

In 1131, Baldwin II died and was succeeded by
his eldest daughter, Melisende, and her husband,

*The embattled piety of the
Crusaders spread to Europe, as
we see in the Templar Church of
Cressac, France, whose walls are
entirely covered with these frescoes
showing the knights riding out to
fight for Jerusalem.*

Fulk, count of Anjou, a formidable warrior who had decided in his middle years to devote his life to the defense of Jerusalem. It was important that the kingdom be seen to have a strong ruler, since for the first time in its history a powerful Muslim leader had risen in the Near East: Imad ad-Din Zangī, the Turkish commander of Mosul and Aleppo. He was determined to impose peace on the region, which had long been torn apart by the internecine wars of the emirs. Slowly and systematically, Zangī began to subdue the local chieftains of Syria and Iraq, and, with the support of Baghdad, he brought them, one by one, under his authority. Zangī was not particularly interested in recovering territory occupied by the Franks: he had his hands full with the recalcitrant Muslim emirs. But the Franks were very conscious of Zangī's growing empire. Fulk fortified the borders of the kingdom more strongly than ever, dispatching a garrison of Hospitalers to the frontier castle of Beth-Gibrin in 1137. That year he also made an alliance with Unur, prince of Damascus, who was determined that his city should not be absorbed into Zangī's empire.

One of the diplomats who negotiated this treaty was the Syrian prince Usāmah ibn Mundiqh, who, after the signing, was taken on a tour of Frankish Palestine and left us, in his memoirs, a valuable glimpse of the way the Muslims regarded the Westerners who had so violently erupted into their region. A cultured, affable man, Usāmah was bemused by the Franks. He admired their physical courage but was appalled by their primitive medicine, their disrespectful treatment of women, and their religious intolerance. He was horribly embarrassed when a pilgrim offered to take Usāmah's son back with him to Europe to give him a Western education. As far as Usāmah was concerned, his son would be better off in prison than in the land of the Franks. Yet he did admit that the Franks who had been born in the East were better than the newcomers, who were still filled with the primitive prejudices of Europe. He illustrated this insight with an instructive anecdote. He had made friends with the Templars in Jerusalem, and whenever he visited them in the Aqsā they put a little oratory at his disposal. One day, when he was praying facing Mecca, a Frank rushed into the room, lifted Usāmah into the air, and turned him forcibly toward the east: "That is the way to pray!" he exclaimed. The Templars hurried in and took the man away, but as soon as their backs were turned, the same thing happened again. The Templars were mortified. "He is a foreigner who has just arrived today from his homeland in the north," they explained, "and he has never seen anyone pray facing any other direction than east." "I have finished my prayers," Usāmah said with dignity and left, "stupefied by the fanatic who had been so perturbed and upset to see someone praying facing the qiblah."[24]

Increasingly the Kingdom of Jerusalem was torn by an internal conflict between those Franks who had been born in Palestine and who could, like the Templars in this story, understand the Muslims' point of view and wanted to establish normal relations with their neighbors, and the newcomers from Europe, who found it impossible to tolerate another religious orientation. This dissension was growing at a time when their Muslim neighbors were at last laying their own destructive factionalism aside and uniting under a strong leader. In 1144 the Franks suffered a blow which showed them how vulnerable they were. In November that year, as part of his campaign against Damascus, Zangī conquered the Crusader city of Edessa and destroyed the Frankish state. There was wild jubilation in the Muslim world, and Zangī, a hard-drinking, ruthless warrior, suddenly found himself a hero of Islam. When he was killed two years later, he was succeeded by his son Mahmoud, who was more generally known by his title Nūr ad-Dīn ("Light of the Faith"). Nūr ad-Dīn was a devout Sunni, determined to wage a holy war against both the Franks and the Shiites. He went back to the spirit of Muḥammad, living frugally and giving large sums of money to the poor. He also initiated an effective propaganda campaign for the jihād. The Qur'ān condemns all war as abhorrent but teaches that, regrettably, it is sometimes necessary to fight oppression and persecution in order to preserve decent values. If people were killed or driven from their homes and saw their places of worship destroyed, Muslims had a duty to fight a just war of self-defense.[25] The Qur'ānic injunction was a perfect description of the Crusaders, who had killed thousands of Muslims, driven them from their homes, and burned their mosques. They had also desecrated the Ḥaram of al-Quds. Nūr ad-Dīn circulated the anthologies of the Praises of Jerusalem (faḍā'il al-quds) and commissioned a beautiful pulpit to be installed in the Aqṣā Mosque when the Muslims liberated Jerusalem from the Franks.

The practice of jihād had died in the Near East. The cruel aggression of the Western Crusaders had rekindled it. But they could make no effective response to Nūr ad-Dīn because of their ingrained prejudice. When the armies of the Second Crusade finally arrived in Palestine in 1148 to relieve the beleaguered Franks, instead of attacking Nūr ad-Dīn in Aleppo the Crusaders turned against their one ally in the Muslim world, Unur of Damascus. This meant that Unur had no option but to ask for the help of Nūr ad-Dīn. The Crusaders then compounded their stupidity by totally mismanaging the siege of Damascus, which was an

THE HOLY SEPULCHER CHURCH

BUILT BY THE CRUSADERS, 1149

1. Tomb Aedicula
2. Rotunda
3. Choir
4. North transept
5. South transept
6. Calvary
7. Main entrance
8. Front courtyard (Parvis)
9. Chapel of the Holy Trinity
10. Chapel of St. John the Baptist
11. Chapel of St. James
12. Belfry
13. Ambulatory
14. Infirmary hall for canons
15. Dormitories for canons
16. Chapter house
17. Kitchen
18. Buttery
19. Refectory
20. Great Cloister
21. Dome of St. Helena's Chapel
22. Shops
23. Patriarchate (now the Salahiyya Khanaqah)

ignominious failure. The Second Crusade showed that the Franks' hostility to the Islamic world could set them on a suicidal course. Their isolation from the region also meant that they had no grasp of the realpolitik of the Near East.

The failure of the Second Crusade must have soured the dedication of the restored Church of the Holy Sepulcher on 15 July 1149, the fiftieth anniversary of the conquest of the city. After the ceremony, the congregation processed to the Temple of the Lord and visited the Kidron Valley, where the Crusaders who had fallen in the battle for Jerusalem were buried. They ended up at the cross in the northern wall which marked the spot where Godfrey's troops had penetrated the city in 1099. The contrast with the recent fiasco must have been painful. The new church was a triumph, however: the Crusaders had brought all the scattered shrines on the site—the tomb of Christ, the rock of Golgotha, and the crypt where Helena was supposed to have found the True Cross—into one large Romanesque building. (See diagram.) They had joined the eleventh-century Rotunda built by Constantine Monomarchus to their new church on the site of the old courtyard, linking the two by means of a high triumphal arch. Yet the Western architecture did not clash with the Byzantine, and the Crusaders had attempted to harmonize with the local style, a feat that they could not achieve in life. What remained of the tomb was covered with a marble slab, to which a gold casing was added later. Mosaics and slabs of colored marble adorned the walls in a way that was both brilliant and elegant, a splendor that is hard to imagine today in the present gloomy building.

Nūr ad-Dīn continued his campaign. His plan was to encircle the Franks with a Muslim empire dedicated to the *jihād*. Yet in the Kingdom of Jerusalem the internal feuds continued. It seemed as though the aggression built into every aspect of life in the Crusader states impelled the Franks to turn against one another. In 1152 the young King Baldwin III had clashed with his mother, Melisende, who started to fortify Jerusalem against her son. There would have been open civil war had not the burgesses of the city forced Melisende to surrender. The Templars and the Hospitalers were also at loggerheads, and neither would submit to the authority of the king and patriarch. The Hospitalers built a tower in their complex that was higher than the Holy Sepulcher Church. It was a deliberate insult and an act of defiance. They also sabotaged services in the Holy Sepulcher. William of Tyre tells us that as soon as the patriarch got up to preach, they would "set their many great bells ringing so loudly and persistently that the voice of the Patriarch could not rise above the din." When the patriarch remonstrated with them, the Hospitalers simply stormed into the Holy Sepulcher Church and let loose a stream of arrows.[26] Clearly, the experience of living in the holy city did not inspire the Crusaders to follow Christ's ethic of love and humility.

The fatal disunity of the Kingdom continued right up to the bitter end, the Christians consumed with internal power squabbles. The Franks tried to forestall Nūr ad-Dīn's plan to conquer Fatimid Egypt, but failed when the kingdom was captured by the Kurdish general Shirkuh. His nephew Yūsuf ibn Ayyūb succeeded him as *wazīr* in 1170 and abolished the Shii caliphate. Yūsuf, usually known in the West as Saladin from his title Ṣalāh ad-Dīn ("the Righteousness of the Faith"), was passionately devoted to the *jihād* but convinced that he and not Nūr ad-Dīn was destined to liberate Jerusalem, and this brought him into conflict with his master. When Nūr ad-Dīn died of a heart attack in 1174, Saladin fought his son for the leadership of his empire. His charisma, kindliness, and evident piety won him the support of the Muslims, and within ten years he was the acknowledged leader of most of the main Muslim cities in the region. The Crusaders found themselves surrounded by a united Muslim empire, led by a devout and charismatic sultan and dedicated to the destruction of their kingdom.

Yet even in the face of this obvious threat, the Franks continued to quarrel among themselves. At a time when strong leadership was essential, their young king, Baldwin IV, had leprosy. The barons of the kingdom backed the regent, Raymund, count of Tripoli, who knew that their only hope was to appease Saladin and try to establish good relations with their Muslim neighbors. They were opposed, however, by a group of newcomers who clustered around the royal family and pursued a policy of deliberate provocation. The most notorious of these hawks was Reynauld of Chatillon, who broke every truce that Raymund made with Saladin by attacking Muslim caravans and, on two occasions, attempted—unsuccessfully—to attack Mecca and Medina. For Reynauld, hatred of Islam and absolute opposition to the Muslim world was a sacred duty and the only true patriotism. The kingdom also lacked spiritual leadership. The patriarch Heraklius, another newcomer, was illiterate and degenerate, and openly flaunted his mistress. The death of the "Leper King" in March 1185 was succeeded the following year by the death of his small son, Baldwin V, and there was almost a civil war for the succession as Saladin prepared to invade the country. Reynauld broke yet another truce, which Raymund had engineered to give the kingdom breathing space, and the barons had no choice but to accept the Leper King's brother-in-law Guy of Lusignan—a weak and ineffective newcomer—as their king. But they were still bitterly divided. The feuding and arguments continued as the whole army prepared to fight Saladin in Galilee in July 1187. The hawkish party prevailed with King Guy and persuaded him to attack the Muslims, even though Raymund urged that it would be much wiser to wait. It was nearly time for the harvest, and Saladin would be unable to keep his large army on foreign soil for much longer. But Guy did not listen to this sensible advice and gave the orders to march and attack. The result was an overwhelming Muslim victory at the battle of Hittin near Tiberias. The Christian Kingdom of Jerusalem was lost.

After Hittin, Saladin and his army marched through Palestine, receiving the submission of one town after another. The Christian survivors took refuge in Tyre, but some went to Jerusalem in a desperate attempt to save the Holy City. Finally the Muslim army encamped on the Mount of Olives and Saladin looked down at the desecrated shrines on the Ḥaram and the cross on the Dome of the Rock. He preached a sermon to his officers, reminding them of the *faḍāʾil al-quds:* Jerusalem was the city of the Temple, the city of the prophets, the city of the Night Journey and the *miʿrāj,* the city of the Last Judgment. He considered it his duty to avenge the massacre of 1099 and was determined to show no mercy to the inhabitants. Inside the city, the Christians were afraid. There was no knight capable of organizing an effective defense. Then, as if in answer to prayer, the distinguished Baron Balian of Ibelin arrived. He had entered the city with Saladin's permission to collect his wife and family and take them to Tyre. He had vowed to spend only one night in Jerusalem. But when he saw the plight of the besieged Christians, he went back to the sultan and asked him to release him from his oath. Saladin respected Balian and agreed, sending an escort to take his family and all their possessions to the coast.

Balian did his best with meager resources, but his task was hopeless. On 26 September 1187, Saladin began his attack on the western gate of the city, and his sappers started to mine the northern wall near St. Stephen's Gate. Three days later, a whole section of the wall—including Godfrey's cross—had fallen into the moat, but the Muslims now had to face the inner defensive wall. Balian, however, decided to sue for peace. At first Saladin would show no mercy. "We shall deal with you just as you dealt with the population when you took [Jerusalem]," he told Balian, "with murder and enslavement and other such savageries."[27] But Balian made a desperate plea. Once all hope was lost, the Christians would have nothing further to lose. They would kill their wives and children, burn their houses and possessions, and pull down the Dome of the Rock and al-Aqsā before coming out to meet Saladin's army; each one of them would kill a Muslim before he died. Saladin consulted his *ʿulamāʾ* and agreed to take the city peacefully. The Franks must not stay in the city, however. They would become his prisoners, though they could be ransomed for a very moderate sum of money.

On 2 October 1187, the day when the Muslims celebrated the Prophet's Night Journey and *miʿrāj,* Saladin and his troops entered Jerusalem as conquerors. The sultan kept his word. Not a single Christian was killed. The barons could easily afford to ransom themselves, but the poor people could not, and they became prisoners of war. Large numbers were released, however, because Saladin was moved to tears by the plight of the families who were being separated when they were taken into slavery. Al-ʿĀdil, Saladin's brother, was so distressed that he asked for a thousand prisoners for his own use and released them on the spot. All the Muslims were scandalized to see the richer Christians escaping with their wealth without making any attempt to ransom their fellow countrymen. When the Muslim historian ʿImād ad-Dīn saw Patriarch Heraklius leaving the city with his chariots groaning under the weight of his treasure, he begged Saladin to confiscate this wealth to redeem the remaining prisoners. But Saladin refused; oaths and treaties must be kept to the letter. "Christians everywhere will remember the kindness we have done them."[28] Saladin was right. Christians in the West were uneasily aware that this Muslim ruler had behaved in a far more "Christian" manner than had their own Crusaders when they conquered Jerusalem. They evolved legends that made Saladin a sort of honorary Christian; some of these tales even asserted that the sultan had been secretly baptized.

The Crusading experiment in Jerusalem was almost over. The Muslims would try to re-create the old system of coexistence and integration in al-Quds, but the violent dislocation of Crusader rule had damaged relations between Islam and the Christian West at a fundamental level. It had been the Muslims' first experience of the Western world, and it has not been forgotten to this day. Their sufferings at the hands of the Crusaders had also affected the Muslims' view of their Holy City. Henceforth, there would be a defensiveness in their devotion to al-Quds, which would become a more aggressively Islamic city than hitherto.

14

JIHAD

O NCE THE FRANKS had all left Jerusalem, the Muslims wandered around the city marveling at the splendors of Crusader Jerusalem. Yet in many ways it felt like a homecoming. Saladin was enthroned in the Hospital, right in the heart of Crusader Jerusalem, to receive the congratulations of his emirs, sufis, and ʿulamāʾ. His face shone with delight, ʿImād ad-Dīn tells us. Poets and Qurʾān reciters declaimed verses in his praise, while others wept and could hardly speak for joy.[1] But the Muslims knew that the jihād for Jerusalem had not ended with the conquest of the city. The word jihād does not mean merely "holy war." Its primary meaning is "struggle," and it is in this sense that it is chiefly used in the Qurʾān. Muslims are urged to "struggle in the way of God," to make their lives a purposeful striving to implement God's will in a flawed, tragic world. A famous ḥadīth has Muḥammad say on returning from a battle: "We are now returning from the lesser jihād to the greater jihād," the more important and exacting struggle to establish justice in one's own society and integrity in one's own heart. Saladin had conducted his jihād in accordance with the Qurʾānic ideal: he had always granted a truce when the Crusaders had asked for one; he had, for the most part, treated his prisoners fairly and kindly. He had behaved with humanity in the hour of triumph. Indeed, some of the Muslim historians believe that he was clement to a fault. Because he allowed the Christians to congregate in Tyre, they had retained a foothold in Palestine and the conflict would continue for over a hundred years. A Third Crusade, led by King Richard I of England and King Philip II of France, failed to reconquer Jerusalem, but it did establish the Franks in a thin coastal state stretching from Jaffa to Beirut.

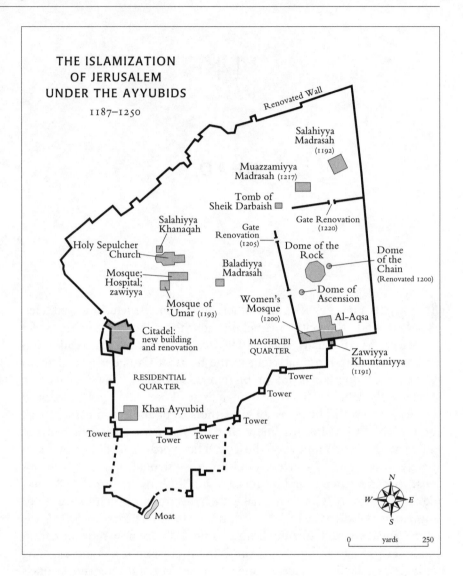

THE ISLAMIZATION
OF JERUSALEM
UNDER THE AYYUBIDS
1187–1250

Renovated Wall

Salahiyya
Madrasah
(1192)

Muazzamiyya
Madrasah (1217)

Tomb of
Sheik Darbaish

Gate Renovation
(1220)

Salahiyya
Khanaqah

Gate
Renovation
(1205)

Dome of the
Rock

Dome
of the
Chain
(Renovated 1200)

Holy Sepulcher
Church

Mosque;
Hospital;
zawiyya

Baladiyya
Madrasah

Dome of
Ascension

Mosque of
'Umar (1193)

Women's
Mosque
(1200)

Al-Aqsa

Citadel:
new building
and renovation

MAGHRIBI
QUARTER

Zawiyya
Khuntaniyya
(1191)

RESIDENTIAL
QUARTER

Tower

Tower

Khan Ayyubid

Tower

Tower

Tower

Tower

Moat

N
W   E
S

0   yards   250

Though their capital was Acre, its rulers wistfully continued to call
themselves "King of Jerusalem." The Crusader dream was not dead, and
as long as the Franks remained in Palestine, the Muslims were wary and
defensive.

But in 1187, Muslim hopes were high. Saladin knew that he now had
to undertake a different kind of *jihād* to make Jerusalem into a truly
Muslim city once again. The first task was to purify the Ḥaram. The
Aqsā Mosque had to be cleared of the Templars' latrines and furniture
and made ready for Friday prayers. The *miḥrāb* indicating the direction

of Mecca had been bricked up and needed to be uncovered. The internal walls built by the Templars were knocked down and the floor covered in rugs. The pulpit commissioned years before by Nūr ad-Dīn was brought from Damascus and installed. In the Dome of the Rock, the pictures and statues were removed, the Qur'ānic inscriptions revealed, and the marble casing over the Rock taken away. Like 'Umar, the Muslim chroniclers tell us, Saladin worked all day beside his men, washing the courts and pavements of the Ḥaram with rose water and distributing alms to the poor. On Friday, 4 Shaban, the Aqsā was filled with Muslim worshippers for the first time since 1099. People wept with emotion as the *qāḍī* of Jerusalem, Muhyi ad-Din al-Qurashi, mounted the new pulpit.

Before the Crusade, Muslim Jerusalem had consisted almost entirely of the buildings on and around the Ḥaram, but Saladin's new building *jihād* demanded that the Christian topography be overlaid with Muslim institutions. Once again, building had become an ideological weapon in the hands of the victors. Instead of being a predominantly Christian city with an important Muslim shrine, Jerusalem was to be an obviously Muslim city. There was a new hostility toward Christianity. Saladin confiscated the residence of the patriarch next to the Holy Sepulcher and with state funds acquired the Convent and Church of St. Anna. He did not simply turn these buildings into mosques, however. As part of their Crusade against the Shiites, both Nūr ad-Dīn and Saladin had endowed Sufi convents (*khawāniq*) and colleges of jurisprudence (*madāris*) in every city they conquered. These were the chief institutions of the reformed Sunnah, as devised by al-Ghazzālī, the great scholar who had lived in the Sufi *khānaqāh* over the Gate of Mercy shortly before the First Crusade. Now Saladin turned the Church of St. Anna into a mosque, while the adjoining convent became a *madrasah;* the patriarch's residence became a *khanaqah*. Both institutions were endowed by the sultan and bore his name. There had been Sufis in Jerusalem from the earliest days, but now Saladin insisted that the Sufis in his new *khanaqah* must not be local people, who might have been infected by the Shiah, but must come from the Sunni heartland.

Sufis and scholars came to live in these new institutions, and *'ulamā'* came to serve on the Ḥaram. After the conquest of Jerusalem, thousands of Muslims came to visit the city that had been for so long in enemy hands. Saladin remained encamped on the Mount of Olives until the city was settled and he had appointed a governor. A garrison was installed in the citadel. Then Saladin returned to Damascus to plan the Muslim riposte to the Third Crusade. The soldiers and civil servants settled in the former Patriarch's Quarter. Soon after the conquest, Muslims also began to arrive in al-Quds from North Africa, which had been overrun by Berber tribes who were savaging the countryside. These Maghribi Muslims settled in the southwest corner of the Ḥaram and retained their own cultural and religious traditions. They were allowed to convert the Templars' refectory on the Ḥaram into a mosque of their own, and the Maghribi Quarter became a new feature of Jerusalem. But Saladin did not intend to exclude Christians and Jews from the city entirely: the old ideal of integration and coexistence persisted. A few thousand Syrian and Armenian Christians asked to stay on as *dhimmis,* and Saladin gave the Greek Orthodox the custody of the Holy Sepulcher Church. These local Christians could not be blamed for the European Crusade. The Holy Sepulcher was now surrounded by the new Islamic buildings. Saladin had also taken over large portions of the Hospital for the governor's residence, a Muslim hospital, and a mosque, endowed by his son al-Afḍal. There was also a new mosque in the Citadel, dedicated to the prophet David. Minarets now bristled around the Christian holy place, and the call to prayer resounded through the streets of the Patriarch's Quarter. Some emirs had wanted to destroy the Holy Sepulcher itself, but Saladin agreed with his wiser officers, who pointed out that it was not the church but the site that was sacred to Christians. After the Third Crusade, even Latin pilgrims from Europe would be permitted to come on pilgrimage to Jerusalem.

Saladin also invited the Jews to come back to Jerusalem, from which they had been almost entirely excluded by the Crusaders. He was hailed throughout the Jewish world as a new Cyrus. The Crusades had not only inspired a new *jihād* in the Muslim world. They had also given rise to a form of Zionism among the Jews of Europe and the Islamic empire. The first stirrings of this new religious Zionism had appeared in the early twelfth century. The Toledan physician Judah Halevi had been caught in the crossfire of the Christian wars of *reconquista* in Muslim Spain. Frequently he had to uproot himself, alternating between Muslim and Christian territory. This experience of dislocation had convinced him that Jews must return to the land of their fathers. That was their true place in the world. The Holy Land did not belong to either the Christians or the Muslims, who were fighting over it at the present time. Jews must stake their claim to Palestine and the Holy City. Jerusalem was the center of the earth, the place where the mundane world opened to the divine. Prayers rose through the Gate of Heaven, which was situated directly over the site of the Devir, and the divine power flowed back through this opening to the people of Israel, filling them with prophetic power. Only in Palestine could the Jews maintain their creative link with the divine world and be truly themselves. They had a duty to make the *aliyah* to Palestine and risk their lives for Zion. Then the Shekhinah would return to Jerusalem and the Redemption would begin. Halevi himself set sail from Spain to make this effort, but almost certainly never reached Jerusalem. He probably died in Egypt in 1141. Few Jews felt inclined to follow him at this stage, but his story was emblematic. When people become alienated from their surroundings and feel that, physically and spiritually, they have no home in the world, they feel drawn to return to their roots to find healing.

Saladin's conquest of Jerusalem was both wonderful and disturbing to the Jewish people. The sultan had brought the Jews home to their Holy City and allowed them to live there in large numbers. In September 1187, Saladin had conquered Ascalon, but when Jerusalem was conquered the following month the Muslims could not defend both cities. Ascalon was, therefore, systematically destroyed, and the inhabitants were taken to safety. The Jews of Ascalon were settled in Jerusalem in 1190 and allowed to build a synagogue. They were assigned a district to the west of the new Maghribi Quarter, with the residential Sharaf Quarter in between. More Jews began to arrive from North Africa in 1198, and in about 1210 three hundred Jewish families made the *aliyah,* in two groups, from France. This return was exciting and inspired some messianic hopes of imminent Redemption. But the Islamization of Jerusalem was also extremely distressing. The sight of the Christians and Muslims battling for the city that the Jews were convinced belonged to *them* was confusing. When the Spanish poet Yehuda al-Harizi made his pilgrimage to Jerusalem in 1217 he found the sight of the Muslim buildings on the Ḥaram profoundly upsetting.

> What torment to see our holy courts converted into an alien temple! We tried to turn our faces away from this great and majestic church now raised on the site of the ancient tabernacle where once Providence had its dwelling.[2]

More and more Jews became convinced that the land was waiting for the return of its true inhabitants. As Halevi had pointed out, neither the Christians nor the Muslims could benefit from its holiness.

The ferment even affected the sober Maimonides, the Jewish philosopher who was one of Saladin's personal physicians. He was convinced that Jerusalem remained the center of gravity for the Jewish people and that a Jewish state founded elsewhere would have no validity. A Jewish kingdom and Jewish law must be based on the Temple. The Temple Mount might be desacralized by the Goyim, but it was still a holy place, because Solomon had consecrated it for all time. The divine Presence could never be banished from the Temple Mount. Consequently, when they visited the Ḥaram, Jews must comport themselves as though the

Temple were still standing. They must not venture into the forbidden areas nor act irreverently when they faced the east, where the Devir had once stood. The Temple had gone, but the sanctity of the place would endure for all time, a symbol of God's continued care for his people.

Saladin died of typhoid fever in 1194. His empire was split up and its various cities ruled by members of his family of Ayyūb, each with its own separate army and administration. But the unity that Saladin had been able to inspire died with him, and soon his heirs were fighting among themselves. Jerusalem would suffer from this internal conflict. Yet their enthusiasm for al-Quds did not diminish. Muslims had also suffered from the loss of Jerusalem, and now that they had returned they were more devoted to it than ever. They continued their building *jihād*. In 1193, Izz ad-Din Jardick, the emir of Jerusalem, rededicated the small mosque near the Holy Sepulcher, which had been dedicated to ʿUmar before the First Crusade; next to this mosque a Qurʾān school was opened. Al-ʾĀfdal endowed the whole Maghribi Quarter so that aid and services could be provided for North African pilgrims and the poor; he also built a *madrasah* where the jurisprudence of the North African Māliki school could be taught and studied and provided it with a permanent endowment.

This is one of the earliest recorded instances of a *waqf* endowment in Jerusalem, whereby a donor would surrender his ownership of an income-producing property, such as a shop, and dedicate the profits (after the running costs had been subtracted) to a good cause. A *waqf* could be used to ransom prisoners of war, fund a soup kitchen, or build a *madrasah*. It was a virtuous act to make such an endowment, especially in al-Quds, where a good deed was thought to be especially meritorious. But there were also practical advantages. Some donors used *awqāf* to provide for their descendants, who could either live in the endowed building or become the salaried inspector of the endowment. Sometimes a *madrasah* or a *khanāqāh* had an apartment for the donor, who planned to retire to Jerusalem. The *waqf* was an act of practical charity: it promoted Islamic learning, offered scholarships to needy students, and provided for the poor. The system thus ensured that the ideal of social justice, which was so crucial to the teaching of the Qurʾān, was central to the *jihād* for Jerusalem. The *waqf* not only contributed to the beauty and fabric of the city but also provided employment. Somebody in straitened circumstances could get a job as the custodian of a *madrasah* or join a Sufi order. Any surplus money of any *waqf* was always given to the poor, so that people who had to live on charity were treated with dignity and respect. Justice and compassion had been central to the holiness of Jerusalem from the very earliest days of the city. It had not been much in evidence in Crusader Jerusalem but had been of great concern to Saladin. Almsgiving had accompanied the purification of the Ḥaram after the Crusaders had left, and now the institution of the *waqf* made the care of the poor and needy an essential part of the Ayyūbid Islamization of Jerusalem.

But the Muslims could not relax as long as the Crusaders remained in Palestine. In fact, the Franks who lived in the Kingdom of Acre were now anxious to keep the peace; they had learned a valuable lesson at the battle of Hittin. But the Christians of the West were more bellicose and continued to send Crusades to liberate Jerusalem. Al-ʿĀdil's son al-Muʿaẓẓam Isa became the Sultan of Damascus in 1200 but was so devoted to al-Quds that he made it his chief residence. He endowed two *madāris:* one, which bore his name, for the Hanifi school of law to the north of the Ḥaram, and the second for the teaching of Arabic over the Gate of Mercy. Al-Muʿaẓẓam also repaired the colonnades around the Ḥaram borders. But in 1218 there was another Crusade from the West.

This time the Crusaders did not sail directly to Palestine but tried to dislodge the Muslims from Egypt, hoping to establish a base there for the reconquest of Jerusalem. The mere presence of Crusaders in the Near East was enough to inspire dread throughout the region. People fearfully recalled the massacre of 1099 and expected new atrocities. Al-Muʿaẓẓam was convinced that the Crusaders would take back Jerusalem, slaughter the population, and dominate the whole Islamic world. In fact, after its initial success, the Crusade made little headway. But the Franks had left such a legacy of terror behind that it was difficult for the Muslims to see the situation objectively. Al-Muʿaẓẓam gave orders that the walls of Jerusalem be dismantled so that the Crusaders would not be able to establish themselves there. It was a drastic step; the emirs of Jerusalem argued that they would be able to ward off a Crusader attack, but al-Muʿaẓẓam waved away their objections and insisted on overseeing the demolition himself. There was huge distress in the city and the region as a whole. From the very beginning, the *raison d'être* of any city was to give its inhabitants security, and when the sultan's engineers, masons, and miners arrived in Jerusalem and began to pull the walls down there was panic. The most vulnerable people in the city—women, girls, and old men—rushed through the streets weeping and tearing their garments. They congregated in the Ḥaram and fled the city for Damascus, Cairo, and Kerak, leaving their families and possessions behind. Eventually the city was left without fortifications and its garrison was withdrawn. Only the Tower of David remained standing.

Al-Quds was no longer a viable city. Now that it had no walls, the Muslims dared not live there while the Franks remained close by in the

Kingdom of Acre. The city became little more than a village, inhabited only by a few devoted ascetics and jurists, who somehow kept the new Ayyūbid institutions going, and state officials and a handful of soldiers. Al-Muʿaẓẓam's decision proved to be premature, since in 1221 the Crusaders were forced to return home. But the Crusades had so profoundly unsettled the region that it seemed impossible for Muslims to contemplate a Western presence with any degree of confidence or equanimity. A new defensiveness had entered the Muslim feeling for Jerusalem, which could be destructive to the city.

Security had become a top priority to the Muslim rulers. In 1229, al-Kāmil, the Sultan of Egypt, was ready to give Jerusalem up rather than face the hideous prospect of fighting a new invasion of Crusaders. Meanwhile Frederick II, the Holy Roman Emperor of Europe, was being pressured by the pope to lead a new expedition to the Holy Land. Known by his contemporaries as Stupor Mundi, the Wonder of the World, Frederick constantly flouted Western expectations. He had been brought up in cosmopolitan Sicily and did not share the usual xenophobia of Europe. He had no hatred of Islam; on the contrary, he spoke fluent Arabic and enjoyed conversing and corresponding with Muslim scholars and rulers. He regarded the Crusade for Jerusalem as a waste of time, but knew that he could not continue to disregard public opinion by putting it off any longer. He rather cynically suggested to al-Kāmil that he simply hand Jerusalem over to him. After all, now that the city had no walls, it was of no use to the sultan, economically or strategically. Al-Kāmil was ready to agree. By this time, he had seriously quarreled with his brother al-Muʿaẓẓam, Sultan of Damascus, and without a united front could not contemplate fighting an army of Crusaders. A Frankish presence in unfortified Jerusalem could pose no military threat, and giving the city back to the Franks might defuse the danger from the West. Frederick would also be a useful ally against al-Muʿaẓẓam.

Eventually, after some hesitation on both sides, Frederick and al-Kāmil signed the treaty of Jaffa on 29 February 1229. There would be a truce for ten years; the Christians would take back Jerusalem, Bethlehem, and Nazareth, but Frederick promised not to rebuild the walls of Jerusalem. The Jews would have to leave the city, but the Muslims would retain the Ḥaram. Islamic worship would continue there without hindrance and the Muslim insignia be displayed.

News of the treaty evoked outrage in both the Muslim and the Christian world. Muslims poured onto the streets of Baghdad, Mosul, and Aleppo in angry demonstrations; imāms mobbed al-Kāmil's camp at Tel al-Ajul and had to be driven away by force. Al-Muʿaẓẓam, who was mortally ill, was so shocked by the news that he insisted on leaving his bed in order personally to supervise the destruction of Jerusalem's last remaining defenses. Crowds sobbed and groaned in the Great Mosque in Damascus as Sheikh Sibt al-Jauzi denounced al-Kāmil as a traitor to Islam. Al-Kāmil tried to defend himself: he had not ceded the sacred shrines of Islam to the Christians; the Ḥaram was still under Muslim jurisdiction; they had merely given up "some churches and ruined houses" of no real value.[3] It would be a simple matter for the Muslims to recover the city at a later date. But after the bloodshed and the wars, Jerusalem had become a symbol of Muslim integrity and no Islamic ruler could easily make concessions about the Holy City.

The Christians were equally shocked. To make such a treaty with the infidel was almost blasphemous. The very notion of allowing the Muslims to remain on the Ḥaram in a Christian city was intolerable. They were utterly scandalized by Frederick's behavior when he visited the Holy City. Because he had recently been excommunicated by the pope, no priest would crown him King of Jerusalem,[4] and the emperor simply placed the crown on his own head at the high altar of the Holy Sepulcher Church. Then he walked to the Ḥaram, joked with the attendants in Arabic, admired the architecture profusely, and beat up a Christian priest who had dared to enter the Aqsā carrying his Bible. He had been most upset when he learned that the *qāḍī* had ordered the muezzin to be silent during his stay and asked that the call to prayer be issued as usual. This was no way for a Crusader to behave! The Templars plotted to have Frederick killed, and he hastily left the country; as he hurried to his ship in the early hours of the morning, the butchers of Acre pelted him with offal and entrails. Jerusalem had now become such a sensitive issue in the Christian world that anybody who fraternized with Muslims or appeared to trifle with the Holy City was likely to be assassinated. The whole story of Frederick's extraordinary Crusade shows that Islam and the West were finding it impossible to accommodate each other: on neither side was there any desire for coexistence and peace.

Nonetheless the truce held for ten years, even though Muslims from Hebron and Nablus raided the city shortly after Frederick's departure and pilgrims were harassed on the road leading to Jerusalem from the coast. But the Christians did not have the resources to defend Jerusalem, which was an isolated enclave in the midst of enemy territory. When the truce expired in 1239, al-Nasir Dāʾūd, governor of Kerak, was able to force the Franks to leave the city after a short siege. But since there was still internecine warfare among the ʿAyyūbids, he gave the city back to the Christians shortly afterward in return for their help against the Sultan of Egypt. This time the Muslims did not hold on to the Ḥaram, and they were horrified to hear that the Christians had hung bells in the

Aqsā Mosque and "set bottles of wine on the Rock" for the celebration of Mass.[5] But their tenure was short-lived. In 1244 an army of Khwarazmian Turks, who were fleeing the Mongol invasion of their own land in Central Asia, burst into Palestine, having been summoned by the Sultan of Egypt to help him with his wars in Syria. They sacked Damascus and devastated Jerusalem, killing the Christians there and violating the shrines, including the Church of the Holy Sepulcher. The city was back in ʿAyyūbid hands, but many of its houses and churches were little more than smoking ruins. After this catastrophe, most of the inhabitants fled to the relative safety of the coastal cities. There was now only a skeleton community of about two thousand Muslims and Christians living on the site of the once-populous metropolis.

A seventh Crusade, led by King Louis IX of France, failed to reconquer Jerusalem; indeed, the whole army was taken prisoner in Egypt for a few months in 1250. While the Crusaders were in captivity, the ʿAyyūbids of Egypt were defeated by a party of disaffected Mamluks, who founded their own kingdom. *Mamālīk* had originally come from the Eurasian steppes, beyond the borders of the Islamic empire. As children they had been enslaved by Muslims, converted to Islam, and then drafted into elite regiments in the Muslim armies. Since their lives had dramatically improved after their capture and conversion, they were usually devoted Muslims, who yet retained a distinct ethnic identity and felt strong solidarity with one another. Now the Bahariyya regiment that had seized control of Egypt would create a new Mamluk state and become a major power in the Near East.

At first the rise of the Mamluks did not affect Jerusalem. The ʿAyyūbids in the rest of Saladin's empire opposed them, and the position of Jerusalem continued to be unstable. But in 1260 the Mamluk sultan al-Zahīr Baybars (1260–76) defeated the invading Mongol army at the battle of Ain Jalut in Galilee. It was a glorious achievement: the Mongols had brought down the ʿAbbasid caliphate; they had sacked and destroyed major Muslim cities, including Baghdad itself. Now Baybars had dispatched them beyond the Euphrates and become a hero of Islam. Since the ʿAyyūbid sultans had also been brought down by the Mongols, Baybars was now the ruler of Syria and Palestine. He still had to deal with occasional Mongol sorties and was determined to eject the Franks from their coastal state, but ultimately the Mamluks brought the region a security and order it had not known for years.

Jerusalem was of no strategic importance to the Mamluks, and they never bothered to rebuild the walls, but they were most impressed by the holiness of the city, whose religious status rose during their tenancy. Nearly all the sultans made a point of visiting Jerusalem and endowing new buildings there. When Baybars visited al-Quds in 1263, besides undertaking restoration work on the Ḥaram, he found an imaginative solution to Jerusalem's security problem. Easter was a particularly dangerous time, because the city was full of Christians. So Baybars founded two new sanctuaries close by: one to the prophet Moses (Nebī Mūsā) near Jericho and the other to the Arab prophet Salih in Ramleh. The festivals of the prophets were held during the week before Easter, so that Jerusalem was surrounded by crowds of devout Muslim pilgrims during this vulnerable season. Nebī Mūsā became particularly important. Pilgrims processed around Jerusalem to the Ḥaram and through the streets, as they had seen the Christians doing for centuries. They were demonstrating their ownership of al-Quds, just as the Christians had done. A special Nebī Mūsā banner was unfurled. When all the pilgrims had gathered in Jerusalem, the crowds left for the shrine, having made sure that the Christians saw how numerous they were. At Nebī Mūsā they spent the week praying, reciting the Qur'ān, taking part in Sufi exercises, and also enjoying themselves, camping out in the courtyards of the shrine and in the surrounding hills. The Christian pilgrims, meanwhile, were celebrating Easter in Jerusalem, knowing that there were crowds of Muslims nearby ready to spring to the defense of al-Quds. It was an ingenious device, but the Nebī Mūsā celebrations together with the other festivals that developed at new shrines in the vicinity demonstrated the new defensiveness in Muslim piety.

A militant element was also creeping into the Jewish devotion to Jerusalem. In 1267, Rabbi Moses ben Nachman, better known as Nachmanides, was exiled from Christian Spain, and made the *aliyah* to Jerusalem. He was appalled by the desolate state of the city, where he found only two Jewish families on his arrival. Undeterred, Nachmanides founded a synagogue in a deserted house with a beautiful arch in the Jewish Quarter. Known as the Ramban Synagogue (after *Rabbi Moses ben Nachman*), it became the center of Jewish life in Mamluk Jerusalem. Students were attracted by Nachmanides's intellectual reputation as a Talmudist and began to settle in Jerusalem to study in his yeshiva. In his new homelessness, Nachmanides found comfort in making physical contact with Jerusalem. He could "caress" and "fondle" its stones and weep over its ruined state.[6] It is almost as though the ruined city had replaced his wife and family, whom he had been obliged to leave behind in Spain. He was convinced that all Jews had a duty to settle in Palestine. The sorry plight of Jerusalem and the surrounding countryside, which had been ravaged by three hundred years of intermittent warfare, seemed evidence that the land would never prosper under Christians or Muslims but was awaiting the return of its true owners. Nachmanides taught that *aliyah* was a "positive precept," an obligatory commandment incumbent upon all Jews of every generation. But the anti-Semitic persecution that Nachmanides had experienced in Spain had put iron in his soul and a new antagonism toward Christians and Muslims, with whom in previous centuries Jews had been able to live together fruitfully when al-Andalus was in the hands of Islam. The words he now addressed to his fellow Jews reflected this new intransigence toward his people's political and religious rivals in Palestine:

> For we were enjoined to destroy those nations if they make war upon us. But if they wish to make peace, we shall make peace with them and let them stay upon certain conditions. But we shall not leave the land in their hands or those of any other nation at any time whatsoever![7]

The Crusades in the East and the *reconquista* in Europe had made a new and permanent rift between the three religions of Abraham.

Nachmanides was a Kabbalist, a practitioner of the esoteric form of mysticism that had developed in Spain during the thirteenth century. Even though few Jews had the capacity to undertake this discipline in its entirety, the spiritual ideas and myths of Kabbalah would become normative in Jewish piety. Indeed, Kabbalah represents the triumph of mythology over the more rational forms of Judaism at this time. In their new distress, Spanish Jews found the God of philosophy too remote from their suffering. They turned instinctively to the old sacred geography, which they internalized and spiritualized still more. Instead of seeing ten degrees of holiness radiating from the inaccessible God in the Devir, Jews now imagined the incomprehensible and utterly mysterious Godhead (which they called *Ein Sof:* "Without End") reaching out toward the world in ten *sefiroth* ("numerations"), each of which represents a further stage in God's unfolding revelation or, as it were, the Godhead's adaptation of itself to the limited minds of human beings. But these ten *sefiroth* also represented the stages of consciousness by which the mystic makes the *aliyah* to God. Yet again, this was an "ascent inward" to the depths of the self. The imagery of Kabbalah, a restatement of the spirituality of the Jerusalem Temple, symbolized the interior life of both God and man. Kabbalah stressed this identity between the emanations of the Godhead and humanity. The last of the *sefiroth* was the Shekhinah, also called Malkhuth ("Dominion"). It represented both the divine Presence and the power that unites the people of Israel. Here below, this last *sefirah* is identified with Zion, which was thus taken up into the divine sphere without losing its earthly reality. The Presence, Israel, and Jerusalem remained in one profound sense inseparable.

Kabbalah made it possible to make the *aliyah* to God in the Diaspora without going to Jerusalem, but it also stressed that the Jews' separation from Zion was a victory for the forces of evil.[8] During the Exodus, Israelites had been forced to wander in the "desert of horrors," doing battle with the demonic powers that haunt the wilderness. As soon as the Israelites had taken possession of the land and inaugurated the liturgy on Mount Zion, order had been restored and everything had fallen into its right place. The Shekhinah had dwelt in the Devir, the source of blessing, fertility, and order for the whole world. But when the Temple was destroyed and the Jews were exiled from Jerusalem, the demonic forces of chaos triumphed. There was now a deep imbalance at the heart of all existence, which could be rectified only when the Jews were reunited with Zion and restored to their proper place. This mythology showed how deeply their geographic displacement had affected the Jewish soul: it symbolized a more profound separation from the source of being. Now that Jews were beginning to be forced out of Spain by the Christians, they felt anew their alienation and anomie. The myths of Kabbalah also spoke to the condition of the Jews in the rest of Europe, whose lives had become intolerable since the repeated pogroms of the Crusaders. This mythology, delineating their interior world, spoke to them at a deeper level than did the more cerebral doctrines of the Jewish philosophers. At this stage, most were content with a symbolic and spiritual return to Zion. Indeed, it was still considered wrong to try to hasten redemption by making the *aliyah* to Palestine. But some Kabbalists like Nachmanides felt impelled to find healing in making physical contact with Jerusalem.

The Christians of the West were having to face the fact that they would probably never regain control of Jerusalem, and to make their own accommodation to this loss. In 1291 the Mamluk sultan Khalil finally destroyed the Kingdom of Acre and expelled the Franks from their coastal state. For the first time in nearly two hundred years, the whole of Palestine was in Muslim hands. From this point, the fortunes of Jerusalem improved. Once the Franks were no longer on the scene, Muslims began to feel safe enough to come back to live there even though the city still had no proper fortifications. But the Christians had not given up. For centuries they would continue to plan new Crusades and dream of liberating the holy city. It seemed crucial that some Western presence be preserved in Jerusalem. Shortly after the fall of Acre, Pope Nicholas IV asked the sultan to allow a group of Latin clergy to serve in the Holy Sepulcher. The sultan agreed, and since the pope was himself a Franciscan, he sent a small group of friars to keep the Latin liturgy going in Jerusalem. They had no convent and no income and had to live in an ordinary pilgrim hostel. In 1300, their plight came to the attention of Robert, King of Sicily, who made the sultan a large gift of

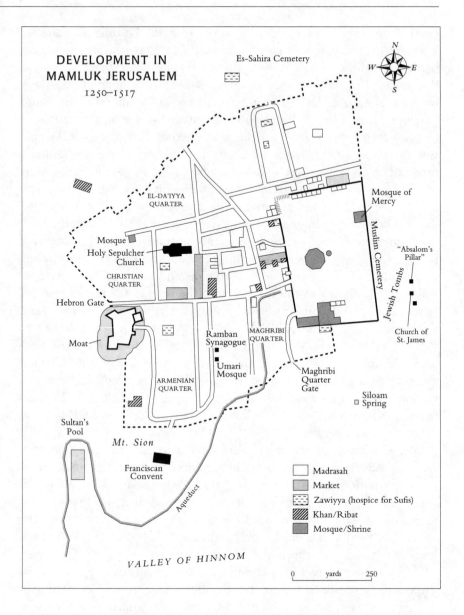

DEVELOPMENT IN
MAMLUK JERUSALEM
1250–1517

Es-Sahira Cemetery

N
W   E
S

EL-DA'IYYA
QUARTER

Mosque of
Mercy

Mosque
Holy Sepulcher
Church

"Absalom's
Pillar"

CHRISTIAN
QUARTER

Hebron Gate

Moat

Ramban
Synagogue

MAGHRIBI
QUARTER

Church of
St. James

Umari
Mosque

ARMENIAN
QUARTER

Maghribi
Quarter
Gate

Siloam
Spring

Sultan's
Pool

Mt. Sion

Franciscan
Convent

Aqueduct

Madrasah

Market

Zawiyya (hospice for Sufis)

Khan/Ribat

Mosque/Shrine

Muslim Cemetery

Jewish Tombs

VALLEY OF HINNOM

0   yards   250

money and asked him to let the Franciscans have the church on Mount
Sion, the Mary Chapel in the Holy Sepulcher Church, and the Nativity
Cave. Again, the sultan agreed. This would be the first of many occasions
when a Western power would use its influence to further the cause of
the Latins in Jerusalem. Henceforth the Sion Church became the Franciscans' new headquarters and the father superior became the *custos* or
guardian of all the Europeans living in the East. He was in effect fulfill-
ing the role of a consul in Jerusalem. The Franciscans had developed

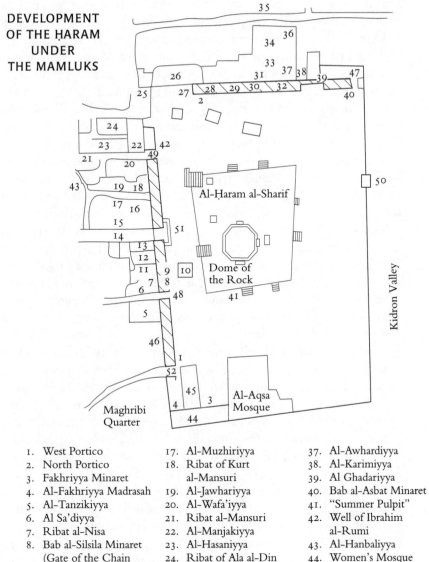

DEVELOPMENT
OF THE HARAM
UNDER
THE MAMLUKS

Al-Haram al-Sharif

Dome of
the Rock

Kidron Valley

Maghribi
Quarter

Al-Aqsa
Mosque

1. West Portico
2. North Portico
3. Fakhriyya Minaret
4. Al-Fakhriyya Madrasah
5. Al-Tanzikiyya
6. Al Sa'diyya
7. Ribat al-Nisa
8. Bab al-Silsila Minaret
   (Gate of the Chain
   Minaret)
9. Al-Ashrafiyya
10. Fountain of Sultan
    Qaytbay
11. Al-Baladiyya
12. Al-'Uthmaniyya
13. Ribat al-Zamani
14. Suq al-Quattanin
    (Cotton Merchants'
    Market)
15. Al-Khatuniyya
16. Al-Arghuniyya

17. Al-Muzhiriyya
18. Ribat of Kurt
    al-Mansuri
19. Al-Jawhariyya
20. Al-Wafa'iyya
21. Ribat al-Mansuri
22. Al-Manjakiyya
23. Al-Hasaniyya
24. Ribat of Ala al-Din
25. Ghawanima Minaret
26. Al-Jawiliyya
27. Al-Subaybiyya
28. Al Is'ardiyya
29. Al-Almalikiyya
30. Al-Farisiyya
31. Al-Aminiyya
32. Al-Basitiyya
33. Al Dawadariyya
34. Al Salamiyya
35. Mu'azzamiyya Minaret
36. Ribat al-Maridini

37. Al-Awhardiyya
38. Al-Karimiyya
39. Al Ghadariyya
40. Bab al-Asbat Minaret
41. "Summer Pulpit"
42. Well of Ibrahim
    al-Rumi
43. Al-Hanbaliyya
44. Women's Mosque
45. Maghribi Mosque
46. Site of the present
    Western Wall
47. Pool of the Sons of
    Israel
48. Gate of the Chain
49. Gate of the Inspector
50. Gate of Mercy
51. Cotton Merchants'
    Gate
52. Maghribi Gate

militant policies toward Islam in other parts of the world, and in Europe their preaching often inspired anti-Semitic pogroms, so they were unlikely to be an altogether soothing influence in Jerusalem.

Now that there was peace in the country, the Mongol and Crusader threat contained, Palestine flourished under the Mamluks. Jerusalem was never an important political center in their empire. It was governed by a low-ranking emir and was chiefly used as a place of exile for officials who were *battal,* out of favor. In this unfortified town, they could do little harm, but many of these exiles were drawn into the religious life of al-Quds. Some were given the prestigious position of superintendent of the two *harams* of Jerusalem and Hebron and many made *waqf* endowments. The building *jihād* continued, and this brought Sufis, scholars, lecturers, jurists, and pilgrims to the town. The Mamluks transformed Jerusalem.[9] Only the sultans were permitted to build on the Haram itself, and most took advantage of this privilege. In 1317, Sultan al-Nasir Muhammad commissioned new colonnaded porches along the northern and western borders, restored the dome of the Aqsā, and regilded the Dome of the Rock. He also built a new commercial center on the site of an old Crusader market. It was a sign of a new prosperity in Jerusalem during the early fourteenth century. Soap, cotton, and linen products were all manufactured in the city, and Haram documents show that foreign traders from the east, especially textile merchants, were often present in the city, though we have no detailed information about the actual volume of trade. The sultan's new market was called Suq al-Qattanin, the Cotton Merchants' Market. He was anxious that it actually made contact with the Haram wall, where he built a magnificent new gate—Bab al-Qattanin—from which twenty-seven steps led up to the Haram platform.

The desire to make physical contact with the holy place had often characterized Jewish and Christian devotion to Jerusalem. During the Mamluk period, this longing to touch the Haram was particularly evident in the new *madāris* that were built around the Haram borders. Often the architects had to be extremely ingenious, since space was at a premium. (See diagram.) It was only possible to build around the northern and western borders of the Haram, because on the eastern and southern sides the ground fell away too sharply. But all the donors wanted their *madrasah* to have a view of the Haram or to touch the sacred ground. One of the earliest of the new buildings was endowed in 1328 by Tanziq, the viceroy of Syria, beside the western supporting wall. He was particularly proud to be building so close to the third-holiest site in Islam. In the mosque of the Tanziqiyya Madrasah an inscription reads: "[God] made his mosque the neighbor of the Aqsā

Mosque and how goodly is a pure neighbor." The building was exquisitely decorated and cruciform in shape: four halls for lectures and communal prayers led off a central courtyard. The Tanziqiyya was not simply a law school, however. It also contained a convent (*khānaqāh*) for eleven Sufis and a school for orphans. Study, mystical prayer, and philanthropy were all conducted under one roof. The plan showed the desire for integration, which was still crucial in the Muslim conception of sacred space. It also showed how central practical charity continued to be in the ongoing Islamization of al-Quds. The architect found, however, that the site was too small to house all the institutions adequately, so he had the inspiration of building the Sufi convent on top of the sultan's new porch on the western border of the Ḥaram. Now when the Sufis made their spiritual exercises, they could look at the Dome of the Rock, a paradigm of their own quest.

Other donors were quick to follow Tanziq's example. The Aminiyya Madrasah (1229–30) had to be crammed into a very narrow site—a mere nine meters—between the eastern spur of the Antonia rock and the street, so they built upward; the third story was constructed on top of the northern portico. The Malikiyya Madrasah

This view of the borders of the Ḥaram al-Sharif shows how it was possible for the Mamluks to build their madāris on top of the porticoes around the edge of the sacred precincts.

adopted the same solution, so that the main floor of the law school over-looked the Ḥaram. The Manjakiyya Madrasah (1361) was built entirely on the porches and over the Inspector's Gate (Bab al-Nasir), one of the busiest entrances of the Ḥaram during the Mamluk period. The Tulu-niyya Madrasah and Faraniyya Madrasah were also built on top of the northern porch, one on either side of the minaret of the Gate of the Tribes (Bab al-Asbat): students had to use the narrow staircase of the minaret, since there was no other entrance.

As in Judaism, the study of law was not a dry, academic discipline but, like mystical prayer, a way of lifting the mind and heart to God. The desire to study with a view of the Dome of the Rock, the great Islamic symbol of spiritual ascent, shows this clearly. But the *madrasah* had acquired a wholly new importance since the Mongol invasions. So many libraries, manuscripts, and artifacts had been sacked and burned that Muslims felt a new urgency about the study of their traditions. It had become a *jihād* to recover what had been lost, and, perhaps inevitably, a new conservatism had entered Islamic thought. These new *madāris,* built protectively around the Ḥaram, can also be seen as an attempt to create a bulwark between the sacred place and a hostile world. They expressed the new defensiveness that the Muslims now felt for Jerusalem. This can also be seen in the austere hospices (*ribāts*) that were being built throughout the city. Originally the *ribāt* had been a military fortress; now it was used to house ascetics, the poor, and the pilgrims.

The new conservatism was countered by the Sufi movement, which enjoyed a great flowering after the Mongol scourge, as Muslims strug-gled to make some ultimate sense of the catastrophe and suffering. More Sufis congregated in al-Quds during the fourteenth century than ever before, some, as we have seen, taking up residence in the new buildings beside the Ḥaram, others in smaller communities scattered over the city. Sufism was not a discipline for the chosen few; it was also a popular movement, and, intensely individualistic, it encouraged the laity to defy the traditional teachings of the *ʿulamā*ʾ, even though some Sufi sheikhs also taught law in the *madāris*. Eventually Sufism would introduce a spirit of freethinking into the Islamic world. Sufis were beginning to form large orders, and several of them were established in Jerusalem at this time. But their members were not taught to turn away from the world, like Christian ascetics. The extremely influential Qadariyya, which had its headquarters in the old Hospital complex, taught that social justice was the highest religious duty. The *jihād* for spirituality and interior prayer had to be combined—yet again—with practical compas-sion. The Bistamiyya, settled in the north of the city, taught yogic disci-plines to help its members pay attention to the deeper currents of the unconscious that surfaced in dreams and visions. But it also promoted a program called *sulh-e kull* ("universal conciliation") to enable the different religious traditions to understand one another. After the centuries of hatred and warfare, it was an attempt to find reconciliation that could have been very valuable in the tense city of al-Quds.

The clash between conservatism and innovation can be seen in the work of the fourteenth-century reformer Taqiyy ad-Dīn ibn Taymiyya, who was alarmed at the new intensity of devotion to Jerusalem, which, he felt, was incompatible with Islamic tradition. During the Mamluk period, at least thirty new anthologies of the *faḍāʾil al-quds* were published, repeating the old traditions in praise of the city's holiness and urging Muslims to make the *ziyāra* ("visit") to Jerusalem. Practices had crept into the Ḥaram devotions that disturbed Ibn Taymiyya. We have seen that for some time Muslims had liked to perform some of the *hajj* rituals in Jerusalem; it was a way of expressing their conviction that al-Quds derived its holiness from Mecca. Ibn Taymiyya insisted that it was important to keep the *ziyāra* to al-Quds quite separate from the *hajj* to Mecca in his brief treatise *In Support of Pious Visits to Jerusalem*. It was wrong to circle the Rock and kiss it as though it were the Kaʿbah. Such shrines as the Cradle of Jesus were pure fabrications, and only fools could give them credence. Ibn Taymiyyah still believed that Jerusalem was the third-holiest city in the Islamic world but wanted to make it clear that the *ziyāra* could only be a private devotion and was not binding upon all Muslims, as was the *hajj*. His zeal to conserve tradition and to stop innovation (*ʿbida*) was characteristic of the time; his austere view of Jerusalem has never been accepted by the majority of Muslims, who still quote the *faḍāʾil al-quds* and regard the cult of Jerusalem as an authentic Muslim devotion.

It was a devotion that was not always easy to cultivate. Some of the *faḍāʾil* see the *ziyāra* as a pious act that needed courage and endurance. "He who lives in Jerusalem is considered a warrior of the *jihād*," Muḥammad is reported to have said in one of the new traditions. Others spoke of the "inconvenience and adversity" of visiting al-Quds.[10] By the second half of the fourteenth century, the first cracks could be seen in the Mamluk system. New sultans were finding it difficult to establish their authority. The Bedouin, who had been too frightened to invade Jerusalem during the Crusader period, had resumed their incursions. In 1348 they had actually driven all the inhabitants out of the city. In the years 1351–53, Jerusalem was badly hit by the Black Death. Then the political instability meant that governors were appointed for only short periods and never gained a sound knowledge of local conditions. By the beginning of the fifteenth century, there were more Bedouin raids, and

Christian pirates attacked the coastal cities of Palestine. The economy was depressed, taxation increased, and there were occasionally riots in the city that resulted in fatalities. The building *jihād* continued, despite these problems. Sultans al-Nasir Hasan (1347–51) and al-Salih Salih (1351–54) completed a major renovation of the Aqsā Mosque, and new *madāris* and *ribāts* were endowed in the city and around the borders of the Haram. Money was pouring into Jerusalem for these foundations, but this did not help the economy of the city, since the *madāris* generated no income.

As always, economic and political problems in Muslim Jerusalem made it harder for Christians and Muslims to live peaceably together. Jews did not feel as hostile toward Islam. Visitors described the Jewish community as prosperous and peaceful during the fourteenth century. But in these hard times most new immigrants preferred to settle in Galilee, where there was more opportunity and which was becoming a rabbinic holy land. Pilgrims now liked to pray at the tombs of the great Talmudic scholars, such as Rabbi Yohanan ben Zakkai and Rabbi Akiva. Safed, near the grave of Rabbi Simeon ben Yohai, the hero of the Kabbalistic classic the *Zohar,* was becoming another holy city, especially to Jews who were mystically inclined. Muslims also honored these tombs, and Jewish visitors noted that Jews and "Saracens" both tended the same country shrines in Palestine. Muslims also enjoyed good relations with the local Christians and the Armenians. The chief problem to disturb the peace of al-Quds was the tension between the Muslims and the Western Christians, a direct legacy of the Crusades.

In 1365, for example, when the Hospitalers attacked Alexandria from their base in Cyprus, the Muslims arrested the whole Franciscan community and closed the Holy Sepulcher. The Franciscans were no passive victims, however. They began to launch an occasional suicide attack, similar to those undertaken by other Franciscans in other parts of the Islamic world, against the Muslim establishment in Jerusalem. On 11 November 1391, a group of them processed to the Aqsā and insisted on an audience with the *qādī.* As soon as they were brought before him, they announced that Muhammad had been "a libertine, a murderer, a glutton, a despoiler who thought that the purpose of human life was eating, whoring, and wearing expensive clothes."[11] The news of this verbal assault spread, and soon an angry mob had gathered at the *qādī*'s door. Since it was a capital offense to insult the Prophet, the *qādī* offered the friars the option of conversion to Islam before sentencing them to death. This had been the Franciscans' intention. By forcing the Muslims to make martyrs of them, they intended to bring "death and damnation on the infidel."[12] There was another, similar incident in 1393 when three friars challenged the *'ulamā'* to a public debate and then proceeded to denounce Muḥammad in the coarsest terms as an impostor. These incidents could not but lead to a deterioration of Muslim-Christian relations. Muslims felt exploited and abused, and the attacks revealed a loathing that made real coexistence impossible.

As a result of this increased tension, the building *jihād* of the Muslims sometimes seemed intended—and was certainly perceived—as an invasion of other people's sacred space. At the end of the fourteenth century, the Muslims rebuilt a minaret which belonged to a mosque adjoining the Ramban Synagogue. This proximity would cause a great deal of trouble in the future. In 1417 the sheikh of the Salihiyya *khanāqāh* built a minaret that towered provocatively above the Holy Sepulcher: Muslims in Jerusalem believed that he would be rewarded for this at the Last Judgment. But, not surprisingly, this clash of interests came most aggressively to the surface at the Franciscans' headquarters on Mount Sion.

When the Franciscans purchased the site of the Sion Church in 1300, it had included the so-called Tomb of David, which had come to light during the Crusader period. It was not one of their major attractions. The Franciscans had little love of Jewish lore, and when they escorted pilgrims around

The so-called Tomb of David on Mount Sion has been the cause of much dispute among Jews, Christians, and Muslims since the fifteenth century. Today Orthodox Jews tacitly make their claim to the site when they celebrate here the first haircut of their sons in a traditional ceremony.

the city, they emphasized its New Testament associations. The Sion Church was principally a monument to the early church: pilgrims were shown the Upper Room, the Pentecost Shrine, the place where St. John used to say Mass for the Virgin Mary, and the place where Mary "fell asleep" at the end of her life on earth. The Tombs of David and the Kings of Judah were often mentioned last in pilgrims' descriptions of Mount Sion. But the Jews of the city had suddenly awakened to the fact that the tomb of the first Jewish king of Jerusalem was in a Christian precinct. They repeatedly asked Sultan Barsbay (1422–37) to hand it over to them. This was a mistake. When Barsbay was told about the Tomb of the Prophet Dā'ūd, he found it intolerable that it should be in the hands of avowed enemies of Islam. He descended upon Mount Sion and locked up the tomb in such a way that the Franciscans could not enter it from their convent. He then dismantled the Christian accouterments of the tomb and turned it into a mosque. Finally he closed the Upper Room, also known as the Cenacle Church, because it was directly above the Tomb of David and it was not suitable for Christians to traipse about in processions on top of the new mosque.[13] As far as the Latin Christians were concerned, the old Muslim ideal of coexistence and integration was crumbling fast.

The *jihād* was continued by Sultan al-Zahir Jaqmaq (1438–53), who decided to apply the letter of the law forbidding *dhimmis* to restore their places of worship without permission. He closed down the rest of the Sion Church and exhumed the bones of the friars buried in the nearby cemetery. A wooden balustrade that had been "illegally" erected in the Holy Sepulcher Church was carried off to the Aqsā, and new buildings were also pulled down in Bethlehem. A Syrian convent was confiscated, but in the main the sultan's offensive was directed solely against the Latins. He issued a special edict in favor of the Armenians, forbidding the emir of Jerusalem to harass them with unnecessary taxation, and an inscription to this effect was engraved on a plaque at the western entrance to the Armenian Quarter. The Armenians had been closely involved with the Crusaders, but they had not followed them in uncritical and fanatical hatred of Islam. They had already learned not to take sides, and as a result, they were the only community that had remained in its own quarter without being dislodged during the upheavals of the previous three hundred years.

Yet despite the tension in the city, huge numbers of Western pilgrims continued to visit the city. Their stay was not always comfortable, but they were allowed to see what they had come to see and their visit was efficiently organized. They spent a whole night in the Holy Sepulcher Church and were escorted around the city in a set tour, which began before daybreak so as not to antagonize the Muslims. The circuit began at the Holy Sepulcher Church, whence pilgrims marched quietly to the eastern gate of the city (known today as the Lion Gate), crossed the Kidron Valley to Gethsemane, and then climbed to the Ascension Church on the Mount of Olives. They returned to the city via the Pool of Siloam and finally visited what they could of Mount Sion. There was also a three-day trip to Bethlehem and the River Jordan. As before, the pilgrims scarcely mention the mosques and *madāris,* though the Franciscans countered the Islamization of the Ḥaram by stressing its exclusively Christian significance. The "Temple of the Lord," as they still called the Dome of the Rock, was important because the Virgin Mary had been presented to God there as a baby; later she had gone to school in the Temple and had wed St. Joseph there. The Christians now proprietorially called the Aqsā Mosque "the Church of Our Lady."

The Franciscans had a special devotion to the Passion of Christ, and they were beginning to point out places connected with Jesus's last painful hours. These were now, as far as the Latins were concerned, nearly all located in the northern districts of Jerusalem. The transfer from Mount Sion, which had begun during the Crusader period, seemed almost complete. Thus James of Verona, who vis-

Today the Franciscans, still the official Roman Catholic guardians of Jerusalem's holy places, process down the Via Dolorosa, regarded somewhat warily by Muslim residents.

ited Jerusalem in 1335, entered the city at the eastern (Lion) gate near the Pool of Beth-Hesda; he passed St. Anna's Church (now the Salihiyya Madrasah) and proceeded down the road known today as the Via Dolorosa. He was shown the house of Annas (now a mosque) and the house of Herod in this street; he saw "Pilate's House" (the "Ecce Homo Arch" of Hadrian's forum), the place where Mary fainted when she saw Jesus carrying the cross, and the ruins of a gate near which Jesus was supposed to have left the city. Once he had entered the Holy Sepulcher precinct, James paused at other "stations." There was a cracked stone in the courtyard where Jesus rested before mounting Golgotha, and a cave inside the church where he had been imprisoned while the cross was being prepared and had been stripped of his garments. Then came Golgotha itself, the Black Stone of Unction, where Jesus had been laid after being taken down from the cross, and, finally, the tomb. Some of these sites would change: this is not yet the devotion known today as the Stations of the Cross. When the Franciscans led the pilgrims down the Via Dolorosa by torchlight, they were taking them in the reverse direction. But the ground had been prepared. Now that the Latin Christians no longer had much space of their own in the Holy Sepulcher Church, they were cultivating other sites outside.

The German Dominican Felix Fabri, who visited Jerusalem in about 1480, has left a vivid account of his pilgrimage. He became aware of the tension that now existed between the Muslim population and the Latins as soon as his ship docked at Jaffa. Muslim officials grabbed each pilgrim roughly, demanding his name and particulars, and then Felix was hurled into a "darksome and decayed dwelling beneath a ruinous vault . . . even as men are wont to thrust a sheep into a stable to be milked."[14] Here he was assigned his dragoman, a guide who would be his only contact with the Muslim world during his stay, and the Franciscan *custos* gave the pilgrims a stern lecture. They must on no account wander around without their dragoman, inscribe graffiti on the walls, look appreciatively at Muslim women, or drink wine in public (it might inflame the Muslims to murderous envy). There must be no fraternization with Muslims at all; the tension was now such that the authorities could no longer guarantee the goodwill of the local population.

This grim reception, however, did not dampen the pilgrims' ardor. As soon as they saw the Holy City, Felix tells us, they leaped from their donkeys and burst into tears. There was more weeping when they first saw the Holy Sepulcher: "such bitter heartfelt groans, such sweet wailings, and such deep sighs, such sorrow, such sobs from the inmost breast, such peace and gladsome solace."[15] Some pilgrims wandered around like zombies, beating their breasts in an uncoordinated manner, as though possessed. Women shrieked as though in labor; some pilgrims simply collapsed and lay on the ground like corpses. Pilgrims were regularly so overcome that they had to be hospitalized. Western devotion to Jerusalem had taken on a hysterical cast. There was no disciplined "ascent" here and no real transcendence. These pilgrims seemed mired in their own neuroses.

Yet Western piety was changing in other ways. Felix examined his own response analytically in a way that would not have occurred to earlier pilgrims. He found that pilgrimage was very hard work. It was not easy to march from place to place in the blazing sun, kneeling and prostrating yourself to the ground and, above all, worrying whether you were responding properly. "To struggle after mental abstraction whilst bodily walking from place to place is exceedingly toilsome."[16] Felix was also worried about the authenticity of some of the sites. How much of the original tomb could remain after all this time? How was it that nobody had discovered the Tomb of David before?[17] A new critical spirit was beginning to appear that would make the traditional pilgrimage impossible for many Western pilgrims.

But perhaps the pilgrimage had already had its day. All the major faiths insist that a true religious experience must issue in practical compassion. That is, as it were, the litmus test of authentic spirituality. In the past, Jerusalem had not helped Christians to be charitable, either to one another or to people of other faiths. The Crusades can be seen as a travesty of religion: an idolatry that regarded the mere possession of a holy place as the ultimate goal. Now, on the brink of modernity, the critical Felix could scarcely find a good word to say about any of the other inhabitants of Jerusalem. The "saracens" are "befouled with the dregs of all heresies, worse than idolaters, more loathsome than the Jews"; the Greek church, once learned, is now "darkened with numberless errors"; the Syrians are the "children of the devil" and the Armenians sunk in diverse heresies; the Jews are justly hated by all the rest, their intellects dulled by the misery and contempt they undergo. Only the Franciscans, of all the citizens of Jerusalem, live a virtuous life, the chief mark of their piety being a longing "with all their hearts" for a new Crusade to conquer the holy city.[18] This dismal catalogue shows that the pilgrimage did nothing to liberate Felix from his projections and prejudices but had simply led him to a dead end of hatred and self-righteousness.

During the reign of Sultan al-Ashraf Qaytbay (1468–96), the Mamluk empire entered its last phase. The armies of the Ottoman Turks of Asia Minor were beginning to encroach on their territory; the Bedouin raids made it dangerous to leave the city: sixty people had been killed by Bedouin in 1461 outside the walls of Jerusalem. Mamluk trade was also damaged by the Portuguese. Yet still the sultan did not neglect Jerusalem but commissioned a new *madrasah* beside the western wall of the Ḥaram. The Ashrafiyya Madrasah is probably the loveliest of all the Mamluk buildings. Mūjīr ad-Dīn called it the third jewel of the Ḥaram. Built partly on the roof of the Baladiyya Madrasah and partly on the Ḥaram portico, its main hall was unique in extending onto the Ḥaram itself. It was as though the last Mamluk rulers were yearning toward the Rock, even as al-Quds was slipping from their grasp. Again, the Ashrafiyyah symbolized the integration of Islam: there were ʿulamāʾ from all four law schools and sixty Sufis. But the sultan also tried to alleviate the religious tensions of Jerusalem. The Franciscans had befriended him in his youth, while he had been banished to Jerusalem, and Qaytbay did not forget this. He allowed them to return to Mount Sion, where they lived rather grimly in cramped quarters, guarded by savage watchdogs. In 1489 they managed, by bribery, to have the Tomb of David and the Cenacle Chapel returned, and they began to rebuild. But the following year an assembly of ʿulamāʾ decreed that since the place had once been a mosque, it was unlawful to return it to the Christians.

Relations between the Muslims and the Jewish community of Jerusalem also took a turn for the worse during these last years. In 1473, part of the Ramban Synagogue collapsed in a heavy rainstorm. When the Jews asked permission to rebuild, the officials of the adjoining mosque protested: they should be able to walk straight into the mosque from the street, without having to pass through the grounds of the synagogue. The Jews offered the appropriate bribes and retained the site, but this so enraged their Muslim neighbors that they invaded the synagogue one night and demolished it. Sultan Qaytbay, however, found for the Jews and gave orders that the synagogue be rebuilt. There were now only about seventy Jewish families in Jerusalem; most were poor, and many lived in ramshackle houses. Yet this was not entirely the fault of the Muslims, the Italian traveler Obadiah da Bertinero pointed out when he visited Jerusalem in 1487. Their chief problem was the bitter discord between the Ashkenazi Jews from Germany and the Sephardi Jews from Spain and the Islamic countries. Jews now refused to set foot in the Ḥaram, Obadiah tells us. Sometimes the Muslims needed repairs there, but Jews would never take these jobs because they were not in the required state of ritual purity. This is the first time we hear of this self-imposed restriction, which some Jews still follow today; when Maimonides, who had similar views, visited Jerusalem he had nonetheless felt able to enter the Ḥaram. Now that the Temple Mount was even more removed from them, the Jews would need a new holy place. Yet when Obadiah passed the western supporting wall of the Ḥaram, he felt no special emotion. The wall was "composed of large, thick stones, such as I have never seen before in an old building, either in Rome or in any other city."[19] The Western Wall was not yet holy to the Jews of Jerusalem. But that would soon change.

The historian Mūjīr ad-Dīn, writing in 1496, gives us a valuable description of Jerusalem in the last days of the Mamluks. During the Mamluk centuries, the holiness of Jerusalem had become more central to the Muslim imagination than ever before. But the city was still without walls and virtually without a garrison. The evening parade at the Citadel had been discontinued, and the governor lived like a private citizen. Even though the Mamluks had lavished so much loving attention on the Ḥaram, they had never bothered to fortify the city, which was completely without strategic importance. The Mamluks had not neglected the city's mundane life, however. Mūjīr tells us that the buildings of the city were solidly constructed and the markets were the finest in the world. Mamluk devotion to the Ḥaram had changed the focus of the city, so that the center of its urban life had shifted back from the Western Hill, which had dominated Jerusalem since the time of Constantine, to the Ḥaram area. When Saladin first conquered Jerusalem, he and his emirs had taken up residence beside the Holy Sepulcher. By Mūjīr's time, the governor lived beside the northern border of the Ḥaram. Like most Oriental cities, Jerusalem was divided into quarters. The inhabitants of Jerusalem tended to settle in different districts according to their religion and ethnic origin. The Armenians and the Maghribis lived together, as did the Muslims from Iran, Afghanistan, and India, beside the northwest corner of the Ḥaram. Yet there was no strict segregation. There were still neighborhoods where Jews and Muslims lived side by side in the south of the city; similarly in the northeastern neighborhood of Bezetha, Christians and Muslims lived together. The divide was not yet total.

During the reign of Sultan al-Ashraf Aqnouk al-Ghuri (1513–16) it became clear that the Mamluks could not keep the Ottomans at bay indefinitely. In 1453 the Ottomans had conquered Constantinople and absorbed the old Christian empire of Byzantium. For a time it seemed as though they would conquer Europe too, but they were driven back from Belgrade by the Hungarian army. Then in 1515 the Ottoman sultan Selim I moved to the offensive. Within two years he had checked the Iranian advance at the battle of Chaldiran and defeated the Mamluks at Merj-Dibik to the north of Aleppo. One more battle outside Cairo brought the Mamluk empire effectively to an end. On 1 December

1516, Selim arrived outside Jerusalem. There was no opposition. The *ʿulamāʾ* went out to meet the sultan and presented him with the keys of the Aqsā and the Dome of the Rock. At once Selim leaped from his horse, prostrated himself in the attitude of Muslim prayer, and shouted: "Thanks be to God! I am the possessor of the sanctuary of the first *qiblah!*"

15

OTTOMAN CITY

T
HE PEOPLE of Jerusalem welcomed the Ottomans with relief. As the Mamluk empire had declined, the city had been neglected: *waqf* endowments had lapsed, the economy was depressed, and the roads were terrorized by the Bedouin. The Ottomans were already experienced empire builders and had established a strong, centralized administration. Like the Mamluks, they were a predominantly military power; at the heart of their army and their state were the Janissaries, an elite infantry corps, whose great strength was their willingness to use firearms. By the mid-sixteenth century, when the empire was at the height of its power, there were between twelve thousand and fifteen thousand Janissaries. The Ottomans brought law and order back to Palestine: the Bedouin were held in check, and once they had stopped wasting the countryside, agriculture could improve. The Ottomans were generous to the Arab provinces in the early years. They introduced an efficient administration, the economy improved, and trade and commerce flourished. Palestine was divided into three districts (*sanjaks*) based on Jerusalem, Nablus, and Gaza. These were all part of the province (*eyālet*) of Damascus. There was no attempt to repopulate Jerusalem with Turks. The Ottomans merely sent a governor (pasha), civil officials, and a small military force which was garrisoned in the citadel.

The fortunes of Jerusalem improved dramatically under Sultan Suleiman the Magnificent (1520–66). He fought wars in Europe, expanded the empire to the west, and then concentrated on its internal development. Under Suleiman, the Ottoman empire enjoyed a cultural revival, and Jerusalem was one of his chief beneficiaries. The Turkish wars had naturally led to a renewal of hatred of Islam in Europe. There was talk of a new Crusade, and it is said that Suleiman had a dream in which the Prophet Muḥammad commanded him to organize the defense of Jerusalem. At all events, in 1536 Suleiman ordered that the city walls be rebuilt. It was a massive project, involving huge expenditure and great skill. There were few other places where the Ottomans built such elaborate fortifications. The wall, which is still standing today, was two miles long and about forty feet high. It completely encircled the city and included thirty-four towers and seven open gates. The great court architect Sinan passed through the city during the construction and is said to have personally designed the Damascus Gate in the north of the city. When the wall was finished in 1541, Jerusalem was properly fortified for the first time in over three hundred years.

Suleiman also invested large sums in Jerusalem's water system. Six beautiful fountains were built in the city, canals and pools were excavated, and the "Sultan's Pool," southwest of the city, was renovated and its aqueducts repaired. To strengthen Jerusalem still further, Suleiman tried to persuade his subjects to settle there, particularly the Jewish refugees who had settled in the Ottoman empire after their expulsion from Christian Spain in 1492. From the population censuses taken by the Ottomans, we can see that the population almost trebled by the mid-sixteenth century. In 1553, there were approxi-

The early Ottoman commitment to Jerusalem is clear in the majestic city walls built by Suleiman; they are still one of the most famous landmarks of the Old City.

mately 13,384 inhabitants. The Jewish and Christian communities each numbered about 1,650 souls. Most of the Muslims were local Arab Sunnis, though there were also Muslims from North Africa, Egypt, Persia, Iraq, Bosnia, India, and Central Asia. The city now enjoyed a new prosperity. The markets had been developed and enlarged; the price of goods increased, a sign of an improvement in the general standard of living. There were five chief industries in the city, involving the manufacture of food, textiles, soap, leather, and metalwork. Soap was exported to Egypt and grain to Egypt, Rhodes, and Dubrovnik. Textiles and rice were imported from Egypt, clothes and coffee from Damascus, and textiles and rugs from Istanbul, China, and the Hijaz. The various industries and professions in Jerusalem were organized into about forty guilds (*taifa*), each with a sheikh and his deputy. Even singers and dancers had their own *taifa*. Because of the increase in population and income and also because of the religious prestige of the city, Jerusalem was promoted administratively in the second half of the sixteenth century. It was now a *mutasarri-flik,* an enlarged administrative unit which included the *sanjaks* of Nablus and Gaza. The pasha who governed Jerusalem had the title *mutasarrif;* the jurisdiction of the *qāḍī* of al-Quds was much larger, stretching from Gaza to Haifa. Consequently these two officials were paid the same salary.

Suleiman did not neglect the Ḥaram. The mosaic on the upper part of the exterior wall of the Dome of the Rock was restored and the lower part encased in marble. The Dome of the Chain was also given a beautiful faience covering, and Suleiman built a superb ablutions fountain in the forecourt of the Aqsā. The *waqf* for the Ḥaram was built up again, as also was that of some of the *madāris*. The sultan waived his claim to the entrance fee paid by pilgrims to finance a year-long reading of the Qurʾān in the Dome of the Rock. The restored and enlarged *waqf* provided jobs and charity, and the sultan's Russian-born wife Roxelana built the Takiyya Hospice in Jerusalem in 1551, a large complex comprising a mosque, a *ribāt,* a *madrasah,* an inn (*khān*), and a kitchen, which provided free meals to students, Sufis, and the poor. Endowed with a very large *waqf,* which included several villages and farms in the Ramallah area, the hospice became the most important charitable institution in Palestine.

The new stability brought by the Ottomans also improved the lot of the *dhimmis.* Most Jews still preferred to settle in Tiberias or Safed, but the Jewish community grew in Jerusalem under Suleiman. There was as yet no official Jewish Quarter. Jews tended to live in three residential districts in the south of the city: the Risha, Sharaf, and Maslakh neighborhoods, where they lived side by side with Muslims. Jewish visitors from Europe were struck by the freedom enjoyed by the Jews of Palestine. In

1535, David dei Rossi, an Italian Jew, noted that Jews even held government positions, something that would be inconceivable in Europe: "Here we are not in exile, as in our own country. Here . . . those appointed over the customs and tolls are Jews. There are no special Jewish taxes."[1] The Ottomans did not apply the strict letter of the *shariʿah* law regarding the fiscal arrangements for Jews. Not all Jews in Jerusalem had to pay the *jizyah* tax, and those that did generally paid at the lowest official rates. The law courts protected Jews and accepted their testimony; the autonomy of the Jewish community was both encouraged and protected by the Ottoman officials.[2]

Their improved status made the Jews extremely wary of a strange young Jew who arrived in Jerusalem in 1523 claiming to be the Messiah: they feared that his activities would be construed as rebellion by the Ottoman authorities and that this would endanger their position. David Reuveni said that he was a prince of a remote Jewish kingdom, the home of the ten lost tribes of Israel. Soon the tribes would return to Jerusalem, but first he had to perform an important task. During the reign of King Solomon, the rebel Jeroboam had put a stone from a pagan temple into the western wall of the Temple Mount. As long as it remained in place, redemption could not come. The Jerusalem Jews would have nothing to do with this highly dangerous and obviously unsound project: the wall in question had not been in existence in Solomon's day. After Reuveni left for Italy, a rabbi of Jerusalem warned the Italian Jews to have nothing whatever to do with him. But there were disturbing rumors of an imminent Jewish exodus from Gaza, Egypt, and Salonica. Jews there were said to be selling all their possessions and preparing to come to Jerusalem for Passover to greet the Messiah. "May God take pity on us!" the rabbi wrote in distress.[3] Not only would this huge influx disturb the authorities, but it would be impossible to house or feed these vast hordes.

In the event, the Jews failed to show up in Jerusalem when Passover came around. But David Reuveni attracted a considerable following in Italy, where he posed as the new King David. He told a fantastic story of his stay in Jerusalem: he had been greeted with honor by the Muslim establishment, he told his disciples, and been escorted onto the Ḥaram. There he had lived in the cave under the Rock for five weeks. This period of prayer and fasting on the site of the Devir had led to a remarkable event. On the first day of Shavuoth, the crescent on top of the Dome of the Rock had turned eastward and could not be righted. David had seen this as a sign that it was time for him to leave for Rome.

David's messianic movement petered out, but it was a symptom of the acute distress in the Jewish world after the expulsion from Spain. Under

Islam, the Jews had enjoyed a golden age in al-Andalus. The loss of Spanish Jewry was mourned throughout the world as the greatest catastrophe to have befallen Israel since the destruction of the Temple. The fifteenth century had also seen an escalation of anti-Semitic persecution in Europe, where Jews had been deported from one city after another. Exile had become the Jewish condition more acutely than ever, and many dreamed of a dramatic end to this painful separation from home and the past. The conquest of Jerusalem by the Ottomans, who had befriended the Jewish exiles, sent a tremor of excitement through the communities of the diaspora that would continue to ferment for over a century.

The mission of David Reuveni in Jerusalem had focused on the western supporting wall of the Ḥaram, which had been built originally by King Herod and was practically the last vestige of the lost Temple. During the Mamluk period, *madāris* had been built all along this wall, except for a stretch of about twenty-two meters between the Street of the Chain (Tariq al-Silsila) and the Maghribi Gate. Jews had never previously shown any particular interest in this portion of the wall. In Herod's day, the place had been part of a shopping center and had no religious significance. Hitherto, Jewish pilgrims had gathered in prayer on the Mount of Olives and at the gates of the Ḥaram. When they were excluded from the city during the Crusader period, they had sometimes prayed at the eastern wall of the Temple Mount.[4] But during the last years of the Mamluk regime, there had been a change. It may be that the increased Bedouin incursions at this time made it unsafe for Jews to congregate on the Mount of Olives outside the city. Instead, they seem to have turned to the vacant stretch of the western wall of the Ḥaram, clinging to it as their last link with the past.

During the construction of the city wall, possibly while Sinan was in residence and working on the Damascus Gate, Suleiman issued an official edict (*firman*) permitting the Jews to have a place of prayer at the Western Wall. Sinan is said to have designed the site, excavating downward to give the wall added height and building a wall parallel to it to separate the Jewish oratory from the Maghribi Quarter.[5] The enclave was very narrow, only about nine feet wide. But this had the advantage of making the wall beetle impressively over the worshippers. The enclave at the Western Wall soon became the center of Jewish religious life in Jerusalem. There were as yet no formal devotions, but Jews liked to spend the afternoon there, reading the psalms and kissing the stones. Suleiman, who had probably merely hoped to attract more Jews to Jerusalem, was hailed as the friend and patron of Israel. In Jewish legend, he was said to have helped to clear the site himself and to have washed

The small prayer-enclave at the Western Wall for which Suleiman gave permission; it is said to have been designed by Sinan, the chief architect at the Ottoman Court in Istanbul.

the wall with rose water to purify it, as ʿUmar and Saladin had done when they reconsecrated the Temple Mount.[6]

The Western Wall soon attracted many of the usual myths connected with a sacred place. It was naturally associated with the traditions in the Talmud about the western wall of the Devir, which, the rabbis had said, the Shekhinah had never abandoned and which God had promised to preserve forever.[7] Now these Talmudic sayings were applied to the western supporting wall of the Ḥaram. As the Presence was thought to linger there, Jews began to remove their shoes when they entered the enclosure. They liked to write petitions on slips of paper and insert them between the stones, so that they might remain continually before God. Because it was so close to the site of the Temple, it was said that the Gate of Heaven was situated directly above the Western Wall and that prayers ascended directly from the enclave to the divine Throne. As the Karaite Moses Yerushalmi wrote in 1658, "a great sanctity rests on the Western Wall, the original sanctity which attached to it then and forever."[8] When they stepped into the narrow enclosure and gazed up at the wall that towered powerfully and protectively over them, Jews felt that they had stepped into the presence of the sacred. The wall had become a symbol of the divine, but also a symbol of the Jewish people. For all its majesty, the wall was a ruin—an emblem of destruction and defeat. As Moses Yerushalmi continued, "one wall and one wall only is left from the Temple."[9] It evoked absence as well as presence. When they clung to the Western Wall and kissed its stones, Jews could feel that they were making contact with past generations and a departed glory. Like the Jews themselves, the wall was a survivor. But it also reminded them of the desecration of their Temple, which itself symbolized the accumulated tragedies of Israel. Weeping over the wall, Jews could cathartically mourn for everything they had lost, in the past and in the present. Like the Temple itself, the Western Wall would come to represent both God and the Jewish self.

Life was not idyllic for Jews in Ottoman Jerusalem. There was still tension with the officials of the al-'Umari mosque adjoining the Ramban Synagogue. Twice during the 1530s and 1540s the Muslims tried to get the synagogue closed, but the *qādī* decided in favor of the Jews. In 1556 there were so many Jewish worshippers in the synagogue that their Muslim neighbors made yet another attempt to have them evicted. They complained that Jews were disobeying the law by aping Muslim dress, covering their heads with their prayer shawls as with a *keffiyeh*. They also accused them of praying so loudly that they disturbed the Muslim worship next door. Eventually in 1587 the synagogue was closed permanently, though it was shut down in an orderly fashion.[10] The Jews were permitted to keep their scrolls and pray in their own houses. There were similar problems at the Tomb of the Prophet Samuel (Nebī Samwīl), nine miles north of Jerusalem, which was revered by both Jews and Muslims. The Jews kept a synagogue there and came frequently on pilgrimage. The local Muslims complained that the Jews took the place over and behaved offensively to Muslim pilgrims to the shrine. This time, however, the *qādī* ruled permanently in the Jews' favor and they kept their synagogue.

The tension revealed a deep-seated insecurity. The proximity of a rival cult at the same holy place can be extremely disturbing. Muslims felt threatened by the large numbers of Jews, whose worship penetrated their personal space. The convergence of two communities at the same site, each insisting that it had the monopoly of truth, raised difficult questions.

Which one of them was right? The complaint about the Jewish prayer shawls showed a desire to establish a clear and distinct Muslim identity and to separate Islam from this confusion. Many similar clashes have developed in the increasingly pluralistic world of the twentieth century, especially when there is also a political quarrel between the religious groups. The most famous case is the current Muslim–Hindu conflict at Ayodhya in the eastern Gangetic plain, which both communities claim as a holy place. Jews were beginning to feel vulnerable in Ottoman Jerusalem. By the end of Suleiman's reign, they were starting to leave the city. They were also abandoning the districts of Risha and Maslakh, where they lived alongside Muslims, and moving into the Sharaf district, which was closer to the Western Wall. A new Jewish enclave was being created. By the end of the sixteenth century, Sharaf was regarded as a distinct Jewish Quarter, quite separate from the surrounding Muslim neighborhoods.

There was also renewed tension between the Muslims and the Western Christians of Jerusalem. The Ottoman conquests had made a great difference to the relative status of the different Christian denominations. The Greek Orthodox, Syrian, and Armenian Christians were all Ottoman subjects, members of a recognized religious *taifa*. But the Franciscans were mere resident aliens. They were still living in their cramped quarters on Mount Sion, and the Cenacle Church, though not the Tomb of David, was in their hands. During the last years of the Mamluk empire, the Franciscans had also managed to move into the Holy Sepulcher Church, and now eight priests and three lay brothers lived in a dark, stuffy underground apartment, constantly suffering from headaches and fever. They had somehow succeeded in gaining control of the chief sites in the Holy Sepulcher Church before the arrival of the Ottomans. We have no record of this transaction, but the Fransciscans had learned the value of documents as a proof of title and had efficiently begun to collect official deeds and *firmans*.

Yet in 1523 their position deteriorated. Suleiman, who was still fighting his wars in Europe, purported to be horrified to hear that some "religious Franks" occupied a church directly above the Tomb of the Prophet David and were tramping over it in the course of their false worship.[11] He issued a *firman* closing the Cenacle Church and transforming it into a mosque. On the eastern wall of the Cenacle an inscription can still be seen stating that: "Suleiman the emperor, offspring of Uthman, ordered this place to be purified and purged of infidels and constructed it as a mosque in which the name of God is venerated." The Franciscans moved into a bakery on Mount Sion. In vain did Francis I, King of France, try to intervene with Suleiman on their behalf, but the sultan did assure him that all the other Christian holy places in Jerusalem were safe and secure.

The support of the great powers of Europe proved to be an important counterweight to the Franciscans' vulnerability in Jerusalem. In 1535, Suleiman made a treaty with Francis I against the European emperor Charles V. As a gesture of goodwill toward France, Suleiman, who represented the stronger power, concluded the Capitulations, which gave French merchants a privileged position in the empire by exempting them from Ottoman jurisdiction. Francis could appoint a French "bailiff" or "consul" to judge civil and criminal cases between merchants and other French subjects in Ottoman territory, without interference from the Muslim legal system. The Capitulations also confirmed the Franciscans as the chief custodians of the holy places in Jerusalem.[12] Very little came of these discussions. It was three hundred years before a Western consul was able to reside permanently in Jerusalem. Suleiman had offered the Capitulations in a spirit of condescension; the Ottoman empire was then at the peak of its power. Later his successors would make similar agreements with France and other Western countries. But Suleiman had miscalculated. When the Ottoman empire was in decline, this type of arrangement gave the West a chance to intervene with impunity in its internal affairs in a way that violated Turkish sovereignty.

Naturally the Franciscans' control of the holy places led to tension with the Greek Orthodox, who since the Crusades had never been able to look kindly upon the Latin church. Not only had the Crusaders usurped their tenure of the Holy Sepulcher, but in 1204 the armies of the Fourth Crusade had sacked Constantinople in one of the most disgraceful incidents in the whole Crusader enterprise; some historians believe that Byzantium never fully recovered from the Crusaders' attack. It is not surprising, then, that the Greeks saw the Latins as their enemies. Yet the Greeks had not yet learned how to manipulate the Ottoman authorities or to exploit the fact that their ecumenical patriarch lived in the Ottoman capital of Istanbul (as Constantinople was now called). In 1541, Patriarch Germanus of Jerusalem instituted the Hellenic Confederacy of the Holy Sepulcher as the official guardians of the holy places on behalf of Orthodox Christendom; at the same time, the Franciscans formed themselves into a national community to guard the holy places on behalf of Latin Christendom. Battle lines had been drawn and preliminary skirmishing began in the long, disedifying fight between Greek and Western Christians for the control of Christ's sepulcher. In 1551 the Franciscans won another victory. The Venetians persuaded Suleiman to let them have a small convent to the west of the Holy Sepulcher, which at the time housed only a few Georgian nuns. The Georgian Christians protested, but money changed hands and the nuns had to leave. In July 1559 the Franciscans moved in and renamed the convent St. Saviour's.

This became their chief headquarters in Jerusalem; they began to acquire some of the neighboring houses, and by 1600 St. Saviour's had become a thriving compound, with a carpenter's shop and a smithy. By 1665 there was also a boys' school, a hospice, a library, and an infirmary that offered the best medical care in the city.

After the death of Suleiman in 1566, his empire began to show signs of weakness. The feudal system gradually deteriorated. Once the wars of conquest came to an end, the *sipāhīs,* the feudal landlords, tried to compensate for the loss of spoils by exploiting the peasantry on their lands. This led to a sharp drop in agricultural production, which precipitated the empire into crisis. Other factors in the Ottoman decline were the loss of trade once the sea routes to India had opened, the depreciation of silver currency after the discovery of the New World, and the growing dissatisfaction of the Janissaries and the peasants in both Turkey and the provinces. Starting with the defeat of the Ottomans at the battle of Lepanto in 1571, the empire also lost its military supremacy. The growing crisis was reflected in the lesser caliber of Ottoman officials in Jerusalem. Pashas began to oppress Muslims and *dhimmis* alike: between 1572 and 1584, Jews, Christians, and Muslims all began to leave the city. There was a marked deterioration in public security, particularly on the roads leading to the city, which once more became the prey of the Bedouin. From the end of the sixteenth century, the Bedouin regularly attacked pilgrims traveling to Hebron and Nebī Mūsā and prevented preachers from delivering their sermons in the mosques. The government tried to find a solution: they took Bedouin hostages, appointed sheikhs as fiefholders, and tried to enlist their support by putting them in charge of pilgrim caravans. They even attempted to create rural settlements for the Bedouin in the countryside. Fortresses were built and garrisoned against them, and in 1630 Sultan Murad IV built large fortresses near Bethlehem and at the Sultan's Pool. But they were fighting a losing battle. Istanbul was now involved with wars in both Europe and Russia and lacked the manpower to enforce law and order in the provinces.

But the sultans did not neglect the Ḥaram. The Dome of the Rock was restored by Sultan Mehmet III in 1597, by Ahmad I in 1603, and by Mustafa I in 1617. They issued frequent *firmans* regarding the holy places. Pashas were to consider it one of their chief duties to keep order on the Ḥaram and to ensure that the shrines were always clean and in good repair. The *waqf* revenues were used for this maintenance, but the government was always ready to share the expense, when necessary.

Even though conditions had begun to deteriorate in Jerusalem during the seventeenth century, the city was still impressive. When the Turkish traveler Evliye Chelebi visited al-Quds in 1648, he was fascinated by the citadel and the Ḥaram and even admired the economy. He found eight hundred salaried imams and preachers employed on the Ḥaram and the surrounding *madāris,* fifty muezzins, and a host of Qur'ān reciters. Muslim pilgrims still processed around the Ḥaram, praying at its various "stations." Chelebi was particularly impressed by the small Dome of the Prophet and was told that its black stone had originally been ruby-red but had been affected by the waters of the Flood. He prayed at the Dome of the Chain, noting its exquisite Kashem tiles, which were the color of lapis lazuli. The Ḥaram was the center of an intense spirituality. The porticoes were crowded with dervishes from India, Persia, Kurdistan, and Asia Minor. All night long they recited the Qur'ān and held *dhikrs,* chanting the names of God as a mantra, in the flickering light of the oil lamps that were placed along the entire length of the colonnades. After the morning prayer another *dhikr* was held in the Mosque of the Maghribis on the south-western corner of the Ḥaram: Chelebi found it a noisy, bewildering affair.

He reported that the pasha of Jerusalem had five hundred soldiers at his command; one of their chief tasks was to escort the *hajj* caravan of the Damascus province to Mecca each year. The *qāḍī* and the pasha still both earned the same salary and got an extra fifty thousand piastres apiece from the pilgrim trade. At Easter alone there could be between five thousand and ten thousand Christian pilgrims in the city, who could not enter the Holy Sepulcher until they had each paid between ten and fifteen piastres as an entrance fee. Muslim pilgrims also had to pay for protection on the roads when they visited Nebī Mūsā or Hebron. Jerusalem, with its fine stone houses and imposing walls, seemed like a fortress town to Chelebi, yet, he said, it had 43,000 vineyards which all Jerusalemites enjoyed for about three months a year, and many flower gardens and vegetable plots. The surrounding mountains were covered in olive groves, the air of the city was fresh, and its waters sweet. Checking the official records of the *muhtasib* (the supervisor of the *sūq*), he noted that Jerusalem had 2,045 shops; it also had six inns, six bathhouses, and several fine markets. But above all it was a religious town. The Armenians had two churches, the Greeks three, and the Jews had two synagogues:

> Although the city appears to be small, it has 240 *mihrābs,* seven schools for the teaching of *hadīth,* ten for the teaching of Qur'ān, forty *madāris* and convents for seventy Sufi orders.[13]

For security reasons, the gates were locked every night, and there were no houses outside the walls except on Mount Sion, which Chelebi called "the suburb of David."[14]

Chelebi was obviously impressed, but after the vibrant developments under Suleiman, the city was beginning to slow down. Most of the

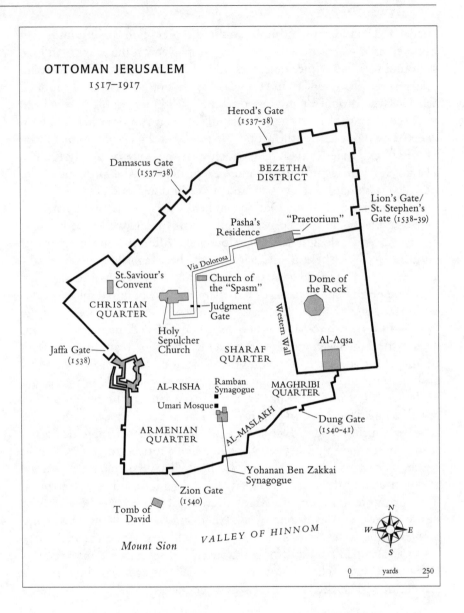

OTTOMAN JERUSALEM
1517–1917

Herod's Gate
(1537-38)

Damascus Gate
(1537-38)

BEZETHA
DISTRICT

Lion's Gate/
St. Stephen's
Gate (1538-39)

Pasha's
Residence

"Praetorium"

Via Dolorosa

St.Saviour's
Convent

Church of
the "Spasm"

Dome of
the Rock

CHRISTIAN
QUARTER

Judgment
Gate

Western Wall

Holy
Sepulcher
Church

Jaffa Gate
(1538)

SHARAF
QUARTER

Al-Aqsa

AL-RISHA

Ramban
Synagogue

MAGHRIBI
QUARTER

Umari Mosque

AL-MASLAKH

Dung Gate
(1540-41)

ARMENIAN
QUARTER

Yohanan Ben Zakkai
Synagogue

Zion Gate
(1540)

Tomb of
David

Mount Sion

VALLEY OF HINNOM

N
W   E
S

0   yards   250

building work was restorative rather than innovative, and because of the
imperial crisis, there was little direct contact with Istanbul. Local Arab
dignitaries were sometimes appointed governor of Jerusalem, a practice
which increased during the eighteenth century. The *qāḍī* usually came
from Istanbul, but the lesser religious posts were usually filled by members of the leading Jerusalem families. Four *muftīs* (*sharīʿah* consultants)
were appointed from the Abu 'l Lutf family and one from the Dajani.

The families also provided personnel for the main teaching posts, which became in effect hereditary. This inevitably led to a drop in standards. In 1670 the traveler al-Khiyari explained that he could not find a reputable scholar in the whole of al-Quds. Yet the *madāris* were still open: Chelebi noted that forty out of the fifty-six Mamluk *madāris* were active. But the strain was evident. The state still paid the salaries of the teachers and officials, but by the seventeenth century these sometimes outnumbered the students. The Aqsā Mosque was in bad repair and had to support the dervishes in residence in the porches. The *waqf* system was beginning to deteriorate: there were cases of neglect, dishonesty, and embezzlement.

The decline of the Ottoman empire was balanced by the rise of the European powers, which were now able to dictate terms to the sultans. This meant that the position of the Franciscans in Jerusalem continued to improve. Nearly every military or trade agreement between the Ottomans and Europe included a clause about the Holy Sepulcher. The kings of Europe could not yet influence the affairs of Jerusalem as much as they would have liked, however. In 1621, following a trade agreement with France and Sultan Mustafa I, M. Jean Lempereur was sent to Jerusalem as the first French consul, his brief to protect the rights of the Franciscans and the Western pilgrims. He did manage to lessen the excessive extortions from the pilgrims in fees, fines, and bribes, and by 1631 the pashas were seriously annoyed. They saw the consul as the thin end of the wedge: the port of Jaffa was only eight hours away. How many more of the Western "consuls" would follow Lempereur and interfere with their customs? The royal decree was canceled and the consul returned home. No other consul was permitted in Jerusalem, but in 1661 the French were able to insist that their consul in Sidon or Acre assume responsibility for the Latins in Jerusalem. They stipulated that he must be permitted to come to Jerusalem every Easter to protect the pilgrims and ensure that the ceremonies were carried out without hindrance.

The Greek Orthodox were beginning to organize their affairs more efficiently. The ecumenical patriarch in Istanbul was well placed to pull strings in the court and to offer bribes to the sultans and the *wazīrs*. In 1634, in an audience with Sultan Murad IV, Patriarch Theophanes of Jerusalem produced the letter which Caliph ʿUmar had given Patriarch Sophronius in 638, granting the Greeks control of the holy places. At once the French ambassador in Istanbul declared that the letter was a forgery, whereupon Theophanes produced more recent Ottoman documents, purporting to be from Selim I and Suleiman, supporting the Greek cause. Sultan Murad issued a *firman* in favor of the Greeks, giving them the Nativity Church in Bethlehem and most of the key sites in the Holy Sepulcher Church. Under pressure from the pope, France, and

Venice, however, the sultan annulled this *firman* following a payment of 26,000 piastres, and the Franciscans were back in power. Not for long, however. The Ottomans had now discovered a valuable source of income: the holy places would henceforth go to the highest bidder, and in 1637 the Greeks were back in control with a new *firman* putting them in the superior position in the Holy Sepulcher.

It was an unseemly struggle for supremacy at a place where, according to Christian belief, the God-man had voluntarily divested himself of power and accepted death. The Franciscans were particularly devoted to Christ's Passion but seemed unable to apply its lessons to their own lives. They continued a vicious campaign against Islam: during the sixteenth century, two more Franciscans had been executed after rushing onto the Ḥaram waving the cross and cursing the Prophet Muḥammad. This aggressive quest for martyrdom was their way of following in Christ's footsteps unto death, even though it was inspired by hatred rather than love. Their other method of identifying with Christ's death was by the new devotion of the Stations of the Cross, which was now part of the Jerusalem scene. By the beginning of the seventeenth century, the Franciscans would lead the pilgrims in a procession down the Via Dolorosa every Friday evening, barefoot; they would pause to say an Ave and a Paternoster at eight "stations" along the route, beginning at the "House of Pilate" at the "Ecce Homo Arch." They would then proceed down the street, stopping at the places where Christ fell under the weight of the cross, met his mother, was helped by Simon of Cyrene, and prophesied the destruction of Jerusalem to the women of the city. Then they visited the "Prison of Christ" in the Holy Sepulcher Church before going to Golgotha itself. Other pilgrims had their own variations of the stations, and some of them reproduced Christ's last journey in their churches back home. Eventually fourteen stations were customarily commemorated in Europe in pictures illustrating the various incidents around the church walls. In the nineteenth century, the six extra stations were added at appropriate points to the stations in the Via Dolorosa in Jerusalem. This was a peculiarly Western devotion. The Greek Orthodox had always emphasized the Resurrection more than the Passion of Christ, but the stations were an attempt to help people get beyond their personal sufferings by identifying themselves with the divine pathos.

Jews were creating similar rituals, based symbolically on Jerusalem. After their expulsion from Spain, many of the Jewish refugees had eventually settled in Safed, and there, under the influence of the Kabbalist Isaac Luria, they developed a new type of mysticism that focused on the experience of exile. The myths of Lurianic Kabbalah suggested that at the very beginning God had, as it were, gone into exile from a part of himself to make room for the created world. There had also been a primal catastrophe, during which the Shekhinah, the bride of God, had been separated from the Godhead; divine sparks were now scattered abroad and imprisoned in base matter. There was thus a displacement at the heart of Being itself. Nothing could be in its right place, and the exile of the Jews symbolized the cosmic homelessness suffered alike by God and humanity. But Jews could end the exile of the Shekhinah by the careful observance of Torah and mystical prayer. These poetic myths—a re-creation of ancient pagan mythology—spoke directly to many of the Jewish people, who had experienced their state of exile anew in these dark years. Cut loose from their roots, Jews experienced the world as a demonic realm and their life as a struggle with evil powers. Luria's imagery helped them to transcend their own misery by imagining a final return to the primal unity that had characterized existence before the beginning of time.

From the middle of the sixteenth century, the Kabbalists of Safed and Jerusalem celebrated the redemption of the Shekhinah in a ritual that—in the time-honored way—was thought to have repercussions in the divine sphere. Every Friday afternoon, they would dress in white and process to the fields outside the city to greet the Shekhinah, the divine bride of God. They would then escort the Presence back to their own homes. In each house, the dining room was decked with myrtle, like a wedding canopy, and loaves, wine, and a candlestick were set out in a way that recalled the Temple. Thus the Shekhinah symbolically reentered the Devir and was also reunited with the Godhead in the Heavenly Sanctuary. Isaac Luria composed a hymn that was always sung after the Sabbath meal:

> To southward I set
> the mystical candelabrum,
> I make room in the north
> for the table with the loaves. . . .
>
> Let the Shekhinah be surrounded
> by six Sabbath loaves
> connected on every side
> with the Heavenly Sanctuary.
>
> Weakened and cast out
> the impure powers,
> the menacing demons
> are now in fetters.[15]

Each home had become a replica of the Temple; each was therefore symbolically linked to the heavenly Jerusalem, the celestial home of God. The ritualized return of the Shekhinah meant that for one night each week, everything was back in its proper place and the demonic powers were under control. The Sabbath therefore became a temporal sanctuary, an image of life as it was meant to be. The Friday-night ritual also looked forward to that final Return to the Source of being—a union suggested by the sexual imagery of Lurianic Kabbalah.

At Safed the old mourning rituals for the Temple acquired a fresh urgency. Abraham Halevi Berukhim, one of Luria's disciples, had once had a vision of the Shekhinah, weeping and dressed in black, imprinted on the Western Wall. Every night he used to rise at midnight and run, sobbing, through the streets of Safed, crying: "Arise in God's name, for the Shekhinah is in exile, the house of our sanctuary is burned, and Israel is in great distress."[16] Others performed a more elaborate midnight ritual. The mystic would rise and dress to perform the "Rite of Rachel," in which he would imaginatively enter into the exile of the Shekhinah. Weeping, like the Shekhinah herself, he would remove his shoes and rub his face in the dust. It was an act of *imitatio Dei* which brought about his participation in this cosmic dislocation. But Luria never left his disciples in misery; he constantly emphasized the importance of joy and celebration. At sunrise, the mystic would perform the "Rite of Leah": he would recite a description of the Shekhinah's final redemption, meditating the while upon her final union with the Godhead until he felt that each organ of his body had formed part of the Chariot-Throne. Each night, therefore, the Kabbalist passed from despair to a joyful reunion with the Source of being. He became himself the human shrine of the divine Presence, an incarnate Jerusalem and a bodily Temple.[17]

Lurianic Kabbalah was a spiritualized version of the old mythology. There was no need to make the physical *aliyah* to Jerusalem. Jews could encounter the reality that gave the city its value in their own homes and in the depths of their own being. Luria was not a Zionist, as Nachmanides had been. His ideas spread like wildfire in Europe, where its vision of divine exile spoke to the suffering and displaced Jews. Like the sacred geography of the ancient world, this type of mysticism was an essentially imaginative exercise. It depended upon the ability to see that the symbols introduced you to the reality that existed ineffably beyond them. They were suffused with the unseen mystery that they imperfectly represented in terms that human beings could apprehend, so that the two became one in the experience of the worshippers. If the myths of Kabbalah, for example, were understood literally, they either were patently absurd or could even lead to catastrophe. This became evident in the affair of Shabbetai Zevi, a disturbed Jew who demonstrated symptoms that we would classify today as manic-depressive.[18] In his "manic" phases, he would break the food laws, utter the forbidden Name of God, and declare that the Torah had been abrogated. These would be succeeded by periods of black despair. In his wanderings, Shabbetai met the young Kabbalist rabbi Nathan of Gaza, who was entranced by him and declared him to be the Messiah. When Shabbetai sank into depression, he had entered the demonic realm to fight the powers of evil; he would raise the Shekhinah from the dust and end the divine exile. His "manic" phases presaged the messianic period after the Redemption, when there would be no need for Torah and nothing would be forbidden.

On 31 May 1665, Shabbetai proclaimed himself the Messiah and announced that he was about to go up to Jerusalem. He chose twelve young rabbis as his disciples, one for each of the tribes of Israel. His plan was to go to the Temple Mount and resume the sacrificial rites: Nathan was appointed high priest. When the news reached the Jews of Jerusalem, there was panic and consternation. Their position was already vulnerable, and if Shabbetai violated the sanctity of the Ḥaram, Muslim vengeance might be terrible indeed. They begged Shabbetai to give up his plan. He was desolate: Redemption had been so near, and now it had been delayed yet again! He did go to Jerusalem, however, where he announced that the Torah had been revoked and declared that he was the King of Israel. The rabbis handed him over to the *qāḍī*, who acquitted him of treason, doubtless seeing that the man was not in his right mind. But Shabbetai saw this as proof of his mission and rode around the city streets on horseback, clad in a green cloak: it was another act of defiance, since *dhimmis* were forbidden to ride horses and green was the color of the Prophet.

Shabbetai left Jerusalem, but frantic enthusiasm for this strange mystical Messiah spread through the Jewish communities of the Ottoman empire, as well as Italy, Holland, Germany, Poland, and Lithuania. But all ended in tears. In January 1666, Shabbetai arrived in Istanbul to ask the sultan to crown him King of the Jews and restore to him the city of Jerusalem. Instead, the sultan, faced with the frightening prospect of a Jewish revolt, gave him the choice of conversion to Islam or death. Shabbetai opted for conversion and lived as an apparently devout Muslim until his death, ten years later. He retained a surprising number of followers, but most Jews, horrified by the scandal of an apostate Messiah, were disillusioned not only with Shabbetai but with the Lurianic mysticism that had been the driving force of his appeal. Yet Lurianic mythology was chiefly concerned with the interior landscape of the soul. It was not meant to be lived out literally in the political world. Luria had not urged Jews to work for a physical return to Zion. Instead he had charted a spiritual path for them, leading from disintegration and displacement to the Source of being. The mythology made no sense if translated into the realm of mundane reality.

Increasingly the people of Europe were discovering for themselves that the old myths of sacred geography no longer appealed to them. They had started a scientific revolution that would eventually transform the world. Seeds of a new rationalism had been planted, which would encourage Catholics and Protestants alike to examine the physical properties of phenomena in and for themselves, instead of seeing them as symbols of the unseen. They must ruthlessly exclude such unproven and unprovable associations and concentrate on the objects themselves and find out what they were literally made of. It was a whole new way of seeing. Their discoveries were leading people to map the world scientifically, and from this perspective it was clearly nonsense to say that Jerusalem was the center of the world. As their outlook changed, Europeans would begin to look for a more rational religion that eschewed myths, fictions, and mystery and concentrated on the so-called facts of the faith that could be demonstrated logically. They had no time for a religion of the imagination. Gradually the traditional symbols and images of the faith ceased to be impregnated with numinous significance, as people examined them critically in the cold light of reason. They became *only* symbols, essentially separate from the unseen reality they represented. Ritual became *mere* ceremony; liturgical gestures were no longer inseparable from the spiritual dynamic they bodied forth. The Protestant reformers had already divorced the symbol from the divine reality. Zwingli saw the bread of the Eucharist as a mere symbol, quite distinct from the body of Christ. The elaborate ceremonies of Catholic liturgy were a meaningless distraction from the truth, not an *imitatio dei* that brought the timeless mystery into the present. The life, death, and resurrection of Jesus were events that had happened in the past, not an eternal dimension of reality.

Naturally this made the old sacred geography meaningless. "Holy places" could not provide a link with the heavenly world. God could not be contained in a mere place, because he was infinite, so a particular location was only "sacred" if it had been set aside for religious purposes. The Puritan John Milton expressed his scorn for pilgrims

> . . . *that strayed so farr to seek*
> *In Golgotha him dead, who lives in Heav'n.*[19]

But Catholics were equally involved in the scientific revolution of Europe, and they would increasingly find that a shrine had a different meaning for them.

Felix Fabri had already revealed the incipient skepticism of the new Europe. By the seventeenth century, Europeans had started to arrive in Jerusalem who were tourists rather than pilgrims. In 1601 the British traveler John Sanderson had not wept or gone into a trance when he saw the Holy Sepulcher. He merely strolled around the church, regarding the fervor of Catholics and Orthodox with detached amusement.[20] When Henry Maundrell, the chaplain of the English Levant Company in Aleppo, visited Palestine in 1697, he was even more scornful of the "rubbish" of "vain apparitions" that had made his ancestors quake. He was as interested in the Greek and Roman antiquities as in the biblical sites. When he attended the ceremony of the Holy Fire, he was horrified by the crowds' ecstasy, which seemed to him pure "madness," "Bedlam itself."[21]

He was especially disgusted by the antagonism of Greeks and Latins at the Tomb of Christ; they demonstrated all the murderous rage and fanaticism that the advocates of cool reason were seeking to transcend. There had recently been yet another change of arrangements in the Holy Sepulcher, following the victory of Austria, Poland, and Venice over the Ottomans at the battle of Belgrade in 1688. The Franciscans were now back in charge. Maundrell explained that they and their Greek Orthodox rivals

> have sometimes proceeded to blows and words, even at the very door of the Sepulchre, mingling their own blood with their sacrifices. As evidence of which fury, the [Franciscan] Father Guardian showed us a great scar upon his arm, which he told us was the mark given him by a sturdy Greek priest in one of these unholy wars.[22]

It was pointless to dream of a new Crusade to liberate these "holy places," since "if they should be recovered, what deplorable contests might be expected to follow about them, seeing even in their present state of captivity they are made the occasion of such unchristian rage and animosity."[23]

By the eighteenth century, the Ottoman empire seemed to have broken down irretrievably. The sultans were weak and devoted themselves to private pleasures, which they financed by the sale of public offices. Governors of the provinces and *sanjaks* were no longer chosen for their ability but because they had bribed their way into power. When the sultans discovered that they had lost control of the pashas, they began to replace them on an almost annual basis. This had serious consequences for the provinces. It was simply not worth repairing buildings or reforming the local administration if you were likely to be replaced the following year. Since a pasha's property was sometimes confiscated at the end of his period of office, governors often tried to make as much money from their district as they could, bleeding it dry with unfair taxation, exploitation, illegal confiscation of land, and other desperate measures. Istanbul had in effect abandoned its empire to unscrupulous officials. Peasants began to leave their villages to escape from rapacious pashas, which added to the dereliction of a land already damaged by the Bedouin raids. In 1660 the French traveler L. d'Arrieux noted that the countryside around Bethlehem was almost completely deserted, the peasants having fled the pashas of Jerusalem.

In 1703 the people of Jerusalem revolted against the cruel taxation of Jurji Muḥammad Pasha, governor of the city. Muḥammad ibn Mustafa al-Husaini led them in an attack upon the citadel. They released all the prisoners and put the pasha to flight. Al-Husaini became governor in his stead, and it was two years before the Turks were able to regain control of the city. Eventually, in November 1705, Jurji Muḥammad, now provincial governor (*wālī*) of Damascus, attacked Jerusalem with two thousand Janissaries. The city was not occupied by the Turks easily: there were hours of fierce and desperate fighting.

The Turkish governors were increasingly powerless. They could not even collect taxes from the recalcitrant population. Each year the *wālī* of Damascus had to come with soldiers to force the people to pay up. Even then they were not always successful. There is virtually no mention of the city's revenues in the Ottoman documents of the eighteenth century, possibly because the returns were so negligible they were not worth recording.[24] The pasha could not move freely about his own *sanjak* without bribing the Bedouin. As a result, Istanbul resorted to the expedient of appointing local Arabs as governors. The Turqan and Nimr families of Nablus both produced governors of Jerusalem. 'Umar al-Nimr (1717–31) was particularly effective and was appointed for a second term in 1733: he cooperated with the notables of Jerusalem, kept the pilgrim roads free of the Bedouin, and even kept the feuds of the Christians within reasonable bounds. But most governors remained impotent. They found it extremely difficult to keep order even within the walls, and Jerusalemites would sometimes refuse to admit a governor to the city who was not to their taste.

As a result of the governors' weaknesses, the main families of Jerusalem rose to fill the power vacuum. The Husainis, the Khālidīs, and the Abu 'l Luṭfs took an increasingly large share of the administration of the city. They were often the sole link between the local population and the ruling power, having made a point of keeping on good terms with influential people in Damascus and Istanbul since the 1703 revolution. They were rewarded with large landholdings and important offices. During the eighteenth century, the Abu 'l Luṭf family continued to provide *muftīs,* while the Husainis held the presidency of the Sharī'ah Court. For several generations, Khālidīs became deputy judges and chief clerks of the Shari'ah Court. Mūsā al-Khālidī (1767–1832), an eminent authority on Islamic jurisprudence, was highly respected in Istanbul and became the chief *qāḍī* of Anatolia, one of the three highest judicial posts in the empire.

Jerusalem still attracted Sufis and scholars from Syria and Egypt. There were actually more *'ulamā'* in the city than there had been in the seventeenth century. Some of the *'ulamā'* developed important private libraries in the city. But the *madāris* were declining fast. By the mid-eighteenth century, there were only thirty-five of them left, and later they would almost all have ceased to exist. The deepening economic plight and impoverishment of the city and its citizens meant that many of the *awqāf* became extinct, and others were dissolved and the assets alienated. Muslims would try to recoup their losses by leasing the *waqf* properties and, later, even selling them to non-Muslims.

The *dhimmis* were as badly off as the Muslims. In the early eighteenth century, the community of Ashkenazic Jews from Europe had grown so rapidly that they bribed the pasha and thus gained permission to build a new synagogue, a yeshiva, and forty dwellings for the poor in the south of Jerusalem. But almost immediately they fell into debt and were charged an exorbitant rate of interest. The Ashkenazim had enough difficulties getting along in Jerusalem anyway, because they did not speak Arabic and had not yet learned their way around the system. Now they scarcely dared to leave their homes lest their creditors seize them and throw them into prison. In 1720 they fell so badly behind in their payments that the Turks confiscated their property and the Ashkenazim were forced to leave the city: two hundred families left for Hebron, Safed, and Damascus, even though conditions were little better in these cities.[25] It would be another century before the Ashkenazim felt able to establish themselves in Jerusalem again. The Jewish *taifa* in Jerusalem was now entirely Sephardic. They lived in the Sharaf neighborhood, which deteriorated considerably as the century wore on and as the Ottoman crisis deepened. The Sephardim worshipped at four interconnected synagogues that were supposedly built on the site of the yeshiva of Rabbi Yohanan ben Zakkai: adjoining the Ben Zakkai Synagogue were the three smaller synagogues of the Prophet Elijah, the Kehal Zion, and the Istanbuli. By the end of the eighteenth century these were in a deplorable state. The whole Jewish Quarter was full of neglected houses, and its streets were filled with decaying rubbish. Disease was rife and mortality high. The synagogues were scarcely standing. The buildings were tumbling down, rain poured in through the roof, and services had to be rushed before the synagogues flooded. It was not uncommon for the congregation to leave in tears.

The Latin Christians were in a better position, because they were supported by rich communities abroad. In 1720, the year the Ashkenazim lost their property, the Franciscans were able to refurbish the mosaics in the Holy Sepulcher Church and enlarge their underground convent there. But, like the Greeks, Copts, and Armenians, who also had apartments in the church, they had become virtual prisoners. The Turkish authorities kept the keys, and the Christians dared not leave the building lest they lose their right of possession. Food was passed in to them through a large hole in the front door. Each sect controlled different parts of the church, and in 1720 the Franciscans still had the choicest sites. In 1732 the French were able to put pressure on the sultan and new Capitulations were granted them in perpetuity. The French were now recognized as the official "protectors" of the Roman Catholics in the Ottoman Empire and the Franciscans' custodianship of the Holy Sepulcher was reconfirmed. In 1757 the Franciscans were also given the Tomb of the Virgin in the Kidron Valley.

The Greek Orthodox had watched all this with ever-increasing fury. Finally they could bear it no more. On the day before Palm Sunday 1757, they stormed into the Rotunda, smashing the Latin vessels and lamps. Blood was shed and several people were seriously injured. The Franciscans took refuge in St. Saviour's, which was besieged by the Greek and Arab members of the Orthodox Church, and the patriarch hurried to the imperial court in Istanbul. Since the French were too busy fighting the Seven Years War in Europe to help the Turks in their war against Russia, the sultan felt free to issue a *firman* in favor of the Greeks. This extremely important document remains in force to the present day, and the Greeks are still the chief custodians of the Holy Sepulcher. In 1774 their hand was further strengthened when Russia was named the official "protector" of Orthodox Christians in the Ottoman empire.

By the end of the eighteenth century, Jerusalem had become an impoverished city. The French traveler Constantin Volney could scarcely believe his eyes when he visited Palestine in 1784 and, two days after leaving Nablus, arrived

> at a town, which . . . presents a striking example of the vicissitudes of human affairs: when we behold its walls levelled, its ditches filled up, and all its buildings embarrassed with ruins, we scarcely can believe we view that celebrated metropolis, which, formerly, withstood the efforts of the most powerful empires . . . in a word, we with difficulty recognize Jerusalem.[26]

Volney was one of the new men of Europe. He came not as a pilgrim but to conduct the first scientific survey of Jerusalem, with a prepared questionnaire. His object was to study the geography, climate, social life, and economy of the city. Its holiness was of interest only insofar as it affected the economy. Volney noted that the Turks had made a huge profit from the stupidity of the Christians. Greeks, Copts, Abyssinians, Armenians, and Franks continually played into the governor's hands by paying large sums in bribes "to obtain some privilege for themselves or to take it from their rivals":

> Each sect is perpetually informing against the other for irregularities. Has a church been clandestinely repaired; or a procession extended beyond the usual limits; has a Pilgrim entered by a different gate from that customary? All these are the subject of accusations to the Government, which never fails to profit from them in fines and extortions.[27]

The barren struggle for possession that now engaged the Christians of Jerusalem was actually eroding their position and standing in the Holy City.

Volney noted that very few pilgrims came to Jerusalem from Europe—a fact that scandalized the other communities in the city. Many travelers would have been deterred by his gloomy account of Jerusalem, which had indeed fallen upon hard times. But the picture was not as bleak as he implied. The walls, for example, had not been leveled as he claimed, though he was right about the blocked valleys surrounding them. There was an inordinate amount of rubbish lying in and around the city. Stones, earth, ashes, shards of pottery, and decayed wood clogged the deep valleys beneath the city, sometimes to a depth of forty feet. Indeed, much of the city had actually been built on the debris that had accumulated over the centuries. To the north of the walled city were several artificial mounds composed of waste from the soap factories.[28] Jerusalem was known to be unhealthy: there was no sanitation, a poor water supply, and a great deal of poverty. But that was not the whole story. There were still about nine soap factories that were fully functioning; ceramics was also becoming an important industry, and the *sūqs* were usually well stocked. Evliye Chelebi had been struck by the number of vineyards and gardens in and around the city, and these were still a feature of Jerusalem, particularly in the Bezetha district in the northeast of the city, which was sparsely settled. The *waqfiyya* of Sheikh Muḥammad al-Khalīlī shows that there were many vineyards and orchards of figs, olives, apples, pomegranates, mulberries, apricots, and almonds inside and outside the walls. Some parts of the town were undoubtedly run-down, but there were also beautiful villas and mansions belonging to the chief families of Jerusalem. The sheikh himself built two large houses outside the city walls and stressed the importance of keeping buildings in good repair and not allowing them to fall into the hands of non-Muslims, who were still eyeing Jerusalem covetously.[29] The more prescient inhabitants were uneasy about these new French and Russian "protectorates"; when the French again attempted to install a consul in Jerusalem, the local Muslims had made sure that he was ejected. But Constantin Volney and his scientific survey had simply been the precursor of a much more formidable Western presence.

In 1798, Napoleon sailed to Egypt with scores of Orientalist scholars, who were charged with the task of making a scientific study of the region as a prelude to colonization. Napoleon's aim was to establish a French presence in the east to challenge the British acquisition of India, and he was prepared to use the new science of "orientalism" to further his political ambitions. In January 1799, Napoleon also dispatched 13,000 French troops to Palestine; they defeated the Ottoman army at al-Arish and Gaza and then began to advance up the coast to Acre, the leading city of Palestine. He had brought map-makers and explorers with his army and they branched out into the hill country on a fact-finding mission, while the soldiers proceeded up the coastal road. In Ramleh, Napoleon called upon Jews, Christians, and Muslims to shake off the Ottoman yoke and accept the *liberté* of revolutionary France. Yet the local inhabitants were not impressed by this promise of freedom, recognizing that it would simply mean subjugation to this western power. There was panic and fury in Jerusalem. The Muslims attacked St. Saviour's and took some of the Franciscans—the clients of the French—as hostages; but the sultan insisted that their churches and property were to be protected as long as they paid the *jizyah*. Sheikh Mūsā al-Khālidī, the Jerusalem-born *qādī* of Anatolia, called upon the people of Palestine to defend their country against the French, and all the able-bodied Arabs of Jerusalem were drafted into the Ottoman army by the *wālī* of Damascus.

Napoleon's army was hit by plague, but he pressed on to Acre, where he was repelled not only by the British fleet but also by the army of Ahmad Jezzar Pasha, the *wālī* of Sidon, which displayed exemplary courage and effectiveness. Napoleon's bid for an eastern empire had failed and he was forced to return to Europe. But his expedition had introduced Western modernity and science to Palestine, which from the start were linked to European dreams of conquest and imperialism. Other colonialists would shortly follow and drag Jerusalem into the modern age.

16

REVIVAL

THE NINETEENTH CENTURY began badly in Jerusalem. There
was poverty and tension in the city. The Ottoman system was still
in disarray, and the people suffered from bad government. Nominally
part of the province of Damascus, the city was actually ruled by the *walī*
of Sidon during the early years of the new century. There were more
Arab governors; one of these, Muḥammad Abu Muraq, was notorious
for his tyranny to Muslims and *dhimmis* alike. There was also friction
between the different communities. In 1800, Jerusalem had about 8,750
inhabitants: 4,000 Muslims, 2,750 Christians, and 2,000 Jews. They all
shared a common *sūq* and lived clustered around their principal shrines.
Some intercommunal relationships were friendly. The Muslims in the
Maghribi Quarter, for example, had a healthy rapport with the Jews,
who had to walk through their district to get to the Western Wall. But
Jews were forbidden to enter the Holy Sepulcher, and relations were so
bad with the Christians that they kept away from their neighborhoods.
The different Christian denominations coexisted in a state of poisonous
animosity that could flare into physical violence at the smallest provocation. In the Jewish Quarter, relations between the Sephardim and the
Ashkenazim, who had returned to Jerusalem between 1810 and 1820,
were strained. The city of peace was seething with frustration and
resentment, and the old ideal of integration seemed a vanished dream.
This anger frequently erupted in riots and uprisings.

In 1808 a fire broke out in the Holy Sepulcher Church. It began in
the Crypt of St. Helena, which was under Armenian aegis, and spread
rapidly. The whole church was gutted, and the pillars supporting the
dome collapsed. Recriminations began immediately as the different

communities blamed one another for the catastrophe. The Armenians were accused of starting the fire deliberately to change the status quo in the church; others said that the Greek Orthodox priests had accidentally set fire to some wood while drunk and had then tried to douse the flames with brandy. Since rebuilding was a mark of legal ownership, there was intense competition to take charge of the restoration, each denomination trying to outbid the others and appealing to their foreign "protectors" for support. Eventually the Greeks succeeded in buying the privilege, and the repairs began in 1819. But building had never been a neutral activity in Jerusalem, and the Muslims had long been uneasy about the Holy Sepulcher Church, particularly in times of economic hardship. Muslims now laid siege to the governor's residence demanding that the work stop; they were joined by the local Janissaries, who were angry that other troops were garrisoned in the citadel. Soon full-scale rebellion had broken out all over the city. The rebels attacked the Greek Orthodox patriarchate and occupied the Citadel, expelling the governor from the city. The uprising was not quelled until the *walī* of Damascus sent a detachment of troops to besiege the Citadel. Forty-six of the ringleaders were decapitated, and their heads sent to Damascus.

The rebuilding of the Holy Sepulcher continued, but the reconstruction itself turned out to be an act of war. The Greeks seized the opportunity of erasing all traces of Latin occupation from the building. They replaced the edicule built by the Franciscans over the tomb during the eighteenth century and threw out the graves of Godfrey of Bouillon and King Baldwin I. Henceforth a Greek monk stood on permanent guard over the sepulcher. They now controlled the tomb and Golgotha; the Franciscans were confined to the north of the building, the Armenians to the Crypt of St. Helena, the Copts to a small chapel west of the tomb, and the Syrians to a chapel on the Rotunda. The Ethiopians would be forced to build their monastery and church on the roof. Christians found it impossible to live together amicably at their holiest shrine: a Muslim family was given possession of the key to the church, and to this day has the privilege of locking and unlocking the church at the direction of the various authorities. This cumbersome arrangement was necessary because no one sect could be trusted to let the others in. The different denominations would take the key in turns to hold services at the tomb, but this frequently led to brawling and incivility. One shocked British visitor described the scene:

> The Copts, say, are standing before the shrine: long before they have finished their service of sixty minutes, the Armenians have gathered in numbers around the choir, not to join in the prayers and genuflections but to hum profane airs, to hiss the Coptic priests, to jabber and jest and snarl at the morning prayer.

Often the worshippers came to blows, and then the Turkish guards, posted permanently outside the church to meet this contingency, thundered in to stop the fighting—"an affair of candles, crooks, and crucifixes."[1] If no blood had been shed, the service would continue, but the soldiers stood on guard, guns at the ready. If charity and loving-kindness were indeed the hallmarks of the faith, Christianity had clearly failed in Jerusalem.

There were further Muslim demonstrations against the Christians in 1821, when the Greeks of the Peloponnese rebelled against the Ottomans. Again the Greek Orthodox patriarchate was attacked, though the *qāḍī* and the leading Jerusalem families, under strict orders from Istanbul, did their best to stop the violence. In 1824 there was a more serious disturbance. Mustafa Pasha, the new *wālī* of Damascus, raised the taxes to ten times their former rate. The peasants in the villages around Jerusalem immediately revolted, and the pasha set out from Damascus to quell the uprising with five thousand soldiers. This time the Jerusalem notables did not support the Ottoman establishment but banded together with the peasants and townsfolk. As soon as the pasha had returned to Damascus, having, as he thought, quashed the revolt, the people of Jerusalem invaded the citadel, drove out the Ottoman garrison, helped themselves to weapons, and threw all the non-Arab citizens out of the city. It was, perhaps, an early expression of Arab solidarity in Jerusalem. The Arabs refused to surrender, even when Abdallah Pasha, governor of Sidon, arrived with two thousand men and seven cannons. The fighting continued for a week, and the city was under continuous bombardment from the Mount of Olives. Eventually the Turks agreed to the rebels' demands: the taxes were reduced, the army undertook not to interfere with the life of the city, and in future all officials in Jerusalem would be Arabs.

But in 1831, Jerusalem came under stronger Turkish rule. Muḥammad ʿAli, an Albanian Turk and Ottoman commander, had fought Napoleon in Egypt. After the departure of the French, he was able to make himself virtually independent of Istanbul; his ambition was to make Egypt a modern state, run on Western lines. There would be a strong central government, and all citizens would be equal before the law, whatever their race or religion. The army was modernized, and by November 1831 it was strong enough to invade Palestine and Syria and wrest these provinces from the Ottomans. It was a turning point in the history of Jerusalem. Muḥammad ʿAli controlled Syria and Palestine until 1840. During those nine years, he applied his modernizing ideas and permanently changed the Jerusalem way of life. His son Ibrāhīm Pasha was able to curb the Bedouin and threatened to draft them into the Egyptian army. He also established a secularized judicial system which effectively undercut the power of the Sharīʿah Court. Henceforth the *dhimmis* would enjoy full equality and personal security of life and property; Jews and Christians were also represented on the Jerusalem *majlis,* a consultative body appointed to advise the governor of the city. Secularism had arrived in Jerusalem, the state and judiciary operating independently of religion.

Naturally there was opposition to these reforms. The main Jerusalem families and the local dignitaries feared the loss of the independence and privilege they had acquired over the years. In 1834 the whole of Palestine and part of the Transjordan rose up in rebellion. Insurgents took control of Jerusalem for five days, the rebels rushing through the streets and smashing and looting the shops of the *dhimmis.* Ibrāhīm Pasha needed the force of his entire army to crush this uprising. When peace was finally restored, the Egyptian government continued to implement the reforms. Ibrāhīm Pasha built the first two windmills in Jerusalem in the hope of introducing modern industrial methods into the city. The *dhimmis* began to enjoy their new freedom: they were now allowed to build and restore their places of worship without needing to resort to bribery and graft.

They immediately took advantage of this privilege. In 1834, many of the Christian monasteries had been damaged in an earth tremor, and the monks were now able to repair them at once. The Franciscans also restored St. Saviour's, which had taken a lot of battering during the recent uprisings. Over the years it had become a large complex. The Franciscans now gave bread to about eight hundred Christians and Muslims each week, and they were the first to offer an education to Arab Christians. Fifty-two boys whose families had converted to Catholicism were taught to read and write in Arabic, Italian, and Latin, though there were as yet no lessons in arithmetic or natural science. There was also a sewing school for Arab girls. In 1839 the Franciscans were able to extend themselves in the city, building a new convent in the Muslim quarter of Bezetha, which was still largely uninhabited. Their Church of the Flagellation was one of the first Christian buildings to be built beside the Via Dolorosa, which gradually became a new Christian street during the nineteenth century.

Jews also took the chance to build. In 1834, Muḥammad ʿAli issued a *firman* giving the Sephardim permission to rebuild the dilapidated Ben Zakkai Synagogue. The Ashkenazic community had increased dramatically in recent years with the influx of new immigrants from Poland, and it also needed a new place of worship. In 1836 the Ashkenazim got permission to build a new synagogue, yeshiva, and *mikveh* on the site which they had been forced to vacate in 1720. The whole community turned out to work on the new building; rabbis, students, and even old people helped to dig the foundations and clear away the piles of refuse. The first wing of the new Hurva Synagogue was consecrated in 1837. But this building proved to be a source of contention. Rabbi Bardaki of Minsk was opposed to the new synagogue, believing that the site should have been used instead for housing: about five hundred new Jewish immigrants were practically destitute. In protest, he and his followers built the Sukkoth Shalom Synagogue, creating a permanent rift in the Ashkenazic community. It was the first of many. During the nineteenth century the Jewish community continued to fragment: Sephardim opposed Ashkenazim, Hasidim fought Mitnaggedim, and sects grew up within these larger groupings. The Jewish Quarter was split into antagonistic *kahals,* each one clustered around its own rabbi and frequently worshipping in a different synagogue.

Almost every new development in Jerusalem seemed doomed to increase the sectarianism and rivalry that now seemed endemic to the city. Muḥammad ʿAli was anxious to gain the support of the West, and he therefore encouraged Europeans to settle in the city. Thus for the first time a Western power was able to establish a consulate in Jerusalem—a step which the local people had fought for so long. In 1839 the English diplomat William Turner Young arrived in Jerusalem as British vice-consul, and within the next fifteen years, France, Prussia, Russia, and Austria all opened consulates in the Holy City. The consuls would become an extremely important presence in Jerusalem. They helped to bring modern medicine, education, and technology to the city. But each one had his own political agenda, and this often led to new conflict in the already divided city. The local people found themselves drawn into the quarrels of the European powers. Thus William Young was told to take a special interest in the Ashkenazic Jews. Britain would have liked to establish a "protectorate" in Jerusalem, as France and Russia had done, but there were no Protestants for the consul to take under his wing. The European Jews, however, had no foreign sponsor, and Young set himself up as their unofficial patron. He was inspired by an old millennial dream. St. Paul had prophesied that all the Jews would be converted to Christ before the Second Coming, and an increasing number of British Christians felt that they had a duty to fulfill this prophecy and clear away this obstacle to the final Redemption. By September 1839, through Young's good offices, the London Society for Promoting Christianity Among the Jews (also known as the "London Jews Society") had been given permission to work in Jerusalem, and the first Protestant missionaries began arriving in the Holy City. But they would clash with both the older denominations and the Jews, who resented this Christian initiative.

Modern ideas had now begun to penetrate Jerusalem, and there was no stopping the process. When the Egyptians were forced out of Palestine in 1840 by the European powers and the Ottomans resumed control, there could be no question of returning to the old system. Istanbul was also bent on modernization, and Sultan Mahmud II was attempting to run a more centralized state with a reformed army. His tanẓīmāt ("regulations") confirmed the new privileges of the *dhimmis*. They still had to pay the *jizyah* for military protection, but they had greater religious freedom and could continue to build and restore their places of worship without hindrance from the local Muslims. The Ottomans now showed more interest in Jerusalem, in part alerted by the Western preoccupation with the holy city. Before the Egyptian invasion, Acre had been considered the chief city of Palestine. Now Jerusalem was taking its place. It was still a *mutaṣarriflik,* coming between a province (*eyālet*) and a district (*sanjak*) on the administrative scale, but the *sanjaks* of Gaza, Jaffa, and (until 1858) Nablus were added to Jerusalem. For a short time in 1872, Jerusalem became independent: no longer subject to the *wālī* of Sidon or Damascus, the governor reported directly to Istanbul. The population was also growing. In 1840 there were 10,750 people in the city, with 3,000 Jews and 3,350 Christians. The population continued to increase dramatically. By 1850 the Jews formed a majority in the city, their numbers having almost doubled in ten years. This trend continued, as the following table makes clear:

YEAR	MUSLIMS	CHRISTIANS	JEWS	TOTAL
1850	5,350	3,650	6000	15,000
1860	6,000	4,000	8,000	18,000
1870	6,500	4,500	11,000	22,000
1880	8,000	6,000	17,000	31,000
1890	9,000	8,000	25,000	42,000
1900	10,000	10,000	35,000	55,000
1910	12,000	13,000	45,000	70,000
1922	13,500	14,700	34,400	62,600[2]

From being a deserted, desperate city, Jerusalem was being transformed by modernity into a thriving metropolis, and for the first time since the destruction of the Temple, Jews were once again gaining an ascendency.

In the meantime, the Western powers were doing their best to extend their influence in the Holy City through the consuls and the churches. Prussia and Britain jointly appointed the first Protestant bishop to Jerusalem, and on 21 January 1842, Bishop Michael Solomon, a Jewish convert, arrived in Jerusalem and announced that his first duty was to bring the Jews of the city to Christ. Naturally this alarmed the Jews. The new Protestant cathedral was called Hebrew Christ Church and was built near the Jaffa Gate, next door to the British consulate. On 21 May 1843, three Jews were baptized in a Hebrew ceremony in the cathedral in the presence of Consul Young. The Jews, not unnaturally, were outraged that these Protestants were blatantly trying to lure their impoverished people into their churches with the promise of welfare and security. Converts, who were cast out of the Jewish community, were usually supported by the Christians whose ranks they had joined. In 1844 there were yet more Jewish baptisms and the Jews realized that they would have to counter this Christian offensive.

Philanthropy had always been crucial to the sanctity of Jerusalem. Now it too was becoming aggressive and divisive. In 1843 the London Jews Society established a hospital offering free medicine on the borders of the Jewish Quarter. When Consul James Finn replaced Young he threw himself into the conversion campaign, offering protection to the Jewish immigrants from Russia at the behest of the consulate in Beirut. In 1850, when the Ottomans gave foreigners permission to buy land in the empire, Finn bought an estate outside the walls a mile to the west of Mount Sion. This became the Talbieh colony, where Jews could be trained in agricultural work. Finn's chief donor was a Miss Cook of Cheltenham, and her money also funded two other farms, one near Bethlehem and the other at Abraham's Vineyard, north of the Jaffa Gate, which employed six hundred Jews. Finn was convinced that if Jews could leave the squalor of the Jewish Quarter and earn their own living, their lot would improve. Most of the Jerusalem Jews lived on the halakka, alms collected in the Diaspora to maintain a community in the Holy City where Jews could study Torah and Talmud. Like the enlightened Jewish philanthropists, Finn believed that it was essential that Jews shake off this unhealthy dependence, which made them particularly vulnerable if, for any reason, the halakka failed to arrive. Education was also important. The new Protestant Bishop Gobat opened two schools, one for each sex, on the northern slope of Mount Sion for Jewish converts and Arab Christians. German deaconesses founded a school for Jews near Christ Church, and the London Jews Society built a House of Industry, also near Christ Church, to teach young Jews a trade. These institutions inevitably attracted poverty-stricken Jews. Clearly the best way to withstand this threat was to open Jewish welfare establishments. In 1843 the British Jewish philanthropist Sir Moses Montefiore set up a Jewish clinic in the city, and in 1854 the Rothschilds established the Misgav Ladach Hospital on the southern slope of Mount Sion together with a fund for schools and a low-interest lending scheme.

The older Christian communities were also spurred on to new philan-
thropic efforts by this Protestant challenge. The Greek Orthodox opened
a school for Arab boys with a broader curriculum than St. Saviour's. The
arrival of the Protestant bishop inspired the Roman Catholic Church to
revive the Latin patriarchate, which had lapsed with the demise of the
Crusader kingdom. The new patriarch moved into a new building near
the Jaffa Gate, which was becoming a modern enclave in Jerusalem. His
presence caused new dissension in the city. He not only offered an obvious challenge to the Greeks but also antagonized the Franciscans of St.
Saviour's, who felt slighted by his appointment. The new patriarchate
meant the introduction of more Catholic orders in the city. Soon the Sis-
ters of Zion—a Roman Catholic version of the London Jews Society—
founded a convent near the Ecce Homo Arch in the Via Dolorosa, where
they opened a school for girls.

Jerusalem was waking up to the modern world. The American archaeologist Edward Robinson had noticed the change as soon as he set foot in
the city in April 1852. He had previously visited Jerusalem in 1838, during
the Egyptian occupation. But this time he was immediately struck by the
modern Anglican church, the consulate, and the coffeehouses at the Jaffa
Gate. "There was a process going on in Jerusalem, of tearing down old
dwellings and replacing them with new ones which reminded me somewhat of New York," he wrote. "There was more activity in the streets;
there were more people in motion, more bustle and more business."[3]
Robinson had come to research ancient Jerusalem, however, but from a
very modern perspective. He wanted to prove the literal truth of the Bible
by scientific, empirical methodology. He was convinced that it was possible to trace the journeys of Abraham, Moses, and Joshua. During his 1838
visit, he had crawled through the water conduit built by Hezekiah. There
had been immense excitement when he published his *Biblical Researches in
Palestine* (1841). It seemed that it really might be possible to demonstrate
the truths of religion and answer some of the worrying criticisms of sci-
entists, geologists, and exegetes who were beginning to call the historical
reliability of the Bible into question. This new "biblical archaeology" was
an expression of the rationalized religion of the modern West based on
facts and reason rather than on imaginative mythology. Yet Jerusalem still
exerted a less cerebral pull that operated independently of theological conviction. During Robinson's first visit to the city, he found himself overwhelmed by emotion. The place had been imaginatively present to him
since infancy, so that even though he had never been there before, he felt
that his visit was a "return" and an encounter with his younger self. The
sites "all seemed familiar to me, as if the realization of a former dream. I
seemed to be again among the cherished scenes of childhood."[4]

When Robinson came back to Jerusalem in 1852 he made an interesting discovery. The year before, the American engineer James Barclay had visited the city as the guest of the Ottomans to advise them about the preservation of the Mamluk *madāris*. At the Western Wall, he had noticed a huge lintel stone which had topped one of the gates to Herod's Temple. Now Robinson caught sight of some large stones protruding at ground level from the southwest face of the Western Wall. When he unearthed them, he realized that this must have been one of the monumental arches spanning the Tyropoeon Valley described by Josephus. "Barclay's Gate" and "Robinson's Arch" were valuable finds, though it is doubtful whether they had any real religious significance. Yet archaeology could fuel its own holy wars, and Catholics felt impelled to challenge these and other Protestant discoveries. In 1850, Felicien de Saulcy, a soldier who had no training in antiquities, claimed that the Herodian walls of the Ḥaram had been built by Solomon and that the "Tomb of the Kings," built in the first century by the Queen of Adiabene, was the Tomb of David and the Kings of Judah. Without offering any proof for these assertions, de Saulcy hoped to discredit the Protestant enterprise (Robinson had believed that David's tomb was on Mount Sion) and thus cast doubt upon Protestant belief in general.

While these more scholarly disputes were in process, the bitter feuding of the Jerusalem Christians led to a full-scale war between the great powers. In 1847 a particularly disreputable brawl had broken out in the Nativity Church between the Greek and Latin clergy. Blood was shed and furious accusations were made about a missing silver star. This led to a clash between France and Russia, the "protectors" of the two communities. France in particular welcomed the chance to reopen the question of the holy places, while Russia replied that the status quo, with the Greeks in pride of place, must be maintained. This quarrel gave Britain and France the pretext they needed to declare war on Russia in order to stop any further Russian advance into Ottoman territory. In 1854 the Crimean War broke out. Despite the new secularism, the issue of Jerusalem could still spur a major confrontation between the Christian powers.

When the war ended with the defeat of Russia in September 1855, Britain and France had greater leverage in Istanbul. The Ḥaram was opened to Christians for the first time for centuries. The duke and duchess of Brabant had been the first Western visitors to the sacred precinct in March 1855, and a few months later, in recognition of Britain's part in the war, Sir Moses Montefiore ascended to the Ḥaram platform reciting Psalm 121, carried in a sedan chair lest his feet inadvertently touch one of the forbidden areas. Other favors were also forthcoming. The sultan returned the Crusader Church of St. Anna, which Saladin had converted into a *madrasah,* to Napoleon III as a gift to the French people, and the British were able to insist that the Jews be allowed to extend the Hurva Synagogue.

Modernization proceeded apace after the war. The Christian churches had all bought printing presses, and by 1862 there were two Jewish presses, which a year later had begun to produce two Hebrew newspapers. The Laemel School was founded to give Jewish boys a modern education: they learned Arabic and arithmetic as well as Torah. This led to more antagonism in the Jewish Quarter, since the more conservative Jews, particularly the Ashkenazim, would have no truck with this *goyische* establishment.[5] More modern buildings had started to appear in the city. The Austrian government had built a hospice for Catholic pilgrims at the intersection of one of the main streets of the *sūq* in 1863. Nearby the Austrian consulate was established in a beautiful house in Bezetha, near the Damascus Gate, which was also beginning to be a center of modernity. The British and French consulates also moved to this district, which was becoming one of the most salubrious areas in town.

Far more momentous, however, was the exodus from the walled city. It began in 1857 when Montefiore got permission to buy a plot of land opposite Mount Sion, several hundred yards nearer to the city than Finn's Talbiyeh estate. He had intended first to found a hospital but changed his mind, building instead a row of almshouses for impoverished Jewish families. He wanted Jews to move out of the overcrowded and unhealthy Jewish Quarter; on top of the hill overlooking the cottages, he built the most advanced windmill in Jerusalem. Like Finn, Montefiore wanted Jews to become self-reliant. Other Jews were attracted by the idea. In 1860, David Yellin, a Russian Jew, bought land near the village of Kalonia, five miles west of the city. By 1880 there were nine of these new Jewish suburbs. One of them was the Ashkenazi colony called Mea Shearim ("Hundred Gates"), half a mile from the Jaffa Gate. It was built strictly according to the rules of the Torah, with its own synagogue, market, and yeshivas. Moving out to these settlements was dangerous. The first families in Montefiore's cottages were so frightened of robbers that they used to creep back into the city at night to sleep in their old hovels. The Ashkenazim were often attacked on their way out to Mea Shearim. Nevertheless, the settlements grew and prospered. Once they started to leave the Jewish Quarter, the health of Jerusalem's Jews began to improve dramatically, and this was one reason for the great increase of the Jewish community during the nineteenth century. Another was the new opportunities to earn a decent living. Life had always been economically difficult for the Jews of Jerusalem, and for this reason many new immigrants had preferred to settle in Safed or Tiberias. Now that obstacle was being removed, Jews naturally wanted to come to their Holy City, and when there was an earthquake or some other disaster in Safed, they instinctively came to settle in Jerusalem.

Arabs had also begun to settle outside the walls, forming Muslim, Christian, and mixed communities. By 1874 there were five Arab residential suburbs at Karim al-Sheikh and Bab al-Zahreb, north of the city; Muresa, four hundred yards northwest of the Damascus Gate; Katamon, a mile from the Jaffa Gate; and Abu Tor, overlooking the Hinnom and Kidron valleys. The Christian communities were also starting to move beyond the walls. In 1860 the Swiss German Brotherhood built an orphanage in the fields outside the Jaffa Gate for Arab children. The German deaconesses built the Talitha Cumi School for girls in the fields south of the Jaffa Road. In 1871, Protestants from Württemberg built the German Colony south of the city, starting with a church,

The Damascus Gate became one of the centers of modern Jerusalem, though for some time old and new methods of transport, style of dress, and architecture continued to exist side by side.

hospice, school, and hospital. In 1880 the Spaffords, an American family, founded a new Protestant mission center north of the Damascus Gate, and this would become the American Colony. Not long afterward the Russians built a huge hospice, capable of housing a thousand pilgrims, west of the city; its distinctive green domes were the first buildings to be seen on arrival from Jaffa. Catholics also opened institutions outside the walls during the 1880s: the Schmidt College, opposite the Damascus Gate, and, at the northwest corner of the walls, the St. Vincent de Paul Monastery, Notre Dame de France, and the Hospital of St. Louis.

Arab Jerusalem was also developing. In 1863 the first municipal council (*baladiyya al-quds*) was established in the city, occupying at first two small rooms off the Via Dolorosa. Jerusalem was probably the first

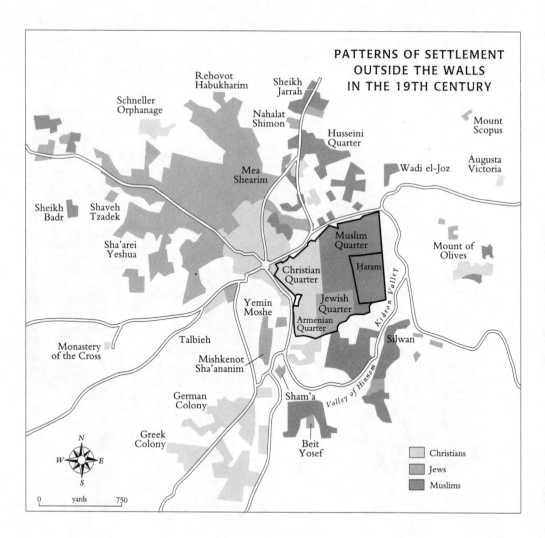

PATTERNS OF SETTLEMENT
OUTSIDE THE WALLS
IN THE 19TH CENTURY

Rehovot Habukharim
Sheikh Jarrah
Schneller Orphanage
Nahalat Shimon
Husseini Quarter
Mount Scopus
Augusta Victoria
Wadi el-Joz
Mea Shearim
Sheikh Badr
Shaveh Tzadek
Sha'arei Yeshua
Muslim Quarter
Mount of Olives
Haram
Christian Quarter
Kidron Valley
Yemin Moshe
Jewish Quarter
Armenian Quarter
Silwan
Monastery of the Cross
Talbieh
Mishkenot Sha'ananim
Sham'a
Valley of Hinnom
German Colony
Beit Yosef
Greek Colony

N
W   E
S

0   yards   750

Christians
Jews
Muslims

Ottoman town after Istanbul to have such a body. The council had ten members: six Muslims, two Christians, and one Jew; the Jewish quota was raised to two in 1908. Despite the tensions in the city, the members of the three faiths were able to work creatively together. The council was elected every four years by male Ottoman citizens who were over twenty-five years old and paid a property tax of at least fifty Turkish pounds per annum. The mayor was chosen by the governor from the elected members. Until 1914 most of the mayors came from the Khālidī, ʿAlami, Husaini, and Dajani families, and the appointment usually reflected the balance of power between the notable families, especially between the Khālidīs and the Husainis. The municipality took an active role in the development of Jerusalem. From the very beginning it tried to improve the infrastructure of Jerusalem, paving and clearing the streets, installing a sewage system, and taking steps to light and clean the city. In the 1890s the council arranged for the streets to be regularly sprinkled with water, arranged for rubbish collection, planted trees along some of the streets, and opened a city park on the Jaffa Road. The council was responsible for introducing a police force, a municipal hospital providing free medical help, and, at the turn of the century, the Museum of Antiquities and a theater near the Jaffa Gate, where plays were performed in Turkish, Arabic, and French. Few other cities of the late Ottoman empire had such an active and committed municipality.

One of its leading lights was Yusuf al-Khālidī, who held the position of mayor for nine years.[6] He was representative of the new Palestinian citizen, being one of the first Arabs of Jerusalem to receive a modern, Western education. Khālidī had no nationalistic aspirations, however. He was a loyal Ottoman citizen and was the Jerusalem delegate to the short-lived Ottoman parliament in 1877–78. Here he spoke out fearlessly against the corruption of the administration and the unconstitutional behavior of Sultan Abdulhamid. He believed that the reformed Ottoman state should establish modern education, an uncorrupt administration, religious toleration, constitutional rights, and an improved infrastructure. He became a local hero in Jerusalem until he was removed from office in 1879 by the governor Rauf Pasha, who wanted to break the power of the local families. This ended the political ascendancy of the Khālidīs in Jerusalem, and henceforth the more conservative and intolerant Husainis tended to take the lead—a development that would not always be helpful as tension increased in Jerusalem.

When Rauf Pasha tried to replace the Khālidīs and other Arab notables with Turkish officials, there was uproar in Jerusalem. The action was seen as an anti-Arab move. This was a new development. Hitherto religion had been far more important as a determinant of identity than race.

The new Arab consciousness that had first surfaced during the 1825 uprising showed the first stirrings of Arab nationalism in Palestine. The consuls noted that increasingly the Turks were resented as usurpers by the Arabs of Jerusalem, who would later take a leading role in the struggle to come. Another sign of this assertion of a distinctly Arab identity came in 1872 when the Arab members of the Greek Orthodox Church started to campaign vehemently for greater participation in their church. They felt despised and marginalized by the elite Greek minority. The quarrel started in Jerusalem but spread to the rest of Palestine, encouraged by the Russian consul, who had his own reasons for challenging the Greek hegemony of Orthodoxy in the Holy Land. At one point, Arab behavior became so violent that the British consul saw it as an incipient revolt. Peace was eventually restored, but Arab discontent smoldered beneath the surface. In 1882 the Arab Christians founded the Orthodox Palestine Society to fight against the foreign control of their church.

The Arabs were trying to form their own plans for their country, but the Europeans were also eyeing Palestine possessively. They tended to see their bringing of modernity to Jerusalem as a "peaceful Crusade," a term which laid bare the desire to conquer and dominate.[7] The French looked forward to Jerusalem and the whole Orient coming under the rule of the cross in a successful Crusade. Their task was to liberate Jerusalem from the sultan, and their new weapon would be colonialism. The Protestants who built the German Colony called themselves the Templars and urged their government to complete the work of the Crusaders. The British had a rather different line. They developed a form of gentile Zionism. Their reading of the Bible convinced them that Palestine belonged to the Jews, and already in the 1870s sober British observers looked forward to the establishment of a Jewish homeland in Palestine under the protection of Great Britain. It was a point of view clearly allied to the policies of the British consuls. It had become a received idea to many people in Protestant England, where the Bible was read rather literally, that the Jews would one day return to Zion and that the Arabs were temporary usurpers.[8]

The Europeans were using the modernization of Jerusalem as a way of taking possession of the country. In 1865, Captain Charles Wilson of the British Royal Engineers arrived in Palestine to study the hydrology of Jerusalem. He would also prepare the first ordnance survey of the Holy City, which, in Western minds, would tend to supersede the old sacred geography. While exploring the underground cisterns of the Ḥaram, Wilson noticed a monumental arch parallel to "Robinson's Arch." "Wilson's Arch" caught the attention of the British public far more than the proposed new water system, and as a result of Wilson's dispatches the Palestine Exploration Fund (PEF) was founded in 1865 to research the archaeology and history of the Holy Land. The inherent possessiveness of this "peaceful Crusade" was voiced by the archbishop of York, president of the new society, at the inaugural ceremony. "The country of Palestine belongs to you and me; it is essentially ours," he announced. "It is the land from which news came of our Redemption. It is the land we turn to as the foundation of all our hopes. It is the land to which we look with as true a patriotism as we do this dear old England."[9] Because Palestine was such an important province of the Christian imagination, it was difficult to see it as objectively as the new scientific disciplines required. It was somehow part of the Christian self and identity, which made it hard to see it as belonging in a wholly different sense to the people who actually lived there and made it their home.

The people of Palestine soon got wind of this new crusading archaeology. When de Saulcy returned to Jerusalem in 1863 to continue his excavations at the Tomb of the Kings, he was confronted by the angry local residents, who demanded financial compensation for their land and possessions, which he had violated. The Jews also accused de Saulcy of desecrating the graves of their ancestors. The Europeans seemed to assume that the land that they were exploring was theirs to do with as they liked. When Charles Warren of the Royal Engineers arrived in Jerusalem in February 1867, he found the authorities unhelpful and suspicious. He was not permitted to dig under the Ḥaram itself: the holy place could not be penetrated by the crowbars, jacks, and blocks of these new Crusaders. To solve the problem, Warren rented private plots of land around the southern end of the Ḥaram, then sank deep shafts and underground passages leading to the base of the walls. What he discovered was that Herod's Temple had been built on top of mounds of loose rubble that had gradually accumulated during the biblical period and filled the Tyropoeon Valley. While digging on the Ophel, he also came across the ancient Jebusite water conduit, which was henceforth known as "Warren's Shaft."

Increasingly, Western travelers arrived in Palestine in search of facts. Unlike the pilgrims of old, they were not there to explore the sacred geography of the spirit but to find historical evidence that their faith was true. The PEF set up a shop and lecture room at the Jaffa Gate, and guides had to pass an examination on the history of Jerusalem, based on the findings of PEF explorers. "Biblical archaeology" had begun as a quest for intellectual certainty, but it was beginning to uncover a more complex reality that made such certainty difficult. It was not really possible to make simple statements about Jerusalem's past. The excavations of the American archaeologist Frederick J. Bliss had unearthed a cuneiform tablet at Tel el-Hesy, some thirty miles south of Jerusalem. The tablet was similar to those recently found at Tel el-Amarna in Egypt. Clearly the history of the "Holy Land" did not begin with the Bible. Bliss discovered a similar complexity in Jerusalem. Although he could not yet prove this, he became convinced that the original City of David had not been on Mount Sion, as people had assumed for centuries, but on the Ophel hill. Did this make nonsense of the struggle for the so-called Tomb of David? When he began to excavate the Ophel, however, Bliss found that it was not possible simply to dig down and uncover the 'Ir David. Many of the ancient structures he found were not at all easy to date, but it was clear that the hill had been inhabited continuously from the Bronze Age to the Byzantine period. The various strata overlapped in a most confusing manner, and it would take years for archaeologists to form an accurate picture of Jerusalem's past. It was far more difficult than the Bible-reading faithful tended to assume.[10]

In 1910 the Dominican archaeologist Hughes Vincent was able to complete Bliss's excavations on the Ophel and showed that the earliest city of Jerusalem had indeed been sited there and not on Mount Sion. He found Bronze Age tombs, water systems, and fortifications that proved that the town had a history that long predated David.[11] It was not possible, therefore, to claim that the city belonged to the Jews because they had been there first. Indeed, the Bible went out of its way to show that the Israelites had taken both Palestine and Jerusalem from the indigenous population. Modern archaeology could therefore threaten some of the simple certainties of faith.

Archaeology was still experienced by the Muslims of Jerusalem as a potentially blasphemous activity that sought to penetrate the mystery of the sacred with crude, aggressive methods. Père Vincent's excavations took place in the context of the disgraceful expedition of Montagu Brownlow Parker, son of the earl of Morley. He had been led to believe that there was buried treasure in the underground vaults of the Haram. Vincent had agreed to help him simply to ensure that the wholly untrained Parker did not destroy valuable evidence. On the night of 17 April 1910, Parker bribed his way onto the Haram and started to explore the cave under the Rock. A Muslim attendant, who had decided to sleep on the Haram, heard noises and rushed to the Dome of the Rock to discover Parker hacking away at the sacred stone with a pickax. The Muslims of Jerusalem were horrified, and there were riots in the city for days. Parker was an example of the worst aspects of Western secularism. He had violated an ancient sanctum and attempted—literally—to undermine the holiness of the site not as part of a noble quest for knowledge but for pure material gain.

Modernity was gradually changing religion. People in Europe and the United States had lost the art of thinking in symbols and images. Instead, they were developing a more linear, discursive mode of thought. New ideologies, such as socialism and nationalism, were beginning to challenge the old religious convictions. Yet the mythology of sacred geography went deep. We have seen that Byzantine Christians, who thought they had outgrown this type of religion, had to revise their ideas when their circumstances changed. Soon after the discovery of the tomb of Christ they had quickly evolved their own mythology of sacred space. During the second half of the nineteenth century, some Jews were beginning to restate the old ideology of Zion in a new way. European Jews had undergone an immense upheaval. In France, Germany, and England they had been emancipated and encouraged to join modern secular society. But though some flourished when they left the ghetto, others felt curiously lost. They had been cut off from their roots and felt adrift, without orientation. What did it mean to be a Jew in the modern world? Was Judaism simply a private affair of the individual? Some Jews developed a demythologized faith that eschewed messianism and the desire to rebuild the Temple; they wanted to separate religion from politics. But others found this solution unsatisfactory. Moreover, they were becoming painfully aware that the new tolerance of Europe was superficial. Anti-Semitism was an ingrained Christian habit and would not easily disappear. Europeans would indeed reinterpret the old myths about Jews in the lights of their new enthusiasms. Increasingly, some Jews felt alienated and vulnerable in the brave new modern world. Without a true place of their own, they turned instinctively to Zion.

As early as 1840, after the first anti-Semitic pogroms in the Islamic world were instigated by Franciscans in Damascus, Yehuda Hai Alchelai, a Sephardic rabbi of Sarajevo, urged Jews to take their destiny into their own hands. They were not as safe in the Islamic world as they had supposed. It was no good sitting back helplessly waiting for the Messiah: "The Redemption will begin by efforts of the Jews themselves," he wrote in his *Minḥat Yehuda*.[12] They must organize, choose leaders, and establish a fund to buy land in Palestine. In 1860 the Ashkenazic rabbi Zvi Hirsch Kalischer had been disturbed to see the new nationalism of his gentile neighbors in Poland. Where would this leave the Jews, who had no land of their own? They must develop their own nationalism. Again, Kalischer taught, it was no good waiting passively for the Messiah. The Montefiores and Rothschilds should form a company for Jewish settlement in Palestine and organize a mass migration of Jews to a place they could really call their own. Most Orthodox rabbis—who, refusing to make any concessions to modernity, maintained a strict observance of traditional practices—would have no part of this new Zionism, which they saw as an impious attempt to precipitate forcibly the Redemption; but Alchelai and Kalischer showed how natural it was for Jews to look to Zion when they felt alienated in a hostile world. Zionism would be a secular movement, inspired for the most part by Jews who had lost faith in religion, but these two rabbis showed that the movement had a religious potential.

The man who has been called the father of Zionism, however, was Moses Hess, a disciple of Marx and Engels, who reinterpreted the old biblical mythology according to the revolutionary ideals of socialism and nationalism. He was one of the first people to see that a new form of anti-Semitism was rising in nationalistic Germany, based on race rather than religion. As Germans became more devoted to the Fatherland, Jews would be hated and persecuted because they did not belong to the Aryan nation and had no land of their own. Few people believed Hess at the time—Germany seemed eager to allow Jews to assimilate—but Hess had sensed the deeper currents that were at work in society. In his Zionist classic *Rome and Jerusalem* (1860) he argued that Jews must establish a socialist society in Palestine. Just as Mazzini would liberate the eternal city on the Tiber, Jews must liberate the eternal city on Mount Moriah. Socialism and Judaism were entirely compatible. The prophets had taught the paramount importance of justice and concern for the poor. Once Jews had established a socialist commonwealth in Jerusalem, the light would go forth once more from Zion. They would thus bring about what Hess called "the Sabbath of history," the utopia prophesied by Karl Marx, which Hess equated with the messianic kingdom.

Those Jews who felt marginalized in Europe were heartened by the German historian Heinrich Graetz, who taught them that Judaism was relevant to the highly politicized world of their day. In his monumental *History of the Jews from the Earliest Times to the Present* (1853–76), Graetz argued that it was no use trying to copy Christianity and separate religion from politics, as Reform Jews advocated. Judaism was an essentially political faith. From the time of King David, Jews had linked politics and religion in a creative synthesis. Even after the Temple was lost, Jews had developed the Talmud as a substitute for the Holy Land. The Torah could "turn every Jewish household anywhere in the world into a precisely defined Palestine."[13] The Holy Land was, therefore, in their blood. "The Torah, the Nation, and the Holy Land stand, one might say, in a mystical relationship with one another, they are inseparably united by an invisible bond."[14] They were sacred values, inextricably bound up with the Jewish identity. Unlike Hess, whose work he admired, Graetz did not advocate migration to Palestine. He had been horrified by the backward-looking Jews of Jerusalem and the squalid Jewish Quarter when he had visited the Holy City. His contribution to the Zionist cause was his *History*, which educated a whole generation of Jews and taught them to rethink their traditions in the light of modern philosophy.

The years 1881–82 were a watershed in the history of Palestine and Jerusalem. First, the British established themselves politically in the region by conquering Egypt. They would play a fateful role in the coming struggle. One of the heroes of the Egyptian campaign was General Charles "Chinese" Gordon, who was killed in the Sudan after the fall of Khartoum. His main contribution to Jerusalem was the discovery of the "Garden Tomb." Many Europeans had become repelled by the Holy Sepulcher Church, finding this musty building filled with angry, rebarbative monks impossible to associate with the limpid mysteries of their faith. When Gordon studied Wilson's ordnance survey of Jerusalem, he noticed that one of the contour lines resembled a woman's body, whose "head" was a little hill north of the Damascus Gate. This must be the "Place of the Skull." With touching faith in his so-called scientific method, when Gordon found an apparently ancient rock tomb there, he immediately identified the hill as Golgotha and the tomb as Christ's. After his death, the Garden Tomb became a Protestant holy place. It was a monument to the British imperialism that would permanently change the history of Jerusalem.

In 1882, following the outbreak of vicious pogroms in Russia, the first Zionist colonies were established in Palestine—not in Jerusalem but in the countryside. These colonies, run according to socialist ideals, were not a success, but the new Jewish enthusiasm that would transform Palestine had been given a local habitation and appeared on the map. Zionism was taking on flesh and substance in the land of the Patriarchs. In 1899, Zionists acquired an international platform when they held their first conference at Basel, Switzerland. Even though many of these early Zionists were secularists who no longer shared the theological beliefs of traditional Judaism, they had called their movement after one of the oldest names of the Holy City, which had for so long been an image of salvation. They also expressed their ideals in conventional Jewish imagery. Thus they were moved to see Theodor Herzl, who had become the spokesman of Zionism, ascend the podium. He looked like "a man of the House of David, risen all of a sudden from his grave in all his legendary glory," recalled Mordechai Ben-Ami, the delegate from Odessa. "It seemed as if the dream cherished by our people for two thousand years had come true at last and Messiah the Son of David was standing before us."[15]

Herzl was not an original thinker, though his book *The Jewish State* (1896) would become a Zionist classic. Nor was he a religious man; he had been committed to the ideal of assimilation and had even toyed with the possibility of converting to Christianity. But then came the shock of France's Dreyfus affair, which showed him the vulnerability of the Jewish people. He foresaw—correctly—an impending anti-Semitic catastrophe and literally worked himself to death in an attempt to find a haven for the Jews. Realizing the importance of public relations, he approached the sultan, the pope, the Kaiser, and the British colonial secretary and thus brought Zionism to the attention of the world's political leaders. Herzl did not believe that the new Jewish state needed to be in Palestine, and he was shocked at the Second Zionist Conference by the depth of opposition to his proposal to establish a state in Uganda. To retain the leadership, Herzl was forced to abandon the idea. He stood before the delegates, raised his right hand, and quoted the words of the psalmist: "If I forget thee, O Jerusalem, may my right hand wither!"

When, however, Herzl actually visited Jerusalem in 1898, he was not favorably impressed. To the contrary, he was appalled by "the musty deposits of two thousand years of inhumanity, intolerance, and foulness" in its "reeking alleys," and resolved that the first thing the Zionists would do if they ever got control of Jerusalem was to clean it up.

> I would clear out everything that is not sacred, set up workers' houses beyond the city, empty and tear down the filthy rat-holes, burn all non-sacred ruins, and put the bazaars elsewhere. Then, retaining as much of the old architectural style as possible, I would build an airy, comfortable, properly sewered, brand new city around the holy places.[16]

A few days later, he changed his mind: he would build the new secular city outside the walls and leave the holy shrines in an enclave of their own. It was a perfect image of the new secularist ideal: religion must be relegated to a separate sphere. The sanctity of Jerusalem played little part in the early Zionist movement. Most of its luminaries preferred to leave the city and its religious communities alone. For Herzl, salvation would not descend from on high: it lay in the brave new city that he would like to build outside the city walls. The "wide, green ring of hillside all around" would be "the location of a glorious New Jerusalem."[17] The old religious traditions of Judaism had been superseded and left behind. Consequently Herzl's chief emotion when he visited the Western Wall was disgust: the squalor, the moaning, and the craven attitudes of the Jews who clung to its stones symbolized everything that Zionism must transcend.

Not all Zionists had that reaction, however. Mordechai Ben Hillel wept like a child when he first caught sight of the Western Wall. It was a survivor, like the Jewish people, its power deriving not from facts and reason but from "legend" that had the power to unleash immense psychic force.[18] The writer A. S. Hirschberg had a similar experience when he visited Jerusalem in 1901. Walking through the Maghribi Quarter, he felt ill at ease and out of place. But as soon as he stood before the Western Wall and took the prayer book offered him by the Sephardic beadle, he started to weep uncontrollably. He was in shock, he recalled later, touched to the depths of his being: "All my private troubles mingled with our nation's misfortunes to form a torrent."[19] The wall had become a symbol that had the power to heal the sense of rootlessness and alienation that afflicted the most secular of Jews. Its power took them by surprise, bringing them up against themselves and reaching hitherto unsuspected areas of their hearts and minds.

In 1902 a new wave of Zionist settlers began to arrive in Israel from Russia and Eastern Europe; they were secular revolutionaries, dedicated to the socialist ideal. One of them was the young David Ben-Gurion. This "Second Aliyah," as the migration was called, would be decisive in the history of the movement. Ben-Gurion was not religious. His New Jerusalem was the socialist vision. To his wife, Paula, he wrote: "Dolorous and in tears you will arise to the high mountain from which one sees vistas of a new world, shining in the glow of an eternally young ideal of supreme happiness and glorious existence."[20] Their secular faith filled these settlers with the kind of exaltation that is usually associated with religion. They called their migration to Palestine an *aliyah,* chiefly because this was the traditional term for return to the Land of Israel, but also because it represented an ascent to a higher plane of being. For them, however, holiness resided in the land, not in heaven. Some of these Zionists did settle in Jerusalem, but many of them shared Herzl's distaste. In 1909, beside the Arab port of Jaffa, they began to build Tel Aviv, which became the showcase city of their new Judaism.

Most of the settlers were such urban types. In the Zionist pantheon, however, they were never as important as the settlers in the *kibbutzim.* The first of these collective farms was established in Degania in the Galilee in 1911. The Zionist theorist Nahum Sokolov remarked: "The point of gravity has shifted from the Jerusalem of the religious schools to the farms and agricultural schools, the fields and the meadows."[21] Just as ancient Israel had come into being outside Jerusalem, the new Israel would be formed not in the holy city but in the *kibbutzim* of Galilee.

Yet Jerusalem was still a symbol that had power to inspire these secular Zionists as they struggled to create a new world, even if they had little time for the city as an earthly reality. Yitzhak Ben-Zvi, who would become the second President of the State of Israel, was converted to

The seeds of the modern confrontation between Arabs and Jews in Jerusalem had already been sown by the early twentieth century.

Zionism while speaking at a revolutionary rally in Russia. Suddenly he felt dissociated from his surroundings and in the wrong place. "Why am I here and not there?" he asked himself. Then he had a vision. There arose "in my mind's eye the living image of Jerusalem, the holy city, with its ruins, desolate of its sons." From that moment he thought no more of revolution in Russia but only of "*our* Jerusalem." "That very hour I reached the absolute decision that our place is the Land of Israel, and that I must go there, dedicate my life to its upbuilding, and as soon as possible."[22] He had discovered his true orientation and his real place in the world.

The trouble was that Jerusalem was not "desolate of its sons." It already had sons, a people who had lived there for centuries and who had their own plans for the city. Nor was the city a ruin, as Ben-Zvi imagined. Fourteen new suburbs had been established since the 1870s. Jerusalem had a modern shopping arcade and hotel at the Jaffa Gate, a brand-new park where the municipal band played in the afternoons, a museum, a theater, a modern post office, and a telegraph system. There was now a carriage road linking the Holy City to Jaffa, and a railway brought visitors from the coast through the Baq'a Valley. Jerusalem had become a city to be proud of. Its Arab residents had come to resent the Turkish occupation and were alarmed by the Zionist settlers. In 1891 a number of Jerusalem notables sent a petition to Istanbul, asking the government to prevent further immigration of Jews and the sale of land to Zionists. The last known political act of Yusuf al-Khālidī had been to write a letter to Rabbi Zadok Kahn, the friend of Herzl, begging him to leave Palestine alone: for centuries, Jews, Christians, and Muslims had managed to live together in Jerusalem, and this Zionist project would end such coexistence. After the Young Turk revolt in 1908, Arab nationalists of Palestine began to dream of a state of their own, free of Turkish control. When the first Arab Congress met in Paris in 1913, a telegram of support was signed by 387 Arabs from the Near East, 130 of them Palestinians. In 1915, Ben-Gurion became aware of these Arab aspirations for Palestine and found them profoundly disturbing. "It hit me like a bomb," he said later. "I was utterly confounded."[23] Yet, the Israeli writer Amos Elon tells us, despite this bombshell, Ben-Gurion continued to ignore the existence of the Palestinian Arabs. Only two years later, he made the astonishing suggestion that in a "historical and moral sense," Palestine was a country "without inhabitants."[24] Because the Jews felt at home there, all other inhabitants of the country were merely the ethnic descendants of various conquerors. Ben-Gurion wished the Arabs well as individuals but was convinced that they had no rights at all as a nation. Like Jerusalem, the Land of Israel had long been a state of mind for Jews. Even a committed atheist like Ben-Gurion found its sacred position on his own emotional map more compelling than the demographic and historical facts that were staring him in the face. Yet this deep denial was destined shortly to run up against some hard realities—perhaps partly because of that denial, a tragic clash of interests between Jews and Arabs was developing.

In 1914 the Great War broke out, Turkey siding with the Germans against the French and the British. Jerusalem became the headquarters of the Turkish VIII Corps. Between 1915 and 1918 a tragedy occurred that presaged a future catastrophe that would have a profound impact on the history of Jerusalem. Official Turkish policy demanded the massacre of the Armenian people. In Jerusalem, where the Armenians had long kept a low profile, the *kaghakatsi* were unmolested, however. Those who had government positions were deprived of their posts, but otherwise family life continued as usual in the Armenian Quarter, except that the young men were drafted into the Turkish army. In other parts of the Ottoman empire, however, Armenians were mercilessly exterminated. The code word for this mass execution would be "deportation," just as it was later in Nazi Germany. Crowds were herded to riverbanks and pushed into the water, the soldiers shooting those who tried to save themselves by swimming. Tens of thousands were driven into the desert without food and water. A million Armenians died in this way; another million went into exile. Some of them arrived in Jerusalem and crowded into the Armenian Quarter. The refugees were allowed to reside in the Convent of St. James with the brotherhood, a privilege usually denied seculars. The first genocide of the twentieth century had led some to seek refuge in the ancient sanctity of Jerusalem.

In 1916 the British decided that a spectacular victory in the Near East would break the stalemate of trench warfare in France. The British Egyptian Expeditionary Force was moved into the Sinai Peninsula, but met determined Turkish resistance in Gaza. General Murray was replaced by General Edward Allenby, who was told by Prime Minister Lloyd George to conquer Jerusalem as a Christmas present for the people of Britain. Allenby carefully studied the PEF publications: as in Napoleon's conquest over a century earlier, scientific study was a prelude to military occupation. In October 1917, Allenby took Gaza and began his advance to Jerusalem. There the governor Djemal Pasha gave orders for the Turks to evacuate the city, and on 9 December, Mayor Hussein Selim al-Husaini was the only authority left in the city. He borrowed a white sheet from an American missionary and left the Old City through the Jaffa Gate with a procession of small boys. He surrendered Jerusalem to two startled British scouts. When Allenby arrived at the Jaffa Gate on 11 December, the bells of the city pealed to welcome him. Out of respect for the holiness of Jerusalem, Allenby dismounted and entered the city on foot, taking his stand on the steps of the Citadel. He assured the inhabitants of "Jerusalem the Blessed" that he would protect the holy places and preserve the religious freedom of all three faiths of Abraham in the name of His Majesty's Government. He had completed the work of the Crusaders.

17

ISRAEL

JERUSALEM had been destroyed and rebuilt many times in its long and often tragic history. With the arrival of the British, the city was about to undergo another painful period of transformation. Apart from the brief interlude of Crusader occupation, Jerusalem had been an important Islamic city for nearly thirteen hundred years. Now that the Ottoman empire had been conquered, the Arabs of the region were about to be given their independence. At first the British and the French established mandates and protectorates in the Near East, but, one by one, new Arab states and kingdoms began to appear: Jordan, Lebanon, Syria, Egypt, and Iraq. Other things being equal, Palestine would probably also have become an independent state, and Jerusalem, now such an important city, might well have been its capital. But this did not happen. During the period of the British Mandate, the Zionists were able to establish themselves in the country and create a Jewish state. Jerusalem remained a religious and a strategic prize, and its ownership was contested by the Jews, the Arabs, and the international community. But eventually in 1967, Jewish military and diplomatic maneuvers would carry the day, and Jerusalem became the capital of the Jewish State of Israel. At the present time, the Arab character of Jerusalem is only a shadow of what it was when Allenby and his troops marched into the city.

The Zionist victory was an extraordinary reversal. In 1917, Arabs formed 90 percent of the total population of Palestine and just under 50 percent of the population of Jerusalem. Both the Jews and the Arabs look back on this process with astonishment. Zionists regard their success in the face of such overwhelming odds as little short of miraculous; Arabs speak of their defeat as *al-nakhbah,* a word which denotes a catastrophe of near-cosmic proportions. It is not surprising that on both sides black-and-white accounts of the struggle have tended to oversimplify the issue, presenting it in terms of villains and heroes, total right and absolute wrong, the will of God or a divine chastisement. But the reality was more complex. In large part, the outcome was determined by the skill and resources of the Zionist leaders, who managed to influence first the British and later the American governments and who showed a canny understanding of the diplomatic process. Whenever they were offered something by the great powers, they nearly always accepted it, even though it often fell short of their needs or requirements. In the end, they got everything. The Zionists were also able to overcome the ideological divisions within their own movement. The Arabs were not so fortunate. Reeling under the shock of the collapse of the Ottoman empire and the arrival of the British, the Arab nationalist movement in Palestine lacked the coherence and sense of realpolitik that was necessary to deal with the Europeans on the one hand and the Zionists on the other. They could not mount a sustained resistance, and, unaccustomed to the methods of Western diplomacy, they continually said no when offered anything at all—hoping that a firm and uncompromising policy of rejection would secure them the right to an independent Arab state in the land which seemed, demographically and historically, to

During the British Mandate, Jerusalem began the slow and painful process that would transform it from an Arab to a predominantly Jewish city.

belong by rights to them. At the start, they were naively convinced of Britain's good intentions toward them. As a result of their oft-repeated veto, they were left with nothing, and with the establishment of the State of Israel in 1948, the dispossessed, uprooted, and wandering Jew was replaced by the homeless, uprooted, and dispossessed Palestinian.

The motivation and policy of the British were also confusing and dubious. Both sides found it hard to work out what the British intended. During the Great War, the British government had made pledges to both the Arabs and the Jews. In 1915, to encourage the Arabs of the Hijaz to rebel against Turkey, Sir Henry McMahon, high commissioner of Egypt, had promised Husain ibn ʿAli, sherif of Mecca, that Britain would recognize the future independence of the Arab countries and that the holy places would remain under the control of an "independent Sovereign Muslim State." Palestine was not explicitly mentioned, nor was Jerusalem, the third-holiest place in Islam. The McMahon Pledge was not a formally ratified treaty, but it had the force of a treaty, especially when Husain decided to act upon it and raised the Arab revolt with the help of T. E. Lawrence in 1916. At the same time as McMahon was negotiating this agreement, Britain and France were negotiating the secret Sykes-Picot Agreement, which divided the whole Arab world north of the peninsula into British and French zones.

Then on 2 November 1917, just over a month before Allenby's conquest of Jerusalem, Prime Minister Lloyd George instructed his foreign secretary, Arthur Balfour, to write a letter to Lord Rothschild, containing this important declaration:

> His Majesty's Government views with favour the establishment in Palestine of a national home for the Jewish people, and will use their best endeavours to facilitate the achievement of this object, it being clearly understood that nothing shall be done to prejudice the civil and religious rights of existing non-Jewish communities in Palestine, or the rights and political status enjoyed by Jews in any other country.[1]

Britain had long entertained the fantasy of returning the Jews to Palestine. In 1917, during a world war, there may also have been strategic considerations. A British protectorate of grateful Jews might counter French ambitions in the region. But Balfour was aware of the essential contradiction of the pledges given by his government. In a memorandum of August 1919, he pointed out that Britain and France had promised to set up national governments in the Near East, based on the free choice of the people. But in Palestine, "we do not propose even to go through the form of consulting the wishes of the present inhabitants of the country."

The Four Great Powers are committed to Zionism. And Zionism, be it right or wrong, good or bad, is rooted in age-long traditions, in present needs and future hopes of far profounder import than the desires and prejudices of the 700,000 Arabs who now inhabit that ancient land.

With astonishing insouciance, Balfour concluded that "so far as Palestine is concerned, the Powers had made no statement of fact that is not admittedly wrong, and no declaration of policy which, at least in the letter, they have not always intended to violate."[2] This was not the stuff of which clear, focused administration is made.

From 1917 until July 1920, Palestine and Jerusalem were under British military control (the Occupied Enemy Territories Administration). The military governor was Lieutenant Colonel Ronald Storrs, who had played a key role in the 1916 Arab uprising. His first duty was to repair the ravages of war in the city. The sewage system had failed, there was no clean water, and the roads were no longer viable. The British were much occupied by the responsibility of administering the holy places, and Storr, a civilized, cultivated man who loved Jerusalem, set up the Pro-Jerusalem Society, composed of the religious leaders of all three faiths and the local notables, to protect its historic sites. The society organized the repairs and renovation of public buildings and monuments; it also financed proposals for urban planning and preserving ancient sites by raising money abroad. One of its most useful rulings ordained that all new buildings in the city must use the local pinkish stone, a directive that is still followed and has helped to preserve the beauty of Jerusalem.

There were tensions, however. The Arabs had not been officially informed about the Balfour Declaration, but the news had been leaked. They were, not surprisingly, suspicious and alarmed. They noted that Hebrew was beginning to be introduced in official notices, along with English and Arabic, and that Jewish bureaucrats and translators were employed by the administration. But they still hoped that the British would acknowledge the justice of their cause. At least, they retained a certain hegemony in the municipal council, which Storrs had reestablished in January 1918. It had six members, two from each religious community, but the mayor was Muslim. Storrs's first appointment to the mayoralty was Musa Kasim al-Husaini: he now had two deputies, one Jewish and one Christian. The Jews were not entirely happy with this arrangement, since they formed 50 percent of the city's population. They were also irritated when it became apparent that the Arab mayors were using the mayoralty as a political platform from which to fight the Balfour Declaration.

There were also rumblings from abroad. The Vatican expressed its concern that Jerusalem, now conquered by the British, should remain in Christian hands. It would be tragic if "the most holy sanctuaries of the

Christian religion were given to the charge of non-Christians."[3] In 1919 the King-Crane Report, commissioned by the new League of Nations, concluded that the Balfour Declaration should not be implemented. Instead, Palestine should be joined with Syria in a united Arab state, under the aegis of a temporary mandatory power. Nothing came of this report, however. When the time came to consider it, President Wilson's attentions were elsewhere and it was quietly shelved.

The tension in the city erupted during the Nebī Mūsā celebrations on 4 April 1920. These had originally been initiated by the Mamluks when Jerusalem was endangered by the Western Crusaders. Since Allenby, the new Crusader, had arrived in the city, the Arabs of Palestine were beginning to think that al-Quds was imperiled again. A new interest in the Crusades began to appear in the Arab world: Saladin, the Kurd, now became an Arab hero and the Zionists were seen as new Crusaders or at least as tools of the Crusading West.[4] The Nebī Mūsā processions had always been regarded as a symbolic way of taking possession of the Holy City, but this year the Muslim crowds broke ranks and stormed through the Jewish Quarter. The Arab police sided with the rioters, the British troops did not come out to quell the violence, and the Jews were forbidden to organize their own defense. Most of the casualties were Jewish: nine people were killed and 244 injured. There had been communal tension and occasional violence in Jerusalem for many years, but the 1920 riots showed that this had taken a terrible turn for the worse. It also created a rift between the Jews and the British. The Zionists immediately blamed Storrs and the administration for the pogrom: they had revealed their partiality for the Arabs. Henceforth both Jews and Arabs would accuse the British of favoring the "other side."

In fact, there was an inherent contradiction in British policy. In April 1920, Britain became the Mandatory power in Palestine. Article 22 of the League of Nations Covenant insisted that Britain apply "the principle that the well-being and development [of the people of Palestine] form a sacred trust of civilization." But the British were also to implement the Balfour Declaration and pave the way for the establishment of a Jewish National Home in Palestine. A Jewish Agency was to be set up as a public body to facilitate this and the development of the country in general (Article 4). The agency was also to work to "facilitate the acquisition of Palestinian citizenship by Jews" (Article 6) and to "facilitate Jewish immigration under suitable conditions" (Article 7). Was there no danger that these measures would prejudice the rights of "the non-Jewish communities" in Palestine?

The first civilian high commissioner to be appointed to Palestine, in July 1920, was Sir Herbert Samuel, who was himself Jewish. It seemed a hopeful sign to the Zionists and ominous to the Arabs. Samuel was committed to the Balfour Declaration, but throughout his five-year term of office he tried to reassure the Arabs. He told them that their land would never be taken away from them and that a Jewish government would never rule the Muslim and Christian Palestinian majority: "This is not the meaning of the Balfour Declaration."[5] But not only did these assurances fail to allay Arab fears, they antagonized the Jews. The White Paper of 1922, written by the British colonial secretary Winston Churchill, advanced a similar argument: there was no question of subjugating the Arab majority. The idea of the Balfour Declaration was simply to create a center *in* (but not in the whole of) Palestine where Jews could live as of right instead of on suffrance. Again, neither side was pleased, and the Arabs rejected the White Paper, though the Zionists accepted it in the hope of gaining more later.

In some ways, however, Jerusalem seemed to prosper under the Mandate. For the first time since the Crusades, it was the capital city of Palestine. During the 1920s, new garden suburbs, similar to those appearing in England, were appearing beyond the municipal borders around Jerusalem. Talpiot, Rehavia, Bayit Vegan, Kiryat Moshe, and Beit Hakerem were Jewish neighborhoods with parks, open spaces, and individual gardens. They had been established to the west of the Old City. A new commercial center was built to the west of the Old City walls on land bought from the Greek Orthodox patriarchate: its main street was named after Eliezar Ben-Yehuda, the philologist who had revived the use of Hebrew as a modern, spoken language. A second commercial center was also starting up at the Maḥaneh Yehudah Market. But there were also elegant Arab suburbs in West Jerusalem at Talbieh, Katamon, and Ba'ka, as well as to the north of the city at Sheikh Jarrah, Wadi al-Joz, and the American Colony. An important day for Jerusalem was the opening of the Hebrew University on Mount Scopus. Lord Balfour came to preside: it was his one and only visit to Palestine. Throughout the ceremony, tears poured openly down his cheeks. Yet he did not seem to notice that the streets of Arab Jerusalem were shuttered and silent and that black flags of mourning hung in the *sūq*.[6]

New leaders had emerged in Jerusalem. One of Samuel's first appointments was Ḥajj Amin al-Husaini to the post of muftī. This appalled the Zionists, since Husaini was an extreme Arab nationalist who had taken a leading role in the 1920 riots. Samuel probably hoped to neutralize Ḥajj Amin by co-opting him, yet like most of the British he was also genuinely impressed by the young man. Courteous, reserved, and dignified, the new muftī did not seem like a rabble-rouser. The following year he was appointed president of the Supreme Muslim Council, a new body which supervised all the Islamic institutions in Palestine. He made this a base from which to fight the Balfour Declaration, starting a building and renovation program on the Ḥaram which he funded by means of a large-scale propaganda campaign. The Zionists were dreaming of rebuilding their Temple, the muftī claimed, and this would inevitably threaten the Muslim shrines on the Ḥaram. These accusations seemed fantastic to the Zionist leaders, most of whom had no interest whatever in the Temple and were not even much moved by the Western Wall. But Husaini's fears were not entirely without foundation, as we can see today.

The appointment of Husaini tended to polarize the Arabs of Jerusalem into two opposing camps. The radicals gravitated toward the muftī, while the moderates grouped themselves around the new mayor, Raghib al-Nashashibi, who was opposed to Zionism but believed in cooperating with the authorities whenever possible. Samuel did seem ready to acknowledge that Jerusalem was a predominantly Islamic city. The municipal council had been expanded and now consisted of four Muslims, three Christians, and three Jews; the mayor continued to be a Muslim. But Samuel had also extended the franchise to allow more Jews to vote. By trying to be fair to both sides, the high commissioner satisfied neither. The Zionists and Arabs had mutually exclusive plans for Palestine and Jerusalem, and conflict was inevitable.

The Zionists naturally had their own heroes and luminaries. The Palestinians did not need to create a new mythology and ideology to fuel their struggle. Palestine was their home; they had lived for centuries in al-Quds, celebrating its holiness. There was no need for them to write books about their land and city: did a man find it necessary to write passionate poems to a beloved wife? But the Zionists did have to attach themselves to Palestine. They had been driven to the country by the desire to find a place of their own in an alien, hostile world. Yet *aliyah* was often a wrenching, painful experience. Most of the new pioneers left the country during the 1920s: life was hard and the place was strange. It did not seem like their homeland. To root themselves spiritually in the land, they needed more than a cerebral ideology, and their ideologues turned instinctively to the old spiritual geography of Kabbalah. The originally secular movement acquired a mystical dimension.

The main protagonist of this Zionistic Kabbalah did not live in Jerusalem, nor did he focus on the Holy City. A. D. Gordon, who had been initiated into Kabbalah in Russia, made the *aliyah* at the quite advanced age of forty-six.[7] At his *kibbutz* in Degania he worked in the fields alongside the young pioneers, with his flowing white beard. He found the migration to Palestine very difficult: he was bitterly homesick for Russia and found the Near Eastern landscape of Palestine alien. Yet in working on the soil, he had experienced what would, he said, in previous times have been called a revelation of the Shekhinah. He felt that he had returned to that primal wholeness which had so often characterized the experience of God in Jerusalem but which had come to Gordon in the Galilee. Jews had lived a wretched and unnatural life in the Diaspora, Gordon taught the young pioneers in his poems and lectures. Landless and cut off from the soil, they had perforce immured themselves in the urban life of the ghetto. But, more important, they had been alienated from both God and themselves. Like Judah Halevi, Gordon believed that the Land of Israel (Eretz Yisrael) had been creative of the uniquely Jewish spirit. It had revealed to them the clarity, infinity, and luminosity of the divine, and it was this that made them truly themselves. Separated from this source of being, they had become damaged and fragmented. Now, in immersing themselves in the land's towering holiness, they had the duty of creating themselves anew. "Every one of us is required to refashion himself," Gordon wrote, "so that the unnatural, defective, splintered person within him may be changed into a natural, wholesome human being who is true to himself."[8] But there was also a hint of aggression in Gordon's mysticism: Jews must reestablish their claim to the land by what he called the Conquest of Labor. Physical toil would return Jews to themselves

The first task of these Zionist settlers in the Negev was to erect a barbed-wire fence around their new kibbutz when they founded it in 1946. Labor Zionism was positive for Jews, but despite its socialist ethic it excluded the Arab population of Palestine. Even A. D. Gordon described the Arabs as "filthy," "degraded," and "contemptible."

and restore Palestine to its true owners, who alone could respond to its holiness.

In ancient times, Jews had sought a similar return to a primal harmony in their Temple in Jerusalem. But Gordon taught the Zionists that the Shekhinah was no longer to be found on Mount Zion but in the fields and mountains of Galilee. In the old days, *avodah* had meant the Temple service: for Gordon, *avodah* was physical labor. A smaller number of Zionists, however, were expecting the imminent return to the Temple Mount. Marginalized and rather ridiculed by the secular leaders of Labor Zionism, religious Zionists formed a group which they called "Mizrachi." They saw Jerusalem as the center of the world in a more conventional sense. Their leader was Rabbi Abraham Isaac Kook, who became the chief rabbi of the Ashkenazim in Jerusalem in 1921. Most Orthodox Jews were strongly opposed to the whole Zionist enterprise, but Kook supported the movement. He believed that the secular Zionists were helping to build God's kingdom even though they did not realize it. The return to the land would inevitably lead them back to Torah. A Kabbalist, Kook believed that the balance of the whole world had been damaged while the Jews had been separated from Palestine. The divinity had been hidden away in synagogues and yeshivas in the Diaspora, which was polluted with the impurity of the gentile world. Now the whole universe would be redeemed: "All the civilizations of the world will be renewed by the renaissance of our spirit. All quarrels will be resolved and our revival will cause all life to be luminous with the joy of fresh birth."[9] Indeed, the Redemption had already begun. Kook could already see, in his mind's eye, the rebuilt Temple revealing the divinity to the world:

> Here stands the Temple upon its foundation, to the honour and glory of all peoples and kingdoms, and here we joyfully bear the sheaves brought forth by the land of our delight, coming, our wine presses filled with grain and wine, our hearts glad over the goodness of this land of delight, and here before us appear the priests, holy men, servants of the Temple of the Lord God of Israel.

This was not a distant dream: "We shall see them again on the mountain of the Lord in the near future, and how shall our hearts swell to see these priests of the Lord and these Levites at their holy service [*avodah*] and at their wonderful singing."[10] It was not a vision that was calculated to bring great joy to the Palestinian Muslims of Jerusalem, however. In his lifetime, Rabbi Kook was generally seen as an eccentric figure: it is only in our own day that his ideas have come into their own.

Under Lord Plumer, who succeeded Herbert Samuel in 1925, Palestine was apparently peaceful. The Jewish community—or Yishuv—was busily creating a para-state within the Mandate, with its own army (the Haganah), a parliamentary body of representatives from the *kibbutzim* and trade unions (the Histadruth), its own taxation, financial institutions, and a range of educational, cultural, and charitable organizations. The Jewish Agency, with its headquarters in Rehavia in West Jerusalem, had become the official representative body of the Yishuv to the British government. The Arabs were less organized, their opposition to Zionism split by the tension between the Husaini and Nashashibi factions. On both sides of the Zionist-Arab conflict, however, extremists were rising to the fore who were unwilling to accept the present situation any longer. Radical Zionists were attracted by the ideas of Vladimir Jabotinsky, while the muftī urged his followers to stop cooperating with the British.

The conflict entered a new and tragic phase in Jerusalem, a city which symbolized the deepest aspirations of both peoples. Since the arrival of the British, the Arabs had become worried about the Jewish devotions at the Western Wall. Montefiore and Rothschild had both tried to buy the prayer enclave during the nineteenth century, and since 1918 the Muslims noticed that the Jews had started to bring more furniture into their oratory: chairs, benches, screens, tables, and scrolls. It seemed as though they might be trying to establish a synagogue there, in violation of the status quo arrangements under the Ottomans. The muftī had alerted his followers to what he perceived as the Zionist design to gain control of the Ḥaram, seeing these Jewish developments at the wall as the thin end of the wedge. The trouble came to a head on the eve of Yom Kippur in 1928. The district commissioner of Jerusalem, Edward Keith Roach, was taking a walk around the Old City with Douglas Duff, the chief of police. They called in at the Muslim Sharī'ah Court in the Tanziqiyya Madrasah, and while they were looking down on the Jewish oratory below, Roach noticed that a bedroom screen had been put up to separate men and women during the services. The Muslim clerics in the room expressed great indignation, and Roach agreed that this was an infringement of the status quo. The next day, which was Yom Kippur, police were sent to remove the screen. They arrived at the most solemn part of the service, when the worshippers stood motionless in silent prayer. Insensitively assuming that the service must be over, the police began to take the screen away; the Jews reacted with dismay to this overt lack of respect. Throughout Palestine, the Yishuv furiously accused the British of blasphemy.

The muftī now began a new campaign, insisting that the status quo be rigidly observed. The wall was part of the Ḥaram and an Islamic *waqf* property. It was the place where Muḥammad had tethered Burāq after the Night Journey. Jews must not treat the holy place as though it belonged to them, bringing in furniture and blowing the *shofar* in such a way as to disturb Muslim prayer on the Ḥaram. They were there on suffrance only. The muftī also began a devotional offensive. There was a Sufi convent nearby, and the *dhikrs* suddenly became very loud and noisy indeed. The muezzin timed the call to prayer precisely to coincide with services at the wall. Finally, the Supreme Muslim Council opened the northern wall of the enclave so that it was no longer a cul-de-sac but now a thoroughfare linking the Maghribi Quarter to the Ḥaram purlieus: Arabs began to lead their animals through the alley during Jewish services and ostentatiously light cigarettes there during the Sabbath. Naturally the Jews of the Yishuv, secular and religious, became increasingly angry and resentful, especially when the British actually endorsed these outrageous arrangements.

In the summer of 1929 the Sixteenth Zionist Conference met at Zurich. On the first day, Jabotinsky made an inflammatory speech calling for the establishment of a Jewish state—not a "homeland"—on both sides of the Jordan. His proposal was soundly defeated by the more moderate Zionists at the conference, but the Arabs were still seriously alarmed. Then, on the Ninth of Av (15 August), a group of young disciples of Jabotinsky demonstrated outside the Mandatory Offices in Jerusalem and afterward proceeded to the Western Wall, where they waved the Jewish national flag and vowed to defend the wall to the

Hajj Amin al-Husaini (center), Grand Muftī of Jerusalem, with members of the Arab League. Uncompromising in his opposition to Zionism, he would ultimately discredit the Palestinian cause in the eyes of many observers by making overtures to Hitler during the Second World War.

death. On both sides tension grew. The next day, when the Arabs began to assemble in the Ḥaram for the Friday prayers, some of the muftī's supporters invaded the Jewish oratory at the wall. This time the police quelled the riot. But later, a tragic incident sparked a major confrontation. A Jewish boy kicked a football into an Arab garden, and during the ensuing brawl the child was killed. Zionists demonstrated angrily at his funeral, and on 22 and 23 August, crowds of Palestinian peasants began to arrive in Jerusalem with clubs and knives. Some even had firearms. The muftī did nothing to dispel the pent-up fury. In his Friday sermon that weekend he said nothing that could actually be called incitement, but afterward the mob rushed from the Ḥaram and started to attack every Jew they met. Again, the British refused to allow the Jews to retaliate in kind, and the British police force, which had been reduced by Lord Plumer, was unable to deal with this crisis adequately. Violence broke out all over Palestine. By the end of August, 133 Jews had been killed and 339 injured. The British police had killed 110 Arabs, and six more had died in a Jewish counterattack near Tel Aviv.

The Western Wall riots led inevitably to an escalation of tension on both sides. Superficially, the Arabs won their fight for the wall. The Shaw Commission appointed to investigate the matter confirmed the status quo arrangements that had been made by the Ottomans. Jews could bring their ritual articles into the prayer enclave, but the scrolls, menorahs, and Arks must not exceed a prescribed size, the *shofar* must not be blown at the wall, and there could be no singing. The Muslims were also forbidden to hold their noisy *dhikrs* and to lead their animals through the area during Jewish services. But it was a hollow victory. Zionism became a more radical, desperate struggle when Hitler came to power. Refugees began to come to Palestine from Germany and Poland in greater numbers than ever before. The old gradualist policies of the Zionists no longer seemed adequate, and more Jews in the Diaspora—though not in the Yishuv—began to veer toward Jabotinsky's Revisionist Party. Radical Jewish groups—some of whom were inspired by the works of Rabbi Kook—were even more extreme and began to form militant organizations. They were not interested in the socialist ideals of Ben Gurion. Their heroes were Joshua and King David, who had used force to establish the Jews in Palestine. The most important of these right-wing groups was the Irgun Zvei Leumi. But still in Palestine only about 10 to 15 percent of the Yishuv inclined to the right. Ben Gurion continued to urge a policy of restraint, realizing that Hitler's rabidly anti-Semitic policies might well help the Zionist cause.

The Arabs were extremely alarmed by the rise in Jewish immigration during the 1930s. They accused the Zionists of exploiting the German danger to further their cause. They asked why they should suffer the loss of their country because of the anti-Semitic crimes of Europe. It was an entirely valid and unanswerable question. Arab anxiety was understandable. In 1933, Jews had constituted only 18.9 percent of the population; by 1936 the percentage had risen to 27.7. Arabs also felt that stronger measures were necessary. More radical parties now started to appear in the Arab camp, though at this stage they were still controlled by the notables: the Defence Party, the Reform Party, and the Pan-Arab Istiqlal. Some of the Palestinians began to join guerrilla organizations to fight the British and the Zionists. In November 1935, Sheikh al-Qassam's guerrillas led a revolt against the British near Jenin during which the sheikh was killed: he became one of the first martyrs for Palestine. In 1936 the Arab Higher Committee was established in Jerusalem under the presidency of the muftī, consisting of the leaders of the new parties. On both sides, therefore, more extreme counsels were beginning to prevail, and Zionists and Arabs were arming themselves for the final confrontation.

Yet despite the growing tension in the city, Jerusalem continued to flourish and develop. Such famous landmarks as the King David Hotel, the imposing YMCA building opposite, the post office, and the Rockefeller Museum began to appear outside the walls. Jerusalem was rapidly expanding far beyond the borders of the metropolitan area. The British had therefore established an extensive Jerusalem Sub-District, which included the new Jewish and Arab suburbs surrounding the Old City. If Jews had begun to pour into Palestine in greater numbers, the Arab population of Jerusalem had also increased. Jews were in a majority within the municipality; there were now 100,000 Jews to 60,000 Arab Muslims and Christians. But in the Sub-District, the Arabs constituted just over half the total population and owned 80 percent of the property. In particular the large middle-class Arab suburbs in West Jerusalem had grown, and others had developed: Katamon, Musrarah, Talbiyeh, Upper and Lower Ba'ka, the Greek and German colonies, Sheikh Jarrah, Abu Tor, Mamillah, Nebī Dāᶜūd, and Sheikh Badr all contained a good deal of valuable Arab real estate. (See map.) Many of these Arab districts were situated in West Jerusalem, which is today a predominantly Jewish area.

Arab discontent exploded into outright civil disobedience during the general strike of 1936. Then came the Arab rebellion against the British from 1936 to 1938, during which Jerusalem suffered greatly. Arab mobs demonstrated angrily, a bomb in a Jewish religious school killed nine children, and forty-six Jews were killed in other terrorist attacks. At one point in 1938, Palestinian rebels briefly seized control of the city. During this crisis, the Zionist leadership still urged a policy of restraint, but the Irgun staged bomb and terrorist attacks in which forty-eight Arabs lost their lives. During the rebellion, Jerusalem lost its place as the leader of the resistance to Zionism. The muftī and the Arab Higher Committee were exiled by the British, and in exile the muftī gravely damaged the Palestinian cause abroad by allying himself with Hitler. In Palestine the leadership passed to the rural sheikhs, who were prepared to use more ruthless methods.

As the violence flared, the British tried to find a solution to the question of Palestine. In 1937 the Peel Committee recommended the partition of the country. There would be a Jewish state in the Galilee and on the coastal plain, but the remaining territory, including the Negev,

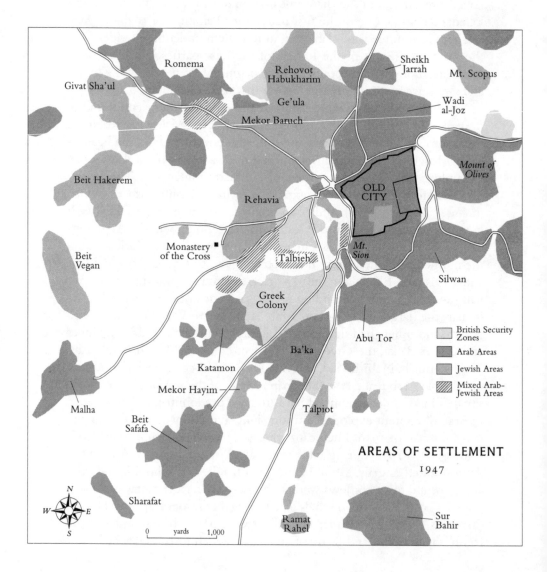

AREAS OF SETTLEMENT
1947

should go to the Arabs. The commissioners also decided that the Jerusalem municipality and Sub-District should form a *corpus separatum,* under the permanent control of the British Mandate. Henceforth most of the plans devised for Palestine by the international community tried to keep Jerusalem out of the conflict to make sure that the holy places— "a sacred trust of civilization," as the Peel commissioners put it—should remain accessible to all.[11] After much anguished debate, the Zionists accepted the Peel plan, though they submitted their own partition scheme. This Zionist plan proposed to divide Jerusalem: the Jews would take the new suburbs of West Jerusalem, while the Old City and East Jerusalem should stay under Mandatory control.

The Arabs said no to the Peel Plan, and in 1939 their firm stand seemed to have paid off. Poised as it was on the brink of the Second World War, the British government was persuaded by several Arab states to reduce its commitment to Zionism. A new White Paper severely limited Jewish immigration to Palestine and revoked the Peel partition plan. Instead, it envisaged the creation of an independent state in Palestine ruled jointly by Arabs and Jews. It was a severe blow to the Zionists, who would never trust Britain again, even though they had no choice but to support Britain against Nazi Germany during the war. This did not apply to the Revisionists, however, who began to mount terrorist attacks against the British. Abraham Stern's Lehi Group, founded in 1940, saw no difference between the British and the Nazis. Two of the leading Jewish terrorists would—years later—become prime ministers of the State of Israel. When Stern was killed during a raid in 1942, Yitzhak Shamir became the leader of the "Stern Gang." In 1942, Menachem Begin, a fervent admirer of Jabotinsky, entered Palestine illegally and became one of the leaders of the Irgun. Even the moderate Ben-Gurion became more radical in 1942 when the first news of the Nazi death camps reached Palestine. The old gradualist policies of the Yishuv were abandoned. There was no more talk of a "homeland." Zionists were convinced that only a fully Jewish state could provide a safe haven for the Jews, even if that meant evicting the Arabs from the country.[12]

The postwar period saw an escalation of terrorism on both sides. The British stubbornly refused the Zionists' request to permit 100,000 refugees, survivors of the Nazi camps, to enter Palestine. In retaliation, the Irgun blew up a wing of the King David Hotel, one floor of which was used as a British army headquarters. Ninety-one people were killed and forty-five more wounded. In these last years the British seem to have lost control. The Mandate had begun in confusion, and by 1947 the British officials in Palestine were demoralized, exasperated, and frustrated by the attempt to implement an impossible policy. They had become harmful to the country and had to go. On 11 February 1947, Foreign Secretary Ernest Bevin referred the Mandate to the new United Nations Organization. The UN then produced a new partition plan, which divided the country in a way that was more advantageous to the Jews than the Peel Plan. There was to be a Jewish state (in eastern Galilee, the Upper Jordan Valley, the Negev, and the coastal plain) and an Arab state in the rest of the country. The *corpus separatum* of Jerusalem and Bethlehem would come under international control. On 29 November 1947, the General Assembly of the UN voted to accept this plan, and a special committee was set up to work out a statute for the international zone of Jerusalem. The Arabs refused to accept the decision of the UN, but the Zionists accepted it with their usual pragmatism. They also agreed to the internationalizing of Jerusalem. In the plan that they had put forward to the United Nations in August 1946, Jerusalem had again been placed in a *corpus separatum*. Possession of the Holy City was not, at this stage, regarded as essential to the new Jewish state.

Fighting broke out in Palestine almost immediately after the passing of the UN resolution. On 2 December an Arab mob streamed through the Jaffa Gate and looted the Jewish commercial center on Ben Yehuda Street. Irgun retaliated by attacking the Arab suburbs of Katamon and Sheikh Jarrah. By March 1948, 70 Jews and 230 Arabs had been killed in the fighting around Jerusalem, even before the official expiration of the British Mandate. Syrian and Iraqi troops entered the country and blocked the roads to Jerusalem. The Haganah began to execute the military Plan Dalet, which eventually succeeded in creating a corridor to Jerusalem from the coast. The British refused to intervene. In February 1948, the Arabs had besieged some of the Jewish suburbs in West Jerusalem, which remained cut off from the rest of the country until the Haganah opened the roads. On 10 April the war entered a new phase when the Irgun attacked the Arab village of Deir Yassin, three miles to the west of Jerusalem: 250 men, women, and children were massacred and their bodies mutilated. On 13 April the Arabs attacked a convoy carrying Irgun terrorists, who had been wounded at Deir Yassin, to the Mount Scopus Medical Center, killing forty innocent Jewish medical staff.

Before the departure of the British on 15 May 1948, the Irgun attacked Jaffa and the specter of Deir Yassin caused the seventy thousand Arab inhabitants of the city to flee. It marked the beginning of the Palestinians' exodus from their country. Some of the refugees sought a haven in Jerusalem. On 26 April, the Haganah began to attack the large, middle-class Arab suburbs in West Jerusalem. Raiding parties cut telephone and electricity wires. Loudspeaker vans drove through the streets blurting such messages as "Unless you leave your houses, the fate of Deir

Yassin will be your fate!" The inhabitants were finally forced out of their homes by the end of May, many taking refuge in the Old City. In early May, UN representatives had arrived in Jerusalem to set up the international administration but were ignored by the British and by both of the contending parties. On 14 May, Ben-Gurion held a ceremony in the Tel Aviv Museum to proclaim the birth of the new State of Israel. When the British finally left the next day, Jewish forces were poised to attack the Old City but were held back by the last-minute arrival of the Jordanian Arab Legion, which set up a military administration in the walled city and in East Jerusalem.

When a truce was arranged by the UN in July 1948, the city had been divided between Israel and Jordan. The city remained split in two, along the western wall of the Old City and a band of wrecked, deserted territory which became No Man's Land. (See map.) The two thousand inhabitants of the Jewish Quarter had been expelled from the Old City and were dispatched across the new border into West Jerusalem, which was now controlled by the Israelis. The thirty thousand Arab residents of West Jerusalem had therefore lost their homes to the State of Israel. The Old City was now crammed with refugees from Jaffa, Haifa, the suburbs, and the villages around Jerusalem. Neither Israel nor Jordan would agree to leave the Jerusalem area. They refused to heed the UN General Assembly Resolution 303, which called upon them to evacuate Jerusalem and its environs to allow it to become an internationalized *corpus separatum* as originally planned. On 15 November, King ʿAbdallah of Jordan was crowned King of Jerusalem in the Old City by the Coptic bishop; East Jerusalem and the West Bank of the Jordan were declared Jordanian territory, and on 13 December the Jordanian parliament approved the union of Jordan and Palestine. There was to be no question of creating an independent Palestinian state. Instead, the king gave the inhabitants of East Jerusalem and the West Bank Jordanian citizenship. Neighboring Arab states protested vehemently against this Jordanian occupation but eventually had to accept it as a *fait accompli*. On the Israeli side, Ben-Gurion announced on 13 December that the Knesset and all the government offices, except for the ministries of defense, police, and foreign affairs, should move to West Jerusalem. On 16 March 1949, Israel and Jordan signed a formal agreement accepting the armistice lines as the legitimate borders between their two states. The UN continued to regard the Israeli/Jordanian occupation of Jerusalem as illegal, but after April 1950 took no further action on the Jerusalem question.

Jerusalem, which had so frequently been divided internally, was now split by more than one and a half miles of fortified frontier, barbed-wire fences, and massive defensive ramparts. On both sides, snipers shot into

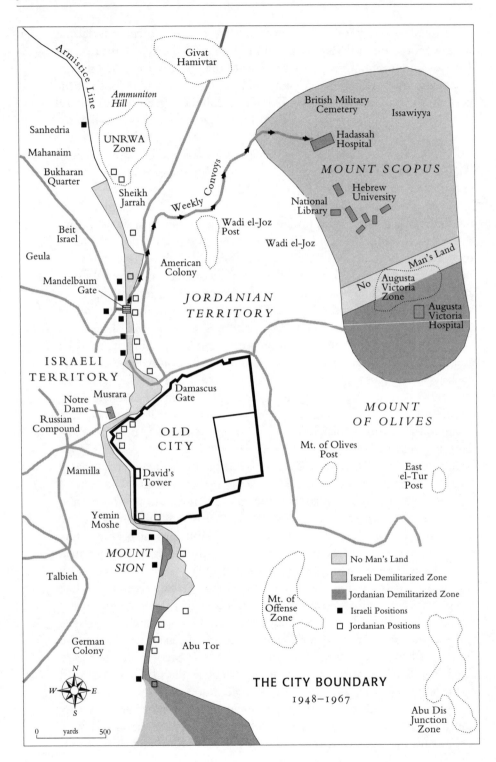

Givat Hamivtar

British Military Cemetery

Issawiyya

Ammuniton Hill

Sanhedria

UNRWA Zone

Hadassah Hospital

Mahanaim

MOUNT SCOPUS

Bukharan Quarter

Sheikh Jarrah

Weekly Convoys

Hebrew University

National Library

Beit Israel

Wadi el-Joz Post

Wadi el-Joz

Geula

No Man's Land

Mandelbaum Gate

American Colony

JORDANIAN TERRITORY

Augusta Victoria Zone

Augusta Victoria Hospital

No Man's Land

ISRAELI TERRITORY

Musrara

Damascus Gate

Notre Dame

Russian Compound

MOUNT OF OLIVES

OLD CITY

Mt. of Olives Post

Mamilla

East el-Tur Post

David's Tower

Yemin Moshe

No Man's Land

Israeli Demilitarized Zone

Jordanian Demilitarized Zone

MOUNT SION

Israeli Positions

Jordanian Positions

Talbieh

Mt. of Offense Zone

German Colony

Abu Tor

THE CITY BOUNDARY

1948–1967

N
W   E
S

0   yards   500

Abu Dis Junction Zone

the territory on the other side of No Man's Land. In No Man's Land itself were deserted streets and 150 abandoned buildings. Three of the gates of the Old City (New Gate, Jaffa Gate, and Zion Gate) were blocked and reinforced by concrete walls. The city was now divided by tall barriers and tens of thousands of mines laid by both sides. The only crossing point was the so-called Mandelbaum Gate, an open roadway near a house belonging to a Mr. Mandelbaum, which now had a barrier across it. Only clergy, diplomats, UN personnel, and a few privileged tourists were permitted to go from one side to the other. The Jordanians required most tourists to produce baptismal certificates—to prove they were not Jewish—before they were allowed to enter East Jerusalem from Israel. They could not then go back into Israel but had to return to their countries of origin from Jordan. Water, telephone, and road systems were split in two. Mount Scopus became a Jewish enclave in Jordanian Jerusalem; and the buildings there of the Hadassah hospital and the Hebrew University were closed and placed under UN auspices; an Israeli convoy was let through the lines to supply the tiny Scopus garrison. On both sides, territory and buildings which had belonged to the enemy before 1948 were entrusted to a custodian. The inhumanity of the partition was especially poignant in the village of Bayt Safafa, which was split in two: one half of the village in Israeli territory, the other in Jordan. Families and friends were cut off from one another, though occasionally people got permission to hold weddings or other gatherings at the railway line on the border and the villagers would shout news and gossip over the divide.

Article 8 of the Israeli-Jordanian Armistice Agreement provided for free access for Israeli Jews to the Western Wall, but Jordan refused to honor this unless Israel was willing to return the Arab suburbs in West Jerusalem. After years of pressure, Arab Christians from Israel were allowed to visit the Holy Sepulcher and the Nativity Church at Christmas and Easter, though not for longer than forty-eight hours. Each side accused the other of violating sacred sites: Israelis blamed Jordan for defiling the Jewish cemetery on the Mount of Olives and for destroying the synagogues in the Jewish Quarter of the Old City, which was now a camp for Palestinian refugees; Arabs complained bitterly of Israel's destruction of their historic cemetery at Mamilla, where many famous scholars, mystics, and warriors were buried.

Jordanian Jerusalem was plagued by many problems.[13] After the 1948 war, the Israelis had a state in Palestine that was significantly larger than that envisaged by the UN. Of all the surrounding Arab states, only Jordan had been able to prevent the advance of the Israeli forces. During the hostilities, some 750,000 Arabs of Palestine, terrified by reports of the

Deir Yassin atrocities, had fled the country. Many of these refugees settled in camps in the surrounding Arab states; none were permitted to
return to their towns and villages. Many Palestinians blamed Jordan for
depriving them of their independence: in Egypt, the muftī formed the
Palestine National Council as a government in exile. King ʿAbdallah
tried to court the influential Arab families, who had traditionally
opposed the muftī: many of them held government posts in Amman and
even had seats in the Jordanian parliament. As a result, many of the notables left Jerusalem to settle in Amman, which entirely altered the ambi-
ence of the city. Most of the Palestinians who remained in Jerusalem
were fiercely resentful of Amman. They were better educated and more
advanced than most of the Arabs on the East Bank and found their political subservience to Jordan intolerable. When the Jordanian government
was in trouble, there were often riots in Jerusalem, which became a center of Palestinian resistance to the Kingdom of Jordan. It often seemed to
the Arabs of al-Quds that having defied the world to gain possession of
the Holy City, King ʿAbdallah now was determined to run it down.

After 1948, Arab Jerusalem had received a serious wound. It had lost
its aristocracy, and to ensure that he had a power base in Jerusalem, the
king had encouraged the people of Hebron, who had supported Jordan,
to settle in al-Quds. The city had a huge refugee problem and had sustained severe damage during the war. Jordan's resources were stretched
to the limit, and the kingdom was not in a position to alleviate the distress of the thousands of uprooted Palestinians who now perforce
crowded into the Jerusalem area. Conditions in the Old City were
appalling for months after the war. Yet the king was also reluctant to
invest in a city which was a center of Palestinian nationalism. Often
ʿAbdallah gave preference to Nablus and Hebron over Jerusalem. Government offices were transferred from Jerusalem to Amman. The city's
relationship with the Jordanian government was not likely to improve
when, in April 1951, the king was assassinated at the entrance of the
Aqsā Mosque by the muftī's agents.

Yet Jordanian Jerusalem did recover. In 1953 the Aqsā Mosque was
restored and the Muslim Charitable Society for the Reconstruction of
Jerusalem was set up to found schools, hospitals, and orphanages. New
homes were built for the refugees during the 1950s on the Ophel hill
and in Wadi Joz, Abu Tor, and Sheikh Jarrah, though the Jordanians still
adhered strictly to the Master Plan for Jerusalem laid down during the
Mandate. To preserve the beauty of the city, they did not develop the
western slopes of Mount Scopus or the Kidron Valley. A new commercial district was built to the north and east of the Old City, and in 1958
a major renovation of the Ḥaram was begun. Gradually the economy

improved. Jerusalem had never been an industrial center, and the government tended to deflect plans to build factories and plants in the Jerusalem outskirts to Amman. But Jordan did develop the tourist industry in Jerusalem, which provided 85 percent of the income of the West Bank. In 1948 there had been only one modern hotel in East Jerusalem, but by 1966 there were seventy. There was a great disparity between rich and poor in the city, but by the 1960s, Arab Jerusalem had sufficiently recovered from its violent partition to become a pleasant place to live. The middle and upper classes probably enjoyed a higher standard of living than their Israeli counterparts in West Jerusalem. Yet the process of modernization had not destroyed the historical and traditional atmosphere of Jerusalem, which retained its distinctively Arab character.

The status of the city also improved. The Israelis were busily making West Jerusalem their capital, in defiance of the international community, and had moved the Knesset there. Jordan felt that it had to respond. In July 1953 the Jordanian cabinet met in Jerusalem for the first time and shortly afterward the whole parliament was convened there. Local government achieved stability when Rauhi al-Khatib became the mayor of Arab Jerusalem at the beginning of 1957. An ascetic, and an excellent administrator, he was able to resolve some of the tension that existed between Amman and the Palestinian nationalists. Relations with Jordan improved, and by 1959 Jerusalem's status was upgraded from *baladiyya* (municipality) to *amāna* (trusteeship), making it equivalent to Amman. King Hussein announced that Jerusalem was the second capital of the Kingdom of Jordan and planned to build a palace to the north of the city.

On the other side of the border, West Jerusalem had many similar problems. In December 1949, Ben Gurion had announced that it was essential for the Jewish state to maintain a presence in Jerusalem:

> Jewish Jerusalem is an organic and inseparable part of the State of Israel, as it is an inseparable part of the history of Israel and the faith of Israel and of the very soul of our people. Jerusalem is the heart of hearts of the State of Israel.[14]

The old Zionist indifference to the city had gone, once the fortunes of war had placed West Jerusalem in Israeli hands. During the 1950s the Israelis had embarked on a determined policy to make West Jerusalem the working capital of Israel, even though it was not recognized as such in international law. The UN still maintained that Jerusalem should be a *corpus separatum,* and the Catholic countries in particular were opposed to the partition of the city. In 1952, Yitzhak Ben-Zvi became the second President of Israel and moved his offices from Tel Aviv to Jerusalem, leaving the foreign ambassadors to Israel with a problem. If they presented their letters of credence to the president in West Jerusalem, this

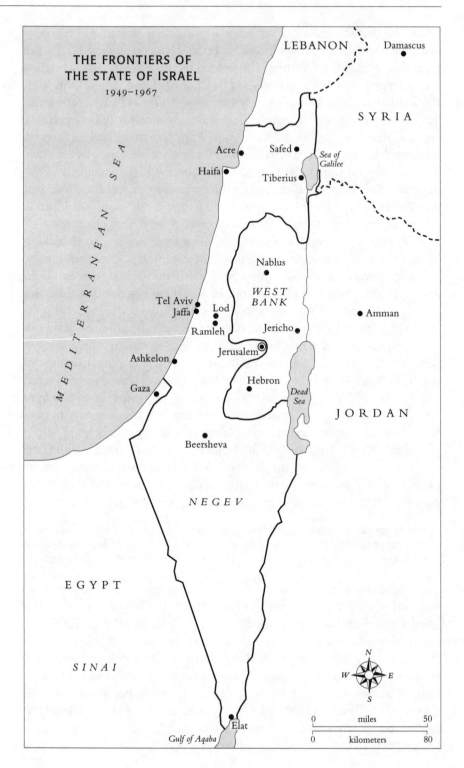

THE FRONTIERS OF
THE STATE OF ISRAEL
1949–1967

LEBANON

Damascus

SYRIA

MEDITERRANEAN SEA

Acre

Safed

Sea of Galilee

Haifa

Tiberius

Nablus

WEST BANK

Tel Aviv

Jaffa

Lod

Ramleh

Jericho

Amman

Jerusalem

Ashkelon

Hebron

Dead Sea

Gaza

JORDAN

Beersheva

NEGEV

EGYPT

SINAI

N

W   E

S

Elat

Gulf of Aqaba

0	miles	50
0	kilometers	80

amounted to a tacit recognition of the city as Israel's capital. Some ambassadors did begin to come to West Jerusalem, however, and when in 1954 the British and American ambassadors both presented their letters to President Ben-Zvi in Jerusalem it was clear that the boycott was being slowly eroded. Both Britain and the United States declared that they still adhered to the UN resolutions, but the Israelis had won the first round, despite these official disclaimers. Then Foreign Minister Moshe Sharett moved his main office to West Jerusalem, and the foreign diplomats also gradually got used to calling on him there. By 1967 nearly 40 percent of the foreign diplomatic establishments of Israel had moved from Tel Aviv to West Jerusalem.

Yet, having defied the world to make West Jerusalem its capital, the Israeli government tended to neglect it. Most members of the Knesset were kibbutzniks who were not very interested in cities and had no clear urban policy.[15] West Jerusalem did not benefit as much as it should have from its capital status. Its economic growth was rather less than that of Israel as a whole. The chief employers were the government and the Hebrew University, but they were not wealth-producing institutions. Not surprisingly, tourism did not flourish in West Jerusalem: by far the most interesting sites were on the other side of No Man's Land. There was little light industry, and prices were high. Some parts of Jewish Jerusalem had become slums, filled with Jewish refugees from the Arab countries who had been ejected after the creation of the State of Israel and the Palestinian exodus in 1948. From the first these Oriental, Sephardi Jews were never fully accepted by the Ashkenazi Zionist establishment. They were housed in the more dangerous districts of Jerusalem, close to No Man's Land, where they were within range of Arab snipers. There was inequality and resentment in the Jewish city.

Indeed, West Jerusalem seemed to have neither coherence nor unity. It was a series of suburbs, each one inhabited by a distinct ethnic or religious group which had its own self-contained life. It was also a city divided against itself: Sephardim against Ashkenazim, religious against secular Jews. The Orthodox, still passionately opposed to the State of Israel, had taken to standing at the street corners of their districts on the Sabbath to throw stones at the passing cars of Israelis who were violating the Sabbath rest. Cut off from its heart in the Old City, West Jerusalem made no sense. It was a dead end, isolated from the rest of Israel and surrounded on three sides by Arab territory. The city had become little more than a terminus of roads from the coast. It was "at the end of a narrow corridor with roads leading nowhere," recalled its future mayor Teddy Kollek. "Half the time you drove down a road or a side street, you ran into a sign reading STOP! DANGER! FRONTIER AHEAD!"[16]

In his classic novel *My Michael,* set in this period, the Israeli writer Amos Oz presented a similar picture of West Jerusalem as a city which had received a mortal wound. Its suburbs were scattered, solitary fortresses, lost and overwhelmed by the menacing landscape where the jackals howled. It was a city of walls, ruins, and waste plots, which continued to shut out its Jewish inhabitants.[17] "Can one ever feel at home in Jerusalem, I wonder, even if one lives here for a century?"[18] asks Oz's heroine, Hannah. It might seem like an ordinary city, but then you would turn a corner and suddenly be brought up against the void:

> If you turn your head, you can see in the midst of all this frantic building a rocky field. Olive trees. A barren wilderness. Thick overgrown valleys. Criss-crossing tracks worn by the tread of myriad feet. Herds grazing round the newly built Prime Minister's office.[19]

The ancient city had been built as an enclave of safety against the demonic realm of the desert, where no life was possible. Now the citizens of West Jerusalem were brought up against the wilderness at every turn and had to face the possibility of mortality and extinction in this dangerous terrain. Indeed, Jerusalem itself had been invaded by the wilderness—the ancient nightmare—and barely seemed to exist. "There is no Jerusalem," says Hannah.[20]

The State of Israel could not escape the void. Had it not been for Hitler's Nazi crusade against the Jews, the Zionist enterprise might never have succeeded. The guilt, shock, and outrage occasioned by the discovery of the camps had evoked a wave of sympathy for the Jewish people after the Second World War which certainly helped the Zionist cause. But how were the Jewish people and the State of Israel to come to terms with the catastrophe of the six million dead? Holy cities had originally been regarded as havens which would protect their inhabitants from destruction. Now the Jews had faced extinction in a near-fatal encounter with the demonic imagination of Europe, which had for centuries been hagridden by fearful fantasies of Jews. In the myth of the Exodus, the people of ancient Israel had recalled their journey through the nothingness of the desert to safety in the Promised Land. The modern State of Israel was a similar creation out of the fearful annihilation of the camps. But in West Jerusalem, the nothingness of the desert could still be found in the midst of the city: there was no escaping the void left by the Holocaust. The Zionist leaders had come largely from Poland, Russia, and Eastern Europe. They had built their state for Jews who were now mostly dead. One of the chief shrines of this new secular Jewish Jerusalem was the Holocaust Memorial at Yad Vashem, with its Ohel Yizkor ("Memorial Tabernacle"), inscribed with the names of twenty-two of the largest death camps. It was little wonder that the New Jerusalem created by the Israelis made no sense. Eventually, as we shall see in the following chapter, some Jews would find healing in the old myths and spirituality of sacred space.

The Palestinians had also suffered, however. They had lost their homeland and been wiped off the map. They too had suffered a form of annihilation. The inhabitants of both East and West Jerusalem were shocked to the core during these years of Jerusalem's partition. Palestinians had to come to terms with their catastrophe; the Israelis had to face the unwelcome fact that they, the victims of Europe, had, in their desperate quest for survival, fatally injured another people. Both tried to blot out the other. Arab tourist maps represented West Jerusalem as a blank white space. In Israel, Prime Minister Golda Meir once famously stated: "The Palestinians do not exist." The educational system encouraged this mutual denial on both sides of the city. Neither Israeli nor Arab children were taught sufficiently about the history, language, and culture of "the other side."[21] Israelis also resented Arab Jerusalem: yet again they were debarred from the city. Centuries before, Jews had mourned their lost Temple from the Mount of Olives. The Israelis could not do this, because the mount was in Jordanian hands. On feast days there would be prayers on top of a high building on Mount Sion, where it was possible to catch a glimpse of the Jewish Quarter.

But in fact the two halves of the city were turning away from each other.[22] Despite the tension with the Jordanian government, Arab Jerusalem was naturally oriented eastward, toward Amman and away from the unacceptable reality of West Jerusalem. In Jewish Jerusalem too, the Israelis inevitably turned away from the perils of No Man's Land toward Tel Aviv and the coast. The districts beside the border were slums, inhabited by the Sephardim. The commercial center at Ben Yehuda Street, which was within range of the snipers, was neglected. New districts were built on hilltops in the west. The geographical center of West Jerusalem was now the Hebrew University at Givat Ram, which was far to the west of the pre-1948 municipality. Had this state of affairs continued, Jerusalem would indeed have become two separate cities, separated by the desolate terrain and barbed wire of No Man's Land.

In 1965, Teddy Kollek, a member of Ben Gurion's new Rafi Labor Party, became the mayor of West Jerusalem. He was as good an influence as Rauhi al-Khatib on the other side of the border. Stocky, blond, and forceful, he gave the Israeli municipality a greater stability than it had ever had before. He tried to correct the orientation of West Jerusalem toward the coast. There had been plans to move the municipality building, which was right on the border, to the western part of the new

Jerusalem. Kollek decided to stay where he was: it would be wrong for the mayor and his council to be seen to be abandoning the Oriental Jews in their border slums. But above all, "by staying put on the frontier, we were giving expression to our faith in the eventual unification of Jerusalem."[23] In the midst of the division and anomie of the postwar years, Israelis had started to dream of wholeness and integration.

In May 1967, Israel and the Arab countries faced the dreadful possibility of another war. On 13 May the Soviets informed Syria that Israel was about to invade its territory. They were probably misinformed, since

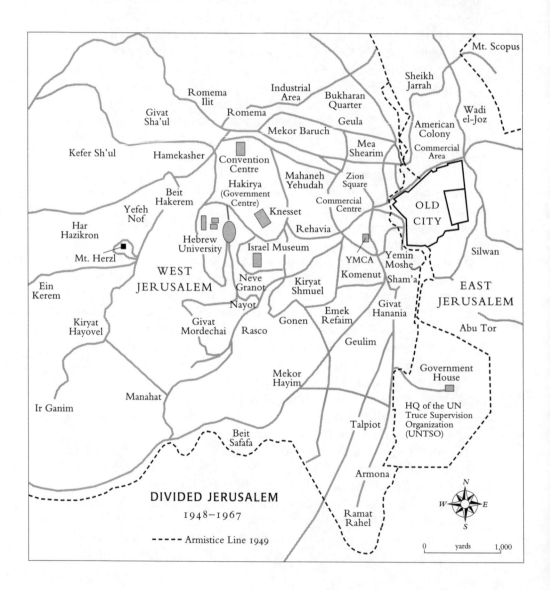

DIVIDED JERUSALEM

1948–1967

- - - - Armistice Line 1949

there was no plan for such an invasion. But President Gamal Abdal Nasser of Egypt responded to this supposed threat against his Arab ally by moving 100,000 troops into the Sinai Peninsula and closing the Gulf of Aqaba to Israeli shipping. On 30 May, King Hussein of Jordan signed a military agreement with Egypt, even though Israel begged Jordan to keep out of the conflict. The great powers took sides, and a terrifying confrontation loomed. The Israelis had to listen to Nasser's impassioned rhetoric, threatening to drive them all into the sea. Inevitably they expected the worst and awaited a new holocaust.

Yet, three weeks before the outbreak of the war, West Jerusalem enjoyed an idyllic day when the Israelis had decided to hold the Independence Day celebrations there. It was a special event: the anniversary was calculated according to the Hebrew calendar, so it rarely coincided with the civil date of 14 May, as it did in 1967. There could be no military parade, since the United Nations would not permit any arms or military equipment in Jerusalem. Instead Kollek suggested that the municipality sponsor a song by the well-known lyricist Naomi Shemer. "Jerusalem of Gold" became an instant hit. It was a love song to a tragic city "with a wall in its heart," but it also revealed the Israeli blind spot:

> *How the cisterns have dried up:*
> *The marketplace is empty*
> *No one visits the Temple Mount in the Old City.*

The city was far from deserted, however: Its *sūq* was crowded and selling luxury goods that were not available to the Israelis in West Jerusalem. The Ḥaram was thronged with pious visitors and worshippers. The song assumed—yet again—that the Palestinians of Arab Jerusalem did not exist. Meanwhile on the other side of West Jerusalem, Rabbi Zvi Yehuda Kook, the son of the eminent chief rabbi of Jerusalem during the British Mandate, was preaching the annual sermon to celebrate the birth of the State of Israel at the Merkaz Harav Yeshiva. Suddenly his quiet voice rose and he seemed to his audience to be possessed by the spirit of prophecy. At one point, he sobbed aloud, yearning for the towns torn from the living body of Eretz Yisrael on the West Bank: Jerusalem, the Temple Mount, Hebron, Shechem, and Jericho—cities and places that were sacred to the Jewish people. It was a sin, the rabbi wept, to leave these holy sites in the hands of the *goyim*.[24] Three weeks later the rabbi was hailed as a true prophet of Israel when the tanks of the Israeli Defence Forces rolled into all these West Bank towns and reunited the Jewish people with the Old City of Jerusalem.

18

ZION?

THE HOLOCAUST that so many of the Israelis had feared in 1967 never, of course, came to pass. On 5 June, the Israeli forces launched a preemptive strike against the United Arab Republic and destroyed almost the entire Egyptian air force on the ground. This inevitably drew Jordan into the war, though Jerusalem was inadequately defended by, perhaps, as few as five thousand troops. They did their best—two hundred died in the defense of the Holy City—but on Wednesday, 7 June, the Israel Defense Forces circled the Old City and entered it through the Lion Gate. Most Israeli civilians were still in their air-raid shelters, but news of the capture of Arab Jerusalem spread by word of mouth and a wondering crowd gathered at the Mandelbaum Gate.

Meanwhile, Israeli soldiers and officers had one objective: to get as quickly as possible to the Western Wall. The men ran through the narrow winding streets and rushed over the Ḥaram platform, scarcely giving the Muslim shrines a glance. It was not long before seven hundred soldiers with blackened faces and bloodstained uniforms had crowded into the small enclave that had been closed to Jews for almost twenty years. By 11:00 a.m., the generals began to arrive, bringing General Shlomo Goren, chief rabbi of the IDF, who had the honor of blowing the *shofar* at the wall for the first time since 1929. A platoon commander also sent a jeep to bring Rabbi Zvi Yehuda Kook to the wall. For all these men, whatever their theological beliefs, confronting the wall was a profound—even shocking—religious experience. Only a few days earlier they had faced the possibility of annihilation. Now they had unexpectedly made contact once again with what had become the most holy place in the Jewish world. Secular young paratroopers clung to the

"This is how the conquering generation looks." Exultant Jewish soldiers pose before the Dome of the Rock after their conquest of the Old City in 1967.

stones and wept: others were in shock, finding it impossible to move. When Rabbi Goren blew the *shofar* and began to intone the psalms, atheistic officers embraced one another, and one young soldier recalled that he became dizzy; his whole body burned. It was a dramatic and unlooked-for return that seemed an almost uncanny repetition of the old Jewish myths. Once again the Jewish people had struggled through the threat of extinction; once again they had come home. The event evoked all the usual experiences of sacred space. The wall was not merely a historical site but a symbol that reached right down to the core of each soldier's Jewish identity. It was both Other—"something big and terrible and from another world"[1]—and profoundly familiar—"an old friend, impossible to mistake."[2] It was *terrible* but *fascinans*; holy, and at the same time a mirror image of the Jewish self. It stood for survival, for continuity, and promised that final reconciliation for which humanity yearns. When he kissed the stones, Avraham Davdevani felt that past, present, and future had come together: "There will be no more destruction and the wall will never again be deserted."[3] It presaged an end to violence, dereliction, and separation. It was what other generations might have called a return to paradise.

Religious Jews, especially the disciples of Rabbi Kook the Younger, were convinced that the Redemption had begun. They recalled their rabbi's words only a few weeks earlier and became convinced that he had been divinely inspired. Standing before the wall on the day of the conquest, Rabbi Kook announced that "under heavenly command" the Jewish people "have just returned home in the elevations of holiness and our own holy city."[4] One of his students, Israel "Ariel" Stitieglitz, left the wall and walked on the Haram platform, heedless of the purity laws and the forbidden areas, bloodstained and dirty as he was. "I stood there in the place where the High Priest would enter once a year, barefoot, after five plunges in the *mikveh*," he remembered later. "But I was shod, armed, and helmeted. And I said to myself, 'This is how the conquering generation looks.' "[5] The last battle had been fought, and Israel was now a nation of priests; all Jews could enter the Holy of Holies. The whole Israeli army, as Rabbi Kook repeatedly pointed out, was "holy" and its soldiers could step forward boldly into the Presence of God.[6]

The phrase "Never again!" now sprang instantly to Jewish lips in connection with the Nazi Holocaust. This tragedy had become inextricably fused with the identity of the new state. Many Jews saw the State of Israel as an attempt to create new life in the face of that darkness. Memories of the Holocaust had inevitably surfaced in the weeks before the Six-Day War, as Israelis listened to Nasser's rhetoric of hatred. Now that they had returned to the Western Wall, the words "Never again!" were immediately heard in this new context. "We shall never move out of here,"[7] Rabbi Kook had announced, hours after the victory. General Moshe Dayan, an avowed secularist, stood before the wall and proclaimed that the divided city of Jerusalem had been "reunited" by the IDF. "We have returned to our most holy places; we have returned and we shall never leave them."[8] He gave orders that all the city gates be opened and the barbed wire and mines of No Man's Land be removed. There could be no going back.

Israel's claim to the city was dubious. At the end of the Six-Day War, Israel had occupied not only Jerusalem but the West Bank, the Gaza Strip, the Sinai Peninsula, and the Golan Heights. (See map.) Neither the Hague Regulations of 1907 nor the Geneva Conventions of 1949 supported Israel's claim. It was no longer permissible in international law

FRONTIERS, 1967

Territory occupied
by Israel during the
Six-Day War

*MEDITERRANEAN
SEA*

LEBANON

◉ Damascus

SYRIA

*Golan
Heights*

*West
Bank*

Amman
◉

Jerusalem ◉

Gaza

*Dead
Sea*

El Arish

I S R A E L

J O R D A N

SUEZ CANAL

Nile River

SINAI

◉ Cairo

Suez ●

E G Y P T

E G Y P T

Gulf of Suez

Gulf of Aqaba

S A U D I
A R A B I A

N
W   E
S

0   miles   50
0   kilometers   80

*Strait
of Tiran*

RED SEA

permanently to annex land conquered militarily. Some Israelis, including
Prime Minister Levi Eshkol, were willing to give back these Occupied
Territories to Syria, Egypt, and Jordan in return for peace with the Arab
world. But there was never any question in 1967 of returning the Old
City of Jerusalem to the Arabs. With the conquest of the Western Wall,
a transcendent element had entered Zionist discourse, once so defiantly

secular. Even the most diehard atheists had experienced their Holy City as "sacred." As Abba Eban, Israel's delegate to the United Nations, expressed it, Jerusalem "lies beyond and above, before and after, all political and secular considerations."[9] It was impossible for Israelis to see the matter objectively, since at the wall they had encountered the Jewish soul.

On the evening of the conquest, Levi Eshkol announced that Jerusalem was "the eternal capital of Israel."[10] The conquest of the city had been such a profound experience that, to many Jewish people, it seemed essentially "right": it was a startling evocation of myths and legends that had nurtured Jews for centuries in the countries of the Diaspora. As Kabbalists would put it, now that Israel was back in Zion, everything in the world and the entire cosmos had fallen back into its proper place. The Arabs of Jerusalem could scarcely share this view of the matter, however.[11] The Israeli conquest was not a "reunification" of the city but its occupation by a hostile power. The bodies of about two hundred soldiers of the Arab Legion lay in the streets; Arab civilians had been killed. Israeli reserve units were searching the houses for weapons and arrested several hundred Palestinians whose names were on a prepared wanted list. The men were marched away from their families, convinced they were going to their deaths. When they were allowed to return that evening, they were greeted with tears as though they had escaped from Hades. Looters had followed behind the troops: some of the mosques had been robbed and the Dead Sea Scrolls had been removed from the Palestine Archaeological Museum. The Palestinian inhabitants of the Old City and East Jerusalem locked themselves fearfully in their houses until Mayor Rauhi al-Khatib walked through the streets with an Israeli officer persuading them to come out and reopen the shops so that people could buy food. On the morning of Friday, 9 June, half the Arab municipal workers reported for duty, and, under the direction of the mayor and his deputy, they began to bury the dead and repair the water systems. They were later joined by Israeli municipal workers in East Jerusalem.

But this cooperation did not last. On the very day of the conquest, Teddy Kollek approached Dayan and promised that he would personally supervise the clearing of No Man's Land, a task of great danger and complexity. Like Dayan, he saw the importance of "creating facts" that would establish a permanent Jewish presence in the Holy City, so that there could be no question of vacating it at the behest of the international community. On the night of Saturday, 10 June, after the armistice had been signed, the 619 inhabitants of the Maghribi Quarter were given three hours to evacuate their homes. Then the bulldozers came in and reduced this historic district—one of the earliest of the Jerusalem *awqāf*—to rubble. This act, which contravened the Geneva Conventions, was supervised by Kollek in order to create a plaza big enough to accommodate the thousands of Jewish pilgrims who were expected to flock to the Western Wall. This was only the first act in a long and continuing process of "urban renewal"—a renewal based on the dismantling of historic Arab Jerusalem—that would entirely transform the appearance and character of the city.

On 28 June, the Israeli Knesset formally annexed the Old City and East Jerusalem, declaring them to be part of the State of Israel. This directly contravened the Hague Convention, and there had already been demands from the Arab countries, the Soviet Union, and the Communist bloc for Israel to withdraw from occupied Arab Jerusalem. Britain had told the Israelis not to regard their conquest of the city as permanent. Even the United States, always kindly disposed toward Israel, had warned against any formal legislation to change the status of the city, since it could have no standing in international law. The Knesset's new Law and Administration Ordinance of 28 June carefully avoided using the word "annexation." Israelis preferred the more positive term "unification." At the same time, the Knesset enlarged the boundaries of municipal Jerusalem, so that the city now covered a much wider area. The new borders skillfully zigzagged around areas that had a large Arab population and included plenty of vacant land for new Israeli settlements. (See map.) This ensured that the voting population of the city would remain predominantly Jewish. Finally, on the day after the annexation, Mayor al-Khatib and his council were dismissed in an insulting ceremony. They were driven by the military police from their homes to the Gloria Hotel near the Municipality Building. There Yaakov Salman, the deputy military governor, read a prepared statement that curtly informed the mayor and his council that their services were no longer required. When al-Khatib asked to have the statement in writing, Salman's assistant, David Farhi, scribbled the Arabic translation on a paper napkin belonging to the hotel.[12] The ceremony had been designed to bid a formal farewell to the mayor, who had cooperated so generously with the Israelis, and to explain the new legal status of Jerusalem to him in person. But this was not done. The bitterness of the former mayor and councillors was not due to their dismissal: that, they knew, was inevitable. What offended them was the humiliating and undignified form of the ceremony, which did not reflect the importance of the occasion. Some members of the Israeli government had thought that the Arab municipality should continue in some form to work side by side with—or under—the municipality of West Jerusalem. Teddy Kollek would have none of this. The Arabs, he said, would "get in the way of my work." "Jerusalem is one city," he told the press, "and it will have one municipality."[13]

At midday on 29 June, the barriers dividing the city came down and Arabs and Israelis crossed No Man's Land and visited the "other side." The Israelis, the conquerors, rushed exuberantly into the Old City, buying everything in sight in the *sūq,* shocked to find that the Arabs had been enjoying luxury food and foreign imports that had been unavailable in West Jerusalem. The Arabs were more hesitant. Some took the keys of their old houses in Katamon and Bakʾa, which they had kept in the family since 1948, and stood staring at their former homes. Some Jews were embarrassed when Arabs knocked at the door and politely asked permission to look inside their family houses. Yet there was no violence, and at the end of the day the Israelis generally believed that the Arabs were beginning to accept the "reunification" of the city. In fact, as events would prove, they were simply in shock. There was no such acceptance. Al-Quds was a holy place to the Arabs too. The Palestinians had suffered their own annihilation in 1948, and now they were beginning to be eliminated from Jerusalem as well. Their former mayor, Rauhi al-Khatib, calculated that by 1967 there were about 106,000 Arab Jerusalemites in exile as a result of the wars with Israel.[14] Now, because of the new gerrymandered boundaries, Arabs would account for only about 25 percent of the city's population. Palestinians were suffering their own exile, homelessness, and separation. They could not share the Kabbalistic dream: as far as they were concerned, everything was in the wrong place. This experience of dislocation and loss would make Jerusalem more precious than ever to the Arabs.

The international community was also unwilling to accept Israel's annexation of Jerusalem. In July 1967, the United Nations passed two resolutions calling upon Israel to rescind this "unification" and to desist from any action that would alter the status of Jerusalem. The war and its aftermath had at last drawn the attention of the world to the plight of the dispossessed Palestinian refugees; now thousands more had fled Israel's Occupied Territories and languished in the camps in the surrounding Arab countries. Finally, on 22 November 1967, the United Nations Security Council passed Resolution 242: Israel must withdraw from the territories it had occupied during the Six-Day War. The sovereignty, territorial integrity, and political independence of all the states in the region must be acknowledged.

But most of the Israelis and many Jews in the Diaspora had been caught up in their new passion for sacred space and could not recognize the validity of these resolutions. Since the destruction of the Temple, Jews had gradually relinquished the notion of physically occupying Jerusalem.

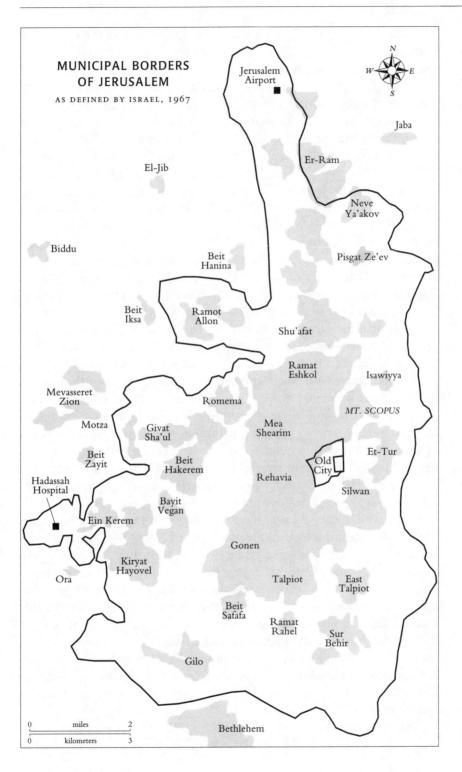

MUNICIPAL BORDERS
OF JERUSALEM

AS DEFINED BY ISRAEL, 1967

Jerusalem
Airport

N
W · E
S

Jaba

Er-Ram

El-Jib

Neve
Ya'akov

Biddu

Beit
Hanina

Pisgat Ze'ev

Beit
Iksa

Ramot
Allon

Shu'afat

Ramat
Eshkol

Isawiyya

Mevasseret
Zion

Romema

MT. SCOPUS

Motza

Givat
Sha'ul

Mea
Shearim

Et-Tur

Beit
Zayit

Beit
Hakerem

Old
City

Hadassah
Hospital

Rehavia

Silwan

Bayit
Vegan

Ein Kerem

Ora

Kiryat
Hayovel

Gonen

Talpiot

East
Talpiot

Beit
Safafa

Ramat
Rahel

Sur
Behir

Gilo

0   miles   2
0   kilometers   3

Bethlehem

The sacred geography had been internalized, and many of the Orthodox still regarded the State of Israel as an impious human creation. But the dramatic events of 7 June were beginning to change this. The situation was not unlike the transformation of the Christian idea of Jerusalem in the time of Constantine. Like the Jews, the Christians had thought that they had outgrown the devotion to holy places, but the unexpected reunion with the tomb of Christ had almost immediately led to a new appreciation of Jerusalem as a sacred symbol. Like the Jews, the Christians of the fourth century had recently emerged from a period of savage persecution. Like the Jews again, they had just acquired an entirely new political standing in the world. The Nazi catastrophe had inflicted a wound that was too deep to be healed by more cerebral consolations. The old myths—an ancient form of psychology—could reach to a deeper, less rationally articulate level of the soul. This new Jewish passion for the holiness of Jerusalem could not be gainsaid by mere United Nations directives nor by logically discursive arguments. It was powerful not because it was legal or reasonable but precisely because it was a myth.

In Constantine's time, the tomb of Christ had been discovered during one of the first-recorded archaeological excavations in history. The process of digging down beneath the surface to a buried and hitherto inaccessible sanctity was itself a powerful symbol of the quest for psychic healing. Fourth-century Christians, no longer a persecuted, helpless minority, were having to reevaluate their religion and find a source of strength as they struggled—often painfully—to build a fresh Christian identity. Freud had been quick to see the connection between archaeology and psychoanalysis. In Israel too, as the Israeli writer Amos Elon has so perceptively shown, archaeology became a quasi-religious passion. Like farming, it was a way for the settlers to reacquaint themselves with the Land. When they found physical evidence in the ground of Jewish life in Palestine in previous times, they gained a new faith in their right to the country. It helped to still their doubts about their Palestinian predecessors. As Moshe Dayan, the most famous of Israel's amateur archaeologists, remarked in an interview, Israelis discovered their "religious values" in archaeology. "They learn that their forefathers were in this country three thousand years ago. This is a value. . . . By this they fight and by this they live."[15] In this pursuit of patriotic archaeology, Elon argues, "it is possible to observe, as of faith or of Freudian analysis, the achievement of a kind of cure; men overcome their doubts and fears and feel rejuvenated through the exposure of real, or assumed, but always hidden origins."[16]

The exhibition hall built to house the Dead Sea Scrolls, which had been captured during the Six-Day War, shows how thoroughly the

Israelis had adapted the old symbols of sacred geography to their own needs. Its white dome has become one of the most famous landmarks of Jewish Jerusalem, and, facing the Knesset, it challenges the Christian and Muslim domes that have in the past been built to embody rival claims to the Holy City. As Elon points out, Israelis tend to regard the scrolls as deeds of possession of this contested country. Their discovery in 1947, almost coinciding with the birth of the Jewish state, seemed perfectly timed to demonstrate the prior existence of Israel in Palestine. The building is known as the Shrine of the Book, a title that draws attention to its sacred significance. The womblike interior of the shrine, entered through a dark, narrow tunnel, is a graphic symbol of the return to the primal peace and harmony which, in the secular society of the twentieth century, has often been associated with the prenatal experience. The phallic, clublike sculpture in the center of the shrine demonstrates the national will to survive—but also, perhaps, the mating of male and female elements that has frequently characterized life in the lost paradise. The holy place had long been seen as a source of fertility, and in the shrine, says Elon, "archaeology and nationalism are united as in an ancient and rejuvenative fertility rite."[17]

But, like the fierce theology of Qumran, this quest for healing and national identity had an aggressive edge. From the first, Moshe Dayan made it clear that Israel would respect the rights of Christians and Muslims to run their own shrines. Israelis would proudly compare their behavior with that of the Jordanians, who had denied Jews access to the Western Wall. On the day after the conquest, the military governor of the West Bank held a meeting to reassure all the Christian sects of Jerusalem, and on 17 June, Dayan told the Muslims that they would continue to control the Ḥaram. He made Rabbi Goren remove the Ark that he had placed on the southern end of the platform. Jews were forbidden by the Israeli government to pray or hold services on the Ḥaram, since it was now a Muslim holy place. The Israeli government has never retreated from this policy, which shows that the Zionist conquerors were not entirely without respect for the sacred rights of their predecessors in Jerusalem. But Dayan's decision immediately enraged some Israelis. A group calling itself the Temple Mount Faithful was formed in Jerusalem. They were not especially religious. Gershom Solomon, one of their leaders, was a member of Begin's right-wing Herut party and was moved more by nationalist than by religious aspirations. He argued that Dayan had no right to prohibit Jewish prayers on the Temple Mount, since the Holy Places Bill guaranteed freedom of access to all worshippers. On the contrary, since the Temple Mount had been the political as well as the religious center of ancient Israel, the Knesset, the President's

Residence, and government offices should move to the Ḥaram.[18] On the major Jewish festivals, the Temple Mount Faithful have continued to pray on the Ḥaram and are regularly ejected by the police. A similar mechanism had inspired the demolition of the Maghribi Quarter: in the eyes of Israel's right, the Jews' return to their holy place involved the destruction of the Muslim presence there.

This became clear in August 1967, when Rabbi Goren and some yeshiva students marched onto the Ḥaram on the Ninth of Av and, after fighting off the Muslim guards and the Israeli police, held a service which ended with Rabbi Goren blowing the *shofar.* Prayer had become a weapon in a holy war against Islam. Dayan tried to reassure the Muslims and closed down the rabbinate offices that Goren had established in one of the Mamluk *madāris.* Just as the agitation was subsiding, however, Zerah Wahrhaftig, minister for religious affairs, published an interview in which he claimed that the Temple Mount had belonged to Israel ever since David had purchased the site from Araunah the Jebusite;[19] Israel had, therefore, a legal right to demolish the Dome of the Rock and the Aqṣā Mosque. The minister, however, did not actually recommend this course of action, since Jewish law stated that only the Messiah would be permitted to build the Third Temple. (It will be recalled that, even though any such new shrine would technically be the fourth Jewish temple, the services had never been interrupted during the construction of Herod's building, so that it too was known as the Second Temple.)

On the day of the conquest, it had seemed to the soldiers who had crowded up to kiss the Western Wall that a new era of peace and harmony had begun. But in fact Zion, the city of peace, was once again the scene of hatred and discord. Not only had the return to the Jewish holy places led to a new conflict with Islam, it had also revealed the deep fissures within Israeli society. Almost immediately the new plaza created by the destruction of the Maghribi Quarter became the source of a fresh Jewish quarrel. Kollek's hasty action appeared to have been not only inhumane but an aesthetic mistake. The confined space of the old narrow enclave had made the Western Wall look bigger than it was. Now it appeared little higher than the walls of the adjoining Tanziqiyya Madrasah or Suleiman's city wall, which were now clearly visible. "Its gigantic stones seemed to have shrunk, their size diminished," a disappointed visitor remarked on the day of the opening. The wall at first glance seemed to be "fusing with the stones of the houses to the left." The intimacy of the narrow enclave had gone. The new plaza no longer "permitted the psychic affinity and the feeling that whoever comes here is, as it were, alone with his Maker."[20]

Soon a most unholy row had erupted between the religious and the secular Jews about the management and conduct of the site.[21] The wall was now a tourist attraction and visitors no longer came solely to pray. The ministry for religious affairs, therefore, wanted to fence off a new praying area directly in front of the wall. Secular Israelis were furious: how dare the ministry deny other Jews access to the wall? They were as bad as the Jordanians! Soon the rabbis were also in bitter conflict about the actual extent of this holy space. Some argued that the whole of the Western Wall was sacred, as well as the plaza in front of it. They started excavating the basements of the Tanziqiyya Madrasah, establishing a synagogue in one of the underground chambers and declaring every cellar or vault they cleared to be a holy place. Naturally Muslims feared that this religious archaeology was radically—and literally—undermining their own sacred precincts. But the rabbis were also trying to liberate Jerusalem from the Jewish secularists, pushing forward the frontiers of sanctity into the godless realm of the municipality. This struggle intensified when the Israeli archaeologist Benjamin Mazar started to excavate the southern end of the Ḥaram. This again alarmed the Muslims, who were afraid that he would damage the foundations of the Aqṣā Mosque. Religious Jews were also enraged at this unholy penetration of sacred space, especially when Mazar edged around the foot of the Western Wall and inched his way up to Robinson's Arch. Within a few months of the "unification" of the city, there was a new "partition" at the Western Wall. The southern end was now a historic, "secular" zone; the old praying area was the domain of the religious; and in between was a neutral zone—a new No Man's Land—which consisted of a few remaining Arab houses. Once these had been demolished, each side looked covetously at the space between them. On two occasions in the summer of 1969, the worshippers actually charged through the barbed-wire fence in order to liberate this neutral area for God.

The Israeli government attempted to keep the peace at the holy places but was fighting its own war for the possession of Jerusalem, resorting to the time-honored weapon of building.[22] Almost immediately, the Israelis began to plan new "facts" to bring more Jews into Jerusalem by constructing a security zone of high-rise apartment blocks around East Jerusalem. These were built at French Hill, Ramat Eshkol, Ramot, East Talpiot, Neve Yakov, and Gilo. (See map.) Several miles farther east, on the hills leading down to the Jordan Valley, an outer security belt was constructed at Ma'alot Adumin. Building proceeded at frantic speed, mostly on expropriated Arab land. Strategic roads linked one settlement to another. The result was not only an aesthetic disaster—the skyline of Jerusalem having been spoiled by these ugly blocks—but an effective destruction of long-established Arab districts. During the first ten years after the annexation, the Israeli government is estimated to have seized some 37,065 acres from the Arabs. It was an act of conquest and destruction. Today only 13.5 percent of East Jerusalem remains in Arab hands.[23] The city had indeed been "united," since there was no longer a clear distinction between Jewish and Arab Jerusalem, but this was not the united Zion for which the prophets had longed. As the Israeli geographers Michael Romann and Alex Weingrod have remarked, the militaristic terminology of the planners, when they speak of "engulfing," "breaching," "penetration," "territorial domination," and "control," reveals their aggressive intentions toward the Arab population in the city.[24]

As they found themselves being squeezed out of al-Quds, the Arabs had to organize their own defense, and though they could do nothing to counter this building offensive, they managed to wrest some significant concessions from the government. In July 1967, for example, they refused to accept the *qāḍīs'* law which had been imposed on the Muslim officials in Israel proper. Nor would the *qāḍīs* of Jerusalem change their rulings to fit Israeli law on such matters as marriage, divorce, the *waqf,* and the status of women. On 24 July 1967 the *'ulamā'* announced that they were going to revive the Supreme Muslim Council, since it was against Islamic law for unbelievers to control Muslim religious affairs. The government responded by expelling some of its more radical Muslim opponents but in the end was forced to recognize, if only tacitly, the existence of the Supreme Muslim Council. Arabs also fought an effective campaign against the imposition of the Israeli educational system in Jerusalem, since it did not do justice to their own national aspirations, language, and history. Only thirty hours a year were devoted to the Qur'ān, for example, compared with 156 hours of Bible, Mishnah, and Haggadah. Students who matriculated from these Israeli schools would not be eligible to study at Arab universities. Eventually the government had to compromise and allow a parallel Jordanian curriculum in the city.

The Israelis were discovering that the Arabs of Jerusalem were not as malleable as the Arabs in Israel proper. In August they began a campaign of civil disobedience, calling for a general strike: on 7 August 1967 all shops, businesses, and restaurants closed for the day. Worse, extremist members of Yasir Arafat's Fatah established cells in the city and began a terror campaign. On 8 October three of these cells tried to blow up the Zion Cinema. On 22 November 1968, the anniversary of UN Resolution 202, a car bomb in the Maḥane Yehudah market killed twelve peo-

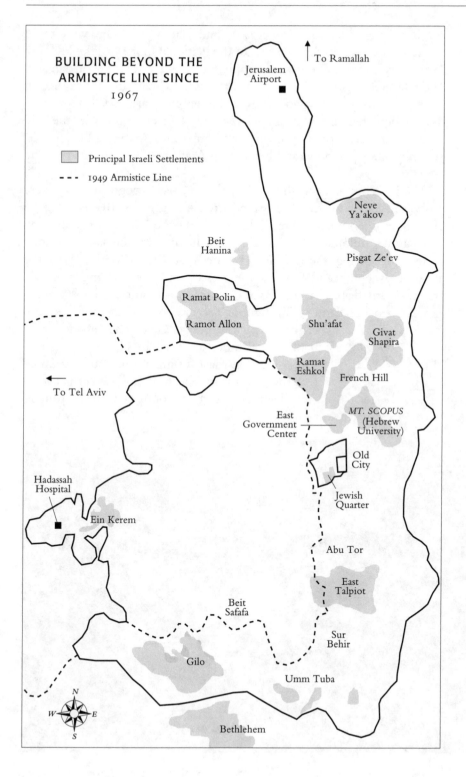

BUILDING BEYOND THE
ARMISTICE LINE SINCE
1967

☐ Principal Israeli Settlements
--- 1949 Armistice Line

To Ramallah

Jerusalem
Airport ■

Neve
Ya'akov

Pisgat Ze'ev

Beit
Hanina

Ramat Polin

Ramot Allon

Shu'afat

Givat
Shapira

Ramat
Eshkol

French Hill

To Tel Aviv

East
Government
Center

MT. SCOPUS
(Hebrew
University)

Old
City

Hadassah
Hospital

Jewish
Quarter

Ein Kerem ■

Abu Tor

East
Talpiot

Beit
Safafa

Sur
Behir

Gilo

Umm Tuba

N
W · E
S

Bethlehem

ple and injured fifty-four. In February and March 1969 there were more
bomb attacks: one in the cafeteria of the National Library of the Hebrew
University injured twenty-six people and did a great deal of damage.
West Jerusalem suffered more terrorist attacks than any other city in
Israel, and, perhaps inevitably, these led to Jewish reprisals. On 18 August
1968 when demolition charges exploded at several points in the city
center, hundreds of young Jewish men burst into Arab neighborhoods,
smashing shop windows and beating up Arabs they encountered on the
streets.

The Israeli public was shocked by this anti-Arab pogrom. They were
also dismayed by the depth of Arab hatred and suspicion that erupted on
21 August 1969 when a fire broke out in the Aqsā Mosque, destroying
the famous pulpit of Nūr ad-Dīn and licking up the large wooden
beams supporting the ceiling. Hundreds of Muslims rushed to the
mosque, weeping and flinging themselves into the burning building.
They screamed abuse at the Israeli firefighters, accusing them of spraying
gasoline on the flames. Throughout the city, Arabs demonstrated and
clashed with the police. Given the inflammatory
behavior of some Israelis in the Ḥaram, it is hardly
surprising that the Muslims immediately assumed
that the arsonist had been a Zionist. Yet it had in
fact been a disturbed young Christian tourist,

*By 1974 the new Jewish settle-
ments dominated the Jerusalem
skyline, surrounding the city like
the old Crusader castles. Once
again, Jerusalem had become a
fortress city, holding antagonistic
neighbors at bay.*

David Rohan of Australia, who had set fire to the mosque in the hope that it would hasten Christ's Second Coming. It took months before the government was able to allay Muslim fears and assure them that Rohan was indeed a Christian and not a Jewish agent and that Jews had no plans to destroy the shrines on the Ḥaram.

Yet during the next four years a sullen calm descended on Jerusalem. There were even signs that Israelis and Arabs were beginning to learn how to live with one another. After the death of Nasser in September 1970, the government gave permission for the Arabs of Jerusalem to hold a mourning procession for this enemy of the State of Israel. On Thursday, 1 October, the whole Arab population of the city assembled quietly and marched to the Ḥaram in perfect order. As agreed, there were no Israeli policemen on the streets, nor was there a single anti-Israeli placard in sight. Yet the Palestinians had not given up during these years of peace, as some Israelis hoped. They had adopted the policy of *sumud* ("steadfastness"), realizing that their physical presence in the city was their chief weapon. They would take advantage of the welfare and economic benefits that Israel was so keen to thrust upon them; they would continue to live in Jerusalem and beget children there. "We shall not give you the excuse to throw us out," one of the Palestinian leaders said. "By the mere fact of being there, we shall remind you every day that the problem of Jerusalem has got to be solved."[25]

In October 1973, Egypt and Syria launched a surprise attack on Israel on Yom Kippur, which changed the mood on both sides. This time the Arabs did much better, and, caught off guard, it took the IDF days to repel the attack. In Jerusalem the morale of the Palestinians improved, and they began to hope that the Israeli annexation of al-Quds might only be temporary. The Israelis had been shocked out of their complacency by this new revelation of their isolation in the Near East. This fear led to a new intransigence in Israel, especially among religious groups. Shortly after the war, disciples of Rabbi Kook founded the Gush Emunim ("Bloc of the Faithful").[26] Their love affair with the Israeli establishment was over: God had offered Israel a magnificent opportunity in 1967, but instead of colonizing the occupied territories and defying the international community, the government had merely tried to appease the *goyim*. The Yom Kippur War had been God's punishment and a salutary reminder. Secular Zionism was dead: instead, the Gush offered a Zionism of Redemption and Torah. After the war, its members began to establish settlements in the occupied territories, convinced that this holy colonization would hasten the coming of the Messiah. The chief focus of Gush activity was not Jerusalem, however, but Hebron, where Rabbi Moshe Levinger, one of the founding members, managed by skillful lobbying to get the Israeli government to found a new town at Kiryat Arba next to Hebron. There the settlers began to agitate for more prayer time in the Cave of the Patriarchs, where Jews were allowed to worship only at certain times. But Levinger was also determined to establish a Jewish base in the city of Hebron itself and to avenge the massacre of Jews there during the riots of 1929. Soon the place where Abraham was said to have genially encountered his God in human form would become the most violent and hate-ridden city in Israel.

When Menachem Begin's new Likud party ousted the Labor government and came to power in 1977, the hopes of the right soared, especially when the new government called for massive settlement on the West Bank. But then, to their horror, Begin, of all people, began to make peace with the Arab world. On 20 December, President Anwar al-Sadat of Egypt made his historic visit to Jerusalem, and the following year, he and Begin signed the Camp David Accords. Egypt recognized the State of Israel, and in return, Begin promised to withdraw from the Sinai Peninsula. This drew him into outright confrontation with the Israeli settlers, who had built the Jewish town of Yamit in the Sinai and fought to the last in an attempt to prevent its dismantling. New right-wing groups were formed to oppose the accords and to fight against the government.

In Jerusalem the new far-right activities centered increasingly on the Temple Mount. In 1978, Rabbi Shlomo Aviner founded the Yeshivat Ateret ha-Kohanim ("Crown of the Priests Yeshiva"), as an annex of Rabbi Kook's Merkaz Harav. One of its objectives was to Judaize the Old City. After the 1967 conquest, the government had restored the old Jewish Quarter, which, during the Jordanian period, had been a refugee camp. The desecrated synagogues were restored, the old damaged houses pulled down, and new houses, shops, and galleries built. In the eyes of the Ateret ha-Kohanim, this was not enough. Funded largely by American Jews, the yeshiva began to buy Arab property in the Muslim Quarter, and within ten years it owned more than seventy buildings.[27]

The chief work of the new yeshiva, however, was to study the religious meaning of the Temple.[28] Rabbi Aviner himself did not believe that Jews should build the Third Temple, a task reserved for the Messiah, but his deputy Rabbi Menachem Fruman wanted his students to be ready to undertake the Temple *avodah* when the Messiah did arrive—an eventuality he expected in the near future. He began to research the rules and techniques of sacrifice and instructed his students in this lore. Rabbi David Elboim began to weave the priests' vestments, following the minute—and frequently obscure—directions of the Torah.

Others believed that more decisive action was necessary. Shortly after Sadat's visit to Jerusalem, two Gush members, Yehuda Etzion and Menachem Livni, began to hold secret meetings with a Jerusalem Kabbalist called Yehoshua Ben-Shoshan. Gradually an underground movement was formed, whose chief object was to blow up the Dome of the Rock. This would certainly halt the peace process and would also shock Jews worldwide into an appreciation of their religious responsibilities. This spiritual revolution, they believed, would compel God to send the Messiah and the final Redemption. Livni, who was an explosives expert, calculated that they would need twenty-eight precision bombs to demolish the Dome of the Rock without damaging its surroundings. They amassed huge quantities of explosives from a military camp in the Golan Heights. But when the moment of decision arrived in 1982, the group could not find a rabbi to bless their enterprise, and since only Etzion and Ben-Shoshan were willing to go ahead without rabbinical sanction, the plan was shelved.

A religious spirit had emerged in Israel which fostered not compassion but murderous hatred. In 1980, Etzion's group was responsible for the plot to mutilate five Arab mayors on the West Bank in order to avenge the murder of six yeshiva students in Hebron. The plot was not entirely successful, since only two of the mayors were horribly crippled. The most complete incarnation of this new Judaism of hatred was Rabbi Meir Kahane. He had begun his career in New York, where he had formed the Jewish Defense League to avenge attacks made on Jews by black youths. When he arrived in Israel, Kahane had organized street demonstrations in Jerusalem in protest against the activities of Christian missionaries: his activities, he believed, were sanctioned by certain rabbinical pronouncements about the presence of *goyim* in the Holy Land. Finally, in 1975, Kahane had moved to Kiryat Arba and changed the name of his organization to Kach ("Thus!"—i.e., by force). His main objective now was to drive Arabs from the State of Israel. In 1980 he was briefly imprisoned for plotting to destroy the Dome of the Rock with a long-range missile.

The people who joined these far-right groups were not primitive or uneducated. Yoel Lerner, who was sent to prison in 1982 for planting a bomb in the Aqsā Mosque, was a graduate of the Massachusetts Institute of Technology and a professor of linguistics. After his release, Lerner began to campaign to restore the Sanhedrin to the Temple Mount. All these activities had a dangerously cumulative effect. More people were getting involved in nefarious activities, some of them holding official positions. At the end of March 1983, Rabbi Israel "Ariel" was arrested with thirty-eight yeshiva students on their way to the Ḥaram. Their intention was to reach the remains of the First Temple, under the Herodian platform, by means of an underground tunnel, to celebrate Passover there, and—perhaps—to establish a subterranean settlement. Their object was to force the Muslims to allow Jews to build a synagogue on the Ḥaram. Rabbi Meir Yehuda Getz, who was in charge of the Western Wall, also conducted secret investigations in the Ḥaram vaults and campaigned for a synagogue on the platform. Until 1984, when the Etzion plot to blow up the Dome of the Rock came to light, the idea of a Third Temple had been taboo. Like the Name of God, it was dangerous to speak of it or to give voice to plans for its rebuilding. But now that taboo was being eroded and people were becoming familiar with the idea as a plausible project. In 1984, "Ariel" founded the periodical *Tzfia* ("Looking Ahead") to discuss the Third Temple publicly. In 1986 he opened the Museum of the Temple in the Old City, where visitors are shown the vessels, musical instruments, and priestly vestments that have already been made. Many come away with the impression that the Jews are waiting in the wings. As soon as the Muslim shrines on the Ḥaram have been destroyed, by fair means or foul, they are ready to step onto Mount Zion and inaugurate a full-blown ceremonial liturgy. The implications are frightening. American strategists calculated that, in terms of the Cold War, when Russia supported the Arabs and America backed the Israelis, had Etzion's plot to blow up the Dome of the Rock succeeded, it could have sparked World War Three.

On 9 December 1987, exactly seventy years after Allenby's conquest of Jerusalem, the popular Palestinian uprising known as the *intifādah* broke out in Gaza. A few days later the hard-liner general Ariel Sharon moved into his new apartment in the Muslim Quarter of the Old City—a symbolic gesture that expressed the determination of the Israeli right-wing to remain in Arab Jerusalem. But by mid-January the *intifādah* had also erupted in East Jerusalem: Israeli troops used tear gas on the Ḥaram to disperse demonstrators. Although the *intifādah* was less intense in Jerusalem than in the rest of the Occupied Territories, there were disturbances and strikes in the city. The Israelis had to accept the fact that twenty years after the annexation of Jerusalem, the Palestinian inhabitants of al-Quds were in total accord with the rebels in the Territories. One practical consequence of the *intifādah* was that Jerusalem became two cities once again. This time there was no barbed wire, no mined No Man's Land between East and West Jerusalem. But Arab Jerusalem became a place that Israelis no longer felt able to enter with impunity. When they crossed the invisible partition line, there was now a possibility that they or their cars would be stoned by Palestinian youths and an incident ensue. East Jerusalem had become enemy territory.

The *intifādah* also achieved striking results internationally. All around the world, the general public became aware of the aggressive nature of the Israeli occupation of Jerusalem and the territories in a new way when they saw armed Israeli soldiers chasing and gunning down stone-throwing children or breaking the bones of their hands. The uprising had been master-minded by the younger generation of Palestinians, who had grown up under the Israeli occupation and had no faith in the PLO's policies, which had so signally failed to achieve results. The *intifādah* also impressed the Arab world. On 31 July 1988, King Hussein made a dramatic declaration in which he relinquished Jordan's claim to the West Bank and East Jerusalem—territory that he now acknowledged to belong to the Palestinian nation. This created a power vacuum which the PLO took advantage of. The leadership of the *intifādah* urged the PLO to renounce its old unrealistic policies: whether the Palestinians liked it or not, Israel and the United States held the chief cards in the Israeli-Palestinian conflict. The PLO must abandon its rejectionist stance and accept UN Resolution 242, recognize the existence of the State of Israel, and renounce terrorism. On 15 November 1988, the PLO took this path and recognized Israel's right to exist and to security. It also issued the Palestinian Declaration of Independence. There would be a Palestinian state in the West Bank, beside the State of Israel, and the capital of the State of Palestine would be Jerusalem [al-Quds al-Sharif].

The *intifādah* also strengthened the hand of the Israeli peace movement. It demonstrated the Palestinians' absolute insistence on achieving national independence and self-determination too eloquently for an increasing number of Israelis to deny. More significantly, perhaps, it also influenced the thinking of some of the more intransigent. Yitzhak Rabin, the minister of defense, had always taken a tough line on the Palestinian question, but the *intifādah* finally convinced him that Israel could not continue to hold the Occupied Territories without losing its humanity. The might of the Israeli army could not be used indefinitely to batter into submission the mothers and children who took part in the *intifādah*. When he became prime minister in 1992, Rabin was prepared to enter into peace negotiations with the PLO. The following year, Israel and the PLO signed the Oslo Agreement, turning over the Gaza Strip and parts of the West Bank (most immediately, the area around Jericho) to a Palestinian administration. Arafat and Rabin shook hands on the lawn of the White House in Washington, D.C.

The Oslo Agreement inspired much opposition. On both sides, people felt that their leaders had made too many concessions. The discussion of the future of Jerusalem was to be postponed until May 1996—a tacit acknowledgment that this would be the most difficult hurdle of all. Just how difficult was shown in the 1993 Jerusalem municipal elections, when Mayor Teddy Kollek was defeated by the conservative Likud candidate Ehud Olmert. Despite his role in the destruction of the Maghribi Quarter and the Arab municipality in 1967, Kollek was regarded as a liberal. He devoted a good deal of time to the Arabs of Jerusalem and sometimes even took their part. He insisted that everything must be done to preserve the Arab way of life in Jerusalem. Nonetheless Kollek was still firmly committed to the "reunification" of the city. All over the world, he fired audiences with his vision of a united city, haunted by the fear of "partition" and barbed-wire boundaries.

Yet the unity of Kollek's Jerusalem had not meant equality. A recent survey shows that of the 64,880 housing units built in Jerusalem since 1967, only 8,800 were for the Palestinians. Of the city's nine hundred sanitation workers, only fourteen were assigned to East Jerusalem. No new roads were built to link up the older Arab districts.[29] Clearly, even an Israeli "liberal" was discriminating in his benevolence. Moreover, the legal planning procedures adopted by the Israeli government have prevented the Palestinians from using 86 percent of the land in East Jerusalem. A study recently commissioned by the municipality shows that, as a result, 21,000 Palestinian families are currently homeless or inadequately housed. Because of the lack of land legally zoned for housing, it is almost impossible for Palestinians to obtain building permits in East Jerusalem. A home built by a family without permission is subject to demolition. Figures obtained in 1994 indicated that since mid-1987, 222 Palestinian homes had been demolished in East Jerusalem, yet the annual report of the municipality showed that a further 31,413 new housing units for Jewish residents were planned to the north, south, and east of Jerusalem.[30] Palestinians have been progressively excluded from al-Quds. Unlike Teddy Kollek, the new mayor, Ehud Olmert, has felt no need to make liberal noises. "I will expand Jerusalem to the east, not to the west," he has declared. "I can make things happen on the ground to ensure the city will remain united under Israeli control for eternity."[31] It is an attitude that does not bode well for peace.

Olmert has no need to woo Israeli liberals. He came to power by making an alliance with the ultra-Orthodox Jews of Jerusalem, who have grown rapidly in number in recent years. No longer confined to the ghetto of Mea Shearim, they have taken over most of the northern districts of the city. In 1994, 52 percent of the Jewish children under ten in Jerusalem belonged to ultra-Orthodox families. They have no interest in seeking peace with the Arabs. Their concern is to make Jerusalem a more observant city and to keep the secular Jews in line. They want fewer nonkosher restaurants, fewer theaters and places of entertainment open on the Sabbath. Olmert's supporters do not believe in any sharing of sovereignty with the Palestinians. For the ultra-Orthodox, as for the far-right groups, sharing means partition, and a divided Jerusalem is a dead Jerusalem.

Repeatedly, Israeli governments have insisted that Jerusalem is the eternal and indivisible capital of the Jewish state, and that there can be no question of sharing its sovereignty. The government continues its efforts to disabuse Palestinians of the idea that their capital will be al-Quds. Yet the mood is changing. Since the *intifādah,* Jerusalem has in effect become a divided city: there are now few places where Arabs and Jews are likely to meet on a normal basis. The main commercial district in West Jerusalem is almost entirely Jewish, the Old City almost entirely Arab. The only point of contact is the belligerently planted ring of Israeli settlements in East Jerusalem. Increasingly, Israelis are coming to accept this as a fact of life. What is the point, some ask, of "controlling" an area that you cannot enter without an armed escort? An opinion poll conducted in May 1995 for the Israel-Palestine Centre for Research and Information revealed that a surprising 28 percent of Israeli Jewish adults were prepared to envisage some form of divided sovereignty in the Holy City, provided that Israel retains control over the Jewish districts.

On 13 May 1995, Feisal Husseini, the PLO representative in Jerusalem, made a speech during a demonstration protesting against the confiscation of Arab land. Standing beneath the walls of the Old City in what had once been No Man's Land, Husseini said: "I dream of the day when a Palestinian will say 'Our Jerusalem' and will mean Palestinians and Israelis, and an Israeli will say 'Our Jerusalem' and will mean Israelis and Palestinians."[32] In response, seven hundred prominent Israelis, including writers, critics, artists, and former Knesset members, signed this joint statement:

> Jerusalem is ours, Israelis and Palestinians—Muslims, Christians, and Jews.
> Our Jerusalem is a mosaic of all the cultures, all the religions, and all the periods that enriched the city, from the earliest antiquity to this very day— Canaanites and Jebusites and Israelites, Jews and Hellenes, Romans and Byzantines, Christians and Muslims, Arabs and Mamelukes, Ottomans and Britons, Palestinians and Israelis. They and all the others who made their contribution to the city have a place in the spiritual and physical landscape of Jerusalem.
> Our Jerusalem must be united, open to all and belonging to all its inhabitants, without borders and barbed wire in its midst.
> Our Jerusalem must be the capital of the two states that will live side by side in this country—West Jerusalem the capital of the State of Israel and East Jerusalem the capital of the State of Palestine.
> Our Jerusalem must be the Capital of Peace.[33]

If Zion is indeed to be a city of peace instead of a city of war and hatred, some form of condominium must be achieved. A number of solutions have been proposed. Should Jerusalem be an internationally ruled *corpus separatum*? Should there be Israeli sovereignty with special privileges for the Palestinian authority, a joint Israel–Palestine administration of an undivided city, two separate municipalities, or one, with two distinct governing bodies? Discussion rages fiercely. But unless the underlying principles are clear, all these solutions remain utopian.

What can the history of Jerusalem teach us about the way forward? In the autumn of 1995, the Israelis opened a year-long festival to celebrate the three-thousandth anniversary of the conquest of the city by King David. The Palestinians objected, seeing the celebrations as propaganda for a wholly Jewish Jerusalem. Yet the story of David's conquest is, perhaps, more expressive of their cause than the more conservative Israelis imagine. We have seen that all monotheistic conquerors have had to face the fact that Jerusalem was a holy city to other people before them. Since all three faiths insist on the absolute and sacred rights of the individual, the way that the victors treat their predecessors in the Holy City must test the sincerity of their ideals. In these terms King David, as far as we can ascertain from our admittedly imperfect records, stands up fairly well. He did not attempt to eject the Jebusite incumbents from Jerusalem; the Jebusite administration remained in place, and there was no expropriation of sacred sites. Under David, Jerusalem remained a largely Jebusite city. The State of Israel has not measured up to his example. In 1948, thirty thousand Palestinians lost their homes in West Jerusalem, and since the 1967 conquest there has been continual expropriation of Arab land and, increasingly, insulting and dangerous attacks on the Ḥaram al-Sharif. The Israelis have not been the worst conquerors of Jerusalem: they have not slaughtered their predecessors, as the Crusaders did, nor have they permanently excluded them, as the Byzantines banned the Jews from the city. On the other hand, they have not reached the same high standards as Caliph ʿUmar. As we reflect on the current unhappy situation, it becomes a sad irony that on two occasions in the past, it was an Islamic conquest of Jerusalem that made it possible for Jews to return to their holy city. ʿUmar and Saladin both invited Jews to settle in Jerusalem when they replaced Christian rulers there.

The 1967 conquest was indeed a mythical occurrence, its symbolism overpowering. Jews had at last truly returned to Zion. Yet from the first, Zion was never merely a physical entity. It was also an ideal. From the Jebusite period, Zion was revered as a city of peace, an earthly paradise of harmony and integration. The Israelite psalmists and prophets also developed this vision. Yet Zionist Jerusalem today falls sadly short of the ideal. Ever since the Crusades, which permanently damaged relations between the three religions of Abraham, Jerusalem has been a nervous, defensive city. It has also, increasingly, been a contentious place. Not only have Jews, Christians, and Muslims fought and competed with one another there, but violent sectarian strife has divided the three main communities internally into bitterly warring factions. Nearly every development in nineteenth-century Jerusalem was either inspired by or led to increased communal rivalry. Today, the Christian sects still snarl at one another over the tomb of Christ, and not long after the emotional conquest of the city during the Six-Day War, religious and secular Israelis were at daggers drawn at the Western Wall. This is not Zion, the haven of rest established by King David.

Constantly Israel insists on the paramount importance of national security. Where the Palestinians want liberation, Israeli Jews want secure borders. Given the atrocities that have scarred Jewish history, this is hardly surprising. Security was one of the first things that people demanded of a city. One of the most important duties of a king in the ancient world was to build powerful fortifications to give people the safety for which they yearned. From its very earliest days, Zion was meant to be such a walled enclave of peace, though from the days of Abdi-Hepa it was also threatened by enemies within and without. Today Jerusalem is once again a beleaguered fortress city, its borders to the east marked by the huge new settlements which crouch around the city like the old Crusader fortifications. But walls are no good if there is deadly trouble within. Pessimistic observers believe that if some equitable solution is not found, Jerusalem is likely to become as violent and dangerous a place for all its inhabitants as Hebron.

Central to the sanctity of Zion from the earliest period was the ideal of social justice. This was one of the chief ways in which an ancient ruler believed that he was imposing the divine order on his city and enabling it to enjoy the peace and security of the gods. The ideal of social justice was crucial to the cult of Baal in Jebusite Jerusalem. The psalmists and prophets insisted that Zion must be a refuge for the poor: the prophets in particular were adamant that devotion to sacred space was pointless if Israelites neglected to care for the vulnerable people in their society. Embedded in the heart of P's Holiness Code was concern and love for the "stranger" whom Israelites must welcome into their midst. Social justice is also at the core of the Qur'ānic message, and in Ayyūbid and Mamluk times, practical compassion was an essential concomitant of the Islamization of Jerusalem. It was also at the root of the socialist Zionism of the veteran pioneers. But sadly the Palestinians have not been made welcome in Zion today, not even under Mayor Teddy Kollek. Israelis often reply that the Palestinians of Jerusalem are treated far better than they would be in an Arab state. This may well be true, but the Palestinians are not comparing themselves with other Arabs but with their Jewish fellow citizens. To insist that a city is "holy" without implementing the justice that is an inalienable part of Jerusalem's sanctity is to embark upon a dangerous course.

We can see, perhaps, how dangerous if we look back on some previous regimes that have stressed the importance of possessing the city but have neglected the duty of compassion. There was little charity in Hasmonean Jerusalem: after a committed struggle to preserve the integrity of Jewish Jerusalem, the Hasmoneans became masters of a kingdom that differed little from the cruel Hellenistic despotisms they had been fighting. Their behavior was such that they alienated the Pharisees, who constantly stressed the primacy of charity and loving-kindness. Eventually the Pharisees on several different occasions asked the Romans to depose Jewish monarchs: foreign rule would be preferable to the regime of these bad Jews.

Christian Jerusalem offers a particularly striking instance of the dangers of leaving compassion and absolute respect for the rights of others out of the picture. The New Testament is clear that without charity, faith is worth nothing. Yet this ideal was never integrated with the Christian cult of Jerusalem, perhaps because devotion to the city came quite late and almost took Christians by surprise. Byzantine Jerusalem was capable of giving Christians a powerful experience of the divine, but it was a most uncharitable city. Not only were Christians at one another's throats but they saw the dismantling and exclusion of paganism and Judaism as essential to the holiness and integrity of their New Jerusalem. Christians gloated over the fate of the Jews; some of the most ascetic monks who had settled in the Judaean desert precisely to be close to the Holy City were murderously anti-Semitic. Eventually the intolerant policies of the Christian emperors so alienated Jews and "heretics" that they became perilously disaffected. Jews greeted the Persian and Muslim invaders of Palestine with enthusiasm and gave them practical help.

Crusader Jerusalem was, of course, an even more cruel city. It was established on slaughter and dispossession. Like the Israelis today, the Crusaders had founded a kingdom that was a foreign enclave in the Near East, dependent upon overseas help and surrounded by hostile states. The entire history of the Crusader kingdom was a struggle for survival. We have seen that the Crusaders shared Israel's passion for security—with good reason. As a result, there could be little true creativity in Crusader Jerusalem, since art and literature cannot really thrive in such an embattled atmosphere. There were Franks in Jerusalem who realized, like many Israelis today, that their kingdom could not survive as a Western ghetto in the Near East. They must establish normal relations with the surrounding Muslim world. But the Crusaders' religion of hatred was ingrained: on one occasion they attacked their sole ally in the Islamic world and also turned venomously on one another. The religion of hatred does not work; it so easily becomes self-destructive. The Crusaders lost their state. The barrenness of a piety that sees the possession of a holy place as an end in itself, neglecting the more important duty of charity, is most graphically shown today in the interminable squabble of the Christian sects in the Holy Sepulcher.

In monotheistic terms, it is idolatry to see a shrine or a city as the ultimate goal of religion. Throughout, we have seen that they are symbols that point beyond themselves to a greater Reality. Jerusalem and its sacred sites have been experienced as numinous. They have introduced millions of Jews, Christians, and Muslims to the divine. Consequently they have for many monotheists been viewed as inseparable from the notion of God itself, as we have seen. And, because the divine is not simply a transcendent reality "out there" but something also sensed in the depths of the self, we have also seen that holy places have been regarded as part of a people's inner world. Sometimes when confronting a shrine, Jews, Christians, and Muslims have felt that they have had a startling and moving encounter with themselves. This can make it very difficult for them to see Jerusalem and its problems objectively. Many of the difficulties arise when religion is seen primarily as a quest for identity. One of the functions of faith is to help us build up a sense of self: to explain where we have come from and why our traditions are distinctive and special. But that is not the sole purpose of religion. All the major world faiths have insisted on the importance of transcending the fragile and voracious ego, which so often denigrates others in its yearning for security. Leaving the self behind is not only a mystical objective; it is required also by the disciplines of compassion, which demand that we put the rights of others before our own selfish desires.

One of the inescapable messages of the history of Jerusalem is that, despite romantic myths to the contrary, suffering does not necessarily make us better, nobler people. All too often, quite the reverse. Jerusalem first became an exclusive city after the Babylonian exile, when the new Judaism was helping Jews to establish a distinct identity in a predominantly pagan world. Second Isaiah had proclaimed that the return to Zion would usher in a new era of peace, but the Golah simply made Jerusalem a bone of contention in Palestine when they excluded the Am ha-Aretz. The experience of persecution at the hands of Rome did not make the Christians more sympathetic to the suffering of others, and al-Quds became a much more aggressively Islamic city after the Muslims suffered at the hands of the Crusaders. It is not surprising, therefore, that

the State of Israel, founded shortly after the catastrophe of the Holocaust, has not always implemented policies of sweetness and light. We
have seen that the fear of destruction and extinction was one of the main
motives that impelled the people of antiquity to build holy cities and
temples. In their mythology the ancient Israelites told the story of their
journey through the demonic realm of the wilderness—a non-place,
where there was no-one and no-thing—to reach the haven of the
Promised Land. The Jewish people had endured annihilation on an
unprecedented scale in the death camps. It is not surprising that their
return to Zion during the Six-Day War shook them to the core and
led some of them to believe that there had been a new creation, a new
beginning.

But today, increasingly, Israelis are beginning to contemplate the possibility of sharing the Holy City. Sadly, however, most of the committed
people who are working for peace are seculars. On both sides of the
conflict, religion is becoming increasingly belligerent. The apocalyptic
spirituality of extremists who advocate suicide bombing, blowing up
other people's shrines, or driving them from their homes is pursued by
only a small minority, but it engenders hatred on a wider scale. On both
sides, attitudes harden after an atrocity, and peace becomes a more distant
prospect. It was the Zealots who opposed the Peace Party in 66 CE who
were chiefly responsible for the destruction of Jerusalem and its Temple,
and it was Reynauld of Chatillon, convinced that any truce with the
infidel was a sin, who brought down the Crusader kingdom. The religion of hatred can have an effect that is quite disproportionate to the
numbers of people involved. Today religious extremists on both sides of
the conflict have been responsible for atrocities committed in the name
of "God." On 25 February 1994, Baruch Goldstein gunned down at
least forty-eight Palestinian worshippers in the Cave of the Patriarchs in
Hebron: today he is revered as a martyr of Israel by the far right. Another
martyr is the young woman member of the Islamic group Hamas, who
died in a suicide bombing of a Jerusalem bus on 25 August 1995, killing
five people and injuring 107. Such actions are a travesty of religion, but
they have been frequent in the history of Jerusalem. Once the possession
of a land or a city becomes an end in itself, there is no reason to refrain
from murder. As soon as the prime duty to respect the divinity
enshrined in other human beings is forgotten, "God" can be made to
give a divine seal of absolute approval to our own prejudices and desires.
Religion then becomes a breeding ground for violence and cruelty.

On 4 November 1995, Prime Minister Yitzhak Rabin was murdered
after speaking at a peace rally in Tel Aviv. To their horror, Israelis learned
that the assassin was another Jew. Yigal Amir, the young student who

fired the fatal shots, declared that he had acted under God's direction and that it was permissible to kill anybody who was prepared to give the sacred land of Israel to the enemy. The religion of hatred seems to have a dynamic of its own. Murderous intransigence can become such a habit that it is directed not only against the enemy but also against co-religionists. Crusader Jerusalem, for example, was bitterly divided against itself, and the Franks were poised on the brink of a suicidal civil war at a time when Saladin was preparing to invade their territory. Their hatred of one another and their chronic feuding was a factor in their defeat at Saladin's hands at the battle of Hattin.

The tragic murder of Rabin was a shocking revelation to many Israelis of the deep fissures in their own society—divisions which till then they had tried to ignore. The Zionists had come to Palestine to establish a homeland where Jews would be safe from the murderous *goyim*. Now Jews had begun to kill one another for the sake of that land. All over the world, Jews struggled with the painful realization that they were not merely victims but could also do harm and perpetrate atrocity. Rabin's death was also a glaring demonstration of the abuse of religion. Since the time of Abraham, the most humane traditions of the religion of Israel had suggested that compassion to other human beings could lead to a divine encounter. So sacred was humanity that it was never right to sacrifice another human life. Yigal Amir, however, subscribed to the more violent ethic of the Book of Joshua. He could see the divine only in the Holy Land. His crime was a frightening demonstration of the dangers of such idolatry.

Kabbalistic myth taught that when the Jews returned to Zion, everything in the world would fall back into its proper place. The assassination of Rabin showed that the return of the Jews to Israel did not mean that everything was right with the world. But this mythology had never been meant to be interpreted literally. Since 1948 the gradual return of the Jewish people to Zion had resulted in the displacement of thousands of Palestinians from their homeland as well as from Jerusalem. We know from the history of Jerusalem that exile is experienced as the end of the world, as a mutilation and a spiritual dislocation. Everything becomes meaningless without a fixed point and the orientation of home. When cut off from the past, the present becomes a desert and the future unimaginable. Certainly the Jews experienced exile as demonic and destructive. Tragically, this burden of suffering has now been passed by the State of Israel to the Palestinians, whatever its original intentions. It is not surprising that Palestinians have not always behaved in an exemplary manner in the course of their own struggle for survival. But, again, there are Palestinians who recognize that compromise may be necessary if they are to regain at least part of their homeland. They have made their own hard journey to the Oslo Accords: that Palestinians should give official recognition to the State of Israel would once have seemed an impossible dream. In exile, Zion became an image of salvation and reconciliation to the Jews. Not surprisingly, al-Quds has become even more precious to the Palestinians in their exile. Two peoples, who have both endured an annihilation of sorts, now seek healing in the same Holy City.

Salvation—secular or religious—must mean more than the mere possession of a city. There must also be a measure of interior growth and liberation. One thing that the history of Jerusalem teaches is that nothing is irreversible. Not only have its inhabitants watched their city destroyed time and again, they have also seen it built up in ways that seemed abhorrent. When the Jews heard of the obliteration of their Holy City, first by Hadrian's contractors and then by Constantine's, they must have felt that they would never win their city back. Muslims had to see the desecration of their beloved Ḥaram by the Crusaders, who seemed invincible at the time. All these building projects had been intent on creating facts, but ultimately bricks and mortar were not enough. The Muslims got their city back because the Crusaders became trapped in a dream of hatred and intolerance. In our own day, against all odds, the Jews have returned to Zion and have

One example of belligerent religion today: members of Hamas, the militant Islamic group which is bitterly opposed to the Oslo Accords, march through Gaza, twirling clubs and chains.

A Palestinian prays beneath a futuristic apartment block, inhabited by ultra-Orthodox Jews, in north Jerusalem. Will construction continue to be used as a weapon of exclusion, or can Jerusalem really become Zion, a city of peace, where Jews and Arabs can encounter the sacred together?

created their own facts in the settlements around Jerusalem. But, as the long, tragic history of Jerusalem shows, nothing is permanent or guaranteed. The societies that have lasted the longest in the holy city have, generally, been the ones that were prepared for some kind of tolerance and coexistence in the Holy City. That, rather than a sterile and deadly struggle for sovereignty, must be the way to celebrate Jerusalem's sanctity today.

Notes

1. ZION

1. Kathleen Kenyon, *Digging Up Jerusalem* (London, 1974), p. 78.
2. *New York Times,* 8 September 1994.
3. "Tyropoeon" has been translated "Cheese-makers": by Josephus's time the original name of the valley may have been corrupted.
4. Benjamin Mazar, *The Mountain of the Lord* (New York, 1975), pp. 45–46; Gosta W. Ahlström, *The History of Ancient Palestine* (Minneapolis, 1993), pp. 169–72.
5. Mazar, *Mountain of the Lord,* p. 11.
6. Mircea Eliade, *The Sacred and the Profane,* trans. Willard J. Trask (New York, 1959), p. 21.
7. Ibid., *passim.* Also Mircea Eliade, *Patterns in Comparative Religion,* trans. Rosemary Sheed (London, 1958), pp. 1–37, 367–88; Mircea Eliade, *Images and Symbols: Studies in Religious Symbolism,* trans. Philip Mairet (Princeton, 1991), pp. 37–56.
8. Eliade, *Sacred and the Profane,* pp. 50–54, 64.
9. Eliade, *Patterns in Comparative Religion,* p. 19.
10. Ibid., pp. 99–101; R. E. Clements, *God and Temple* (Oxford, 1965), pp. 2–6; Richard J. Clifford, *The Cosmic Mountain in Canaan and the Old Tes*tament (Cambridge, Mass., 1972), pp. 4–10.
11. Clifford, *Cosmic Mountain,* p. 4.
12. Eliade, *Sacred and the Profane,* p. 33.
13. Eliade, *Patterns in Comparative Religion,* pp. 382–85.
14. Ahlström, *History of Ancient Palestine,* pp. 248–50.
15. J. B. Pritchard, ed., *Ancient Near Eastern Texts Relating to the Old Testament* (Princeton, 1969), pp. 483–90.
16. Ahlström, *History of Ancient Palestine,* pp. 279–81.
17. Ronald de Vaux, *The Early History of Palestine,* 2 vols., trans. David Smith (London, 1978), 1:6–7.
18. H. J. Franken, "Jerusalem in the Bronze Age: 3000–1000 BC," in K. J. Asali, ed., *Jerusalem in History* (New York, 1990), p. 39.
19. Kenyon, *Digging Up Jerusalem,* p. 95.
20. Ibid., p. 100.
21. Pritchard, *Ancient Near Eastern Texts,* p. 483.
22. Clifford, *Cosmic Mountain,* pp. 57–59.
23. John C. L. Gibson, *Canaanite Myths and Legends* (Edinburgh, 1978), p. 66.
24. Ibid., p. 50.
25. Clifford, *Cosmic Mountain,* pp. 57–68; cf. Psalm 47.

26. Ibid., p. 68.
27. Ibid., p. 77.
28. Ibid., p. 72.
29. *Epic of Gilgamesh* 1:15–18. See also Jonathan Z. Smith, "Wisdom's Place," in John J. Collins and Michael Fishbane, eds., *Death, Ecstasy and Other Worldly Journeys* (Albany, 1995), pp. 3–13.
30. Pritchard, *Ancient Near Eastern Texts*, p. 164.
31. Ibid., p. 178.
32. Gibson, *Canaanite Myths*, pp. 102–7.
33. John Gray, "Sacral Kingship in Ugarit," *Ugaritica* 6 (1969), pp. 295–98.
34. Clifford, *Cosmic Mountain, passim.*; Clements, *God and Temple*, p. 47; Ben C. Ollenburger, *Zion, the City of the Great King: A Theological Symbol of the Jerusalem Cult* (Sheffield, 1987), pp. 14–16; Margaret Barker, *The Gate of Heaven: The History and Symbolism of the Temple in Jerusalem* (London, 1991), p. 64; Hans-Joachim Kraus, *Worship in Israel: A Cultic History of the Old Testament* (Oxford, 1966), pp. 201–4.

2. ISRAEL

1. Joshua 10:40. Biblical quotations are from the Jerusalem Bible (London, 1966).
2. Ibid., 15:63; cf. Judges 1:21.
3. Robin Lane Fox, *The Unauthorized Version: Truth and Fiction in the Bible* (London, 1991), pp. 225–33.
4. Joshua 17:11–18; Judges 1:27–36.
5. J. Alberto Soggin, *A History of Israel from the Beginnings to the Bar Kochba Revolt AD 135,* trans. John Bowden (London, 1984), pp. 141–43; Gosta W. Ahlström, *The History of Ancient Palestine* (Minneapolis, 1993), pp. 347–48.
6. Ahlström, *History of Ancient Palestine,* pp. 234–35, 247–48; Amnon Ben Tor, ed., *The Archeology of Ancient Israel,* trans. R. Greenberg (New Haven and London, 1992), p. 213.
7. G. E. Mendenhall, *The Tenth Generation* (Baltimore, 1973); N. P. Lemche, *Early Israel: Anthropological and Historical Studies of the Israelite Society Before the Monarchy* (Leiden, 1985); D. C. Hopkins, *The Highlands of Canaan* (Sheffield, 1985); R. B. Coote and K. W. Whitelam, *The Emergence of Early Israel in Historical Perspective* (Sheffield, 1987); James D. Martin, "Israel as a Tribal Society," in R. E. Clements, ed., *The World of Ancient Israel: Sociological, Anthropological and Political Perspectives* (Cambridge, 1989), pp. 94–114; H. G. M. Williamson in Clements, *World of Ancient Israel,* pp. 141–42.
8. This accounts for the traditional distinction between the "Rachel" and the "Leah" tribes.
9. Genesis 12:1.
10. See Genesis 23:5.
11. Genesis 12:7.
12. Popular etymology sees the name deriving from '*aqeb* ("heel"), but in Genesis 27:36 the name means "supplanted" (*'aqab*). "Yaakov" probably meant "May God protect!"
13. Exodus 6:3, from the Priestly (P) source.
14. Genesis 28:11–17.
15. Genesis 18:1–15.
16. Genesis 22:2.
17. 2 Chronicles 3:1.
18. Genesis 22:14.
19. Genesis 17:20.
20. Harold H. Rowley, *Worship in Ancient Israel: Its Forms and Meaning* (London, 1967), pp. 17–19, sums up the main arguments. Other suggested sites are Shechem, Mount Tabor, and Mount Gerizim.
21. Benjamin Mazar, *The Mountain of the Lord* (New York, 1975), p. 157.
22. Flavius Josephus, *The Antiquities of the Jews,* 1:40.
23. Psalm 110:4.
24. R. E. Clements, *God and Temple* (Oxford, 1965), p. 43.
25. Ibid., pp. 44–47.
26. Jonathan Z. Smith, "Earth and Gods," in *Map Is Not Territory: Stud-*

ies in the History of Religions (Leiden, 1973), p. 110.

27. Mircea Eliade, *Patterns in Comparative Religion,* trans. Rosemary Sheed (London, 1958), pp. 118–226.

28. Smith, "Earth and Gods," p. 109.

29. Deuteronomy 32:10.

30. Jeremiah 2:2; Job 38:26; Isaiah 34:12.

31. Isaiah 34:11; Jeremiah 4:25.

32. Deuteronomy 10:1–8; Exodus 25:10–22.

33. Numbers 10:35–36.

34. 1 Samuel 3:3.

35. Judges 5:4–5; Deuteronomy 33:2; Psalm 68:8–11. See Richard J. Clifford, *The Cosmic Mountain in Canaan and the Old Testament* (Cambridge, Mass., 1972), pp. 114–23.

36. Clements, *God and Temple,* pp. 25–28.

37. 1 Samuel 7:2–8:22; 10:11–27; 12.

38. Keith W. Whitelam, "Israelite Kingship: The Royal Ideology and Its Opponents," in Clements, ed., *World of Ancient Israel,* pp. 119–26.

39. 1 Samuel 4:1–11; 5; 6:1–7:1.

40. 2 Samuel 1:23.

41. Actual location of Ziklag is obscure: some identify it with Tel as-Sahara, forty-eight km from Beersheva.

3. CITY OF DAVID

1. 2 Samuel 5:6.

2. A suggestion of the Israeli archaeologist Yigal Yadin; the point of the story is to explain why blind and lame people were later forbidden to enter the Temple.

3. The word *tsinur* could mean "pipe," but this is by no means certain. 2 Samuel 5:8; 1 Chronicles 11:4–7.

4. 2 Samuel 5:9. Perhaps the phrase should be translated "the Fortress of David."

5. 2 Samuel 5:8; 1 Chronicles 11:5.

6. Joshua 15:8.

7. See R. E. Clements, *Abraham and David* (London, 1967).

8. 1 Kings 4:3.

9. G. E. Mendenhall, "Jerusalem from 1000–63 BC," in K. J. Asali, ed., *Jerusalem in History* (New York, 1990), p. 45.

10. 1 Chronicles 21:9. Cf. Gosta W. Ahlström, *The History of Ancient Palestine* (Minneapolis, 1993), pp. 504–05.

11. Gosta W. Ahlström, "Der Prophet Nathan und der Tempelban," *Vetus Testamentum* 11 (1961); R. E. Clements, *God and Temple* (Oxford, 1965), p. 58.

12. Harold H. Rowley, *Worship in Ancient Israel: Its Forms and Meaning* (London, 1967), p. 73; Clements, *God and Temple,* pp. 42–43; cf. Roland de Vaux, *Ancient Israel: Its Life and Institutions,* trans. John McHugh (New York and London, 1961), pp. 114, 311.

13. 1 Chronicles 6.

14. 2 Samuel 6.

15. 2 Samuel 7:6–16.

16. 1 Chronicles 28:11–19.

17. 2 Samuel 24.

18. Benjamin Mazar, *The Mountain of the Lord* (New York, 1975), p. 52; Clements, *God and Temple,* pp. 61–62; Ahlström, *History of Ancient Palestine,* p. 471; Hans-Joachim Kraus, *Worship in Israel: A Cultic History of the Old Testament* (Oxford, 1966), p. 186.

19. 1 Chronicles 28:11–19.

20. 1 Chronicles 28:19.

21. The Temple took eight years to build, the palace thirteen years.

22. David Ussishkin, "King Solomon's Palaces," *Biblical Archeologist* 36 (1973).

23. 1 Kings 6:1–14; 2 Chronicles 3:1–7.

24. Numbers 21:8–9; 2 Kings 18:14.

25. The meaning of these names is obscure. Perhaps they are the opening words of two benedictions, linking them with the Davidic dynasty: *Yakhin YHWH et kisei David l'olam va'ed* ("The Lord will establish the throne of David forever") and *Boaz Yahweh* ("By the Power of YHWH"). Boaz is also the quasi-mythical ancestor of King David in the Book of Ruth. Or these could have been cosmic pillars, forming a

gateway for the sunlight to enter the Temple area at dawn.

26. 1 Kings 6:15–38; 2 Chronicles 3:8–13.

27. Margaret Barker, *The Gate of Heaven: The History and Symbolism of the Temple in Jerusalem* (London, 1991), pp. 26–29; Clements, *God and Temple*, p. 65.

28. Genesis 11:4–9.

29. Clements, *God and Temple*, pp. 64, 69–72; Norman Cohn, *Cosmos, Chaos and the World to Come: The Ancient Roots of Apocalyptic Faith* (New Haven and London, 1993), p. 138; Richard J. Clifford, *The Cosmic Mountain in Canaan and the Old Testament* (Cambridge, Mass., 1972), pp. 177–78.

30. Psalm 2:6–12.

31. Psalm 72:4.

32. Psalm 9:10, 16.

33. Psalm 48:8.

34. Cohn, *Cosmos, Chaos and the World to Come*, p. 139.

35. 1 Kings 11:4–8.

36. 1 Kings 4:18–19.

37. 1 Kings 8:15–24.

38. 1 Kings 11:26–40.

4. CITY OF JUDAH

1. 1 Kings 12:11.

2. Isaiah 27:1; Job 3:12, 26:13; Psalm 74:14.

3. Job 38:10.

4. Psalm 89:10.

5. Psalm 48:1–3. This translation is not from the Jerusalem Bible but by Jonathan Z. Smith in "Earth and Gods," in *Map Is Not Territory: Studies in the History of Religions* (Leiden, 1978), p. 112. Many translators prefer to translate *tspn* as "north," but it clearly makes no sense to speak of Mount Zion, in southern Palestine, as being "in the far north," as the Jerusalem Bible has it.

6. Psalm 48:12–14.

7. Psalm 46:5, 9.

8. Psalm 46:1.

9. Psalm 99.

10. Psalm 47:5–6.

11. Psalm 97:2–6; Isaiah 6:4.

12. Psalms 47:2, 99:1–4.

13. Psalm 97:9.

14. Psalm 84:5–7.

15. Psalm 84:3.

16. 2 Samuel 7:10–12.

17. Psalm 84:1–2.

18. Psalm 84:10.

19. The dates of King Uzziah, like those of several other kings, are differently calculated by the Deuteronomist and the Chronicler. Uzziah's case is especially complicated because while he was ill his son Jotham served as regent.

20. Isaiah 6:3.

21. Isaiah 2:2–3.

22. Isaiah 11:6–9.

23. Isaiah 1:11–12.

24. Isaiah 1:16–17.

25. Amos 5:25–27.

26. Amos 1:2.

27. Psalms 9:10–13; 10. Ben C. Ollenburger, *Zion, the City of the Great King: A Theological Symbol of the Jerusalem Cult* (Sheffield, 1987), pp. 58–69.

28. Isaiah 7:14–17.

29. 2 Chronicles 29, 30.

30. Micah 3:12.

31. 2 Kings 29:34.

32. 2 Chronicles 32:21.

33. 2 Kings 21:1–18; 2 Chronicles 33:1–10.

34. 1 Kings 8:27.

35. Deuteronomy 16:13–15.

36. This ideal is enshrined in the Sh'ma, the Jewish profession of faith: "Hear, Israel, Yahweh is our *elohim;* Yahweh alone!" (Deuteronomy 6:4).

37. Deuteronomy 12:1–4. Harold H. Rowley, *Worship in Ancient Israel: Its Forms and Meaning* (London, 1967), pp. 106–7; E. Nielsen, *Shechem* (London, 1955), pp. 45, 85.

38. 2 Kings 22; 2 Chronicles 34:8–28.

39. 2 Kings 23:10–14.

40. Jeremiah 7:3–7.

41. There are discrepancies concerning the actual numbers of deportees in the different accounts. Jeremiah says

that only 3,023 people were sent to Babylon. But they may have left Judah in three groups.

42. 2 Maccabees 2:4–5; B. Yoma 52B; Horayot 12A; J. Shekalim 6:1.
43. Jeremiah 29:5–10.
44. Jeremiah 3:16.
45. Jeremiah 32:44.

5. EXILE AND RETURN

1. Jeremiah 4:23–26.
2. Psalm 74:3–7.
3. Psalm 137:9.
4. Psalm 79:4.
5. Jeremiah 41:4–6.
6. Lamentations 4:5–10.
7. Lamentations 1:8–9.
8. 2 Kings 25:27–30.
9. Ezra 2.
10. Elias J. Bickermann, *The Jews in the Greek Age* (Cambridge, Mass., and London, 1988), pp. 47–48.
11. Quoted in Jonathan Z. Smith, "Earth and Gods," in *Map Is Not Territory: Studies in the History of Religions* (Leiden, 1978), p. 119.
12. Psalm 137:4.
13. Bickerman, *The Jews in the Greek Age,* pp. 241–42.
14. Ezekiel 1:26–28.
15. Ezekiel 43:1–6.
16. Ezekiel 31:34–36.
17. Ezekiel 40:2, 48:35.
18. Ezekiel 47:11–12.
19. Ezekiel 40:48–41:4.
20. Ezekiel 40:17–19, 28–31.
21. Ezekiel 47:13–23.
22. Ezekiel 48:9–29.
23. Ezekiel 43:11.
24. Mary Douglas, *Purity and Danger* (London, 1966).
25. Leviticus 19:11–18.
26. Leviticus 19:33–34.
27. Ezekiel 44:11–16.
28. Ezekiel 44:16–31.
29. Jeremiah 31:31–34; Ezekiel 36:26–27.
30. Isaiah 40:3–4, 41:19–20, 44:20.
31. Isaiah 52:10.
32. Isaiah 46:1.
33. Isaiah 45:14.
34. Isaiah 54:13–15.

35. Ezra 2:64.
36. Haggai 2:6–9.
37. Ezra 3:12–13.
38. Haggai 2:6–9, 20:3.
39. Zachariah 2:9, 4:14, 8:3.
40. Ezra 4:1–3.
41. Ezra 4:4.
42. Isaiah 66:1.
43. Isaiah 66:2.
44. Isaiah 65:16–25.
45. Isaiah 56:9–12, 65:1–10.
46. Isaiah 56:7.
47. Nehemiah 1:3–2:8.
48. Nehemiah, for example, castigates all the previous governors of Jerusalem, and it is unthinkable that he would have included Ezra in this stricture; also, when Ezra arrives, the city is thriving and populous—a state it did not enjoy until after Nehemiah had worked there.
49. Nehemiah 2:3.
50. Nehemiah 4:11–12.
51. Nehemiah 7:4–5.
52. Nehemiah 5.
53. Seth Kunin, "Judaism," in Jean Holm with John Bowker, eds., *Sacred Place* (London, 1994), pp. 121–22.
54. Ezra 7:6.
55. Ezra 7:14.
56. Ezra 7:21–26; Bickerman, *Jews in the Greek Age,* p. 154.
57. Nehemiah 8.
58. Ezra 10.
59. Isaiah 63:10, 19.

6. ANTIOCH IN JUDAEA

1. Josephus, *Antiquities of the Jews* 11:7.
2. Ibid., 12:175–85.
3. Ben Sira 50:5–12.
4. Ben Sira 45:17.
5. Ben Sira 45:7.
6. Ben Sira 50:1–4.
7. Ben Sira 13:20–27.
8. Ben Sira, Introduction, v. 12.
9. The terms used in the Book of Daniel to refer to the "abomination" are all distortions of *Baal* ("Lord") and *Shemesh* ("Sun").
10. Martin Hengel, *Judaism and Hellenism, Studies in Their Encounter in*

Palestine During the Early Hellenistic Period (2 vols., trans. John Bowden, London, 1974), I, pp. 294–300; Elias J. Bickerman, From Ezra to the Last of the Maccabees (New York, 1962), pp. 286–89; The Jews in the Greek Age (Cambridge Mass. and London, 1988), pp. 294–96.

11. Corpus Hermeticum 16:2, in A. J. Festugiere, La Révélation d'Hermès Trismégiste (4 vols., Paris, 1950–54), 1:26.

12. Hai Gaon (939–1038), in Louis Jacobs (trans. and ed.), The Jewish Mystics (Jerusalem, 1076, London 1990), p. 23.

13. I Enoch 4.

14. 2 Maccabees 5:27.

15. I Maccabees 2:44–48.

16. I Maccabees 4:36–61.

17. I Maccabees 8:17–32.

18. I Maccabees 10:17–21.

19. I Maccabees 13:49–53.

20. Josephus, Antiquities 2:190.

21. Historia de Legis Divinae Translatione 5 in Extracts from Aristeas Hecataeus and Origen and Other Early Writers (trans. Aubrey Stewart (London, 1895; New York, 1971).

22. Ibid., p. 3.

23. Ibid., p. 4.

24. Josephus, The Jewish War 1:67–69.

25. Josephus, Antiquities 13:372.

26. Josephus, Antiquities 13:38, Jewish War 1:97.

27. Josephus, Antiquities 13:401.

28. Josephus, Jewish War 1:148.

29. Latinization of "Philistia."

7. DESTRUCTION

1. Josephus, The Jewish War 5:146.

2. Sukkot 51B.

3. Josephus, Jewish War 5:210.

4. Josephus, Antiquities of the Jews 15:396.

5. Josephus, Jewish War 5:224–25.

6. B. Batria 3B.

7. Josephus, Jewish War 5:211–17.

8. Philo, The Special Laws 1:66.

9. Philo, Questions on the Exodus 2:95.

10. Josephus, Jewish War 5:19.

11. Philo, Special Laws 1:96–97.

12. E. P. Sanders, Judaism: Practice and Belief, 63 BCE to 66 CE (London and Philadelphia, 1992), p. 128.

13. Josephus, Antiquities 4:205; Philo, Special Laws 1:70.

14. Raphael Patai, Man and Temple in Ancient Jewish Myth and Ritual (London, 1967), Chapter 3.

15. The origins of the synagogue are obscure and much disputed. They started in the Diaspora, though we are not exactly sure when. The synagogue was a unique religious institution in the ancient world, since it seemed more like a school of philosophy than a religious building. It was the scene of study and prayer rather than sacrificial liturgy. By the first century BCE there were many synagogues in Jerusalem, some established by particular Diaspora communities.

16. See, for example, Avot 1:12–13; Sifra 109B; B. Batria 9A,B; Avot de Rabba Nathan 7:17A,B; B. Tanhuma Noah 16A.

17. Sanders, Judaism: Practice and Belief, p. 441.

18. II QPS 22, translated in Geza Vermes, The Dead Sea Scrolls in English (London, 1987), p. 212.

19. Josephus, Jewish War 1:650–52.

20. Josephus, Antiquities 17:206–18.

21. Ibid., 8:3.

22. Mark 11:15–18; cf. Isaiah 56:7, Jeremiah 7:11.

23. Mark 13:1–2.

24. Luke 22:28–30.

25. Acts 5:34–40.

26. Acts 2:44–47; Matthew 5:25–34. Matthew was sympathetic to the ideals of the Jewish Christians and is a source for their views; Jewish Christians used to use a version of his gospel.

27. Galatians 2:6.

28. Matthew 5:17–42.

29. Acts 6:1.

30. Acts 7:1–49.

31. Acts 8:1.

32. Acts 11:26.

33. Romans 7:14–20; Galatians 3:10–22.

34. Jonathan Z. Smith, "The Temple and the Magician," in *Map Is Not Territory: Studies in the History of Religions* (Leiden, 1978).

35. Philippians 2:5–11.

36. Mircea Eliade, *Patterns in Comparative Religion,* trans. Rosemary Sheed (London, 1958), pp. 26–28.

37. Galatians 2:10; Romans 15:25–27.

38. Acts 21:26–40.

39. Ephesians 2:14–21.

40. Hebrews 5:17, 12:22–23.

41. Josephus, *Antiquities* 18:261–72.

42. Josephus, *Jewish War* 6:98.

43. Dio Cassius, *History* 66:6.

44. Josephus, *Jewish War* 6:98.

45. Lamentations Rabbah 1:50.

8. AELIA CAPITOLINA

1. Benjamin Mazar, *The Mountain of the Lord* (New York, 1975), p. 113.

2. Antoine Duprez, *Jésus et les Dieux Guérisseurs à la propos de Jean V* (Paris, 1970).

3. Quoted in F. E. Peters, *Jerusalem: The Holy City in the Eyes of Chroniclers, Visitors, Pilgrims and Prophets from the Days of Abraham to the Beginnings of Modern Times* (Princeton, 1985), p. 125.

4. Eusebius, *Ecclesiastical History* 4:5.

5. Origen notes this legend in the *Sermon in Honor of Matthew,* 12B.

6. 2 Baruch 10.

7. Yalkut Song of Songs 1:2.

8. Avot de Rabbi Nathan 6.

9. Sifre on Leviticus 19:8.

10. Mekhilta on Exodus 21:73.

11. Sanhedrin 4:5.

12. Baba Metzia 58B.

13. M. Berakoth 4:5.

14. Fourteenth Benediction.

15. Yalkut on I Kings 8.

16. Pesikta de Rabbi Kahana 103A.

17. 2 Baruch 4.

18. 4 Enoch 7:26.

19. 4 Enoch 8:5, 2–3.

20. Revelation 2:10.

21. Revelation 22:1–2.

22. Luke 24:52–53.

23. Acts of the Apostles 1:8.

24. Matthew 24:1–3.

25. John 1:1–5, 14.

26. See John 7:38–39, where Jesus uses the phrase "I AM" to describe himself in the Temple on Sukkoth; W. D. Davies points out that the phrase "I AM" (*Ani Waho*) was used in the liturgy during Sukkoth and could have been a term for the Shekhinah. *The Gospel and the Land: Early Christianity and Jewish Territorial Doctrine* (Berkeley, 1974), pp. 294–95.

27. John 2:19–21.

28. John 4:20–24.

29. John 8:57. See note 26 above. When Jesus left the Temple, it was equivalent to the Shekinah departing from the site. Davies, *Gospel and the Land,* p. 295.

30. Dio Cassius, *History* 69:12.

31. Ibid.

32. See Vergil, *Aeneid* 5:785–86.

33. Micah 3:12.

34. John Wilkinson, however, believes that the arch is Herodian; see "Jerusalem Under Rome and Byzantium 63 BC to 637 AD," in K. J. Asali, ed., *Jerusalem in History* (New York, 1990), p. 82.

35. J. Berakoth 1:4A, line 27; B. Keuboth 17A.

36. T. Avodah Zarah 1:19.

37. Genesis Rabbah a:18.

38. T. B. Megillah 29A.

39. Mekhilta Visha 14.

40. T. B. Berakoth 6A; Numbers Rabbah 11:2.

41. Numbers Rabbah 1:3.

42. Song of Songs Rabbah 8:12.

43. M. Kelim 1:6–9.

44. Pirqe Rabbi Eliezer 31.

45. J. Berakoth 9:3, 13D.

46. Michael Avi-Yonah, *The Jews of Palestine: A Political History from the Bar Kokhba War to the Arab Conquest* (Oxford, 1976), pp. 80–81.

47. Robert L. Wilken, *The Land Called Holy: Palestine in Christian History*

and Thought (New Haven and London, 1992), p. 106.

48. Eusebius, *Ecclesiastical History* 4:6.
49. Eusebius, *Onomastikon* 14:19–25.
50. Melito, "Paschal Sermon."
51. Eusebius, *The Proof of the Gospel* 6:18–23.
52. Melito, "Paschal Sermon."
53. Irenaeus, *Heresies* 5:35:2; Justin, *Dialogue with Trypho the Jew* 80:5; Origen, *First Principles* 4:2:1.
54. Origen, *Against Celsus* 3:34, 7:35.
55. Origen, *First Principles* 4:2:1.
56. Eusebius, *Proof of the Gospel* 1:1:2, 3:2:47, 7:2:1.
57. Acts of John 97.
58. Matthew 24:3.
59. Origen, *First Principles* 4:1:3.
60. Eusebius, *Proof of the Gospels* 6:18:23.
61. Ibid., 3:2:10.

9. THE NEW JERUSALEM

1. Eusebius, *Ecclesiastical History* 9:9.
2. Ibid., 1:4; Eusebius, *The Proof of the Gospel* 1:6:42.
3. Eusebius, *Proof of the Gospel* 1:6:42.
4. Ibid., 8:3:11–12.
5. Ibid., 5, Preface 29.
6. Ibid., 1:6:40.
7. Ibid., 406 B–C.
8. Proverbs 8:22.
9. Philippians 2:8–11.
10. Eusebius, *Proof of the Gospel* 6, Preface 1.
11. Ibid., 5, Preface 2.
12. Eusebius, *The Life of Constantine* 3:27.
13. Ibid., 3:28, 3:30:1.
14. Ibid., 3:36.
15. Ibid., 3:28.
16. Ibid., 3:26.
17. Eusebius, *Theophany* 3:61.
18. Eusebius, *Life of Constantine* 3:28.
19. Eusebius, *Sermon on Psalm 87.*
20. Eusebius, *Life of Constantine* 4:33.
21. Ibid., 3:53.
22. 2 Chronicles 24:19–22.
23. *Itinerary from Bordeaux to Jerusalem,* trans. Aubrey Stewart, (London 1887, New York, 1971), p. 22.

24. Matthew 4:5.
25. *Itinerary,* p. 23.
26. Ibid., pp. 23–24.
27. Cyril, *Catechetical Lectures* 3:7, 17:13.
28. Ibid., 13:30, 19:22.
29. Ibid., 14:16.
30. Ibid., 16:26; 12:16.
31. Ibid., 13:22.
32. John Chrysostom, *Against the Jews,* 5:11.
33. Michael Avi-Yonah, *The Jews of Palestine: A Political History from the Bar Kokhba War to the Arab Conquest* (Oxford, 1976), pp. 160–173.
34. Ibid., p. 176.
35. A. Hayman (ed.), *Disputation of Sergius the Stylite Against a Jew* (Louvain, 1973), p. 67.

10. CHRISTIAN HOLY CITY

1. John Chrysostom, *Against the Jews* 5:11.
2. Quoted in Yohan (Hans) Lewy, "Julian the Apostate and the Building of the Temple," in L. I. Levine, ed., *The Jerusalem Cathedra: Studies in the History, Geography and Ethnography of the Land of Israel,* 3 vols. (Jerusalem, 1921–83), 3:86. The other main account of this strange episode is in Michael Avi-Yonah, *The Jews of Palestine: A Political History from the Bar Kokhba War to the Arab Conquest* (Oxford, 1976), pp. 185–204.
3. Rufinus, *Ecclesiastical History* 10:38.
4. There are virtually no references to Julian's plan in the Talmud.
5. Ammianus Macellinus, *Rerum Gestarum* 28:1–2.
6. Lamentations Rabbah 1:17–19A.
7. Commentary on Zephaniah 1:15.
8. Commentary on Jeremiah 31:38–40.
9. Jerome, Epistle 46:10, 108:33.
10. Jerome, Epistle 54:12:5.
11. Jerome, Epistle 58:4:4.
12. For Egeria's pilgrimage, see *The Pilgrimage of St. Silvia of Aquitania to the Holy Places,* trans. and ed. John H. Bernard (London, 1891; New York, 1971), pp. 11–77.

13. Ibid., p. 62.
14. Jerome, Epistle 108:6.
15. Paulinus of Nola, Epistle 49:402.
16. Gregory of Nyssa, *Encomium on St. Theodore.*
17. Gregory of Nyssa, Epistle 3:4.
18. Jerome, *Against Vigilantius* 5.
19. Avi-Yonah, *Jews of Palestine,* pp. 225–29.
20. *Epistle of Lucian* 8.
21. Peter Brown, *The Cult of the Saints: Its Rise and Function in Classical Antiquity* (London, 1981), pp. 81–82.
22. This was not Spain but an area to the north of Armenia.
23. Cyril of Scythopolis, *Lives of the Monks* 24–5.
24. *Life of Sabas* 90:5–10.
25. F. Nau, "Deux épisodes de l'histoire juive sous Theodose II (423 et 438) d'après la vie de Barsauma le Syrien," *Revue des études juives* 83 (1927).
26. It has been argued that these "walls" were in fact simply Eudokia's church buildings, the confusion—if such there be—arising from a quotation used to compliment the empress: "In thy good pleasure [Greek: *eudokia*] build up the walls of Jerusalem" (Psalm 51:18).
27. Epistles 113, 123.
28. Michael Avi-Yonah, *The Madaba Mosaic Map with Introduction and Commentary* (Jerusalem, 1954).
29. Cyril of Jerusalem, *Discourse on the Theotokos.*
30. Robert L. Wilken, *The Land Called Holy: Palestine in Christian History and Thought* (New Haven and London, 1992), pp. 168–69.
31. Antoninus Martyr, *On the Holy Places Visited,* trans. Aubrey Stewart, ed. C. W. Wilson (London, 1896), p. 23.
32. Theodosius, *On the Topography of the Holy Land,* trans. J. H. Bernard, (London, 1893), p. 45.
33. Antoninus, *On the Holy Places,* pp. 24–27.
34. Cyril Mango, *The Art of the Byzantine Empire, 312–1453: Sources and*

Documents (Englewood Cliffs, N.J., 1972), p. 173.
35. *The Breviary or Short Description of Jerusalem c. 530,* trans. Aubrey Stewart, with notes by C. W. Wilson (London, 1890), pp. 14–15; Theodosius, *Topography,* p. 40; Antoninus, *On the Holy Places,* p. 19.
36. Strategos, *Conquest of Jerusalem* 14:14–16.
37. *Book of Zerubbabel* 11:67–71; *Mishna Geula* 78:1:69.
38. *Anacreontics,* Canto 20, PPTS, Vol. 11, p. 30.

11. BAYT AL-MAQDIS

1. Qur'ān 3:65–68. All quotations from the Qur'ān are taken from the translation of Muhammad Asad, *The Message of the Qur'ān* (Gibraltar, 1980).
2. Qur'ān 29:46. The more usual translation of *ahl al-kitāb* is "the People of the Book." Asad, however, points out that a more accurate rendering is "people of an earlier revelation."
3. See, for example, Qur'ān 2:129–32, 35:22, 61:6.
4. Qur'ān 2:30–37.
5. Qur'ān 2:125. See also the entry for "Kaabah" in the *Encyclopaedia Islamica,* 2nd ed.
6. Qur'ān 6:159, 161–63.
7. Qur'ān 17:1.
8. Clinton Bennet, "Islam," in Jean Holm with John Bowker, eds., *Sacred Place* (London, 1994), pp. 88–89.
9. The actual date of the conquest is uncertain.
10. Eutyches, *Annals* 16–17.
11. Quoted in Guy Le Strange, *Palestine Under the Moslems: A Description of Syria and the Holy Land from AD 650 to 1500* (London, 1890), p. 141.
12. Muthir al-Ghiram, 5; Shams ad-Din Suyuti; al-Walid ibn Muslim. Traditions quoted in Le Strange, *Palestine Under the Moslems,* pp. 139–43.
13. Hisham al-Ammor. Tradition quoted in Le Strange, *Palestine Under the Moslems,* p. 142.

14. Adamnan, *The Pilgrimage of Arculfus in the Holy Land*, trans. and ed. James Rose Macpherson, (London, 1895; New York, 1971), pp. 4–5.

15. Tabarī, *Ta'rikh ar-Rusul wa'l-Muluk* 1:2405.

16. Moshe Gil, *A History of Palestine, 634–1099*, trans. Ethel Broido (Cambridge, 1992), pp. 143–48.

17. *History* 3:226, quoted in Joshua Prawer, *The Latin Kingdom of Jerusalem, European Colonialism in the Middle Ages* (London, 1972), p. 216.

18. Robert L. Wilken, *The Land Called Holy: Palestine in Christian History and Thought* (New Haven and London, 1992), pp. 241–49.

19. The Greeks had called the Arabs of the peninsula "Sarakenoi" (*Saraceni* in Latin); they had previously been called "Scenite Arabs": the Arabs who dwell in tents (from the Greek *skēnē*, a tent).

20. The use of the term *al-ḥaram al-sharif* ("the Noble Sanctuary") may not have been in general use to describe the entire precinct until the Ottoman period. Until then the whole sacred area was known as *al-masjid al-aqsā* ("the Distant Mosque"). But to avoid confusion with the mosque of that name on the Ḥaram, I have used the term in current use throughout.

21. Gil, *History of Palestine*, pp. 70–72, 636–38.

22. Ibid., p. 72.

23. F. E. Peters, *Jerusalem: The Holy City in the Eyes of Chroniclers, Visitors, Pilgrims and Prophets from the Days of Abraham to the Beginning of Modern Times* (Princeton, 1985), p. 192.

24. "Book of Commandments" in Gil, *History of Palestine*, p. 71.

25. Isaac Hasson, "Muslim Literature in Praise of Jerusalem," in L. I. Levine, ed., *The Jerusalem Cathedra: Studies in the History, Geography and Ethnography of the Land of Israel*, 3 vols. (Jerusalem, 1981–83), 1:170.

26. Muqaddasī, *Description of Syria, Including Palestine*, trans. and ed. Guy le Strange (London, 1896; New York, 1971), pp. 22–23.

27. Adamnan, *Pilgrimage of Arculfus*, p. 24.

28. Gil, *History of Palestine*, p. 92.

29. Benjamin Mazar, *The Mountain of the Lord* (New York, 1975), p. 98.

30. F. E. Peters, "Who Built the Dome of the Rock?" *Graeco-Arabica* 2 (1983); Meir Ben Dov, *The Western Wall* (Jerusalem, 1983), p. 57.

31. Qur'ān 4:171; inscription also includes 4:172; 19:34–37.

32. Oleg Grabar, "The Umayyad Dome of the Rock in Jerusalem," *Ars Orientalis* 3:33 (1959); *The Formation of Islamic Art* (New Haven and London, 1973), pp. 49–74.

33. Bernard Lewis, "An Apocalyptic Vision of Islamic History," *Bulletin of the School of Oriental and African Studies* 13 (1950). The caliph mentioned in this text is Muᶜāwiya, who may indeed have originally planned the Dome of the Rock.

34. *History* 2:311.

35. Bennett, "Islam," pp. 106–7.

36. Meir Kister, "A Comment on the Antiquity of Traditions Praising Jerusalem," in Levine, *Jerusalem Cathedra*, 1:185–86.

37. F. E. Peters, *The Distant Shrine: The Islamic Centuries in Jerusalem*, (New York, 1993), p. 60.

38. Mujīr ad-Dīn, *Histoire de Jérusalem et d'Hébron, Fragments of the Chronicle of Mujir ad-Din*, trans. and ed. Henry Sauvaire (Paris, 1876), p. 57.

12. AL-QUDS

1. Muqaddasī, *Description of Syria, Including Palestine*, trans. and ed. Guy Le Strange (London, 1896; New York, 1971), p. 41.

2. Qur'ān 17:1.

3. These small shrines are mentioned in texts of the early tenth century as established holy places. We cannot be absolutely certain of their location on the Ḥaram: they may not be in the same places as the shrines of the

same name today. There was a break in continuity at the time of the Crusades, after which some of the locations may have changed.

4. Qurʾān 3:35–38.

5. Qurʾān 57:13.

6. Notker, *De Carolo Magno,* in Einard and Notker the Stammerer, *Two Lives of Charlemagne,* trans. and ed. Lewis Thorpe (London, 1969), p. 148.

7. William, Archbishop of Tyre, *A History of Deeds Done Beyond the Sea,* 2 vols., trans. E. A. Babcock and A. C. Krey (New York, 1943), 1:65.

8. F. E. Peters, *Jerusalem: The Holy City in the Eyes of Chroniclers, Visitors, Pilgrims and Prophets from the Days of Abraham to the Beginnings of Modern Times* (Princeton, 1985), p. 261.

9. Mujīr ad-Dīn, *Histoire de Jérusalem et d'Hébron, Fragments of the Chronicle of Mujir ad-Din,* Trans. and ed. Henry Sauvaire (Paris, 1876), p. 689.

10. Moshe Gil, *A History of Palestine, 634–1099,* trans. Ethel Broido (Cambridge, 1992), p. 618.

11. Ibid., p. 325.

12. Ibid., p. 326.

13. Muqaddasī, *Description of Syria,* p. 37.

14. Ibid.

15. Ibid., pp. 67–68.

16. Ibn al-Qalanisi, *Continuation of the Chronicle of Damascus: The Damascus Chronicle of the Crusades,* ed. and trans. H. A. R. Gibb (London, 1932), p. 66.

17. Ibid.

18. Charles Coüasnon, O. P., *The Church of the Holy Sepulchre in Jerusalem* (London, 1974), p. 19.

19. Gil, *History of Palestine,* p. 167.

20. Muqaddasī, *Description of Syria,* p. 36.

21. Gil, *History of Palestine,* p. 151.

22. Isaac Hasson, "Muslim Literature in Praise of Jerusalem," in L. I. Levine, *The Jerusalem Cathedra: Studies in the History, Geography and Ethnography of the Land of Israel,* 3 vols. (Jerusalem, 1981–82), I, p. 182.

23. Guy Le Strange, *Palestine Under the Moslems: A Description of Syria and the Holy Land from AD 650 to 1500* (London, 1890), pp. 164–65.

24. William of Tyre, *History* 1:406–8.

25. Glaber, *History* 3:1.

26. Revelation 20:1–3.

27. Glaber, *History* 4:6.

28. Gil, *History of Palestine,* p. 400.

29. Ibid., p. 627.

30. *Rihla* 66–67, quoted in Mustafa A. Hiyari, "Crusader Jerusalem, 1099–1187 AD," in K. J. Asali, ed., *Jerusalem in History* (New York, 1990), p. 131.

13. CRUSADE

1. *Alexiad* 10:5, 7.

2. *The Deeds of the Franks and the Other Pilgrims to Jerusalem,* trans. R. Hill (London, 1962), p. 91.

3. Fulcher of Chartres, *History of the Expedition to Jerusalem, 1095–1127,* trans. F. R. Ryan, 3 vols. (Knoxville, 1969), 1:19.

4. August C. Krey, *The First Crusade: The Accounts of Eye Witnesses and Participants* (Princeton and London, 1921), p. 266.

5. Ibid.

6. Robert the Monk quoted in Jonathan Riley-Smith, *The First Crusade and the Idea of Crusading* (London, 1987), p. 143.

7. Baldric of Bourgeuil in ibid.

8. Ibid., p. 140.

9. Krey, *First Crusade,* p. 38.

10. William, Archbishop of Tyre, *A History of Deeds Done Beyond the Sea,* 2 vols., trans. E. A. Babcock and A. C. Krey (New York, 1943), 1:368.

11. Fulcher of Chartres, *History,* 1:33.

12. F. E. Peters, *Jerusalem: The Holy City in the Eyes of Chroniclers, Visitors, Pilgrims and Prophets from the Days of Abraham to the Beginnings of Modern Times* (Princeton, 1985), p. 292.

13. William of Tyre, *History,* 1:507.

14. Joshua Prawer, "The Settlement of the Latins in Jerusalem," *Speculum* 27 (1952).

15. Joshua Prawer, *The Latin Kingdom of Jerusalem: European Colonialism in the Middle Ages* (London, 1972), p. 214.

16. Daimbert was deposed in 1102, convicted of simony and embezzlement.

17. For the military orders, see Prawer, *Latin Kingdom,* pp. 253–79; Jonathan Riley-Smith, *The Knights of St. John in Jerusalem and Cyprus, 1050–1310* (London, 1967).

18. Jonathan Riley-Smith, "Crusading as an Act of Love," *History* 65 (1980).

19. Sylvia Schein, "Between Mount Moriah and the Holy Sepulchre: The Changing Traditions of the Temple Mount in the Central Middle Ages," *Traditio* 40 (1984).

20. Fulcher of Chartres, *History,* 3:307.

21. Theoderich, *Description of the Holy Places,* trans. and ed. Aubrey Stewart, (London, 1896; New York, 1971), p. 44.

22. The chapel was given this name because after the Resurrection, Jesus told the women that he would meet his disciples in Galilee (Matthew 28:7).

23. F. E. Peters, *Jerusalem,* p. 330.

24. *Kitab al I'tibir,* in Francesco Gabrieli, trans. and ed., *Arab Historians of the Crusades,* trans. from the Italian by E. J. Costello (London, 1969), p. 80.

25. Qur'ān 22:40–42.

26. William of Tyre, *History,* 2:240–41.

27. Ibn al-Athir, *Kamil at-Tawarikh,* in Amin Maalouf, *The Crusades Through Arab Eyes,* trans. Jon Rothschild (London, 1973), p. 198.

28. Imad ad-Din al-Isfahani, *al-Fath al-qussi fi l'Fath al-qudsi,* in ibid., p. 200.

14. JIHAD

1. Imad ad-Din al-Isfahani, *al-Fath al-qussi f l'Fath al-qudsi,* in Francesco Gabrieli, trans. and ed., *Arab Historians of the Crusades,* trans. from the Italian by E. J. Costello (London, 1969), p. 182.

2. M. Schwab, "Al-Harizi et ses pérégrinations en Terre Sainte (vers 1217)," in *Archives de l'Orient Latin,* ed. Ernest Leroux, 2 vols. (Paris, 1881, 1884), 2:239.

3. Ibn Wasil, *Mufarrij al-Kurub fi akhbar Bani Ayyub,* in Gabrieli, *Arab Historians of the Crusades,* p. 271.

4. Frederick had married Yolanda, the heiress to the throne of the Kingdom of Acre, so he was entitled now to be crowned in Jerusalem.

5. Al-Maqrizi, *History,* 272, in Donald P. Little, "Jerusalem Under the Ayyubids and the Mamluks, 1187–1516," in K. J. Asali, *Jerusalem in History* (New York, 1990), p. 185.

6. F. Kobler, ed., *Letters of Jews Through the Ages from Biblical Times to the Middle of the Eighteenth Century,* 2 vols. (New York, 1978), 2:227.

7. Joshua Prawer, *The Latin Kingdom of Jerusalem: European Colonialism in the Middle Ages* (London, 1972), pp. 247–48.

8. Eliezer Schweid, *The Land of Israel: National Home or Land of Destiny,* trans. Deborah Greniman (London and Toronto, 1985), pp. 71–81.

9. Michael Hamilton Burgoyne and D. S. Richards, *Mamluk Jerusalem: An Architectural Survey* (London, 1987).

10. E. Sivan, *L'Islam et la Croisade: Idéologie et propagande dans les réactions musulmans aux Croisades* (Paris, 1968), p. 118. These *ahadith* were probably composed during the post-1244 period.

11. P. Durrien, "Procès-verbale du martyre des quatre frères Mineures en 1391" in *Archives de l'Orient Latin,* I (1910).

12. For other such suicidal attacks on the Muslim world in Spain and North Africa, see Benjamin K. Kedar, *Crusade and Mission: European Approaches Towards the Muslims* (Princeton, 1984), pp. 125–26.

13. Felix Fabri, *The Book of the Wanderings of Brother Felix Fabri,* trans. and ed. Aubrey Stewart (London, 1887–97; New York, 1971), pp. 304–5.

14. Ibid., p. 224.

15. Ibid., p. 283.

16. Ibid., p. 299.

17. Ibid., pp. 304, 408–16.

18. Ibid., pp. 384–91.

19. E. N. Adler, *Jewish Travellers: A Treasury of Travelogues from Nine Centuries* (New York, 1966), p. 240.

15. OTTOMAN CITY

1. F. E. Peters, *Jerusalem: The Holy City in the Eyes of Chroniclers, Visitors, Pilgrims and Prophets from the Days of Abraham to the Beginnings of Modern Times* (Princeton, 1985), p. 484.
2. Amnon Cohen, *Jewish Life Under Islam: Jerusalem in the Sixteenth Century* (Cambridge, Mass., and London, 1984), pp. 119, 123–25.
3. K. Wilhelm, *Roads to Zion: Four Centuries of Travellers' Reports* (New York, 1946), pp. 50–51.
4. E. N. Adler, *Jewish Travellers: A Treasury of Travelogues from Nine Centuries* (New York, 1966), p. 21.
5. On the creation of the Western Wall in the sixteenth century: F. E. Peters, *Jerusalem and Mecca: The Typology of the Holy City in the Near East* (New York and London, 1986), pp. 126–31; Meir Ben Dov, *The Western Wall* (Jerusalem, 1983), pp. 33–36, 60.
6. Ben Dov, *Western Wall*, p. 108.
7. Song of Songs Rabbah 2:9.
8. Ben Dov, *Western Wall*, p. 69.
9. Ibid.
10. Cohen, *Jewish Life Under Islam*, pp. 75–85.
11. F. E. Peters, *The Distant Shrine: The Islamic Centuries in Jerusalem* (New York, 1993), p. 223.
12. Peters, *Jerusalem*, p. 483.
13. *Siyahatnemesi* 13:253.
14. Ibid., 8:156.
15. Gershom Scholem, *On the Kabbalah and Its Symbolism* (New York, 1965). p. 144.
16. Ibid., p. 149.
17. Ibid., pp. 149–50.
18. Gershom Scholem, *Sabbetai Sevi* (Princeton, 1931).
19. *Paradise Lost* 3:476–77.
20. John Sanderson, *The Travels of John Sanderson in the Levant,* ed. W. Forster (London, 1931), p. 107.

21. Henry Maundrell, *A Journey from Aleppo to Jerusalem in 1697,* intro. by David Howell (Beirut, 1963), pp. 127–30.
22. Ibid., p. 94.
23. Ibid.
24. Amnon Cohen, *Palestine in the Eighteenth Century: Patterns of Government and Administration* (Jerusalem, 1973), p. 169.
25. Peters, *Jerusalem,* pp. 532–34.
26. C-F. Volney, *Travels Through Syria and Egypt in the years 1783, 1784 and 1785,* 2 vols. (London, 1787), 2:302–3.
27. Ibid., p. 305.
28. Thomas Chaplin, M.D., "The Fevers of Jerusalem," *Lancet* 2 (1864).
29. K. J. Asali, "Jerusalem Under the Ottomans," in Asali, ed., *Jerusalem in History* (New York, 1990), p. 219.

16. REVIVAL

1. W. H. Dixon, *The Holy Land* (London, 1865), pp. 238–40.
2. Y. Ben-Arieh, "The Growth of Jerusalem in the Nineteenth Century," *Annals of the Association of American Geographers* 65 (1975), p. 262. Ottoman sources give very different figures. In particular, the number of Jews noted is far smaller. This is largely because only a small proportion of the Jewish residents of Jerusalem were Ottoman citizens during the nineteenth century.
3. Martin Gilbert, *Jerusalem, Rebirth of a City* (London, 1985), p. 65.
4. Neil Asher Silberman, *Digging for God and Country: Exploration, Archeology and the Secret Struggle for the Holy Land 1799–1917* (New York, 1982), p. 42.
5. Gilbert, *Jerusalem,* pp. 166–67, 182.
6. Alexander Scholch, *Palestine in Transformation 1856–1882: Studies in Social, Economic and Political Development,* trans. William C. Young and Michael C. Gerrity (Washington, D.C., 1986), pp. 241–52.
7. Ibid., p. 60.

8. Albert M. Hyamson, *British Projects for the Restoration of the Jews* (Leeds, 1917), pp. 22–36.

9. Silberman, *Digging for God and Country*, p. 86.

10. Ibid., pp. 155–58.

11. Ibid., p. 185.

12. Arthur Hertzberg, *The Zionist Idea* (New York, 1969), p. 106.

13. Heinrich Graetz, *The Structure of Jewish History*, trans. Ismar Schorsch (New York, 1975), p. 95.

14. Ibid., p. 71.

15. Conor Cruise O'Brien, *The Siege: The Saga of Israel and Zionism* (London, 1986), p. 78.

16. Theodor Herzl, *The Complete Diaries of Theodor Herzl*, ed. R. Patai, 2 vols. (London and New York, 1960), p. 745.

17. Ibid., p. 793.

18. Meir Ben Dov, *The Western Wall* (Jerusalem, 1983), p. 73.

19. Ibid.

20. Amos Elon, *The Israelis: Founders and Sons* (London and Tel Aviv, 1981), p. 134.

21. Gilbert, *Jerusalem*, p. 214.

22. Elon, *The Israelis*, pp. 77–78.

23. Ibid., p. 155.

24. Ibid., p. 156.

17. ISRAEL

1. Christopher Sykes, *Crossroads to Israel* (London, 1965), p. 15.

2. Ibid., pp. 16–17.

3. H. Eugene Bovis, *The Jerusalem Question 1916–1968* (Stanford, 1971), p. 7.

4. E. Sivan, *Modern Arab Historiography of the Crusades* (Tel Aviv, 1973).

5. Sykes, *Crossroads to Israel*, p. 71.

6. B. S. Vester, *Our Jerusalem: An American Family in the Holy City* (Garden City, N.Y., 1950), p. 318.

7. For A. D. Gordon, see Eliezer Schweid, *The Land of Israel: National Home or Land of Destiny*, trans. Deborah Greniman (London and Toronto, 1985), pp. 142–45, 156–70; Shlomo Avineri, *The Making of Modern Zionism: The Intellectual Origins of the Jewish State* (London, 1981), pp. 152–54.

8. Arthur Hertzberg, *The Zionist Idea* (New York, 1969), p. 377.

9. Ibid., p. 423.

10. Schweid, *Land of Israel*, pp. 181–82.

11. Bovis, *Jerusalem Question*, p. 24.

12. Michael Palumbo, *The Palestinian Catastrophe: The 1948 Expulsion of a People from Their Homeland* (London, 1987), pp. 1–4.

13. Joel L. Kraemer, ed., *Jerusalem: Problems and Perspectives* (New York, 1980), pp. 88–94; Meron Benvenisti, *Jerusalem: The Torn City* (Jerusalem, 1975), pp. 22–60; Michael C. Hudson, "The Transformation of Jerusalem, 1917–1987," in K. J. Asali, *Jerusalem in History* (New York, 1990), pp. 263–67.

14. Benvenisti, *Jerusalem*, pp. 11–12.

15. Ibid., Chap. 3; Teddy Kollek, *For Jerusalem: A Life*, with Amos Kollek (London, 1978), p. 182.

16. Kollek, *For Jerusalem*, p. 182.

17. Amos Oz, *My Michael*, trans. Nicholas de Lange (London, 1984), pp. 85–88.

18. Ibid., p. 87.

19. Ibid., p. 210.

20. Ibid., p. 87.

21. Benvenisti, *Jerusalem*, pp. 50–52, 36–37.

22. Ibid., pp. 39–40.

23. Kollek, *For Jerusalem*, p. 183.

24. Raphael Mergui and Philippe Simonnot, *Israel's Ayatollahs: Meir Kahane and the Far Right in Israel* (London, 1987), p. 125.

18. ZION?

1. Meir Ben Dov, *The Western Wall* (Jerusalem, 1983), p. 146.

2. Ibid., p. 148.

3. Ibid.

4. Ehud Sprinzak, *The Ascendance of Israel's Radical Right* (Oxford and New York, 1991), p. 44.

5. Ibid., p. 262.

6. Ibid., p. 46.

7. Ibid., p. 44.

8. Meron Benvenisti, *Jerusalem: The Torn City* (Jerusalem, 1975), p. 84.

9. Ibid., p. 119.

10. Ibid., p. 81.

11. Ibid., pp. 86–88.

12. Ibid., pp. 104–5.

13. Ibid., p. 115.

14. David Hirst, *The Gun and Olive Branch* (London, 1977), p. 237.

15. Amos Elon, *The Israelis, Founders and Sons* (London and Tel Aviv, 1981), p. 281.

16. Ibid., p. 282.

17. Ibid., p. 286.

18. Sprinzak, *Israel's Radical Right,* pp. 280–81.

19. Benvenisti, *Jerusalem,* pp. 288–89.

20. Ibid., pp. 306–07.

21. Ibid., pp. 308–15.

22. Ibid., pp. 239–55; Michael Romann and Alex Weingrod, *Living Together Separately: Arabs and Jews in Contemporary Jerusalem* (Princeton, 1991), pp. 32–61.

23. Paul Goldberger, "Whose Jerusalem Is It?," *New York Times,* 10 September 1995.

24. Romann and Weingrod, *Living Together Separately,* p. 56.

25. Benvenisti, *Jerusalem,* pp. 253–54.

26. Sprinzak, *Israel's Radical Right,* pp. 47, 60–99; Gideon Aron, "Jewish Zionist Fundamentalism," in Martin E. Marty and R. Scott Appleby, *Fundamentalisms Observed* (Chicago, 1991), pp. 265–345.

27. Robert I. Friedman, *Washington Post,* 2 June 1987.

28. For the Third Temple enthusiasm, see Sprinzak, *Israel's Radical Right,* pp. 94–99, 253–71, 279–88.

29. Goldberger, "Whose Jerusalem Is It?"

30. Anne Kindrachuk and Jan Abu Shakrah, "The Eviction of Jerusalem's Palestinians," *Middle East International,* 485, 7 October 1994.

31. Ghada Karmi, "Must the Palestinians Lose East Jerusalem?" *Middle East International,* 500, 26 May 1995.

32. *The Other Israel,* 67–68, August/September 1995, p. 24.

33. Ibid.

Bibliography

Ackroyd, Peter R. *Exile and Restoration: A Study of Hebrew Thought in the Sixth Century* BCE. Philadelphia, 1975.

Adamnan. *The Pilgrimage of Arculfus in the Holy Land.* Trans. and ed. James Rose Macpherson. London, 1895; New York, 1971.

Adler, C. *Memorandum on the Western Wall Prepared for the Special Commission of the League of Nations.* Philadelphia, 1930.

Adler, E. N. *Jewish Travellers: A Treasury of Travelogues from Nine Centuries.* New York, 1966.

Ahlström, Gosta W. "Der Prophet Nathan und der Tempelban." *Vetus Testamentum* 11 (1961).

———. *The History of Ancient Palestine.* Minneapolis, 1993.

Alon, Gedaliah. *The Jews in Their Land in the Talmudic Age.* Jerusalem, 1980.

Alt, A. *Essays in Old Testament History and Religion.* Trans. R. A. Wilson. Oxford, 1966.

Alter, Robert, and Frank Kermode, eds. *The Literary Guide to the Bible.* London, 1987.

Anati, Emmanuel. *Palestine Before the Hebrews: A History from the Earliest Arrival of Man to the Conquest of Canaan.* New York, 1963.

Antoninus. *Of the Holy Places Visited.* Trans. Aubrey Stewart, ed. C. W. Wilson. *Palestine Pilgrims' Text Society,* vol. 2. London, 1986; New York, 1971.

Asali, K. J., ed. *Jerusalem in History.* New York, 1990.

Ashtor, L. "Saladin and the Jews." *Hebrew Union College Annual* 27 (1956).

Avigad, N. *Discovering Jerusalem.* New York, 1983.

Avineri, Shlomo. *The Making of Modern Zionism: The Intellectual Origins of the Jewish State.* London, 1981.

Avi-Yonah, Michael. *The Jews of Palestine: A Political History from the Bar Kokhba War to the Arab Conquest.* Oxford, 1976.

———. *The Madaba Mosaic Map with Introduction and Commentary.* Jerusalem, 1954.

———. *The Holy Land: From the Persian to the Arab Conquests.* Grand Rapids, Mich., 1977.

———, with Zvi Baras, eds. *The Herodian Period.* New Brunswick, N.J., 1975.

Bahat, Dan, with Chaim T. Rubinstein. *An Illustrated Atlas of Jerusalem.* Trans. Shlomo Ketko. New York, 1990.

Baldwin, M. W. *Raymund III of Tripoli and the Fall of Jerusalem 1140–1187*. Princeton, N.J., 1936.

Baltzer, K. "The Meaning of the Temple in the Lukan Writings." *Harvard Theological Review* 58 (1967).

Barker, Margaret. *The Gate of Heaven: The History and Symbolism of the Temple in Jerusalem*. London, 1991.

Barnes, Timothy D. *Constantine and Eusebius*. Cambridge, 1981.

Baron, Salo Wittmayer. *A Social and Religious History of the Jews*. 16 vols. New York, 1952.

Bartsch, H. W. *Kerygma and Myth: A Theological Debate*. London, 1953.

Ben-Ami, Aharon. *Social Change in a Hostile Environment: The Crusaders' Kingdom of Jerusalem*. New Haven, Conn., 1969.

Ben-Arieh, Yehoshua. *Jerusalem in the Nineteenth Century: The Old City*. Jerusalem and New York, 1984.

Ben Dov, Meir. *The Western Wall*. Jerusalem, 1983.

Benjamin of Tudela. *The Itinerary of Benjamin of Tudela*. Trans. and ed. M. N. Adler. London, 1907.

Ben-Tor, Amnon, ed. *The Archeology of Ancient Israel*. Trans. R. Greenberg. New Haven, Conn., and London, 1992.

Benvenisti, Meron. *Jerusalem: The Torn City*. Jerusalem, 1976.

Bernard, J. H., trans. and ed. *Guide Book to Palestine, Circa AD 1350*. Palestine Pilgrims' Text Society, vol. 6. London, 1894; New York, 1971.

Betz, O. *What Do We Know About Jesus?* London, 1968.

Bickerman, Elias J. *From Ezra to the Last of the Maccabees*. New York, 1962.

———. *The Jews in the Greek Age*. Cambridge, Mass., and London, 1988.

Bordeaux Pilgrim. *Itinerary from Bordeaux to Jerusalem*. Trans. Aubrey Stewart. Palestine Pilgrims' Text Society, vol. 1. London, 1887; New York, 1971.

Bovis, H. Eugene. *The Jerusalem Question 1917–1968*. Stanford, Calif., 1971.

Bowker, John. *The Religious Imagination and the Sense of God*. Oxford, 1978.

Braude, B., and B. Lewis. *Christians and Jews in the Ottoman Empire*. New York, 1982.

Bright, J. *A History of Israel*. London, 1960.

Brooks, N. C. *The Sepulchre of Christ in Art and Liturgy, with Special Reference to the Liturgic Drama*. Urbana, Ill., 1921.

Brown, Peter. *The Making of Late Antiquity*. Cambridge, Mass., and London, 1978.

———. *The Cult of the Saints: Its Rise and Function in Classical Antiquity*. London, 1981.

———. *Society and the Holy in Late Antiquity*. London, 1982.

Buber, Martin. *On Zion: The History of an Idea*. Trans. Stanley Godman. Edinburgh, 1952.

Burchard of Mount Sion. *A Description of the Holy Land*. Trans. Aubrey Stewart. Palestine Pilgrims' Text Society, vol. 12. London, 1986; New York, 1971.

Burchardt, Titus. *Art of Islam: Meaning and Message*. London, 1976.

Burgoyne, Michael Hamilton, and D. S. Richards. *Mamluk Jerusalem: An Architectural Survey*. London, 1987.

Campbell, Joseph, with Bill Moyers. *The Power of Myth*. New York and London, 1988.

Canaan, Taufik. *Mohammedan Saints and Sanctuaries in Palestine*. London, 1927.

Canard, Marius. "Destruction de L'Eglise de la Résurrection." *Byzantion*, 12, 1965.

Carroll, M. P. "One More Time: Leviticus Revisited." *Archives européennes de sociologie* 99 (1978).

Catsen, C. "An Introduction to the First Crusade." *Past and Present* 6 (1954).

———. "En Quoi la conquête turque appelait-elle la Croisade?" *Bulletin de la Faculté des Lettres de Strasbourg* 29 (1950).

Chadwick, Henry. *The Circle and the Ellipse: Rival Concepts of Authority in the Early Church*. Oxford, 1959.

Chaplin, Thomas, M.D. "The Fevers of Jerusalem," *Lancet* 2 (1864).

Charles, R. H., ed. *Apocrypha and Pseudepigrapha of the Old Testament.* 2 vols. Oxford, 1913.

Clark, K. W. "Worship in the Jerusalem Temple After 70 AD." *New Testament Studies* 6 (1960).

Clements, R. E. *Abraham and David.* London, 1967.

———. *God and Temple.* Oxford, 1965.

———, ed. *The World of Ancient Israel: Sociological, Anthropological and Political Perspectives.* Cambridge, 1989.

Clifford, Richard J. *The Cosmic Mountain in Canaan and the Old Testament.* Cambridge, Mass., 1972.

Cohen, Amnon. *Jewish Life Under Islam: Jerusalem in the Sixteenth Century.* Cambridge, Mass., and London, 1984.

———. *Palestine in the Eighteenth Century: Patterns of Government and Administration.* Jerusalem, 1973.

Cohen, M. A. "The Role of the Shilonite Priesthood in the United Monarchy of Ancient Israel." *Hebrew Union College Annual* 36 (1965).

Cohn, Haim. *The Trial and Death of Jesus.* New York, 1977.

Cohn, Norman. *The Pursuit of the Millennium: Revolutionary Millenarians and Mystical Anarchists of the Middle Ages.* London, 1957.

———. *Cosmos, Chaos and the World to Come: The Ancient Role of Apocalyptic Faith.* New Haven, Conn., and London, 1993.

Collins, John J., and Michael Fishbane, eds. *Death, Ecstasy and Other Worldly Journeys.* Albany, N.Y., 1995.

Conant, K. J. "The Original Buildings at the Holy Sepulchre in Jerusalem." *Speculum* 31 (1956).

Conder, C. R., trans and ed. *The City of Jerusalem.* London, 1896; New York, 1971.

Conybeare, F. "Antiochus Strategos' Account of the Sack of Jerusalem in 614." *English Historical Review* 25 (1910).

Conzelmann, H. *The Theology of St. Luke.* London, 1960.

Coote, R. B., and K. W. Whitelam. "The Emergence of Israel: Social Transformation and State Formation Following the Decline in Late Bronze Age Trade." *Semeia* 37 (1986).

———. *The Emergence of Early Israel in Historical Perspective.* Sheffield, 1987.

Coüasnon, Charles, O. P. *The Church of the Holy Sepulchre in Jerusalem.* London, 1974.

Creswell, K. A. C. *Early Muslim Architecture.* Oxford, 1969.

Critchlow, Keith. *Islamic Patterns: An Analytical and Cosmological Approach.* London, 1976.

Cross, F. M. *Canaanite Myth and Hebrew Epic.* Cambridge, Mass., 1973.

Crowfoot, J. W. *Early Churches in Palestine.* London, 1941.

Danell, G. A. *Studies in the Name Israel in the Old Testament.* London, 1946.

Daniel. *The Pilgrimage of the Russian Abbot Daniel in the Holy Land.* Trans. and ed. Sir Charles W. Wilson. London, 1895; New York, 1971.

Daniel, Norman. *Islam and the West: The Making of an Image.* Edinburgh, 1960.

———. *The Arabs and Medieval Europe.* London and Beirut, 1975.

Danielou, Jean. *The Theology of Jewish Christianity.* London, 1964.

Davies, W. D. *The Territorial Dimension of Judaism.* Berkeley, Calif., and Los Angeles, 1982.

———. *The Gospel and the Land: Early Christianity and Jewish Territorial Doctrine.* Berkeley, Calif., 1974.

———, with Louis Finkelstein, eds. *The Cambridge History of Judaism.* 2 vols. Cambridge, 1984.

Detienne, Marcel, and Jean-Pierre Vernant. *The Cuisine of Sacrifice Among the Greeks.* Trans. Paula Wissing. Chicago and London, 1989.

De Vaux, Ronald. *Ancient Israel: Its Life and Institutions.* Trans. John McHugh. New York and London, 1961.

———. *The Early History of Israel.* 2 vols. Trans. David Smith. London, 1978.

———. "Les textes de Ras Shamra et L'Ancien Testament." *Revue Biblique* 46 (1937).

————. "Jerusalem and the Prophets." In H. M. Orlinski, ed., *Interpreting the Prophetic Tradition*. Cincinnati, 1969.

Dixon, W. H. *The Holy Land*. London, 1965.

Dodd, C. H. *The Interpretation of the Fourth Gospel*. Cambridge, 1953.

————. *Historical Tradition in the Fourth Gospel*. Cambridge, 1963.

Dodds, E. R. *Pagan and Christian in an Age of Anxiety*. Cambridge, 1965.

Douglas, Mary. *Purity and Danger*. London, 1966.

————. *Implicit Meaning: Essays in Anthropology*. London, 1975.

Dressaire, L. "La Basilique de Ste. Marie le Neuve à Jérusalem." *Echos d'Orient* 15 (1912).

Drory, Joseph. "Jerusalem During the Mamluk Period (1250–1517)." In L. I. Levine, *The Jerusalem Cathedra: Studies in the History, Geography and Ethnography of the Land of Israel*, vol. 1. 3 vols. Jerusalem, 1981–83.

Dubois, Pierre. *The Recovery of the Holy Land*. Trans. W. I. Brandt. New York, 1956.

Duby, Georges. *The Chivalrous Society*. Trans. C. Postan. London, 1977.

————. *L'An Mil*. Paris, 1980.

————. "Les Pauvres de campagnes dans l'Occident médiéval jusqu'au XIII siècle." *Revue d'Histoire de l'Eglise de France* 52 (1966).

Duckworth, H. T. F. *The Church of the Holy Sepulchre*. London, 1922.

Durraq, A. *L'Egypte sous le Règne de Barsbay 1422–1438*. Damascus, 1961.

Duprez, Antoine. *Jesus et les Dieux Guérisseurs à la propos de Jean V*. Paris, 1970.

Durrien, P. "Procès-verbale du martyre du quartre frères Mineures en 1391." *Archives de l'Orient Latin* 1, 1910.

Dussaud, René. *Les origines cananéennes du sacrifice Israelite*. Paris, 1921.

Eaton, J. H. *Kingship and the Psalms*. London, 1978.

Edbury, Peter W., ed. *Crusade and Settlement*. Cardiff, 1985.

Einard and Notker the Stammerer. *Two Lives of Charlemagne*. Trans. and ed. Lewis Thorpe. London, 1969.

Eisenman, Robert, and Michael Wise, trans. and ed. *The Dead Sea Scrolls Uncovered*. London, 1992.

Elad, Amikam. *Medieval Jerusalem and Islamic Worship: Holy Places, Ceremonies, Pilgrimage*. Leiden and New York, 1994.

Eliade, Mircea. *The Myth of the Eternal Return, or, Cosmos and History*. Trans. Willard J. Trask. Princeton, N.J., 1954.

————. *The Sacred and the Profane*. Trans. Willard J. Trask. New York, 1959.

————. *Patterns in Comparative Religion*. Trans. Rosemary Sheed. London, 1958.

————. *Images and Symbols: Studies in Religious Symbolism*. Trans. Philip Mairet. Princeton, N.J., 1991.

Elon, Amos. *The Israelis: Founders and Sons*. London and Tel Aviv, 1981.

————. *Jerusalem, City of Mirrors*. London, 1989.

Fabri, Felix. *The Book of the Wanderings of Brother Felix Fabri*. Trans. Aubrey Stewart. 1887–97; New York, 1971.

Festugière, A. J. *La Révélation d'Hermès Trismegiste*. 4 vols. Paris, 1950–54.

Fischel, H. A., ed. *Essays in Greco-Roman and Related Talmudic Literature*. New York, 1977.

Fishbane, Michael. *Text and Texture: Close Readings of Selected Biblical Texts*. New York, 1979.

Flight, J. W. "The Nomadic Idea and Ideal in the Old Testament." *Journal of Biblical Literature* 43 (1923).

Focillon, Henri. *L'An Mil*. Paris, 1952.

Franken, H. J. "Jerusalem in the Bronze Age, 3000–1000 BC." In K. J. Asali, ed., *Jerusalem in History*. New York, 1990.

Frankfort, H. *Kingship and the Gods*. Chicago and London, 1948.

Fulcher of Chartres. *A History of the Expedition to Jerusalem 1095–1127*. 3 vols. Trans. F. R. Ryan. Knoxville, Tenn., 1969.

Gabrieli, Francesco. *Muhammad and the Conquests of Islam*. Trans. Virginia Luling and Rosamund Linell. London, 1968.

————, trans. and ed. *Arab Historians of the Crusades*. Trans. from the Italian by E. J. Costello. London, 1969.

Gaston, Lloyd. *No Stone on Another: Studies in the Significance of the Fall of Jerusalem in the Synoptic Gospels.* Leiden, 1970.

Geertz, Clifford. *Islam Observed.* New Haven, Conn., 1968.

Gellner, Ernest. *Muslim Society.* Cambridge, 1981.

Gibb, H. A. R., and H. Bowen. *Islamic Society and the West.* London, 1957.

Gibson, John C. L. *Canaanite Myths and Legends.* Edinburgh, 1978.

Gil, Moshe. *A History of Palestine 634–1099.* Trans. Ethel Broido. Cambridge, 1992.

———. "Aliya and Pilgrimage in the Early Arab Period." In L. I. Levine, *The Jerusalem Cathedra: Studies in the History, Geography and Ethnography of the Land of Israel,* vol. 3. Jerusalem, 1983.

Gilbert, Martin. *Jerusalem, Rebirth of a City.* London, 1985.

Gilsenan, Michael. *Recognizing Islam.* London, 1990.

Goitein, S. D. *A Mediterranean Society.* 5 vols. Berkeley, Calif., 1967–88.

———. "The Sanctity of Jerusalem in Moslem Piety." *Bulletin of the Jewish Palestine Exploration Society* 12 (1946).

———. "Contemporary Latin Letters on the Capture of Jerusalem by the Crusaders." *Journal of Jewish Studies* 3 (1952).

Goldstein, David, trans. and ed. *The Jewish Poets of Spain 900–1250.* Harmondsworth, England, 1965.

Goodenough, E. R. *Jewish Symbols in the Greco-Roman Period: Symbolism in the Dura Europos Synagogue.* New York, 1964.

Gottwald, N. K. *The Tribes of Yahweh: A Sociology of the Religion of Liberated Israel.* Maryknoll, N.Y., 1979.

Goulder, Michael. *A Tale of Two Missions.* London, 1994.

Grabar, Oleg. "The Umayyad Dome of the Rock in Jerusalem." *Ars Orientalis* 3:33 (1959).

———. *The Formation of Islamic Art.* New Haven, Conn., and London, 1973.

Graetz, Heinrich. *The Structure of Jewish History.* Trans. Ismar Schorsch. New York, 1975.

Grant, Michael. *The Emperor Constantine.* London, 1993.

Gray, G. B. *Sacrifice in the Old Testament.* Oxford, 1925.

Gray, John. *The Canaanites.* London, 1964.

———. "Sacral Kingship in Ugarit." *Ugaritica* 6 (1969).

Green, Arthur, ed. *Jewish Spirituality.* 2 vols. London and New York, 1986, 1988.

Griffith, S. H. "Stephen of Ramlah and the Christian Kerygma in Arabic in Ninth Century Palestine," *Journal of Ecclesiastical History* 36 (1985).

Guillaume, A. "Where Was al-Masjid al-Aqsa?" *Andalus* 18 (1953).

———, trans. and ed. *The Life of Muhammad: A Translation of Ishaq's Sirat Rasul Allah.* London, 1955.

Gunkel, Hermann. *The Psalms: A Form Criticism Introduction.* Trans. Thomas M. Horner. Philadelphia, 1967.

Gutmann, Joseph. *Sacred Images: Studies in Jewish Art from Antiquity to the Middle Ages.* Northampton, Mass., 1989.

Halbwachs, Maurice. *La Topographie Légendaire des Evangiles en Terre Sainte.* Paris, 1971.

Hamilton, B. *The Latin Church in the Crusader States.* London, 1980.

Hamilton, R. W. *The Structural History of the Aqsa Mosque: A Record of Archeological Gleanings from the Repairs of 1938–1942.* London, 1949.

———. "Jerusalem, Patterns of Holiness." In Roger Moorey and Peter Parr, eds., *Archeology in the Levant: Essays for Kathleen Kenyon.* Warminster, England, 1978.

Hanson, P. D. *The Dawn of Apocalyptic: The Historical and Sociological Roots of Jewish Apocalyptic Eschatology.* Philadelphia, 1979.

Haran, Menahem. *Temples and Temple-Service in Ancient Israel: An Inquiry into the Character of Cult Phenomena and the Historic Setting of the Priestly School.* Oxford, 1978.

al-Harawi, Abu al-Hasan. *Guide des Lieux de Pélérinage.* Trans. Janine Sourdel-Thomime. Damascus, 1957.

Harper, R. F., ed. and trans. *The Code of Hammurabi.* London, 1904.

Harvey, A. E. "Melito and Jerusalem." *Journal of Theological Studies* 17 (1966).

Harvey, W. *Church of the Holy Sepulchre: Structural Survey.* London, 1935.

Hasson, Isaac. "Muslim Literature in Praise of Jerusalem." In L. I. Levine, *The Jerusalem Cathedra: Studies in the History, Geography and Ethnography of the Land of Israel,* vol. 1. Jerusalem, 1981.

Hayes, J. H., "The Tradition of Zion's Inviolability," *Journal of Biblical Literature* 82 (1963).

Hayman, A., ed. *Disputation of Sergius the Stylite Against a Jew.* Louvain, Belgium, 1973.

Helzer, M. *The Rural Community in Ancient Ugarit.* Wiesbaden, Germany, 1976.

———. *The Internal Organization of the Kingdom of Ugarit.* Wiesbaden, Germany, 1982.

Hengel, Martin. *Judaism and Hellenism: Studies in Their Encounter in Palestine During the Early Hellenistic Period.* 2 vols. Trans. John Bowden. London, 1974.

———. *The Zealots: Investigations into the Jewish Freedom Movement in the Period from Herod I Until 70 AD.* Trans. David Smith. Edinburgh, 1989.

Hertzberg, Arthur, ed. *The Zionist Idea.* New York, 1969.

Herzl, Theodor. *The Complete Diaries of Theodor Herzl.* Ed. R. Patai. 2 vols. London and New York, 1960.

Heschel, Abraham. *The Prophets.* 2 vols. New York, 1962.

Hess, Moses. *Rome and Jerusalem.* New York, 1943.

Hill, Rosalind, trans. and ed. *The Deeds of the Franks and the Other Pilgrims to Jerusalem.* London, 1962.

Hoade, E., trans. and ed. *Visit to the Holy Places of Egypt, Sinai, Palestine and Syria.* Jerusalem, 1948.

Hodgson, Marshall G. S. *The Venture of Islam, Conscience and History in a World Civilization.* 3 vols. Chicago and London, 1974.

Holm, Jean, with John Bowker, eds. *Sacred Place.* London, 1994.

Holtz, A., ed. *The Holy City: Jews on Jerusalem.* New York, 1971.

Holum, Kenneth G., Robert L. Hohlfelder, Robert J. Bull, and Avner Raban. *King Herod's Dream: Caesarea on the Sea.* New York and London, 1988.

Homolka, Walter, and Albert H. Friedlander. *The Gate to Perfection: The Idea of Peace in Jewish Thought.* Providence, R.I., 1994.

Hooke, S. H., ed. *Myth and Ritual.* London, 1933.

———. *Myth, Ritual and Kingship.* Oxford, 1958.

———, ed. *The Labyrinth.* London and New York, 1935.

Hopkins, D. C. *The Highlands of Canaan.* Sheffield, England, 1985.

Hunt, E. D. *Holy Land Pilgrimage in the Later Roman Empire AD 312–460.* Oxford, 1982.

Hyamson, Albert M. *British Projects for the Restoration of the Jews.* Leeds, England, 1917.

Ibn al-Qalanisi. *Continuation of the Chronicle of Damascus: The Damascus Chronicle of the Crusades.* Ed. and trans. H. A. R. Gibb. London, 1932.

Idinopulos, Thomas A. *Jerusalem: A History of the Holiest City as Seen Through the Struggles of Jews, Christians and Muslims.* Chicago, 1991.

Jacobson, M. D. "Ideas Concerning the Place of the Herodian Temple." *Palestine Exploration Quarterly,* 1980.

James, E. O. *The Ancient Gods: The History and Diffusion of Religion in the Ancient Near East and the Eastern Mediterranean.* London, 1960.

Jeremias, Joachim. *Jerusalem in the Time of Jesus: An Investigation into Economic and Social Conditions During the New Testament Period.* Trans. F. H. Cave and C. H. Cave. London, 1969.

———. *The Proclamation of Jesus.* London, 1971.

John of Würzburg. *Description of the Holy Land.* Trans. and ed. Aubrey Stewart.

Palestine Pilgrims' Text Society, vol. 5. London, 1896; New York, 1971.

Johnson, A. R. *Sacral Kingship in Israel.* London, 1955.

Jones, Douglas. "The Cessation of Sacrifice After the Destruction of the Temple." *Journal of Theological Studies* 14 (1963).

Keck, L. E., and J. L. Martyn, eds. *Studies in Luke-Acts.* Nashville, Tenn., 1966.

Kedar, Benjamin, K. *Crusade and Mission: European Approaches Towards the Muslims.* Princeton, 1984.

Kenyon, Kathleen. *Jerusalem: Excavating 3000 Years of History.* New York and London, 1967.

Digging Up Jerusalem (London, 1974).

Kister, Meir. "A Comment on the Antiquity of Traditions Praising Jerusalem." In L. I. Levine, ed., *The Jerusalem Cathedra: Studies in the History, Geography and Ethnography of the Land of Israel,* vol. 1. Jerusalem, 1981.

———. "You Shall Only Set Out for Three Mosques." *Le Muséon* 82 (1969).

Knibb, Michael A. *The Qumran Community.* Cambridge, 1987.

Kobler, F., ed. *Letters of Jews Through the Ages from Biblical Times to the Middle of the Eighteenth Century.* 2 vols. New York, 1978.

Kollek, Teddy. "Jerusalem." *Foreign Affairs,* July 1977.

———, with Amos Kollek. *For Jerusalem: A Life.* London, 1978.

Kostoff, Spiro. *The City Shaped: Urban Patterns and Meanings Through History.* London, 1991.

Kraemer, Joel L., ed. *Jerusalem: Problems and Perspectives.* New York, 1980.

Kraus, Hans-Joachim. *Worship in Israel: A Cultic History of the Old Testament.* Oxford, 1966.

Krautheimer, R. *Early Christian and Byzantine Architecture.* Baltimore, 1965.

Krey, August C. *The First Crusade: The Accounts of Eyewitnesses and Participants.* Princeton and London, 1921.

Lacquer, Walter, and Barry Rubin, eds. *The Israel-Arab Reader: A Documentary History of the Middle East Conflict.* 4th edn. London, 1984.

Lane Fox, Robin. *Pagans and Christians in the Mediterranean World from the Second Century AD to the Conversion of Constantine.* London, 1986.

———. *The Unauthorized Version: Truth and Fiction in the Bible.* London, 1991.

Lane-Poole, Stanley. *Saladin and the Fall of Jerusalem.* London and New York, 1898.

Lang, B., ed. *Anthropological Approaches to the Old Testament.* London, 1985.

———. *Monotheism and the Prophetic Minority.* Sheffield, England, 1983.

Lassner, J. *The Shaping of Abbasid Rule.* Princeton, 1980.

Lawlor, Hugh Jackson, and John Ernest Leonard Oulton. *Eusebius, Bishop of Caesarea: The Ecclesiasstical History and the Martyrs of Palestine.* 2 vols. London, 1957.

Lemche, N. P. *Early Israel: Anthropological and Historical Studies on the Israelite Society Before the Monarchy.* Leiden, 1985.

Le Strange, Guy. *Palestine Under the Moslems: A Description of Syria and the Holy Land from AD 650 to 1500.* London, 1890.

Levenson, Jon D. *Theology of the Program of Restoration in Ezekiel 40 to 48.* Missoula, Mont., 1976.

———. *Sinai and Zion.* Minneapolis, 1985.

———. "The Jerusalem Temple in Devotional and Visionary Experience." In Arthur Green, ed., *Jewish Spirituality,* vol. 1. London and New York, 1986.

Levine, L. I., ed. *The Jerusalem Cathedra: Studies in the History, Geography and Ethnography of the Land of Israel.* 3 vols. Jerusalem, 1981–83.

Lewis, Bernard. *The Arabs in History.* London, 1950.

———. *The Jews of Islam.* New York and London, 1982.

———. "An Apocalyptic Vision of Islamic History." *Bulletin of the School of Oriental and African Studies* 13 (1950).

Lightfoot, R. H. *Locality and Doctrine in the Gospels.* New York, 1937.

Lings, Martin. *Muhammad: His Life Based on the Earliest Sources.* London, 1983.

Loew, Cornelius. *Myth, Sacred History and Philosophy.* New York, 1967.

Lucas, Noah. *The Modern History of Israel.* London, 1974.

Ludolph von Suchem. *Description of the Holy Land and the Way Thither.* Ed. and trans. Aubrey Stewart. London, 1895; New York, 1971.

Lyons, M. C., and D. E. P. Jackson. *Saladin: The Politics of the Holy War.* Cambridge, 1982.

Maalouf, Amin. *The Crusades Through Arab Eyes.* Trans. Jon Rothschild. London, 1973.

Mackowski, R. M. *Jerusalem, City of Jesus: An Exploration of the Traditions, Writings and Remains of the Holy City from the Time of Christ.* Grand Rapids, Mich., 1980.

Maimonides. *The Code of Maimonides.* Book 8, *The Book of Temple Service.* Trans. M. Lewittes. New Haven, 1957.

Malina, B. J. *The New Testament World: Insights from Cultural Anthropology.* Atlanta, Ga., and London, 1981–83.

Mango, Cyril. *The Art of the Byzantine Empire, 312–1453: Sources and Documents.* Englewood Cliffs, N.J., 1972.

———. *Byzantium: The Empire of the New Rome.* London, 1994.

Mann, J. *The Jews in Egypt and Palestine Under the Fatimid Caliphs.* 2 vols. New York, 1970.

Ma'oz, Moshe, ed. *Studies on Palestine During the Ottoman Period.* Jerusalem, 1975.

Matthews, Charles D. *Palestine— Mohammedan Holy Land.* New Haven, Conn., and London, 1949.

———. "A Muslim Iconoclast: Ibn Taymiyya on the 'Merits' of Jerusalem." *Journal of the American Oriental Society* 56 (1936).

Maundrell, Henry. *A Journey from Aleppo to Jerusalem in 1697.* With introduction by David Howell. Beirut, 1963.

Mayer, L. A. "A Sequel to Mujîr ad-Dîn's Chronicle." *Journal of the Palestine Oriental Society* 11:2 (1931).

Mazar, Benjamin. *The Mountain of the Lord.* New York, 1975.

Melville, Herman. *Journal of a Visit to Europe and the Levant, October 11, 1856–May 6, 1857.* Ed. Howard C. Horsford. Princeton, N.J., 1955.

Mendenhall, G. E. "The Hebrew Conquest of Palestine." *Biblical Archeologist* 25 (1962).

———. *The Tenth Generation.* Baltimore, 1973.

Miller, P. D. *The Divine Warrior in Early Israel.* Cambridge, Mass., 1973.

Moorey, Roger, and Peter Parr, eds. *Archeology in the Levant: Essays for Kathleen Kenyon.* Warminster, England, 1978.

Mujîr ad-Dîn. *Histoire de Jérusalem et d'Hébron: Fragments of the Chronicle of Mujir al-Din.* Trans. and ed. Henry Sauvaire. Paris, 1876.

Muqaddasî. *Description of Syria, Including Palestine.* Trans. and ed. Guy Le Strange. *Palestine Pilgrims' Text Society,* vol. 3. London, 1896; New York, 1971.

Nasir-i-Khusrau. *Diary of a Journey Through Syria and Palestine.* Trans. and ed. Guy Le Strange. *Palestine Pilgrims' Text Society,* vol. 4. London, 1893; New York, 1971.

Nasr, Sayyid Hossein. *Ideals and Realities of Islam.* London, 1966.

———. *Islamic Spirituality.* 2 vols. Vol. 1, *Foundations.* London, 1987. Vol. 2, *Manifestations.* London, 1991.

———. *Traditional Islam in the Modern World.* London, 1987.

Nau, F. "Deux épisodes de l'histoire juive sous Théodose II (423 et 438) d'après la vie de Barsauma le Syrien." *Revue des études juives* 83 (1927).

Neher, Andre. *Moses and the Vocation of the Jewish People.* New York, 1959.

Nelson, H. H. "The Significance of the Temple in the Ancient Near East." *Biblical Archeologist* 7 (1944).

Neusner, Jacob. *The Rabbinic Traditions About the Pharisees Before 70.* 3 vols. Leiden, 1971.

———. *From Politics to Piety: The Emergence of Pharisaic Judaism.* Englewood Cliffs, N.J., 1973.

———. *Messiah in Context: Israel's History and Destiny in Formative Judaism.* Philadelphia, 1984.

———. *Judaism in the Beginning of Christianity.* Philadelphia, 1984.

———. "Map Without Territory: Mishnah's System of Sacrifice and Sanctuary." *History of Religions,* November 1979.

Niccolo of Poggibonsi. *A Voyage Beyond the Sea (1346–50).* Trans. T. Bellorini and E. Hoade. Jerusalem, 1945.

Nicholson, E. W. *God and His People: Covenant and Theology in the Old Testament.* Oxford, 1986.

Nicholson, Reynold A. *The Mystics of Islam.* London, 1963.

Nielson, E. *Shechem.* London, 1955.

Norwich, John Julius. *Byzantium: The Early Centuries.* London, 1988.

Noth, M. *Exodus.* London, 1962.

O'Brien, Conor Cruise. *The Siege: The Saga of Israel and Zionism.* London, 1986.

Ollenburger, Ben C. *Zion, the City of the Great King: A Theological Symbol of the Jerusalem Cult.* Sheffield, England, 1987.

Orlinsky, H. M., ed. *Interpreting the Prophetic Tradition.* Cincinnati, 1969.

Otto, Rudolf. *The Idea of the Holy: An Inquiry into the Nonrational Factor in the Idea of the Divine and Its Relation to the Rational.* Trans. John W. Harvey. Oxford, 1923.

Ousterhout, Robert, ed. *The Blessings of Pilgrimage.* Urbana, Ill., and Chicago, 1990.

Oz, Amos. *My Michael.* Trans. Nicholas de Lange. London, 1984.

Paetow, L. J. *The Crusades and Other Historical Essays Presented to Dana C. Monro.* New York, 1928.

Palumbo, Michael. *The Palestinian Catastrophe: The 1948 Expulsion of a People from Their Homeland.* London, 1987.

Parrot, A. *Golgotha et Saint-Sépulchre.* Neufchatel and Paris, 1955.

Patai, Raphael. *Man and Temple in Ancient Jewish Myth and Ritual.* London, 1947.

Peake, A. S., ed. *The People and the Book.* London, 1925.

Pederson, J. "Canaanite and Israelite Cultus." *Acta Orientalia* 18 (1940).

Pernoud, Regine. *The Crusaders.* Trans. Enid Grant. Edinburgh and London, 1963.

Peters, F. E. *Jerusalem: The Holy City in the Eyes of Chroniclers, Visitors, Pilgrims and Prophets from the Days of Abraham to the Beginnings of Modern Times.* Princeton, N.J., 1985.

———. *Jerusalem and Mecca: The Typology of the Holy City in the Near East.* New York and London, 1986.

———. *The Distant Shrine: The Islamic Centuries in Jerusalem.* New York, 1993.

———. *The Hajj: The Muslim Pilgrimage to Mecca and the Holy Places.* Princeton, N.J., 1994.

———. *Mecca: A Literary History of the Muslim Holy Land.* Princeton, 1995.

Prawer, Joshua. *The Latin Kingdom of Jerusalem: European Colonialism in the Middle Ages.* London, 1972.

———. "The Settlement of the Latins in Jerusalem." *Speculum* 27 (1952).

———. "The Jerusalem the Crusaders Captured: A Contribution to the Medieval Topography of the City." In Peter W. Edbury, ed., *Crusade and Settlement.* Cardiff, 1985.

Pritchard, J. B., ed. *Ancient Near Eastern Texts Relating to the Old Testament.* Princeton, N.J., 1969.

Prittie, Terence. *Whose Jerusalem?* London, 1981.

Procopius. *Of the Buildings of Justinian.* Trans. Aubrey Stewart. Ed. C. W. Wilson and Hagler Lewis. London, 1896; New York, 1971.

Raphael, Chaim. *The Walls of Jerusalem: An Excursion into Jewish History.* London, 1968.

Redford, D. B. *Canaan and Israel in Ancient Times.* Princeton, N.J., 1992.

Rhoads, David M. *Israel in Revolution, 6–74 CE: A Political History Based on the Writings of Josephus.* Philadelphia, 1976.

Richmond, E. T. *The Dome of the Rock in Jerusalem.* Oxford, 1924.

Riley-Smith, Jonathan. *The Knights of St. John in Jerusalem and Cyprus 1050–1310.* London, 1967.

———. *The Feudal Nobility and the Kingdom of Jerusalem 1174–1277.* London, 1973.

———. *The First Crusade and the Idea of Crusading.* London, 1986.

———. "Crusading as an Act of Love." *History* 65 (1980).

Robinson, Edward. *Biblical Researches in Palestine, Mount Sinai and Arabia Petraea.* Boston, 1841.

Romann, Michael, and Alex Weingrod. *Living Together Separately: Arabs and Jews in Contemporary Jerusalem.* Princeton, 1991.

Rowley, Harold H. *Worship in Ancient Israel: Its Forms and Meaning.* London, 1967.

———. *The Relevance of Apocalyptic.* London, 1963.

———. "Zadok and Nehushtan." *Journal of Biblical Literature* 58 (1939).

Runciman, Steven. *A History of the Crusades.* 3 vols. Cambridge, 1951–54.

———. "The Byzantine 'Protectorate' in the Holy Land." *Byzantium* 18 (1948).

———. "Charlemagne and Palestine." *English Historical Review* 1 (1935).

Ryce-Menuhin, Joel. *Jung and the Monotheisms: Judaism, Christianity and Islam.* London and New York, 1994.

Saewulf. *Pilgrimage to Jerusalem and the Holy Land.* Trans and ed. Rt. Rev. Bishop of Clifton. London, 1896; New York, 1971.

Samuel, M. D. *The World of Sholem Aleichem.* New York, 1965.

Sandars, N. K. *Poems of Heaven and Hell from Ancient Mesopotamia.* Harmondsworth, England, 1971.

Sanders, E. P. *Paul and Palestinian Judaism.* London, 1977.

———. *Jesus and Judaism.* London, 1984.

———. *Judaism: Practice and Belief, 63 BCE to 66 CE.* London and Philadelphia, 1992.

———. *The Historical Figure of Jesus.* London, 1993.

Sanderson, John. *The Travels of John Sanderson in the Levant.* Ed. W. Forster. London, 1931.

Sanuto, Marino. *Secrets for True Crusaders to Help Them Recover the Holy Land.* Trans. Aubrey Stewart. London, 1896; New York, 1971.

Saperstein, Marc, ed. *Essential Papers on Messianic Movements and Personalities in Jewish History.* New York and London, 1992.

Schacht, Joseph, with C. E. Bosworth. *The Legacy of Islam.* Oxford, 1974.

Schein, Sylvia. "Between Mount Moriah and the Holy Sepulchre: The Changing Traditions of the Temple Mount in the Central Middle Ages." *Traditio* 40 (1984).

Schimmel, Annemarie. *And Muhammad Is His Messenger: The Veneration of the Prophet in Islamic Piety.* Chapel Hill, N.C., and London, 1985.

Schlumberger, G. *Renaud de Chatillon.* Paris, 1898.

Scholch, Alexander. *Palestine in Transformation 1856–1882: Studies in Social, Economic and Political Development.* Trans. William C. Young and Michael Gerrity. Washington, D.C., 1986.

Scholem, Gershom. *Major Trends in Jewish Mysticism.* London, 1955.

———. *The Messianic Idea in Judaism and Other Essays on Jewish Spirituality.* New York, 1970.

———. *On the Kabbalah and Its Symbolism.* New York, 1965.

———. *Sabbeti Sevi.* Princeton, 1973.

Schwab, M. "Al-Harizi et ses pérégrinations en Terre Sainte (vers 1217)." In *Archives de l'Orient Latin.* Ed. Ernest Leroux. 2 vols. Paris, 1881, 1884.

Schweid, Eliezer. *The Land of Israel: National Home or Land of Destiny.* Trans. Deborah Greniman. London and Toronto, 1985.

Scully, R. A. *The Earth, the Temple and the Gods.* New Haven, 1979.

Segal, Peretz. "The Penalty of the Warning Inscription from the Temple in

Jerusalem." *Israel Exploration Journal* 39 (1989).

Segev, Tom. *The Seventh Million: The Israelis and the Holocaust*. Trans. Haim Wetzman. New York, 1993.

Setton, Kenneth M., ed. *A History of the Crusades*. 6 vols. Madison, Wis., and London, 1976–87.

Sharon, Moshe, ed. *The Holy Land in History and Thought: Papers Submitted to the International Conference on the Relations Between the Holy Land and the World Outside It*. Johannesburg, 1986; Leiden, 1988.

Sidersky, D. *Les Origines des légendes musulmans dans le Coran et dans les vies des prophètes*. Paris, 1933.

Silberman, Neil Asher. *Digging for God and Country: Exploration, Archeology and the Secret Struggle for the Holy Land, 1799–1917*. New York, 1982.

Sivan, Emmanuel. *L'Islam et la Croisade: Idéologie et propagande dans les réactions musulmans aux Croisades*. Paris, 1968.

———. "Le caractère sacré de Jérusalem dans l'Islam aux XII–XIII siècles." *Studia Islamica* 27 (1967).

———. *Modern Arab Historiography of the Crusades*. Tel Aviv, 1973.

Smith, Jonathan Z. *Map Is Not Territory: Studies in the History of Religions*. Leiden, 1973.

———. *To Take Place: Toward Theory in Ritual*. Chicago and London, 1987.

Smith, R. H. "Abraham and Melchizedek." *Zeitschrift für der Alttestamentlische Wissenschaft* 78 (1965).

Smooha, S. *Israel: Pluralism and Conflict*. London, 1978.

———. *The Orientation and Politicization of the Arab Minority in Israel*. Haifa, 1984.

Soggin, J. Alberto. *A History of Israel from the Beginnings to the Bar Kochba Revolt AD 135*. Trans. John Bowden. London, 1984.

Speiser, E. A. "The Hurrian Participation in the Civilizations of Mesopotamia, Syria and Palestine." *Journal of World History* 1 (1953).

Sprinzak, Ehud. *The Ascendence of Israel's Radical Right*. Oxford and New York, 1991.

Stanley, Arthur. *Sinai and Palestine in Connection with Their History*. London, 1856.

Steiner, George. *Real Presences: Is There Anything in What We Say?* London and Boston, 1989.

Storme, Albert. *The Way of the Cross: A Historical Sketch*. Trans. Kieran Dunlop. Jerusalem, n.d.

Sykes, Christopher. *Cross Roads to Israel*. London, 1965.

Sylvia (or Egeria). *The Pilgrimage of S. Sylvia of Aquitania to the Holy Places*. Trans. John Bernard. London, 1891; New York, 1971.

Terrien, S. "The Omphalos Myth and Hebrew Religion." *Vetus Testamentum* 20 (1970).

Theoderich. *Description of the Holy Places*. Trans. and ed. Aubrey Stewart. London, 1896; New York, 1971.

Theodosius. *On the Topography of the Holy Land*. Trans. John Bernard. London, 1893; New York, 1971.

Thompson, T. L. *The Historicity of the Patriarchal Narratives: The Quest for the Historical Abraham*. Berlin, 1974.

———. *The Origin Traditions of Genesis and Exodus 1–23*. Sheffield, England, 1987.

Tibawi, A. L. *Anglo-Arab Relations and the Question of Palestine, 1914–1921*. London, 1978.

———. *The Islamic Pious Foundations in Jerusalem: Origins, History and Usurpation by Israel*. London, 1978.

———. *Jerusalem: Its Place in Islam and Arab History*. Beirut, 1967.

Toynbee, J. M. C. *The Hadrianic School: A Chapter in the History of Greek Art*. Cambridge, 1934.

Tshelebi, Evlya. *Evliya Tshelebi's Travels in Palestine*. Trans. St. H. Stephan. Jerusalem, 1980.

Twain, Mark. *The Innocents Abroad*. New York, 1911.

Ussishkin, David. "King Solomon's Palaces." *Biblical Archeologist* 36 (1973).

Van Seters, J. *Abraham in History and Tradition*. New Haven, 1975.

———. *In Search of History: Historiography in the Ancient World and the Origins of Biblical History*. New Haven, 1983.

Vermes, Geza. *The Dead Sea Scrolls: Qumran in Perspective*. London, 1977.

———, ed. and trans. *The Dead Sea Scrolls in English*. London, 1987.

Vester, B. S. *Our Jerusalem: An American Family in the Holy City*. Garden City, N.Y., 1950.

Vilnay, Zev. *The Sacred Land: Legends of Jerusalem*. Philadelphia, 1973.

Vincent, H., and F. M. Abel. *Jerusalem: Récherches de Topographie d'archéologie et d'histoire*. 2 vols. (Paris, 1912, 1926).

Volney, C.-F. *Travels Through Syria and Egypt in the Years 1783, 1784 and 1785*. 2 vols. London, 1787.

Von Harff, Arnold. *The Pilgrimage of Arnold Von Harff 1496–1499*. London, 1946.

Von Rad, G. *The Problem of the Hexateuch and Other Essays*. Trans. E. W. T. Dicken. New York, 1966.

Walker, P. W. L. *Holy City, Holy Places? Christian Attitudes to Jerusalem and the Holy Land in the Fourth Century*. Oxford, 1990.

Warren, Charles, *Underground Jerusalem* (London, 1876).

Watt, W. Montgomery. *Muhammad at Mecca*. Oxford, 1953.

———. *Muhammad at Medina*. Oxford, 1956.

———. *Muhammad's Mecca: History in the Qur'an*. Edinburgh, 1988.

Weiden, Naphtali. *The Judaean Scrolls and Karaism*. London, 1962.

Welch, A. C. *The Code of Deuteronomy*. London, 1924.

Wilhelm, K. *Roads to Zion: Four Centuries of Travellers' Reports*. New York, 1946.

Wilken, Robert L. *The Land Called Holy: Palestine in Christian History and Thought*. New Haven and London, 1992.

Wilkinson, John. *Jerusalem as Jesus Knew It: Archeology as Evidence*. London, 1978.

———. *Jerusalem Pilgrims Before the Crusade*. Jerusalem, 1977.

———. *Egeria's Travels*. London, 1971.

———. *Jerusalem Pilgrimage: 1095–1185*. London, 1988.

———. "Architectural Procedures in Byzantine Palestine." *Levant* 13 (1981).

William, Archbishop of Tyre. *A History of Deeds Done Beyond the Sea*. 2 vols. Trans. E. A. Babcock and A. C. Krey. New York, 1943.

Williams, Stephen, and Gerard Friell. *Theodosius: The Empire at Bay*. London, 1994.

Wilson, Charles. *Ordnance Survey of Jerusalem Made in the Years 1864–5*. Southampton, England, 1866.

Wilson, Robert. *Prophecy and Society in Ancient Israel*. Philadelphia, 1980.

Wright, G. E. *Biblical Archeology*. Philadelphia, 1967.

———. "Pre-Israelite Temples in the Land of Canaan." *Palestine Exploration Quarterly* 103 (1971).

Zaidman, Louise Bruitt, and Pauline Schmitt Pantel. *Religion in the Ancient Greek City*. Trans. Paul Cartledge. Cambridge, 1994.

Zander, W. *Israel and the Holy Places of Christendom*. London, 1970.

Index

Page numbers in *italics* indicate illustrations.

PICTURE ACKNOWLEDGMENTS

Abbas/Magnum Photos NY: 81, 201, 219.
Archives Nationales, Paris: 280.
Associated Press: 381.
Micha Bar-Am/Magnum Photos NY: 29, 43, 61, 192, 368.
René Burri/Magnum Photos NY: 317.
Cornell Capa/Magnum Photos NY: 399.
Raymond Depardon/Magnum Photos NY: 20, 412.
Stuart Franklin/Magnum Photos NY: 283.
Leonard Freed/Magnum Photos NY: 32, 50, 144, 324.
Israel Museum, Jerusalem: 162.
Mansell Collection, London: 67, 328, 357.
Peter Marlow/Magnum Photos NY: 427.
Inge Morath/Magnum Photos NY: 182, 311.
Fred Mayer/Magnum Photos NY: xviii, 101, 112, 123, 131, 167, 211, 236, 240, 262, 315.
James Nachtway/Magnum Photos NY: 378.
Chris Steele-Perkins/Magnum Photos, NY: xiv, 248.
Larry Towell/Magnum Photos NY: 426.
Private Collections: 16, 378.

COLOR SECTION

British Library: Add Mss 28681 folio 9, page 1; Or Mss 2265 folio 195 recto, page 3.
J.P. Laffont/Sygma: pages 4–5.
Fred Mayer/Magnum Photos NY: pages 2 above, 6 above, 7.
James Nachtway/Magnum Photos NY: page 6 below.
Chris Steele-Perkins/Magnum Photos NY: page 2 below.

Picture Research: Juliet Brightmore, London.

A NOTE ABOUT THE AUTHOR

Karen Armstrong spent seven years as a Roman Catholic nun. After leaving her order in 1969 she took a B.Litt. at Oxford, taught modern literature at the University of London, and headed the English department of a public girls' school. In 1982 she became a free-lance writer and broadcaster. She has long been one of the foremost British commentators on religious affairs and is well on her way to a similar status in the United States. In 1983 she worked in the Middle East on a six-part documentary television series on the life and works of St. Paul. Her other television work has included "Varieties of Religious Experience" (1984) and "Tongues of Fire" (1985); the latter resulted in an anthology by that name on religious and poetic expression. In 1996 she participated in Bill Moyers's television series "Genesis." She teaches at the Leo Baeck College for the Study of Judaism and the Training of Rabbis and Teachers and is also an honorary member of the Association of Muslim Social Sciences. Her published works include *Through the Narrow Gate* (1981), *The Gospel According to Woman* (1987), *Holy War: The Crusades and Their Impact on Today's World* (1991), *The English Mystics of the Fourteenth Century* (1991), *Muhammad: A Biography of the Prophet* (1992), and *A History of God: The 4000-Year Quest of Judaism, Christianity and Islam* (1993). She is also a regular contributor of reviews and articles to newspapers and journals.